Research Anthology on Usage and Development of Open Source Software

Information Resources Management Association
USA

Volume I

Published in the United States of America by
    IGI Global
    Engineering Science Reference (an imprint of IGI Global)
    701 E. Chocolate Avenue
    Hershey PA, USA 17033
    Tel: 717-533-8845
    Fax: 717-533-8661
    E-mail: cust@igi-global.com
    Web site: http://www.igi-global.com

Library of Congress Cataloging-in-Publication Data

Names: Information Resources Management Association, editor.
Title: Research anthology on usage and development of open source software
    / Information Resources Management Association, editor.
Description: Hershey, PA : Engineering Science Reference, [2021] | Includes
    bibliographical references and index. | Summary: "This comprehensive
    reference book covers the latest and most emerging research, concepts,
    and theories for those working with open source software with the goal
    of demonstrating various ways of its tremendous potential with room for
    improvement and advancement, though it has faced challenges and issues
    throughout the years"-- Provided by publisher.
Identifiers: LCCN 2021030071 (print) | LCCN 2021030072 (ebook) | ISBN
    9781799891581 (hardcover) | ISBN 9781799891598 (ebook)
Subjects: LCSH: Shareware (Computer software) | Open source software. |
    Computer software--Development.
Classification: LCC QA76.76.S46 R47 2021 (print) | LCC QA76.76.S46
    (ebook) | DDC 005.3--dc23
LC record available at https://lccn.loc.gov/2021030071
LC ebook record available at https://lccn.loc.gov/2021030072

British Cataloguing in Publication Data
A Cataloguing in Publication record for this book is available from the British Library.

For electronic access to this publication, please contact: eresources@igi-global.com.

List of Contributors

Table of Contents

Section 2
Multi-Industry Applications

Volume II

Preface

Great emphasis has recently been placed on the accessibility of all research. From the Open Access movement that is driving authors to ensure that their research is openly available without purchase to the open collaboration ideals of open source software, it is clear that researchers recognize the importance that openly available content has on the advancement and innovation of society. Open source software is growing as the world increasingly implements new technology into all aspects of life; open source software is one of many innovations that has become more popular as it continues to grow and offers benefits in a wide range of areas. Allowing users to use, study, change, and distribute the software and its source code, open source software has allowed for the improvement and efficiency of systems in a variety of industries, including education, finance, waste reduction, and more.

Thus, the *Research Anthology on Usage and Development of Open Source Software* seeks to fill the void for an all-encompassing and comprehensive reference book covering the latest and emerging research, concepts, and theories for those working with open source software. This two-volume reference collection of reprinted IGI Global book chapters and journal articles that have been handpicked by the editor and editorial team of this research anthology on this topic will empower computer scientists, programmers, developers, systems engineers, designers, industry professionals, teachers, academicians, researchers, and students with an advanced understanding of critical issues and advancements of opensource software.

The *Research Anthology on Usage and Development of Open Source Software* is organized into three sections that provide comprehensive coverage of important topics. The sections are:

1. Development, Standards, and User Expectations;
2. Multi-Industry Applications; and
3. Prediction Models, Big Data, and Statistics.

The following paragraphs provide a summary of what to expect from this invaluable reference tool.

Section 1, "Development, Standards, and User Expectations," provides investigations on the development and design of open source software, challenges to its standardization, and what users expect from adopting open source software into their systems. The first chapter of this section, "A Systematic Review of Attributes and Techniques for Open Source Software Evolution Analysis," by Profs. Munish Saini and Kuljit Kaur Chahal of Guru Nanak Dev University, India, uses various techniques for understanding the OSS evolution process from different perspectives and reports a meta-data analysis of the systematic literature review on the topic in order to understand its current state and to identify opportunities for the future. The following chapter, "Exploratory Analysis of Free and Open Source Software Ecology," by Prof. K.G. Srinivasa of Chaudhary Brahm Prakash Government Engineering College, India and Profs.

Ganesh Chandra Deka and Krishnaraj P.M. from M. S. Ramaiah Institute of Technology, India, confirms the existence of power law in Sourceforge.net and reveals that there is a separate core and are periphery groups of developers in Sourceforge.net, as well as in other forges like Freecode and Rubyforge. The next chapter, "Open Source Software Development Challenges: A Systematic Literature Review on GitHub," by Profs. Abdulkadir Seker and Halil Arslan of Sivas Cumhuriyet University, Turkey and Profs. Banu Diri and Mehmet Fatih Amasyalı from Yıldız Technical University, Turkey, conducts a literature review on studies that used GitHub data based on a GitHub dataset source study instead of a keyword-based search in digital libraries. Another chapter in this section, "On Challenges for Implementing ISO Standards in Software: Can Both Open and Closed Standards Be Implemented in Open Source Software?" by Profs. Björn Lundell and Jonas Gamalielsson of the University of Skövde, Sweden and Prof. Andrew Katz of the University of Skövde, Sweden and Moorcrofts LLP, UK, elaborates on the implications and suggests ways of addressing the challenges of implementing standards in software. Another chapter in this section, "Analysis of Free and Open Source Software (FOSS) Product in Web Based Client-Server Architecture," by Prof. Pushpa Singh of Accurate Institute of Management and Technology, Greater Noida, India and Prof. Narendra Singh from G. L. Bajaj Institute of Management and Research, Greater Noida, India, studies FOSS products used in web-based client server architecture and provides information about FOSS product such as FireFox (web browser), Apache (web server), and MySQL (RDBMS). An additional chapter, "Strategy of Good Software Governance: FLOSS in the State of Turkey," by Prof. Hüseyin Tolu of Recep Tayyip Erdogan University, Turkey, discusses in what matters and for what reasons software governance of Turkey has locked into the ecosystems of PCSS; considers causes, effects, and potential outcomes of not utilizing FLOSS in the state of Turkey; and argues that Turkey has taken a pragmatic decision-making process of software in the emerging cybernetics that leads and contributes to techno-social externality of PCSS hegemonic stability. Following this chapter is "On Solving the Multi-Objective Software Package Upgradability Problem" by Profs. Noureddine Aribi and Yahia Lebbah of Lab. LITIO, University of Oran 1, Oran, Algeria, which proposes a Leximax approach based on mixed integer linear programming (MILP) to tackle the upgradability problem while ensuring efficiency and fairness requirements between the objective functions. The next chapter, "Finding Influential Nodes in Sourceforge.net Using Social Network Analysis," by Prof. K.G. Srinivasa of Chaudhary Brahm Prakash Government Engineering College, India and Profs. Ganesh Chandra Deka and Krishnaraj P.M. from M. S. Ramaiah Institute of Technology, India, studies the contribution of volunteers in the development of Free and Open Source Software in Sourceforge.net and discovers the small set of developers who can maximize the information flow in the network. An additional chapter in this section, "The Cultural and Institutional Barrier of Knowledge Exchanges in the Development of Open Source Software," by Prof. Ikbal Maulana of Indonesian Institute of Sciences, Indonesia, discusses the diffusion and development of OSS in Indonesia after the government took "Indonesia, Go Open Source" (IGOS) initiative, which initiative united government organizations, communities, R&D institutions, and universities. A concluding chapter, "Understanding Users' Contributions in Open Source Software Communities: A Social Influence Perspective," by Prof. Tao Zhou of Hangzhou Dianzi University, China, examines user contributions in OSS communities and indicates that contribution intention is significantly affected by social identity, which includes cognitive, affective and evaluative identity, as well as that the subjective norm has a negative effect on contribution intention. The next chapter, "Trust in Open Source Software Development Communities: A Comprehensive Analysis," by Prof. Amitpal Singh Sohal of IKG Punjab Technical University, Kapurthala, Punjab, India; Prof. Sunil Kumar Gupta from Beant College of Engineering and Technology, Gurdaspur, Punjab, India; and Prof. Hardeep Singh of Guru

Nanak Dev University, Amritsar, Punjab, India, presents the significance of trust for the formation of an Open Source Software Development (OSSD) community and offers an overview of various existing trust models, which aids in the development of a trust evaluation framework for OSSD communities. Another concluding chapter, "The Impact of Project Initiators on Open Source Software Project Success: Evidence From Emerging Hosting Platform Gitee," by Prof. Ling Wang of China University of Political Science and Law (CUPL), Beijing, China and Prof. Jinxiao Wang from Tsinghua University, Beijing, China, focuses on studying the role of open source software project initiator in affecting the OSS project success from the perspective of individual and collective behaviors. The next chapter, "Does an Open Source Development Environment Facilitate Conventional Project Management Approaches and Collaborative Work?" by Prof. Richard Garling of American Military University, USA, focuses on how an open source development environment facilitates conventional Waterfall project management approaches and how an open source development environment facilitates Agile project collaborative work. The final chapter in this section, "Prospects of Open Source Software for Maximizing the User Expectations in Heterogeneous Network," by Prof. Pushpa Singh of Accurate Institute of Management and Technology, Greater Noida, India and Prof. Rajeev Agrawal from G.L. Bajaj Institute of Technology and Management, Greater Noida, India, focuses on the prospects of open source software and tools for maximizing the user expectations in heterogeneous networks.

Section 2, "Multi-Industry Applications," considers the various uses and benefits of applying open source software in different fields from education to banking. The opening chapter in this section, "Open Source Software Usage in Education and Research: Network Traffic Analysis as an Example," by Profs. Vladimir V. Syuzev, Ark M. Andreev, and Samih M. Jammoul of Bauman Moscow State Technical University, Russia, presents the trend of using open source software in higher education, discusses pros and cons of using open source software in engineering education, presents network traffic analysis as an example of recent effective research topics, and provides a set of open source tools to perform the research's practical steps. Another opening chapter in this section, "Open Sourcing the Pedagogy to Activate the Learning Process," by Prof. Alan Rea of Western Michigan University, Kalamazoo, USA and Prof. Nick Yeates from UMBC, Baltimore, USA, describes how 19 undergraduates in a web development and design course at a Midwest university worked collaboratively with leading open source software provider, Red Hat, to revamp the Teaching Open Source website. Another chapter, "Optimization Scenarios for Open Source Software Used in E-Learning Activities," by Prof. Utku Köse of Suleyman Demirel University, Turkey, discusses some possible applications of artificial intelligence to include optimization processes within open source software systems used in e-learning activities, focuses on using swarm intelligence and machine learning techniques for this aim, and expresses some theoretical views for improving the effectiveness of such software for a better e-learning experience. The following chapter, "DuBot: An Open-Source, Low-Cost Robot for STEM and Educational Robotics," by Profs. Michail Kalogiannakis and Stamatios Papadakis of the University of Crete, Greece; Profs. Avraam Chatzopoulos and Michail Papoutsidakis of the University of West Attica, Greece; Prof. Sarantos Psycharis of the School of Pedagogical and Technological Education, Greece; and Dethe Elza from Richmond Public Library, Canada, presents the design and development of an open source, low-cost robot for K12 students, suitable for use in educational robotics and science, technology, engineering, mathematics (STEM). The next chapter, "Open Source Online Learning in Rural Communities," by Prof. Gary L. Ackerman of Windsor (Vermont) School, USA, focuses on three cases in which open source technology was installed to support teaching and learning in three rural communities by detailing the projects, assessing the method of technology planning, and addressing unanswered questions. Another chapter,

"Open Source Software Virtual Learning Environment (OSS-VLEs) in Library Science Schools," by Prof. Rosy Jan of the University of Kashmir, India, discusses some of the most used OSS VLEs, determines the suitability of a VLE for higher education, and explores and identifies the recent contributions to the concept by analyzing ongoing virtual learning initiatives and projects by different organizations and information centres to stimulate future Research and development trend in the field. The next chapter, "A Multi-Step Process Towards Integrating Free and Open Source Software in Engineering Education," by Prof. K.G. Srinivasa of Chaudhary Brahm Prakash Government Engineering College, India and Profs. Ganesh Chandra Deka and Krishnaraj P.M. from M. S. Ramaiah Institute of Technology, India, presents a three-stage process which can be adopted by teachers and institutes to utilize the benefits of FOSS to the fullest. An additional chapter, "Development of Assessment Criteria for Various Open Sources GIS Software Packages," by Prof. Shahriar Shams of Institut Teknologi Brunei, Brunei, focuses on the assessment criteria enabling developers, researchers, and GIS users to select suitable OGIS software to meet their requirements for analysis and design of geospatial application in multidisciplinary fields, and highlights the importance of assessment criteria, followed by an explanation of each criteria and their significance with examples from existing OGIS software. Another chapter, "Transmission Line Routing Using Open Source Software Q-GIS," by Prof. Sandeep Chakravorty of Indus University, Ahmedabad, India; Prof. Amitava Ray from Jalpaiguri Government Engineering College, Jalpaiguri, India; and Profs. Shabbir Uddin and Karma Sonam Sherpa of Sikkim Manipal Institute of Technology, Sikkim Manipal University, Rangpo, India, contends that planning for power systems is essentially a projection of how the system should grow over a specific period of time, given certain assumptions and judgments about the future load and the size of investment in generating capacity additions, transmission facilities expansion, and reinforcements. Another chapter in this section, "An Open Source Software: Q-GIS Based Analysis for Solar Potential of Sikkim (India)," by Profs. Dipanjan Ghose, Sreejita Naskar, Shabbiruddin, and Amit Kumar Roy of Sikkim Manipal Institute of Technology, Sikkim Manipal University, East Sikkim, India, investigates the land suitability for medium-scale solar power installations in Sikkim by using open source software Quantum-Geographic Information System (Q-GIS) combined with multi-criteria decision making (MCDM) techniques. The next chapter, "Role of Free and Open Source GIS in River Rejuvenation," by Profs. Smart Kundassery and Babu C. A. of Cochin University of Science and Technology, India, focuses on the possibilities emerging out of integration of free and open source GIS that can eventually succeed in bringing forth a ray of hope to the forlorn riverine ecosystem. The following chapter, "Designing a Framework of Ethnomedicinal Plant Knowledge Integration Using OSS," by Prof. Piyali Das of MUC Women's College, Burdwan, India, provides a framework for design an information retrieval system for ethnomedicine or knowledge on medicinal plants that are used to manage human ailments. Another chapter, "Critical Barriers to Business Intelligence Open Source Software Adoption," by Prof. Placide Poba-Nzaou of the University of Quebec in Montreal, Montreal, Canada; Prof. Sylvestre Uwizeyemungu from the University of Quebec in Trois-Rivières, Trois-Rivières, Canada; and Mariem Saada of DiCentral, Montreal, Canada, proposes a framework that categorizes and structures 23 barriers to OSBI adoption by organizations including 4 that were identified by BI Experts but not explicitly found in the literature and contributes to OSS and Information Systems (IS) research literature on BI adoption in general, as well as provides specific insights to practitioners. Another chapter, "Open Source Software in Financial Auditing," by Prof. Tânia Correia of Instituto Politécnico de Coimbra, Portugal; Prof. Isabel Pedrosa from Instituto Politécnico de Coimbra, Portugal & Instituto Universitário de Lisboa, Portugal; and Prof. Carlos J. Costa of the Universidade de Lisboa, Portugal, focuses on which factors affect open source software adoption by carrying out a survey aimed at financial auditors. The following chapter in this section, "Application of Quality in Use Model to Evaluate the User Experience of Online Banking Software," by Profs. Manar Abu Talib, Areej Alsaafin, and Selma Manel Medjden of the University of Sharjah, Sharjah, UAE, compares two pieces of banking software that show the great potential of OSS, especially in the banking field: one open source and one closed source. One of the final chapters in this section, "Challenges and Trends in Home Automation: Addressing the Interoperability Problem With the Open-Source Platform OpenHAB," by Profs. Cristina Portalés and Sergio Casas of the University of Valencia, Spain and Dr. Kai Kreuzer of openHAB Foundation e.V., Germany, analyzes current trends and challenges in HA and proposes a way to deal with the interoperability problem by means of the open source platform openHAB. Another concluding chapter, "Enhancing Information Retrieval System Using Change-Prone Classes," by Prof. Deepa Bura of Manav Rachna International Institute of Research and Studies, India and Prof. Amit Choudhary from Maharaja Surajmal Institute, India, aims to find the association between changes and object-oriented metrics using different versions of open source software using execution time, frequency, run time information, popularity, and class dependency in prediction of change-prone classes. The final chapter in this section, "Optimized Test Case Generation for Object Oriented Systems Using Weka Open Source Software," by Profs. Rajvir Singh and Anita Singhrova of Deenbandhu Chhotu Ram University of Science and Technology, Haryana, India and Prof. Rajesh Bhatia of PEC University of Technology, Chandigarh, India, presents a novel technique for an optimized test case generation for ant-1.7 open source software.

Section 3, "Prediction Models, Big Data, and Statistics," investigates prediction models including fault prediction in open source software, as well as its connection to Big Data. The opening chapter of this section, "Demography of Open Source Software Prediction Models and Techniques," by Profs. Kaniz Fatema and M. M. Mahbubul Syeed of American International University, Bangladesh and Prof. Imed Hammouda of South Mediterranean University, Tunisia, reports on a systematic literature survey aimed at the identification and structuring of research that offers prediction models and techniques in analyzing OSS projects and provides insight into what constitutes the main contributions of the field, identifies gaps and opportunities, and distils several important future research directions. Another opening chapter, "Predicting Change Prone Classes in Open Source Software," by Prof. Amit Choudhary of Maharaja Surajmal Institute, Delhi, India and Profs. Deepa Godara and Rakesh Kumar Singh from Uttarakhand Technical University, Sudhowala, India, focuses on the association between changes and object-oriented metrics using different versions of open source software. The next chapter, "Predicting the Severity of Open Source Bug Reports Using Unsupervised and Supervised Techniques," by Profs. Pushpalatha M. N. and Mrunalini M. of Ramaiah Institute of Technology, Bengaluru, India, uses unsupervised and supervised learning algorithms to automate the prediction of bug report severity. The next chapter, "Ensemble Techniques-Based Software Fault Prediction in an Open-Source Project," by Prof. Wasiur Rhmann of Babasaheb Bhimrao Ambedkar University, Amethi, India and Prof. Gufran Ahmad Ansari from B. S. Abdur Rehman Crescent Institute of Science and Technology, India, uses ensemble models for software fault prediction, collects change metrics-based data for an open source android project from GIT repository, obatins code-based metrics data from PROMISE data repository, and uses datasets kc1, kc2, cm1, and pc1 for experimental purposes. Another chapter, "Generalized Multi-Release Framework for Fault Prediction in Open Source Software," by Profs. Shozab Khurshid and Javaid Iqbal of the University of Kashmir, Srinagar, India and Prof. A.K. Shrivastava of International Management Institute, Kolkata, West Bengal, India, presents a general framework for multi-release OSS modeling incorporating imperfect debugging and change points. The following chapter in this section, "Logging

Analysis and Prediction in Open Source Java Project," by Profs. Sangeeta Lal and Neetu Sardana of Jaypee Institute of Information Technology, India and Prof. Ashish Sureka of Ashoka University, India, performs an in-depth, focused, and large-scale analysis of logging code constructs at two levels: the file level and catch-blocks level and answers several research questions related to statistical and content analysis. The next chapter, "Using Design of Experiments to Analyze Open Source Software Metrics for Change Impact Estimation," by Profs. Miloud Dahane and Mustapha Kamel Abdi of the Université Oran 1, Oran, Algeria; Profs. Mourad Bouneffa and Henri Basson of the Université du Littoral Côte d'Opale, Dunkirk, France; and Dr. Adeel Ahmad from Laboratoire d'Informatique Signal et Image de la Côte d'Opale, Calais, France, describes the use of the design of experiments method to evaluate the influence of variations of software metrics on the change impact in developed software. Another chapter, "Introduction to the Popular Open Source Statistical Software (OSSS)," by Prof. Gao Niu of Bryant University, USA; Prof. Zhijian Wu from New York University, USA; and Prof. Zichen Zhao of Yale University, USA, introduces the two most popular Open Source Statistical Software (OSSS), R, and Python, along with their integrated development environment (IDE) and graphical user interface (GUI). A concluding chapter, "What Is Open Source Software (OSS) and What Is Big Data?" by Prof. Richard S. Segall of Arkansas State University, USA, discusses what Open Source Software is and its relationship to Big Data and how it differs from other types of software and its software development cycle. One of the final chapters in this section, "Open Source Software (OSS) for Big Data," by Prof. Richard S. Segall of Arkansas State University, USA, discusses Open Source Software and associated technologies for the processing of Big Data. The final chapter in this section, "Role of Open Source Software in Big Data Storage," by Profs. Rupali Ahuja, Jigyasa Malik, Ronak Tyagi, and R. Brinda of the University of Delhi, India, discusses the role of open source software in big data storage and how various organizations have benefitted from its use and provides an overview of popular open source big data storage technologies existing today.

Although the primary organization of the contents in this work is based on its three sections offering a progression of coverage of the important concepts, methodologies, technologies, applications, social issues, and emerging trends, the reader can also identify specific contents by utilizing the extensive indexing system listed at the end. As a comprehensive collection of research on the latest findings related to open source software, the *Research Anthology on Usage and Development of Open Source Software* provides computer scientists, programmers, developers, teachers, academicians, researchers, students, and all audiences with a complete understanding of the challenges that face those working with open source software. Given the need for a comprehensive guide on the latest issues, challenges, advancements, and overall history of open source software, this extensive book presents the latest research to address the challenges and provide further opportunities for improvement.

Section 1
Development, Standards, and User Expectations

Chapter 1
A Systematic Review of Attributes and Techniques for Open Source Software Evolution Analysis

Munish Saini

https://orcid.org/0000-0003-4129-2591

Guru Nanak Dev University, India

Kuljit Kaur Chahal

Guru Nanak Dev University, India

ABSTRACT

Many studies have been conducted to understand the evolution process of Open Source Software (OSS). The researchers have used various techniques for understanding the OSS evolution process from different perspectives. This chapter reports a meta-data analysis of the systematic literature review on the topic in order to understand its current state and to identify opportunities for the future. This research identified 190 studies, selected against a set of questions, for discussion. It categorizes the research studies into nine categories. Based on the results obtained from the systematic review, there is evidence of a shift in the metrics and methods for OSS evolution analysis over the period of time. The results suggest that there is a lack of a uniform approach to analyzing and interpreting the results. There is need of more empirical work using a standard set of techniques and attributes to verify the phenomenon governing the OSS projects. This will help to advance the field and establish a theory of software evolution.

1. INTRODUCTION

Due to the rising dominance of Open Source Software (OSS) in the software industry; not only are practitioners, but researchers as well as academicians also keen to understand the OSS development and evolution process. OSS development involves various stakeholders ranging from contributing volunteers

DOI: 10.4018/978-1-7998-9158-1.ch001

to commercial software vendors. There is need to understand the OSS development model in general and OSS evolution in particular so that the evolution process can be improved, if need be, for the future systems.

OSS evolution has attracted a lot of attention in the last decade. Easy and free availability of data on open source projects has resulted in a splurge of studies in this domain. As a result, the number of empirical studies related to OSS is much more in number in comparison to other topics in the field (Stol and Babar, 2009). Various methods have been employed in the past for analysis and prediction of OSS evolution. It is necessary to systematically summarise the empirical evidence obtained on these methods from the existing literature so that it is easy to comprehend the research work in this area, and reveal gaps in the existing work. As per the existing work in this direction, a few studies focusing on the survey of literature in the domain have been published. Fernandez- Ramil et al. (2008) discuss, in an informal way, a small sample (seven in numbers) of OSS evolution studies. Breivold et al. (2010) carry out a systematic literature review of OSS evolution studies (41 in numbers) focusing only on the evolvability characteristic of OSS systems. Syeed et al. (2013) follows a systematic literature review protocol to analyze studies on OSS Evolution. They present review of 101 research papers but their focus is on a limited set of categories of studies. Stol and Babar (2009) reviewed empirical studies reported in four International OSS conferences to assess quality of the papers from the perspective of the way they report the empirical research in OSS. Unlike the present study, their target is not review of studies on OSS evolution but assessment of quality of empirical research papers involving OSS systems. This chapter presents a systematic literature review of an extensive list of research papers published on the subject between the period of 1997 and 2016.

A number of research publications on OSS evolution have explored the phenomenon from different dimensions using different approaches. Broadly two dimensions are taken: Evolution in OSS structure, and Evolution in OSS community. Software structure exploration includes source code analysis, version history analysis, and repository information analysis. Community structure exploration includes social network analysis. Both the dimensions cannot be isolated from each other. They are useful when put together, and complement each other in answering questions regarding the OSS development and evolution process. Analyzing the links between the software structure and the developer community helps in improving software evaluation and quality.

In this chapter, we report a meta-data analysis on comprehensive review on OSS evolution published in the time period of 1997 to 2016 along with discussion on the project attributes and techniques used for analyzing software evolution (Chahal and Saini, 2016a; 2016b).

The rest of the paper is organized as follows: Section 2 presents the research questions that are addressed in this systematic review and the research criteria followed in this study for selection of primary studies. Section 3 presents the answers to the research questions identified in this work. Section 4 gives conclusions and future directions obtained from this systematic review.

2. RESEARCH METHODOLOGY

The review process follows a systematic review protocol (Kitchenham, 2007) so as to reduce the research bias. The review process included the following steps: 1) Defining the research questions, 2) Choosing a search strategy and study selection criteria, and 3) Data Extraction and Synthesis.

To begin with, research questions set the motivation for collection of relevant research studies. An objective quality assessment criterion helps in deciding the selection of studies as per their focus on research questions and quality of presentation as well. OSS evolution studies are categorized under various heads to put the related work at one place for easy understanding. The chapter summarizes the techniques and the empirical evidence available in the reviewed papers. A set of 9 different categories (see Table 1), with further subcategories, are identified for understanding the variety of techniques and methods for OSS evolution.

Table 1. Research questions

Sr. No.	Research Question
1.	Which attributes and techniques have been used for OSS evolution analysis?
2.	Which attributes and techniques have been used for OSS evolution prediction?
3.	Is there any evidence of difference in the evolution of OSS v/s CSS?
4.	How do artifacts, other than source code, evolve in OSS systems?
5.	How has the choice of programming languages changed over the period of time in OSS evolution?
6.	What is the state of software development paradigms such as software reuse in the OSS evolution?
7.	How has the community contribution evolved?
8.	What part of the software evolution process has been automated?
9.	What is the state of the theory of OSS evolution?

For detailed review methodology refer to our previous publications (Chahal and Saini, 2016a; 2016b).

3. RESULTS AND DISCUSSION

This section presents the details of the studies focusing on evolution of OSS systems. After a thorough analysis, 190 studies are selected for discussion here. All these studies address different aspects of the OSS evolution. First, we describe the meta-analysis of the research studies discussing their publication sources, and publication year. Then the results for each research question are discussed in the subsequent sections.

3.1. The Meta-Data Analysis

This section presents the meta-data analysis of the research studies identified for discussion in this chapter.

3.1.1. Publication Sources

Table 2 summarizes the details of the publications in top journals, conferences, workshops, and symposium along with the number indicating the count for studies (the table shows only the publications with count more than 3). Majority of the publications are in the International Conference on Software

Maintenance (ICSM),IEEE Transactions on Software Engineering, International Conference on Software Engineering, International Workshop on Principles of Software Evolution, and Journal of Software Maintenance and Evolution: Research and Practice. A significant portion of the studies is published as conference papers with the ICSM attracting most of the work in this domain. Interestingly, International Conference on Open Source Systems lags way behind ICSM for giving space to studies on OSS evolution, despite its focus on the core domain. It has been observed that researchers prefer to publish their work in conferences as compared to journals (Hermenegildo, 2012). Perhaps the reason is that journal papers are long and take more time to get the work published, whereas conferences let a researcher present, and publish work quickly. Conferences also provide opportunities for social/professional networking with other researchers in the field. Unfortunately, in some countries publishing work in conference proceedings is not encouraged. The University Grants Commission, India in its latest guidelines for promotion of university/college teachers does not assign any API (Application Performance Indicators) score for research publications in conferences. Only the paper presenter can claim the score, not the co-authors.

Table 2. A summary of top publications

Publication Name	Type	Number
International Conference on Software Maintenance	Conference	18
IEEE Transactions on Software Engineering	Journal	8
International Conference on Software Engineering	Conference	7
International Workshop on Principles of Software Evolution	Workshop	7
Journal of Software Maintenance and Evolution: Research And Practice	Journal	6
Journal of Systems and Software	Journal	4
Journal of Empirical Software Engineering	Journal	4
Working Conference on Reverse Engineering	Conference	4
International Conference on Open Source Systems	Conference	4
International Workshop on Mining Software Repositories	Conference	4
Journal of Software: Evolution and Process	Journal	4
Journal of Information and Software Technology	Journal	3
Conference on Software Maintenance and Reengineering	Conference	3
International Workshop on Emerging Trends in Software Metrics	Workshop	3
International Software Metrics Symposium	Symposium	3
IEEE Software	Journal	3

Figure 1 indicates that the journals have the second highest count in the total number of publication sources. Moreover, the research in this domain is not limited to journals or conferences; there are symposiums, workshops, book chapters, technical reports, and other forms of publication as well.

We further explored and found that majority of the publications (Journals/proceedings) are in IEEE (see Figure 2). Next is the ACM for sponsoring conferences alone or with IEEE (ACM/IEEE). In others category, there are publishers like Academia, IGI global, SECC, SERSC, Pearson, Science Direct etc., where publications related to software evolution can be found.

Figure 1. Type of Publication

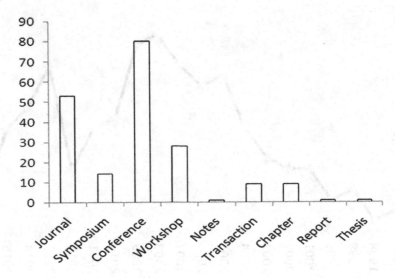

Figure 2. Top Publishers for OSS evolution Studies

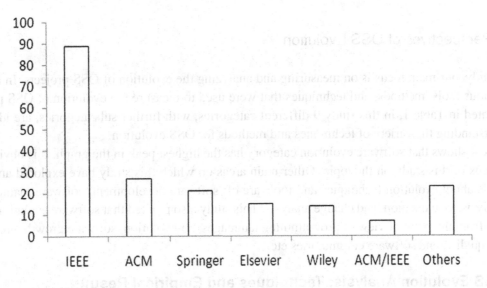

3.1.2. Year Wise Distribution

Figure 3 indicates that in almost all the years (from 1997-2016), there is a study on the software evolution. Therefore, it has been consistently a topic of active interest for the research community. Figure 3 shows that number of research studies increased continuously until 2009. After that the number dropped. It may be attributed to the shift in focus from evolution of single systems (reviewed in this chapter) to evolution of OSS eco systems (out of scope of this study (see section 2 Table 1). The significant drop in the year 2016 may be due to the fact that data for the complete year is not recorded in the study (as it may not be available online at the time of data collection).

Figure 3. Year wise distribution of studies

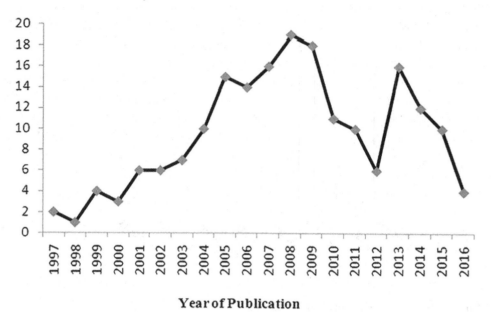

Year of Publication

3.1.3. Perspectives of OSS Evolution

In this study, our main focus is on measuring and analyzing the evolution of OSS projects. In addition to it, various tools, methods, and techniques that were used to measure the evolution of OSS projects. As indicated in Table 1, in this study 9 different categories, with further subcategories, are identified for understanding the variety of techniques and methods for OSS evolution.

Figure 4 shows that software evolution category has the highest peak in the graph. It is obvious due to the focus of this study on the topic. Other main areas on which this study have explored and given the details about evolution techniques and tools are of: software development, software maintenance, code analysis, visualization, and change analysis. This study also pointed that software evolution can be analyzed from the point of view of programming languages, co-evolution, software growth, prediction, software quality, and software communities etc.

3.2. OSS Evolution Analysis: Techniques and Empirical Results

Taking research questions as the points of reference, this section presents the various studies selected in this SLR to analyze their contribution in advancing the state of the art. It summarizes the techniques and the empirical evidence available in the reviewed papers. For a detailed discussion, please refer to these papers (Chahal and Saini, 2016a; 2016b).

Figure 4. Various perspectives of OSS evolution

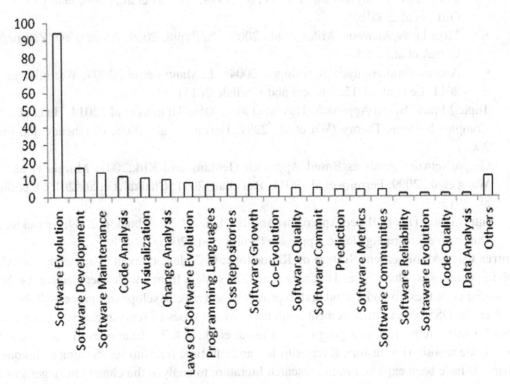

3.2.1. RQ 1: Which Attributes and Techniques Have Been Used for OSS Evolution Analysis?

Based on the studies, we identified the following categories to understand the attributes and techniques the researchers used to analyze OSS evolution.

Broadly, the data is extracted from the following sources, and researchers employ various techniques for analyzing the data:

- **Source Code Analysis:** Measuring different aspects of code has been of interest of researchers as well as practitioners in the software engineering field since long time back, when software measurement was looked up to as a tool to make software development a scientific process. The idea was to make progress in the software development measurable, so that it can be monitored and controlled. Moreover, code quality was thought of as a basis to ensure quality of a software product. Therefore, source code measurement attracted a lot of attention. Among the traditional set of source code metrics, we can include size, complexity, coupling and cohesion metrics. As the paradigms change, more metrics are added to measure the new features such as inheritance in Object Oriented Systems. After extracting the source code, it is analyzed from various perspectives. We noticed the following techniques for analyzing the software evolution in the review papers:
    - Using Metrics
        - Growth Analysis (Godfrey and Tu, 2000; Lehman et al., 2001; Robles et al., 2005; Koch, 2007)

- Complexity Analysis (Tahvildari et al., 1999; Stewart et al., 2006; Darcy et al., 2010; Girba et al.,2005b)
- Modularity Analysis (Milev et al., 2009; Capiluppi, 2009; Alenezi and Zarour, 2015; Olszak et al., 2015)
- Architectural Analysis (Capiluppi, 2004a; LaMantia et al., 2008; Wermilinger et al., 2011; Le et al., 2015; Alenezi and Khellah, 2015)
  - Topic Models Based Approach (Hassan et al., 2005a; Thomas et al., 2014, Hu et al., 2015)
  - Complex Systems Theory (Wu et al., 2007; Herraiz et al., 2008; Gorshenev and Pismak, 2003)
  - Graph/Network Analysis Based Approach (Jenkins and Kirk,2007; Murgia et al., 2009; Wang et al., 2009; Ferreira et al., 2011; Pan et al., 2011; Chaikalis et al., 2015; Kpodjedo et al., 2013)
  - Information Theory Based Approach (Abd-El-Hafiz, 2004; Arbuckle, 2009; Arbuckle, 2011)
  - Qualitative Reasoning Based Approach (Smith et al., 2005)
- **Source Code Management System or Repository:** OSS development is a complex activity involving volunteers. There is need to analyze an OSS system from a wider perspective, i.e. beyond its source code files, to understand and improve the software development process (Robles et al., 2006a). An OSS project management team uses several types of repositories to track the activities of a software project as it progresses (Hassan et al., 2005b). Examples of such repositories are – Code repositories, historical repositories, and run-time repositories. Several techniques and attributes have been explored in the research literature to analyze the change management information available in a code repository.
  - Change analysis (Gefen and Schneberger, 1996; Kemerer and Slaughter, 1997; Schach et al.,2003; Barry et al., 2003; Gupta et al., 2008; Ali and Maqbool, 2009; Hindle et al., 2009a; Meqdadi et al., 2013; Saini and Kaur, 2014a; Ahmed et al., 2015)
  - Change request analysis (Herraiz et al., 2007a; Goulão et al., 2012)
  - Commit analysis (Hattori and Lanza, 2008; Hindle et al., 2009a; Alali et al., 2008; Agrawal et al., 2015; Santos et al., 2016)

3.2.2. RQ2: Which Attributes and Techniques Have Been Used for OSS Evolution Prediction?

Prediction or forecast states the way things are going to occur in future. Time series analysis is the most commonly used tool (Yuen, 1985; 1987; 1988) to predict future attributes, e.g. size, defects of software systems.The software evolution metrics (based on project/process attributes) undertaken for prediction include

- Monthly number of changes (Herraiz, 2007a; Kemerer and S. Slaughter, 1999),
- Change requests (Goulão et al.,2012; Kenmei et al.,2008),
- Size & complexity (Caprio et al., 2001; Fuentetaja et al. 2002),
- Defects (Kläs et al., 2010; Raja et al., 2009),
- Clones (Antoniol et al., 2001), and
- Maintenance effort (Yu, 2006).

Various techniques used for software evolution prediction include. The review studies explore the following models for OSS evolution prediction:

- ARIMA (Caprio et al., 2001; Kenmei et al., 2008)),
- ARMA models (Zhongmin et al., 2010),
- Hybrid models such as ARIMA and SVN (Kemerer and Slaughter,1999; Goulão et al., 2012),
- Data mining techniques (Ratzinger et al., 2007; Siy et al., 2007),
- Signal processing techniques (Dalle et al., 2006),
- Linear regression models (Zimmermann et al.,2007),
- Simulation tools (Smith et al., 2006; Lin, 2013).

A perusal of the existing research in this area shows ARIMA modelling as the most frequently used prediction procedure. However, OSS development is a wobbly process. Unlike the traditional development in which the environment is controlled, OSS development is based on contributions from volunteers who could not be forced to work even if something is of high priority for the project (Godfrey et al., 2000). Along with this unplanned activity, there is a lack of planned documentation related to requirements, and detailed design (Herraiz et al., 2007c). Classical time series techniques are inappropriate for analysis and forecasting of the data which involve random variables (Herraiz et al., 2007b; Kemerer et al., 1999). Fuzzy time series can work for domains which involve uncertainty. Saini and Kaur (2014b) propose to use a computation method of forecasting based on fuzzy time series (Singh, 2008) to predict the number of commits in OSS projects. Fuzzy time series can work for domains which involve uncertainty. Open source projects, sans any tight organizational support, face many uncertainties. Uncertainty lies in uncontrolled development environment such as availability of contributors at any point of time. Due to uncertainty, there is a large fluctuation in consecutive values. Analysis of monthly commits of three OSS projects, Eclipse, PostgreSQL, and Wildfly, indicates that the computation method outperforms the naive random walk model. When the study was expanded to seven OSS projects, the computation method did even better than the ARIMA models (Saini and kaur, 2016).

3.2.3. RQ 3: Is There Any Evidence of Difference in the Evolution of OSS v/s CSS?

Proprietary systems or Closed Source Systems (CSS) are developed following a strict organizational control. With OSS systems getting popular, a comparison of the CSS development process model with the new bazaar style development approach is but natural.

Based on the review, some studies have focused on the comparison of characteristics of OSS with CSS from their evolutionary behavior point of view. They pointed that the evolution of OSS and CSS may or may not vary in terms of

- Growth rate (Paulson et al., 2004); Robles et al., 2003; Capiluppi et al., 2004b; Xie et al., 2009; Neamtiu et al., 2013; Ferreira et al., 2011).
- System features (Mockus et al., 2002)
- Quality of code (Stamelos et al., 2002)
- Creativity (Paulson et al., 2004)
- Changing rate (Paulson et al., 2004)
- Modularity (Paulson et al., 2004)

- Effort estimation models (Fernandez- Ramil et al., 2008)
- Bug-fixing process and release frequency (Rossi et al., 2009)

Unlike CSS systems, OSS systems do not have a constrained growth due to increasing complexity as they evolve. However, software evolution is a discontinuous phenomenon in both the cases.

3.2.4. RQ 4: How Do Artifacts, Other Than Source Code, Evolve in OSS Systems?

Several software artifacts co-evolve with source code. The researchers have studied the evolution of source code with various artifacts, such as

- Build systems (Robles et al., 2006b; Adams et al., 2008; McIntosh et al., 2012)
- Comments (Fluri et al., 2009)
- Test-code (Marsavina et al., 2014)
- Changes related to database schema (Qiu et al., 2013)
- Database related activities (Goeminne et al., 2014)

There are a few studies in which artifacts other than source code are studied together

- Test-code and production code (Zaidman et al., 2011)
- Infrastructure as Code (IaC) files along with three other types of files – source code, test, and build files (Jiang and Adams, 2015)

3.2.5. RQ 5: How Has the Choice of Programming Languages Changed Over the Period of Time in the OSS Evolution?

The development of OSS has initiated a revolution in the development process of software, as most of the software systems nowadays are developed with the support for multiple programming languages (Delorey et al., 2007). However, the choice of programming languages has changed over the period of time.

- Trend in the popularity of different set of programming languages (Karus and Gall, 2011; Bhattacharya et al., 2011)
  - Scripting and Interpreter based (platform independent) languages are more popular (Robles et al., 2006b)
- Choice of language viz-a-viz developer productivity, and defect density (Phipps, 1999; Myrtveit et al., 2008)
- Choice of language and gender of the developers (Dattero and Galup, 2004)

3.2.6. RQ 6: What Is the State of Software Development Paradigms Such as Software Reuse in the OSS Evolution?

Software reuse is a means for overcoming software crisis (Pressman, 2010). McIlroy (1968) pointed towards the reuse of code to build large reliable software systems in a controlled and cost effective way.

It has been observed that OSS projects make extensive use of (third party) reusable software components (Zaimi et al., 2015). A few other papers that studied software reuse aspects in OSS projects are as follows:

- Developers' choice of evolutionary reuse for cost efficiency (Capra, 2006).
- Differences in the nature of evolution of libraries v/s applications (Vaucher and Sahraoui, 2007).
- The effect of reuse based development style on the evolution of software systems (Gupta et al., 2008).
- The evolutionary aspects of reusable software components (Kaur, 2013).

3.2.7. RQ 7: How Has the Community Contribution Evolved?

The development of OSS is not a well-planned activity (Goulão et al., 2012). A few people start an OSS project, users of the OSS system contribute to make changes to satisfy their own requirements, and the system starts evolving. Users and developers of an OSS project are called the OSS community. Community drives the evolution of OSS (Girba et al., 2005a). Research studies discussed the OSS community from different points of view:

- To identify reasonable community size to sustain an OSS project (Mockus et al., 2002; Capiluppi, 2003).
- The community dynamics (Nakakoji et al., 2002).
- Stability of the Community support (Robles et al., 2005).
- Developer productivity (Capiluppi et al., 2004b).
- Inequality in work distribution in OSS projects (Koch et al., 2007; Mockus et al., 2002)
- Team profile and structure in large vs small OSS projects (Xu et al., 2005)
- The deadline effect (Lin et al., 2013).
- Predicting next release date on the basis of community activity (Weicheng et al., 2013).

3.2.8. RQ 8: What Part of the Software Evolution Process Has Been Automated?

Automated support for a software engineering task is always appreciated as it can not only help to handle large volumes of data but also makes the task easily repeatable. Several tools have been created to handle comparison of successive versions of OSS systems, and to answer software evolution related questions. Some of these tools are

- Beagle (Tu and Godfrey, 2002)
- Kenyon (Bevan et al., 2005)
- Ferret (Rainer et al., 2008).
- Churrasco (D'Ambros and Lanza, 2010)
- CodeVizard (Zazworka and Ackermann, 2010).
- Replay (Hattori et al., 2013)

3.2.9. RQ 9: What Is the State of Theory of OSS Evolution?

In software evolution, Lehman's laws (1974, 1978, 1996) can be the best (and the only) example of a theory, though many empirical studies have refuted these laws in the context of OSS evolution. Several studies checked the applicability of Lehman's laws:

- Anomaly in the applicability of the laws (Godfrey and Tu, 2000, Robles et al., 2005).
- Confirmed the two laws related to continuous change (1st law), and continuous growth (6th law) (Godfrey and Tu, 2000, 2001; Bauer and Pizka, 2003; Wu and Holt, 2004; Robles et al., 2005; Herraiz et al., 2006; Koch, 2005, 2007; Mens et al., 2008; Israeli and Feitelson, 2010; Vasa, 2010; and Neamtiu et al., 2013).
- The fourth law confirmed only in (Israeli and Feitelson, 2010).
- The fifth law confirmed only in (Vasa, 2010).
- Only Bauer and Pizka (2003) confirm all the eight laws.
- Lehman's laws for small v/s large systems (Roy and Cordy, 2006; Koch, 2007).

All these studies lack a uniform approach to analyze and interpret the results. There are multiple interpretations of the statements defining the laws. The metrics for measuring the constructs to validate the laws are defined differently in different studies.

With the availability of tools and data resources in the public domain, researchers can now repeat experiments and build empirical evidence to confirm/refute the laws. However, collecting empirical evidence is only the first stage for theory building. It has to be followed by hypothesis formulation, testing, and then optimization (Godfrey and German, 2008). In the new context, laws should be reformulated to suit the changing software development paradigms as they have not been since 1996.

4. CONCLUSION AND FUTURE GUIDELINES

Open Source Software has been able to get a lot of attention of the research community as it is easy not only to prove a new concept, but also to repeat the experiments on OSS data sets available in the public domain. The meta-data analysis depicts valuable facts such as:

- Most of the contributors prefer to publish their work in conferences as compared to journals.
- The evolution of OSS is measured by using different methods, tools and techniques.
- IEEE and ACM are among the publishers who published research related to OSS evolution.

Some of the other major revelations of the review results are as follows:

- Software size has been the most common attribute to analyze evolution of OSS projects. Several types of metrics have been employed to measure software size. These metrics range from coarse grained level metrics such as number of files, modules, and functions, to fine grained level metrics such as number of LOC, methods, and classes. Several approaches, other than source code analysis using metrics, to analyze OSS evolution have also been employed in the research literature.

- Lately, metrics related to change activity have also been included to understand OSS evolution. These metrics measure changes in source code such as number of program elements (functions/classes/methods) changed in consecutive versions. Change activity as recorded in SCM systems is also used in a few cases. Most of the work deals with finding change size, change effort distributions. A few studies do change profile analysis as OSS systems evolve. But that is restricted to a few of the change categories e.g. adaptive v/s non-adaptive changes, or corrective v/s non-corrective changes. A fine-grained view of the changes can help to answer amount of progressive/ regressive work performed in a software system as it evolves. It can also be used to validate Lehman's 2nd law as Gonzalez-Barahona (2014) points to the lack of information available in this regard in their study of the glibc system.

- Herraiz et al. (2007c) observed that there are no long term correlations in the time series representing OSS activity. There is need to explore other alternative methods for time series analysis (rather than ARIMA) to deal with the uncertain evolutionary behavior of OSS systems.

- A shift in the programming languages, from procedural to object oriented, has been noticed as OSS systems, as subject systems in the corresponding studies, evolved over the period of time.

- Techniques and tools have been devised to tackle large amounts of data generated in software evolution analysis and prediction. Software evolution automation offers to collect volumes of data in a consistent manner. Software evolution visualization helps in understanding the transitions in complex and large systems in an easy way. Big data analytics can also help to analyze large sets of data generated during software evolution. Data analytics can be used to manage and understand the complex web of software evolution as it happens in source code and other related repositories.

REFERENCES

Abd-El-Hafiz, S. (2004). *An Information Theory Approach to Studying Software Evolution. Alexandria Engineering Journal, 43*(2), 275–284.

Adams, B., De Schutter, K., Tromp, H., & De Meuter, W. (2008). The evolution of the Linux build system. *Electronic Communications of the EASST, 8.*

Agrawal, K., Amreen, S., & Mockus, A. (2015). Commit quality in five high performance computing projects. In *International Workshop on Software Engineering for High Performance Computing in Science* (pp. 24-29). IEEE Press. 10.1109/SE4HPCS.2015.11

Ahmed, I., Mannan, U., Gopinath, R., & Jensen, C. (2015). An Empirical Study of Design Degradation: How Software Projects Get Worse over Time. *Proceedings of the 2015 ACM/IEEE International Symposium on Empirical Software Engineering and Measurement*, 1 – 10. 10.1109/ESEM.2015.7321186

Alali, A., Kagdi, H., & Maletic, J. (2008). What's a Typical Commit? A Characterization of Open Source Software Repositories. In *Proceedings of the 16th International Conference on Program Comprehension* (pp. 182-191). IEEE. 10.1109/ICPC.2008.24

Alenezi, M., & Khellah, F. (2015). Architectural Stability Evolution in Open-Source Systems. In *Proceedings of the International Conference on Engineering & MIS 2015 (ICEMIS '15)*. ACM. 10.1145/2832987.2833014

Alenezi, M., & Zarour, M. (2015). Modularity Measurement and Evolution in Object-Oriented Open-Source Projects. In *Proceedings of the International Conference on Engineering & MIS (ICEMIS '15)*. doi:10.1145/2832987.2833013

Ali, S., & Maqbool, O. (2009). Monitoring Software Evolution Using Multiple Types of Changes. In *Proceedings of the 2009 International Conference on Emerging Technologies* (pp. 410-415). IEEE. 10.1109/ICET.2009.5353135

Antoniol, G., Casazza, G., Penta, M., & Merlo, E. (2001). Modeling Clones Evolution through Time Series. In *Proceedings of the IEEE International Conference on Software Maintenance* (pp. 273-280). IEEE.

Arbuckle, T. (2009). Measure Software and its Evolution-using Information Content. In *Proceedings of the joint international and annual ERCIM workshops on Principles of Software Evolution (IWPSE) and Software Evolution (Evol) Workshops* (pp. 129-134). ACM. doi:10.1145/1595808.1595831

Arbuckle, T. (2011). Studying Software Evolution using Artifacts Shared Information Content. *Science of Computer Programming*, *76*(12), 1078–1097. doi:10.1016/j.scico.2010.11.005

Barry, E., Kemerer, C., & Slaughter, S. (2003). On the Uniformity of Software Evolution Patterns. *Proceedings of the 25th International Conference on Software Engineering*, 106-113. 10.1109/ICSE.2003.1201192

Bauer, A., & Pizka, M. (2003). The Contribution of Free Software to Software Evolution. In *Proceedings of the Sixth International Workshop on Principles of Software Evolution* (pp. 170-179). IEEE. 10.1109/IWPSE.2003.1231224

Bevan, J., Whitehead, E. Jr, Kim, S., & Godfrey, M. (2005). Facilitating Software Evolution Research with Kenyon. *Software Engineering Notes*, *30*(5), 177–186. doi:10.1145/1095430.1081736

Bhattacharya, P., & Neamtiu, I. (2011). Assessing Programming Language Impact on Development and Maintenance: A Study on C and C++. In *Proceedings of the 33rd International Conference on Software Engineering (ICSE)* (pp. 171-180). IEEE. 10.1145/1985793.1985817

Breivold, H., Chauhan, M., & Babar, M. (2010) A Systematic Review of Studies of Open Source Software Evolution. *Proceedings of the 17th Asia Pacific Software Engineering Conference (APSEC)*, 356-365. 10.1109/APSEC.2010.48

Capiluppi, A. (2003). Models for the Evolution of OS Projects. In *Proceedings of International Conference on Software Maintenance (ICSM)*. IEEE. 10.1109/ICSM.2003.1235407

Capiluppi, A. (2009). Domain Drivers in the Modularization of FLOSS Systems. Open Source EcoSystems: Diverse Communities Interacting. In C. Boldyreff, K. Crownston, B. Lundell et al. (Eds.), *Proceedings of the 5th IFIP WG 2.13 International Conference on Open Source Systems OSS '09*. Skovde, Sweden: Springer. 10.1007/978-3-642-02032-2_3

Capiluppi, A., Morisio, M., & Ramil, J. (2004a). The Evolution of Source folder structure in actively evolved Open Source Systems. In *Proceedings of the 10th International Symposium on Software metrics (METRICS '04)* (pp. 2-13). IEEE Computer Society, 10.1109/METRIC.2004.1357886

Capiluppi, A., Morisio, M., & Ramil, J. (2004b). Structural Evolution of an Open Source System: A case study. *Proceedings of the International Workshop on Program Comprehension.* 10.1109/WPC.2004.1311059

Capra, E. (2006). Mining Open Source web repositories to measure the cost of Evolutionary reuse. In *Proceedings of the 1st International Conference on Digital Information Management* (pp. 496-503). IEEE.

Caprio, F., Casazza, G., Penta, M., & Villano, U. (2001). Measuring and predicting the Linux kernel Evolution. *Proceedings of the Seventh Workshop on Empirical Studies of Software Maintenance*, 77.

Chahal, K. K., & Saini, M. (2016a). Open Source Software Evolution: A Systematic Literature Review (Part 1). *International Journal of Open Source Software and Processes*, 7(1), 1–27. doi:10.4018/IJOSSP.2016010101

Chahal, K. K., & Saini, M. (2016b). Open Source Software Evolution: A Systematic Literature Review (Part 2). *International Journal of Open Source Software and Processes*, 7(1), 28–48. doi:10.4018/IJOSSP.2016010102

Chaikalis, T., & Chatzigeorgiou, A. (2015). Forecasting Java Software Evolution Trends Employing Network Models. *IEEE Transactions on Software Engineering*, 41(6), 582–602. doi:10.1109/TSE.2014.2381249

D'Ambros, M., & Lanza, M. (2010). Distributed and Collaborative Software Evolution Analysis with Churrasco. *Science of Computer Programming*, 75.

Dalle, J. M., Daudet, L., & den Besten, M. (2006). Mining CVS signals. *Proceedings of the Workshop on Public Data about Software Development*, 12-21.

Darcy, P., Daniel, L., & Stewart, K. (2010). Exploring Complexity in Open Source Software: Evolutionary Patterns, Antecedents, and Outcomes. In *Proceedings of the 2010 43rd Hawaii International Conference on System Sciences (HICSS)*. IEEE Press. 10.1109/HICSS.2010.198

Dattero, R., & Galup, S. (2004). Programming languages and Gender. *Communications of the ACM*, 47(1), 99–102. doi:10.1145/962081.962087

Delorey, D., Knutson, C., & Giraud-Carrier, C. (2007). Programming language trends in Open Source development: An evaluation using data from all production phase Sourceforge Projects. *Proceedings of the Second International Workshop on Public Data about Software Development (WoPDaSD'07)*.

Fernandez-Ramil, J., Lozano, A., Wermilinger, M., & Capiluppi, A. (2008). Empirical Studies of Open Source Evolution. In T. Mens & S. Demeyer (Eds.), *Software Evolution* (pp. 263–288). Berlin: Springer. doi:10.1007/978-3-540-76440-3_11

Ferreira, K., Bigonha, A., Bigonha, S., & Gomes, M. (2011). Software Evolution Characterization-a Complex Network Approach. *Proceedings of the X Brazilian Symposium on Software Quality-SBQS*, 41-55.

Fluri, B., Würsch, M., Giger, E., & Gall, H. (2009). Analyzing the Co-Evolution of Comments and Source code. *Software Quality Journal, 17*(4), 367–394. doi:10.100711219-009-9075-x

Fuentetaja, E., & Bagert, D. (2002). Software Evolution from a Time-series Perspective. In *Proceedings International Conference on Software Maintenance* (pp. 226-229). IEEE. 10.1109/ICSM.2002.1167769

Gefen, D., & Schneberger, S. (1996). The Non-homogeneous Maintenance Periods: a Case Study of Software Modifications. In *Proceedings International Conference on Software Maintenance* (pp. 134-141). IEEE. 10.1109/ICSM.1996.564998

Girba, T., Kuhn, A., Seeberger, M., & Ducasse, S. (2005a). How Developers Drive Software Evolution. In *Proceedings of the Eighth International Workshop on Principles of Software Evolution* (pp. 113-122). IEEE. 10.1109/IWPSE.2005.21

Girba, T., Lanza, M., & Ducasse, S. (2005b). Characterizing the Evolution of Class Hierarchies. In *Proceedings of the Ninth European Conference on Software Maintenance and Reengineering (CSMR)* (pp. 2-11). IEEE. 10.1109/CSMR.2005.15

Godfrey, M., & German, D. (2008). Frontiers of software maintenance track. In *International Conference on Software Engineering* (pp. 129-138). IEEE.

Godfrey, M., & Tu, Q. (2000). Evolution in Open Source Software: A case study. In *Proceedings of the International Conference on Software Maintenance* (pp. 131–142). IEEE. 10.1109/ICSM.2000.883030

Godfrey, M., & Tu, Q. (2001). Growth, Evolution, and Structural Change in Open Source Software. In *Proc. of the 2001 Intl. Workshop on Principles of Software Evolution (IWPSE-01)* (pp. 103-106). IEEE.

Goeminne, M., Decan, A., & Mens, T. (2014). Co-evolving Code-related and Database-related Changes in a Data-intensive Software System. *Proceedings of the IEEE Conference on Software Maintenance, Reengineering and Reverse Engineering (CSMR-WCRE)*, 353–357. 10.1109/CSMR-WCRE.2014.6747193

Gonzalez-Barahona, J. M., Robles, G., Herraiz, I., & Ortega, F. (2014). Studying the laws of software evolution in a long-lived FLOSS project. *Journal of Software: Evolution and Process, 26*(7), 589–612. PMID:25893093

Gorshenev, A., & Pismak, M. (2003). Punctuated Equilibrium in Software Evolution. *Physical Review E: Statistical, Nonlinear, and Soft Matter Physics, 70*(6). PMID:15697556

Goulão, M., Fonte, N., Wermelinger, M., & Abreu, F. (2012). Software Evolution Prediction Using Seasonal Time Analysis: A Comparative Study. *Proceedings of 16th European Conference Software Maintenance and Reengineering (CSMR)*, 213-222. 10.1109/CSMR.2012.30

Gupta, A., Cruzes, D., Shull, F., Conradi, R., Rønneberg, H., & Landre, E. (2008). An examination of Change Profiles in reusable and non-reusable Software Systems. *Journal of Software Maintenance and Evolution: Research and Practice, 22*(5), 359–380.

Hassan, A., Mockus, A., Holt, R., & Johnson, P. (2005b). Special issue on Mining Software Repositories. *IEEE Transactions on Software Engineering, 31*(6), 426–428. doi:10.1109/TSE.2005.70

Hassan, A., Wu, J., & Holt, R. (2005a). Visualizing Historical Data Using Spectrographs. In *Proceedings of the 11th IEEE International Software Metrics Symposium (METRICS '05)*. IEEE Computer Society. 10.1109/METRICS.2005.54

Hattori, L., D'Ambros, M., Lanza, M., & Lungu, M. (2013). Answering Software Evolution Questions: An Empirical Evaluation. *Information and Software Technology, 55*(4), 755–775. doi:10.1016/j.infsof.2012.09.001

Hattori, L., & Lanza, M. (2008). On the Nature of Commits. In *Proceedings of the 23rd IEEE/ACM International Conference on Automated Software Engineering-Workshops* (pp. 63-71). IEEE.

Hermenegildo, M. V. (2012). *Conferences vs. journals in CS, what to do? Evolutionary ways forward and the ICLP/TPLP model*. Leibniz-ZentrumfürInformatik.

Herraiz, I., Gonzalez-Barahona, J., & Robles, G. (2007a). Forecasting the Number of Changes in Eclipse using Time Series Analysis. In *Proceedings of the 2007 Fourth International Workshop on Mining Software Repositories MSR'07* (pp. 32-32). IEEE. 10.1109/MSR.2007.10

Herraiz, I., Gonzalez-Barahona, J., & Robles, G. (2007b). Towards a Theoretical Model for Software Growth. In *Proceedings of the Fourth International Workshop on Mining Software Repositories* (p. 21). IEEE Computer Society. 10.1109/MSR.2007.31

Herraiz, I., Gonzalez-Barahona, J., Robles, G., & German, D. (2007c).On the prediction of the Evolution of libre Software Projects. In *Proceedings of the 2007 IEEE International Conference on Software Maintenance (ICSM '07)* (pp. 405-414). IEEE. 10.1109/ICSM.2007.4362653

Herraiz, I., Gonzlez-Barahona, J., & Robles, G. (2008). Determinism and Evolution. In A. Hassan, M. Lanza, & M. Godfrey (Eds.), *Mining Software Repositories*. ACM. doi:10.1145/1370750.1370752

Herraiz, I., Robles, G., González-Barahona, J., Capiluppi, A., & Ramil, J. (2006). Comparison between SLOCs and Number of files as Size Metrics for Software Evolution analysis. In *Proceedings of the 10th European Conference on Software Maintenance and Reengineering (CSMR '06)* (p. 8). IEEE. 10.1109/CSMR.2006.17

Hindle, A., German, D., Godfrey, M., & Holt, R. (2009a). Automatic Classification of Large Changes into Maintenance Categories. In *Proceedings of the 17th International Conference on Program Comprehension ICPC'09* (pp. 30-39). IEEE.

Hu, J., Sun, X., Lo, D., & Bin, L. (2015). Modeling the Evolution of Development Topics using Dynamic Topic Models. *Proceedings of the 2015 IEEE 22nd International Conference on Software Analysis, Evolution and Reengineering*, 3-12. 10.1109/SANER.2015.7081810

Israeli, A., & Feitelson, D. (2010). The Linux Kernel as a Case Study in Software Evolution. *Journal of Systems and Software, 83*(3), 485–501. doi:10.1016/j.jss.2009.09.042

Izurieta, C., & Bieman, J. (2006). The Evolution of FreeBSD and Linux. In *Proceedings of the 2006 ACM/IEEE international symposium on Empirical Software engineering* (pp. 204-211). ACM. 10.1145/1159733.1159765

Jenkins, S., & Kirk, S. (2007). Software Architecture Graphs as Complex Networks: A Novel Partitioning Scheme to Measure Stability and Evolution. *Information Sciences*, *177*(12), 2587–2601. doi:10.1016/j. ins.2007.01.021

Jiang, Y., & Adams, B. (2015). Co-Evolution of Infrastructure and Source Code: An Empirical Study. In *Proceedings of the 12th Working Conference on Mining Software Repositories (MSR '15)* (pp. 45-55). Piscataway, NJ: IEEE Press. 10.1109/MSR.2015.12

Karus, S., & Gall, H. (2011). A Study of Language Usage Evolution in Open Source Software. In *Proceedings of the 8th Working Conference on Mining Software Repositories* (pp. 13-22). ACM. 10.1145/1985441.1985447

Kaur, K. (2013). Analyzing Growth Trends of Reusable Software Components. In H. Singh & K. Kaur (Eds.), *Designing, Engineering, and Analyzing Reliable and Efficient Software*. Hershey, PA: IGI Global; doi:10.4018/978-1-4666-2958-5.ch003

Kemerer, C., & Slaughter, S. (1997). A Longitudinal Analysis of Software Maintenance Patterns. In *Proceedings of the eighteenth international conference on Information Systems* (pp. 476-477). Association for Information Systems.

Kemerer, C., & Slaughter, S. (1999). An Empirical Approach to Studying Software Evolution. *IEEE Transactions on Software Engineering*, *25*(4), 493–509. doi:10.1109/32.799945

Kenmei, B., Antoniol, G., & Penta, M. (2008). Trend Analysis and Issue Prediction in Large-scale Open Source Systems. In *Proceedings of the 12th European Conference on Software Maintenance and Reengineering (CSMR'08)* (pp. 73-82). IEEE. 10.1109/CSMR.2008.4493302

Kitchenham, B. (2007). *Guidelines for Performing Systematic Literature Review in Software Engineering*. Technical report EBSE-2007-001.

Kläs, M., Elberzhager, F., Münch, J., Hartjes, K., & Von Graevemeyer, O. (2010). Transparent Combination of Expert and Measurement Data for Defect Prediction: an Industrial Case Study. In *Proceedings of the 32nd ACM/IEEE International Conference on Software Engineering* (Vol. 2, pp. 119-128). ACM. 10.1145/1810295.1810313

Koch, S. (2005). Evolution of Open Source System Software Systems - a Large Scale Investigation. *Proceedings of the First International Conference on Open Source Systems*.

Koch, S. (2007). Software Evolution in Open Source Projects—a Large-scale Investigation. *Journal of Software Maintenance and Evolution: Research and Practice*, *19*(6), 361–382. doi:10.1002mr.348

Kpodjedo, S., Ricca, F., Galinier, P., & Antoniol, G. (2013). Studying Software Evolution of Large Object Oriented Software Systems using an etgm Algorithm. *Journal of Software: Evolution and Process*, *25*(2), 139–163.

LaMantia, M., Cai, Y., MacCormack, A., & Rusnak, J. (2008). Analyzing the Evolution of large-scale Software Systems using Design Structure Matrices and Design Rule Theory: Two Exploratory Cases. In *Proceedings of theSeventh Working IEEE/IFIP Conference on Software Architecture (WICSA '08)* (pp. 83-92). IEEE. doi:10.1109/WICSA.2008.49

Le, D., Behnamghader, P., Garcia, J., Link, D., Shahbazian, A., & Medvidovic, N. (2015). An Empirical Study of Architectural Change in Open-Source Software Systems. In *Proceedings of the 12th Working Conference on Mining Software Repositories (MSR '15)* (pp. 235-245). IEEE. 10.1109/MSR.2015.29

Lehman, M. (1996). Laws of Software Evolution Revisited. In *Proceedings of the European Workshop on Software Process Technology* (pp. 108-124). Springer-Verlag. 10.1007/BFb0017737

Lehman, M., Ramil, J., & Sandler, U. (2001). An Approach to Modeling Long-term Growth Trends in Software Systems. In *Proceedings of the International Conference on Software Maintenance* (pp. 219–228). IEEE.

Lin, S., Ma, Y., & Chen, J. (2013). Empirical Evidence on Developer's Commit Activity for Open-Source Software Projects. *Proceedings of the 25th International Conference on Software Engineering and Knowledge Engineering*, 455-460.

Marsavina, C., Romano, D., & Zaidman, A. (2014). Studying Fine-Grained Co-Evolution Patterns of Production and Test Code. *Proceedings of the 2014 IEEE 14th International Working Conference on Source Code Analysis and Manipulation (SCAM)*, 195-204. 10.1109/SCAM.2014.28

McIntosh, S., Adams, B., & Hassan, A. (2012). The Evolution of Java build Systems. *Empirical Software Engineering*, *17*(4), 578–608. doi:10.100710664-011-9169-5

McIlroy, M. (1968). *Mass Produced Software Components*. Keynote address in NATO Software Engineering Conference.

Mens, T., Fernández-Ramil, J., & Degrandsart, S. (2008). The Evolution of Eclipse. In *Proceedings of the 2008 IEEE International Conference on Software Maintenance (ICSM)* (pp. 386-395). IEEE. 10.1109/ICSM.2008.4658087

Meqdadi, O., Alhindawi, N., Collard, M., & Maletic, J. (2013). Towards Understanding Large-scale Adaptive Changes from Version Histories. In *Proceedings of the 2013 IEEE International Conference on Software Maintenance* (pp. 416-419). IEEE. 10.1109/ICSM.2013.61

Milev, R., Muegge, S., & Weiss, M. (2009). Design Evolution of an Open Source Project using an Improved Modularity Metric. In *Proceedings of the 5th IFIP WG 2.13 International Conference on Open Source Systems OSS '09*. Skovde, Sweden: Springer. 10.1007/978-3-642-02032-2_4

Mockus, A., Fielding, R., & Herbsleb, J. (2002). Two case studies of Open Source Software development: Apache and Mozilla. *ACM Transactions on Software Engineering and Methodology*, *11*(3), 309–346. doi:10.1145/567793.567795

Murgia, A., Concas, G., Marchesi, M., Tonelli, R., & Turnu, I. (2009). Empirical study of Software Quality Evolution in Open Source Projects using Agile Practices. *Proceedings of the International symposium on Emerging Trends in Software Metrics (ETSM)*.

Myrtveit, I., & Stensrud, E. (2008). *An Empirical Study of Software development Productivity in C and C++*. Presented at NIK-2008 conference. Retrieved from www.nik.no

Nakakoji, K., Yamamoto, Y., Nishinaka, Y., Kishida, K., & Ye, Y. (2002). Evolution Patterns of Open-Source Software Systems and Communities. In *Proceedings of the international workshop on Principles of Software Evolution* (pp. 76-85). ACM. 10.1145/512035.512055

Neamtiu, I., Xie, G., & Chen, J. (2013). Towards a Better Understanding of Software Evolution: An Empirical Study on Open-Source Software. *Journal of Software: Evolution and Process, 25*(3), 193–218.

Olszak, A., Lazarova-Molnar, S., & Jørgensen, B. (2015). Evolution of Feature-Oriented Software: How to Stay on Course and Avoid the Cliffs of Modularity Drift. In *Proceedings of the 9th International Joint Conference Software Technologies, CCIS* (Vol. 555, pp. 183-201). Springer.

Pan, W., Li, B., Ma, Y., & Liu, J. (2011). Multi-Granularity Evolution Analysis of Software. *Journal of Systems Science and Complexity, 24*(6), 1068–1082. doi:10.100711424-011-0319-z

Paulson, J., Succi, G., & Eberlein, A. (2004). An Empirical Study of Open-Source and Closed-Source Software products. *IEEE Transactions on Software Engineering, 30*(4), 246–256. doi:10.1109/TSE.2004.1274044

Phipps, G. (1999). Comparing Observed Bug and Productivity Rates for Java and C++. *Software, Practice & Experience, 29*(4), 345–358. doi:10.1002/(SICI)1097-024X(19990410)29:4<345::AID-SPE238>3.0.CO;2-C

Pressman, R. (2010). *Software Engineering – A Practitioner's Approach* (7th ed.). McGraw Hill Education.

Qiu, D., Li, B., & Su, Z. (2013). An Empirical Analysis of the Co-Evolution of Schema and Code in Database Applications. In Meeting on Foundations of Software Engineering, ser. ESEC/FSE 2013 (pp. 125–135). ACM. doi:10.1145/2491411.2491431

Rainer, A., Lane, P., Malcolm, J., & Scholz, S. (2008). Using N-grams to Rapidly Characterise the Evolution of Software code. In *Proceedings of the 23rd IEEE/ACM International Conference on Automated Software Engineering Workshops* (pp. 43-52). IEEE. 10.1109/ASEW.2008.4686320

Raja, U., Hale, D., & Hale, J. (2009). Modeling Software Evolution Defects: A Time Series Approach. *Journal of Software Maintenance and Evolution: Research and Practice, 21*(1), 49–71. doi:10.1002mr.398

Ratzinger, J., Gall, H., & Pinzger, M. (2007). Quality Assessment Based on Attribute Series of Software Evolution. In *Proceedings of the 14th Working Conference on Reverse Engineering WCRE '07* (pp. 80-89). IEEE. 10.1109/WCRE.2007.39

Robles, G., Amor, J., Gonzalez-Barahona, J., & Herraiz, I. (2005). Evolution and Growth in Large Libre Software Projects. In *Proceedings of the International Workshop on Principles in Software Evolution* (pp. 165-174). IEEE. 10.1109/IWPSE.2005.17

Robles, G., Gonzalez-Barahona, J., & Merelo, J. (2006a). Beyond Source Code: The Importance of other Artifacts in Software Development. *Journal of Systems and Software, 79*(9), 1233–1248. doi:10.1016/j.jss.2006.02.048

Robles, G., Gonzalez-Barahona, J., Michlmayr, M., & Amor, J. (2006b). Mining Large Software Compilations over Time: Another Perspective of Software Evolution. In *Proceedings of the 2006 international workshop on Mining Software repositories (MSR'06)* (pp. 3-9). ACM 10.1145/1137983.1137986

Robles-Martinez, G., Gonzlez-Barahona, J., Centeno-Gonzalez, J., Matellan-Olivera, V., & Rodero-Merino, L. (2003). Studying the Evolution of Libre Software Projects using Publicly Available Data. *Proceedings of the 3rd Workshop on Open Source Software Engineering*.

Rossi, B., Russo, B., & Succi, G. (2009) Analysis of Open Source Software Development Iterations by Means of Burst Detection Techniques, In Open Source EcoSystems: Diverse Communities Interacting. In *Proceedings 5th IFIP WG 2.13 International Conference on Open Source Systems* (pp. 83-93). Springer.

Roy, C., & Cordy, J. (2006). *Evaluating the Evolution of Small Scale Open Source Software Systems*. Academic Press.

Saini, M., & Kaur, K. (2014a). Analyzing the Change Profiles of Software Systems using their Change Logs. International Journal of Software Engineering, 7(2), 39-66.

Saini, M., & Kaur, K. (2014b). Software Evolution Prediction using Fuzzy Analysis. In *Proceedings of International Conference on Emerging Applications of Information Technology, organized by Computer Society of India at Indian Institute of Science*. Kolkata, India: IEEE Computer Society Press.

Saini, M., & Kaur, K. (2016). Fuzzy analysis and prediction of commit activity in open source software projects. *IET Software*, *10*(5), 136–146. doi:10.1049/iet-sen.2015.0087

Santos, E. A., & Hindle, A. (2016). Judging a commit by its cover; or can a commit message predict build failure?. *PeerJ PrePrints, 4*, e1771v1.

Schach, S., Jin, B., Yu, L., Heller, G., & Offutt, J. (2003). Determining the Distribution of Maintenance Categories: Survey versus Measurement. *Empirical Software Engineering*, *8*(4), 351–365. doi:10.1023/A:1025368318006

Singh, S. (2008). A Computational Method of Forecasting Based on Fuzzy Time Series. *Journal of Mathematics and Computers in Simulation*, *79*(3), 539–554. doi:10.1016/j.matcom.2008.02.026

Siy, H., Chundi, P., Rosenkrant, D., & Subramaniam, M. (2007). Discovering Dynamic Developer Relationships from Software Version Histories by Time Series Segmentation. In *Proceedings of the 2007 IEEE International Conference on Software Maintenance* (pp. 415-424). IEEE. 10.1109/ICSM.2007.4362654

Smith, N., Capiluppi, A., & Fernandez-Ramil, J. (2006). Agent-based Simulation of Open Source Software Evolution. *Software Process Improvement and Practice*, *11*(4), 423–434. doi:10.1002pip.280

Smith, N., Capiluppi, A., & Ramil, J. (2005). A Study of Open Source Software Evolution Data using Qualitative Simulation. *Software Process Improvement and Practice*, *10*(3), 287–300. doi:10.1002pip.230

Stamelos, I., Angelis, L., Oikonomou, A., & Bleris, G. L. (2002). Code quality analysis in open source software development. *Information Systems Journal*, *12*(1), 43–60. doi:10.1046/j.1365-2575.2002.00117.x

Stewart, K., Darcy, D., & Daniel, S. (2006). Opportunities and Challenges Applying Functional Data Analysis to the Study of Open Source Software Evolution. *Statistical Science*, *21*(2), 167–178. doi:10.1214/088342306000000141

Stol, K., & Babar, M. (2009). Reporting Empirical Research in Open Source Software: the State of Practice. In *Proceedings 5th IFIP WG 2.13 International Conference on Open Source Systems OSS '09.* Skovde, Sweden: Springer. 10.1007/978-3-642-02032-2_15

Syeed, M., Hammouda, I., & Systa, T. (2013). Evolution of Open Source Software Projects: A Systematic Literature Review. *Journal of Software, 8*(11).

Tahvildari, L., Gregory, R., & Kontogiannis, K. (1999). An Approach for Measuring Software Evolution using Source Code Features. In *Proceedings of the Sixth Asia Pacific Software Engineering Conference (APSEC '99)* (pp. 10-17). IEEE. 10.1109/APSEC.1999.809579

Thomas, S., Adams, B., Hassan, A., & Blostein, D. (2014). Studying Software Evolution using Topic Models. *Science of Computer Programming, 80,* 457–479. doi:10.1016/j.scico.2012.08.003

Tu, Q., & Godfrey, M. (2002). An Integrated Approach for Studying Architectural Evolution. In *Proceedings of the 10th International Workshop on Program Comprehension* (pp. 127-136). IEEE.

Turski, W. (1996). Reference Model for Smooth Growth of Software Systems. *IEEE Transactions on Software Engineering, 22*(8), 599–600.

Vasa, R. (2010). *Growth and Change Dynamics in Open Source Software Systems* (Ph.D. thesis). Swinburne University of Technology, Melbourne, Australia.

Vaucher, S., & Sahraoui, H. (2007). Do Software Libraries Evolve Differently than Applications?: An Empirical Investigation. In *Proceedings of the 2007 Symposium on Library-Centric Software Design* (pp. 88-96). ACM. 10.1145/1512762.1512771

Wang, L., Wang, Z., Yang, C., Zhang, L., & Ye, Q. (2009). Linux Kernels as Complex Networks: A Novel Method to Study Evolution. In *Proceedings of the 25th International Conference on Software Maintenance* (pp. 41-51). IEEE. 10.1109/ICSM.2009.5306348

Weicheng, Y., Beijun, S., & Ben, X. (2013). Mining GitHub: Why Commit Stops -- Exploring the Relationship between Developer's Commit Pattern and File Version Evolution. *Proceedings of the 20th Asia-Pacific Software Engineering Conference, 2,* 165–169. 10.1109/APSEC.2013.133

Wermilinger, M., & Ferreira, H. (2011). Quality Evolution track at QUATIC 2010. *Software Engineering Notes, 36*(1), 28–29. doi:10.1145/1921532.1960273

Wu, J., & Holt, R. (2004). Linker Based Program Extraction and its use in Software Evolution. *Proceedings of the International Workshop on Unanticipated Software Evolution,* 1-15.

Wu, J., Holt, R., & Hassan, A. (2007). Empirical Evidence for SOC Dynamics in Software Evolution. In *Proceedings of the International Conference on Software Maintenance* (pp. 244-254). IEEE. 10.1109/ICSM.2007.4362637

Xie, G., Chen, J., & Neamtiu, I. (2009). Towards a Better Understanding of Software Evolution: An Empirical Study on Open Source Software. In *Proceedings of the International Conference on Software Maintenance* (pp. 51-60). IEEE. 10.1109/ICSM.2009.5306356

Xu, J., Gao, Y., Christley, S., & Madey, G. (2005). A Topological Analysis of the Open Source Software Development Community. In *Proceedings of the 38th Annual Hawaii International Conference on System Sciences (HICSS'05)*. IEEE.

Yu, L. (2006). Indirectly Predicting the Maintenance Effort of Open-Source Software. *Journal of Software Maintenance and Evolution: Research and Practice, 18*(5), 311–332. doi:10.1002mr.335

Yuen, C. (1985). An empirical approach to the study of errors in large software under maintenance. *Proc. IEEE Int. Conf. on Software Maintenance*, 96–105.

Yuen, C. (1987). A statistical rationale for evolution dynamics concepts. *Proc IEEE Int. Conf. on Software Maintenance*, 156–164.

Yuen, C. (1988). On analyzing maintenance process data at the global and detailed levels. *Proc. IEEE Int. Conf. on Software Maintenance*, 248–255.

Zaidman, A., Rompaey, B., Deursen, A., & Demeyer, S. (2011). Studying the Co-Evolution of Production and Test Code in Open Source and Industrial Developer Test Processes through Repository Mining. *Empirical Software Engineering, 16*(3), 325–364. doi:10.100710664-010-9143-7

Zaimi, A., Ampatzoglou, A., Triantafyllidou, N., Chatzigeorgiou, A., Mavridis, A., & Chaikalis, T. (2015). An Empirical Study on the Reuse of Third-Party Libraries in Open-Source Software Development. In *Proceedings of the 7th Balkan Conference on Informatics Conference* (pp. 4). ACM. 10.1145/2801081.2801087

Zazworka, N., & Ackermann, C. (2010). CodeVizard: a Tool to Aid the Analysis of Software Evolution. In *Proceedings of the 2010 ACM-IEEE International Symposium on Empirical Software Engineering and Measurement (ESEM '10)*. ACM 10.1145/1852786.1852865

Zhongmin, C., & Yeqing, W. (2010,). The application of theory and method of time series in the modeling of software reliability. In *Proceedings of the 2010 Second International Conference on Information Technology and Computer Science (ITCS)* (pp. 340-343). IEEE. 10.1109/ITCS.2010.89

Zimmermann, T., Premraj, R., & Zeller, A. (2007). Predicting Defects for Eclipse. *Proceedings of the Third International Workshop on Predictor Models in Software Engineering (Promise '07)*. 10.1109/PROMISE.2007.10

This research was previously published in Optimizing Contemporary Application and Processes in Open Source Software; pages 1-23, copyright year 2018 by Engineering Science Reference (an imprint of IGI Global).

Chapter 2
Exploratory Analysis of Free and Open Source Software Ecology

K.G. Srinivasa
Chaudhary Brahm Prakash Government Engineering College, India

Ganesh Chandra Deka
M. S. Ramaiah Institute of Technology, India

Krishnaraj P.M.
M. S. Ramaiah Institute of Technology, India

ABSTRACT

Shared repositories provide a host of services to start and sustain a FOSS project. They also share the details of projects with researchers. Sourceforge.net is a popular and populous forge with total number of projects exceeding 400,000 and developers counting more than 3 million as of Jan 2015. The evolution of this forge is studied and it was found that there is a small slide in the number of developers since September 2011. The existence of power law in Sourceforge.net is confirmed. The visualisation of developer relations reveal that there is a separate core and periphery groups of developers in Sourceforge.net and this trend was found to repeat in other forges like Freecode and Rubyforge.

INTRODUCTION

Free and Open Source Software (FOSS) is characterised mainly by its licensing terms. The Free Software licences and Open Source licences, though different in their relationship with commercial software, together provides an alternate model of software distribution. But FOSS is also important for the development model it follows. The success of FOSS lies in demonstrating the feasibility of developing a complex artefact like software by involving global set of volunteers and using Internet as a communication medium. Ranging from a lone developer to literally tens of thousands of people and organisation, FOSS ecology today is probably world's largest virtual software development entity. But it is not necessary that

DOI: 10.4018/978-1-7998-9158-1.ch002

any person or organisations who want to develop FOSS must follow this process. They can develop the software in-house without involving public but still release the software under FOSS licences.

Given the advantages of public participation model as demonstrated by success of GNU-Linux, many FOSS projects are developed in similar way. In the early days of GNU project and even during the initial stages of GNU-Linux development, the project leader would normally release the source code to public. Interested people would download, use, test, find bugs and then either reported or send fixes to the leader. The leader would have final say regarding the inclusion of bug fixes and new features. This model of development is still followed today but in place of a single leader there is a team which is normally formalised in all mature FOSS projects.

One of the major contributions of FOSS which is normally understudied is how much it has contributed towards the system and software development tools. Given the fact that most developers are mainly involved in FOSS to write software for their own use, this is quite natural. The growth of Internet coupled with the spread of computers during late 1990's enabled much larger participation in FOSS projects. This necessitated a mechanism which can automate the build and release processes. Separately there was a need for a communication platform beyond usenet and irc which could connect developers and end users. Bug reporting, feature request and general support also needed to be supported. Therefore, FOSS projects slowly started moving away from niche environments to public platform like Internet.

Mature and popular projects mostly host their projects in dedicated websites which support a range of features for efficient project management. Almost all technical and pubic communication details of the projects hosted in these sites are available for researchers. But given the fact that many FOSS projects start with single developer, it is not practical for every project to have its own website with all features. Also, the visibility of a project decreases if it works independently. Therefore, there exists multiple repositories which provide common facilities required to start and sustain a software project. They also provide a platform for developers to interact with projects they are interested. This multiplicity effect attracts many developers and organisations to host their projects in such repositories which are also called as forges.

In accordance with the promise of public development model of FOSS, such forges make the data regarding the projects hosted by them available for researchers. Mining Software Repositories has become a standard research topic providing a host of interesting issues to work upon. The software engineering researchers have access to such exhaustive data sets for first time and there are many opportunities to learn about software development process. Design, quality assurance and project management studies today include data from FOSS forges. The richness of data which include communication details is attracting researchers from rainbow domains like anthropology, sociology, economics, law and political science. Together they are trying to interpret this wonder phenomenon where gifted programmers seem to work without pay to create industry grade software and then distribute it at no cost along with source code without any restrictions on further use, modification and redistribution.

Evolution of Sourceforge.net

Sourceforge.net is probably more well known and one of the biggest FOSS repositories. As on Jan 2015 it hosts 400,000 projects and has 3 million registered users. Several high-profile projects like Vlc player, eMule are hosted in this site. It shares the data regarding projects hosted in the site with researchers through University of Norte Dam, USA.

SourceForge.net uses relational databases to store project management activity and statistics. There are over 100 relations (tables) in the data dumps provided to Notre Dame. Some of the data have been removed for security and privacy reasons. The Notre Dame researchers have built a data warehouse comprised of these monthly dumps, with each stored in a separate schema. Thus, each monthly dump is a snapshot of the status of all the SourceForge.net projects at that point in time.

The data dump of each month is identified as sfmmyy. Therefore, the dump of Jan 2013 is referred as sf0113. The tables in each dump are referred by the dump identifier and table name. So, the table 'artifact' for the month Oct 2013 should be referred as 'sf0913.artifact'. To facilitate the access of data, University of Notre Dame has provided a web access for the researchers to run sql queries on the data and download the result files in many formats.

For the purpose of present study, the data from Feb 2005 to Feb 2013 (sf0205-sf0213) is considered. Therefore, total of 96 datasets each containing around 100 tables is analysed. In some cases, the datasets for July 2007 (sf0707) and August 2007 (sf0807) were not considered because the data for these months were not in line with the historical trend. Repeated attempts to extract data from the data warehouse of University of Notre Dame gave the same erroneous results.

Figure 1. Developer and project growth in Sourceforge.net

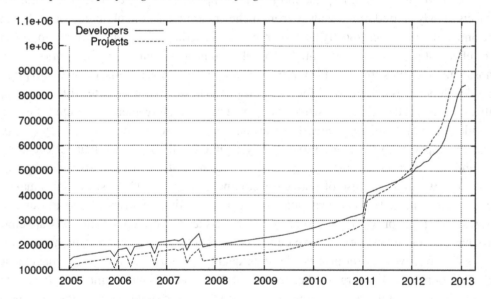

Therefore, it was concluded that these data are corrupted and should not be considered for present work.

The growth of projects and developers in Sourceforge.net is shown in Figure 1. The evolution of Sourceforge.net can be traced in three stages. The first period was 2005-2008 when the developers and projects were growing at a steady rate. 2009-2011 was the second period when there was a rapid growth of developers and projects. During September 2011, there was a dramatic shift in Sourceforge.net. For first time, the numbers of projects outnumbered the developers. It is beyond the scope of the present work to analyze the reasons behind this shift but we note that this is an important event which deserves much closer examination. One of the reasons for this trend may be the emergence of newer forges like github which began to attract more attention since 2010 onwards. But what is perplexing is the growth of projects. If developers are deserting Sourceforge.net why are the projects increasing at a healthy rate? Will be an interesting question to investigate further.

Visualisations of Developer Relations in Source-Forge.net

The Principle Component Analysis of Sourceforge.net as shown in Figure 2 confirms that number of developers in a project is an important measure of its success. Figure 3 shows that there exists power law in Sourceforge.net meaning there is a large set of developers working on small number of projects. Or in other words there is large number of projects which have small number of developers. To study this matter further there is a need to understand developer relations in Sourceforge.net.

Figure 2. Principle component analysis of Sourceforge.net

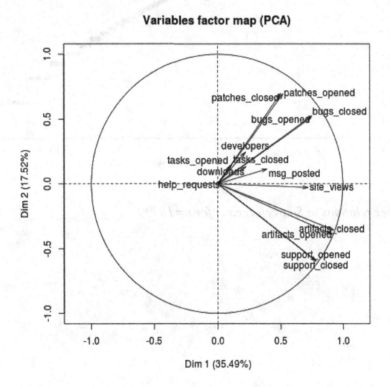

Sourceforge.net maintains the developer and project details in the relation USER GROUP. The attribute USER ID is the unique code assigned to each registered user who is labelled as developer in present work and GROUP ID is the unique code of project to which the developer has subscribed. In order to visualise Sourceforge.net as a social network, developers were considered as nodes. An edge was present between two developers if they worked on same project. The resulting graphs are shown in Figure 4, Figure 5, Figure 6 and Figure 7. The complete network diagram consisting of 67565 developers and 643204 relations is shown in Figure 8. A simplified version of the same is shown in Figure 9.

All these figures suggest that there exists a central core team of developers who heavily interact with each other working in each others project. In the outer periphery, there exist isolated teams who work on their projects independently. The core and periphery teams who seldom interact with each other are the main characteristic of FOSS ecology. Surprisingly this resembles the Onion Model which is used to describe the structure of individual FOSS projects. This trend is also seen in other forges like Rubyforge (Figure 10) and Freecode (Figure 11).

Figure 3. Power law in Sourceforge.net

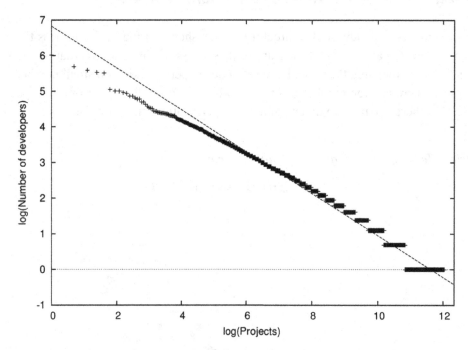

Figure 4. Developer relations in Sourceforge.net for n=10000

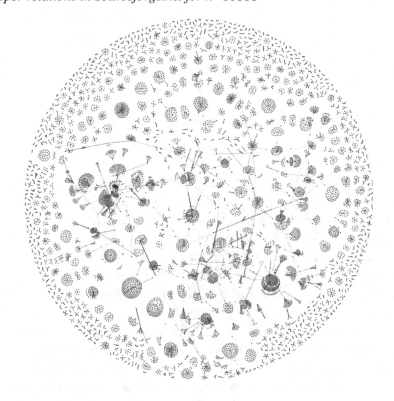

Figure 5. Developer relations in Sourceforge.net for n=20000

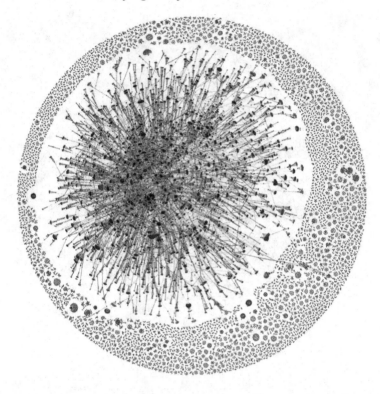

Figure 6. Developer relations in Sourceforge.net for n=30000

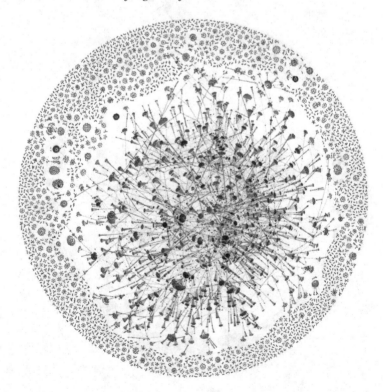

Figure 7. Developer relations in Sourceforge.net for n=40000

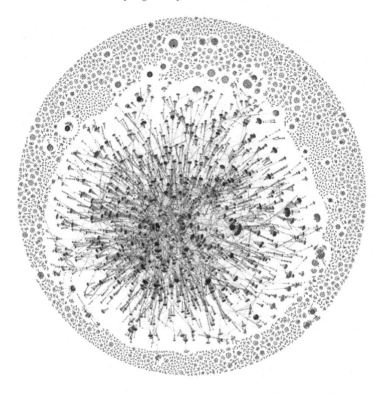

Figure 8. Developer relations in Sourceforge.net for n=67565

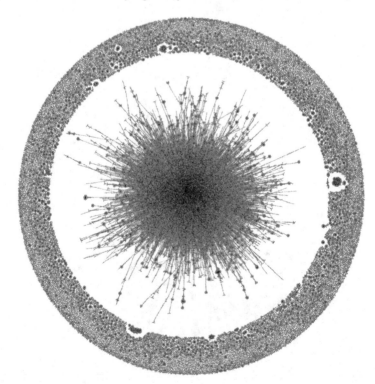

Figure 9. Refined developer relations in Sourceforge.net for n=67565

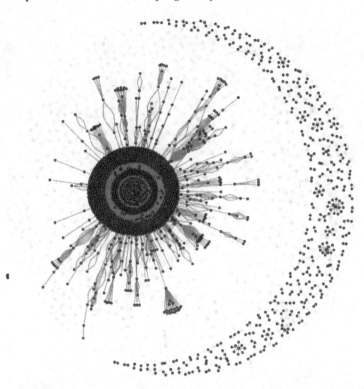

Figure 10. Developer relations in rubyforge

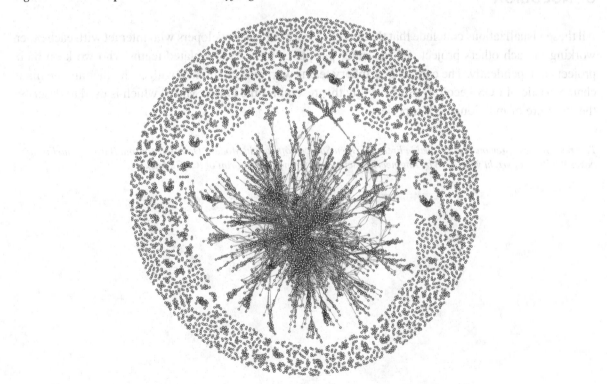

Figure 11. Developer relations in freecode

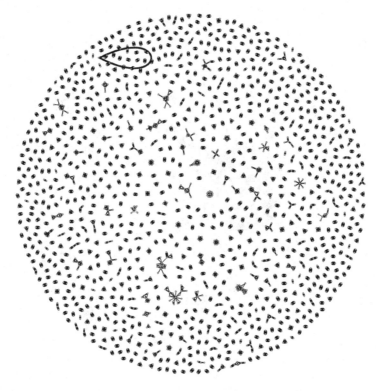

CONCLUSION

All these visualizations conclude that there exists a core team of developers who interact with each other working in each others project and the outer periphery there exist isolated teams who work on their projects independently. The core and periphery teams who seldom interact with each other are the main characteristic of FOSS ecology. Surprisingly this resembles the Onion Model which is used to describe the structure of individual FOSS projects.

This research was previously published in Free and Open Source Software in Modern Data Science and Business Intelligence; pages 93-103, copyright year 2018 by Engineering Science Reference (an imprint of IGI Global).

Chapter 3
Open Source Software Development Challenges:
A Systematic Literature Review on GitHub

Abdulkadir Seker
Sivas Cumhuriyet University, Turkey

Banu Diri
Yıldız Technical University, Turkey

Halil Arslan
Sivas Cumhuriyet University, Turkey

Mehmet Fatih Amasyalı
Yıldız Technical University, Turkey

ABSTRACT

GitHub is the most common code hosting and repository service for open-source software (OSS) projects. Thanks to the great variety of features, researchers benefit from GitHub to solve a wide range of OSS development challenges. In this context, the authors thought that was important to conduct a literature review on studies that used GitHub data. To reach these studies, they conducted this literature review based on a GitHub dataset source study instead of a keyword-based search in digital libraries. Since GHTorrent is the most widely known GitHub dataset according to the literature, they considered the studies that cite this dataset for the systematic literature review. In this study, they reviewed the selected 172 studies according to some criteria that used the dataset as a data source. They classified them within the scope of OSS development challenges thanks to the information they extract from the metadata of studies. They put forward some issues about the dataset and they offered the focused and attention-grabbing fields and open challenges that we encourage the researchers to study on them.

DOI: 10.4018/978-1-7998-9158-1.ch003

INTRODUCTION

Thanks to distributed version control systems such as Git, Mercurial, etc., open-source development platforms have reached a considerable number of users. The most common of these platforms is GitHub (based on git). GitHub has become the world's largest code server with more than 40 million developers hosting and collaborating over 100 million repositories.

On platforms such as GitHub, the development process is distributed. Developers can participate in a project, contribute, discuss bugs with each other, and write comments about code from various locations. In this way, a considerable amount of textual, numerical and network or collaboration-based features about the projects and developers are extracted from the platform. Besides, GitHub includes many social relations among users or projects. GitHub is the most common code hosting and repository service for open-source software projects. For the researchers that focus on software engineering, the content of this platform provides many valuable sources. Most of the studies about this domain use GitHub as a data source because of easy to access, amount of data, and diversity of features. In this context, we think that is important to conduct a literature review on studies that used GitHub data.

There are several options to reach GitHub data. In a survey study which is given the usage rates of GitHub dataset, they addressed that the most used dataset is GHTorrent (34%) in the articles that are reviewed according to the certain criteria (Cosentino, Luis, & Cabot, 2016). In Cosentino's systematic mapping study, the GHTorrent dataset is in the lead with a 41\% use rate (Badashian, Shah, & Stroulia, 2015; Cosentino, Canovas Izquierdo, & Cabot, 2017). In the another study, GHTorrent is the most cited dataset (Kotti & Spinellis, 2019). The GHTorrent dataset was developed by Georgios Gousios in the software engineering department at Delft University of Technology(Gousios, 2013). The dataset is generated by systematically crawling with the GitHub API and includes information about all public projects and users on the platform. GHTorrent stores some information about repositories, projects, issue descriptions, comments, and pull request (PR) conversations in 26 relational tables totally.

We saw from other systematic literature review (SLR) papers that some studies can be missed when reviewing with a text-based (keyword) search from search engines or digital libraries. Because of that, to reach the studies, we conducted this literature review based on a GitHub dataset source study instead of a keyword-based search in digital libraries. Due to GHTorrent is the most widely known and used GitHub dataset according to the literature, we considered the studies which cite this dataset for the systematic literature review.

In this study, we offered to find out the topics of all studies and classified them. We focused on the studies with the context of open-source software development. We divided the studies into some categories and challenges. Besides, some distributions (type, venue, year, method, data, topic) have been obtained from the studies that used the dataset. We show which challenges are mentioned in the studies and how each study is using the dataset. Thus, we hope the study guided the researchers who interest in software engineering challenges with open-source systems. We formed this review following these research questions:

RQ1: What are the trends of open-source software development challenges?
RQ2: What are the handicaps/cons of GHTorrent?
RQ3: What are the open challenges that have not yet been studied with this dataset?

In this context, we reviewed the articles which use GHTorrent and offered a systematic mapping study. We applied 3 phased systematic literature review protocol as suggested by Kitchenham (Brereton, Kitchenham, Budgen, Turner, & Khalil, 2007). Firstly, we developed a review method using citations of the main paper of the dataset. Then, we conducted a review as extract trend topics from metadata of studies and made assessments. Finally, we revealed some discussions and open challenges. The protocol and details are given Figure 1. We used a cross-checked mechanism (two of the authors) while finding studies and classifying them.

Figure 1. Systematic literature review protocol

Conduct Review

Determine exclusion criteria.
Find relevant studies.
Extract features from metadata.
Analyze Studies.

Phase 1

Phase 3

Develop Review

Determine research question.
Find citations of main study.
Validate citations.

Phase 2

Document Review

Write conclusion with trend topics.
Extract the pros-cons of the dataset
Determine open challenges.

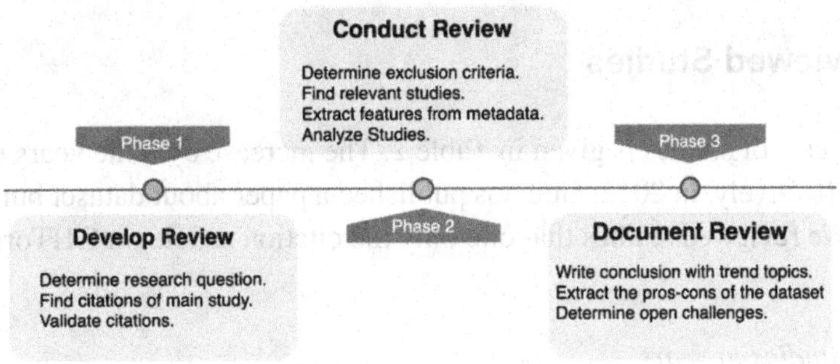

METHODOLOGY

Developing Review

In these other SLR studies, they noticed that some studies can be missed when reviewing with a keyword based search from digital libraries (Khan & Keung, 2016; Schreiber & Zylka, 2020). Because of that, we followed the citation of the main study of the dataset. We used an application[1] to extract all citations of the GHtorrent's study. All 332[2] studies which cited the main study of GHTorrent (Gousios, 2013) were reviewed. We applied exclusion criteria similar to the recently published an SLR study (Schreiber & Zylka, 2020). We exclude the studies that were written in any language other than English, paid studies, and reports/books/theses (Table 1). In addition, the articles refer GHTorrent only as related works or similar dataset were also eliminated.

Table 1. Selecting studies with some criteria

Exclusion Criteria	Amount	Total
Language problem	25	
Paid/non-accessible article	18	
Book/thesis	49	
Refers it as related work	47	160
Refers as similar dataset	16	
Report/speech etc.	5	

After we applied the exclusion protocol, we reviewed 172 studies. 49 of the studies were published in journals, and the remaining 123 were published in conferences.

Firstly, we started to review as extracting some features from the metadata of studies.

- Title, authors, keywords, and abstract.
- The aim, methods, and research questions
- The datasets that were used alongside GHTorrent
- The date of used dataset dump
- Publishing venue information
- Citation counts

Overview of Reviewed Studies

The distribution by years of studies is given in Table 2. The increase over the years is an indication that the data set is used effectively. In 2012, Gousios published a paper about dataset but the source paper is published in 2013. We reviewed studies that cite only the citation article on GHTorrent website.

Table 2. Number of studies in years

Year	2012	2013	2014	2015	2016	2017	2018	2019
Amount	1	1	22	26	28	36	41	17

The source journal distribution of the studies is given in Table 3. The highest number of publications (8 papers) were in "Empirical Software Engineering" (Excluding ArXiv papers). Only 1 study was published in the journals labeled "Others".

Table 3. Number of studies in journals

Journal Name	Amount
Empirical Software Engineering	8
Information and Software Technology	6
IEEE Transactions of Software Engineering	4
Journal of System and Software	2
Physica A	2
IEEE Access	2
PeerJ	2
ArXiv	10
Others	13

Apart from journals, most of the articles were published in various conferences (Table 4). The foremost among them were the MSR and ICSE. Conferences with 1–2 publications are labeled "Others".

Apart from using the dataset, some extended datasets were generated by adding various features to GHTorrent. Furthermore, some studies produced sub/derivative datasets from GHTorrent by filtering some features. In this context, the most common derivative dataset is TravisTorrent. The dataset that was used for the continuous integration challenge was produced with some features from GHTorrent and information extracted from Travis CI. Moreover, information obtained from various platforms, such as Stackoverflow and Twitter, were used in some studies. While 133 (77\%) of papers used only GHTorrent, the remaining 39 were used other datasets with GHTorrent. Table 5 shows the usage rates of datasets with GHTorrent. Most of the studies that used extra dataset addressed the GitHub users' activities in other social networks.

Table 4. Number of studies in conferences

Conference Name	Amount
Int. Conf. on Mining Soft. Repository (MSR)	40
Int. Conf. on Soft. Eng. (ICSE)	9
Int. Conf. on Soft. Eng. Knowledge Eng. (SEKE)	5
Int. Conf. on Soft. Analysis, Evolution and Reengineering (SANER)	5
Int. Conf. on Soft. Maintenance and Evolution (ICSME)	3
Asia-Pacific Soft. Eng. Conference (APSEC)	3
Symposium on the Foundations of Soft. Eng. (FSE)	3
Int. Conf. on Connected Health: App., Systems and Eng. (CHASE)	3
Int. Workshop on Emotion Awareness in Soft. Eng. (SEmotion)	3
Others	49

Table 5. Number of studies according to usage dataset

Dataset	Amount
GHTorrent	133
GHTorrent + Stackoverflow	15
GHTorrent + TravisTorrent	13
GHTorrent + Twitter	2
GHTorrent + Others	9

The methods used in all studies were also extracted (Table 6). The category labeled "statistics" is the most used method group. This group includes statistical, mathematical, and probabilistic methods, etc. Text mining studies are relatively less than other methods despite the dataset includes rich textual features. In this regard, we thought using text mining methods based on deep learning with the dataset will be worthwhile and distinctive. The studies that contain topics such as data visualization, use of the dataset, or creating a new dataset are in the "Others" category.

Table 6. Number of studies according to usage methods

Dataset	Amount
Statistic	68
Machine Learning	41
Survey	25
Text Mining	25
Others	34

The words in the abstracts of an article roughly give information about its topic. Starting from this point of view, another important feature extracted from these studies was relation of words in the abstracts. The cluster density graph[3] was created by use frequency of these words (Figure 2). The clusters and underlined words were played crucial roles on separating studies into categories.

Figure 2. The cluster density graph of words in abstracts

RESULTS

RQ1: What are the trends of open-source software development challenges?

Firstly, to group studies on domains, we used the nature of GitHub itself. "User" (developer) and "project" are the backbones of open-source software platforms. Secondly, in considerations of the density graph (Figure 2), apart from these it is seen that the "development" topic is also at the center. Besides, the "dataset" topic is added because some of the studies are related to the dataset directly. Thus, the studies have been separated into 4 domains. In order to determine challenges under these domains, we appealed to Cosentino's GitHub review article (Cosentino et al., 2017) and the cluster density graph. We chose the most inclusive ones while determining the challenges. After all processes, the software engineering challenges were separated into 16 challenges under four domains.

The studies were split into four domains, User (USR), Development (DEV), Project (PRO), and Dataset (DAT). The challenges of these domains and related studies are given in Table 7. The reason the total numbers in the table are greater than the total number of studies is that some of them focus on more than one challenge. The abbreviations of these challenges that are going to use following tables are given in this table. We used the cluster density graph and chose the most inclusive ones while determining the challenges.

Table 7. Number of studies in domains and challenges

Domains	Amount	Challenges	Amount	Alias
USER	69	Activity	39	ACTV
		Interaction	39	INTR
		Revision-Assignment	9	REVI
		Characterization	35	CHAR
DEVELOPMENT	59	Pull Request	18	PREQ
		Source Code	35	CODE
		Continuous Integrations	17	CONT
		Quality	12	QUAL
PROJECT	63	Issue/bug	24	ISSU
		Team-Member	11	TEAM
		Dependency	9	DEPE
		Characterization	36	CHAR
DATASET	28	Definition-Usage	4	DEFI
		Subsets	4	SUBS
		Augments-Derivatives	7	AUGM
		Helper	13	HELP

In addition to these numbers, the detailed information about each domain is given in Tables 8–11 below. The given tables for each domain contain the reference id of studies and related challenges ("x" in a cell indicates that the study focuses on a challenge in this column).

User

GitHub users are the main roles in software projects positioned as contributors (with codes or comments), developers, project managers, etc. to perform all activities in the software life cycle. In this context, a lot of studies have been published about user's domain. The user domain challenges were divided into four topics, activity, interaction, revision/assignee, and characterization (Table 8).

- *ACTY(Activity):* In general terms, it covers the GitHub developers' contributions such as coding history, comments, like/star, developer performances, and other past activities.
- *INTR (Interaction):* It is related to users' interactions both within the GitHub environment and on other platforms such as Stackoverflow and Twitter. Events such as following or watching among users, forking projects, etc. come under this topic.
- *REVI (Revision-Assignment):* The studies about pull request reviewer, issue or bug assignment problems are in this topic.
- *CHAR(Characterization):* Out of the topics above, the studies interest in behavior of user's emotional activity, classifying the developers according to features such as gender, activity, tenure/ volunteer were analyzed under this title.

Table 8. Challenges in the USER domain

References of Studies	Amount	ACTV	INTR	REVI	CHAR
(Cosentino, Izquierdo, & Cabot, 2014; Horschig, Mattis, & Hirschfeld, 2018; Rahman & Roy, 2014; Saito, Fujiwara, Igaki, Yoshida, & Iida, 2016)	4	x			
(Abdalkareem, Shihab, & Rilling, 2017; Alves, Brandão, Santana, Silva, & Moro, 2016; Batista, Brandão, Alves, da Silva, & Moro, 2017; Calefato, Lanubile, & Novielli, 2017; Komamizu, Hayase, Amagasa, & Kitagawa, 2017; Kopczyński & Celińska-Kopczyńska, 2017; J. Liu, Li, Wang, Yu, & Yin, 2018; Sheoran, Blincoe, Kalliamvakou, Damian, & Ell, 2014; Silvestri, Yang, Bozzon, & Tagarelli, 2015; Yan & Wang, 2017; Yang, Martins, Saini, & Lopes, 2017; Yu, Yin, Wang, & Wang, 2014)	12		x		
(Badashian, Hindle, & Stroulia, 2015; de Lima Júnior, Soares, Plastino, & Murta, 2015)	2			x	
(Bayati, 2018; Brokmeier, 2017; Cassee, Pinto, Castor, & Serebrenik, 2018; Hauff & Gousios, 2015; Lu et al., 2019; Ortu, Hall, et al., 2018; Ortu, Pinna, et al., 2018; Qiu, Nolte, Brown, Serebrenik, & Vasilescu, 2019; Saha, Muradul Bashir, Raihan Talukder, Karmaker, & Saiful Islam, 2018; Terrell et al., 2017)	10				x
(Badashian, Esteki, Gholipour, Hindle, & Stroulia, 2014; Baltes, Knack, Anastasiou, Tymann, & Diehl, 2018; Constantinou & Kapitsaki, 2016b; Constantinou & Mens, 2017a; Destefanis, Ortu, Bowes, Marchesi, & Tonelli, 2018; Y. Hu, Wang, Ren, & Choo, 2018; Jiang, Feng, Lian, & Zhang, 2016; Lee & Lo, 2018; Manes & Baysal, 2019; Vasilescu, Filkov, & Serebrenik, 2013)	10	x	x		.
(Jarczyk, Jaroszewicz, Wierzbicki, Pawlak, & Jankowski-Lorek, 2018; Júnior, Soares, Plastino, & Murta, 2018; Xavier, Macedo, & Maia, 2014)	3	x		x	
(Baltes & Diehl, 2018a, 2018b; Brunet, Murphy, Terra, Figueiredo, & Serey, 2014; Burlet & Hindle, 2015; Jaruchotrattanasakul, Yang, Makihara, Fujiwara, & Iida, 2016; C. Liu, Yang, Zhang, Ray, & Rahman, 2018; Sayagh, Kerzazi, Adams, & Petrillo, 2018; Vasilescu, Filkov, & Serebrenik, 2015; Yamashita, McIntosh, Kamei, Hassan, & Ubayashi, 2015; Yan, Wei, Han, & Wang, 2017; P. Zhang, Xiong, Leung, & Song, 2018)	11	x			x
(Blincoe, Sheoran, Goggins, Petakovic, & Damian, 2016; Middleton et al., 2018; Rastogi & Nagappan, 2016b; Sun, Xu, Xia, Chen, & Li, 2018; Wisse & Veenman, 2015; Yan, Li, & Wang, 2017)	6		x		x
(Ying, Chen, Liang, & Wu, 2016; Yu, Wang, Yin, & Ling, 2014; Yu, Wang, Yin, & Wang, 2016)	3	x	x	x	
(Bao, Xia, Lo, & Murphy, 2019; Bayati, 2019; Casalnuovo, Vasilescu, Devanbu, & Filkov, 2015; Constantinou & Kapitsaki, 2016a; Jiang, Lo, Yang, Li, & Zhang, 2019; Nielek et al., 2016; Z. Wang, Wang, & Redmiles, 2018)	7	x	x		x
(Daricélio M. Soares, de Lima Júnior, Plastino, & Murta, 2018)	1	x	x	x	x

The most studied challenges in the user domain are activity and interaction, as seen in Table 8. This trend can be interpreted as a natural consequence of GitHub being an open-source, community-oriented project repository service.

Development

The basic activity that affects the performance of its targeted product in software projects can be considered as the development process. The challenges in the development domain were divided into four topics, pull request, source code, continuous integration, and quality (Table 9).

- *PREQ (Pull Request (PR))*: It covers some problems about PR classifications or prioritization, PR description and comment contents, and PR acceptance/rejection and reasons for them.
- *CODE (Source Code):* It is about topics such as the programming languages of projects, connections between codes (referring to original source code, code cloning), refactoring, tactic codes, and code conflict on PR.
- *CONT (Continuous Integration (CI)):* It is related to the use of CI, the effect of CI quality, build breakage problems, test cases, automatizations of CI process.
- *QUAL (Quality):* It contains all studies which aim at increasing software quality as the main purpose.

Table 9. Challenges in the DEVELOPMENT domain

References of Studies	Amount	PREQ	CODE	CONT	QUAL
(Brokmeier, 2017; Calefato et al., 2017; Chen, Stolee, & Menzies, 2017; El Mezouar, Zhang, & Zou, 2019; Pletea, Vasilescu, & Serebrenik, 2014; Rahman & Roy, 2014; Saito et al., 2016; Daricélio M. Soares et al., 2018; Daricélio Moreira Soares, de Lima Júnior, Murta, & Plastino, 2015; Daricelio Moreira Soares, Junior, Murta, & Plastino, 2015; Terrell et al., 2017; Y. Zhang, Yin, Yu, & Wang, 2014)	12	x			
(Cassee et al., 2018; Celińska & Kopczyński, 2017; Coelho, Almeida, Gousios, Deursen, & Treude, 2017; Coelho, Almeida, Gousios, & Van Deursen, 2015; Constantinou & Mens, 2017a; Gharehyazie, Ray, & Filkov, 2017; Gharehyazie et al., 2019; Gonzalez, Prentice, & Mirakhorli, 2018; Guzman, Azócar, & Li, 2014; Horschig et al., 2018; D. Li et al., 2016; X. Liu, Shen, Zhong, & Zhu, 2016; Lopes et al., 2017; Martins, Achar, & Lopes, 2018a; Saha et al., 2018; Wisse & Veenman, 2015; Wittern, Suter, & Rajagopalan, 2016; Yang et al., 2017)	18		x		
(Baltes, Knack, et al., 2018; Beller, Gousios, & Zaidman, 2017b; Hilton, Tunnell, Huang, Marinov, & Dig, 2016; Madeyski & Kawalerowicz, 2017; Ortu, Pinna, et al., 2018; Vassallo, Proksch, Gall, & Di Penta, 2019; Xia & Li, 2017)	7			x	
(Hata, Treude, Kula, & Ishio, 2019; Flávio Medeiros et al., 2018; Veen, Gousios, & Zaidman, 2015)	3	x	x		
(Yu, Yin, Wang, Yang, & Wang, 2016; Zhao, da Costa, & Zou, 2019)	2	x			x
(Beller, Gousios, & Zaidman, 2017a; Dimitropoulos, Aung, & Svetinovic, 2017; Gonzalez, Santos, Popovich, Mirakhorli, & Nagappan, 2017; Luo, Zhao, Ma, & Chen, 2017; Muylaert & De Roover, 2017; Muylaert, Meuter, & Roover, 2016)	6		x	x	
(Baltes & Diehl, 2018b; Kikas, Gousios, Dumas, & Pfahl, 2017; Flavio Medeiros et al., 2018; Mujhid, S. Santos, Gopalakrishnan, & Mirakhorli, 2017; Santos, Campbell, Hindle, & Amaral, 2017; Sharma, Fragkoulis, & Spinellis, 2016; Tomasdottir, Aniche, & Van Deursen, 2018)	7		x		x
(Urli, Yu, Seinturier, & Monperrus, 2018; Vasilescu, Van Schuylenburg, Wulms, Serebrenik, & van den Brand, 2014; Vasilescu, Yu, Wang, Devanbu, & Filkov, 2015)	3			x	x
(Yu, Wang, Filkov, Devanbu, & Vasilescu, 2015)	1	x	x	x	

In this domain, most studies are about source code. GHTorrent does not contain features directly related to source code. However, the other datasets used with GHTorrent, such as StackOverflow, give rise to this result.

Project

The essential motivation of distributed version control systems is the development of targeted products on the basis of public projects. The project domain challenges were divided into four topics, issue/bug, team/ members, dependency, and characterization (Table 10).

Table 10. Challenges in the PROJECT domain

References of Studies	Amount	ISSU	TEAM	DEPE	CHAR
(Abdalkareem et al., 2017; Alonso-Abad, López-Nozal, Maudes-Raedo, & Marticorena-Sánchez, 2019; Badashian, Hindle, et al., 2015; Cabot, Canovas Izquierdo, Cosentino, & Rolandi, 2015; Destefanis et al., 2018; Fan, Yu, Yin, Wang, & Wang, 2017; Guzman et al., 2014; D. Hu, Wang, Chang, Zhang, & Yin, 2018; Jarczyk et al., 2018; Karampatsis & Sutton, 2019; Kikas, Dumas, & Pfahl, 2016; D. Li et al., 2016; X. Liu et al., 2016; Murgia et al., 2014; Pletea et al., 2014; Saha et al., 2018; Werder & Brinkkemper, 2018)	17	x			
(El Mezouar et al., 2019; Middleton et al., 2018; Qiu et al., 2019; Vasilescu, Filkov, et al., 2015; Vasilescu, Serebrenik, & Filkov, 2015)	5		x		
(Gharehyazie et al., 2017)	1			x	
(Aggarwal, Hindle, & Stroulia, 2014; Bayati, 2019; Burlet & Hindle, 2015; Cheng, Li, Li, & Liang, 2018; Constantinou & Mens, 2017b; Cosentino et al., 2014; Eck & Uebernickel, 2016; Fernández, Robles, Libresoft, Rey, & Carlos, 2017; Gharehyazie et al., 2019; Knauss, Damian, Cleland-Huang, & Helms, 2015; Kovalenko, Palomba, & Bacchelli, 2018; Lakkundi, Agrahari, & Chimalakonda, 2019; C. Liu et al., 2018; J. Liu et al., 2019; Ma et al., 2018; Miranda, Lins, Klosowski, & Silva, 2018; Onoue, Hata, & Matsumoto, 2014; Onoue, Kula, Hata, & Matsumoto, 2017; Raghuraman, Ho-Quang, V Chaudron Chalmers, Serebrenik, & Vasilescu, 2019; Rastogi & Nagappan, 2016a; Robles, Ho-Quang, Hebig, Chaudron, & Fernandez, 2017; W. Wang, Poo-Caamano, Wilde, & German, 2015; Yamashita, McIntosh, Kamei, & Ubayashi, 2014)	24				x
(Ortu et al., 2017; Ortu, Hall, et al., 2018)	2	x	x		
(Blincoe, Harrison, Kaur, & Damian, 2019; Izquierdo, Cosentino, Rolandi, Bergel, & Cabot, 2015)	2	x		x	
(Kalliamvakou et al., 2014; P. Zhang et al., 2018)	2	x			x
(Constantinou & Mens, 2016; Low, Yathog, & Svetinovic, 2015; Matragkas, Williams, Kolovos, & Paige, 2014; Werder, 2018)	4		x		x
(Aue, Haisma, Tomasdottir, & Bacchelli, 2016; Hata, Todo, Onoue, & Matsumoto, 2015; Liao et al., 2019; Padhye, Mani, & Sinha, 2014; Yamashita, Kamei, McIntosh, Hassan, & Ubayashi, 2016)	5			x	x
(Blincoe, Harrison, & Damian, 2015)	1	x		x	x

- *ISSU (Issue/bug):* It includes topics such as open and closed issues (commits, tasks) in a project, bugs occurrence, and bug triaging. Moreover, the differences, characterization, and classification of the trio of issue-bug-feature are under this topic.
- *TEAM (Team/member):* It contains the challenges about the team diversity in terms of some features (location, gender, tenure, permanence, etc.), the actions as a team, joining or leaving behaviors, core and other members, and the effect of teams on software quality.

- *DEPE (Dependency):* It includes topics about project dependencies. Varied types of dependencies in GitHub projects were examined with regards to programming languages, codes, problems, forking cases, and code clones. In addition, the relationships between projects and the parameters related to project survival are other challenges under this topic.
- *CHAR (Characterization):* It involves some topics such as GitHub repository features, the unique parts of projects, the diversity of projects in terms of some parameters such as language or design, features of public projects, matters about the GitHub ecosystem, repository artifacts, forking, and branching.

Most studies under the project domain were related to characterization. The rich features of the GH-Torrent about projects are thought to have a positive impression on this result.

Dataset

Apart from using the dataset, some extended datasets were generated by adding various features to GHTorrent. In the dataset domain, there were four sub-topics such as; definition, usage, extended-sub datasets, and helper (Table 11).

- *DEFI (Definition-Usage):* It is about the description of GHTorrent dataset. Besides, it covers the studies that contain dataset obtaining methods, dataset usage tips and tools.
- *SUBS (Subsets):* It is about the studies that created by some filtering process on GHTorrent. Most of studies filter dataset according to features of developers or projects.
- *AUGM (Augments-Derivatives):* It covers the studies that produce new datasets based upon GHTorrent (TravisTorrent, SOTorrent, etc.) and extended datasets created via data fusion from social media data.
- *HELP (Helper):* Apart from above, some papers interest in dissimilar problems via only a few features (user mail, project language, etc.) extracted from GHTorrent. These studies were brought together under this title.

Table 11. Papers about the dataset

References of Studies	Amount	DEFI	SUBS	AUGM	HELP
(Badashian, Shah, et al., 2015; Gousios, Pinzger, & Deursen, 2014; Gousios & Spinellis, 2012; Markovtsev & Long, 2018)	4	x			
(Cheng et al., 2018; Gousios & Zaidman, 2014; Karampatsis & Sutton, 2019; Lakkundi et al., 2019; Martins et al., 2018a; Robles et al., 2017; Vasilescu, Serebrenik, et al., 2015)	7		x		
(Baltes, Dumani, Treude, & Diehl, 2018; Batista et al., 2017; Beller et al., 2017b; Komamizu et al., 2017)	4			x	
(Baltes & Diehl, 2016; Filippova & Cho, 2016; Gousios, Storey, & Bacchelli, 2016; Gousios, Zaidman, Storey, & Deursen, 2015; Jaffe, Lacomis, Schwartz, Goues, & Vasilescu, 2018; Y. Li, Katsipoulakis, Chandramouli, Goldstein, & Kossmann, 2017; Martins, Achar, & Lopes, 2018b; Munaiah, Kroh, Cabrey, & Nagappan, 2017; Sawant, Robbes, & Bacchelli, 2016, 2018; van der Bent, Hage, Visser, & Gousios, 2018; Vasilescu, 2014; Vasilescu, Posnett, et al., 2015)	13				x

Many datasets have been created by using GHTorrent. Besides, there is a lot of software engineering studies that benefit from some features of GHTorrent. It is clearly understood from the studies under this topic that GHTorrent (hence GitHub data) how has rich features.

RQ2: What are the handicaps/cons of GHTorrent?

GitHub data retrieves with the GitHub API as fast response and consistent data. However, its 5000 requests per hour limit is a crucial problem when retrieving large data[4]. Thereagainst, GHTorrent presents up to date data thanks to downloadable dumps without any restriction.

GHTorrent provides flexibility by presenting data in different types. It presents raw JSON data in MongoDB database and relational tables in MySQL database. You can use whichever format that suitable for your environment.

MongoDB Format

1. You can download previous bi-monthly MongoDB collections from the website (until 2015 / by collections.).
2. You can download daily collections from the website (from 2015/ all collections are included.)
3. You can connect to the remote MongoDB server with the instructions on the website. The remote MongoDB server's data may not up to date.

MySQL Format
1. You can download all relational tables in a single MySQL dump file. (until 2015).
2. You can download all relational tables as separate CSV files containing a table in each. (from 2015).
3. You can query the online SQLite tool from the latest dump of MySQL database. (We couldn't try this because of login problem.)

Although the GHTorrent publishes as up to date, it is seen from our review that most of the researchers (including in recent years) use the older versions of the dataset (Table 12). In this table, it is given that the dates of dataset dump which studies published in the last two years. In 25 of 55 studies, it was not explicitly stated which dump was used.

Table 12. Older dumps usages

Dataset Dumps	2019 Studies	2018 Studies
2016 and older	5	5
2017	5	4
2018	4	1
2019	1	0
unknown	6	19

In order to use up to date data, there is two possible option.

- Download huge MySQL dumps and import all CSV files to local database environments.
- Download all daily MongoDB dumps and restore them to local environments according to instructions on the website.

In both of the above two options, processing and transferring these large files is taken serious time and effort (Badashian, Shah, et al., 2015). We think that this situation prompts researchers to use older and smaller dumps. This may not a problem, however, it is a matter of curiosity why they use older data.

Besides the advantages, GHTorrent has some cons and problems. The problems reported from reviewed studies and experienced by us are given below list.

- It is reported in some studies that GHTorrent have duplicated data (Martins et al., 2018a; Werder & Brinkkemper, 2018). We noticed this problem in the collections of *repos* and *users*, too. (There are several docs have same *id* and *url* field.)
- Another problem is that some fields that can be used as a linkage between data are missing. For instance, there is no *repo id* or *full name* in *commits* and *commits comments* collections. You have to parse the *url* field to generate them.
- It is reported that GHTorrent does not provide correct data on whether developer accounts are members of teams on GitHub (Middleton et al., 2018).
- Sun et al. have also stated that GHTorrent did not have data on who edited what file (Sun et al., 2018).

It is thought that a topic is also missing about the dataset. We have also extracted dataset usage criteria from studies. Except studies that few related to data visualization or extending the dataset, almost all them use data by applying particular filters to the dataset. Commonly they use filters based on user or project metrics (number of commit/pull request/followers, code language, etc.) However, since each study has its own subset, it is not possible to compare success-even on similar subjects. In this context, it is also important to publish domain-based subsets that can be used for specific challenges. Actually, this is necessary for software engineering challenge studies that use not only GHTorrent but also all GitHub dataset.

RQ3: What are the open challenges that have not yet been studied with this dataset?

We extract top-10 studies according to citations on Google Scholar to find attention-grabbing publications. As seen Table 13, the prominent domain is Development (DEV). Besides, the studies about the dataset (DAT) domain are among to influential ones. Starting from this point of view, we aimed to find open challenges under these domains.

Assignee feature used for assign to pull requests or issues to someone in Git-based platforms such as GitHub, GitLab, Bitbucket, etc. Much as some projects don't use this feature effectively, this is crucial for project management (Jiang, Lo, Ma, Feng, & Zhang, 2017). To automate the assigning process, issues are classified with some labels or tags, then match to suitable developers. It is seen in Table 8 that only 12% of the studies in the user domain are related to revision/assignee problems. However, it is expected that more studies can be done with GHTorrent about task or reviewer assignment, which is one of the major challenges of software engineering (Hoda & Murugesan, 2016).

Table 13. Top 10 studies according to citation count

Title	Citation	Year	Domain
The promises and perils of mining GitHub	442	2014	PRO
Work practices and challenges in pull-based development: the integrator's perspective	217	2015	DAT
Quality and productivity outcomes relating to continuous integration in GitHub	212	2015	DEV
Gender and tenure diversity in GitHub teams	188	2015	DAT
Usage, costs, and benefits of continuous integration in open-source projects	169	2016	DEV
Sentiment analysis of commit comments in GitHub: an empirical study	169	2014	DEV
Work practices and challenges in pull-based development: the contributor's perspective	142	2016	DAT
Reviewer recommendation for pull-requests in GitHub: What can we learn from code review and bug assignment?	120	2016	USR
Wait for it: Determinants of pull request evaluation latency on GitHub	113	2015	DEV
Curating GitHub for engineered software projects	111	2017	DAT

New trends in software developments are aimed at automating everything from issue assignment to test and deploy. DevOps is used for this purpose. DevOps process means that to integrates developments and operations via increasing communications and automatizations. All processes such as continuous integrity, automated testing or deploying, performance managements, etc. can handle with DevOps pipelines. In the studies we reviewed, it was observed that the researchers focused on a few of the DevOps processes such as continuous integrity, testing or revision. The data provided by GHTorrent has the necessary elements to contribute to all these steps.

Due to the rapid increase of open-source software projects, developers miss some of the projects in their areas of interest. This led to the need to recommend projects to users in environments such as GitHub. In this context, one of the recent studied hot topics related to project dependency is project recommendation to users (for following or contribution) (C. Liu et al., 2018; Nielek et al., 2016; Sun et al., 2018). New recommend models and metrics can develop with GHTorrent.

CONCLUSION

Most of the studies that focus on software engineering, use GitHub as a data source because of easy to access, amount of data, and diversity of features. Thanks to the great variety of features, researchers benefit from GitHub to solve a wide range of open-source software development challenges. In this context, we thought that is important to conduct a literature review on studies that used GitHub data. In conclusion, we constructed this study in light of three research questions. Firstly, we explored trend challenges in open-source software development, and we found the most popular challenge is related to characterizing developers (users) and projects. Secondly, we analyzed the most common GitHub dataset and we put forward some issues and problems. Lastly, we investigated whether is there any challenges that have not yet been studied much yet and we discovered some open challenges such as GitHub project recommendation, and automatic assignment to pull requests or issues reviewer.

In this SLR study, we classified the open-source software development studies under 4 domains and 16 challenges via the information that we extract from words in abstracts. Unlike the existing SLR, we used the dataset citation-based review method owing to some problems may occur text-based search such a wide range of field. Hereby, we presented a filtered and classified SLR to researchers who interest in open-source software development challenges.

Our results showed that most of the studies swarm to the user and project domains. The researchers specifically focused on the *characterization* challenges under both of the two domains. In the user domain, one of the trending topics is classifying users according to some features and activities to use for other challenges. Besides, analyzing users' past activities and their relationships with each other (in GitHub or other social networks) stood out as other challenges. The topics such as features of repositories, diversity, and relations are prominent ones in project *characterization* challenges. The great majority of studies related to the development domain directed to the *source codes* of projects in order to used extract some metrics such as number of code lines in a commit, programming languages, number of contributors per code line, etc. Lastly, in the dataset domain, most studies under the *helper* challenge focus on dissimilar problems via only a few features (user mail, project language, etc.) extracted from the dataset.

We presented some issues about GHTorrent as another contribution. Missing and duplicate data should be fixed by the creators of the dataset. Besides, we showed that each researcher uses an ad-hoc sub-dataset (filtering data in a different way in each study) in their studies. This situation makes comparing studies with each other difficult. In this regard, we want to cooperate with the creators of GHTorrent to take the whole dataset and present common domain-based datasets for specific challenges.

In another result of this study, we explored that some challenges are rarely studied although they are crucial for open-source software development. For instance, in terms of distributed development, assigning a reviewer to "pull requests" or "issues" fast as possible to maintain software projects is very important. In this context, we think that revision is a crucial challenge to focus on. Moreover, the project recommendation is another important challenge in GitHub. In early this year, GitHub released the "Explore" page to recommend the project to developers based on their activities. We realized that also there are only a few studies about the project recommendation. We encourage the researchers to focus on this challenge.

Lastly, when we analyzed the methods of studies, we noticed that mostly the researchers used surveys (questionnaire, crowdsourcing, manual labeling, etc.) to evaluate their results. We think that the researchers refer to this method due to there is no labeled data on most challenges.

We plan to conduct other SLR's specific to the most studied challenges in future works. Besides, we want to research the methods of reviewed studies comprehensively to analyze which methods used why.

REFERENCES

Abdalkareem, R., Shihab, E., & Rilling, J. (2017). What Do Developers Use the Crowd For? A Study Using Stack Overflow. *IEEE Software*, *34*(2), 53–60. doi:10.1109/MS.2017.31

Aggarwal, K., Hindle, A., & Stroulia, E. (2014). Co-evolution of project documentation and popularity within github. *Proceedings of the 11th Working Conference on Mining Software Repositories - MSR 2014*, 360–363. 10.1145/2597073.2597120

Alonso-Abad, J. M., López-Nozal, C., Maudes-Raedo, J. M., & Marticorena-Sánchez, R. (2019). Label prediction on issue tracking systems using text mining. *Progress in Artificial Intelligence*, 8(3), 325–342. doi:10.100713748-019-00182-2

Alves, G. B., Brandão, M. A., Santana, D. M., da Silva, A. P. C., & Moro, M. M. (2016). The Strength of Social Coding Collaboration on GitHub. *SBBD 2016*. Retrieved from https://www.semanticscholar.org/paper/The-Strength-of-Social-Coding-Collaboration-on-Alves-Brandão/15dc574702e4e61233e04b1e8ea3f5ad38dc0cc6

Aue, J., Haisma, M., Tomasdottir, K. F., & Bacchelli, A. (2016). Social Diversity and Growth Levels of Open Source Software Projects on GitHub. *Proceedings of the 10th ACM/IEEE International Symposium on Empirical Software Engineering and Measurement - ESEM '16*, 1–6. 10.1145/2961111.2962633

Badashian, A. S., Esteki, A., Gholipour, A., Hindle, A., & Stroulia, E. (2014). Involvement, contribution and influence in GitHub and stack overflow. *Proceedings of 24th Annual International Conference on Computer Science and Software Engineering*, 19–33. Retrieved from https://dl.acm.org/citation.cfm?id=2735527

Badashian, A. S., Hindle, A., & Stroulia, E. (2015). Crowdsourced bug triaging. *2015 IEEE 31st International Conference on Software Maintenance and Evolution, ICSME 2015 - Proceedings*, 506–510. 10.1109/ICSM.2015.7332503

Badashian, A. S., Shah, V., & Stroulia, E. (2015). GitHub's big data adaptor: an eclipse plugin. *CASCON 15*, 265–268. Retrieved from https://dl.acm.org/citation.cfm?id=2886490

Baltes, S., & Diehl, S. (2016). Worse Than Spam: Issues In Sampling Software Developers. *Proceedings of the 10th ACM/IEEE International Symposium on Empirical Software Engineering and Measurement - ESEM '16*, 1–6. 10.1145/2961111.2962628

Baltes, S., & Diehl, S. (2018a). Towards a theory of software development expertise. *Proceedings of the 2018 26th ACM Joint Meeting on European Software Engineering Conference and Symposium on the Foundations of Software Engineering - ESEC/FSE 2018*, 187–200. 10.1145/3236024.3236061

Baltes, S., & Diehl, S. (2018b). Usage and attribution of Stack Overflow code snippets in GitHub projects. *Empirical Software Engineering*, 1–37. doi:10.100710664-018-9650-5

Baltes, S., Dumani, L., Treude, C., & Diehl, S. (2018). *The Evolution of Stack Overflow Posts: Reconstruction and Analysis*. Retrieved from https://arxiv.org/abs/1811.00804

Baltes, S., Knack, J., Anastasiou, D., Tymann, R., & Diehl, S. (2018). (No) influence of continuous integration on the commit activity in GitHub projects. *Proceedings of the 4th ACM SIGSOFT International Workshop on Software Analytics - SWAN 2018*, 1–7. 10.1145/3278142.3278143

Bao, L., Xia, X., Lo, D., & Murphy, G. C. (2019). A Large Scale Study of Long-Time Contributor Prediction for GitHub Projects. *IEEE Transactions on Software Engineering*, 1–1. doi:10.1109/TSE.2019.2918536

Batista, N. A., Brandão, M. A., Alves, G. B., da Silva, A. P. C., & Moro, M. M. (2017). Collaboration strength metrics and analyses on GitHub. Proceedings of the International Conference on Web Intelligence - WI '17, 170–178. 10.1145/3106426.3106480

Bayati, S. (2018). Understanding newcomers success in open source community. *Proceedings of the 40th International Conference on Software Engineering Companion Proceeedings - ICSE '18*, 224–225. 10.1145/3183440.3195073

Bayati, S. (2019). Effect of newcomers supportive strategies on open source projects socio-technical activities. *Proceedings of the 12th International Workshop on Cooperative and Human Aspects of Software Engineering CHASE*, 49–50. 10.1109/CHASE.2019.00020

Beller, M., Gousios, G., & Zaidman, A. (2017a). Oops, My Tests Broke the Build: An Explorative Analysis of Travis CI with GitHub. *2017 IEEE/ACM 14th International Conference on Mining Software Repositories (MSR)*, 356–367. 10.1109/MSR.2017.62

Beller, M., Gousios, G., & Zaidman, A. (2017b). TravisTorrent: Synthesizing Travis CI and GitHub for Full-Stack Research on Continuous Integration. *2017 IEEE/ACM 14th International Conference on Mining Software Repositories (MSR)*, 447–450. 10.1109/MSR.2017.24

Blincoe, K., Harrison, F., & Damian, D. (2015). Ecosystems in GitHub and a Method for Ecosystem Identification Using Reference Coupling. *2015 IEEE/ACM 12th Working Conference on Mining Software Repositories*, 202–211. 10.1109/MSR.2015.26

Blincoe, K., Harrison, F., Kaur, N., & Damian, D. (2019). Reference Coupling: An exploration of inter-project technical dependencies and their characteristics within large software ecosystems. *Information and Software Technology, 110*, 174–189. doi:10.1016/j.infsof.2019.03.005

Blincoe, K., Sheoran, J., Goggins, S., Petakovic, E., & Damian, D. (2016). Understanding the popular users: Following, affiliation influence and leadership on GitHub. *Information and Software Technology, 70*, 30–39. doi:10.1016/j.infsof.2015.10.002

Brereton, P., Kitchenham, B. A., Budgen, D., Turner, M., & Khalil, M. (2007). Lessons from applying the systematic literature review process within the software engineering domain. *Journal of Systems and Software, 80*(4), 571–583. doi:10.1016/j.jss.2006.07.009

Brokmeier, P. (2017). Project level effects of gender on contribution evaluation on GitHub. *PeerJ PrePrints, 5*(e2989v1). doi:10.7287/peerj.preprints.2989v1

Brunet, J., Murphy, G. C., Terra, R., Figueiredo, J., & Serey, D. (2014). Do developers discuss design? *Proceedings of the 11th Working Conference on Mining Software Repositories - MSR 2014*, 340–343. 10.1145/2597073.2597115

Burlet, G., & Hindle, A. (2015). An Empirical Study of End-User Programmers in the Computer Music Community. *2015 IEEE/ACM 12th Working Conference on Mining Software Repositories*, 292–302. 10.1109/MSR.2015.34

Cabot, J., Canovas Izquierdo, J. L., Cosentino, V., & Rolandi, B. (2015). Exploring the use of labels to categorize issues in Open-Source Software projects. *2015 IEEE 22nd International Conference on Software Analysis, Evolution, and Reengineering (SANER)*, 550–554. 10.1109/SANER.2015.7081875

Calefato, F., Lanubile, F., & Novielli, N. (2017). A Preliminary Analysis on the Effects of Propensity to Trust in Distributed Software Development. *2017 IEEE 12th International Conference on Global Software Engineering (ICGSE)*, 56–60. 10.1109/ICGSE.2017.1

Casalnuovo, C., Vasilescu, B., Devanbu, P., & Filkov, V. (2015). Developer Onboarding in GitHub: The Role of Prior Social Links and Language Experience. *2015 10th Joint Meeting of the European Software Engineering Conference and the ACM SIGSOFT Symposium on the Foundations of Software Engineering, ESEC/FSE 2015 - Proceedings*, 817–828. 10.1145/2786805.2786854

Cassee, N., Pinto, G., Castor, F., & Serebrenik, A. (2018). How swift developers handle errors. *Proceedings of the 15th International Conference on Mining Software Repositories - MSR '18*, 292–302. 10.1145/3196398.3196428

Celińska, D., & Kopczyński, E. (2017). Programming Languages in GitHub: A Visualization in Hyperbolic Plane. *11. International AAAI Conference on Web and Social Media*. Retrieved from https://www.aaai.org/ocs/index.php/ICWSM/ICWSM17/paper/viewPaper/15583

Chen, D., Stolee, K. T., & Menzies, T. (2017). *Replicating and Scaling up Qualitative Analysis using Crowdsourcing: A Github-based Case Study*. Retrieved from https://arxiv.org/abs/1702.08571

Cheng, C., Li, B., Li, Z., & Liang, P. (2018). *Automatic Detection of Public Development Projects in Large Open Source Ecosystems: An Exploratory Study on GitHub*. doi:10.18293/SEKE2018-085

Coelho, R., Almeida, L., Gousios, G., van Deursen, A., & Treude, C. (2017). Exception handling bug hazards in Android Results from a mining study and an exploratory survey. *Empirical Software Engineering*, *22*(3), 1264–1304. doi:10.100710664-016-9443-7

Coelho, R., Almeida, L., Gousios, G., & Van Deursen, A. (2015). Unveiling exception handling bug hazards in android based on GitHub and Google code issues. *IEEE International Working Conference on Mining Software Repositories*. 10.1109/MSR.2015.20

Constantinou, E., & Kapitsaki, G. M. (2016a). Developers Expertise and Roles on Software Technologies. *2016 23rd Asia-Pacific Software Engineering Conference (APSEC)*, 365–368. 10.1109/APSEC.2016.061

Constantinou, E., & Kapitsaki, G. M. (2016b). Identifying Developers' Expertise in Social Coding Platforms. *2016 42th Euromicro Conference on Software Engineering and Advanced Applications (SEAA)*, 63–67. 10.1109/SEAA.2016.18

Constantinou, E., & Mens, T. (2016). Social and technical evolution of software ecosystems: A Case Study of Rails. *Proceedings of the 10th European Conference on Software Architecture Workshops - ECSAW '16*, 1–4. 10.1145/2993412.3003384

Constantinou, E., & Mens, T. (2017a). An empirical comparison of developer retention in the RubyGems and npm software ecosystems. *Innovations in Systems and Software Engineering*, *13*(2–3), 101–115. doi:10.100711334-017-0303-4

Constantinou, E., & Mens, T. (2017b). Socio-technical evolution of the Ruby ecosystem in GitHub. *2017 IEEE 24th International Conference on Software Analysis, Evolution and Reengineering (SANER)*, 34–44. 10.1109/SANER.2017.7884607

Cosentino, V., Canovas Izquierdo, J. L., & Cabot, J. (2017). A Systematic Mapping Study of Software Development With GitHub. *IEEE Access: Practical Innovations, Open Solutions*, *5*, 7173–7192. doi:10.1109/ACCESS.2017.2682323

Cosentino, V., Izquierdo, J. L. C., & Cabot, J. (2014). *Three Metrics to Explore the Openness of GitHub projects*. Retrieved from https://arxiv.org/abs/1409.4253

Cosentino, V., Luis, J., & Cabot, J. (2016). Findings from GitHub: methods, datasets and limitations. *Proceedings of the 13th International Workshop on Mining Software Repositories*, 137–141. 10.1145/2901739.2901776

de Lima Júnior, M. L., Soares, D. M., Plastino, A., & Murta, L. (2015). Developers assignment for analyzing pull requests. *Proceedings of the 30th Annual ACM Symposium on Applied Computing - SAC '15*, 1567–1572. 10.1145/2695664.2695884

Destefanis, G., Ortu, M., Bowes, D., Marchesi, M., & Tonelli, R. (2018). On measuring affects of github issues' commenters. *Proceedings of the 3rd International Workshop on Emotion Awareness in Software Engineering - SEmotion '18*, 14–19. 10.1145/3194932.3194936

Dimitropoulos, P., Aung, Z., & Svetinovic, D. (2017). Continuous integration build breakage rationale: Travis data case study. *2017 International Conference on Infocom Technologies and Unmanned Systems (Trends and Future Directions) (ICTUS)*, 639–645. 10.1109/ICTUS.2017.8286087

Eck, A., & Uebernickel, F. (2016). Reconstructing Open Source Software Ecosystems: Finding Structure in Digital Traces. *ICIS*. Retrieved from https://www.semanticscholar.org/paper/Reconstructing-Open-Source-Software-Ecosystems%3A-in-Eck-Uebernickel/60ace7d37a292da6b40e0ac468b326f2e0f524af

El Mezouar, M., Zhang, F., & Zou, Y. (2019). An empirical study on the teams structures in social coding using GitHub projects. *Empirical Software Engineering*, 24(6), 1–34. doi:10.100710664-019-09700-1

Fan, Q., Yu, Y., Yin, G., Wang, T., & Wang, H. (2017). Where Is the Road for Issue Reports Classification Based on Text Mining? *2017 ACM/IEEE International Symposium on Empirical Software Engineering and Measurement (ESEM)*, 121–130. 10.1109/ESEM.2017.19

Fernández, M. A., Robles, G., Libresoft, G., Rey, U., & Carlos, J. (2017). Extracting software development information from FLOSS Projects in GitHub. *SATToSE*. Retrieved from http://ghtorrent.org/

Filippova, A., & Cho, H. (2016). The Effects and Antecedents of Conflict in Free and Open Source Software Development. *Proceedings of the 19th ACM Conference on Computer-Supported Cooperative Work & Social Computing - CSCW '16*, 703–714. 10.1145/2818048.2820018

Gharehyazie, M., Ray, B., & Filkov, V. (2017). Some from Here, Some from There: Cross-Project Code Reuse in GitHub. *2017 IEEE/ACM 14th International Conference on Mining Software Repositories (MSR)*, 291–301. 10.1109/MSR.2017.15

Gharehyazie, M., Ray, B., Keshani, M., Zavosht, M. S., Heydarnoori, A., & Filkov, V. (2019). Cross-project code clones in GitHub. *Empirical Software Engineering*, 24(3), 1538–1573. doi:10.100710664-018-9648-z

Gonzalez, D., Prentice, S., & Mirakhorli, M. (2018). A fine-grained approach for automated conversion of JUnit assertions to English. *Proceedings of the 4th ACM SIGSOFT International Workshop on NLP for Software Engineering - NL4SE 2018*, 14–17. 10.1145/3283812.3283819

Gonzalez, D., Santos, J. C. S., Popovich, A., Mirakhorli, M., & Nagappan, M. (2017). A Large-Scale Study on the Usage of Testing Patterns That Address Maintainability Attributes: Patterns for Ease of Modification, Diagnoses, and Comprehension. *2017 IEEE/ACM 14th International Conference on Mining Software Repositories (MSR)*, 391–401. 10.1109/MSR.2017.8

Gousios, G. (2013). The GHTorrent dataset and tool suite. *Proceedings of the 10th Working Conference on Mining Software Repositories*, 233–236. 10.1109/MSR.2013.6624034

Gousios, G., Pinzger, M., & Van Deursen, A. (2014). An exploratory study of the pull-based software development model. *Proceedings - International Conference on Software Engineering*, (1), 345–355. 10.1145/2568225.2568260

Gousios, G., & Spinellis, D. (2012). GHTorrent: Github's data from a firehose. *2012 9th IEEE Working Conference on Mining Software Repositories (MSR)*, 12–21. 10.1109/MSR.2012.6224294

Gousios, G., Storey, M.-A., & Bacchelli, A. (2016). Work practices and challenges in pull-based development: The Contributor's Perspective. *Proceedings of the 38th International Conference on Software Engineering - ICSE '16*, 285–296. 10.1145/2884781.2884826

Gousios, G., & Zaidman, A. (2014). A dataset for pull-based development research. *Proceedings of the 11th Working Conference on Mining Software Repositories - MSR 2014*, 368–371. 10.1145/2597073.2597122

Gousios, G., Zaidman, A., Storey, M.-A., & van Deursen, A. (2015). Work Practices and Challenges in Pull-Based Development: The Integrator's Perspective. *2015 IEEE/ACM 37th IEEE International Conference on Software Engineering*, 358–368. 10.1109/ICSE.2015.55

Guzman, E., Azócar, D., & Li, Y. (2014, May 31). Sentiment Analysis of Commit Comments in GitHub. *An Empirical Study, 352–355*, 352–355. Advance online publication. doi:10.1145/2597073.2597118

Hata, H., Todo, T., Onoue, S., & Matsumoto, K. (2015). Characteristics of Sustainable OSS Projects: A Theoretical and Empirical Study. *2015 IEEE/ACM 8th International Workshop on Cooperative and Human Aspects of Software Engineering*, 15–21. 10.1109/CHASE.2015.9

Hata, H., Treude, C., Kula, R. G., & Ishio, T. (2019). 9.6 Million Links in Source Code Comments: Purpose, Evolution, and Decay. *International Conference on Software Engineering*. 10.1109/ICSE.2019.00123

Hauff, C., & Gousios, G. (2015). Matching GitHub Developer Profiles to Job Advertisements. *2015 IEEE/ACM 12th Working Conference on Mining Software Repositories*, 362–366. 10.1109/MSR.2015.41

Hilton, M., Tunnell, T., Huang, K., Marinov, D., & Dig, D. (2016). Usage, costs, and benefits of continuous integration in open-source projects. *Proceedings of the 31st IEEE/ACM International Conference on Automated Software Engineering - ASE 2016*, 426–437. 10.1145/2970276.2970358

Hoda, R., & Murugesan, L. K. (2016). Multi-level agile project management challenges: A self-organizing team perspective. *Journal of Systems and Software, 117*, 245–257. doi:10.1016/j.jss.2016.02.049

Horschig, S., Mattis, T., & Hirschfeld, R. (2018). Do Java programmers write better Python? Studying off-language code quality on GitHub. *Conference Companion of the 2nd International Conference on Art, Science, and Engineering of Programming - Programming'18 Companion*, 127–134. 10.1145/3191697.3214341

Hu, D., Wang, T., Chang, J., Zhang, Y., & Yin, G. (2018). Bugs and features, do developers treat them differently? *2018 International Conference on Artificial Intelligence and Big Data (ICAIBD)*, 250–255. 10.1109/ICAIBD.2018.8396204

Hu, Y., Wang, S., Ren, Y., & Choo, K.-K. R. (2018). User influence analysis for Github developer social networks. *Expert Systems with Applications*, *108*, 108–118. doi:10.1016/j.eswa.2018.05.002

Izquierdo, J. L. C., Cosentino, V., Rolandi, B., Bergel, A., & Cabot, J. (2015). GiLA: GitHub label analyzer. *2015 IEEE 22nd International Conference on Software Analysis, Evolution, and Reengineering, SANER 2015 - Proceedings*. 10.1109/SANER.2015.7081860

Jaffe, A., Lacomis, J., Schwartz, E. J., Le Goues, C., & Vasilescu, B. (2018). Meaningful variable names for decompiled code: a machine translation approach. *Proceedings of the 26th Conference on Program Comprehension - ICPC '18*, 20–30. 10.1145/3196321.3196330

Jarczyk, O., Jaroszewicz, S., Wierzbicki, A., Pawlak, K., & Jankowski-Lorek, M. (2018). Surgical teams on GitHub: Modeling performance of GitHub project development processes. *Information and Software Technology*, *100*, 32–46. doi:10.1016/j.infsof.2018.03.010

Jaruchotrattanasakul, T., Yang, X., Makihara, E., Fujiwara, K., & Iida, H. (2016). Open Source Resume (OSR): A Visualization Tool for Presenting OSS Biographies of Developers. *2016 7th International Workshop on Empirical Software Engineering in Practice (IWESEP)*, 57–62. 10.1109/IWESEP.2016.17

Jiang, J., Feng, F., Lian, X., & Zhang, L. (2016). Long-Term Active Integrator Prediction in the Evaluation of Code Contributions. *International Conference on Software Engineering and Knowledge Engineering (SEKE)*, 177–182. 10.18293/SEKE2016-030

Jiang, J., Lo, D., Ma, X., Feng, F., & Zhang, L. (2017). Understanding inactive yet available assignees in GitHub. *Information and Software Technology*, *91*, 44–55. doi:10.1016/j.infsof.2017.06.005

Jiang, J., Lo, D., Yang, Y., Li, J., & Zhang, L. (2019). A first look at unfollowing behavior on GitHub. *Information and Software Technology*, *105*, 150–160. doi:10.1016/j.infsof.2018.08.012

Júnior, M. L. de L., Soares, D. M., Plastino, A., & Murta, L. (2018). Automatic assignment of integrators to pull requests: The importance of selecting appropriate attributes. *Journal of Systems and Software*, *144*, 181–196. doi:10.1016/j.jss.2018.05.065

Kalliamvakou, E., Gousios, G., Blincoe, K., Singer, L., German, D. M., & Damian, D. (2014). The promises and perils of mining GitHub. *Proceedings of the 11th Working Conference on Mining Software Repositories - MSR 2014*, 92–101. 10.1145/2597073.2597074

Karampatsis, R.-M., & Sutton, C. (2019). *How Often Do Single-Statement Bugs Occur? The ManyS-tuBs4J Dataset*. Retrieved from https://arxiv.org/abs/1905.13334

Khan, A. A., & Keung, J. (2016, October 1). Systematic review of success factors and barriers for software process improvement in global software development. *IET Software*, *10*(5), 125–135. doi:10.1049/iet-sen.2015.0038

Kikas, R., Dumas, M., & Pfahl, D. (2016). Using dynamic and contextual features to predict issue lifetime in GitHub projects. *Proceedings of the 13th International Workshop on Mining Software Repositories - MSR '16*, 291–302. 10.1145/2901739.2901751

Kikas, R., Gousios, G., Dumas, M., & Pfahl, D. (2017). Structure and Evolution of Package Dependency Networks. *2017 IEEE/ACM 14th International Conference on Mining Software Repositories (MSR)*, 102–112. 10.1109/MSR.2017.55

Knauss, E., Damian, D., Cleland-Huang, J., & Helms, R. (2015). Patterns of continuous requirements clarification. *Requirements Engineering, 20*(4), 383–403. doi:10.100700766-014-0205-z

Komamizu, T., Hayase, Y., Amagasa, T., & Kitagawa, H. (2017). Exploring Identical Users on GitHub and Stack Overflow. *SEKE*, 584–589. doi:10.18293/SEKE2017-109

Kopczyński, E., & Celińska-Kopczyńska, D. (2017). *Hyperbolic triangulations and discrete random graphs.* Retrieved from https://arxiv.org/abs/1707.01124

Kotti, Z., & Spinellis, D. (2019). Standing on shoulders or feet?: the usage of the MSR data papers. *Proceedings of the 16th International Conference on Mining Software Repositories*, 565–576. 10.1109/MSR.2019.00085

Kovalenko, V., Palomba, F., & Bacchelli, A. (2018). Mining file histories: should we consider branches? *Proceedings of the 33rd ACM/IEEE International Conference on Automated Software Engineering - ASE 2018*, 202–213. 10.1145/3238147.3238169

Lakkundi, C. S., Agrahari, V., & Chimalakonda, S. (2019). *GE852: A Dataset of 852 Game Engines.* Retrieved from https://arxiv.org/abs/1905.04482

Lee, R. K.-W., & Lo, D. (2018). Wisdom in Sum of Parts: Multi-Platform Activity Prediction in Social Collaborative Sites. *Proceedings of the 10th ACM Conference on Web Science - WebSci '18*, 77–86. 10.1145/3201064.3201067

Li, D., Li, L., Kim, D., Bissyandé, T. F., Lo, D., & Le Traon, Y. (2016). *Watch out for This Commit! A Study of Influential Software Changes.* Retrieved from https://arxiv.org/abs/1606.03266

Li, Y., Katsipoulakis, N. R., Chandramouli, B., Goldstein, J., & Kossmann, D. (2017). Mison: A Fast JSON Parser for Data Analytics. *Proceedings of the VLDB Endowment International Conference on Very Large Data Bases, 10*(10), 1118–1129. doi:10.14778/3115404.3115416

Liao, Z., Wang, N., Liu, S., Zhang, Y., Liu, H., & Zhang, Q. (2019). Identification-Method Research for Open-Source Software Ecosystems. *Symmetry, 11*(2), 182. doi:10.3390ym11020182

Liu, C., Yang, D., Zhang, X., Ray, B., & Rahman, M. M. (2018). Recommending GitHub Projects for Developer Onboarding. *IEEE Access: Practical Innovations, Open Solutions, 6*, 52082–52094. doi:10.1109/ACCESS.2018.2869207

Liu, J., Li, Z., Wang, T., Yu, Y., & Yin, G. (2018). Adaptive software search toward users' customized requirements in GitHub. *SEKE*, 143–181. doi:10.18293/SEKE2018-064

Liu, X., Shen, B., Zhong, H., & Zhu, J. (2016). EXPSOL: Recommending Online Threads for Exception-Related Bug Reports. *2016 23rd Asia-Pacific Software Engineering Conference (APSEC)*, 25–32. 10.1109/APSEC.2016.015

Lopes, C. V., Maj, P., Martins, P., Saini, V., Yang, D., Zitny, J., ... Vitek, J. (2017). DéjàVu: a map of code duplicates on GitHub. *Proceedings of the ACM on Programming Languages, 1*, 1–28. 10.1145/3133908

Low, J. F., Yathog, T., & Svetinovic, D. (2015). Software analytics study of Open-Source system survivability through social contagion. *2015 IEEE International Conference on Industrial Engineering and Engineering Management (IEEM)*, 1213–1217. 10.1109/IEEM.2015.7385840

Lu, Y., Mao, X., Wang, T., Yin, G., Li, Z., & Wang, W. (2019). Studying in the "Bazaar": An Exploratory Study of Crowdsourced Learning in GitHub. *IEEE Access: Practical Innovations, Open Solutions, 7*, 1–1. doi:10.1109/ACCESS.2019.2915247

Luo, Y., Zhao, Y., Ma, W., & Chen, L. (2017). What are the Factors Impacting Build Breakage? *2017 14th Web Information Systems and Applications Conference (WISA)*, 139–142. 10.1109/WISA.2017.17

Ma, Y., Fakhoury, S., Christensen, M., Arnaoudova, V., Zogaan, W., & Mirakhorli, M. (2018). Automatic classification of software artifacts in open-source applications. *Proceedings of the 15th International Conference on Mining Software Repositories - MSR '18*, 414–425. 10.1145/3196398.3196446

Madeyski, L., & Kawalerowicz, M. (2017). Continuous Defect Prediction: The Idea and a Related Dataset. *2017 IEEE/ACM 14th International Conference on Mining Software Repositories (MSR)*, 515–518. 10.1109/MSR.2017.46

Manes, S. S., & Baysal, O. (2019). How often and what StackOverflow posts do developers reference in their GitHub projects? *Proceedings of the 16th International Conference on Mining Software Repositories*, 235–239. 10.1109/MSR.2019.00047

Markovtsev, V., & Long, W. (2018). Public git archive: a big code dataset for all. *15th International Conference on Mining Software Repositories*, 34–37. Retrieved from https://dl.acm.org/citation.cfm?id=3196464

Martins, P., Achar, R., & Lopes, C. V. (2018a). 50K-C a dataset of compilable, and compiled, Java projects. *Proceedings of the 15th International Conference on Mining Software Repositories - MSR '18*, 1–5. 10.1145/3196398.3196450

Martins, P., Achar, R., & Lopes, C. V. (2018b). *The Java Build Framework: Large Scale Compilation.* Retrieved from https://arxiv.org/abs/1804.04621

Matragkas, N., Williams, J. R., Kolovos, D. S., & Paige, R. F. (2014). Analysing the "biodiversity" of open source ecosystems: the GitHub case. *Proceedings of the 11th Working Conference on Mining Software Repositories - MSR 2014*, 356–359. 10.1145/2597073.2597119

Medeiros, F., Lima, G., Amaral, G., Apel, S., Kästner, C., Ribeiro, M., & Gheyi, R. (2018). An investigation of misunderstanding code patterns in C open-source software projects. *Empirical Software Engineering*, 1–34. doi:10.100710664-018-9666-x

Medeiros, F., Ribeiro, M., Gheyi, R., Apel, S., Kastner, C., Ferreira, B., Carvalho, L., & Fonseca, B. (2018). Discipline Matters: Refactoring of Preprocessor Directives in the #ifdef Hell. *IEEE Transactions on Software Engineering*, *44*(5), 453–469. doi:10.1109/TSE.2017.2688333

Middleton, J., Murphy-Hill, E., Green, D., Meade, A., Mayer, R., White, D., & McDonald, S. (2018). Which contributions predict whether developers are accepted into github teams. *Proceedings of the 15th International Conference on Mining Software Repositories - MSR '18*, 403–413. 10.1145/3196398.3196429

Miranda, F., Lins, L., Klosowski, J. T., & Silva, C. T. (2018). TopKube: A Rank-Aware Data Cube for Real-Time Exploration of Spatiotemporal Data. *IEEE Transactions on Visualization and Computer Graphics*, *24*(3), 1394–1407. doi:10.1109/TVCG.2017.2671341 PMID:28221997

Mujhid, I. J. S., Santos, J. C., Gopalakrishnan, R., & Mirakhorli, M. (2017). A search engine for finding and reusing architecturally significant code. *Journal of Systems and Software*, *130*, 81–93. doi:10.1016/j.jss.2016.11.034

Munaiah, N., Kroh, S., Cabrey, C., & Nagappan, M. (2017). Curating GitHub for engineered software projects. *Empirical Software Engineering*, *22*(6), 3219–3253. doi:10.100710664-017-9512-6

Murgia, A., Concas, G., Tonelli, R., Ortu, M., Demeyer, S., & Marchesi, M. (2014). On the influence of maintenance activity types on the issue resolution time. *Proceedings of the 10th International Conference on Predictive Models in Software Engineering - PROMISE '14*, 12–21. 10.1145/2639490.2639506

Muylaert, W., & De Roover, C. (2017). Prevalence of Botched Code Integrations. *2017 IEEE/ACM 14th International Conference on Mining Software Repositories (MSR)*, 503–506. 10.1109/MSR.2017.40

Muylaert, W., De Meuter, W., & De Roover, C. (2016). An Exploratory Study Into the Prevalence of Botched Code Integrations. *SATToSE*. Retrieved from http://sattose.wdfiles.com/local--files/2016:alltalks/SATTOSE2016_paper_8.pdf

Nielek, R., Jarczyk, O., Pawlak, K., Bukowski, L., Bartusiak, R., & Wierzbicki, A. (2016). Choose a Job You Love: Predicting Choices of GitHub Developers. *2016 IEEE/WIC/ACM International Conference on Web Intelligence (WI)*, 200–207. 10.1109/WI.2016.0037

Onoue, S., Hata, H., & Matsumoto, K. (2014). Software population pyramids: The Current and the Future of OSS Development Communities. *Proceedings of the 8th ACM/IEEE International Symposium on Empirical Software Engineering and Measurement - ESEM '14*, 1–4. 10.1145/2652524.2652565

Onoue, S., Kula, R. G., Hata, H., & Matsumoto, K. (2017). *The Health and Wealth of OSS Projects: Evidence from Community Activities and Product Evolution*. Retrieved from https://arxiv.org/abs/1709.10324

Ortu, M., Destefanis, G., Counsell, S., Swift, S., Tonelli, R., & Marchesi, M. (2017). How diverse is your team? Investigating gender and nationality diversity in GitHub teams. *Journal of Software Engineering Research and Development*, *5*(1), 9. doi:10.118640411-017-0044-y

Ortu, M., Hall, T., Marchesi, M., Tonelli, R., Bowes, D., & Destefanis, G. (2018). Mining Communication Patterns in Software Development: A GitHub Analysis. *Proceedings of the 14th International Conference on Predictive Models and Data Analytics in Software Engineering - PROMISE'18*, 70–79. 10.1145/3273934.3273943

Ortu, M., Pinna, A., Tonelli, R., Marchesi, M., Bowes, D., & Destefanis, G. (2018). Angry-builds: An Empirical Study Of Affect Metrics and Builds Success on GitHub Ecosystem. *Proceedings of the 19th International Conference on Agile Software Development Companion - XP '18*, 1–2. 10.1145/3234152.3234160

Padhye, R., Mani, S., & Sinha, V. S. (2014). A study of external community contribution to open-source projects on GitHub. *Proceedings of the 11th Working Conference on Mining Software Repositories - MSR 2014*, 332–335. 10.1145/2597073.2597113

Pletea, D., Vasilescu, B., & Serebrenik, A. (2014). Security and emotion: sentiment analysis of security discussions on GitHub. *Proceedings of the 11th Working Conference on Mining Software Repositories - MSR 2014*, 348–351. 10.1145/2597073.2597117

Qiu, H. S., Nolte, A., Brown, A., Serebrenik, A., & Vasilescu, B. (2019). Going farther together: the impact of social capital on sustained participation in open source. *41st ACM/IEEE International Conference on Software Engineering, (ICSE2019)*, 688–699. Retrieved from https://research.tue.nl/en/publications/going-farther-together-the-impact-of-social-capital-on-sustained-

Raghuraman, A., Ho-Quang, T. V., Chaudron Chalmers, M. R., Serebrenik, A., & Vasilescu, B. (2019). Does UML Modeling Associate with Lower Defect Proneness? A Preliminary Empirical Investigation. *16th International Conference on Mining Software Repositories*. Retrieved from https://pypi.org/project/langdetect/

Rahman, M. M., & Roy, C. K. (2014). An insight into the pull requests of GitHub. *Proceedings of the 11th Working Conference on Mining Software Repositories - MSR 2014*, 364–367. 10.1145/2597073.2597121

Rastogi, A., & Nagappan, N. (2016a). Forking and the Sustainability of the Developer Community Participation -- An Empirical Investigation on Outcomes and Reasons. *2016 IEEE 23rd International Conference on Software Analysis, Evolution, and Reengineering (SANER)*, 102–111. 10.1109/SANER.2016.27

Rastogi, A., & Nagappan, N. (2016b). On the Personality Traits of GitHub Contributors. *2016 IEEE 27th International Symposium on Software Reliability Engineering (ISSRE)*, 77–86. 10.1109/ISSRE.2016.43

Robles, G., Ho-Quang, T., Hebig, R., Chaudron, M. R. V., & Fernandez, M. A. (2017). An Extensive Dataset of UML Models in GitHub. *2017 IEEE/ACM 14th International Conference on Mining Software Repositories (MSR)*, 519–522. 10.1109/MSR.2017.48

Saha, S., Muradul Bashir, G. M., Raihan Talukder, M., Karmaker, J., & Saiful Islam, M. (2018). Which Programming Language and Platform Developers Prefer for the Development? A Study Using Stack Overflow. *2018 International Conference on Innovations in Science, Engineering and Technology (ICISET)*, 305–310. 10.1109/ICISET.2018.8745630

Saito, Y., Fujiwara, K., Igaki, H., Yoshida, N., & Iida, H. (2016). How do GitHub Users Feel with Pull-Based Development? *2016 7th International Workshop on Empirical Software Engineering in Practice (IWESEP)*, 7–11. 10.1109/IWESEP.2016.19

Santos, E. A., Campbell, J. C., Hindle, A., & Amaral, J. N. (2017). Finding and correcting syntax errors using recurrent neural networks. *PeerJ* Preprints. doi:10.7287/peerj.preprints.3123v1

Sawant, A. A., Robbes, R., & Bacchelli, A. (2016). On the Reaction to Deprecation of 25,357 Clients of 4+1 Popular Java APIs. *2016 IEEE International Conference on Software Maintenance and Evolution (ICSME)*, 400–410. 10.1109/ICSME.2016.64

Sawant, A. A., Robbes, R., & Bacchelli, A. (2018). On the reaction to deprecation of clients of 4 + 1 popular Java APIs and the JDK. *Empirical Software Engineering, 23*(4), 2158–2197. doi:10.100710664-017-9554-9

Sayagh, M., Kerzazi, N., Adams, B., & Petrillo, F. (2018). Software Configuration Engineering in Practice: Interviews, Survey, and Systematic Literature Review. *IEEE Transactions on Software Engineering*, 1–1. doi:10.1109/TSE.2018.2867847

Schreiber, R. R., & Zylka, M. P. (2020, March 1). Social Network Analysis in Software Development Projects: A Systematic Literature Review. *International Journal of Software Engineering and Knowledge Engineering, 30*(03), 321–362. doi:10.1142/S021819402050014X

Sharma, T., Fragkoulis, M., & Spinellis, D. (2016). Does your configuration code smell? *Proceedings of the 13th International Workshop on Mining Software Repositories - MSR '16*, 189–200. 10.1145/2901739.2901761

Sheoran, J., Blincoe, K., Kalliamvakou, E., Damian, D., & Ell, J. (2014). Understanding watchers on GitHub. *Proceedings of the 11th Working Conference on Mining Software Repositories - MSR 2014*, 336–339. 10.1145/2597073.2597114

Silvestri, G., Yang, J., Bozzon, A., & Tagarelli, A. (2015). Linking Accounts across Social Networks: the Case of StackOverflow, Github and Twitter. *KDWeb*. Retrieved from https://www.semanticscholar.org/paper/Linking-Accounts-across-Social-Networks%3A-the-Case-Silvestri-Yang/351b86ffc19cb02e51466522a0b4b199ac1dbd06

Soares, D. M., & de Lima, J. (2018). What factors influence the reviewer assignment to pull requests? *Information and Software Technology, 98*, 32–43. doi:10.1016/j.infsof.2018.01.015

Soares, D. M., & de Lima, J. M. L., Murta, L., & Plastino, A. (2015). Acceptance factors of pull requests in open-source projects. *Proceedings of the 30th Annual ACM Symposium on Applied Computing - SAC '15*, 1541–1546. 10.1145/2695664.2695856

Soares, D. M. Jr., Murta, L., & Plastino, A. (2015). Rejection Factors of Pull Requests Filed by Core Team Developers in Software Projects with High Acceptance Rates. *2015 IEEE 14th International Conference on Machine Learning and Applications (ICMLA)*, 960–965. 10.1109/ICMLA.2015.41

Sun, X., Xu, W., Xia, X., Chen, X., & Li, B. (2018). Personalized project recommendation on GitHub. *Science China. Information Sciences, 61*(5), 1–14. doi:10.100711432-017-9419-x

Terrell, J., Kofink, A., Middleton, J., Rainear, C., Murphy-Hill, E., Parnin, C., & Stallings, J. (2017). Gender differences and bias in open source: Pull request acceptance of women versus men. *PeerJ. Computer Science, 3*, e111. doi:10.7717/peerj-cs.111

Tomasdottir, K. F., Aniche, M., & Van Deursen, A. (2018). The Adoption of JavaScript Linters in Practice: A Case Study on ESLint. *IEEE Transactions on Software Engineering*, 1–1. doi:10.1109/TSE.2018.2871058

Urli, S., Yu, Z., Seinturier, L., & Monperrus, M. (2018). How to design a program repair bot? Insights from the Repairnator Project. *Proceedings of the 40th International Conference on Software Engineering Software Engineering in Practice - ICSE-SEIP '18*, 95–104. 10.1145/3183519.3183540

van der Bent, E., Hage, J., Visser, J., & Gousios, G. (2018). How good is your puppet? An empirically defined and validated quality model for puppet. *2018 IEEE 25th International Conference on Software Analysis, Evolution and Reengineering (SANER)*, 164–174. 10.1109/SANER.2018.8330206

Vasilescu, B. (2014). Human aspects, gamification, and social media in collaborative software engineering. *Companion Proceedings of the 36th International Conference on Software Engineering - ICSE Companion 2014*, 646–649. 10.1145/2591062.2591091

Vasilescu, B., Filkov, V., & Serebrenik, A. (2013). StackOverflow and GitHub: Associations between Software Development and Crowdsourced Knowledge. *2013 International Conference on Social Computing*, 188–195. 10.1109/SocialCom.2013.35

Vasilescu, B., Filkov, V., & Serebrenik, A. (2015). Perceptions of diversity on GitHub: a user survey. *Proceedings of the 8th International Workshop on Cooperative and Human Aspects of Software Engineering*, 50–56. Retrieved from https://dl.acm.org/citation.cfm?id=2819330

Vasilescu, B., Posnett, D., Ray, B., van den Brand, M. G. J., Serebrenik, A., Devanbu, P., & Filkov, V. (2015). Gender and Tenure Diversity in GitHub Teams. *Proceedings of the 33rd Annual ACM Conference on Human Factors in Computing Systems - CHI '15*, 3789–3798. 10.1145/2702123.2702549

Vasilescu, B., Serebrenik, A., & Filkov, V. (2015). A Data Set for Social Diversity Studies of GitHub Teams. *2015 IEEE/ACM 12th Working Conference on Mining Software Repositories*, 514–517. 10.1109/MSR.2015.77

Vasilescu, B., Van Schuylenburg, S., Wulms, J., Serebrenik, A., & van den Brand, M. G. J. (2014). Continuous Integration in a Social-Coding World: Empirical Evidence from GitHub. *2014 IEEE International Conference on Software Maintenance and Evolution*, 401–405. 10.1109/ICSME.2014.62

Vasilescu, B., Yu, Y., Wang, H., Devanbu, P., & Filkov, V. (2015). Quality and productivity outcomes relating to continuous integration in GitHub. *Proceedings of the 2015 10th Joint Meeting on Foundations of Software Engineering*, 805–816. 10.1145/2786805.2786850

Vassallo, C., Proksch, S., Gall, H. C., & Di Penta, M. (2019). Automated reporting of anti-patterns and decay in continuous integration. *Proceedings of the 41st International Conference on Software Engineering ICSE*, 105–115. 10.1109/ICSE.2019.00028

van der Veen, E., Gousios, G., & Zaidman, A. (2015). Automatically Prioritizing Pull Requests. *2015 IEEE/ACM 12th Working Conference on Mining Software Repositories*, 357–361. 10.1109/MSR.2015.40

Wang, W., Poo-Caamano, G., Wilde, E., & German, D. M. (2015). What Is the Gist? Understanding the Use of Public Gists on GitHub. *2015 IEEE/ACM 12th Working Conference on Mining Software Repositories*, 314–323. 10.1109/MSR.2015.36

Wang, Z., Wang, Y., & Redmiles, D. (2018). Competence-confidence gap: a threat to female developers' contribution on github. *Proceedings of the 40th International Conference on Software Engineering Software Engineering in Society - ICSE-SEIS '18*, 81–90. 10.1145/3183428.3183437

Werder, K. (2018). The evolution of emotional displays in open source software development teams: An Individual Growth Curve Analysis. *Proceedings of the 3rd International Workshop on Emotion Awareness in Software Engineering - SEmotion '18*, 1–6. 10.1145/3194932.3194934

Werder, K., & Brinkkemper, S. (2018). MEME - Toward a Method for EMotions Extraction from GitHub. *Emotion 2018 : 2018 ACM/IEEE 3rd International Workshop on Emotion Awareness in Software Engineering*. Retrieved from https://ieeexplore.ieee.org/document/8595354/keywords#keywords

Wisse, W., & Veenman, C. (2015). Scripting DNA: Identifying the JavaScript programmer. *Digital Investigation*, *15*, 61–71. doi:10.1016/j.diin.2015.09.001

Wittern, E., Suter, P., & Rajagopalan, S. (2016). A look at the dynamics of the JavaScript package ecosystem. *Proceedings of the 13th International Conference on Mining Software Repositories*, 351–361. 10.1145/2901739.2901743

Xavier, J., Macedo, A., & Maia, M. de A. (2014). Understanding the popularity of reporters and assignees in the Github. *International Conference on Software Engineering and Knowledge Engineering (SEKE)*, 484–489. Retrieved from https://www.semanticscholar.org/paper/Understanding-the-popularity-of-reporters-and-in-Xavier-Macedo/a113516ff1ca5ff4ebdbb4a2b90c972158cc3763

Xia, J., & Li, Y. (2017). Could We Predict the Result of a Continuous Integration Build? An Empirical Study. *2017 IEEE International Conference on Software Quality, Reliability and Security Companion (QRS-C)*, 311–315. 10.1109/QRS-C.2017.59

Yamashita, K., Kamei, Y., McIntosh, S., Hassan, A. E., & Ubayashi, N. (2016). Magnet or Sticky? Measuring Project Characteristics from the Perspective of Developer Attraction and Retention. *Journal of Information Processing*, *24*(2), 339–348. doi:10.2197/ipsjjip.24.339

Yamashita, K., McIntosh, S., Kamei, Y., Hassan, A. E., & Ubayashi, N. (2015). Revisiting the applicability of the pareto principle to core development teams in open source software projects. *Proceedings of the 14th International Workshop on Principles of Software Evolution - IWPSE 2015*, 46–55. 10.1145/2804360.2804366

Yamashita, K., McIntosh, S., Kamei, Y., & Ubayashi, N. (2014). Magnet or sticky? an OSS project-by-project typology. *Proceedings of the 11th Working Conference on Mining Software Repositories - MSR 2014*, 344–347. 10.1145/2597073.2597116

Yan, D.-C., Li, M., & Wang, B.-H. (2017). Dependence centrality similarity: Measuring the diversity of profession levels of interests. *Physica A*, *479*, 118–127. doi:10.1016/j.physa.2017.02.082

Yan, D.-C., & Wang, B.-H. (2017). *Collaborative similarity analysis of multilayer developer-project bipartite network*. Retrieved from https://arxiv.org/abs/1703.03093

Yan, D.-C., Wei, Z.-W., Han, X.-P., & Wang, B.-H. (2017). Empirical analysis on the human dynamics of blogging behavior on GitHub. *Physica A*, *465*, 775–781. doi:10.1016/j.physa.2016.08.054

Yang, D., Martins, P., Saini, V., & Lopes, C. (2017). Stack Overflow in Github: Any Snippets There? *2017 IEEE/ACM 14th International Conference on Mining Software Repositories (MSR)*, 280–290. 10.1109/MSR.2017.13

Ying, H., Chen, L., Liang, T., & Wu, J. (2016). EARec: Leveraging Expertise and Authority for Pull-Request Reviewer Recommendation in GitHub. *Proceedings of the 3rd International Workshop on CrowdSourcing in Software Engineering - CSI-SE '16*, 29–35. 10.1145/2897659.2897660

Yu, Y., Wang, H., Filkov, V., Devanbu, P., & Vasilescu, B. (2015). Wait for It: Determinants of Pull Request Evaluation Latency on GitHub. *2015 IEEE/ACM 12th Working Conference on Mining Software Repositories*, 367–371. 10.1109/MSR.2015.42

Yu, Y., Wang, H., Yin, G., & Ling, C. X. (2014). Who Should Review this Pull-Request Reviewer Recommendation to Expedite Crowd Collaboration. *2014 21st Asia-Pacific Software Engineering Conference*, 335–342. 10.1109/APSEC.2014.57

Yu, Y., Wang, H., Yin, G., & Wang, T. (2016). Reviewer recommendation for pull-requests in GitHub: What can we learn from code review and bug assignment? *Information and Software Technology*, *74*, 204–218. doi:10.1016/j.infsof.2016.01.004

Yu, Y., Yin, G., Wang, H., & Wang, T. (2014). Exploring the patterns of social behavior in GitHub. *Proceedings of the 1st International Workshop on Crowd-Based Software Development Methods and Technologies - CrowdSoft 2014*, 31–36. 10.1145/2666539.2666571

Yu, Y., Yin, G., Wang, T., Yang, C., & Wang, H. (2016). Determinants of pull-based development in the context of continuous integration. *Science China. Information Sciences*, *59*(8), 080104. doi:10.100711432-016-5595-8

Zhang, P., Xiong, F., Leung, H. K. N., & Song, W. (2018). FunkR-pDAE: Personalized Project Recommendation Using Deep Learning. *IEEE Transactions on Emerging Topics in Computing*, 1–1. doi:10.1109/TETC.2018.2870734

Zhang, Y., Yin, G., Yu, Y., & Wang, H. (2014). Investigating social media in GitHub's pull-requests: a case study on Ruby on Rails. *Proceedings of the 1st International Workshop on Crowd-Based Software Development Methods and Technologies - CrowdSoft 2014*, 37–41. 10.1145/2666539.2666572

Zhao, G., da Costa, D. A., & Zou, Y. (2019). Improving the Pull Requests Review Process Using Learning-to-rank Algorithms. *Empirical Software Engineering*, *24*(4), 1–31. doi:10.100710664-019-09696-8

ENDNOTES

[1]   Harzing's Publish or Perish
[2]   Last check was done on 24 July 2019
[3]   https://www.vosviewer.com
[4]   https://developer.github.com/v3/\#rate-limiting

This research was previously published in the International Journal of Open Source Software and Processes (IJOSSP), 11(4); pages 1-26, copyright year 2020 by IGI Publishing (an imprint of IGI Global).

Chapter 4
On Challenges for Implementing ISO Standards in Software:
Can Both Open and Closed Standards Be Implemented in Open Source Software?

Björn Lundell
University of Skövde, Sweden

Jonas Gamalielsson
University of Skövde, Sweden

Andrew Katz
University of Skövde, Sweden & Moorcrofts LLP, UK

ABSTRACT

Over the years, the importance of open standards has been acknowledged in EU and national policies. Formal (e.g., ISO) standards are often referred to in software development and procurement. Use of formal (ISO) standards and to what extent ISO standards can be implemented in open source software is considered, with particular reference to patent licensing. It is shown that not all formal standards are open standards and that FRAND commitments may impose major challenges for use of such standards. Further policies and procedures set by standards setting organisations (SSOs) regarding the notification of standards-essential patents (SEPs) present challenges for organisations wishing to implement standards in software. This chapter elaborates implications and suggests ways of addressing the challenges identified. Use of formal standards may create barriers for implementation in open source software and inhibit an open and inclusive business-friendly ecosystem.

DOI: 10.4018/978-1-7998-9158-1.ch004

INTRODUCTION

'Openness' including open standards and open source software is increasingly prevalent, but presents a number of challenges requiring effective policy and strategic initiatives. The European Commission (EC, 2013a, 2013b) and countries, such as the Netherlands (NOC, 2007), Portugal (Ballard, 2012), and the U.K. (UK, 2012a, 2015), have acknowledged the importance of open standards and have implemented initiatives accordingly.

Open standards have been discussed by researchers (e.g. Bird, 1998) and policy makers in the EU and different member countries (EU, 2004; SOU, 2009; EC, 2016; Permanent Representatives Committee, 2016) for a long time. Some member countries mandate use of open standards, based on definitions which require that standards are provided on royalty-free conditions, as part of national policy (e.g. NOC, 2007; UK, 2012a). Such policies aim to promote use of standards which have certain open properties and can thereby be used as a basis for implementation in software under different (proprietary and open source) software licenses. For example, the U.K. Government has a national policy which promotes and mandates use of specific open standards (UK, 2012a, 2012b, 2014, 2015). In Sweden, the minister responsible for municipalities has expressed support for the definition of 'open standard' set out in the European Interoperability Framework version 1.0 (Odell, 2009) and national framework agreements for public sector procurement of software in Sweden refer to open standards (EU, 2004; SOU, 2009; Kammarkollegiet, 2013, 2014a, 2014b, 2016) in relation to the standards which can be referenced in procurement. Further, in a response to the view that ICT standardisation needs an IPR policy which is "based on FRAND licensing terms" (EC, 2016) within the EU there are also seven EU members which express concerns and instead emphasise the importance of Open Standards "relying on Royalty Free intellectual property models in regard to software" (Permanent Representatives Committee, 2016) as a strategy for removing "barriers to innovation, particularly for SMEs" (Permanent Representatives Committee, 2016).

At the same time, there is confusion related to use of the term 'standard' and research shows that practitioners may regard products and applications (e.g. Microsoft Word) as standards (e.g. Lundell, 2011; Lundell et al., 2016). The study by Lundell et al. (2016) which is commissioned by the Swedish Competition Authority "found that many IT-projects in the Swedish public sector refer to closed standards which cannot be implemented in open source software" (Lundell et al., 2017). Further, the Director General for the Swedish Competition Authority expresses concerns for closed standards, as follows: "From a competition perspective it is often problematic when public sector organisations conduct IT procurement and express requirements for closed standards" (Lundell et al., 2016 (our translation)).

It has also been shown that there is confusion amongst policy makers between the two concepts of open standard and open source software (e.g. Egyedi & Enserink, 2013). Previous research results also show that many standardisation organisations neglect implementation issues and conclude that standards development and implementation activities "cannot be meaningfully separated" (Egyedi, 2007, p. 612). In particular, implementation of standards for representation of data over long life-cycles, beyond the life-cycle for any specific software, is of particular importance for long-term maintenance of data (Lundell, 2012). For these reasons, this study considers standards for representation of data and the potential for implementation of such standards in software, with a specific focus on the extent to which different standards can be implemented in open source software (i.e. software provided under a license which is recognised by Open Source Initiative (OSI, 2017)).

Previous research shows various positive effects from use of open standards (e.g. Friedrich, 2011; Ghosh, 2005; Krechmer, 2005; Lundell, 2012; Simcoe, 2006) and its potential for promotion of innovation has been stressed in recent research (e.g. Lundell, 2012; Lundell et al., 2016; Lundell et al., 2017). Further, reports from the European Commission (EC, 2013a) and the U.K. Government (UK, 2012a, 2012b, 2015) show considerable potential for innovation from the use of open standards, which can also reduce certain risks, for example to enable interoperability and prevent different kinds of lock-in effects with associated unwanted dependencies on suppliers and proprietary technologies. Friedrich (2011) states that the "prime example for how Open Standards can boost innovation are the internet and the world wide web". Open standards facilitate collaboration in development of software which can be provided under different types of licenses, including open source software. Such open collaboration represents an early exemplar of open innovation (Lundell & van der Linden, 2013) and open standards and open source software are used by most innovative organisations. For example, on 5 May 2014 Rachael King reported in the Wall Street Journal that a Samsung representative stated during an open source business conference: "Today, you can't build a product without using Open Source"[1].

It is noted that "standards are subject to legal rights which impact upon, not only their development, but also their implementation" (Fitzgerald & Pappalardo, 2009, p. 467). Specifically, writing software to implement the technical specifications embodied in standards also requires addressing a number of legal issues since "technical standards may incorporate patented technologies, while the specification documents of standards are protected by copyright" (Fitzgerald & Pappalardo, 2009, p. 467). Legal experts have argued that some commonly used (F)RAND licences are incompatible with open source licensing owing to the inability of the licensee to sub-licence to downstream recipients (EC, 2012) and the European Commission acknowledges that such licensing conditions for standards "create barriers for Open Source projects to implement the technical specification" (EC, 2013b). Further, in a public response to an open consultation concerning establishment of a national open standards policy representatives for the World-Wide-Web Consortium argued: "If a standard is covered by a patent or is in a FRAND system potentially covered by a patent, an open source developer risks his/her economic survival by implementing it because the patent owner can always go back and ask for past royalties." (Dardailler et al., 2012)

There has been a long tradition of using and referencing formal standards when developing and procuring software. For many years it has been permitted to explicitly reference formal standards (as opposed to informal standards) in public sector procurement (Lundell, 2011). However, there is limited knowledge concerning the relationship between formal and open standards, despite inclusion of requirements for open standards in policies in several countries.

The *overarching goal* of our study is to clarify and characterise use of formal and open standards in national policy and implications for implementation in software. Based on this, the study addresses *three specific objectives*. First, we review and report on conditions for use of ISO standards which are to be implemented in software. Second, we report on insights concerning open and formal standards, and elaborate on conditions for use of formal standards in scenarios when national policy imposes requirements for use of open standards. Third, we establish under what conditions open standards can be implemented in open source software, and contrast this with conditions for implementation of formal standards in open source software with a view to suggest ways for resolving potential inhibitors.

Specifically, the chapter makes *three novel contributions*. First, we elaborate conditions for use of ISO standards and highlight inhibitors for their implementation in software. Second, we elaborate conditions for use of open standards and formal standards, and present a conceptual model which can be used as an analytical device for analysis of specific standards. Third, we elaborate conditions for implementation of specific open and formal standards in open source software and thereby illuminate why certain formal standards are not open standards, and based on this elaboration suggest a number of ways of resolving certain inhibitors to implementation.

ON FORMAL AND OPEN STANDARDS

Definitions of 'standards' and the potential business benefit from use of standards in various contexts have been issues for ongoing discussion in the IT-field since the 1990s (e.g. Bird, 1998). Standards have a function of creating norms and can thereby "establish requirements that, though not expressed in formal legal instruments, are in practice mandatory and must be implemented by participants in certain fields of technical or business activity" (Fitzgerald & Pappalardo, 2009, p. 473). Formal standards are provided by organisations recognised as formal standardisation organisations (SSOs) (de Vries, 2006), which include ISO (International Organization for Standardization), ITU (International Telecommunication Union), ETSI (European Telecommunication Standards Institute), and national standardisation organisations (e.g. British Standards Institute). Industry consortia and other bodies (e.g. W3C (World Wide Web Consortium) which do not have the status of formal standardisation organisations also create standards which are adopted *de facto* by industry. Some of these informal standards are submitted to formal SSOs and each such standard may become a formal standard if the standard is adopted by a formal SSO. Broadly, formal standards[2] may, in accordance with relevant legislation[3], be specified as part of a procurement process, whereas informal standards do not automatically have this status[4] (although there exist circumstances in which informal standards may be specifically referenced).

Over the past decades, many consortia and industry fora have become involved in ICT standards setting (Jakobs & Mora, 2008). During this period there has also been a shift of control concerning content in technical standards from government to industry, something which in turn has led to difficulties in distinguishing IT-standards from proprietary technology controlled by individual companies. As stated by Krechmer (2001): "At the end of the nineteenth century, governments controlled the technical standards domain. In the past 100 years, the voluntary consensus standards process has developed and expanded to the point that we have difficulty distinguishing between a standard and a vendor's proprietary technology" (Krechmer, 2001, p. 100).

It has been argued that openness (as the term is used in relation to standards) "describes the fairness of the standardization process to all possible interest groups" (Krechmer, 2001). Further, Bird (1998, p. 76) states that "accessibility of the standard and the control of the standard" are two key principles for any definition of an open standard. First, concerning the principle for accessibility of a standard, it is argued that "any standard must be available to be implemented in product without encumbrance, no royalties, no excessive charges to gain access to the document" (Bird, 1998, p. 76). Second, concerning the principle for control of a standard, it is argued that the "standard must be evolved through a known and predictable process that is open to input and influence by all interested parties" (Bird, 1998, p. 76). However, we contend that these are not the only criteria determining openness. A further crucial criterion concerns its licensing conditions.

Besides copyright for "legal protection to access the standard documentation, there could also be some industrial property rights (that is, patents) on the technical solutions included and described in the standard itself. Therefore whoever acquires such documentation could still be prevented from adopting and implementing the standard, unless by paying another royalty to the possible patent holders." (Aliprandi, 2011, p. 12) In some cases, patentees are willing to license their patents impacting on a particular standard under so called (F)RAND ('(fair,) reasonable and non-discriminatory') licensing terms, something which would imply that all would be allowed licences on supposedly fair royalty terms (Lea & Hall, 2004).

As stated by Contreras (2015): "FRAND commitments are made voluntarily by participants in standards-development activities, among other things, to induce others to adopt their patented technology in a standard". Licensing of patented technology may involve significant revenues for companies. For example, Jakobs (2017) reports that: "Ericsson, Microsoft, and Nokia, with a combined annual income of over $1 billion from the licensing of patents, are examples of firms benefitting from the licensing of IP." (p. 85) Different SSOs have established their "own terms for a FRAND commitment, which could be phrased as an offer to negotiate a license on fair and reasonable terms – it is not a commitment to negotiate a contract at a set rate." (Pentheroudakis & Baron, 2017, p. 33) However, it should be noted that 'fairness' in specific licensing terms for IT-standards are context-dependent and often cannot be assessed a-priori since "the license terms are usually kept secret" (Lea & Hall, 2004, p. 83). For this reason, when an IT-standard is provided under such unknown (F)RAND licensing terms it seems clear that an organisation which plans to use such a standard for implementation in software will face significant challenges.

Based on a comprehensive analysis of cases, a study which analysed interpretation of FRAND commitments and the definition of FRAND royalties found that "Most cases before courts and competition authorities concerning SEPs are related to patent infringement damages, injunctions or antitrust." (Pentheroudakis & Baron, 2017, p. 10). Further, Lerner & Tirole (2015) found that declarations of SEPs that companies do to SSOs contributes to disputes between companies and it is claimed that many of "the critical assertions in these disputes relate to the commitments that firms have made to standard-setting bodies during the standard-setting process." (Lerner & Tirole, 2015, p. 548)

There are several factors which may contribute to significant uncertainty related to implications of FRAND commitments for different parties (e.g. Contreras, 2015, 2017; EC, 2012; ECSIP, 2014; Pentheroudakis & Baron, 2017). For example, when SEPs are transferred to new owners this contributes to increased difficulty in clarifying conditions for use of standards in that some new owners may be difficult or impossible to identify and reach. This may be due to the fact that declarations of SEPs to a patent database maintained by an SSO (e.g. the ISO patent database) are rarely updated, something which contributes to uncertainty concerning FRAND commitments. Concerns related to transfer of SEPs have been analysed in a commissioned study published by the EC (ECSIP, 2014), which found that: "SEP transfers contribute to the lack of transparency about SEP ownership, because their occurrence and the identity of new owners are not public information. A possible means to address this problem is the notification of SEP transfers by recordation." (ECSIP, 2014, p. 189) Further, in a situation where a patent owner decides to sell, or in some other way, transfer, a SEP that has previously been declared in a patent database maintained by one (or several) SSOs this introduces uncertainty concerning the applicability of the commitment made by the initial declarant to their successors in title with respect to the relevant SEPs, something which has been elaborated as follows by Contreras (2017): "When a SEP holder makes a commitment to license SEPs to manufacturers of standardized products, it is not always clear whether that commitment applies only to the SEP holder making the commitment, or whether it binds subsequent holders of the SEP." (Contreras, 2017, p. 38, 39)

It should be noted that not all informal standards bodies work on a Royalty-Free (RF) basis and many have adopted a RAND-based IPR-policy (e.g. OMA[5] and SMPTE[6]). Further, some standards bodies (e.g. OASIS and GS1) allow for both Royalty-Free and RAND-conditions. For example, OASIS allows for different IPR-models and when a Technical Committee (TC) is established the TC selects to operate under one of four different IPR-modes[7] (including RF and RAND terms). Similarly, the GS1 Intellectual Property (IP) Policy[8] states that "GS1 seeks to develop standards that can be practised on a royalty-free basis to the greatest extent possible", even if they also allow for RAND-based licensing commitments from companies.

Standardisation organisations have recently shown an increased interest in exploring the potential for strategic adoption of open source development practices and utilising open source projects for development and provision of standards. For example, several SSOs have organised workshops in order to scrutinise the potential adoption of open source in the traditional SSO contexts in order to improve standardisation processes. These workshops have led to various experiences and suggestions being discussed (e.g. Clark, 2016; Lundell et al., 2016b). From investigation of a specific example, it should be noted that it has been found that open source work practices may contribute to improved standardisation processes (Lundell & Gamalielsson, 2017).

RESEARCH APPROACH

For addressing the *first objective*, we reviewed conditions for use of ISO standards with a view to specifically considering implementation of standards in software. We considered patent policy and other information provided by ISO, such as information related to the ISO patent database. For addressing the *second objective*, we reviewed conditions for use of formal standards in scenarios when national policy imposes requirements for use of open standards. In so doing, we present a conceptual model aimed to clarify the dimensions openness and formality of standards. For addressing the *third objective*, we identified and analysed a relevant set of specific standards for populating and characterising the conceptual model to thereby establish insights and report on conditions (and potential inhibitors) for implementation of standards in open source software. To elaborate on the dimensions openness and formality of standards we undertook a review of conditions for use of standards provided by different formal and informal organisations (including ISO, IETF, W3C, etc.) in order to identify a relevant set of standards for analysis. To this end, our review considered information provided by standardisation organisations (ISO, IETF, W3C, etc.) concerning patent disclosures related to different standards and the extent to which specific standards have been recognised as open standards according to national policy. Our goal was to cover a representative set of standards which have either been recognised as open standards according to national policy (NOC, 2007; Standaardisatie, 2014; Standardisation Forum, 2011), or not so recognised, and within that set, to include standards provided by formal standards organisations on the one hand, and informal standards organisations on the other. Further, within the subset of formal standards, we focus on those for which declarations of patents have been made to the relevant SSO. Further, the study focused on standards for representation of graphics as such constitute a relevant group of (similar) standards for representation of data. An investigation of this type of standards is important for a number of reasons, including the fact that these constitute a basis for maintenance of valuable data for many organisations, sometimes over very long life-cycles. As an outcome of this, the analysis includes three specific examples of formal (ISO) standards (PNG[9], JPEG 2000[10], and TIFF/EP[11]). The analysis also includes a standard (PNG) which in addition to recognition by ISO is also provided as a W3C standard and one specific informal (W3C) standard (SVG[12]) which is not recognised by ISO. By inclusion of these four standards for analysis we cover examples of formal standards (PNG, JPEG 2000, and TIFF/EP), open standards (SVG and PNG), and standards which are both formal and open (PNG).

Specifically, we reviewed patent disclosures for all four selected standards provided by ISO and W3C. For the two standards provided by W3C (SVG and PNG) we investigated specific statements concerning patent disclosures provided at the W3C website[13]. Further, for the three ISO standards we reviewed the content in the ISO patent database[14] related to specific formal standards and collect data from all organisations that have declared patents related to specific standards. Data collection was undertaken by sending letters[15] (with reminders sent more than one month after initial requests) to organisations that have declared IPR related to the specific standard documents using contact information provided for each organisation. Responses led to additional requests for clarifications in several cases and in one case a conference call involving the researchers and legal representatives from the organisation controlling IPR related to specific standard documents.

RESULTS

On Conditions for Use of ISO Standards

ISO (International Organization for Standardization) is a formal standards body that has "published over 19 500 International Standards that can be purchased from the ISO store or from our members" (ISO, 2015a). A standard is defined by ISO as follows: "A standard is a document that provides requirements, specifications, guidelines or characteristics that can be used consistently to ensure that materials, products, processes and services are fit for their purpose." (ISO, 2015a)

The three formal standardisation organisations ISO, IEC and ITU have adopted a common patent policy which is applicable for ISO deliverables, IEC deliverables, ITU-T Recommendations, and ITU-R Recommendations. From their common patent policy, it follows that "a patent embodied fully or partly in a Recommendation | Deliverable must be accessible to everybody without undue constraints" (ISO, 2007, 2012, 2015d). In other words, the patent policy and associated guidelines clarify that a patent which impacts on use of a standard must be accessible to everybody. However, the standardisation organisations are not in any way involved in such arrangements, which is clarified as follows: "The detailed arrangements arising from patents (licensing, royalties, etc.) are left to the parties concerned, as these arrangements might differ from case to case." (ISO, 2007, 2012, 2015d) It follows that an organisation wishing to use a specific standard from any of these formal standardisation organisations must identify and obtain all necessary rights which are required for all patents impacting on the standard.

Patent databases are provided by the formal standardisation organisations as a means for clarifying which organisations control patents related to specific standards. The content in each database is based on information provided in patent declarations provided by patent holders and submitted to the standardisation organisation (ISO, 2012). For example, the ISO patent database contains 2854 declarations (24 October 2015) from organisations that control patents related to specific standards (ISO, 2015b). It should be noted that several of these declarations cover several patents impacting on a specific standard and that patent declarations made for one (or several) normative references are not visible when searching for patent declarations made for a specific standard number in the ISO patent database[16]. Further, most organisations have not disclosed the granted patent number(s) (or application number(s) if pending).

The patent databases are populated from data provided by organisations which make declarations to ISO. The current patent statement and licensing declaration form (which is uniform across ISO, ITU-T, ITU-R and IEC) currently allows the declarant to select one of three options. The options are numbered

1, 2 and 3, with the first being most favourable to a potential licensee, and the third being least favourable. The options are:

- **Option 1 ('Free of Charge'):** The Patent Holder is prepared to grant a Free of Charge license to an unrestricted number of applicants on a worldwide non-discriminatory basis and under other reasonable terms and conditions to make, use and sell implementations of the [standard]. [There are, further, two reciprocity options not discussed in this section of the chapter].
- **Option 2 ('RAND'):** The Patent Holder is prepared to grant a license to an unrestricted number of applicants on a worldwide non-discriminatory basis and under other reasonable terms and conditions to make, use and sell implementations of the [standard]. [There is a further reciprocity option not discussed in this section of the chapter].
- **Option 3 ('Unwilling to Grant'):** The Patent Holder is unwilling to grant licenses in accordance with the provisions of either 1 or 2 above. [In this case, the ISO strongly desires the declarant to notify ISO of relevant patents].

The ISO patent policy only impinges on parties which are involved in the standards-setting process. For this reason, it is possible that relevant patents held by other non-involved organisations may exist which are not reported (and hence not contained in the ISO database).

On Conditions for Use of Open and Formal Standards

This sub-section elaborates on use of open standards in national policy and reports on potential inhibitors for use of formal standards. In so doing we present a conceptual model aimed to clarify the dimensions openness and formality of standards.

The national policy in the Netherlands adopted the same definition of an open standard as the European Interoperability Framework (EU, 2004). According to the definition adopted in the Netherlands, a "standard is fully 'open' if:

1. The standard is adopted and will be maintained by a not-for-profit organisation, and its ongoing development occurs on the basis of an open decision-making procedure available to all interested parties (consensus or majority decision etc.).
2. The standard has been published and the standard specification document is available either freely or at a nominal charge. It must be permissible to all to copy, distribute and use it for no fee or at a nominal fee.
3. The intellectual property – i.e. patents possibly present – of (parts of) the standard is made irrevocably available on a royalty-free basis.
4. There are no constraints on the re-use of the standard." (NOVFS, 2011)

An important principle underlying the idea of an open standard is that it ensures that data can be interpreted independently of the software which generated it (Lundell, 2012). Further, a central characteristic of "open standards is that there are no restrictions regarding their use by ICT users and providers. Open standards are the opposite of closed standards, which do have restrictions" (NOVFS, 2011). Hence, of particular importance with open standards is that a standard which conforms to this definition can be implemented in software that is provided under different proprietary and open source software licenses.

In addition to including a definition of open standard (e.g. EU, 2004) in national policies, some countries also provide specific guidance to their agencies. For example, based on the same definition (EU, 2004) the "Swedish National Procurement Services has published a list of open standards (see Kammarkollegiet, 2016), which all can be referenced as mandatory requirements in public procurement" (Lundell et al., 2017, p. 82). Further, all these "standards can be implemented and distributed under different licenses" for proprietary software and under all licenses approved by the Open Source Initiative for open source software (Lundell et al., 2017).

If a standard is open, both in the sense that the process leading to its adoption is open to all, and that the ability to implement it is not encumbered by difficult or expensive access to the standards documentation itself, as well as challenges raised by obtaining licences to patents which are required to implement the standard without infringing, then the largest number of actors, from small companies through to multinational organisations, will be able to be involved in implementation of the standard.

A number of initiatives from government (for example, in the UK the G-Cloud/Digital Marketplace project is intended to attract the maximum number of potential suppliers for cloud-based services to the public sector) (UK, 2012c) are based on the premise that increasing the number of actors, and levelling the playing field to ensure that SMEs are not excluded from the procurement process because of barriers that are not explicit, but implicit in the complexity of the process, will increase competition, and therefore lower the cost to purchasing organisations. Likewise, where the standards are able to be implemented by the widest possible range of organisations, this can be expected to have a similar pro-competitive effect. Naturally, these arguments do not apply solely in the public sector procurement process, and a recognition that open standards have the potential to lower costs for all purchasers, from individuals to private organisations to the public sector, will be welcomed by many organisations.

Even though organisations that control patents which they believe impact on specific standards are encouraged to declare details of such it is important to note that declarations are voluntary and that not all organisations that control patents impacting on specific standards are involved in a process with the standardisation organisations. In addition, there may also be several other organisations that control patents which impact on a specific standard that cannot be found in the database, perhaps because these organisations have no interest in standardisation and therefore have not declared that they control patents to the standardisation organisation. Further, to maintain an up-to-date content in the patent database the guideline stresses the importance of providing "contact information that will remain valid over time" (ISO, 2012, 2015d) and that contact information therefore "should be generic" (ISO, 2012, 2015d). However, timeliness and the validity of the content in a patent database is considered as a challenge for a standardisation organisation: "The ITU Telecommunication Standardization Bureau (TSB), the ITU Radiocommunication Bureau (BR) and the offices of the CEOs of ISO and IEC are not in a position to give authoritative or comprehensive information about evidence, validity or scope of patents or similar rights" (ISO, 2007, 2012, 2015d).

Figure 1 presents a conceptual model aimed to provide support for analysis of specific standards. The model consists of two orthogonal dimensions. One dimension in the model concerns openness of standards (open vs. closed standard), whereas the other dimension is formality of standards (formal vs. informal standard). For example, the ISO standard PNG (ISO/IEC 15948:2004) is considered to be an open standard in the Netherlands (by the Forum Standaardisate) according to the outcome of specific assessments (NOVFS, 2011) which require that a specific standard conforms to their definition of an open standard (EU, 2004). Hence, based on the outcome of their assessment, some ISO standards (e.g. PNG) belong in the upper right quadrant, whereas other ISO standards (e.g. JPEG 2000) belong in the upper left part of the conceptual model (see Figure 1). On the other hand, some industry consortia use closed processes for development and maintenance of standards (e.g. MXF-standards from SMPTE) which clearly do not fulfil the definition of an open standard (EU, 2004). Such standards belong in the lower left quadrant in Figure 1, and are therefore unsuitable for use in the public sector according to national policy in EU countries that have adopted policy for use of open standards. Hence, it follows that not all informal standards are open standards.

Note that both axes are continuous: a standard may be more or less open depending on any one of the applicable criteria. All other things being equal, a standard, the documentation for which is available free of charge, will be regarded as more open than a standard which costs EUR 5,000 to obtain, and there is clearly a gradation in between. Likewise, the degree of formality varies from standards bodies. For example, previous research indicate that informal processes utilised by consortium SSOs (e.g. OASIS and IETF) are feasible for small companies (e.g. Gamalielsson et al., 2015, p. 41) as contributing to such typically involves remote participation via the web compared to participation in formal standardisation which typically involves additional need for travel.

Figure 1. Openness vs. Formality of standards

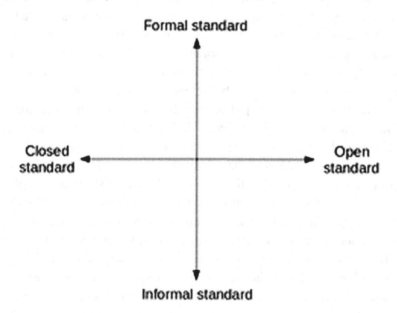

Conditions for Implementing Open and Formal Standards in Software

In this sub-section we present a review of four specific standards with respect to the definition of an open standard and populate the conceptual model with these standards. Of the four specific standards analysed, one informal (consortium) standard (SVG) is provided as a W3C standard (but not as an ISO standard). Further, one formal (ISO) standard (PNG) is included[17] in the explicit list of open standards published in the Netherlands (Standaardisatie, 2014), whereas two other formal (ISO) standards (JPEG 2000 and TIFF/EP) are not included in the explicit list and are consequently considered to be closed standards.

The SVG (Scalable Vector Graphics) standard ("Scalable Vector Graphics (SVG) 1.1 (Second Edition)", W3C Recommendation 16 August 2011[18]) is an informal (W3C) standard for representation of graphics included in the list of open standards in the Netherlands (Standaardisatie, 2014). SVG has been developed and maintained by the W3C SVG Working Group since 1998 and reached standard status (as "W3C recommendation") in 2001 (version 1.0). The current version (1.1) was released in 2011, and is currently widely deployed.

The outcome of the assessment made in the Netherlands implies that the informal (W3C) standard for the SVG standard is considered as an open standard and therefore belongs in the upper right quadrant of the conceptual model (see Figure 1). Considering the third criterion in the definition of an open standard (EU, 2004) and based on the outcome from our own analysis of patent disclosures provided by W3C it seems reasonable that the informal (W3C) standard has been included in the list of open standards (Standaardisatie, 2014).

The information provided by W3C concerning patents disclose that: "the SVG Working Group participants and the W3C are not aware of any royalty-bearing patents that are essential to implement the deliverables of the SVG Working Group, which includes all versions of the SVG specification and the SVG Mobile Profiles." Further, the same web page clarifies that one patent has been disclosed by one company and also acknowledges that the company does not believe it currently has any essential claims that fall within the specification of the recommendation as currently understood and interpreted by the company for implementors of SVG. Further, from information provided by W3C it is clear that several widely deployed (proprietary and open source licensed) software projects have implemented support for SVG[19], including several projects provided under the GPL license (e.g. Blender, Inkscape, and Scribus[20]). For these reasons it may be unsurprising that SVG is recommended for use in national policy concerning open standards, such as in the Netherlands.

The PNG (Portable Network Graphics) standard (ISO/IEC 15948:2004) is a formal (ISO) standard for representation of graphics included in the list of open standards in the Netherlands (Standaardisatie, 2014). Before accepted as an ISO standard, PNG was initially published in 1996 by the Internet Engineering Task Force (as RFC 2083) and soon after as a W3C standard (also in 1996).

The outcome of the assessment made in the Netherlands implies that the formal (ISO) standard for the PNG standard is considered as an open standard and therefore belongs in the upper right quadrant of the conceptual model (see Figure 1). Further, it should be noted that PNG is also provided as a W3C standard[21] (as "W3C recommendation" since 1 October 1996, i.e. before PNG was adopted as an ISO standard) and therefore also belongs in the lower right quadrant of the conceptual model (see Figure 1). Hence, based on adoption by both ISO and W3C, PNG belongs in both the upper right quadrant and the lower right quadrant of Figure 1. Considering the third criterion in the definition of an open standard (EU, 2004) and based on the outcome from our own analysis of the content in the ISO patent database it seems reasonable that the formal (ISO) standard has been included in the list of open standards (Standaardisatie, 2014). We note that no organisation is listed in the ISO patent database for the PNG standard (ISO/IEC 15948:2004).

The information provided by W3C concerning patents disclose that[22]: "the International Standards Organisation (ISO), the PNG Development Group and the W3C are not aware of any royalty-bearing patents that are essential to implement the Portable Network Graphics specification." Like for SVG, it is clear that several widely deployed (proprietary and open source licensed) software projects have implemented support for PNG[23], including several projects provided under the GPL license (e.g. GIMP,

Inkscape, and TuxPaint[24]). For these reasons it may be unsurprising that PNG is recommended for use in national policy concerning open standards, such as in the Netherlands.

The JPEG 2000 standard[25] is a formal (ISO) standard for the representation of graphics which has not been included in the list of open standards in the Netherlands (Standaardisatie, 2014). The JPEG 2000 standard is developed by the Joint Photographic Experts Group[26] (i.e. a joint committee between ISO/IEC JTC1 and ITU-T). The standard consists of 14 parts (parts 1-6 and 8-15 since part 7 has been abandoned) and a number of technical corrigendum have been published for several parts. For example, part 1 of the ISO standard for JPEG 2000 (ISO/IEC 15444-1:2004) with all technical corrections and amendments consists of 12 standard documents in total and the other 12 parts consist of 33 standard documents in total which implies that the entire ISO standard for JPEG 2000 currently consists of 45 standard documents[27]. The total price for buying the 12 standard documents related to part 1 of the ISO standard is 310 CHF, whereas the total price for buying all parts (i.e. the 45 standard documents) of the ISO standard from ISO will be 2718 CHF. With this, the total cost for all these standard documents may be perceived as an inhibitor for adoption, in particular for small companies wishing to bid for contracts involving implementation of this standard. Further, in this case, the cost may seem to exceed what may be considered as reasonable for a "nominal charge" according to the second criterion in the definition of an open standard (EU, 2004).

Since the ISO standard JPEG 2000 is not included in the list of open standards (Standaardisatie, 2014) it is clear that the formal (ISO) standard for the JPEG 2000 standard is considered as a closed standard and therefore belongs in the upper left quadrant of the conceptual model (see Figure 1). Considering the third criterion in the adopted definition of an open standard (EU, 2004) and based on the outcome from our own analysis of the content in the ISO patent database it is clear that the formal (ISO) standard should not be considered an open standard and it is therefore not surprising that it is has not been included in the list of open standards (Standaardisatie, 2014). We note that nine organisations are listed in the ISO patent database for part 1 of the JPEG 2000 standard (ISO/IEC 15444-1:2004) and that, in total, 16 organisations are also listed in the ISO patent database for all parts of the standard. Further, no information is provided in the database for most of these organisations concerning which patents these organisations control and some organisations even declare that they are willing to provide patent licenses under conditions which are not compatible with open source software.

To investigate the situation further we undertook a specific analysis aimed to clarify under which conditions the ISO standard can be used. This involved contacting each organisation listed in the ISO patent database with a set of questions sent in a letter[28] (sent via air-mail since email addresses were not available for most organisations in the database). In total, we sent questions to 16 organisations and after reminders (sent more than one month later) we have received some responses from three organisations. In total, letters from five organisations have so far been returned[29] since the contact information provided in the ISO patent database was incorrect or outdated (with the message "recipient unknown").

Amongst received responses, one organisation responded that they were unwilling to grant a license for their patents that would allow implementation in software to be provided under the GPLv3 license (i.e. a license which is recognised by both Open Source Initiative (OSI, 2017) and Free Software Foundation (FSF, 2017)). Another organisation explicitly stated that they decline to respond, whereas another declined to provide us information concerning which patents they control (the response was "we have at least 3 patents" on the specific standard). It should be noted that an annex in part 1 of the ISO standard (ISO/IEC 15444-1:2004) explicitly lists several organisations which have mentioned that they are willing to provide their patents (for part 1) free-of-charge but also that the patent database contains information with additional organisations since new patents have been declared after the publication of the ISO standard. Further, in one case the organisation that had declared patents declined to clarify conditions for use of the standard and instead referred our request to ISO. However, from a dialogue with ISO representatives we note that ISO as an organisation does not engage in clarifying conditions for use of standards for which patents have been declared. Hence, in this case specific questions concerning conditions for implementation of the standard were left unanswered (as one organisation controlling patent(s) for JPEG 2000 referred to ISO, and vice versa). In addition, it should also be noted that the ITU-T patent database contains information about a different set of organisations which have declared patents.

The TIFF/EP standard[30] is another of the formal (ISO) standards for representation of graphics which has not been included in the list of open standards in the Netherlands (Standaardisatie, 2014). The TIFF/EP (Tag Image File Format / Electronic Photography) standard is developed and maintained by the International Organization of Standardization (ISO). We note that 19 organisations are listed in the ISO patent database for the TIFF/EP standard. From this it follows that TIFF/EP is a closed standard according to the third criterion in the definition (EU, 2004) and that it therefore belongs in the upper left quadrant of the conceptual model (see Figure 1).

To investigate the situation further we undertook a specific analysis aimed to clarify under which conditions the ISO standard for TIFF/EP can be used. This involved contacting each organisation listed in the ISO patent database with a set of questions sent in a letter (sent via air-mail since email addresses were not available for most organisations in the database). In total, we sent questions to 19 organisations and after reminders (sent more than one month later) we did not receive any responses. In total, letters from four organisations were returned[31] since the contact information provided in the ISO patent database was incorrect or outdated (with the message "recipient unknown").

ANALYSIS

First, as one objective for our study involves analysing the conditions for use of formal (ISO) standards where national policy imposes requirements for use of open standards, it seems clear that the conceptual model presented can also support an analysis of the situation with respect to informal standards (e.g. those developed and maintained by various consortia, such as the W3C). However, it should be noted that several standards are recognised and maintained by more than one organisation. For example, the PNG standard is maintained both by ISO and by the W3C which implies that this specific standard could be seen as both a formal standard and an informal standard. Further, previous research shows that there are "many misconceptions and significant unawareness" concerning differences between standards for representation of data and their implementation in software amongst decision makers in public sector organisations (Lundell & Gamalielsson, 2013). By way of example, the Dutch Parliament requested in 2010 the Court of Audit to undertake an assessment of the benefits of open standards and open source software in the government IT which resulted in a criticised report that was published in March 2011 (Egyedi & Enserink, 2013). According to a critical review by Egyedi and Enserink (2013), the assessment was criticised for omitting to address effects of open standards on the market.

Second, our results show that the third criterion (about IPR) in the definition of an open standard adopted in the Netherlands brings with it several complexities for any organisation wishing to use a specific standard. Since different organisations developing and maintaining standards have different policies concerning patents it is important to realise that not all formal standards are open standards. Lea and Hall (2004) bring clarity to this complex issue as follows: "At the time patent policies first emerged, it was clear that few patentees would be willing to license on a 'royalty-free' (RF) basis in the sense of absolutely free: therefore, in some quarters, royalty-free came to mean 'for a lump sum up front' and, subsequently, the alternative concept of '[fair,] reasonable and non-discriminatory' ([F]RAND) licensing was developed, whereby all-comers would be allowed licenses but on royalty terms supposedly both fair across the industry as a whole and as between each of the licensees. This latter often cannot be proven, since the license terms are usually kept secret)." (Lea & Hall, 2004, p. 83)

Third, our results clearly illuminate differences between the investigated formal standards. Our results show clear differences between formal standards which are also 'open' compared to those which are also closed standards (e.g. the ISO standard for JPEG 2000). Our results show that a key issue impacting on the conditions under which formal standards can (or cannot) be implemented in open source software concern the third criterion in the definition of an open standard that has been adopted in the Netherlands (EU, 2004). From this, it is clear that while some formal (ISO) standards (e.g. the ISO standard for PNG) can (and have been) implemented in a variety of different open source software applications, it is also evident that for other formal (ISO) standards (e.g. the ISO standard for JPEG 2000) it is not possible to obtain licenses for the standard to permit implementation in open source software. For the investigated standards, our results clearly illuminate that amongst organisations which control patents impacting on the standard there is no interest in providing licences for those patents which would allow implementation in software to be provided under the GPLv3 licence. Further, given that the vast majority of organisations that have declared that they control patents impacting on the investigated standards either cannot be reached or decline to respond it is clear that any organisation considering an implementation of the standard under any open source software license would face significant risks. Hence, implementing a standard without first having obtained all necessary rights for use of the standard cannot be recommended to anyone.

Fourth, our results show that for several formal (ISO) standards a number of organisations have voluntarily declared that they control patents which are believed to impact on conditions for use of the specific ISO standard and also that investigations for clarifying the conditions are not easy to do in practice since several organisations cannot even be reached. As most organisations that have declared patents in the ISO database related to JPEG 2000 and TIFF/EP cannot be reached, it is implied that there is considerable uncertainty concerning conditions for use of such standards. Further, the complexity related to RAND conditions has been elaborated in previous research (e.g. Fomin et al., 2008). For example, in their study they report that: "Another expert elaborates on why (F)RAND issues, mentioned above, are important. He notes that IPR is the secret (in many senses of the word) tool of vendors to manipulate the standards process. The patent process can be easily manipulated to exclude competition, and flagrant abuses of it can be used to preclude challenge by smaller companies who cannot afford the fight even when they are right" (Fomin et al., 2008). Further, the same study argues that "without meaningful policies on IPR, operating on a global basis, standardization will be manipulated" using such business strategies (Fomin et al., 2008).

Fifth, adoption of requirements for use of standards in national policy may have a number of different effects for different stakeholder groups. Our results show that some formal (ISO) standards are provided under conditions that are unclear even after significant efforts for clarifying conditions for use of such standards. Such uncertainty may inhibit competition and impose challenges related to requirements expressed in public sector procurement. In the European context, legislation and directives for public procurement (Directives 2004/17/EC and 2004/18/EC) aim to achieve procurement practices that stimulate a fair and competitive market based on the important principles of transparency, non-discrimination and equal treatment (Lundell, 2011). Specifically, references to a technical specification "shall not refer to a specific make or source, or to a particular process, or to trade marks, patents, types or a specific origin or production with the effect of favouring or eliminating certain undertakings or certain products." (Directive 2004/17/EC (Article 34) and Directive 2004/18/EC (Article 23)). For this reason, results from an analysis of current practices in Swedish public sector organisations show significant lock-in and illuminate inclusion of requirements for specific standards which refer to specific products, trademarks and imply dependencies to access of specific patent licenses (Lundell, 2011; Wessman, 2013). Further, results from an analysis published by the Swedish competition authorities (Wessman, 2013) show that only a minority of decisions impacting on procurement consider any strategy for avoiding lock-in effects.

Finally, based on our results it is evident that some formal (ISO) standards analysed in this study cannot be implemented and deployed as open source software because of lack of clarity concerning IPRs. Further, when conditions for use of specific ISO standards cannot be clarified and all necessary patent licenses therefore cannot be obtained (as experienced in this study), it follows that such standards cannot be used for implementation in software under any software license without significant risks.

IMPLICATIONS FOR USE OF ISO STANDARDS AND IMPACT ON POLICY

Based on the analysis of our results, from having investigated the process of obtaining information on the conditions for use of specific standards from W3C and ISO, this section elaborates on the implications of our findings for practice. First we elaborate on the implications for small companies[32] wishing to implement ISO standards in software, and second, we suggest how the ISO declaration form can be improved to allow a further option for holders of standards-essential patents (SEPs), to avoid some of the problems identified.

Implications for Companies Wishing to Implement Standards in Software

A small company wishing to implement a standard in software will typically have one or more of the following characteristics:

1. It will not have or control patents of its own;
2. It will not be party to any patent pool arrangement[33];
3. It will not have access to an in-house legal department or have in-depth knowledge of the patent landscape;
4. It will not be actively involved in any standards setting process; and
5. It will wish to implement the standard using open source software components, which may include software licensed under the GPL family.

In seeking to implement an ISO standard in software, a prudent company may take the following steps, each of which raises a potential barrier to such a company implementing a standard, the implementation of which is dependent on patents:

1. The company must acquire a copy of the standard (the cost of which may itself be prohibitive, especially where the standard contains multiple parts and normative references to other standards copies of which themselves may need obtaining in a similar way. By way of example, the results of our analysis show that the cost to acquire the JPEG 2000 standard documentation, even without considering the cost of documentation relating to normative references, would be 2718 CHF per copy);

2. It must review the ISO database to determine whether the standard (including other standards it relies on, such as normative references) is subject to declared patents;

3. It must attempt to determine what patents are included in each declaration covering the standard (including other standards it relies on), OR if that is not possible, it must determine whether it is going to engage in a negotiation for licences as another way of reducing potential risk;

4. It must determine whether its own implementation of the standard covers the patents in question, and if so, it must contact, and engage in negotiations with, the declarant organisation (or, to the extent that it is possible to do so, decide to exclude provision of its software from the specific market(s) in which relevant patents are registered).

Steps 3 and 4 must be repeated for every declaration contained in the database which is listed against the standard (including those listed against relevant and normative references referred to in the standard) which the company wishes to implement. Clearly, a failure to reach an agreement with the declarant organisation in even one case where the relevant patent impinges on the standard will potentially render the implementing company open to a patent infringement claim.

The above steps present a number of challenges in terms of cost and risk to the implementing company, which we call 'process barriers'. We elaborate further on some of these issues.

To obtain a licence, the implementing company first needs to know what the relevant patents are. Several SSOs (including ISO) have databases populated by organisations which have taken part in the standards setting process, and which have declared that they hold patents which are essential in implementing the standards. They do not necessarily declare (and it is not required as part of the ISO declaration process to declare) which specific patents they hold.

From our experience during the data-gathering process, it is by no means straightforward to obtain the information necessary to enable identification of the relevant patents. We even had problems in many cases eliciting any form of response from organisations listed in the database which claim they are in control of SEPs. We found that contact information provided in the database was no longer accurate for some of the declarations, leading to bounced emails and undelivered airmail letters.

The SSOs are clear that all patent licence negotiations are strictly between the company seeking a licence, and the organisation making the declaration, with the SSO taking no part in that process. However, where it is impossible even to engage the vast majority of declaring organisations, this process is clearly not fit for purpose.

As identified in this study, in the case of the ISO standard TIFF/EP, none of the 19 organisations identified in the ISO database responded to our questions. In the case of JPEG 2000, we were able to establish contact with three organisations from the 16 identified in the database, all of which we attempted to contact.

From the information provided in the dialogues where we were able to engage with the declaring organisations, we were able to establish that one referred us to ISO (which, as we have established, is not prepared to become part of licensing discussions between parties), one was prepared to license, in theory, on RAND terms (but did not provide a draft license), and the third was not prepared to grant a licence which was compatible with the GPLv3 licence. Even if we had received licences from the three respondents that we were able to engage in a dialogue, in the absence of licences from the other declarants (and assuming that those declarants genuinely held SEPs), we would still have been unable to implement the standard without infringing.

Were an enquiring organisation to proceed to implement the standard in software without a complete set of appropriate licences to SEPs, it would be at risk of patent claims from the holders of the SEPs (other than those from whom it had received licences). Those claims could lead to monetary damages (which may, under the US patent regime, have been tripled, given that disclosure on the database would put the enquirer on notice that patents potentially existed) and an injunction restraining any further use or distribution of the software. It is no guarantee of safety that a company is operating solely in one jurisdiction where no SEPs exist. Since software development practices currently tend to involve US based repositories such as GitHub, and since, in any event, exploitation and marketing of the software is likely to occur on the internet and hence worldwide, claims may arise from any jurisdiction where SEPs are registered.

SSOs do not, in general, guarantee completeness of the database or that it is up to date. For example, ISO (2015c) states that "ISO does not verify the veracity or accuracy of the information nor the relevance of the identified patents/patent applications to ISO Standards."

Even assuming that the database is comprehensive, it will not be clear to the implementing company whether:

1. The (part of the) standard it wants to implement is covered by a patent held by the disclosing company or not;
2. The patent(s) in question are still in force, or have expired;
3. The patent(s) in question in fact impinge on the implementation of the standard at all.

Assuming that implementation of the standard in question will infringe a patent which is disclosed, the implementing company will have to enter into negotiations with the declarant organisation, on the basis, as selected by that organisation of either Option 1 (Free of Charge) or Option 2 (RAND) (as such terms are set out in section 4.1).

This process is expected to occur outside the context of ISO. It also assumes that the company wishing to implement is, in practice, able to find, and successfully engage with, the declarant organisation.

If, on the other hand, the company wishing to implement is a larger organisation, by reason of its greater resources, it may, in practice, have a number of other options open to it. It may be able to:

1. Determine that the means by which it wishes to implement the standard does not, in fact, infringe any patent, (or modify the means of implementation to avoid the patent) and so no licence is required;
2. Determine that it already has access to a licence to the relevant patent, either through a patent pool arrangement, or through a pre-existing licence or cross-licence;
3. Negotiate with the patent holder outside the scope of the free-of-charge or RAND option, possibly by cross licensing its own patents, or by joining a relevant patent pool;
4. Seek to invalidate the patent; or
5. Assess the risk that there may be a successful patent claim, and determine it is prepared to accept that risk.

Options a, d and e (above) are also potentially accessible to the smaller company, but are likely to be at a disproportionate cost.

In either case, the implementing company has the option to implement the standard and risk a claim from a patent holder (option e above). If that occurs, the larger company will have the advantage of:

1. Using its own patent portfolio to offer a cross-licensing deal;
2. Using its superior resources to fight the claim, either by invalidating the patent or demonstrating that its implementation does not infringe the underlying patent.

An organisation will experience minimal process barriers where it is possible for that organisation to implement the standard in software without concern for patent infringement, and be permitted to use software which is covered by any of the entire range of licenses approved by OSI (2017) and FSF (2017). It is the case that companies, even where they have no desire to supply software under an open source licence, will nonetheless frequently use open source code as a component in their product as a consequence of near-universal modern software development practices. Hardly any new system is built without using the high quality, easily accessible code which is often available as part of open source development projects (Simeonova, 2015; Milinkovich, 2015). Barriers to entry are likely to impact smaller companies disproportionately[34].

For a company wishing to implement a standard in software it is critical that it can obtain all necessary licenses to do so. In seeking to implement a standard, such a company should initially review the relevant SSO's database to determine whether its implementation is likely to infringe any patents which have been declared by a declarant organisation.

Since details of the specific patents declared by the declarants are not necessarily disclosed in the database (although the declarants are encouraged by the SSO to do so), further investigation may be necessary to even determine what patents may possibly be infringed. For example, previous research shows that it is not uncommon for companies to declare that they own essential patents without specifying any details about these patents (Bekkers & West, 2009, p. 83).

If a company is comfortable that its implementation will not require a licence under a particular patent – perhaps because

- It is not implementing the part of the standard which is covered by the patent, or
- The patent has expired, or
- It does not wish to implement or provide the software product in the jurisdiction where the patent is registered, or
- On close reading of the patent, it is not essential in implementing the standard

then it will, naturally, not need to approach the relevant declarant. In all other cases, to minimise its risk of infringement in implementing the standard, it will need to ensure that relevant licences are in place and engage with the patent holder accordingly.

If any patents are declared under Option 3, this presents a serious risk to a company wishing to implement the standards (in practice, this is unlikely to occur, as the ISO's wider patent policy excludes from the standardisation process essential patents which are unavailable under RAND, or Free of Charge terms). Where patents are declared under Options 2 or 1, the company wishing to implement will need to engage with each relevant declarant organisation to negotiate a patent licence (on RAND or Free of Charge terms).

It is important to recognise that when an organisation declares to ISO that it is willing to provide its patents related to the specific standard at hand according to Option 1 (or indeed Option 2) this does not imply that the organisation *has* provided a license for these patents or that a license is automatically available on defined terms. A declaration under Option 1 implies that the organisation has declared that it is committed to provide its patents on Free of Charge terms and that it is willing to engage in a negotiation with the organisation which wishes to use the standard on that basis.

For many companies it is important to be able to implement the standard in open source software that is to be provided under common open source licences, including licences from the GPL-family. As GPL-licensed open source software is the most common type of open source software (under various accepted measures), and previous research from the embedded systems domain has showed that this is particularly essential for consultant companies, it is important for many companies to be able to use and implement standards in software that is provided under the GPL and its family of licences (Lundell et al., 2011).

Towards an Improved Standardisation System for Stakeholders

The standards ecosystem involves a number of different stakeholder groups. These include: legislators; SSOs; organisations which are involved in the standards setting process (and which may hold patents which impinge on the standards); and companies which wish to implement the standards.

For companies wishing to implement standards it would clearly be of significant benefit if the friction inherent in this process could be reduced by minimising the number of decision points that occur in the process. As our results have shown, one set of decision points arises in relation to the implementation of ISO standards at the stage where the implementing company undertakes an analysis of the patents which may possibly be infringed by the implementation of the standard in software, based on the data disclosed in the ISO database (or possibly elsewhere), and entering into negotiations with the parties it identifies as (possibly) having relevant patents to obtain appropriate licences. Any initiative which simplifies this process and brings clarity will be welcomed by the implementing company by both reducing the time and effort involved in the process, and providing improved data on which the company can assess its commercial risk.

One way forward would be to introduce a mechanism whereby a relevant licence may, if selected by the patent holder as part of the patent declaration process applicable to a specific standard, automatically be available on suitable terms covering patents which may possibly impinge on an implementation of the standard. In such a case, the implementing company would no longer need to:

- Assess whether the declared patent did cover its implementation of the standard;
- Consider not trading in a jurisdiction where a relevant patent was registered, if it perceives negotiating the licence to be too complex (to the extent that it is possible to do so, given the global reach of the internet, and its almost universal role in software distribution);
- Assess the risk of implementing the standard without a suitable licence;
- Enter into negotiations with the declaring body;
- Reject methods of implementation (for example, the use of GPL code) which may be incompatible with any licence granted;

all of which potentially represent a significant investment and time and, possibly (for small companies in particular), the purchase of external professional advice.

To minimise friction, and maximise the ability for all companies, including SMEs, to implement standards under transparent conditions in a way which enables them to more accurately assess and manage risk (thus encouraging competition and innovation by allowing more actors with diverse interests to enter the market), we propose that an additional option for patent-holders declaring their approach to patent licensing with respect to a specific standard may be offered to patent-holders as follows (we call this 'Option Zero'):

1. By selecting this box, the declarant agrees to license, perpetually, and irrevocably except as specifically set out below, on a worldwide, royalty-free, non-exclusive basis to all third parties ('licensee') seeking to make, use and sell software implementations of the above document solely to the extent that such software implements the standard;

2. The licence set out in (1) above arises automatically in favour of all licensees without the need to execute any document;

3. The licence set out in (1) above may only be revoked against a specific licensee where the licensee is in breach of the licence set out in (1) above, and, having received notice specifying such breach fails to cure it within 30 days.

The most significant characteristics of Option Zero, in contrast with Option 1, are:

*   An Option Zero licence is automatically available. There is no need to negotiate it;
*   An Option Zero licence is explicitly perpetual and irrevocable, except in specified circumstances. As well as protecting the licensees' investment in development of a compatible solution, this is intended to aid compatibility with various definitions of 'open standard' (including version 1 of the European Interoperability Framework); and
*   An Option Zero licence is explicitly designed to be compatible both with a proprietary software development model, and an open source development model.

This last point is somewhat problematic as regards certain open source licences. It has been noted (Mitchell & Mason, 2010), that there may be a fundamental mismatch between the requirements of some open source software licences (notably those of the GPL family), and parallel patent licences, unless the terms of those licences are extremely liberal.

In brief, as an analysis of this point is beyond the scope of this chapter, there is a spectrum of opinion as to the interaction between the GPL and typical patent licensing structures. On the one hand, the least problematic view is that so long as the implementer of a standard using software licensed under a GPL family licence can distribute that software in such a way that the recipient has no fewer rights that the implementer has, then there is no problem (in other words, if the implementer has the benefit of a specific patent licence, any recipient of the implementer's code will also need to have the benefit of a patent licence on the same terms, either directly from the licensor, or as a sub-licence from the implementer). On the other hand, a more problematic view is that the implementer of a standard containing third party GPL code has to cause any recipient of that code to receive a licence (including a patent licence) which would enable the recipient to exercise *all* rights permitted under the GPL, including the right to modify the code so that it no longer implements the standard, but nonetheless still has the benefit of a relevant patent licence. Clearly, such a broadly drafted patent licence would render the economic value of the patent close to zero, so it would be unlikely to be acceptable.

The approach we have taken falls midway between these two extremes and is guided by the scope of the patent licence in GPLv3 (which does not expect a distributor of GPL software to provide a blanket patent licence to recipients covering all possible modifications of the code transferred). If the ISO were to adopt something similar to Option Zero, we would expect this to follow consultation with relevant stakeholders in the worlds of both proprietary and open source software, and, in particular, seek assurances from organisations like the Free Software Foundation (custodian of the GPL family of licences) that an approach like this would be compatible with both the spirit and the legal terms of the relevant licence (noting that such organisations' comments are at best only persuasive: legal interpretation of the licence is ultimately the responsibility of the courts of any jurisdiction in which the licence is litigated).

Many companies involved in the standards setting process are also companies which are heavily involved in the development of open source code, and will be familiar with the concept of licensing their patents on a royalty-free basis (e.g. HP, 2015) in a way which is typically compatible with open source licences. Many licences (GPLv3 and LGPLv3, Mozilla 2.0 and Apache 2.0) contain widely accepted and understood patent licensing clauses, which typically limit the licence granted to the scope of the claims implemented by the version of the software as distributed by the patent licensor. In other words, and by way of example, if a recipient received some word-processing software from the licensor, the recipient cannot expect the patent licence to cover the recipient's use of it should the recipient choose to modify the word processing software to act as a control system for a nuclear power plant. Any open source licence will grant the recipient under its copyright provisions the freedom to make those changes, the patent sections of the same licence may not. By analogy, we believe it is within the scope of acceptable open source practice to limit the scope of the patent licence granted to implementations of the standard. The recipient may, under the open source licence, modify the software so that its functionality no longer meets the requirements of the standard, but, should Option Zero apply, it will not receive the benefit of the patent licence in so doing.

By adopting a mechanism which is similar to that which organisations, including those with large patent portfolios, are already employing to license their patents under various open source licences, we believe that the introduction of similar licence terms as an option in the ISO patent declaration would not be an unusual step. We stress that Option Zero is, as the name implies, only an option which the patent-holder may select, and there is no compulsion in selecting Option Zero. For the many organisations which already license software under licences such as GPLv3 or the Apache licence which contain a similar patent licensing clause, we submit that this option is entirely consistent with, and readily reconcilable with, their current patent licensing policies.

Option Zero does raise a number of interesting issues, which could be considered as sub-options. The patent sections of open source licences frequently contain provisions which are intended to foster reciprocity by ensuring that any actor taking advantage of such a patent licence loses the licence if they themselves assert patent rights against a third party in certain circumstances. We would suggest that suitable wording to implement this would be to allow the declarant to terminate the licence against a specific licensee where:

the licensee asserts any patent claim against a third party, where that third party is implementing the standard and the patent claim covers the implementation of that standard (where 'implementation' includes distribution and importation of software which implements the standard)[35].

In other words, where someone takes the benefit of an Option Zero licence, that licence will terminate if that person starts issuing claims for infringement of its own patents where the claim covers the alleged infringer's implementation of the relevant standard.

Note that the currently-existing Options 1 and 2 also contain sub-options which allow (in the case of Option 1) the declarant to specify that it is only prepared to grant a licence to entities which are prepared to grant a similar Free of Charge licence themselves. Similarly, in the case of Option 2, there is an equivalent sub-option which allows the declarant to specify that it is only prepared to grant a licence to those entities which are prepared to grant a RAND licence (which may not be Free of Charge) themselves.

Another way of achieving a similar aim, which may be neater conceptually, is to state that the Option Zero reciprocity sub-option requires that any licensee taking the declarant's licence is itself deemed to have granted a licence to its own SEPs under Option Zero.

Notwithstanding these suggestions, we have identified two further issues which may impose risk for potential standards-implementing entities.

The first issue involves reliance on the information contained in the patent disclosure database itself. The second issue involves patent ambush, where an organisation initiates a patent claim relating to an implementation of a standard, where that patent has not been disclosed at all. We acknowledge that for the ISO standards investigated in this research, the question of undisclosed patents did not become relevant (because, as our results show, we were unable even to establish contact with many declarant organisations). However, this is an issue which is commonly understood in this field (see, for example, Baird (2007); EC (2007, 2009); Updegrove (2009)), and in the interests of complete disclosure we consider it appropriate to refer to this issue and the extent to which it impacts on our proposals.

In relation to the first issue, we have found that the content in the ISO database is not always accurate or up to date, and, at the very least, ISO should (1) take steps to check the content of its database from time to time, and/or (2) consider implementing sanctions on declarants which fail to keep their entries up to date. To improve the situation, one possibility would be to implement a rule that if a declarant fails to notify ISO on an annual basis that its information remains the same, or if it has changed, the nature of the changes, then that declarant is deemed to have selected Option Zero. Note that once an option has been selected, ISO's rules state that it may only be reclassified to a lower number (e.g. a declarant may make a submission that it is selecting Option 1 in relation to a specific disclosure, only where it has already made an Option 3 or 2 disclosure, or none at all). To retain consistency with this rule, an Option Zero selection would be perpetual (at least until all potentially relevant patents have expired). Note that an inaccuracy in an Option Zero declaration (given that it contains the licence itself, and not an invitation to negotiate a licence), is less impactful on licensees and potential licensees than any of the other options.[36]

From the declarants' perspective, an Option Zero may be attractive (compared to Option 1 – given that both Options Zero and 1 bear no fee or royalty), for reasons of reducing the time and effort involved in responding to, and negotiating individual licences. Further, Option Zero may also have the positive effect of creating an ad-hoc patent pool since declarants are themselves likely to be implementing the standard, and will therefore require their own licences from the other declarants. However, if Option Zero is selected, there may also be possible disadvantages for the declarant:

- The declarant loses the opportunity to negotiate individual terms with the implementer;
- The declarant will not automatically have a list of implementing companies.

These issues also arise when comparing Option Zero with Option 2. In this case, there is the additional disadvantage, from the declarant's perspective, that it will be unable to charge a fee to the licensee.

In relation to the second problematic issue, we have identified concerns relating to patent ambush. Patent ambush occurs when an organisation initiates patent litigation in relation to implementations of a standard, where is has not disclosed those patents during the standards-setting process, either because the entity in question chooses not to disclose the patent in breach of the relevant SSO's rules, or because the entity in question is not part of the standards setting process itself in the first place. The only solutions to this issue which present themselves to us require either the non-trivial implementation of legislation, which, because of the international nature of standardisation would necessarily require a treaty, or some form of international concerted effort requiring states to coordinate approaches in competition/antitrust law. One form of international legislation may provide that entities which hold a patent which impinges on a proposed standard, drafts of which standard have been made publicly available through ISO or another recognised international SSO, are deemed, unless they respond to the standards setting organisation and select a specific option in the patent declaration, to have granted an Option Zero licence in respect of that patent. Alternatively, it may be that competition or anti-trust law provides a solution, possibly by mandating compulsory licensing in this context (but see Chronopoulos (2009), which also covers a number of other possible solutions, analysis of which is beyond the scope of this chapter). We are under no illusion as to the significant challenges raised in implementing these suggestions.

CONCLUSION

Our study highlights that open standards are important for a number of different reasons, both in private and public sectors, something which is apparent in some countries based on recognition and adoption in national policy.

The study shows that while some formal (ISO) standards (e.g. the ISO standard for PNG) are also considered open standards according to the definition adopted in several national policies (including the one adopted in the Netherlands), it is also clear that other formal (ISO) standards (e.g. the ISO standard for JPEG 2000) are not considered open standards by the same policies. Further, from our analysis of the unclear situation related to patents which several organisations have declared related to the ISO standard for JPEG 2000 it is clear from this example that some ISO standards cannot be considered open standards.

Findings from the study contribute to reducing confusion concerning the use of standards in software. In particular, the conceptual model aimed to clarify the dimensions 'openness' and 'formality' of standards may provide an important means for analysing specific standards. Further, it seems apparent that any decision maker involved in specification of requirements for development and procurement of software in which standards are implemented needs to understand and account for conditions under which formal and open standards can be used.

Our study has identified a number of issues for any company wishing to implement an ISO standard. These issues include the ability to determine which organisations hold patents which may impinge on the standard, the complexity of the process under which such a company is expected to engage with the patent-declaring organisation. We found that information contained in ISO's database was, for two of the ISO standards investigated, so inaccurate as to cause attempts even to contact the relevant patent-declaring organisation to fail. In considering these issues, we suggest a number of ways in which they can be effectively addressed.

Our research has shown that there are significant risks associated with use of formal (ISO) standards for which conditions for use are unclear. For any organisation it is essential to clarify conditions for use of any standard before undertaking efforts to implement such in software, irrespectively under which license the software is to be provided. In situations when most organisations that have declared patents related to a specific standard do not respond and cannot be reached (as in the case of JPEG 2000 and TIFF/EP), it seems clear that the content of the patent database (as currently structured) provides limited support for any organisation wishing to clarify conditions for implementation of the standard in software. Our research has elaborated on the implications of the implementation of standards in software for which the patent landscape is unclear. Further, our contribution proposes a mechanism for addressing challenges related to unclear patents by suggesting the addition of an Option Zero to the ISO patent policy and associated patent declaration form.

In practice, as shown through this study, it is evident that FRAND commitments may involve a number of significant challenges for any organisation wishing to obtain all necessary rights to allow for implementation of file formats standards in software. In particular, the study shows that for some ISO standards it may even be impossible to clarify conditions and obtain all necessary rights that allow for implementation of file format standards (provided under ISO IPR rules) in software. There are a number of implications from this which in turn inhibit implementations in open source software (it being a fundamental principle of open source licensing that software under such a licence *must* be capable of distribution to a third party). In light of the observations from practice concerning file formats, with identified challenges concerning FRAND commitment due to unclear conditions for use of file format standards that may be critical for many organisations and the broader society, the situation may call for serious consideration amongst all stakeholders involved that need to maintain their own data in these formats over long life-cycles. From an organisational and broader societal perspective, to be dependent upon file formats which cannot be implemented in open source software may constitute a serious risk. As such situations may inhibit fundamental requirements concerning longevity of data and mission-critical digital assets that need to be maintained over very long life-cycles, envisaged proposals for standardisation (such as 'option zero') may be one way forward to improve the situation, at least for some types of file formats and standards that are either business critical or otherwise important for broader societal reasons. Increased transparency and predictability concerning declared SEPs may improve the situation, especially since transfers of SEPs may take place after[37] the publication of a standard. In order to achieve sustainable IT solutions, that allow for software provided under open source licenses, it is critical that file formats allow for implementation in open source software, which can be transferred to third party without any additional restriction[38]. We conjecture that a future standardisation landscape, with numerous declarations and transfer of SEPs in increasingly complex networks that involve many individuals and organisations, may call for file formats provided under option zero, as outlined for ISO standards in this chapter. Through implementation of option zero amongst SSOs, this will ensure that fundamental data which needs to be maintained over long life-cycles through software solutions that implement file formats can effectively address societal needs.

In summary, the study shows that some formal standards create barriers for implementation in open source software, a finding which confirms previous observations expressed in reports from the European Commission. Thereby, the results from this study provide an important contribution to a more comprehensive understanding concerning conditions (and inhibitors) for implementation of standards in open source software. From these results it follows that inclusion of explicit requirements for use of some formal standards in development and procurement of software may significantly inhibit an open and inclusive business friendly ecosystem. In contrast, a relatively simple change to the process by which patent holders declare patents to the ISO and other SSOs may have the effect of promoting such an open and inclusive ecosystem, something which is of particular importance for small companies that are essential players in an innovative and international society.

REFERENCES

Aliprandi, S. (2011). Interoperability And Open Standards: The Key To True Openness And Innovation. *International Free and Open Source Software Law Review, 3*(1), 5–24. doi:10.5033/ifosslr.v3i1.53

Baird, S. (2007). The Government at the Standards Bazaar. *Stanford Law & Policy Review, 18*(1), 35–100.

Ballard, M. (2012). Portugal's prescribed open standards - full list. *Computer Weekly*. Retrieved from http://www.computerweekly.com/blogs/public-sector/2012/11/-tablemytable-border-collapsec.html

Bekkers, R., & West, J. (2009). The limits to IPR standardization policies as evidenced by strategic patenting in UMTS. *Telecommunications Policy, 33*(1-2), 80–97. doi:10.1016/j.telpol.2008.11.003

Bird, G. B. (1998). The Business Benefit of Standards. *StandardView, 5*(2), 76–80. doi:10.1145/301688.301691

Chronopoulos, A. (2009). Patenting Standards - A case for US Antitrust Law or a Call for Recognizing Immanent Public Policy Limitations to the Exploitation Rights Conferred by the Patent Act? *International Review of Intellectual Property and Competition Law, 40*(7), 782–816.

Clark, J. (2016). *Convergence, Collaboration and Smart Shopping in Open Standards and Open Source.* In Open Source and Standards in 5G, ITU / NGMN Joint Workshop on OS, San Diego, CA. Retrieved from http://www.itu.int/en/ITU-T/Workshops-and-Seminars/itu-ngmn/Documents/Abstracts_and_Presentations/Jamie_Clark_v2.pdf

Contreras, J. L. (2015). A Brief History of FRAND: Analyzing Current Debates in Standard Setting and Antitrust Through a Historical Lens. *Antitrust Law Journal, 80*(1), 39–120.

Contreras, J. L. (2017). *Technical Standards, Standards-Setting Organizations and Intellectual Property: A Survey of the Literature (with an Emphasis on Empirical Approaches).* Utah Law Faculty Scholarship 11. Retrieved from http://dc.law.utah.edu/scholarship/11

Dardailler, D., Archer, P., & Wenning, R. (2012). *W3C Response to UK Cabinet Office Open Standards Consultation.* Retrieved from http://www.w3.org/2012/04/openstandards.html

de Vries, H. J. (2006). IT Standards Typology. In K. Jakobs (Ed.), *Advanced Topics in Information Technology Standards and Standardization Research* (Vol. 1, pp. 1–26). Hershey, PA: Idea Group Publishing. doi:10.4018/978-1-59140-938-0.ch001

EC. (2007). *Antitrust: Commission confirms sending a Statement of Objections to Rambus.* MEMO/07/330, European Commission.

EC. (2009). *Antitrust: Commission accepts commitments from Rambus lowering memory chip royalty rates.* IP/09/1897, European Commission.

EC. (2012). *Implementing FRAND standards in Open Source: Business as usual or mission impossible?* Report summary from a workshop organised by the European Commission (EC) and the European Patent Office.

EC. (2013a). *European Commission: Press Release, Digital Agenda: Open standards would save public sector €1 billion a year.* Retrieved from http://europa.eu/rapid/press-release_IP-13-602_en.htm

EC. (2013b). *Commission staff working document: Guide for the procurement of standards-based ICT — Elements of Good Practice.* SWD(2013) 224 final, European Commission. Retrieved from http://ec.europa.eu/information_society/newsroom/cf/dae/document.cfm?doc_id=2326

EC. (2016). *ICT Standardisation Priorities for the Digital Single Market.* Communication from the Commission to the European Parliament, the Council, the European Economic and Social Committee and the Committee of the regions, COM(2016) 176 final, European Commission.

ECSIP. (2014). Patents and Standards: A modern framework for IPR-based standardization. Final Report: A study prepared for the European Commission Directorate-General for Enterprise and Industry, European Competitiveness and Sustainable Industrial Policy Consortium, Ref. Ares(2014)917720 – 25/03/2014.

Egyedi, T. (2007). Standard-compliant, but incompatible?! *Computer Standards & Interfaces, 29*(6), 605–613. doi:10.1016/j.csi.2007.04.001

Egyedi, T. & Enserink, B. (2013). Measuring the Benefits of Open Standards: A Contribution to Dutch Politics. *Standards Today, 12*(1).

EU. (2004). *European Interoperability Framework for pan-European eGovernment Services, Version 1.0.* European Commission. Retrieved from http://ec.europa.eu/idabc/servlets/

Fitzgerald, A., & Pappalardo, K. (2009). Moving Towards Open Standards. *SCRIPted, 6*(2), 467–483.

Fomin, V. V., Pedersen, M. K., & de Vries, H. J. (2008). Open Standards and Government Policy: Results of a Delphi Survey. *Communications of the Association for Information Systems, 22*(1), 25.

Friedrich, J. (2011). Making Innovation Happen: The Role of Standards and Openness in an Innovation-Friendy Ecosystem, In *Proceedings of 7th International Conference on Standardization and Innovation in Information Technology (SIIT).* IEEE Computer Society. 10.1109/SIIT.2011.6083609

FSF. (2017). *Free Software Foundation.* Retrieved from www.fsf.org

Gamalielsson, J., Lundell, B., Feist, J., Gustavsson, T., & Landqvist, F. (2015). On organisational influences in software standards and their open source implementations. *Information and Software Technology, 67*(Nov), 30–43. doi:10.1016/j.infsof.2015.06.006

Ghosh, R. A. (2005). *An Economic Basis for Open Standards.* FLOSSPOLS. Retrieved from http://www.flosspols.org/deliverables/FLOSSPOLS-D04-openstandards-v6.pdf

HP. (2015). *HP Response to Consultation on Patents and Standards.* Hewlett-Packard.

ISO. (2007). *ISO/IEC/ITU common patent policy.* Retrieved from http://isotc.iso.org/livelink/livelink/fetch/ 2000/2122/3770791/Common_Policy.htm

ISO. (2012). *Guidelines for Implementation of the Common Patent Policy for ITU-T/ITU-R/ISO/IEC, Revision 1*. Retrieved from http://isotc.iso.org/livelink/livelink/fetch/2000/2122/3770791/Common_Guidelines_01_March_07.pdf

ISO. (2015a). *Standards: What is a standard?* Retrieved from http://www.iso.org/iso/home/standards.htm

ISO. (2015b). *Patent declarations submitted to ISO*. Retrieved from http://isotc.iso.org/livelink/livelink/13622347/Patents_database.xls?func=doc.Fetch&nodeId=13622347

ISO. (2015c). *ISO Standards and Patents*. Retrieved from http://www.iso.org/iso/standards_development/patents

ISO. (2015d). *Guidelines for Implementation of the Common Patent Policy for ITU-T/ITU-R/ISO/IEC, Revision 2*. Retrieved from http://www.itu.int/dms_pub/itu-t/oth/04/04/T04040000010004PDFE.pdf

Jakobs, K. (2017). Two dimensions of success in ICT standardization – A review. *ICT Express*, *3*(2), 85–89. doi:10.1016/j.icte.2017.05.008

Jakobs, K. & Mora, M. (2008). Co-ordinating Rule Setters – Co-operation in ICT Standards Setting. *CONF-IRM 2008 Proceedings*, Paper 17.

Kammarkollegiet (2013). Programvaror och tjänster 2013, Statens Inköpscentral, Kammarkollegiet, 5 February, Dnr. 96-40-2013.

Kammarkollegiet (2014a). Programvaror och tjänster 2014 - Kontorsstöd, Dnr 96-33-2014, 2014-09-11.

Kammarkollegiet (2014b). Programvaror och tjänster 2014 - Grundläggande it, Dnr 96-34-2014, 2014-09-11.

Kammarkollegiet. (2016). *Open IT-standards, National Procurement Services (Kammarkollegiet), 7 March, Dnr 96-38-2014*. Retrieved from http://www.avropa.se/globalassets/open-it-standards.pdf

Krechmer, K. (2001). The Need for Openness in Standards. *IEEE Computer*, *34*(6), 100–101.

Krechmer, K. (2005). The Meaning of Open Standards, In *Proceedings of the 38th Hawaii International Conference on System Sciences*. IEEE Computer Society. 10.1109/HICSS.2005.605

Lea, G., & Hall, P. (2004). Standards and intellectual property rights: An economic and legal perspective. *Information Economics and Policy*, *16*(1), 67–89. doi:10.1016/j.infoecopol.2003.09.005

Lerner, J., & Tirole, J. (2015). Standard-Essential Patents. *Journal of Political Economy*, *123*(3), 547–586. doi:10.1086/680995

Lundell, B. (2011). e-Governance in public sector ICT-procurement: what is shaping practice in Sweden? *European Journal of ePractice, 12*(6), 66-78.

Lundell, B. (2012). Why do we need Open Standards? In M. Orviska & K. Jakobs (Eds.), *Proceedings 17th EURAS Annual Standardisation Conference 'Standards and Innovation'* (pp. 227-240). The EURAS Board Series.

Lundell, B., Marr, D., Opie, E., Piana, C., & van Rooijen, A. (2016b). *Panel discussion @ Workshop on Open source and standardization: Legal interactions*. ETSI, Sophia Antipolis, France.

Lundell, B., & Gamalielsson, J. (2013). Usage of Open Standards and Open Source in Swedish schools: On Promotion of Openness and Transparency, In E. Petrinja et al. (Eds.), Open Source Software: Quality Verification (pp. 207-221). IFIP Advances in Information and Communication Technology.

Lundell, B., & Gamalielsson, J. (2017). On the potential for improved standardisation through use of open source work practices in different standardisation organisations: How can open source-projects contribute to development of IT-standards? In *Digitalisation: Challenge and Opportunity for Standardisation: Proceedings of the 22nd EURAS Annual Standardisation Conference*. EURAS Contributions to Standardisation Research.

Lundell, B., Gamalielsson, J., & Tengblad, S. (2016). IT-standarder, inlåsning och konkurrens: En analys av policy och praktik inom svensk förvaltning. *Uppdragsforskningsrapport, 2016*(2). (in Swedish)

Lundell, B., Gamalielsson, J., Tengblad, S., Hooshyar Yousefi, B., Fischer, T., Johansson, G., . . . Lönroth, E. (2017). Addressing lock-in, interoperability, and long-term maintenance challenges through Open Source: How can companies strategically use Open Source? In *The 13th International Conference on Open Source Systems (OSS 2017), IFIP AICT 496*. Springer.

Lundell, B., Lings, B., & Syberfeldt, A. (2011). Practitioner perceptions of Open Source software in the embedded systems area. *Journal of Systems and Software, 84*(9), 1540–1549. doi:10.1016/j.jss.2011.03.020

Lundell, B., & van der Linden, F. (2013). Open Source Software as Open Innovation: Experiences from the Medical Domain. In J. S. Z. Eriksson & ... (Eds.), *Managing open innovation technologies* (pp. 3–16). Berlin: Springer. doi:10.1007/978-3-642-31650-0_1

Milinkovich, M. (2015). *How the Eclipse community works*. Keynote presentation @ the 11th International Conference on Open Source Systems, Florence, Italy.

Mitchell, I. G., & Mason, S. (2010). Compatibility Of The Licensing Of Embedded Patents With Open Source Licensing Terms. *International Free and Open Source Software Law Review, 3*(1), 25–58. doi:10.5033/ifosslr.v3i1.57

NOC. (2007). *The Netherlands in Open Connection: An action plan for the use of Open Standards and Open Source Software in the public and semi-public sector*. Ministry of Economic Affairs. Retrieved from https://www.ictu.nl/archief/noiv.nl/files/2009/12/Action_plan_english.pdf

NOVFS. (2011). *Open Document Standards for the Government Guide*. Programma Nederland Open in Verbinding & Forum Standaardisatie. Retrieved from https://www.forumstandaardisatie.nl/fileadmin/os/documenten/Handreiking_ODF_Engelse_versie.pdf

Odell, M. (2009). European Public Sector Award. Public speech by Swedish minister, Maastricht.

OSI. (2017). *Open Source Initiative*. Retrieved from opensource.org

Pentheroudakis, C., & Baron, J. A. (2017). *Licensing Terms for Standard Essential Patents: A Comprehensive Analysis of Cases*. JRC Science for policy report, European Commission.

Permanent Representatives Committee. (2016). Draft Council conclusions on the "Digital Single Market Technologies and Public Services Modernisation" package. Statement by the United Kingdom, Estonia, Belgium, Slovenia, Poland, Latvia and Malta, 8735/16 ADD 1, 26 May, Brussels.

Simcoe, T. S. (2006). Open Standards and intellectual property rights. In H. Chesbrough & ... (Eds.), *Open Innovation researching a new paradigm*. Oxford, UK: Oxford University Press.

Simeonova, D. (2015). *Digital Solutions: Can we 'Open Source' the Future? Commission en direct #21*. European Commission.

SOU. (2009). *Strategi för myndigheternas arbete med e-förvaltning*. Statens Offentliga Utredningar: SOU 2009:86, e-Delegationen, Finansdepartementet, Regeringskansliet, Stockholm. (in Swedish)

Standaardisatie. (2014). *Lijst met open standaarden, Forum Standaardisatie*. Retrieved from https://lijsten.forumstandaardisatie.nl/lijsten/open-standaarden/

Standardisation Forum. (2011). *A guide for government organisations Governance of Open Standards*. The Standardisation Forum, The Hague.

UK. (2012a). *Open Standards Principles: For software interoperability, data and document formats in government IT specifications*. HM Government, UK. Retrieved from https://www.gov.uk/government/uploads/ system/uploads/attachment_data/file/183962/Open-Standards-Principles-FINAL.pdf

UK. (2012b). *Open Standards in Government IT: A Review of the Evidence*. HM Government, UK. Retrieved from https://www.gov.uk/government/uploads/system/uploads/attachment_data/file/78891/Review-of-the-Evidence_CIPPM.pdf

UK. (2012c). *CloudStore opens for business, Cabinet Office and The Rt Hon Lord Maude of Horsham*. Retrieved from https://www.gov.uk/government/news/cloudstore-opens-for-business

UK. (2014). *Standards Hub*. CabinettOffice, UK Government. Retrieved from http://standards.data.gov.uk/

UK. (2015). *Open Standards Principles, Updated 7 September 2015*. HM Government, UK. Retrieved from https://www.gov.uk/government/uploads/system/uploads/attachment_data/file/459075/OpenStandardsPrinciples2015.pdf

Updegrove, A. (2009). *The EC Settlement: Rambus, Writs and the Rule of Law*. Retrieved from http://www.consortiuminfo.org/standardsblog/article.php?story=20090622043038212

Wessman, R. (2013). *Upphandling av IT - inlåsningseffekter och möjligheter, Uppdragsforskningsrapport 2013:2, ISSN-nr 1401-8438*. Swedish Competition Authorities.

KEY TERMS AND DEFINITIONS

Formal/Informal Standard: Formal standards are provided by organisations which are recognised as formal standardisation organisations, whereas information standards are provided by organisations which are recognised as informal (or consortia) standardisation organisations. For example, an ISO standard that is provided by ISO (International Organization for Standardisation) is considered as a formal standard, whereas a W3C standard that is provided by W3C (the World-Wide-Web consortium) is considered as an informal (or consortia) standard.

FRAND: An acronym for "fair reasonable and non-discriminatory" terms on a similar (or identical) basis to RAND: it is debated whether there is a material difference between RAND and FRAND.

Open Source Software (OSS): Software made available under a software license which has been approved by the Open Source Initiative (see: opensource.org).

Open/Closed Standard: Open standards are standards which are provided on royalty-free terms and such standards can be implemented in open source software without restriction, whereas closed standards are provided on RAND (or other) terms that cannot be implemented in open source software. For example, the W3C standard SVG is considered an open standard, whereas the ISO standard JPEG2000 is considered a closed standard.

RAND: An acronym for "reasonable and non-discriminatory terms." It is used by standardisation organisations to describe a form of licensing commitment. A patent owner that has agreed with a standardisation organisation to provide their patents which impinge on a standard on RAND terms is bound by an offer from any prospective licensee to negotiate a license on reasonable and non-discriminatory terms.

Royalty: A payment made by the licensee to the licensor for the right to use an asset. For example, a payment made by a user of a standard to the owner of a standard-essential-patent. It may be one-off, periodic, or based on another metric (for example, per licensed unit sold).

Royalty-Free: Refers to the right to use an asset (e.g., copyright or patent) without the need for payment. For example, a licensor of a standard-essential patent which provide the patent on royalty-free terms allows a user of the standard to use the patent without payment.

Standard Essential Patent: Refers to a patent which impinges on the conditions for use of a standard. A patent which impinges on a standard is a standard essential patent in case it is necessarily infringed when the technical specification of the standard cannot be implemented without infringing on the patent (i.e. if the technical specification of the standard cannot be implemented without infringing the standard essential patent).

ENDNOTES

[1] http://blogs.wsj.com/cio/2014/05/05/open-source-eating-software-world-samsung/

[2] It should be noted that active participation in international meetings organised in standardisation projects (e.g. ISO and SMPTE) may constitute major inhibitors for a small company, as experienced by representatives from small companies in previous collaborative research involving authors of this manuscript (e.g. Gamalielsson et al., 2015).

[3] See Directive 2014/24/EU, http://eur-lex.europa.eu/legal-content/EN/TXT/PDF/?uri=CELEX: 32014L0024&from=EN; Regulation (EU) No 1025/2012, http://eur-lex.europa.eu/LexUriServ/ LexUriServ.do?uri=OJ:L:2012:316:0012:0033:EN:PDF

[4] For example, the Regulation (EU) No 1025/2012 (EC, 2012) clarifies that consortia standards must not "limit the possibilities for implementers" to use the standard. Further, this EU regulation states that some consortia developing 'informal standards' do not fulfil requirements according to this regulation: "Some ICT technical specifications are not developed in accordance with the founding principles" (i.e. "coherence, transparency, openness, consensus, voluntary application, independence from special interests and efficiency"). From this it follows that 'informal standards' from such consortia cannot be referenced in public sector procurements according to this regulation. However, a legal review of this regulation is beyond the scope of this chapter.

5   Open Mobile Alliance (OMA), http://openmobilealliance.org/, clarifies that "No license to any patent, trademark, copyright or other proprietary right is granted under this Agreement or through any disclosure hereunder except as expressly stated in this Agreement", see http://openmobilealliance.org/about-oma/policies-and-terms-of-use/use-agreement/

6   Society of Motion Picture & Television Engineers (SMPTE), https://www.smpte.org/, clarifies that documents "may include technology that is subject to Essential Claims" only "if all known patent holders are prepared to agree to terms that are RAND for all Essential Claims" (i.e. a claim which "is necessarily infringed by implementing the Normative Text of that Engineering Document and is 'necessarily infringed' only when there is no commercially-reasonable non-infringing alternative for implementing the Engineering Document"), see https://www.smpte.org/sites/default/files/SMPTE_IP_Policy_2013-08.pdf.

7   The OASIS IPR-rules clarifies that when a TC is established it can chose to operate under one (of four different) IPR Modes. At time of initial data collection and analysis, we note that for the 89 currently active TC:s in OASIS we find that: 52 have selected to operate under the mode "RF on Limited Terms"; 18 have selected to operate under the mode "RF on RAND Terms"; 18 have selected to operate under the mode "Non-Assertion"; and 1 has selected to operate under the mode "RAND" (for an overview of the 4 models, see further https://www.oasis-open.org/policies-guidelines/ipr#tcformation). In addition, there are also additional "Legacy IPR rules" for other OASIS TC:s (e.g. see https://www.oasis-open.org/committees/tc_home.php?wg_abbrev=wss; https://www.oasis-open.org/committees/wss/ipr.php).

8   The OASIS IPR-rules clarifies that when a TC is established it can chose to operate under one (of four different) IPR Modes. At time of initial data collection and analysis, we note that for the 89 currently active TC:s in OASIS we find that: 52 have selected to operate under the mode "RF on Limited Terms"; 18 have selected to operate under the mode "RF on RAND Terms"; 18 have selected to operate under the mode "Non-Assertion"; and 1 has selected to operate under the mode "RAND" (for an overview of the 4 models, see further https://www.oasis-open.org/policies-guidelines/ipr#tcformation). In addition, there are also additional "Legacy IPR rules" for other OASIS TC:s (e.g. see https://www.oasis-open.org/committees/tc_home.php?wg_abbrev=wss; https://www.oasis-open.org/committees/wss/ipr.php).

9   ISO/IEC 15948, "Information technology -- Computer graphics and image processing -- Portable Network Graphics (PNG)", ISO/IEC JTC1/SC24.

10   ISO/IEC 15444, "Information technology -- JPEG 2000 image coding system", ISO/IEC JTC1/SC29.

11   ISO 12234-2, "Electronic still-picture imaging -- Removable memory -- Part 2: TIFF/EP image data format", ISO/TC 42.

12   W3C Recommendation, "Scalable Vector Graphics (SVG) 1.1 (Second Edition)", 16 August 2011.

13   www.w3.org

14   http://www.iso.org/iso/standards_development/patents

15   Initial letters (air-mail) were sent in May 2014. Further, requests were also sent via email to all organisations that included email addresses as part of their contact details in the patent database.

16   For example, the ISO standard PDF/A-2 (ISO 19005-2:2011) contains several normative references to other standards (maintained by ISO and other SDOs) which thereby constitute inherent parts of the ISO 19005-2:2011 standard. One of these normative references is Part 2 of the ISO/IEC standard JPEG 2000 for which several patent declarations can be identified in the ISO patent

database. However, the same declarations cannot be found when searching for declarations made for ISO 19005-2:2011 in the ISO patent database (and it is instead necessary to manually search the ISO patent database for all normative references at all levels). Hence, it follows that a simple search in the ISO patent database gives a misleading indication of the scope of how patents declared for the investigated standards impact on other standards.

[17] It should be noted that PNG is also provided as a W3C standard, but it is only included as an ISO standard in the explicit list of open standards in the Netherlands.

[18] http://www.w3.org/TR/2011/REC-SVG11-20110816/

[19] http://www.w3.org/Graphics/SVG/WG/wiki/Implementations

[20] http://www.blender.org/; https://inkscape.org; http://wiki.scribus.net

[21] http://www.w3.org/TR/2003/REC-PNG-20031110/

[22] http://www.w3.org/Graphics/PNG/Disclosures

[23] http://www.w3.org/TR/PNG/; http://www.libpng.org/pub/png/png-sitemap.html

[24] http://www.gimp.org/; https://inkscape.org; http://www.tuxpaint.org/

[25] For the rest of this chapter, we write "JPEG 2000" when referring to the complete ISO standard ISO/IEC 15444.

[26] For an overview of the JPEG 2000 standard as presented by the JPEG committee, see http://jpeg.org/jpeg2000/index.html

[27] In addition, there are a number of draft specifications and several outdated standard documents, which also may be relevant for implementation in software in different usage scenarios (e.g. for scenarios with long life-cycles)

[28] For the six organisations that provided email addresses as part of their contact details in the patent database related to JPEG 2000 we observed that the email addresses to four organisations were invalid (most likely outdated) which implied that we used air mail addresses instead.

[29] We consider data collection to be finished since more than 3 years have elapsed since the initial request. Further, the most recently returned letter was received in March 2015 (i.e. more than eight months after the last reminder).

[30] For the rest of this chapter, we write "TIFF/EP" when referring to the complete ISO standard ISO 12234-2:2001.

[31] We consider data collection to be finished since more than 3 years have elapsed since the initial request. Further, the most recently returned letter was received in March 2015 (i.e. more than eight months after the last reminder).

[32] In this section, we use the terminology 'companies' and 'implementing companies', but this term should be understood to embrace other organisations, such as open source projects, which may also want to implement software which implements the standard, and many of the issues investigated will also impact larger companies.

[33] Organisations exist, such as the Open Invention Network (OIN), which act as the nexus of cross-licensing arrangements between their member organisations, typically in relation to a specific application or vertical market (in the case of the OIN, this covers the various components that they define as the 'Linux System'). Essentially, this enables the members to pool their patent portfolios. The pool may also assist members when third parties claim that the relevant technology infringes their own patents. The OIN, in addition to holding licences from members, also holds patents that it licenses to members.

34   It should be noted that decisions concerning whether or not small companies will participate in international standardisation is also affected by (perceived and experienced) barriers to entry, as indicated by experiences from previous research published by authors of this chapter: "From our own experiences of participation in IETF and W3C standardisation it is highly feasible for small companies to contribute due to low barriers for participation" (Gamalielsson et al., 2015, p. 41).

35   This mechanism, and to a lesser degree, the specific wording, implements a mechanism which will be familiar to many organisations of all sizes which are involved in the licensing of open source software, given that a similar mechanism appears in many common open source licences.

36   One would hope that such a declaration would remain, under all relevant jurisdictions, both irrevocable and also pass with the underlying patent, should the patent be assigned to a third party. The legal analysis of these points will vary from jurisdiction to jurisdiction and is beyond the scope of this chapter. In most common-law jurisdictions (Ireland being an exception that immediately comes to mind), the ISO rules could be amended to render potential licensees under Option Zero third party beneficiaries. There are other possible mechanisms to facilitate transfer of the commitment alongside the patent (deed poll, promissory estoppel, for example), but an analysis of them is beyond the scope of this chapter.

37   For example, concerning transfer of SEPs it has been reported that "A large majority of the transfers (83.5%) took place after standard release." (ECSIP, 2014, p. 190)

38   The first principle of the Open Source Definition states: "The license shall not restrict any party from selling or giving away the software...The license shall not require a royalty or other fee...". For any licence to qualify as an Open Source Licence, it must adhere to this principle. https://opensource.org/osd-annotated

Chapter 5
Analysis of Free and Open Source Software (FOSS) Product in Web Based Client–Server Architecture

Pushpa Singh

Accurate Institute of Management &Technoloy, Greater Noida, India

Narendra Singh

G L Bajaj Institute of Management & Research, Greater Noida, India

ABSTRACT

Free and open source software (FOSS) differs from proprietary software. FOSS facilitates the design of various applications per the user's requirement. Web applications are not exceptional in this way. Web-based applications are mostly based on client server architecture. This article is an analytical study of FOSS products used in web-based client server architecture. This article will provide information about FOSS product such as FireFox (web browser), Apache (web server) and MySQL (RDBMS). These reveal that various FOSS products such as Apache server covers 65% of the market share, while MySQL covers 58.7% market share and hold the top-most rank.

INTRODUCTION

Free and open source software (FOSS) is one of the effective tools that can be easily utilized in business, research and academia. FOSS is a movement started way back in 1980 to provide reliable software at low cost/free of cost to the users (FOSS A General Introduction, 2018). This software could be used, modified, redistributed without any permission required. FOSS insists on ethical and moral importance of users' freedom and hence has strict norms on how to aggregate free and proprietary software together. The proprietary software provides the user right to use the software under certain conditions without

DOI: 10.4018/978-1-7998-9158-1.ch005

any knowledge of how the software is designed and without any access to its source code (Andersson & Laurell, 2003).

FOSS consists two terms: "free" software and "open source" software. The Free Software Foundation (FSF, www.fsf.org) has introduced a definition of "free software". 'Free' does not define software as 'free' in terms of free-of-cost, but in referring to the four freedoms of use to that software. The four freedoms means that it respects the users' essential freedoms(Srinivasa & Deka, 2017) such as:

- Freedom to use for any purpose, including academic or industry (freedom 0)
- Freedom to modify the source code according your own need (freedom 1)
- Freedom to redistribute the code (freedom 2)
- Freedom to improve and release it for everyone use (freedom 3)

A program is called as a 'free' software if users have all stated freedoms(freedom 0 to 3). The General Public License (GPL) and Lesser General Public License(LGPL) are two well known licences which comply these definition (Andersson & Laurell, 2003). These freedoms are absolutely necessary not just for the individual users' sake, but also for society because they promote social solidarity—that is, sharing and collaboration. They become even more important as our culture and life activities are increasingly digitized.

The term 'open source' gives nourish the sense of 'freedom' that makes it qualifying it: open for learning and sharing the knowledge for each and everyone (Wynants & Cornelis, 2005). The term "open source" rapidly became related to thoughts and arguments based only on practical values, such as making a powerful and reliable software. Most of the supporters of open source have come to it since then, and they make the same association."Open" Source Software (OSS) has a pragmatic view on this matter and allows proprietary software to be easily aggregated with open source software. The distribution terms of open-source software must conform to the criteria discussed in reference (The open source definition (annotated), 2016). GPL, LGPL, BSD, MIT and MPL are some popular licenses, which conform to the definition.

These two terms (free and open source) are used for the unique development model and innovative distribution policy of software and often considered as the same thing (Feller and Fitzgerald, 2002; Feller, et al., 2005; Koch, 2005). Both the terms, free and open source is different with regards to the licenses to the respective software(Scacchi, 2007). 'Free' means freedom, not just free of cost. A software that is available free of cost called Freeware which may be copyrighted by its developer, who has the rights to modify, redistribute and improve in the future. Open source is a development methodology to allow the business use of free codes while free software is a social movement and promoted intellectual freedom. FOSS provides both free and open source software for the use of people. FOSS has drawn the attention of people from various backgrounds who have labelled it as an opportunistic software development model (Umarji, Sim & Lopes, 2008).

Undoubtedly, FOSS development has produced software of high quality and functionality. The Linux operating system has recently gained significant commercial success and great competitor to commercial operating systems such as Windows.

The IT and web landscape is really developing fast. IT vendors are most benefited from free and open source software. FOSS developers have a strong track record and market share in consulting and services and it stand to gain market share from the open source contracts. IT vendors that rely heavily on revenues from proprietary software that have strong competitors in the open source marketplace are most at risk (Appelbe, 2003). The GNU project has laid out a basis and motivation for more than thousands of projects that focus to develop Free and Open Source Software (FOSS).

It is obvious that open source is the foundation for the next generation digital revolution. Digital revolution is leading Website Design, Website Development or web based application or 'App' for smaller sized devices(smart phone) or larger sized devices (laptop etc.). A web application presents dynamically tailored content based on request parameters, tracked user behaviors, and security considerations.

Web based applications are generally based on client server architecture.This paper aims to address free and open source software that support web-based client server architecture to prove the success story of open source project.

RELATED WORK

Richard Stallman, researchers at MIT, founded the 'Free Software Foundation' (FSF) to develop and distribute software under the GPL while Bruce Perens defined a set of guidelines that a software license must grant its user, and he called this Open Source Initiative (OSI) (Potdar & Chang, 2004). An open source approach is well-established to provide improved product innovation over proprietary techniques of technical development (Deek, & McHugh, 2007; Lakhani & Von Hippel, 2003; Söderberg, 2015).

The existence of many FOSS products provides a possibility for developers/users to change the way of software development. Proprietary software is not feasible to maintain due to unavailability of source code. The vendor company maintains and upgrades the software and customer has to pay/purchase software upgrades at regular intervals. Open source offers upgradation of software at little or no cost. The customer can select when and where to make upgrades and install as in case of multiple versions of supported Linux (Appelbe, 2003).

The Linux operating system has recently enjoyed major commercial success, and is regarded by many as a serious competitor to commercial operating systems such as Windows (Gaedke & Rehse, 2000).

Steiniger and Hay (2009), reviewed the use of GIS (Geographic Information Systems) and GI tools in landscape ecology, with an emphasis on free and open source software (FOSS). Kitchenham et al. focused the research on adoption of OSS in organizations. With little or no marketing, open source software is finding its way into the information technology (IT) shops of a variety of companies and has been able to gain dominant market shares in several categories for many classes of business applications (Borrell, 2001; Sullivan, 2001).

There are now widely used, open-source programs of all types, including operating systems, databases, web servers, web browsers, word processors, spreadsheets etc. that support a new innovation in various applications including web application. Schwarz (2013) examined times and results for various open source web applications written in Java Servlets and JSP and found the approach was effective for helping the programmer detect client-state manipulation vulnerabilities. The simplest web application involves at least two computers: the one hosting the web server and the one hosting the browser.

There are many successful FOSS based software products/applications are being developed, distributed, and supported by and for the users themselves – no supplier required. A web application is an application that is invoked with a web browser over the internet. Web-based application is based on client server architecture in which servers store documents and client access documents (Jazayeri, 2007). Swain et al. (2015) focused on the challenges of identifying FOSS software to provide a web framework and spatial data capabilities for water resources web apps. Web applications are continuously taking advantages of open source project. This motivates the author to analyze FOSS based product. In this paper we have analyzed FOSS products that involved in web based client server architecture which can be linked to the success and popularity of FOSS.

WEB BASED CLIENT SERVER ARCHITECTURE

The client server architecture, uses, a web browser as its client program, and performs an interactive service by connecting to servers over the internet. Hypertext transfer protocol (HTTP), simple mail transfer protocol (SMTP) and file transfer protocol (FTP) are some standard protocols that client and servers use to communicate with them. Web based client server architecture consists of 2-tier, 3-tier and n-tier architecture. The most commonly used client server architecture is 3 tiers. Three tier architecture is a unique system of developing web database applications which work around the 3 tier model, comprising of the client tier at the first position, the application tier in the middle and the database tier at the last position as shown in Figure 1.

Figure 1. Three-tier client-server architecture

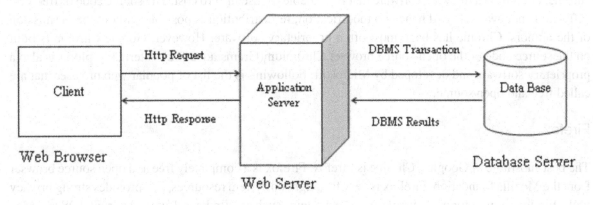

Working of Web Based Client-Server Architecture:

1. A client machine by using a web browser sends a request for a particular HTML text file over the Internet viva HTTP protocol to the web server.
2. The web server interprets the request as a command to run a particular server-side process. The server initiates the server-side process.
3. The server-side process logs into the DBMS and executes a data manipulation or query language command and sends DBMS results to the web server.
4. The web server sends the new HTML page to the web browser as a response equivalent to DBMS result. Depending on the action that the user originally chose and the results of the server-side process, the browser could display an HTML page containing actual data retrieved from the DBMS.

Thus, a client server system can be defined as software architecture made up of both the client and server. A client and a server are two parts of a connection, these are two distinct machines, web client requests information, and the web server is basically a PC that is designed to accept requests from remote computers and send in the information requested. In order to couple the server and client parts from heterogeneous environments in an efficient way, the basic client server architecture is extended by a new component i.e. middleware an integrating resource between the clients and servers.

Middleware is used to perform tasks such as: translation between the different protocols, optimization of the load-balancing, security control and management of the connections. Further, we will discuss the FOSS based product for each different tier as mention in figure 1.

FOSS for Web Client/Browser

A web browser is a program on your computer that allows you to access websites on the internet. Web browser to access and manipulate dynamic information, stored in a centrally controlled DBMS, over the Internet. Web clients can be said as an application or web browser (like Google Chrome, Internet Explorer, Opera, Firefox, Safari) which is installed in a computer and used to interact with Web servers upon user's request. It is basically a consumer application which collects processed data from servers. Today, web browsers support not only HTTP, FTP, and local file access, but e-mail and netnews as well.

There are several web browsers are available as a web browser/client. The best choice is google's chrome. Chrome is a freeware software that is available for use in zero cost. The source code of freeware software is not available and hence no modification, re-distribution is possible without the permission of the authors. Chrome has been most often proprietary software. However, Google Chrome is built on the source code of the open-source browser Chromium(Gramstad, 2012). Internet Explorer is also a proprietary software and developed by Microsoft. Following is the list of popular web browser that are called free and open source.

Firefox

The best substitute of Google's Chrome is Firefox. Firefox is a completely free and open source browser from the Mozilla foundation. FireFox is very fast, light on system resources, and provides strong privacy tools. Firefox support for majority of operating systems such as Windows, Linux, Android, IOS and Mac desktops. Firefox is written in C++, JavaScript, HTML, C, and Rust.

Chromium

Chromium browser is FOSS, So, there is possibility of source code modification and can make closed source. Chromium is an open source software project started by Google.Chromium support almost all of the feature of the Chrome browser. Chromium support for Windows 7 and later, Android 4.1 and later; OS X 10.9, MAC and Linux. Chromium browser is a default browser for a lot of Linux distributions. It is written in C, C++, Java, JavaScript, and Python.

Midori

Midori is also a FOSS browser. Midori is a lightweight browser and utilizes low resource. It is suitable when computer lacking in processing speed, then it will provide maximum performance. It's a minimalistic browser that only has built-in features that are absolutely necessary. Midori is written in C and Vala. Midori supports for Linux and windows.

Brave

Another FOSS based browser is Brave. Brave browser focus to block website trackers and also remove intrusive Internet advertisements. Brave blocks advertisements by default. Its support Windows, Linux, Andriod and IOS. It is written in C, C++ and JavaSript.

FOSS for Web Server

The web server uses to respond the client or web browser. It can be the combination of the hardware (the computer) or the software (computer application programs). The most common use of web server is to deliver the web content on request through the Internet. The Web Server is also used in gaming, storage, FTP, email, etc. Internet Information Server (IIS) is a proprietary server, means the user need to purchase a license to use it. Following are the list of popular web servers.

Apache Server

Apache Server is the most common and popular web server which is developed by Apache Software Foundation (ASF). Apache web server is a free and open source software. It's supports almost all the operating systems, including Linux, UNIX, Windows, FreeBSD, Mac OS X and more. Apache web server business captures the market slowly from Internet Information Server (IIS): a product of Microsoft. It's known for its reliability, an impressive range of features and support for numerous server-side programming languages. It is written in XML and C.

NGINX

NGINX is a free, open-source, high-performance HTTP server and reverse proxy, as well as an IMAP/POP3 proxy server. NGINX is written to address the C10K problem. C10K problem was a challenge for web servers to begin handling ten thousand concurrent. NGINX is known for its high performance, scalability, rich feature set, simplicity, and low resource consumption. NGINX is written in C.

Lighttpd

"Lighttpd" is a free and open source software and popular for its speed, flexibility, security and stability. It is a lightweight server so best suited to those servers which are highly loaded. It is also written to solve the C10K problem. Lighttpd consumes less memory and CPU. It is also written in C.

NGINX and Lighttpd both consists almost similar features. The difference between these two are lighttpd runs as a single process with a single thread and non blocking I/O whereas NGINX has one master process and delegates its work as worker process.

Cherokee

Cherokee is another FOSS cross platform web server. Focus of Cherokee web server is to provide fast and lightweight services to its client. Major features of Cherokee include a graphical administration interface named cherokee-admin, and a modular light-weight design. It is written in C, JavaScript and Python.

Following graph has shown in figure 2, how the FOSS web server is dominating over proprietary software such as Microsoft IIS web server.

Figure 2. Comparison of FOSS Web server to proprietary server (source: Netcraft survey)

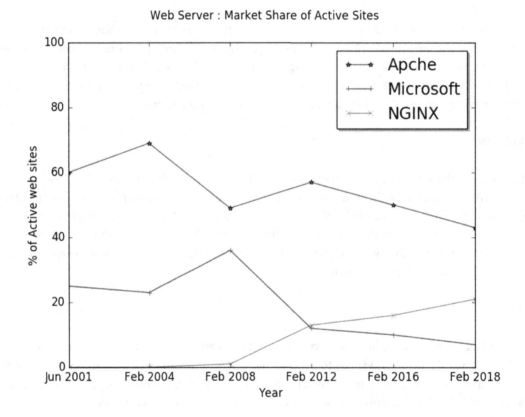

Figure 2, conclude that Apache server is, according to the Netcraft survey (Netcraft Web Server Survey, 2018) the most widely used web server. Data related to figure 2 is given in table 1 and based on Netcraft survey.

FOSS Data Base (DB)

MySQL, Oracle and MS SQL Server are widely used enterprise database systems. MySQL is an open source RDBMS, whereas MS SQL and Oracle Server is a proprietary software product. Following are the list of FOSS data base product:

Table 1. Web Server Developers:Market share of active sites

Year	% of the Active websites by using various mention servers		
	Apache Server	Microsoft IIS Server	NGINX Server
Jun 2001	60%	25%	0%
Feb 2004	69%	23%	0%
Feb 2008	49%	36%	1%
Feb 2012	57%	12%	13%
Feb 2016	50%	10%	16%
Feb 2018	43%	7%	21%

MySQL

MySQL is the world's most popular open source, multi-threaded, multi-user relational database management system. While open source, there are also several paid editions available that offer additional features, like cluster geo-replication and automatic scaling. MySQL provides server as a separate program for client-server networked environment. It supports almost every operating system such as FreeBSD, Linux, OS X, Solaris and Windows. It is written in C and C++. It used master-master and master-slave replication method for redundantly storing data on multiple nodes.

PostgreSQL

PostgreSQL is an open source object-relational database system that provides reliability, data integrity, and correctness. PostgreSQL supports major operating system. It used master-slave replication for redundantly storing data on multiple nodes. It is implemented in C.

MongoDB

MongoDB is also free and open source software based database system. It is schema free, document-oriented, scalable NoSQL database system (Deka, 2014). It supports Windows Vista and later, Linux, OS X 10.7 and later, Solaris, FreeBSD etc. operating system. It is written in C, C++ and JavaScript. MongoDB provided lower execution times than MySQL in all four basic operations: insert, select, update and delete. One can opt MongoDB instead of MySQL if the application is data intensive and stores many data and queries lots of data (Győrödi, 2015).

To compare the popularity of the three FOSS database engine with proprietary database engine, we have used DB ranking method which calculates score of database (solidIT, 2018). It is very clear from the graph as shown in figure 3 that MySQL which is a FOSS gaining or reaching his popularity compare to proprietary database engine Oracle and MS SQL.

Figure 4, shown a recent score gain by the DB engine in June 2018 (solid IT, 2018). The score is represented as a logarithmic scale. Data related to figure 4 is shown in table 2.

Figure 3. Comparison of DB Engine (source: https://db-engines.com/en/ranking_trend)

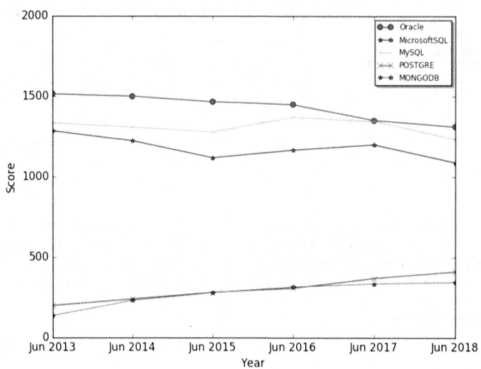

Table 2. Data associated as a scores of DB Engine

Year	Score of Data Base (DB) Engine				
	Oracle	Microsoft SQL	Mysql	PostGRE	MongoDB
Jun 2013	1514.89	1286.222	1334.944	199.386	137.492
Jun 2014	1500.918	1223.786	1309.554	239.985	231.443
Jun 2015	1466.361	1118.05	1278.357	280.905	279.051
Jun 2016	1449.248	1165.809	1370.134	306.609	314.622
Jun 2017	1351.762	1198.965	1345.307	368.544	335.001
Jun 2018	1311.252	1087.731	1233.688	410.669	343.785

DISCUSSION

Commercial, proprietary products are typically designed with a smaller scope of features and abilities. Much of the client-server architecture supported software is successfully based on open-source product. These software became milestone in the success story of FOSS. It is also considered that there will be a wide global demand for development and support of FOSS based web applications. Major product in FOSS based client server architecture is shown in Figure 4.

Figure 4. FOSS product used in client server architecture

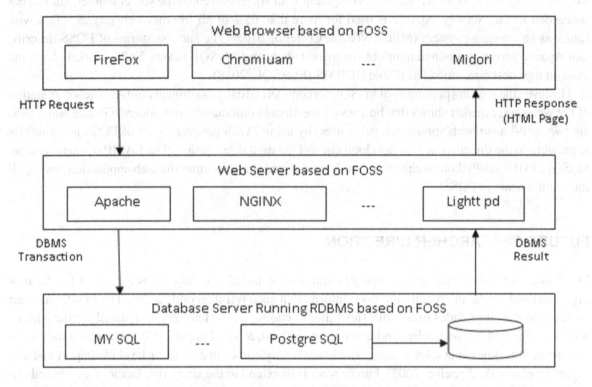

Earlier, chrome browser was considered as on top position, but now a days Firefox is Chrome's biggest contender if we ignore Internet Explorer (mainly used in business environments unwillingly). Firefox can do mostly what chrome can do and became a popular client browser in client server architecture. And over the past year, Firefox usage has risen quite a bit — from 7.7 percent in August 2016 to 12.0 percent in May 2017 (Bye Bye Chrome! Why We Switched to Firefox, 2017). This is all due to the advantages of FOSS. Firefox has several advantages presented over chrome:

- Better Battery life
- Better for heavy tab users.
- Having all features of true open source project and hence provides more customization facility.
- Better privacy

Firefox has two available plugins, which are particularly useful for literature reviews (Pearce, 2018). Firefox has found its way into millions of desktops reducing Microsoft's Internet Explorer's market by significant percentages. Internet Explorer has been losing popularity to FOSS web browsers and Firefox and Chromium are gaining popularity. Google also offered its chromium browser which is the part of open source product. This shows the increasing popularity of FOSS browser in a client-server environment.

There are many successful open source products and Apache web server is one of the most popular web servers in the world. In 2009 it passed a huge milestone, becoming the first web server to be used by more than 100 million websites. The biggest advantage in Apache Server is its open source nature and hence it becomes the cost effective web server in the market. PayPal, Apple, Adobe is some popular websites using the Apache server. IIS is competing with Apache to catch the server market, but has not succeeded so far. Notably, Apache is used for more than 65% of all Internet web servers, often with Linux as an operating system (Miller, Voas & Costello, 2010). The success stories of FOSS describe that Apache server covers maximum of the market share and MySQL covers 58.7% market share and exist on top most rank among available RDBMS (EverSQL, 2018).

However, the growing popularity of MySQL for commercial database projects and Apache's domination of the web server market shows that businesses are already embracing open source. Google and Yahoo are two well-known web application (web sites) by using FOSS product. A set of FOSS technologies is growing in the direction of web development and the digital revolution. The LAMP (Linux, Apache, MySQL, PHP/Perl/Python) architecture for designing and implementing the web application having all four components as FOSS.

FUTURE RESEARCHER DIRECTION

FOSS does not only focus on the software perspectives, but also in its role as a catalyst for the new organizational model in creating the open information society(Fitzgerald, 2005). The FOSS has been so successful as it provides users with flexibility to choose the technology best suited for their needs without being tied to a particular vendor solution (Lakhani, & Von Hippel, 2003). An open source solution generally comes in at a lower cost, but also generally comes in at a lower level of support and at a higher level of risk (Appelbe, 2003). Future work is to extend to the study risk factor of web based client server architecture which is based on FOSS. Future work is needed to determine the most effective methods to reduce risk factor and increase higher level of support to adopt the open source approach in future applications.

CONCLUSION

Free and open source software (FOSS) is an alternative approach for developing large software applications in perspective of the digital revolution. The existence of many popular FOSS projects in web based client server architecture provides an opportunity for developers to change the way of web application. In this paper, we made a comparative study of various FOSS based client, FOSS based server and FOSS based RDBMS. FireFox, as a web browser, Apache as web server and MySQL as an RDBMS is identified as a most popular FOSS products. LAMP architecture is a most popular architecture which is widely used for web applications.

Future developments in web applications will be driven by advances in FOSS technologies due to its advantages and features that provides users to use, change, share and improved.

REFERENCES

Andersson, I., & Laurell, T. (2003). Free and open source software-a feasibility study, Appendix 1: Extensive survey.

Appelbe, B. (2003). The future of open source software. *Journal of Research and Practice in Information Technology, 35*(4), 227.

Borrell, J. (2001). Changing mankind. *Upside,* (January), 68–74.

Deek, F. P., & McHugh, J. A. (2007). *Open source: Technology and policy.* Cambridge University Press. doi:10.1017/CBO9780511619526

Deka, G. C. (2014). A survey of cloud database systems. *IT Professional, 16*(2), 50–57. doi:10.1109/MITP.2013.1

EverSQL Team. (2018, March 13). Most popular databases in 2018 according to Stack Overflow survey. Retrieved from: https://www.eversql.com/most-popular-databases-in-2018-according-to-stackoverflow-survey/

Feller, J., & Fitzgerald, B. (2002). *Understanding Open Source Software Development.* NY: Addison-Wesley.

Feller, J., Fiztgerald, B., Hissam, S., & Lakhani, K. (Eds.). (2005). *Perspectives on Free and Open Source Software.* Cambridge, MA: MIT Press.

Fitzgerald, B. (2005). Has open source software a future. *Perspectives on free and open source software, 1,* 93-106.

Gaedke, M., & Rehse, J. (2000, March). Supporting compositional reuse in component-based Web engineering. In *Proceedings of the 2000 ACM symposium on Applied computing* (*Vol. 2*, pp. 927-933). ACM. 10.1145/338407.338691

Gramstad, A. R. (2012). *Proprietary Software, Free and Open-Source Software, and Piracy: An Economic Analysis: A theoretical approach to competition between free and non-free software in the presence of unauthorised copying and network externalities* [Master's thesis].

Győrödi, C., Győrödi, R., Pecherle, G., & Olah, A. (2015, June). A comparative study: MongoDB vs. MySQL. In *2015 13th International Conference on Engineering of Modern Electric Systems (EMES),* (pp. 1-6). IEEE.

OS Initiative. (2016). The open source definition (annotated).

Jazayeri, M. (2007, May). *Some trends in web application development. In 2007 Future of Software Engineering* (pp. 199–213). IEEE Computer Society.

Kitchenham, B., Brereton, O. P., Budgen, D., Turner, M., Bailey, J., & Linkman, S. (2009). Systematic literature reviews in software engineering–a systematic literature review. *Information and Software Technology, 51*(1), 7–15. doi:10.1016/j.infsof.2008.09.009

Koch, S. (Ed.). (2005). *Free/Open Source Software Development.* Hershey, PA: IGI Global. doi:10.4018/978-1-59140-369-2

L33TDAWG. (2017, June 20). Bye Bye Chrome! Why We Switched to Firefox. Retrieved from https://news.hitb.org/content/bye-bye-chrome-why-we-switched-firefox

Lakhani, K. R., & Von Hippel, E. (2003). How open source software works:"free" user-to-user assistance. *Research Policy*, *32*(6), 923–943. doi:10.1016/S0048-7333(02)00095-1

Miller, K. W., Voas, J., & Costello, T. (2010). Free and open source software. *IT Professional*, *12*(6), 14–16. doi:10.1109/MITP.2010.147

Netcraft. (2018). Netcraft Web Server Survey. Online document. Retrieved from https://news.netcraft.com/archives/2018/02/13/february-2018-web-server-survey.html

Pearce, J. M. (2018). How to Perform a Literature Review with Free and Open Source Software. *Practical Assessment, Research & Evaluation*, *23*(8), 2.

Potdar, V., & Chang, E. (2004, May). Open source and closed source software development methodologies. In *26th International Conference on Software Engineering* (pp. 105-109).

Scacchi, W. (2007). Free/open source software development: Recent research results and methods. *Advances in Computers*, *69*, 243–295. doi:10.1016/S0065-2458(06)69005-0

Schwarz, M. (2013). *Design and Analysis of Web Application Frameworks* [Doctoral dissertation]. Datalogisk Institut, Aarhus Universitet.

Söderberg, J. (2015). *Hacking capitalism: The free and open source software movement* (Vol. 9). Routledge. doi:10.4324/9780203937853

Solid, I. T. (2018). Method of calculating the scores of the DB-Engines Ranking. Retrieved from https://db-engines.com/en/ranking_trend

Srinivasa, K. G., & Deka, G. C. (Eds.). (2017). *Free and Open Source Software in Modern Data Science and Business Intelligence: Emerging Research and Opportunities: Emerging Research and Opportunities*. IGI Global.

Steiniger, S., & Hay, G. J. (2009). Free and open source geographic information, tools for landscape ecology. *Ecological Informatics*, *4*(4), 183–195. doi:10.1016/j.ecoinf.2009.07.004

Swain, N. R., Latu, K., Christensen, S. D., Jones, N. L., Nelson, E. J., Ames, D. P., & Williams, G. P. (2015). A review of open source software solutions for developing water resources web applications. *Environmental Modelling & Software*, *67*, 108–117. doi:10.1016/j.envsoft.2015.01.014

Umarji, M., Sim, S. E., & Lopes, C. (2008, September). Archetypal internet-scale source code searching. In *IFIP International Conference on Open Source Systems* (pp. 257-263). Boston, MA: Springer.

Wynants, M., & Cornelis, J. (Eds.). (2005). *How open is the future?: economic, social & cultural scenarios inspired by free & open-source software*. ASP/VUBPRESS/UPA.

This research was previously published in the International Journal of Open Source Software and Processes (IJOSSP), 9(3); pages 36-47, copyright year 2018 by IGI Publishing (an imprint of IGI Global).

Chapter 6
Strategy of Good Software Governance:
FLOSS in the State of Turkey

Hüseyin Tolu
https://orcid.org/0000-0003-0769-6779
Recep Tayyip Erdogan University, Turkey

ABSTRACT

To chapter concerns emerging cybernetics, which is the school of "meaning to lead" and is particularly associated with the idea of dominations and controls. This chapter initially anatomizes the sociology of software cybernetics into two broad movements—free/libre and open source software (FLOSS) and proprietary close source software (PCSS)—to argue a good software governance approach. This chapter discusses (a) in what matters and (b) for what reasons software governance of Turkey has locked into the ecosystems of PCSS and, in particular, considers causes, effects, and potential outcomes of not utilizing FLOSS in the state of Turkey. The government has continuously stated that there are no compulsory national or international conventions(s) and settlement(s) with the ecosystems of PCSS and that there is no vendor lock-in concern. Nevertheless, the chapter principally argues that Turkey has taken a pragmatic decision-making process of software in the emerging cybernetics that leads and contributes to techno-social externality of PCSS hegemonic stability.

INTRODUCTION

"You never change things by fighting the existing reality. To change something, build a new model that makes the existing model obsolete"; as B. Fuller (1895-1983), believed that in the system of monetary capitalism, it is practically meaningless to fight forces. So, smashing burgeoning technology for putting them out of their particular works is no longer the case of matter in the era of singularity. Nevertheless, this is not meant that the public ought not to have a particular criticism to technological singularity; or at least, no particular ethical concerns about its possible prospective and retrospective memory in the global

DOI: 10.4018/978-1-7998-9158-1.ch006

(capitalist) system. The burgeoning technology is peculiar and mostly irregular, as W. Mossberg states that "why shouldn't a PC work like a refrigerator or a toaster?" Or "I'm an enemy of what I call 'computer theology.' There's a class conflict out there. There's a techno-elite that lives in a different world". These quotations are what makes us concerned about cybernetics which is the school of 'meaning to lead', and particularly associated with the idea of dominations and controls, characteristically regarding criticism against doctrine of technological totalitarianism, existing mechanisms (machines and humans and their commissure), in which known and/or unknown one group control another. So, cybernetic is for the purpose of revealing its orchestrating mechanisms. "It is no longer a question of predicting the future, but of reproducing the present. It is no longer a question of static order, but of a dynamic self-organization" (Tiqqun, 2010, p.18). In this sense, cybernetics refers to an emergent governance of technology, policy and management, in which each element has actual persistence(s) of reality, but when they are merged together, multiplicities of reasonably complex interactions are arisen.

To study concerns of emerging cybernetics, interestingly enough, present software is escalating in order to sell hardware - e.g. present technology has no responsive meaning at all without software applications, such as Operating Systems (OSs) or the Internet. This makes software an interesting but sophisticated phenomenon. It is thereby initially essential to anatomize sociology of software cybernetics into two broad movements: Free/Libre and Open Source Software (FLOSS) and Proprietary Close Source Software (PCSS), to argue how our new technological revolution (e.g. innovations) exposures new concerns of our good governance approach in the capitalist democratic systems. This chapter broadly highlights why not to put technological movements into the same vein at all, because some of burgeoning technology should benefits public as a whole, in the prime imaginable way, as FLOSS movements seek. Then, this chapter compares the sociology of PCSS with those of FLOSS, highlighting their consequences as hegemonic totalitarianism with PCSS versus flexible emancipation with FLOSS. As the "control is as much an effect as a cause, and the idea that control is something you exert is a real handicap to progress" (Grand, 2003). So, it is actually essential to have the core knowledge of sociological of education and technology, in particular neither Utopian nor Luddite approach of Technorealism to conceptualise our new social goods, because

information is the vital element in a 'new' politics and economy that links space, knowledge and capital in networked practices. Freedom is an essential ingredient in this equation if these network practices develop or transform themselves into knowledge cultures. (Peters and Besley, 2008, p.186)

To comprehend these objects, the chapter is organized into seven sections. In the second and third sections, Actor Network Theory (ANT) and then the data collection method are introduced, to begin with, that there is an explicit good governance approach for the current software cybernetics, in particular sociology of education and technology, which crucially anatomizes the movements of FLOSS and PCSS. In this anatomization, the fourth and fifth sections inquire whether or not Turkey has locked-in into the ecosystems of PCSS. If Turkey has been, (a) in what matters and (b) in what reasons has software governance of Turkey locked-in into the ecosystems of PCSS, and in particular it considers causes, effects, potential outcomes for not utilizing FLOSS in the state of Turkey in order to reveal the cybernetics of Turkey. Therefore, the overall aim and contribution of the chapter is to increase an understanding of the underlying socio-political imperatives behind the cybernetics of Turkey in the specific context of PCSS. In the sixth section, it is argued that while the government has constantly stated that there are no compulsory national or international conventions(s) and settlement(s) with the ecosystems of PCSS and there are no vendor lock-in concerns, what does the data analysis principally indicate? Has Turkey actually taken pragmatic decision-making process of software (e.g. de-facto governance) in the emerging cybernetics? And does this negative externality which is certainly driven by state-scapegoatism, builds-in obsolescence and so leads and contributes to PCSS hegemonic stability (e.g. its own dominations and controls) in the era of technological singularity? Before the conclusion remark, the last section particularly focuses on good software governance which is not actually about providing 'correct' decisions, but about the 'best' possible judgment process for developing and implementing these decisions. It is focused that governing current burgeoning technology in specific state structures and regulatory frameworks is crucial for imagining a new sort of 'good software governance' that specific society for the best of the present.

ACTOR NETWORK THEORY

In the literature, ANT is considered as both a theory and a method in which "truth and falsehood. Large and small. Agency and structure. Human and non-human. Before and after. Knowledge and power. Context and content. Materiality and sociality. Activity and passivity. In one way or another all of these divides have been rubbished, in work undertaken in the name of" ANT (Law, 1999, p.3). In spite of this ontological complication, ANT has been applied to many literatures of education and technology. Latour illuminated the motive for ANT popularity as the progression of emerging "an alternative social theory to deal with the new puzzles uncovered after carrying out our fieldwork in science and technology" (2005, p.2). In methodology, the approach of ANT is "through the back door of science in the making, not through the more grandiose entrance of ready made science" (Latour, 1987, p.4) in where technology and science become a reality, for example public and private institutions, labs, etc. ANT's approach is to 'follow actors'. There may be many actors within any obvious network, but some actors may be subsequently excluded or misplaced before the conclusion of the process; the importance of these actors / networks input absence is an unidentified variable (e.g. bureaucrats). So, ANT approach is to highlight the key actors and sub networks, critical to the particular study. ANT, similar to other Science and Technology Studies (STS) approaches, uses 'open black box' technology and science, through evaluating complex associates that might be in presence between various agencies, such as governments, private sectors, etc. Through exploring and highlighting these associates, it becomes clear to realise how and why technology and science harmonize within/between each other; nevertheless,

the actor network is reducible neither to an actor alone nor to a network. Like a network it is composed of a series of heterogeneous elements, animate and inanimate, that have been linked to one another for certain period of time. ... An actor network is simultaneously an actor whose activity is networking heterogeneous elements and a network that is able to redefine and transform what it is made of. (Callon, 1987, p.93)

ANT is taking into consideration of both human and nonhuman actualities as an equilibrium within/between a particular network(s) (but not necessarily an equally shared power relationship), and symmetrically titled them as an 'actant'. This perspective is called under 'the principle of generalized symmetry' by Callon (1986). ANT approaches human and nonhuman facts as meaningful behaviours, including moral distributed agencies by 'seamless web'. Latour argued that "an 'actor' in ANT is a semiotic definition-an actant-, that is, something that acts or to which activity is granted by others. It implies no special motivation of human individual actors, nor of humans in general. An actant can literally be anything provided it is granted to be the source of an action" (1996, p.373). The important point in ANT is 'follow actors' in order to study mutual and elective associations between actants, because an individual actant has not necessarily and inevitably the acting ability. For semiotic, a 'thing' has a meaning associatively with interactions with other things. ANT approaches both human and nonhuman actants; seeing their identities through their interactive relationships within/between networks.

So materials become resources or constraints; they are said to be passive; to be active only when they are mobilized by flesh and blood actors. But if the social is really materially heterogeneous then this asymmetry doesn't work very well. Yes, there are differences between conversations, texts, techniques and bodies. Of course. But why should we start out by assuming that some of these have no active role to play in social dynamics?" (Callon and Law, 1997, p.168)

ANT scholars highlighted that the network, they would like to seek, is different than traditional technological and sociological disciplines. The approach of ANT is concerned with defining key actors, identifying their roles, and investigating their mobilising roles. For power and connectivity relationships, ANT proposes 'heterogeneous actors' though associations. To do this, ANT does not ask which networks are bigger, wider, longer, faster, etc. than others. Rather, which associations are stronger and powerful than others within/between networks? Actors are not simply stable from one situation to another, rather moving and transforming between practises. For heterogeneous, ANT scholars argue that any social contents are the result of interaction within/between heterogeneous networks. That result may become another effect of the same and/or other heterogeneous networks due to associations within/between heterogeneous networks. ANT scholars perceive the power of social actors from the arisen outcome of actors' interactions. However, for ANT, there is no priority allocation between macro and micro social analyses in actor-networks due to 'the principles of generalised symmetry', which agnostically refuse dichotomies and distinctions. Nevertheless, there are some other concepts that make us think that some networks are more crucial than others; mainly influencing powers of associations that might exist due to various reasons such as, size, nostalgia, legislations, formal/informal structures, etc. The important point is, again, studying how these associations (interactions and connections) are performed.

Literally there is nothing but networks, there is nothing in between them, or, to use a metaphor from the history of physics, there is no aether in which the networks should be immersed. In this sense ANT is a reductionist and relativist theory, but, as I shall demonstrate, this is the first necessary step towards an irreductionist and relationist ontology. (Latour, 1996, p.4)

ANT scholars argue that there are advantages in considering heterogeneous networks in the fields of social science and technology studies. (a) 'The tyranny of distance' is not really a concern anymore. In ANT, there are only networks, which are not defined in terms of proximity between actors, as in geography, but rather meanings of associations between actors within network is the main concern. (b) The concept of networks also solves the distinction between micro and macro scale priorities within networks. (c) And, there are no inclusion/exclusion boundaries, because the concern is whether or not there are interactions and connections, there is no such thing as an outsider.

DATA COLLECTIONS

These key principles of ANT are helpful to begin the construction of establishing good governance approach for the process of planning and implementing software decisions making; because, it is not about constructing 'correct' decisions, but about defining the best imaginable process. Hence, as this chapter argues that the current approach to cybernetics is based on pragmatic techno-sociological perspective (e.g. de-facto governance). Many pragmatist' computer scientists may postulate that pragmatism is essential in the sociology of software cybernetics because it is "a philosophical movement that includes those who claim that an ideology or proposition is true if it works satisfactorily, that the meaning of a proposition is to be found in the practical consequences of accepting it, and that unpractical ideas are to be rejected" (McDermid, 2006). Nevertheless, 'an ideology is true if it works satisfactorily' is not meant that there are no negative outcomes or consequences. More generally, as many economists argue, the related arguments under the title of negative externality in which PCSS might be seen as forms of progress that are not only prone to unavoidably failure (e.g. lock-in), but that also inhibit other, more positive forms of 'Progress' (e.g. collaboration) (Boyle, 2008). And importantly, the philosophy of FLOSS is in an indignation commissure and a powerful phenomenon as artefact and human re-shaped each other to lead a better future (Weber, 2004). Consequently, this study inquires whether or not Governments in Turkey should be guilty of what is analogous to cybernetics, namely the rejection of valid technological knowledge between FLOSS and PCSS since their approaches to cybernetics is based on pragmatic techno-sociological perspective (e.g. de-facto governance), but negative externality of that perspective is certainly driven by state-scapegoatism that builds-in obsolescence.

From this standpoint, the data is obtained from Turkey's public reports, in particular over three hundred parliamentary written and verbal questions and responses reports, five parliamentary investigation proposals reports, thousand minutes of general assembly meeting reports, produced in the years of 2005-2006, 2008-2009 and 2013-2017, as secondary sources and studied by under the principles of ANT. All sources are available in the Grand National Assembly of Turkey (TBMM) website, as typing the basic number (e.g. TBMM, Year, No. 7/1540) in the form of 'written oral questions proposals query'; 'parliament general discussion suggestion query form' and 'parliamentary research proposals inquiry form'. To comprehend the software decision-making process of Ministries or the cybernetics of Turkey, additional documentary sources such as national and international reports were also gathered. Unfortunately, the Prime Ministry and the Minister of Science, Industry and Technology (SIT), which are the highest authorities regarding technological related projects, have not responded to certain questions.

"Documents, both historical and contemporary, are a rich sources of data for education and social research" (Punch, 2009, p.158). Notably, it is impossible to merely demarcate cybernetics as policy, technology and management. To avoid repetition, some of the most significant but repeated concepts are addressed only once. So, the chapter may provide generalizability through collected data since it is simply a snapshot which is not aimed at stating an external truth, but to rather present movements of cybernetics. So, this chapter puts forth a generic argument without focusing on a particular Ministry, since each Ministry has its own characters and settings; this could be useful in the scoping of technology in a particular national-state. The chapter sought to interpret the implementation of different policies of different institutions at different times to illustrate cybernetics of Turkey. Therefore, contemporaneousness, which is the reading of historical information; such as, initiating, remaining or happening in the similar time, does not the limitation of the chapter, is just another signification.

MATTERS OF SOFTWARE GOVERNANCE

Initially, Turkey had an original and innovative Linux project. The Scientific and Technological Research Council of Turkey, Turkish National Academic Network and Information Centre (TUBITAK-ULAKBIM) initiated the Pardus-Linux Project for the purpose of establishing a nationally distributed Linux-Based OSs in 2003, but withdrew its financial and political supports in 2012. Within ten years, the project of Pardus-Linux failed to achieve its targets and intentions defined in 2004 and 2011. Afterwards this failure, TUBITAK has intentionally and hiddenly distorted Pardus-Linux into (forked) Pardus Fraud-Debian within a single day in 2014. Since, it has been claimed that Pardus Fraud-Debian is a sufficient ecosystem of FLOSS in Turkey. There have been many instances where Pardus-Linux has been publicly used as leverage to obtain better fiscal deals from Giants, mostly Microsoft (Tolu, 2016).

Before illustrating (a) in what matters software governance of Turkey has locked-in the ecosystems of PCSS, in particular Microsoft OSs, all these parliamentary concerns (e.g. questions, answers, etc.), have some significant misconceptions that provide an insight into the genetic parliamentary' perspectives upon FLOSS. The critical misconception is the focus of 'national' FLOSS and Pardus-Linux, instead of global FLOSS and Linux (Globalness) as an entire concept. Globalness is the mission, "to preserve, protect and promote the freedom to use, study, copy, modify, and redistribute computer software, and to defend the rights of Free Software users" (Stallman, 2013). In this sense, in the ecosystem of FLOSS, there is no 'national' energy or nationalism, all matter is us. Nevertheless, Ministries and/or Governments of Turkey have mainly postulated Pardus-Linux issues (they see them as issues) rather than evaluating themselves based on FLOSS and Linux. This might be the impulse of not mentioning the real issues of FLOSS in Turkey such as the low level of FLOSS localisation or the failure of Pardus-Linux project, etc.

Technological Mechanism

In the literature of software development, a mechanism is an eco-friendly platform that can be joint with other mechanisms in the same or other computers in a distributed network to perform an application. There are mainly two crucial complexes in the technological mechanisms of particular organizations or systems: (a) compatibility refers studying how well applications function within different OSs and/or Internet browsers and (b) interoperability refers studying how well a system under assessment performs while interacting with something else. In this sense, in Turkey, the Centre of High Performance Computing (Ulusal Yüksek Başarımlı Hesaplama Uygulama ve Araştırma Merkezi) is the only public institution that is mainly based on FLOSS. Other institutions, even TUBITAK itself, have adapted software applications and services derived from Microsoft ecosystems, such as active directory, e-mail, libraries, etc. So, Ministries declared that 'Linux does not support (contribute to) their structural compatibility and interoperability' and additional support services are thereby needed. In this regard, the absurdity is that 'Linux does not support' implies supporting technologies developed by Ministries for Ministries is Linux ecosystem responsibility and accountability. Nevertheless, Ministries should have confessed that the current technologies they operate have not been developed based on recommendations (*OS or browser Agnosticism*) from the Guides of Information Communication Technology (ICT) Project Preparation Annual Reports (since 2005; see the subtitle of software[1] by the State Planning Organization (SPO) in the Prime-Ministry. The guides crucially underline Compatibility and Interoperability to be ensured *Open Standard* and *Avoidance Dependence* which refers *Writes Once and Runs Anywhere*; operating software in different OSs or browsers without rewriting it.

Admittedly, each Ministry has its own priorities and so use various and particular software(s), e.g. the Ministry of Environment and Forestry declared that Computer Assisted Design (CAD) and Geographic Information System (GIS) software are used because they are perceived as more 'useful' and 'functional' for Windows compared to their versions for Linux! (TBMM, 2008, No.7/1727) In 2008, this perspective could have been feasible and reasonable because the primary focus in the Ministry was not technology. However within ten years, there have been so many FLOSS alternative projects for CAD and GIS. If the Ministry were to web search 'FLOSS for CAD and GIS', there are so many Turkish and English academic articles highlighting how to use FLOSS for CAD and GIS in public, or asked an expert in Turkey (e.g. Yener, 2017). In fact, whether or not this information presents a particular response to a particular Ministry's problem depends on a particular cybernetics (e.g. software culture), as argued further. Still, the Ministry had not changed its perspective after four years (TBMM, 2012, No.7/5322) and still argues the same reasons. Panoptically, Ministries should have shifted between FLOSS and PCSS alternatives as their needs and requirements modified to keep up with technological acceleration.

Consequently, the lack of compatibility and interoperability arguments (e.g. Linux does not support) has become an unprofessional misconception of FLOSS due to the fact that the principles of *OS Agnosticism* are already noticed by the authorities.

Platform Dependent

At this juncture of OS or browser Agnosticism, few other Ministries have used Linux/Pardus not only in their personal computers (PCs) but also in their servers. E.g. the Ministry of National Defence (MoND) earlier declared that Pardus-Linux and FLOSS office applications played in 48% of PCs and 84% of servers in 2012 (TBMM, 2012, No.7/5316). Under 'the Turkey's 2016-2019 Cyber Security Strategy and Action Plan', MoND have already had new nine different collaborative protocols with TUBİTAK in order to expand the usage of Pardus and FLOSS (MoND, 2017). Evidently they have overcome the lack of compatibility and incompatibility, but still it does not mean they (e.g. MoND) have solved all issues. Nevertheless, compatibility and interoperability is not FLOSS and Linux's issue but Ministries' issues, such as how to establish technological mechanism. Importantly, Ministries are responsible for shaping their ICT projects and then obtaining all software codes when projects are finalised, so Ministries should have ensured platform independency. There are always Interoperability Framework Guide (IFG) Reports (Version 1 - 2005; Version 2 - 2009 and Version 2.1 – 2012); however, the Prime Minister 2012 E-State: Concept and General Issues Report recognized that IFG Reports are also not followed by most Ministries, not even the Prime-Ministry itself. The current situation is still not changed or improved, since then.

Most Ministries thereby preferred to compare Windows and Linux through the technological infrastructure they currently have. For instance, the Turkish Statistical Institute argued that Microsoft Outlook software is required for exchanging mails elementarily ('trouble-free' and 'full functional') with an institutional email server, e.g. Microsoft Exchange 2010 (TBMM, 2012, 7/5284 and 7/5283). This is an unfortunate reality and internationally problematic issue which has been systematically argued since the Microsoft Antitrust Cases in the USA in 1998 and the EU in 2003-04 (e.g. European Commission, 2004), because Microsoft has not provided complete information (also called interoperability information) that would enable other OSs to interoperate with Windows for exchanging essential data between servers and servers/clients. Concordantly, some Ministries have also complained about office applications issues; even in 2017 there are some interoperability issues between Microsoft Office and LibreOffice. Therefore, Ministries postulated that migrating LibreOffice is 'unnecessary' and 'time-consuming'.

This kind of techno-social mobility may be multiplied in the past decade, and has been extensively argued by the literature of Social-Shaping of Technology Theory, Social Construction of Technology Approach, Socio-Technical Systems, etc., because technology is not, either the only end of its wise choices of techno-social mobility, or essentially just sociologically 'social', it is in fact *both*! Therefore, the relationship between 'compatibility and interoperability' and 'platform independency' is actually an international issue and should be decided upon. Yet, over the past decade, there has been no conclusive global consensus about the definition of *Open Standard* and *Implementation of its Definition*. There are just best practices highlighted by the digital single market strategies (see, the document of 'Open Standard' and 'Against lock-in: building open ICT systems by making better use of standards in public' by European Commission, 2013). Consequently, it is essential either to prepare a new agreed IFG report (definitive enduring solution) or wait PCSS's and so Microsoft's compromise (provisional ephemeral solution). In this sense, Ministries of Turkey have presented the reality, but argued absurdly because it is not logical to protest that Linux ecosystem does not have 100% compatibility and interoperability with Windows ecosystem without presenting (signifying) an argumentation of global IFG report.

Globally, the latest argument of platform independency has been 'Secure-Boot' (also called 'Restricted-Boot') which thought as either provides a *complete* solution of compatibility and interoperability issues or *ensures* that there will be no FLOSS, or at least no Linux, in our own products. "'Secure boot' is a technology described by recent revisions of the [Unified Extensible Firmware Interface] UEFI specification; it offers the prospect of a hardware-verified, malware-free OS bootstrap process that can improve the security of many system deployments. Linux and other open OS will be able to take advantage of secure boot if it is implemented properly in the hardware" (Bottomley & Corbet, 2011). Nevertheless, since 2010, the secure golden key system, such as secure-boot, has not been satisfactorily worked out and leads to new concerns for PCSS ecosystems, such as surveillance (e.g. Hruska, 2016). Besides, there are currently many technological alternatives to overcome these kinds of issues in particular for Linux ecosystems, such as Libreboot, MCUBoot, etc.

Network Effects

In the literature of economic and business, a network effect (also titled network externality) is the effect that one end-user of a good has on the value of that good to other people. More and more end-users who own good, more and more valuable the good is to each owner. As, Robert Kiyosaki states that "the richest people in the world look for and build networks; everyone else looks for work." In this sense, the applications of the Ministry of Justice (MoJ) have been developed through OS agnosticism. Therefore, in the '15th MoJ Coordination and Executive Board Meeting' held in June 2007, it was decided to use Pardus-Linux. It was argued that migrating Pardus-Linux was challenging because installing Pardus-Linux is not sufficient; there are other concerns; authorisations, authentications, etc. (TBMM, 2008, No.7/00731). Without technical supports and consulting services, migration is too difficult for one particular Ministry, even if all software applications are developed as OS agnosticism. Hence, all Ministries protested that in the market, there are insufficient numbers of qualified people and companies specialized in Linux, particularly Pardus-Linux. Although, on the face of OSs, it is free (as freedom) and open to use, taking technical supports and services from these companies are much more 'expensive' than imported OSs. For instance, the Ministry of Environment and Forestry (MoEF) earlier claimed that 800,000 companies across the world and 7,000 companies in Turkey provide Windows products and supports (TBMM, 2008, No.7/1727). It was concluded that this kind of platform in Linux ecosystems is not available and cannot be successfully managed by volunteers. For taking and providing FLOSS supports/services, it is essential to make exact actions by public authorities to ample effective migrations.

In the matter of the belief of suddenly being aphasia (ignorant of ICT), FLOSS literature argues that lack of technical supports and services in Linux ecosystems is a misunderstanding due to an intentional and/or unintentional fear. Nowadays, in FLOSS there are extensive communities who provide instant supports and services. There are thousands of forums, blogs, etc. available online to get appropriate information and formal private support corporations that all depend on a particular strategy (see, the open source observatory community and the open source software strategy 2014-2017 at the EC by the European Commission (2017) or Swedish policy makers want end to IT vendor lock-in (Hillenius, 2017). There might be a lack of on-going technical knowledge in Turkish if technological acceleration is considered, but knowing how to speak English is one of the criteria of ICT specialists in Ministries. So, the question has become how software culture is shaped in the Ministries; what is the Government's responsibility regarding to establishing Linux ecosystems and how should the Government play its role, etc.

The majority of end-users and technical support specialists are familiar with Windows platforms; that is one of the most important obstacles to migrating Linux. Therefore, the use of Linux and FLOSS may cause 'workforce loss!' in Ministries. Besides, for end-users, all service providers offer applications with Windows platforms. So, the Ministry of European Union (MoEU) believed that end-users have access to Windows without requiring any expertise, additional time and effort and end-users can use them with minimal effort (TBMM, 2012, No.7/5212). Nevertheless, what does this information tell us? Most Ministries stated that taking technical specialist preferences, skills and knowledge into consideration, migration to Linux was challenging. The reason for this is because of the criteria for contracting ICT specialist in Ministries; e.g., being a system expert in the Ministry of Science, Industry and Technology (MoSIT), specialists must be Microsoft Certified Technology Specialist, Microsoft Certified Database Administrator, and Microsoft Certified Systems Engineer or have Microsoft Certified IT Professional, etc. Additionally specialists must also have Linux, Unix/BSD and Windows platforms experiences. There is only statement of Linux experience! What does experience mean in there, no specification at all (2017) these requirements are so similar and to be become a sort of informal standard for appointing a public worker in Turkey. Most government apparatus have been using the similar requirements, as they use a 'Copy Policy Strategy', as argued in the following section of software culture.

Nevertheless, if end-users' habits and technical support teams' knowledge and skill are one of the most important obstacles, simply it can be argued how Ministries have decided to use LibreOffice in the Fatih project which is the latest educational technology project in Turkey, and how end-users, who already got familiar with Windows platforms through the history by mainly Ministries training services, will gradually get used to using LibreOffice in schools, even without LibreOffice in-service training and LibreOffice's curriculum in the Ministry of National Education (NoNE, 2014-2017[2]). Thus, Ministries underlined crucial points; knowledge and skill (and so habits); however, the points are unacceptable pretexts, because these are invented by Ministries themselves, so they manipulated the reasoning. Ministries have attempted to minimise their responsibilities to shape *Windows Societies* but the concern should be shaping *Digital Societies* in the *Knowledge-Based Economy* (OECD, 1996). Ministries do not fear of suddenly being ignorant of technology. Sometimes, it is necessary to put law when required, regardless of considering condition of society (e.g. readiness level). Make a law, the law enters into force, and society obeys. Indeed, "writing laws is easy, but governing is difficult." Leo Tolstoy (1828-1910)

The MoEU further instructed that if unwillingness is considered due to average-age and digital-literacy, end-users, who use Windows at home, should be persuaded to use Pardus-Linux at work, by receiving in-service voluntary-based trainings. This however is not the case. When E-Transformation Turkey Project (E-TTP) was launched in 2003, the Government did not ask citizens of Turkey to volunteer. In the project, nearly all public sectors' services have become digitalised and none of them is to be voluntary. Is Information Systems of MoNE (MEBBIS) voluntary for teachers? No! Is using F keyboard voluntary in MoNE? (MoNE, 2001, 2005, 2013) No! So, the discourse of Ministries is that when the concept is nurtured by Government's concerns, it is imperative; on the other hand, others are optional or simply voluntary. Nevertheless, imperative ICT legislations and regulations in Ministries are also problematic because they are not followed by Ministries, such as IFG Reports, F keyboard regulation, etc. Thus, some formal rules have become ineffective and inefficient because of neglecting the role of informal rules due to the fact that pragmatic techno-sociological perspective (e.g. de-facto software governance) has been taken by the relative authorities, as thinking today legal technological practice but not governing its future design! But "He who controls the past controls the future. He who controls the present controls the past" George Orwell (1903-1950). Theoretically, North argued that "we need to know much more about" (informal rules) and "how they interact with formal rules" (1990, p.140) to comprehend the mobility from governing political activities to actual performing activities, "the consequence of small events and chance circumstances can determine solutions that, once they prevail, lead one to a particular path" (ibid, p.4).

Many Ministries believed that if Linux becomes a common OS and developed applications become compatible with Linux, there is no obstacle to migrate to Linux. The absurd discourse of Ministries emphasized one reality in the Linux ecosystem, but they have deliberately ignored the main responsibility of the Governments, and their contributions for this outcome such as tender specifications, planning ICT projects, etc. In this sense, the MoEU has become a Microsoft spokesperson because it simply expects Linux to be Windows and to make FLOSS and Linux a scapegoat.

Sublation of FLOSS

The term of sublation has been clarified as abolish, cancel, preserve, and transcend. In the literature of philosophy, 'aufheben' was used by Hegel to illuminate what occurs when a thesis and antithesis relate, and in this sense is interpreted primarily as "sublate". As in the concept of FLOSS, Turkey has been constantly confusing what FLOSS is and what FLOSS is not. The Ministry of Development (MoD) stated that the aim of Pardus project should be transformed from the project supported by TUBITAK to competitive and sustainable OSs. To expand the use and development of FLOSS, the aim is to establish a Pardus-Linux ecosystem that would increasingly meet the demands of public and private sectors. Therefore, Pardus-Linux should be supported until developing a certain level of maturity. After this level, various services such as maintenance, sustainable technical support etc., should be given to commercial firms within the frame of a business plan for establishing Pardus Solution Partners (PSP) (TBMM, 2012, 7/5284 and 7/5283), since the concept of matters are the same[3]. Nevertheless, this business plan contradicts with Linux's philosophy because FLOSS is not a pure business, is also fun and science driven mainly by voluntaries. Ministries understood that today, making Pardus-Linux and office application obligatory for all public institutions and organizations is not 'practicable' because it is needed to be sure that TUBITAK, universities and private sectors should provide education and support activities, otherwise creating an ecosystem is not 'plausible'. However, there is no particular Ministry which is responsible for preparing these related projects.

Currently in Turkey, there is lack of available technical and vocational qualifications and ICT occupational standards. The Professional Competency Board in the Ministry of Labour and the Social Security Department has just developed these standards since 2013[4]. So, why would TUBITAK and Ministries (2008-2012-2017) claim there would be technical standards for PSP?[5] Throughout history, ICT markets and its international standards (Career-Space, SIFA, NWCET, European SOCs, etc.) have controlled ICT occupational standards in Turkey and many other nations. So, the MoD is either mistaken or intentionally misguiding the general public. The related literature is argued under the title of *Glocalization* which is a portmanteau of *Globalisation* and *Localisation*[6]. There are so many national and international bodies that offer standards through Windows ecosystem based on local language, norms etc. The European Centre for the Development of Vocational Training earlier stated that

The ICT sector provides a particular example of task and technology-related certificates and licences. They are in most cases awarded by multinational companies (Apple, Cisco, Microsoft, Oracle, Sun) and exemplify the role of private companies in certifying skills and competences. We also find ICT certification developed outside multinational companies. The European computer driving licence (ECDL) is currently the best known and widely used of these. (2012, p.16)

The aims of the Pardus-Linux project were declared by the MoD in 2012. Yet, these aims are not new. They have been declared repeatedly by TUBITAK since 2005. So, it can be asked whether or not TUBITAK appropriately supported the Pardus project since TUBITAK stated that political decision making is not included in the duties and authorities of TUBITAK (TBMM, 2008, No.7/00731 and No.7/1368). In TUBITAK, while Pardus-Linux was used in all PCs, but not in the intranet system. TUBITAK declared that there are some applications developed for various purposes, and Pardus-Linux migration plans had been prepared and conversion studies had been continuing. After completing all these studies, TUBITAK would use Pardus-Linux in all hardware, and then recommend using Pardus-Linux to all public sectors. Interestingly, the development of Pardus-Linux was started in 2003, in 2008-12, 2012-2017, TUBITAK has not defined and clarified its position. According to Akgül who is an academician and president of Internet Technologies Association (INETD),

Everyone looks positively on FLOSS; however the use of FLOSS is negligible.... So nearly all public talk about the intention of Pardus' usage, but none of them use it. Migration to FLOSS relies on being ready for change by a social leader. In Turkey, I cannot say that Turkey has a study of leadership. TUBITAK, which funds the Pardus project, does not use Pardus appropriately. E.g., in one period, the licence cost of office applications was very costly and TUBITAK was not willing to pay it. When they were just migrating to StartOffice/OpenOffice, Microsoft let the software free of charge. Instantly TUBITAK returned to Microsoft Office. (2008, p.36-37)

After ten years past, Akgül restates that

State wants to use Pardus as a national OS, but Information and Communication Technologies Authority (BTK)... does not mention (recommend) Pardus to public at all, why in this world! (2017[7])

Admittedly, TUBITAK should not be locked-in to one particular PCSS application, because its R&D centre is in charge of keeping up to date with technological acceleration. Notably, commercial 'gift giving' (free of charge) at this financial level, would be recognized as illegal in global competition law: that, however still academically and/or non-academically disputable[8].

REASONS OF SOFTWARE GOVERNANCE

Due to these above four matters of FLOSS, it can be claimed that Turkey does not misapply FLOSS; in reality it does not apply FLOSS whatsoever that has governed (resulted in) unfair competition and barriers to entry, but there are further reasons of software governance.

Total Cost of Ownership (TCO)

"The only thing more expensive than commercial software is free software" Microsoft[9]

The State Planning Organization (SPO) in the Prime-Ministry which is one of the highest level public institutions declared that there is no delimitative agreement and/or protocol between Microsoft and Governments in the matter of software (TBMM, 2008, No.7/1779). While SPO's point might be accurate and acceptable, each Ministry however has its own method of handling ICT projects that is also problematic because Ministries would not acted in harmony, (e.g. in MoNE, there have been Microsoft Partners in Learning Protocols (MPLPs); 2004/2009). For instance, since 2015, the General Directorate of Lifelong Learning in the MoNE and Microsoft has just launched a Business Association Project (BAP) aimed at developing the technology skills of young people in Turkey in line with the requirements of the 21st century (MoNE, 2015). The perspective of SPO is that individual-national states make strategic collaborations with international corporations for different reasons, including the reduction of license fees. These agreements should only be considered with regard to their duration and scope. Nevertheless and evidently, since MPLPs and BAP are not only covered for purchasing Windows licences, what do the protocols and projects actually mean? No particular information is introduced or elucidated.

In terms of software, Ministries desire either annual agreements or whole sale tenders and these agreements include free updates and important basic training. Most Ministries declared that when training cost is taken into consideration, TCO of purchased software is generally and relatively cheaper than other options. Comparing hardware and OS licence costs for each device, the institutional license is significantly lower. So, Ministries prefer bundle tenders or what is also called turn-key solution. Thus, SPO declared that making regulation for the use of Linux OSs as 'imperative' in all public institutions is not considered in a short period because it is noticed as 'nonenforceable' (TBMM, 2008, No.7/1779). The turn-key solution has still been preferred by Ministries based on irrational pretexts for ensuring interoperability instead of separating budgets according to software and hardware. However that preference has evidently become an inconsistency with the Circular Letters of 1998 & 2008 'Use of Licensed Software' by the Prime Ministry which strictly compel public institutions to separate their software purchasing budges as software and hardware. So, Ministries have accomplished *a legally illegal act* with the Prime Ministry itself; and, their accomplishments have become *legally invalid* or at least *in legal conflict of interest*. Nevertheless, that leads unfair competitions for FLOSS's and even PCSS's sectors as we (who analyses the decision-making process) do not have a particular information about what they (e.g. Ministries) do inconsistently. Ministries purchased software which is mainly provided by hardware vendors. So, individual-national software corporations have been forced to be in line with international software and hardware corporations. Since 1993, the Word Bank advised Governments in

Turkey against software 'barriers to entry and competition' and hardware vendors are willing to create their own propriety software systems that result in unfair competition on the market. However even until now, the purchasing process is still in the same inconsistency.

IBM was by far the leading player on the market. Clearly, hardware vendors provide a significant transfer of know-how to the software industry through training, quality standards and procedures, and exposure to best international practice. However, these benefits need to be balanced against the barriers to entry and competition that hardware vendors often create through proprietary software and systems. (World Bank, 1993, p.65)

Disinformation and Misinformation

In the software governance, there are many disinformation and misinformation stated by the Government apparatuses. Disinformation refers to intended information that is wrong, with a deceiving approach behind its wrongness and misinformation is modest information that is unintentionally wrong, or incorrect. Under the reason of TCO, most Ministries stated that if TCO is considered, Linux, which is thought at no cost, is a mistake and inaccurate. In servers, the issue of 'sustainability' and 'supportability' is essential to use OS which already provides 'interoperability' guarantee from server manufacturers to ensure 'smooth' and 'reliable' operation. The MoEU postulated that almost all serious Linux versions supported by server manufacturers are commercial-based, and for versions used in public institutions, there are paid supports and update services on yearly basis (TBMM, 2012, No.7/5212). Preference for Linux, which is less costly, is a decision that must be taken on account of TCO duration in whole projects cycles (infrastructure). The MoEF also claimed that international independent supervision and research institutions such as Gartner, Forrester, Yankee, IDC have revealed that TCO of Linux is much more than TCO of Windows (TBMM, 2008, No:7/1727). The perspective of the Ministries is misleading and misdirect because the literature has shown that comparing Linux to Windows in the sense of TCO is not considered useful and advisable that it all depends on strategic plan(s) (e.g. Russo, 2009, Rentocchini, 2010, Wheeler, 2014). So, no endorsed conclusion can be made based on such assertion due to nature of technology. Thus, Ministries provided their perspectives without providing an appropriate argumentation scheme that would also submit their further un-professionalism and so disinformation. This is the case of, "politically protected monopoly rents are at the heart of profitability in the most advanced sectors of the global neo-liberal economy. Profitability for everyone from Big Pharma and their proprietary drugs to Microsoft and its monopoly on Windows depends on gaining and maintaining monopoly control over intangible assets, which can be achieved only by political means" (Evans, 2008, p.278).

Regarding un-professionalism, the MoD also argued that public institutions have been migrated onto Linux because they are either in the process of renewing their own ICT infrastructures or establishing new additional ICT infrastructure in the direction of expanding their FLOSS's policy (e.g. MoND, the Radio and Television High Council- TBMM, 2012, 7/5284 and 7/5283). From the Ministry's perspective, it is not a logical expectation from institutions which have already established stable and continuing ICT infrastructures, to migrate totally onto different systems due to TCO. This is indeed a wise and admirable perspective; however, it is not an exact case. According to the 23(8) of Directive 2004/18/EC which is consolidated by the European Court of Justice's (ECJ) jurisprudence on the matter, it indicates that "technical specifications shall not refer to a specific make or source, or a particular process, or to trademarks, patents, types or a specific origin or production with the effect of favouring or eliminating certain undertakings or certain products"[10]. Nevertheless, Ministries of Turkey have already ill-guided the relevant arguments.

One-Size-Fits-All-Software

Due to various parliamentary questions, Ministries and Governments presented over three hundreds parliamentary reports and all other hundred formal documents. However, none of them states Free Libre Open Source Software, all of them rather state Open Source Software and/or National Software. In this regard, Free is translated in Turkish as *Özgür-Freedom*, so there is no confusion in Turkish as in English as Stallman (2002) elucidates that 'free as in free speech, not as in free beer'. Therefore, *Freedom* in FLOSS has not been elucidated appropriately in Turkey.

On the subject of PCSS philosophies, the MoEF believed that Linux software applications are still in the development process. Providing such considerable effort and letting this software free of charge as a public good (General Public Licence) is still controversial (TBMM, 2008, No.7/1727); but, the Ministry is misleading and/or being misled because of PCSS (see more the discussion of European Union Public Licence (EUPL)[11]. The literature argues why OS should be signified as a public good because it has a feature of an intellectual good and PCSS model intentionally controlled (e.g. restrained) the potential for innovation and invention. Admittedly there is a crucial distinction between *innovation* and *invention*. This distinction actually generates more arguments than it solves. For instance, what kind of world are we living in if we agree (to some extent) that technologies are some sort of phenomenology, as such a *digital good*, or at least a *knowledge development cycle*? Menell anticipates that "patent protection would lead to an overinvestment in research and development that could result in discoveries that fell within the patent domain, wastefully diverting resources from more appropriate endeavours"(1999, p.132). In the sociology of technology, Proprietary OS actually contradicts itself; because, "it is impossible to keep them secret anyway. The source code--the original lines of text written by the programmers--can be kept secret. But an OS as a whole is a collection of small subroutines that do very specific, very clearly defined jobs. ... It is the fate of operating systems to become free" (Stephenson, 2004, p.19-20).

It appears Ministers neither support nor appreciate philosophy of FLOSS. The Ministry of Agriculture and Rural Affairs stated that it is crucial to perceive that not all Linux-based software are 'reliable' and 'costless' (TBMM, 2008, No.7/1727). This is a valid perspective, and acceptable. The Ministry believed that the methods of software licensing are independent of OS and yet various. Here the important point is: it should be known that there is no such 'free' software which presents 24/7 guarantees for uninterrupted service and provides necessary supports. Interestingly, the discourse of the Ministry is so aggressive and protective that it gives a lesson to MPs who asked the parliamentary questions such as MoEU (2012, No.7/5212). The Ministry clearly puts its pragmatic perspective as a Microsoft Spokesman and protests against FLOSS as a kind of (*negative*) social movement, as being voluntary-based and being not viable in ICT sectors. However, contrary to what is believed in Ministries, software and by extension, FLOSS and PCSS platforms are not simply an artefact. Evidently, each of these has its own technological, political, economical, philosophical and even cultural powers to shape societies or shaped by societies (see, the literature of Social-Shaping of Technology Theory), but the question is to where (*Linux-Societies* versus *Windows-Societies*), as Alice asks 'would you tell me, please, which way I ought to go from here?' Cheshire cat answers 'that depends a good deal on where you want to get to,' crucially, the sophistry of PCSS perception ultimately seeks to keep controlling societies without a tipping point! We cannot be free at all unless we can control our destiny and realise our own power or the power of our capacities. If we signify the sociology of technology, we readjust techno-human interactions and then we may remedy the division between one and another which could be end-users' interests or giant corporations' interests, but in FLOSS, everything is all about our common interests without controlling one to another. The key point is thereby the Freedom of End-Users.

Due to technological promises, services of public and private sectors (e.g. communication channels) have been digitized in recent times. Currently, all digital services in any institution entirely rely upon ICT in which there are four concepts: *infrastructure, hardware, software* and *format* that are all compatibly integrated (interpretability) into each other. Since OS is an essential part in these mechanisms, used computing mechanism cannot stand-alone, rather complex system mechanisms. In this sense, most Ministries highlighted that one particular OS (Linux), which stably works, is not, in principle, sufficient for public institutions' needs and requirements. Ministries postulated that they should have used the 'same' and 'common' technologies with the 'same' and 'common' language to ensure 'integrity' and 'cohesion', and to establish 'proper' and 'suitable' ICT mechanisms. The postulations of sameness and commonness have been still argued by Ministries; such as, see discourse of the 25th Meeting of the High Council of Science and Technology by TUBITAK, 2013. If any institution has an intention of migrating to Linux platforms, they have to modify all their ICT mechanisms, including the incumbent ICT-culture. Consequently, all Ministries have denied Linux migration studies and declared their unwillingness to risk the possibility of 'interruption' and 'disputation' of the current ICT mechanisms.

The above discourse is indeed a *one-size-fits-all-software-system* as a *Procrustean bed system* (identical and pure technological-determination). Nonetheless, certainly a one-size-fits-all-software-system cannot be *realistic* and *useful* for ICT, and is not *the solution* in ICT mechanisms because in reality, there can be no one-size-fits-all in ICT. It is obviously *unsteady* and *uncontrollable*; dissimilar software may work better in dissimilar mechanisms, and there are always lock-in issues, see the 'Guide for the Procurement of Standards based ICT Elements of Good Practice by the Commission of the European Union, 2017'. In particular, FLOSS is not a one-size-fits-all system. It would be agreeable for all these needs and requirements, yet the 'sameness' and 'commonness' of technological platforms (insensible singleness, oneness and/or one-sidedness) cannot constantly assure *integrity* and *cohesion* into public and private institutions without precise on-going interoperability reports, like the European Interoperability Framework (EIF) Version 1.0. (2004-2009). Nonetheless, technology improves from variety of areas for various purposes, so there are always accessible technologies to overcome interoperability issues, such as software and hardware virtualizations, rather than simply locked-in.

Hypengyophobic Software Culture

If there is no comprehensible ICT Policy, Software Policy and so FLOSS Policy, there is one crucial thing left– software culture! The MoNE summarised software culture explicitly and similarly for all Ministries,

The basic principle of the Ministry is to integrate hardware and software technologies, which have demonstrated their reliability at national and international level, into educational practices with being an independent on a particular product and service. This basic principle is avoidance of monopolization in public and private sectors with creating competitive market environments. In line with this principle, in the Ministry, either in central institutions or other sub-institutions, the best and most consistent technology is under consideration from national and/or international corporations, which have the most common technical service networks, within the lowest prices, as the widest range of different platforms. So, the

Ministry do intentional consistency. Whilst ICT market changes rapidly, the main principle is to present the most excellent ICT culture to students, with maintaining Open Source Software (OSS) solution as equilibrium to likely the extent. Despite the fact that Windows platforms are being used in the Ministry, there are continuing activities to support improving Linux's usage in some other institutions, to support OSS. The main principle of these activities is the achievement of OSS culture for not only students but also staff in the Ministry. (TBMM, 2012, No.7/5313; 2008, No.7/1540 and No.7/1315).

Whether the software is stable, reliable, supported, and updated might be arguable because of the nature of ICT. However, being under the guarantee of compatibility and providing solutions for all compatibility and interoperability, FLOSS cannot answer and meet the software culture in Ministries. For FLOSS and Linux, end-users initially should know that FLOSS is not PCSS, and shall not be. With regard to initiatives of Ministries, a fact, or simply, a matter of fact might be understood as just happening because of our needs and requirements. On the other hand, for others (e.g. FLOSS supporters) it might be a threat (e.g. surveillance) and even the reason of something else, as in this instance negative externality (e.g. locked-in). Agreeably, the purposes of ICT projects should not be in the centre for all Ministries; however, the outcomes of the ways of accomplishing these purposes should be anticipated by a particular Ministry due to unintended consequences. The Ministries have underestimated software culture. There is always lock-in, and national security issues. We should remember that "a computer will do what you tell it to do, but that may be much different from what you had in mind" Joseph Weizenbaum (1923-2008)

The MoNE clearly underlined the best and most reliable products with the best price regarding OSS (not FLOSS) in the balance of creating software culture for all, the same as other Ministries that may be called as 'copy policy strategy'. However, FLOSS is never perceived as a real alternative to PCSS. According to MP Erdal Aksünger, in 2012, the strange bureaucratic chain of command is the first main obstacle for the Pardus-Linux development. In his speech in the parliament, he stated that bureaucrats are interrupting to use Pardus-Linux in institutions because of their own un-acceptance and anxiety. In public procurement authority, bureaucrats perceive PCSS as a *commodity* and FLOSS as a *service* only. Ministries, as other state apparatus (e.g. public bodies and authorities) are bound to pursue certain rules whilst procuring goods, services and works. This procurement process should also apply to the procurement of software. For instance, the Article 5 of Public Procurement Law in Turkey compels that "in tenders to be conducted in accordance with this Law, the contracting authorities are liable for ensuring transparency, competition, equal treatment, reliability, confidentiality, public supervision, and fulfilment of needs appropriately, promptly, and efficient use of resources" (issued in January 2012, p.16). These are governing principles of public procurement and the main pillars of the decision-making process. Considering the fact that failing to respect these principles of procurement could result in administrative/ criminal liability. Also, institutions may delay their preference for ICT mechanisms which if they are unfamiliar and require a substantial upgrading before implementation can be justified from the public policy or legal perspective. "'If your attitude to IT is 'Who do I sue when things go wrong?' the document concludes, then perhaps" [FLOSS] "is not for you." (International Development Association, 2003) This is unfortunately replicable from other developed nations, such as in the UK,

We have standardised on Company X's Products; we therefore purchase from Company X; and we have a long term licensing agreement with Company X – and will adapt our own business logic and standards to fit their application. Within such arrangements, government is purchasing (technology) inputs rather than (service) outputs, and it becomes locked in to proprietary standards and processes controlled by the supplier, with whom it occupies a correspondingly weak commercial position. [12]

In Turkey, there have been studies carried out by private and public sectors, to develop Linux-based OSs, e.g. the Pardus-Linux project. While such studies are seen with appreciation by most Ministries, based on Laws of Ministries, it is not considered that constituting ICT and so software policy, in particular FLOSS is within the jurisdiction of Ministries. In this sense, there is no particular Ministry that takes *responsibility* and *obligation* for FLOSS, except TUBITAK which is not a Ministry and has no political power to recommend or criticise Governments and Ministries. Besides, 'bestness', 'mostness', 'cheapestness', as declared by Ministries are sensitive to providing uninterrupted service to 80 million citizens. This perspective might be disputable through comparative studies between FLOSS and PSCC; and Linux and Windows in terms of technological point of view. However, more importantly, it is simply intriguing to fathom how Ministries take a hypengyophobic software culture, and solely relied on Windows platforms to provide their services (e.g. 'the document management system in MoNE has crashed, so there is no paperwork' while 'RedHack hacked the presidency of telecommunication, communication'). There are several websites on Google representing these crashes and hacks. Thus, purchasing variable 'X-NESS' is clearly not eligible and desirable for promising to provide uninterrupted services. Software culture which is based on factors such as lifelong learning, knowing how to know for problem solving and on-going knowledge management, and so forth should be formed by/within Ministries. It must be emphasised that while software culture can be argued with the literature, yet, an analysis of these arguments is beyond the scope of this study. So, software culture should be that "today's technological transformations hinge on each country's ability to unleash the creativity of its people, enabling them to understand and master technology, to INNOVATE and to ADAPT technology to their own needs and opportunities" (United Nations, 2001, p.29), because "the world of the future will be an even more demanding struggle against the limitations of our intelligence, not a comfortable hammock in which we can lie down to be waited upon by our robot slaves." (Wiener, 1950)

GOOD SOFTWARE GOVERNANCE

[1] the power of the state depends upon the scapegoat, whose presence is necessary to disguise and diffuse the conflicts, corruption, and contradictions that underlie all political systems. ... [2] The scapegoat need not be innocent of any wrongdoing. It is only essential that the substitute be seen as a wrongdoer, and that his or her role not be attributed to any established institutional interests. (Shaffer, 2012)

Although, in the 63. State action plan, September 2014, or 2015-2018 Information Society Strategy and Action Plan, March 2015, it was constantly re-announced that FLOSS and Pardus-Linux will be used in public institutions in future (MoD, 2017), as history indicates that there are so many *however* and *nevertheless* (mostly pretexts), as realised from the beginner to end of this paper, as a great precedent for state-scapegoatism. Nearly all Ministries claim the principles of Ministries are 'effective' and 'efficient' in terms of using state's public resources. Ministries have interoperated with national software corporations, except OSs, system security, and some other software applications. The discourse signifies that national techno-social economy is one of the main concerns for Ministries, but for another concerns, there is no choice for them. When Pardus-Linux reaches a sufficient level of development, it can be thought as a *useable OS*, because continuity and maintenance is crucial to provide services without interruptions and distractions.

In specific, the MoD has clarified the satisfactory level as; to use Pardus-Linux in servers; (1) services of database, application server, web and virtualization become entirely stable and easy management tools added into the package repository; (2) migration tools developed for database and application server and educational videos prepared; (3) 24/7 technical support unit established by TUBITAK; and (4) educational programs are prepared and implemented. Nevertheless, there are other Linux distros that can meet these requirements. Besides, Pardus Debian might also now meet these requirements in terms of a technological point of view. To use Pardus-Linux in PCs; (1) Wine software which is a FLOSS compatibility level software application to allow applications considered for Microsoft, is improved for maintaining continuity of current ad-hoc software; (2) technical software, such as process management (activity - business process management platform), remote sensing/geographical information system, data mining, engineering, CAD are added into the package repository; (3) conversion problems in LibreOffice are solved (TBMM, 2012, No.7/5284 and No.7/528). Technologically, there is no issue because it depends on how the migration plan is prepared. However, interestingly, migrating Linux is considered if and only if there are no *interoperability* and *sustainability* issues with Windows platforms. Ministries' approaches to FLOSS, in particular Linux platforms, are a *mirror/clone* of PCSS, in particular Windows platforms. In other words, the Ministries' argument indicates that Ministries should initially establish Windows platforms, to migrate Linux. Regarding these, what does it mean if Pardus-Linux can answer all requirements and needs of institutions? If it is the initial point, Ministries should not use Linux because it will not answer what Ministries are seeking for. Being a part of the FLOSS community means that we exercise responsibility and accountability.

If the aim is full control of cybernetics, has Governments of Turkey issued scapegoatism to cover their failures? We are in the imagination world of knowledge-based economy, which is significantly different from a tradition-based economy. However, the majority of Ministries who frequently responded to parliamentary questions either based on 'article (x) of the questions above is concerned with Ministry/Institutions, so it is approved to answer the question(s) as follows' and ignoring the other questions and/or 'article (y) of the questions above is not concerned with the Ministry/Institutions, so it is not approved to answer the question(s)'. So, there is a broad definition of *transparency* among Ministries even though there is no *responsibility* and *accountability* engaged by Ministries. Transparency is important for the Government; however, the decision making process should also be applied and shared. Consequently, for Ministries, FLOSS and Linux can/cannot answer all needs and requirements but the question is that should Ministries consider FLOSS, if so how? To answer this question, there are some examples, such as the Turkey Radio and Television Corporation (TRT), which has used different Linux options for different purposes. For instance, regarding OSs, Debian, Redhat and Fedora OSs based on Linux, AIX OS based on UNIX are used. To shape ICT mechanisms in the direction of unpredictable technological changes, there is only one thing left -*Written Policies*. However, Turkey has failed to govern written ICT Policies and to ascertain pervasive and trustworthy (flexible) ICT ecosystems which identify either a balanced progress between FLOSS and PCSS or a FLOSS favourable system (Tolu, 2013). FLOSS should be interiorised due to the rationalist desideratum of cybernetics, because "when you simply have power – in potentia – nothing happens and you are powerless; when you exert power – in actu – others are performing the action and not you. ... Power is not something you may possess and hoard. Either you have it in practice and you do not have it –others have– or you simply have it in theory and you do not have it" (Latour, 1986, p.264).

According to the FSFeurope, governments should adapt FLOSS due to three fundamental justifications. The first is the *viral effect* which is proclivity to press citizens to use the same software and platform as the government use. The usage of FLOSS within government applications provides avoidance of proprietary monopoly and lock-in issue. The second is the *squandered resource* which is the lack of local government connections, and their low possibility of obtaining mass information. Any large scale issues at local level could be solved in a similar way through FLOSS. The third is the *role model* which is to illustrate the government's position. FLOSS creates social and cultural values to establish and support the brand equity in the software market (2003). When governments take the side of FLOSS, PCSS's corporations are inevitably affected. However, fourth, government is the most significant influencer upon the software market, the biggest software consumer. Fifth, government and universities can cooperatively develop their own software solution in R&D centres. Sixth, in developing countries, especially governments are responsible to obtain new revolutions of information technologies. Seventh, indisputably, decision-makers have responsibility of eliminating lock-in issue, (*PCSS's hegemony*, and particularly *Microsoft's monopoly*) and finding the best way of spending public money, because

the market has no inherent tendency to 'self-regulation'. Markets in fact generate inequality and encourage competition instead of co-operation as the central structuring norm of the community. In this sense, while markets are an important mechanism for the efficient performance and growth of the economic lives of individuals and communities, they must in their own right be regulated and controlled by the state. (Olssen, et al. 2004)

CONCLUSİVE REMARKS

"Policymaking is best seen as an interactive process in which different actors exchange resources in a series of trust-based relationships in order to achieve their goals" (Daugbjerg, 2011, p.4). For cybernetics, the concepts are more than *trust-based* relationships; these are techno-politically supported *PCSS' hegemony*, particularly *Microsoft's monopoly*. Consequently, the current approach to technology (*de-facto governance*) is certainly driven by *state-scapegoatism* that builds-in *obsolescence* (invisible of market forces), so it has become covertly unfeasible now and in the future. Turkey's pragmatic technological vision on cybernetics and its inconsistencies between needs and requirements of cybernetics and its acknowledgment of locked-in confirms us where the misconceptions and discriminations are. Perhaps, it has become seemingly unfeasible in meeting present and future needs. Indeed, someone may still postulate that Turkey never wants to be *a controller of her cybernetics* (adapters) and remain *a pure controlled* (adopter), as many other similar individual-nations. However, cybernetics is not just for Turkey, it is a global archaic provision and the similar for many developed and developing nations. For instance, the failure and/or success of Government Open Source Policies can be globally achieved from the literature (see, Lewis, 2010, Redhat, 2010). In this regards, OpenForum Europe Procurement Monitoring Report states that "engaging in a more comprehensive and global analysis of the EU's procurement market would show that the use of discriminatory technical specifications is a widespread practice within the EU" (2013, p.1).

Ever since each generation in a particular society has its own particular faith, beliefs, and agreements with its own particular notices, it has to look its own unique issues and efforts, and even its own impasses. Nevertheless, what is clear is that a new cybernetics is urgently needed. According to Yücel 'there is no solution other than the enlargement of the FLOSS ecosystem in Turkey, considering that TÜBİTAK or Pardus is alone limited to doing it alone' (2017). Yet, PCSS' interests are globally protected from *No-National-Law Concept* by PCSS's hegemony and governments' patronages within flagrant injustices; e.g., by approving exclusive rights to offer PCSS only, there is no global dirigisme for software that speaks of an illusionist legal egalitarianism to wit '*Let me issue and control a nation's money and I care not who writes the law*' by Mayer Amschel Rothschild. In this sense, '*give someone (giants) control of global technology, and no one cares that it controls all of us*' (modern libertarianism and clandestine control) (e.g. Bogard, 1996).

To elaborate, by going back to the introductory question, *movements of cybernetics* have philosophically become a '*phenomenon*' (a fact and/or an observable circumstance), as the opposite of '*naumenon*' (incapable of being known and/or inobservable circumstance), in which there is no *democratic-decision making process*, there is indeed techno-politically supported *PCSS' hegemony*. This negative externality certainly driven by state-scapegoatism, builds-in obsolescence and so leads and contributes to PCSS hegemonic stability (e.g. its own dominations and controls) in the era of technological singularity. Hegemonic stability is international system, more likely to remain stable when a particular PCSS ecosystem is the dominant world power, or hegemon. According to Tiemann, there is a powerful and rising global FLOSS's economy, but "18% of all IT projects are abandoned before production while 55% of all IT projects are "challenged" (late, broken, or both)"; also, "proprietary software model destroys 85% of the global innovation potential" (2010). Consequently, there is an *adventurous legal liaison* between Governments and PCSS, while many connexionists from PCSS may dispute differently! Ultimately, there is a *negative externality of cybernetics* (tragedy of the commons- unsustainable development without any reasonable elucidation) especially when "a decision can be rational without being right and right without being rational" (Peterson, 2009, p.4), and "one of the penalties for refusing to participate in politics is that you end up being governed by your inferiors" Plato.

REFERENCES

Akgül, M. (2008). Özgür Yazılım Dünyası Ne İster? *Bilisim ve Hukuk Dergisi*. Retrieved 25/06/2017 from http://www.ankarabarosu.org.tr/Siteler/1944-2010/Dergiler/BilisimveHukukDergisi/2008-4.pdf

Aksünger, E. (2012). Türkiye Büyük Millet Meclisi (TBMM) Genel Kurul Tutanağı; 24. Dönem 2. Yasama Yılı 68. Birleşim; 2012, February 21. *TBMM*. Retrieved 25/06/2017 from https://www.tbmm.gov.tr/develop/owa/tutanak_sd.birlesim_baslangic?P4=21133&P5=B&page1=65&page2=65&web_user_id=14953822

Bottomley, J., & Corbet, J. (2011). Making UEFI Secure Boot Work With Open Platforms. *The Linux Foundation*. Retrieved 25/06/2017 from https://www.linuxfoundation.org/sites/main/files/lf_uefi_secure_boot_open_platforms.pdf

Boyle, J. (2008). *The Public Domain: Enclosing of the Commons of the Mind*. Yale University Press.

Callon, M. (1987). Society in the Making: The Study of Technology as a Tool For Sociological Analysis. In W. Bijker, T. Hughes, & T. Pinch (Eds.), *The Social Construction of Technological Systems*. Cambridge, MA: MIT Press.

Callon, M., & Law, J. (1997). After the Individual in Society: Lessons on Collectivity from Science, Technology and Society. *Canadian Journal of Sociology*, *22*(2), 165–182. doi:10.2307/3341747

Daugbjerg, C. (2001). *Governance Theory And The Question of Power: Lesson Drawing from The Governance Network Analysis Schools.* Paper to the 61st Political Studies Association Annual Conference, London, UK.

European Centre for the Development of Vocational Training (Cedefop). (2012). *International Qualifications.* Luxembourg: Publications Office of the European Union.

European Commission. (2004). *Commission concludes on Microsoft investigation, imposes conduct remedies and a fine.* Retrieved 25/06/2017 from http://europa.eu/rapid/press-release_IP-04-382_en.htm

European Commission. (2009). *European Interoperability Framework for pan-European eGovernment services, the European Interoperability Framework (EIF) Version 1.0.* Retrieved 25/06/2017 from http://ec.europa.eu/idabc/en/document/2319/5644.html

European Commission. (2013a). *Against lock-in: building open ICT systems by making better use of standards in public.* Retrieved 25/06/2017 from http://cordis.europa.eu/fp7/ict/ssai/docs/study-action23/d3-guidelines-finaldraft2012-03-22.pdf

European Commission. (2013b). *Open Standard.* Retrieved 25/06/2017 from http://ec.europa.eu/digital-agenda/en/open-standards

European Commission. (2017). *Strategy for internal use of OSS.* Retrieved 25/06/2017 from http://ec.europa.eu/dgs/informatics/oss_tech/index_en.htm

Evans, P. (2008). Is an Alternative Globalization Possible? *Politics & Society*, *36*(2), 271–305. doi:10.1177/0032329208316570

Grand, S. (2003). *Creation: Life and How to Make It.* Harvard University Press.

Hillenius, G. (2017). Swedish policy makers want end to IT vendor lock-in. *Joinup.* Retrieved 25/06/2017 from https://joinup.ec.europa.eu/community/osor/news/swedish-policy-makers-want-end-it-vendor-lock

Hruska, J. (2016). Microsoft leaks Secure Boot credentials, shows why backdoor 'golden keys' can't work. *Extremetech.* Retrieved 25/06/2017 from https://www.extremetech.com/computing/233400-microsoft-leaks-secure-boot-credentials-demonstrates-why-backdoor-golden-keys-cant-work

International Development Association (IDA). (2003). *IDA issues Open Source Migration Guidelines.* Retrieved 25/06/2017 from http://ec.europa.eu/idabc/en/document/1921.html

Law, J. (1999). After ANT: Complexity, Naming and Topology. In J. Hassard & J. Law (Eds.), *Actor-Network Theory and After.* Oxford, UK: Blackwell Publishers. doi:10.1111/j.1467-954X.1999.tb03479.x

Latour, B. (1986). The Powers of Association. In J. Law (Ed.), *Power, Action and Belief: A New Sociology of Knowledge* (pp. 264–280). London: Routledge & Kegan Paul.

Latour, B. (1996). On Actor-Network Theory: A Few Clarifications. *Soziale Welt*, 369–381.

Latour, B. (2005). *Reassembling the Social: An Introduction to Actor -Network Theory*. New York: Oxford University Press.

McDermid, D. (2006). *Pragmatism*. Retrieved 25/06/2017 from http://www.iep.utm.edu/pragmati/

Menell, P. S. (1999). *Intellectual Property: General Theories*. Berkeley Center for Law and Technology University of California at Berkeley.

Ministry of Science, Industry and Technology (MoSIT). (2017). *T.C. Bilim, Sanayi ve Teknoloji Bakanlığı Sözleşmeli Bilişim Personeli Alım İlanı*. Retrieved 25/06/2017 from http://bid.sanayi.gov.tr/Dokuman-GetHandler.ashx?dokumanId=2071cce7-3a6d-48a9-a59d-fad83972c9eb

Minister of Development. (2017). *2015-2018 Bilgi Toplumu Stratejisi ve Eylem Planı*. retrieved 25/06/2017 from http://www.kalkinma.gov.tr/Pages/EylemVeDigerPlanlar.aspx

Ministry of National Education (MoNE). (2001, 2001, 2005, 2013). *Standart Türk Klavyesi*. Retrieved 25/06/2017 from http://www.resmigazete.gov.tr/eskiler/2013/12/20131210-9.htm

Ministry of National Education (MoNE). (2015). *MEB ile Microsoft Türkiye'den iş birliği projesi*. Retrieved 25/06/2017 from http://www.meb.gov.tr/meb-ile-microsoft-turkiyeden-is-birligi-projesi/haber/8695/tr

North, D. C. (1990). *Institutional Change, and Economic Performance*. Cambridge, UK: Cambridge University Press. doi:10.1017/CBO9780511808678

Olssen, M., Codd, J., & O'Neill, A. (2004). *Education Policy: Globalization, Citizenship and Democracy*. Thousand Oaks, CA: Sage.

OpenForum Europe. (2013). *OFE Procurement Monitoring Report 2013 – 1st Snapshot*. Retrieved 25/06/2017 http://www.openforumeurope.org/library/ofe-procurement-monitoring-report-2013-1st-snapshot/

Organisation for Economic Co-operation and Development (OECD). (1996). *The Knowledge Based Economy*. Paris: Author.

Peters, M. A., & Besley, T. (2008). *Building Knowledge Cultures: Education and Development in the Age of Knowledge Capitalism*. Rowman & Littlefield Publishers.

Peterson, P. (2009). *An Introduction to Decision Theory*. Cambridge University Press. doi:10.1017/CBO9780511800917

Punch, K. (2009). *Introduction to Research Methods in Education*. London: Sage.

Minister, P. (2012). *E-Devlet: Kavram ve Genel Sorunlar* [E-State: Concept and General Issues Report]. Retrieved 25/06/2017 from https://www.tbmm.gov.tr/arastirma_komisyonlari/bilisim_internet/docs/sunumlar/Koordinasyon_Calismasi_Sunum-ea_06062012_1045.pdff

Public Procurement Authority of Turkey. (2012). *Public Procurement Law*. Retrieved 25/06/2017 from, http://www2.ihale.gov.tr/english/4734_English.pdf

Shaffer, B. (2012). The Importance of Free Minds. *Lewrockwell*. retrieved 25/06/2017 from http://archive.lewrockwell.com/shaffer/shaffer250.html

Sondakika News. (2013). *E Okul VBS girişi çöktü MEB sitesine girilmiyor*. Retrieved 25/06/2017 from, http://www.ihlassondakika.com/haber/E-Okul-VBS-girisi-coktu-MEB-sitesine-girilmiyor_568692.html#

Stallman, R. (2002). *Free Software, Free Society: Selected Essays of Richard M. Stallman*. Retrieved 25/06/2017 from http://www.gnu.org/philosophy/fsfs/rms-essays.pdf

Stallman, R. (2013). FLOSS and FOSS. *Free Software Foundation*. Retrieved 25/06/2017 from https://www.gnu.org/philosophy/floss-and-foss.en.html

Stephenson, N. (2004). *In the Beginning was the Command Line*. Retrieved 25/06/2017 from http://introcs.cs.princeton.edu/java/15inout/command.txt

Scientific and Technological Research Council of Turkey (TUBITAK). (2013). *25th Meeting of the High Council of Science and Technology Report*. Retrieved 25/06/2017 from http://www.tubitak.gov.tr/sites/default/files/btyk25_yeni_kararlar_toplu.pdf

Rentocchini, F., & Tartari, D. (2010). An Analysis of the Adoption of Open Source Software by Local Public Administrations: Evidence from the Emilia-Romagna Region of Italy. *International Journal of Open Source Software and Processes*, 2(3), 1–29. doi:10.4018/jossp.2010070101

Russo, B., & Succi, G. (2009). A Cost Model of Open Source Software Adoption. *International Journal of Open Source Software and Processes*, 1(3), 60–82. doi:10.4018/jossp.2009070105

Tiemann, T. (2010). *Growing an Open Source Economy With Competence at the Centre*. Open Source Initiative Vice President, Open Source Affairs, Red Hat Inc.

Tiqqun. (2010). *The Cybernetic Hypothesis*. The Anarchist Library Anti-Copyright.

Tolu, H. (2013). Expendable 'Written' ICT Policies in a Digital Era, No Broken Promise. *International Free and Open Source Software Law Review*, 5(2), 79–104. doi:10.5033/ifosslr.v5i2.86

Tolu, H. (2016). Techno-Social Policy of Free Open Source Software in Turkey, A Case Study on Pardus. *Journal of Software*, 11(3), 287–311. doi:10.17706/jsw.11.3.287-311

United Nations. (2001). *Human Development Report*. Retrieved 25/06/2017 from http://hdr.undp.org/en/reports/global/hdr2001/chapters/

Weber, S. (2004). *The Success of Open Source*. Cambridge, MA: Harvard University Press.

Wiener, N. (1950). *The Human Use Of Human Beings: Cybernetics And Society*. Houghton Mifflin.

Wheeler, A. D. (2014). *Why Open Source Software / Free Software (OSS/FS)? Look at the Numbers!* Retrieved 25/06/2017 from http://www.dwheeler.com/oss_fs_why.html

World Bank. (1993). *Turkey: Informatics and Economic Modernization, A World Bank Country Study*. The World Bank. Retrieved 25/06/2017 from http://www-wds.worldbank.org/external/default/WDSContentServer/IW3P/IB/1993/03/01/000009265_3970128104047/Rendered/INDEX/multi0page.txt

Yener, D. (2017). *Handbook of Research on Geographic Information Systems Applications and Advancements*. IGI Global.

Yücel, N. (2017). *Pardus: Dünü Bugünü*. Retrieved 25/06/2017 from http://www.pardus.org.tr/forum/t/pardus-dunu-bugunu/1592

ENDNOTES

[1]   http://www.bilgitoplumu.gov.tr/yayinlar/.

[2]   http://fatihprojesi.meb.gov.tr/.

[3]   http://www.pardus.org.tr/#.

[4]   See, professional competency board, at http://www.myk.gov.tr/index.php/en/ulusal-meslek-standard-ana.

[5]   Notably, since 2015, the Pardus team has just released two books; (a) Pardus OS and (b) Pardus (Linux Professional Institute) Certification.

[6]   See, 2016 European inventory on national qualifications frameworks, retrieved 25/06/2017 from http://www.cedefop.europa.eu/en/news-and-press/news/2016-european-inventory-national-qualifications-frameworks-just-released.

[7]   Akgül, M. (2017) twitted that "Devlet, Pardus'u Milli İşletim sistemi olarak kullanmak istiyor, ama BTK, US yurttaşlara önerilerinde Pardus'dan bahsetmiyor. Niye acaba" retrieved 25/06/2017 from https://twitter.com/akgul/status/864489144407425029.

[8]   To obtain the on-going argumentation, see, Journal of International Free and Open Source Software Law Review, at http://www.ifosslr.org/ifosslr or the Reports of the Global Competition Review, at http://globalcompetitionreview.com/.

[9]   Cited in Friedman, T. (2005) *The World Is Flat: A Brief History of the Twenty-First Century,* Farrar, Straus and Giroux Hardcover. See, p.21.

[10]   Cf. Cases C-359/93 Commission of the European Communities v. Kingdom of the Netherlands (UNIX) [1995] ECR I-157 and C-59/00 Bent Mousten Vestergaard v. Spøttrup Boligselskab [2001] ECR I-9505.

[11]   https://joinup.ec.europa.eu/community/eupl/og_page/eupl.

[12]   Cited in Thompson, M. (2014). Open standards are about the business model, not the technology ComputerWeekly.com, retrieved 25/06/2017 from http://www.computerweekly.com/opinion/Open-standards-are-about-the-business-model-not-the-technology.

This research was previously published in Optimizing Contemporary Application and Processes in Open Source Software; pages 198-221, copyright year 2018 by Engineering Science Reference (an imprint of IGI Global).

Chapter 7
On Solving the Multi–Objective Software Package Upgradability Problem

Noureddine Aribi
Lab. LITIO, University of Oran 1, Oran, Algeria

Yahia Lebbah
Lab. LITIO, University of Oran 1, Oran, Algeria

ABSTRACT

Free and open source software (FOSS) distributions are increasingly based on the abstraction of packages to manage and accommodate new features before and after the deployment stage. However, due to inter-package dependencies, package upgrade entails challenging shortcomings of deployment and management of complex software systems, inhibiting their ability to cope with frequent upgrade failures. Moreover, the upgrade process may be achieved according to some criteria (maximize the stability, minimize outdated packages, etc.). This problem is actually a multi-objective optimization problem. Throughout the article, the authors propose a Leximax approach based on mixed integer linear programming (MILP) to tackle the upgradability problem, while ensuring efficiency and fairness requirements between the objective functions. Experiments performed on real-world instances, from the MANCOOSI project, show that the authors' approach efficiently finds solutions of consistently high quality.

1. INTRODUCTION

Free and Open Source Software (FOSS) distributions (Di Cosmo, Zacchiroli, & Trezentos, 2008) are among the most complex software systems known, being made of tens of thousands deployment units known as packages. These packages evolve rapidly and are developed and released independently without a priori coordination or central authority able to control the involved parties (Di Cosmo et al., 2008; Michlmayr, Hunt, & Probert, 2007). Owing to this situation, difficult issues are raised for both software editors and system administrators. For instance, system upgrade in a GNU/Linux distribution

DOI: 10.4018/978-1-7998-9158-1.ch007

may proceed on different paths and requires the presence of a set of previously installed packages, and the absence of another set of packages. Hence, in some cases, it is not possible to install or upgrade all the desired packages and possible failures can occur during upgrades.

Research works (cf., (Argelich & Lynce, 2008)) developed in the context of the MANCOOSI [1] (Managing the Complexity of the Open Source Infrastructure) project, aim at developing tools for the system administrator in order to handle complex inter-package dependencies and frequently available package upgrades. These tools are used regularly to address security issues, bug fixes or to add new features that respect user's preferences. Besides, the predecessor EDOS project (Treinen & Zacchiroli, 2008b) had focused on tools for the distribution editor. When performing packages upgrade, user's preferences are expected to be handled in a consistent and efficient way, which is a current hot topic in Artificial Intelligence with active research lines in constraint satisfaction and optimization (Junker, 2004; Rossi, Venable, & Walsh, 2008). When upgrading packages, for instance, one can choose to minimize the whole size of the packages to install, to minimize the number of packages to install, to install the recent versions of packages. All these criteria are objective functions, subject to constraints stating the dependency and avoiding conflicts. By this way, upgrading packages comes back to a multi-objective optimization problem, which has been tackled by the MANCOOSI project. In optimization problems with a single criterion, the goal is to find an optimal solution such that the objective function is minimized or maximized. Hence, the problem is said to be well defined. Alternatively, if the optimization problem comprises more than one criterion (which is the case of most real-world optimization problems), then the solution of the problem becomes difficult to characterize. In fact, we cannot find (in general) a feasible solution that optimizes the whole criteria at the same time. Therefore, what we need is an efficient ordering method that aggregates all these objective functions (aka criteria) into a single and global objective function, which is the strategy, adopted in most optimization methods (Argelich & Lynce, 2008; Argelich, Lynce, & Silva, 2009).

Mixed Integer Programming (MIP) (Wolsey, 1998) is one of the most important techniques for solving complex optimization problems. In this paper, the authors propose a linear *Leximax* approach tailored for solving the upgradability problem, while ensuring efficiency and fairness (equity) requirements. The main intuition behind the equity criterion refers to the idea of selecting solutions that fairly share satisfaction between objective functions (Sen and Foster, 1997). The proposed approach is modeled as a MIP model. Next, this approach is applied on the package upgradability problem (using benchmarks coming from the MANCOOSI project), where the criteria and constraints are linear on boolean domains.

The rest of this paper is organized as follows. Section 2 provides some necessary preliminaries. Section 3 describes the package upgradabiliy problem. Section 4 illustrates our approach on a practical example. Section 5 highlights the contribution of this paper. Sections 6 describe with details the proposed approach. Experimental results are given and discussed in Section 7. We present some related works in Section 8. Section 9 concludes the paper.

2. PRELIMINARIES

Before discussing our approach, we provide some necessary background.

2.1. FOSS Architecture, Packages, Upgrade Process, and Failures Management

Actually, architectures of FOSS distributions are quite similar. A distribution is a collection of (ideally) coherent components provided in packaged form by distribution editors. Packages are abstractions that define the granularity at which end users can manage (e.g. install, remove, and upgrade). Packages are handled using an application coined "package manager" (e.g. *apt* (Trezentos et al., 2007), *rpm*, *yum*, *dpkg*, *Apache Maven*[2]). The package manager is responsible to deploy and alter packages on the file-system, retrieve packages from remote repositories when needed and possibly cope with encountered installation issues due to, for example, some missed dependencies or conflicts (the inability of being co-installed) with existing packages.

2.1.1. Packages

They deðne the granularity at which software components are managed. A package is a bundle of three main parts (see Figure 1 - (a)): (1) a set of ðles, which involves binaries, documentation, data, etc.; (2) a set of meta-data (see Figure 1 - (b)) that describes the package version, inter-package relationships, including: dependencies, conflicts and feature provisions (Di Cosmo, Zacchiroli, & Trezentos, 2008); (3) maintainer scripts (a.k.a. executable configuration scripts) which are executed during the upgrade process. These scripts customize parts of the package to be installed using data that is available only on the target machine. Executable actions usually come as *POSIX* shell scripts to finalize component configuration.

Figure 1. (a) Package structure (b) Meta-data for package aterm

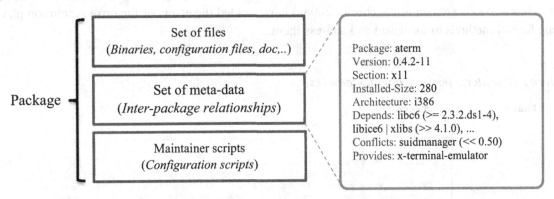

2.1.2. Upgrades

The upgrade process goes through several steps. Figure 2 shows an example of the whole upgrade phases of the *aterm* package using the *apt* meta-installer (aka package manager), usually runs with system administrator rights. Phase (1) starts the process after a user upgrade request. We note that the expressiveness of the requests changes according to the meta-installer, but the actions (install, remove, upgrade, etc.) are ubiquitously supported (Treinen & Zacchiroli, 2008a). Phase (2) verifies whether the package satisfies its dependencies and resolves any conflicts that might arise with other existing packages. This problem is proven to be at least NP-complete (EDOS Project Workpackage 2 Team, 2006). If all the upgrade constraints are satisfied, the new package becomes ready to deploy on the target machine, which consists to package retrieval (phase (3)) and unpacking, phase (4). Unpacking phase results in changing both the package status (in order to keep track of installed packages), and the current filesystem. We note here that package retrieval and unpacking may be intertwined as there can be several configuration phases, (highlighted by phases (5a) and (5b) in Figure 2), where maintainer scripts get executed (Cicchetti, Ruscio, Pelliccione, Pierantonio, & Zacchiroli, 2009). The details depend on the available hooks; *dpkg* offers: pre/post-installation, pre/post-removal, and upgrade to some version (Jackson & Schwarz, 2008).

2.1.3. Failures

Actually, each phase of an upgrade process can fail (which actually happens quite often). Moreover, in state-of-the-art distributions, knowing if the installation process terminate without errors is undecidable (Mancinelli et al., 2006). Thus, efforts should be made to identify errors as early as possible. Interestingly, upgrade runs, in which they fail, trigger upgrade failures and are usually detected via inspection of the configuration script exit code (Cicchetti, Ruscio, Pelliccione, Pierantonio, & Zacchiroli, 2009). For instance, dependency resolution can fail either because the user request is unsatisfiable, or because the meta-installer (e.g. *apt*) is unable to find a solution. Package deployment may also fail, e.g., network or disk shortages, can be easily dealt with when considered in isolation: the completely upgrade process can be aborted and unpack can be undone, since all the involved files are known, no upgrade is performed so, the system remains unchanged (Di Cosmo, Zacchiroli, & Trezentos, 2008). However, maintainer script failures cannot be as easily undone, nor prevented. Therefore, undetected failures can take very long (weeks, months) before being discovered. The EDOS and MANCOOSI projects (EDOS Project Workpackage 2 Team, 2006; Treinen & Zacchiroli, 2008a) have tackled the errors of the error resolution phase, using formal methods to formalize and address them.

Figure 2. The aterm package upgrade process

```
Phase                Trace
   (1)               # apt-get install aterm
User request         ------------------------------------------------------------
                     Reading package lists... Done
                     Building dependency tree... Done
   (2)               The following extra packages will be installed:    libafterimage0
Constraint           The following NEW packages will be installed:    aterm libafterimage0
resolution           0 upgraded, 2 newly installed, 0 to remove and 1786 not upgraded.
                     Need to get 386kB of archives.
                     After unpacking 807kB of additional disk space will be used.
                     Do you want to continue [Y/n]? Y
                     ------------------------------------------------------------
   (3)               Get: 1 http://debian.ens-cachan.fr testing/main libafterimage0 2.2.8-2
Package              [301kB]
retrieval            Get: 2 http://debian.ens-cachan.fr testing/main aterm 1.0.1-4 [84.4kB]
                     Fetched 386kB in 0s (410kB/s)
   (5a)              ------------------------------------------------------------
Pre-configuration    ------------------------------------------------------------
   (4)               Selecting previously deselected package libafterimage0.
Unpacking            (Reading database ... 294774 files and directories currently installed.)
                     Unpacking libafterimage0 (from .../libafterimage0_2.2.8-2_i386.deb) ...
   (5b)              ------------------------------------------------------------
Configuration        Setting up libafterimage0 (2.2.8-2) ...
                     Setting up aterm (1.0.1-4) ...
```

2.2. Multi-Objective Discrete Optimization

A Multi-Objective Discrete Optimization (MODO) problem (Tanino, Tanaka, & Inuiguchi, 2003) is defined by a set of n objective functions $f_j : \mathbb{R}^m \to \mathbb{R}$, for $j=1\ldots n$ and a discrete set $\mathcal{X}$ of feasible solutions (a.k.a *decision space*). For simplification we assume, without loss of generality, that the objective functions are linear, i.e. $\forall j \in [1\ldots n]$, $f_j(x) = \sum_{i=1}^{m} c_i^j x_i$ and are to be minimized (unless otherwise mentioned). Let us consider F as the vector-function $F : \mathbb{R}^m \to \mathbb{R}^n$. Each $x \in \mathcal{X}$ is a feasible solution and is mapped by F into the corresponding objective vector $y = F(x) \in \mathbb{R}^n$. The resulting set of objective vectors $\mathcal{Y} = \{F(x) \mid x \in \mathcal{X}\}$ defines the *objective space*. The MODO problem can be formulated as follows:

Minimize $\{F(x) \mid x \in \mathcal{X}\}$

Objective vectors are commonly compared using the Pareto dominance relation (*P*-dominance). The weak-*P*-dominance $\precsim_P$ between two objective vectors y, y' is defined as: $y \precsim_P y' \Leftrightarrow \{\forall i \in [1\ldots n], y_i \leq y'_i\}$, whereas the strict *P*-dominance $\prec_P$ between y and y' is given by:

$$y \prec_P y' \Leftrightarrow \{y \precsim_P y' \wedge not(y' \precsim_P y)\}.$$

A solution y^* is Pareto-optimal (aka efficient) if and only if there is no solution y that dominates y^*. The set of all efficient solutions (non-dominated set) is coined $\mathcal{X}_E$, while its image is given by $\mathcal{Y}_E = \{y \mid y = F(x), x \in \mathcal{X}_E\}$.

An important step in optimization process of the MODO problem (1) focuses on transforming this multi-objective problem, into a single-objective problem by mean of an aggregation function. This last enables the decision maker (DM) to find a good compromise solution, according to his/her preferences. The DM's preferences are expressed as parameters (c.f., (Boutilier, Regan, & Viappiani, 2010; Delecroix, Morge, & Routier, 2012; Escoffier, Lang, & Öztürk, 2008; Roy & Bouyssou, 2002)). Then, the aggregation function is combined with the acquired parameters to solve the multi-objective problem and meet the decision maker viewpoint. Many multi-objective aggregation methods exist for solving MODO problems, and it is not so simple to choose an appropriate method, well adapted to a given problem.

From the literature, we may highlight two main approaches related to two opposite points of view: classical utilitarianism and egalitarianism. The utilitarian approach deals with the MODO aspect of the problem, by mean of a simple and effective scalarization approach, which combines all the objective functions to form a single objective aggregation function. One of the most common scalarization approaches is the weighted-sum method given as follows:

Minimize $\quad F(x) = \sum_{i=1}^{n} w_i f_i(x)$

where w_i is a coefficient associated to the ith objective function (cf., (Kessler et al., 2005)). However, this kind of aggregation functions is not suitable in the context of "fair aggregation" (Nieto, 1992). The second (egalitarian) approach amounts to compare the objective vectors by comparing their maximal components. This corresponds, indeed, to the *Max*-based aggregation function, and is used, in particular, for optimization problems where fairness is essential. Nevertheless, this aggregation function is hampered by the drowning effect issue (Bouveret and Lema∈tre, 2007), since it cannot distinguish between objective vectors having the same maximal value. An important clue to overcome this issue lies in proposing some refinements of the *Max* operator, in the aim to restrict the set of incomparable objective vectors. In the following, we discuss the Lexicographic Ordering (LO) method, and the *Leximax* method[3]. This work focuses on these specific operators, without being exhaustive. For more details, we refer the reader to (Collette & Siarry, 2002; Dubois & Prade, 1984, 1985; Figueira, Greco, & Ehrgott, 2005; Grabisch et al., 1998; Marichal, 1998; Vincke, 1992; R. R. Yager, 1991).

2.2.1. Lexicographic Ordering

It is usually difficult to determine the best coefficients of the weighted-sum function, since (i) the objective functions are not based on a uniform scale; (ii) the objective functions conflict with each other; and (iii) the consequences of a given tradeoff cannot be quantitatively known prior to the optimization. Lexicographic ordering method appears to be an interesting alternative to avoid the use of weights. This multi-objective method requires an explicit priority order between the objective functions (where $f_1(x)$ being the most important objective function). The lexicographic method solves a sequence of optimization problems by ordering objective functions as follows:

$$
\begin{aligned}
&Minimize && f_i(x) \\
&subject\ to && f_j(x) \le f_j(x_j^*) \\
& \quad \text{for } i = 1, 2, ..., n, && j = 1, ..., i-1 \quad \text{if} \quad i > 1
\end{aligned}
$$

From the second optimization problem (i.e., *i=2...n*), the preceding objective functions are converted to inequality constraints (Jee, McShan, & Fraass, 2007). These new constraints are formulated using the optimal objective values $f_j(x_j^*)$ subject to the underlying constraint system, where $x_j^* = \arg \min f_j(x)$.

2.2.2. Fair Aggregation Using the Leximax Function

A usual way to compare objective vectors consists to aggregate the individual objective values (a.k.a *utilities*) using a *collective utility function* (CUF) (Moulin, 1989) $G : \mathbb{R}_+^n \to \mathbb{R}_+$, which improves the overall welfare by $min\{G(x) : x \in \mathcal{X}\}$. The *G* function can be a linear combination of individual utilities (i.e. *G(x)= sum(x)*), which does not capture properly the idea of fairness. Another way to build *G* is based on the maximum function (i.e. *G(x)= sum(x)*). This approach consists to minimize the most unsatisfied objective function and appears as the simplest alternative to the linear model.

However, focusing on the worst case (i.e. minimizing the maximum) is not always sufficient to guarantee fairness. Indeed, we may encounter undesirable drowning effect (Dubois & Fortemps, 1999) situations that prevent this aggregation function to discriminate between objective vectors. For instance, objective vectors (10, 10, 10) and (10, 1, 1) are indistinguishable according to the min*max* aggregation function.

Other refinements of the maximum function exist, such as the *Leximax* method, which is implemented in the proposed approach. This method has been used successfully on a number of industrial problem (Burkard, Dell'Amico, & Martello, 2009; Lian, Mattei, Noble, & Walsh, 2018), where fairness and efficiency requirements must be met (e.g., assignment problems, nurse rostering problem, etc.).

Definition 1 (Leximax): Let us consider a discrete set of alternatives (solutions) A, such that

$$A \subset F = f_1(x) \times ... \times f_n(x), x \in \mathcal{X}.$$

Now, let $a = \langle a_1, ..., a_i, ..., a_n \rangle$ and $b = \langle b_1, ..., b_i, ..., b_n \rangle$ be two alternatives of the same size, where a_i (respectively b_i) denotes the objective value of the ith objective function. We make the assumption that elements of a and b are commensurate (belong to a linearly ordered scale, e.g. [0, 1]). The *Leximax* ordering (Moulin, 1989) is as a refinement of the maximum ordering. It is based on the idea of eliminating tied elements, once each alternative has been sorted[4] in a decreasing order. Next, a lexicographic ordering is applied on the sorted alternatives. A formal definition of the *Leximax* ordering is given as follows:

$$a \prec_{leximax} b \Leftrightarrow \exists k \leq n, \forall i \in \{1,...,k-1\}, a_{(i)} = b_{(i)}, \text{and } a_{(k)} < b_{(k)}$$

where $a_{(1)} \geq a_{(2)} \geq ... \geq a_{(n)}$, and $b_{(1)} \geq b_{(2)} \geq ... \geq b_{(n)}$.

Note that the symbol $\precsim$ denotes a preference relation. Thus, the relation $a \precsim b$ means that the alternative a is "at least as good as" the alternative b over all the criteria. We suppose that $\precsim$ is a binary relation taking its values in $\{0,1\}$. We define the relation $\prec$ as the asymmetric part of the preference relation $\precsim$.

Example 1: Let us consider the following two alternatives:

a $= \langle 0.2, 0.6, 0.3, 0.4, 0.8 \rangle$ and

b $= \langle 0.2, 0.3, 0.5, 0.6, 0.8 \rangle$.

According to the *Leximax* method, comparing a and b results in the lexicographic comparison of a' and b' such that:

a$' = \langle 0.8, 0.6, 0.4, 0.3, 0.2 \rangle$ and

b$' = \langle 0.8, 0.6, 0.5, 0.3, 0.2 \rangle$.

since $a'_{(1)} = b'_{(1)} = 0.8$ and $a'_{(2)} = b'_{(2)} = 0.6$, we would ignore $\langle 0.8, 0.6 \rangle$ from both vectors a and b, yielding $a \prec_{leximax} b$ since $a' \prec_{leximax} b'$ (i.e., 0.4<0.5).

3. PACKAGE UPGRADABILITY PROBLEM (PUP)

The packages installation problem consists to find the "best" answer to the question: *"can we install a new package p* in an operating system, having an installation profile P and a package repository R?" This problem had been proven to be an NP-complete problem[5] (Mancinelli et al., 2006), especially in modern operating systems, which contain a huge number of packages (usually exceeding 20,000 packages in a Linux distribution). In addition, this problem had been broadly investigated in Edos project (cf., (Argelich et al., 2009; Mancinelli et al., 2006; Tucker, Shuffelton, Jhala, & Lerner, 2007)).

Apart of the installation problem, the upgradeability problem has recently raised interest of software engineering researchers (cf., (Michel & Rueher, 2010; Trezentos, Lynce, & Oliveira, 2010)). This last encompasses the installation problem, and thus being at least NP-complete. Formally, we define the upgradeability problem as follows: let P be a set of installed and uninstalled packages, p_b be a set of packages to be installed, removed or upgraded. The upgradeability problem consists in finding the optimal solution S according to some optimization criteria such as,

- **Stability:** Minimizing the number of changes in the previous installation;
- **Disk Space Efficiency:** Minimizing the size of the newly installed packages;
- **Network Efficiency:** Minimizing the size of the downloaded packages.

4. A PRACTICAL EXAMPLE

Let us consider a simple example of a package upgradability problem taken from Mancoosi project. This problem is defined by a triple (p, D, C) where p is the package to install, D is the set of all dependency clauses of the package p, so that each dependency clause is a disjunction of packages, and C the set of packages in conflict with p.

$$
\begin{cases}
(p_1, \{p_2, p_5 \lor p_6\}, \varnothing), \\
(p_2, \varnothing, \{p_3\}), \\
(p_4, \varnothing, \{p_5, p_6\})
\end{cases}
$$

We model each package p_i with a Boolean decision variable x_i. This variable is set to *true* if and only if p_i is installed. Hence, for each clause $d \in D$, we generate the clause $\neg x_i \lor d$ (i.e. $x_i \triangleright d$), which means that d should be installed prior to install p_i. Similarly, for each package c belonging to C, we generate the clause $\neg x_i \lor \neg c$. By this way, we generate a SAT model in Conjunctive Normal Form (CNF), along with its equivalent MIP model, related to the package upgradability problem (see formulas (5)). We notice that a real MIP instance of a sample upgradability problem generated from a Debian distribution contains 47 956 variables and 254 529 clauses.

$$(p_1, \{p_2, p_5 \lor p_6\}, \varnothing) \overset{CNF}{\Leftrightarrow} \begin{cases} \neg x_1 \lor x_2 \\ \neg x_1 \lor x_5 \lor x_6 \end{cases} \overset{MIP}{\Leftrightarrow} \begin{cases} 1 - x_1 + x_2 \geq 1 \\ 1 - x_1 + x_5 + x_6 \geq 1 \end{cases}$$

$$(p_2, \varnothing, \{p_3\}) \overset{CNF}{\Leftrightarrow} \neg x_2 \lor \neg x_3 \overset{MIP}{\Leftrightarrow} 1 - x_2 + 1 - x_3 \geq 1$$

$$(p_3, \{p_4\}, \{p_1\}) \overset{CNF}{\Leftrightarrow} \begin{cases} \neg x_3 \lor x_4 \\ \neg x_3 \lor \neg x_1 \end{cases} \overset{MIP}{\Leftrightarrow} \begin{cases} 1 - x_3 + x_4 \geq 1 \\ 1 - x_3 + 1 - x_1 \geq 1 \end{cases}$$

$$(p_4, \varnothing, \{p_5, p_6\}) \overset{CNF}{\Leftrightarrow} \begin{cases} \neg x_4 \lor \neg x_5 \\ \neg x_4 \lor \neg x_6 \end{cases} \overset{MIP}{\Leftrightarrow} \begin{cases} 1 - x_4 + 1 - x_5 \geq 1 \\ 1 - x_4 + 1 - x_6 \geq 1 \end{cases}$$

In an upgrade process, we can choose to optimize some user defined objective functions (*preferences*), such as:

1. Emphasize small packages compared to large packages (i.e. minimize the amount of disk space needed for the update). This is modeled with the following objective function

Minimize $500x_3 + 100x_4 + 200x_5 + 700x_6$

where 500 (resp. 100, 200, and 700) is the size of the package p_3 (resp. p_4, p_5 and p_6).

2. A second objective function aims at minimizing the impact of introducing new packages in the current operating system:

$$Minimize \sum_{i=1}^{6} x_i$$

In the literature, several preference-based approaches were proposed in order to solve this kind of multi-objective problems, especially in the synthesis of (Junker, 2004). We have modeled this optimization problem using a linear *Leximax* approach, and solved it using a standard mixed integer programming solver, thus yielding the optimal solution $\langle x_1, x_2, x_5 \rangle$, which corresponds to the objective vector $\langle f_1(x), f_2(x) \rangle = \langle 200, 3 \rangle$. This makes sense, since we wanted to install package p_1, which requires packages, p_2 and p_5 or p_6 to be installed. Here, the package p_5 was selected because it requires less disk space (200 KB). However, package p_3 was not installed because it falls into conflict with the package p_2.

5. CONTRIBUTION

As discussed above, the problem of maintaining FOSS upgradability is far from trivial. In particular, current package managers are not able to predict upgrade failures, since package managers rely on package meta-information only, which are not expressive enough to detect failures. The contribution of the paper is fivefold:

1. It models the package upgradability problem in a FOSS distribution as a multi-objective problem; This model is also able to detect predictable upgrade failures before the system is affected;
2. It is based on a scalable exact approach based on MIP programming to solve efficiently the package upgradability problem;
3. It ensures equity (balancing) requirement between the objective functions. This criterion is leveraged by implementing a *Leximax* based linear aggregation;
4. It ensures the efficiency (i.e. Pareto-optimality) of the computed solutions, using the *Leximax* aggregation;
5. It provides a promising declarative model, which is expressive enough to integrate and handle complex user preferences for software upgrade. Example of preferences are policies (Jackson & Schwarz, 2008; Trezentos et al., 2007), like minimizing the download size or prioritizing popular packages, and also more specific requirements such as blacklisting packages maintained by an untrusted maintainer.

6. PROPOSED LINEAR LEXIMAX APPROACH

The proposed MIP model of the *Leximax* method relies on a linear formulation of a Constraint Programming (CP) model introduced by Bouveret and Lemaître (2007). This CP model is based on the *Atleast* global constraint (Régin, 2011). We show in the next section how to rewrite this constraint in linear form and how to prove the equivalence between both versions.

6.1. Linearizing the Atleast Constraint

As described in Section 2.2, the *Leximax* method requires a fully sorted set of feasible objective vectors, which is, in our context, challenging due to the presence of objective functions given in comprehension. Solving this issue requires resorting to a set of (declarative) sorting constraints. This is why we need the *Atleast* global constraint, coming from a Constraint Programming framework (Rossi, van Beek, & Walsh, 2006). In this paper, we propose a mixed integer linear reformulation of this constraint toward usage in the *Leximax* MIP model.

Definition 2 (Atleast constraint):

Consider a set of p constraints, and an integer value $k \in [1,p]$. The meta-constraint[6] Atleast(Γ,k) holds if and only if at least k constraints among the set of available constraints Γ are satisfied. This constraint is derived from the *cardinality combinator* introduced in (Hentenryck, Simonis, & Dincbas, 1992).

Proposition 1:

The constraint Atleast($\{y_i \geq f_1(x), \ldots, y_i \geq f_n(x)\}, k$) is equivalent to the following linear constraints, where $D_{p_j} = \{0,1\}, \forall j \in [1,n]$.

$$Atleast\_lp \begin{cases} y_i \geq f_1(x) - M \times p_1 \\ y_i \geq f_2(x) - M \times p_2 \\ \cdots \\ y_i \geq f_n(x) - M \times p_n \\ \sum_{j \in 1..n} (1 - p_j) \geq k \end{cases}$$

Proof:

The Atleast($\{y_i \geq f_1(x), \ldots, y_i \geq f_n(x)\}$, k) constraint holds if and only if at least k among n constraints are satisfied, where n is the number of criteria, i.e. $\sum_j (y_i \geq f_j(x)) = k$. In order to get the equivalent linear model, we need to keep track of the set of satisfied constraints. This can be achieved by introducing additional binary variables p_j, $j=1,\ldots,n$, one for each linear equation. Therefore, each equation $y_i \geq f_j(x)$ is rewritten as: $y_i \geq f_j(x) - M \times p_j$, where M is a large enough constant:

$$\begin{cases} (p_j = 0) \Rightarrow y_i \geq f_j(x) \\ \vee \\ (p_j = 1) \Rightarrow y_i \geq f_j(x) - M \end{cases}$$

To ensure that at least k constraints are satisfied, we introduce the equation $\sum_{j \in 1..n} (1 - p_j) \geq k$, to enforce k constraints to hold. Similar reasoning can be followed to prove that the linear program (6) is equivalent to the *Atleast* constraint. Indeed, the *Atleast* constraint holds by fixing k binary variables to zero and this can only be fulfilled if $\sum_{j \in 1..n} (1 - p_j) \geq k$.

6.2. Proposed Algorithm

In this section, we propose an algorithm (see Figure (1)) that constructs a linear *Leximax* model, in order to solve the multi-objective package upgradability problem (PUP). The resulting model addresses both efficiency and fairness requirements when solving the PUP with a standard MIP solver. The proposed algorithm is described as follows: The first instruction checks for the satisfiability of the linear constraint system *Lin* (*inst.* 1). If no solution is found, then the algorithm returns "*Inconsistent*" (*inst.* 2), otherwise, it proceeds by n single objective optimizations, to compute the *Leximax*-optimal solution[7] $\hat{v}(X)$, thereby proving the non-existence of a feasible solution $v(X)$, such that

$$\langle \hat{v}(f_1(X)), \ldots, \hat{v}(f_n(X)) \rangle \succ_{leximax} \langle v(f_1(X)), \ldots, v(f_n(X)) \rangle.$$

More precisely, each iteration i of the *for* loop (5–13) optimizes the ith objective function $f_i(X)$ of the *Leximax* objective vector[8]. In the first iteration, we add one additional decision variable y_1 (*inst.* 6). Then, we extend the constraint system with some reified[9] linear constraints (*inst.* 10), such that each linear constraint is associated with one objective function. In addition, we have $\sum_i (y_1 \geq f_i(X)) = n$, meaning that the sum of the truth-values of those reified constraints is equal to the number of objective functions, where $y_1 \geq f_i(X)$ is set to *true* if this equation is satisfied and false otherwise. At the end of this first iteration, a MODO model is built as a single-objective MIP model (see Equations (7)), with a cost function having a single variable y_1 to be minimized (*inst.* 11). This model is solved in order to compute the first *Leximax*-optimal objective value $\hat{v}(y_1)$ (*inst.* 11). After each iteration, a new constraint (*inst.* 12) is introduced into the linear system Lin_i, in order to fix the decision variable y_i with the computed optimal solution $\hat{v}(y_i)$.

$$
\begin{aligned}
&\textit{Minimize} && y_1 \\
&\textit{subject to} && y_1 \geq f_j(x) - M \cdot p_{1,j}, && \textit{for } j = 1, \ldots, n \\
& && \sum_{j=1,\ldots,n} (1 - p_{1,j}) \geq (n-1) + 1 \\
& && p_{1,j} \in \{0,1\} && \textit{for } j = 1, \ldots, n
\end{aligned}
\tag{7}
$$

Starting from the second iteration, instruction (8) attempts to shrink the initial domains of the decision variables (i.e., y_i, $i = 2 \ldots n$), that are processed in the next MIP model. As long as the resulting *Leximax* objective vector is necessarily ordered, we specify the upper bound (*ub*) of the next decision variable y_2, using the previous optimal value $\hat{v}(y_1)$. After fixing the value of y_1, this algorithm solves the second optimization problem, and computes the optimal value $\hat{v}(y_2)$, such that $\sum_i (y_2 \geq f_i(X)) \geq n - 1$, and so on, until it finds the optimal value $\hat{v}(y_n)$ of the last variable, which satisfies $\sum_i (y_n \geq f_i(X)) \geq 1$. This constraint is coined *Atleast* in Algorithm (1). Once all components of the *Leximax*-optimal vector have been computed (i.e., $\hat{v}(y_1), \hat{v}(y_2), \ldots, \hat{v}(y_n)$), the algorithm returns $\hat{v}(X)$ as the *Leximax*-optimal solution of the resulting optimal objective vector (*inst.* 14).

Figure 3. The Leximax algorithm for solving a MODO problem

Algorithm 1 LEXIMAX - finds the Leximax-optimal solution of the MODO problem

---

Input: A set of linear constraints Lin, and a set of objective functions $F(X) = \{f_1(X), \ldots, f_n(X)\}$.
Output: A Leximax-optimal solution $\hat{v}(X)$ of the MODO problem.

1   **if** SOLVE(Lin) = *"Inconsistent"* **then**
2 | **return** *"Inconsistent"*
3   **end**
4   $Lin_0' \leftarrow Lin$

5   **for** $i \leftarrow 1$ ***to*** n **do**
6 | $X^i \leftarrow X^{i-1} \cup \{y_i\}$

7 | **if** $i \neq 1$ **then**
8 | | $ub(y_i) \leftarrow \hat{v}(y_{i-1})$
9 | **end**

10 | $Lin_i \leftarrow Lin_{i-1}' \cup \left\{ \text{ATLEAST}(\{y_i \geq f_1(X), \ldots, y_i \geq f_n(X)\}, n - i + 1) \right\}$

11 | $\hat{v}(y_i) \leftarrow \text{MINIMIZE}(y_i, Lin)$

12 | $Lin_i' \leftarrow Lin_i \cup \{\hat{v}(y_i) \leq y_i \leq \hat{v}(y_i)\}$
13   **end**
14   **return** $\hat{v}(X)$

6.3. Size of the Resulting Leximax MIP Model

Algorithm (1) generates a MIP model having $n \times (n+1)$ new linear constraints (i.e., for each iteration, $(n+1)$ additional constraints are introduced to linearize the *Atleast* constraint, *inst.* 10), and $n+n^2$ new decision variables (i.e., n decision variables $y_1, \ldots, y_n$, and in the ith iteration, n binary variables $p_{i1}, \ldots, p_{in}$ are created to linearize the *Atleast* constraint, *inst.* 6 & 10), where n is the number of criteria. Trivially, at the first iteration of Algorithm (1), (when $i = 1$), the parameter of the *Atleast* constraint is equal to n, where n is the number of criteria. This means that all the constraints of the *Leximax* model must be satisfied. Thus, a direct improvement in this step consists in not creating n additional decision variables p_{ij}, j=1...n, which are used for the linearization of the *Atleast* constraint (see Formulae (6)). As a result, the constraint $\sum_{j \in 1, \ldots, n} (1 - p_j) \geq (n - i + 1 = n)$ becomes pointless at this step.

6.4. Correctness of the Proposed Algorithm

It is important to note that Algorithm (1) generates a MIP model based on the original Constraint Programming model proposed in (Bouveret & Lemaître, 2007), which was already proven to be correct. So, the correctness of our algorithm is maintained by construction; since (i) the linearization of the *Atleast* global constraint is correct, and (ii) the introduced domain shrinking constraints (see Algorithm (1), inst. 8) preserves the correctness of the MIP model. Indeed, according to the *Leximax* formula (see Definition (1)), each optimal objective value $\hat{v}(y_i)$, $i = 2..n$ is necessarily less or equal to the previous optimal solution $\hat{v}(y_{i-1})$. As a result, the algorithm always calculates *Leximax*-optimal solutions.

Example 2: Let us consider a multi-objective problem with three cost functions to minimize $\{f_1(x), f_2(x), f_3(x)\}$. For the sake of simplicity, we consider a finite set of six feasible solutions (objective vectors) $\{s_1, \ldots, s_6\}$ shown in Figure (4). As long as we have three objective functions, Algorithm (1) will proceeds by three steps. Each step performs a single objective linear optimization and serves to calculate one component of the *Leximax*-optimal objective vector.

Figure 4. Sample solutions of a three-objective problem

	s_1	s_2	s_3	s_4	s_5	s_6
f_1	8	8	7	7	5	5
f_2	1	3	8	3	8	1
f_3	9	5	9	8	5	8

Step 1: We introduce one decision variable y_1, and we look for its minimal value $\hat{v}(y_1)$ such that *at least* three (i.e. all) objective functions $f_i(x)$, i=1...3 get at most y_1. We find $\hat{v}(y_1) = 8$, and then we fix y_1 to this value (see Algorithm (1), *inst.* 11), implicitly removing solutions s_1 and s_3 (see Figure 5 (a)).

Step 2: We add a second decision variable y_2, and we search for its minimal value $\hat{v}(y_2)$, such that at least two objective functions get at most y_2. We find $\hat{v}(y_2) = 5$ and the variable y_2 is set to this value, implicitly deleting the solution s_4 (see Figure 5 (b)).

Step 3: At this final step, we inject the third decision variable y_3, and we investigate the minimal value $\hat{v}(y_3)$ such that at least one objective function gets at most y_3. We find $\hat{v}(y_3) = 1$. In this example, there exists only a single instantiation s_6, that brings the variable y_3 to its minimal value, thereby leading to the *Leximax*-optimal solution $s_6(\langle f_1(x), f_2(x), f_3(x) \rangle = \langle 5,1,8 \rangle)$ of the initial three-objective problem (see Figure 5 (c)).

Figure 5. Sample solutions for a MODO problem

	s_2 s_4 s_5 s_6		s_2 s_5 s_6		s_6
$\xrightarrow{Step1}$	f_1 8 7 5 5 f_2 3 3 8 1 f_3 5 8 5 8	$\xrightarrow{Step2}$	f_1 8 5 5 f_2 3 8 1 f_3 5 5 8	$\xrightarrow{Step3}$	f_1 5 f_2 1 f_3 8
	(a)		(b)		(c)

Interestingly, if we replace the second objective vector $s_2 = \langle 8,3,5 \rangle$ with $\langle 1,3,5 \rangle$, then we can find the *Leximax*-optimal solution (s_2 in this case), after only *one iteration*. Hence, we do not need to proceed by the remaining two iterations to compute values of both y_2 and y_3. Nevertheless, even if we consider the remaining iterations, the returned optimal solution will be the same (i.e. s_2).

7. EXPERIMENTS AND RESULTS

The experimental evaluation is designed to address the following questions:

1. How do the linear approaches compare and scale on several challenging benchmarking instances?
2. How do the resulting solutions to the upgradability problem compare qualitatively in term of fairness?
3. How (in terms of CPU-times) does the proposed *Leximax* approach compares with the Lexicographic approach?

7.1. Experimental Protocol

The proposed MIP model is generated using the algorithm described in Figure (3). This model is designed to find the *Leximax*-optimal solution to a multi-objective problem. By construction, this model provides efficient solutions, while emphasizing a fair compromise between the objective functions. Algorithm (1) was implemented using SCIP framework[10]. This framework is currently one of the fastest non-commercial mixed integer-programming solver. It adopts an approach that integrates Constraint Programming, and Integer Linear Programming techniques in a single framework (Achterberg, Berthold, Koch, & Wolter,

2008). This algorithm is compared with an implementation of a lexicographic method (Marler & Arora, 2004) based on the SCIP solver.

7.1.1. Computational Environment

All experiments were carried out on an x64 Linux machine with Intel® Xeon (x5460) quad Core at 3.16 GHz and 8 GB of RAM. A time limit of 3 600 seconds was fixed for all benchmarks.

7.1.2. Test Instances

In the context of this paper, the proposed *Leximax* model tackles the package upgradability problem (see Section 3), as well as the underlying *stability* requirement (minimize the number of changes in the previous installation). The tests have been conducted on a set of 100 real-world instances, coming from the MANCOOSI benchmarking[11] database. Each instance comprises (in average) 47 900 variables, and 254 000 linear constraints.

7.1.3. Optimization Criteria

Two optimization criteria[12] were defined in MANCOOSI project. Both are combinations of different criteria, which are described below. In this paper, we are interested in the first optimization criterion (*Paranoid*), which is a variant of the *stability* criterion. The second criterion can actually be handled in the same way.

1. **Paranoid:** we want to answer the user request: *do fewer changes as possible* and is a combination of two objective functions. The first objective function tends to minimize the number of packages removed in the proposed solution w.r.t. the original installation.

2. $$Minimize \sum_{p \in F_{Installed}} -p$$

where $F_{installed}$ is the set of installed functionalities. While the second objective function tends to minimize the number of packages with a modified (set of) version(s) in the proposed solution w.r.t. the original installation;

$$Minimize \sum_{p_i \in P_{Installed}} -p_i + \sum_{p_u \in P_{Uninstalled}} p_u$$

where $P_{installed} P_{Installed}$ is the set of installed versioned packages[13] and $P_{uninstalled}$ is the set of uninstalled versioned packages.

3. **Trendy:** we want to answer the user request: *do more updates as possible*, i.e., (a) minimizing the number of packages removed in the solution; (b) minimizing the number of outdated packages in the solution; (c) minimizing the number of unsatisfied recommendations; and (d) minimizing the number of extra packages installed.

7.1.4. Qualitative Measures

This paper investigates the capabilities of MIP approaches to handle the upgradability problem. The qualitative comparison is based on the following two measures:

1. **Overall Software Changes:** This criterion assesses the quality of the resulting upgradability solution, by summing the overall package removes and upgrades.
2. **Standard Deviation:** It is used to compare qualitatively the resulting solutions in term of equilibrium between the objective function values.

7.2. Scale-Up Property Analysis

Empirical results are shown in Figure (6), where columns # and Instance name respectively indicate the benchmark number and the name of the instance to be solved. In the same figure, two main columns can be distinguished:

1. **Leximax Column:** Which brings together the results of our approach (with respect to the following utility vector[14] $u = \langle u_1 = f_1(x), u_2 = 5 \times f_2(x) \rangle$). Note that a decision maker (an expert) has provided this utility vector.
2. **Lexico Column:** Which gathers the results of the **lexico**graphic ordering method.

Both columns report the following information:

- T_x: The solving time (in seconds) of the x approach, where $x=leximax$ (i.e. the *Leximax* approach) or $x=lex$ (i.e. the lexicographic approach);
- Cr_1: The optimal objective value of the first criterion (see Formula (8));
- Cr_2: The optimal objective value of the second criterion (see Formula (9));
- S_i, $i=1,2$: This column is used to compare between the two approaches based on total *changes* made on the operating system (i.e., $Cr_1 + Cr_2$), in order to fulfill the user's installation request.

The last column (i.e., $S_2 - S_1$) illustrates the difference between the two approaches in term of the *number of changes*, to see in what extent our approach is qualitatively better.

It is unsurprising that both optimization approaches compute efficient solutions. For example, the *Leximax*-optimal solution of the first benchmark (#1) is $\langle 47,9 \rangle$, which does not dominate the lexicographic solution on the same instance (i.e., $\langle 43,13 \rangle$), since 47>43, but 9<13. As we are dealing with the stability criterion (see *Paranoid* criterion defined above), it is of interest to note that the *Leximax*-optimal solutions are at least as good as the lexicographic-optimal solutions for all benchmarks (see columns S_1 and S_2, instances #1–7; #91 and #94–96). Additionally, the *Leximax*-based approach is noticeably better for benchmarks #8–9; #92–93 and #97–100, since it generates fewer changes with respect to the *stability criterion* (see column S_2–S_1). By examining the results in columns Lexico/Cr_1 and Leximax/Cr_1, we can observe that the objective values of the lexicographic method are always better (on the first criterion) than the corresponding objective values of the *Leximax* approach. The reason is that the lexicographic method optimizes the first criterion alone, without taking into account the second criterion, thus, $Cr_1 = Cr_1^*$, where $Cr_1^* = min\{f_1(x) \mid x \in X\}$.

In contrast, according to columns Lexico/Cr_2 and Leximax/Cr_2, we observe that the objective values of the *Leximax* order are always better (on the second criterion) than the corresponding objective values of the lexicographic order, specifically because the solutions of both approaches are efficient (non-dominated). Here, we notice that values in column Leximax/Cr_2 are not necessarily equal to Cr_2^*, where $Cr_2^* = min\{f_2(x) \mid x \in X\}$.

In term of CPU times, it is worth observing from Figure 6 (columns $T_{leximax}$ and T_{lexico}) and Figure 7 (full results), that the lexicographic approach outperforms the *Leximax* approach by several orders of magnitude on all instances. This is partly explained by the fact that the *Leximax* approach take into account all the criteria within each optimization step, and in each iteration, it extends the constraint system with additional variables and constraints (in order to ensure the fairness). However, the lexicographic method suggests a process of successive optimizations, and optimizes a single criterion at a time. It follows that the performance of this lexicographic approach was actually rather good against the performance of the *Leximax* approach.

Figure 6. Experimental results for Leximax and lexicographic approaches

	Leximax				Lexico			
# Instance name	$T_{leximax}$	Cr_1	Cr_2	S_1	T_{lex}	Cr_1	Cr_2	S_2	S_2-S_1
1 hal-cups-utils	100.8	47	9	56	29.6	43	13	56	0
2 hellanzb	102.6	50	10	60	25.1	47	13	60	0
3 help2man	100.8	45	9	54	33.8	41	13	54	0
4 hgsvn	99.0	48	9	57	31.5	44	13	57	0
5 hpijs	103.8	44	9	53	30.4	40	13	53	0
6 hplip	104.4	44	9	53	31.1	40	13	53	0
7 i2e	109.8	85	17	102	29.8	73	29	102	0
8 install-info	98.4	47	9	56	30.6	40	21	61	5
9 iotop	135.0	109	19	128	50.9	98	46	144	16
⋮			⋮						⋮
91 libalgorithm-dep	105.0	50	9	59	25.8	46	13	59	0
92 libapache2-pyth	391.2	57	9	66	33.1	44	40	84	18
93 libapache2-cgi	154.8	112	19	131	35.4	98	45	143	12
94 libaprutil-mysql	141.6	65	13	78	48.5	64	14	78	0
95 libapt-pkg-dev	131.4	64	12	76	32.2	56	20	76	0
96 libapt-pkg-perl	345.6	44	9	53	30.2	40	13	53	0
97 libarchive-zip	389.4	140	26	166	42.0	135	51	186	20
98 libaudio-cd-perl	336.6	141	26	167	42.8	136	51	187	20
99 libaudio-header	279.0	140	26	166	45.9	135	51	186	20
100 libaudio-muse	325.8	142	26	168	47.2	137	51	188	20

Figure 7. Solving time of the Leximax and Lexico approaches, using 100 real-world instances of the package upgradability problem

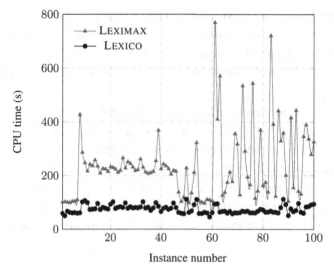

7.3. Qualitative Analysis

When examining the results provided in Figure 6 (column Leximax/Cr_1 and Leximax/Cr_2), along with utility vector $u = \langle u_1 = f_1(x), u_2 = 5 \times f_2(x) \rangle$, we can observe that the *Leximax* approach agree on the best equitable values between criteria, while maintaining the efficiency (Pareto-optimality) of the solutions. In addition, according to the last column ($S_2 - S_1$) of Figure 6, the optimal solutions found by the *Leximax* approach tend to offer better compromises in term of number of changes in package upgrades.

Figure 8. Quality of balancing of the two approaches: Leximax and Lexico, using 100 real-world instances of the package upgradability problem

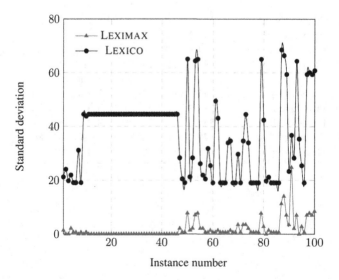

Interestingly, if we consider the standard deviation measure (see Figure 8), the *Leximax* approach clearly achieves the lowest (best) values on all instances. This is indicative of better equilibrium between criteria, which is consistent with our previous conclusion regarding the stability criterion (minimizing the number of changes).

8. RELATED WORKS

The management of upgrades in FOSS distributions raises serious difficulties, because it depends on the maintainer scripts, which can have system-wide side effects, and thus it cannot be narrowed to the involved packages only. We note that the installation problem has been investigated in EDOS project, while the MANCOOSI project had focused on improving the stability of a Linux distribution from the distribution editor's point of view. In this context, a proposal like (Mancinelli et al., 2006) represents a first attempt to formalize the package upgrade problem as a SAT problem; whereas Josep Argelich and Inês Lynce handled the installation problem as a maximum satisfiability (Max-SAT) problem (Argelich et al., 2009). Besides, Tucker et al. (2007) addressed the minimal install/uninstall problem. They developed a tool (coined Opium) that uses Pseudo Boolean and ILP (Integer Linear Program) solvers and can optimize a user-provided *single* objective function. Additionally, Josep Argelich et al. also succeeded to apply a Boolean Multilevel Optimization (BMO) approach to tackle the upgradeability problem. They used two different techniques to solve the BMO problem: (i) by iteratively rescaling the weights of their MaxSAT formulation, (ii) as a sequence of Pseudo Boolean problems. WMaxSatz (Argelich & Manyà, 2007), the tool they developed, could handle problems with up to 4 000 packages, and with which they obtained the best results in a couple of seconds. Paulo Trezentos et al. in (Trezentos et al., 2010) also investigated this technique. However, this approach could not solve most of the upgradability problems.

An interesting proposal to support the upgrade of a system is presented in (Michel & Rueher, 2010); they have succeeded to handle the upgradability problem with a multi-objective MIP approach, where they used the weighted sum approach. However, a linear combination of objective functions using a weighted sum aggregation function is not suitable in fairness context; this suggests resorting to non-linear function (e.g. *Leximax*). Therefore, the main contribution of our work consists to guarantee the *fairness* requirement between the objective functions using a MIP formulation of the *Leximax* method that fully solves the upgradability problems while focusing on *efficiency* and *equity* criteria.

9. CONCLUSION

In this work, the authors proposed a MIP-based *Leximax* approach to address the package upgradability problem in FOSS distribution, while ensuring stability, fairness and efficiency criteria. We have formulated this multi-objective decision problem as a linear single-objective optimization model, implementing an equitable aggregation function using the *Leximax* method. We have compared our approach with a MIP implementation of the lexicographic ordering method. Experiments carried on several real-world multi-objective problems, coming from MANCOOSI project, showed that both approaches were effective. However, for most upgradability problems, the *Leximax* approach has yielded better results according to the stability criterion. Unlike the lexicographic approach, we highlighted that the *Leximax* approach has the ability to ensure fairness between the objective functions. We have also showed that from the CPU time point of view, our approach remains competitive.

Possible future work includes improving the solving performance and the scalability of our approach, by optimizing the number of iterations required by our algorithm in order to compute the *Leximax*-optimal solutions.

REFERENCES

Achterberg, T., Berthold, T., Koch, T., & Wolter, K. (2008). Constraint integer programming: A new approach to integrate cp and mip. In L. Perron & M. A. Trick (Eds.), International Conference on Integration of Artificial Intelligence (AI) and Operations Research (OR) Techniques in Constraint Programming (pp. 6–20). Springer. doi:10.1007/978-3-540-68155-7_4

Argelich, J., & Lynce, I. (2008). Cnf instances from the software package installation problem. In M. Gavanelli & T. Mancini (Eds.), *15th RCRA workshop on experimental evaluation of algorithms for solving problems with combinatorial explosion.*

Argelich, J., Lynce, I., & Silva, J. P. M. (2009). On solving boolean multilevel optimization problems.

Argelich, J., & Manyà, F. (2007). Partial max-sat solvers with clause learning. In J. Marques-Silva & K. A. Sakallah (Eds.), *Sat* (Vol. 4501, pp. 28–40). Springer.

Boutilier, C., Regan, K., & Viappiani, P. (2010, July). Simultaneous elicitation of preference features and utility. In *Proceedings of the twenty-fourth AAAI conference on artificial intelligence (AAAI-10)* (p. 1160-1167). Atlanta, GA, USA:AAAI press.

Bouveret, S., & Lema∈tre, M. (2007). New constraint programming approaches for the computation of leximin-optimal solutions in constraint networks. In M. M. Veloso (Ed.), *IJCAI 2007, proceedings of the 20th international joint conference on artificial intelligence*, Hyderabad, India, January 6-12 (pp. 62–67).

Bouveret, S., & Lema∈tre, M. (2009). Computing leximin-optimal solutions in constraint networks. *Artificial Intelligence, 173*(2), 343–364. doi:10.1016/j.artint.2008.10.010

Burkard, R. E., Dell'Amico, M., & Martello, S. (2009). *Assignment problems*. SIAM. doi:10.1137/1.9780898717754

Cicchetti, A., Ruscio, D. D., Pelliccione, P., Pierantonio, A., & Zacchiroli, S. (2009). Towards a model driven approach to upgrade complex software systems ENASE (pp. 121–133). INSTICC Press.

Delecroix, F., Morge, M., & Routier, J.-C. (2012, November). An algorithm for active learning of lexicographic preferences. In M. Pirlot, & V. Mousseau (Eds.), *Proc. of the workshop from multiple criteria decision aiding to preference learning* (pp. 115-122).

Di Cosmo, R., Zacchiroli, S., & Trezentos, P. (2008). Package upgrades in foss distributions: details and challenges. In *Proceedings of the 1st international workshop on hot topics in software upgrades* (pp. 7:1–7:5). New York, NY: ACM. 10.1145/1490283.1490292

Dubois, D., & Fortemps, P. (1999). Computing improved optimal solutions to max-min flexible constraint satisfaction problems. *EJOR, 118*(1), 95–126. doi:10.1016/S0377-2217(98)00307-5

Dubois, D., & Prade, H. (1984). Criteria aggregation and ranking of alternatives in the framework of fuzzy set theory. In H. Zimmermann, L. Zadeh, & B. Gaines (Eds.), Fuzzy sets and decision analysis (p. 209-240).

Dubois, D., & Prade, H. (1985). A review of fuzzy set aggregation connectives. *Information Sciences, 36*(1-2), 85–121. doi:10.1016/0020-0255(85)90027-1

EDOS Project Workpackage 2 Team. (2006, March). *Report on formal management of software dependencies* (EDOS Project Deliverable Nos. Work Package 2, Deliverable 2).

Escoffier, B., Lang, J., & Öztürk, M. (2008). Single-peaked consistency and its complexity. In *Proceedings of the 2008 conference on ECAI 2008: 18th European conference on artificial intelligence* (pp. 366–370). Amsterdam, The Netherlands: IOS Press.

Figueira, J., Greco, S., & Ehrgott, M. (2005). *Multiple criteria decision analysis: State of the art surveys.* Boston, Dordrecht, London: Springer Verlag. doi:10.1007/b100605

Grabisch, M., Orlovski, S. A., & Yager, R. R. (1998). *Fuzzy aggregation of numerical preferences* (pp. 31–68). Norwell, MA, USA: Kluwer Academic Publishers.

Hentenryck, P. V., Simonis, H., & Dincbas, M. (1992). Constraint satisfaction using constraint logic programming. *Artificial Intelligence, 58*(1-3), 113–159. doi:10.1016/0004-3702(92)90006-J

Jackson, I., & Schwarz, C. (2008). *Debian policy manual.* Retrieved from http://www.debian.org/doc/debian-policy/

Jee, K.-W., McShan, D. L., & Fraass, B. A. (2007). Lexicographic ordering: Intuitive multicriteria optimization for imrt. *Physics in Medicine and Biology, 52*(7), 1845–1861. doi:10.1088/0031-9155/52/7/006 PMID:17374915

Junker, U. (2004). Preference-based search and multi-criteria optimization. *Annals OR, 130*(1-4), 75–115. doi:10.1023/B:ANOR.0000032571.68051.fe

Kessler, M. L., McShan, D. L., Epelman, M. A., Vineberg, K. A., Eisbruch, A., Lawrence, T. S., & Fraass, B. (2005). Costlets: A generalized approach to cost functions for automated optimization of IMRT treatment plans. *Optimization and Engineering, 6*(4), 421–448. doi:10.100711081-005-2066-2

Lian, J. W., Mattei, N., Noble, R., & Walsh, T. (2018). The conference paper assignment problem: Using order weighted averages to assign indivisible goods. AAAI Press.

Mancinelli, F., Boender, J., Cosmo, R. D., Vouillon, J., Durak, B., Leroy, X., & Treinen, R. (2006, September). Managing the complexity of large free and open source package-based software distributions. In *21st IEEE/ACM International Conference on Automated Software Engineering ASE'06* (pp. 199–208). Tokyo, Japan: IEEE CS Press. doi:10.1109/ASE.2006.49

Marichal, J.-L. (1998). *Aggregation operators for multicriteria decision aid.* Unpublished doctoral dissertation, Institute of Mathematics, University of Liège, Liège, Belgium.

Marler, R., & Arora, J. (2004). Survey of multi-objective optimization methods for engineering. *Structural and Multidisciplinary Optimization*, 26(6), 369–395. doi:10.100700158-003-0368-6

Michel, C., & Rueher, M. (2010). Handling software upgradeability problems with milp solvers. In I. Lynce & R. Treinen (Eds.), *Lococo* (Vol. 29, pp. 1–10). doi:10.4204/EPTCS.29.1

Michlmayr, M., Hunt, F., & Probert, D. (2007). Release management in free software projects: Practices and problems. In J. Feller, B. Fitzgerald, W. Scacchi, & A. Sillitti (Eds.), IFIP International Conference on Open Source Systems (pp. 295-300). Springer.

Moulin, H. (1989). Axioms of cooperative decision making. Cambridge University Press.

Nieto, J. (1992). The lexicographic egalitarian solution on economic environments. *Social Choice and Welfare*, 9(3), 203–212. doi:10.1007/BF00192878

ollette, Y., & Siarry, P. (2002). *Optimisation multiobjectif*. Eyrolles.

Régin, J.-C. (2011). Global constraints: a survey, in hybrid optimization. In Hybrid optimization (p. 63-134). Springer.

Rossi, F., van Beek, P., & Walsh, T. (Eds.). (2006). *The handbook of constraint programming*. Elsevier.

Rossi, F., Venable, K. B., & Walsh, T. (2008). Preferences in constraint satisfaction and optimization. *AI Magazine*, 29(4), 58–68. doi:10.1609/aimag.v29i4.2202

Roy, B., & Bouyssou, D. (2002). *Aiding decisions with multiple criteria: Essays in honor of Bernard Roy*. Springer.

Sen, A., & Foster, J. (1997). *On economic inequality*. Oxford: Clarendon Press.

Tanino, T., Tanaka, T., & Inuiguchi, M. (2003). *Multi-objective programming and goal programming: Theory and applications*. Springer. doi:10.1007/978-3-540-36510-5

Treinen, R., & Zacchiroli, S. (2008a, November). *Description of the CUDF format* (Mancoosi project deliverable No. D5.1).

Treinen, R., & Zacchiroli, S. (2008b, November). *Solving package dependencies: from edos to mancoosi* (Tech. Rep.). arXiv:0811.3620

Trezentos, P., Lynce, I., & Oliveira, A. L. (2010). Apt-pbo: solving the software dependency problem using pseudo-boolean optimization. In C. Pecheur, J. Andrews, & E. D. Nitto (Eds.), Proceedings of the IEEE/ACM international conference on Automated software engineering (pp. 427–436). ACM. doi:10.1145/1858996.1859087

Tucker, C., Shuffelton, D., Jhala, R., & Lerner, S. (2007). Opium: Optimal package install/uninstall manager. In *29th international conference on software engineering (ICSE 2007)*, Minneapolis, MN, May 20-26 (p. 178-188). IEEE Computer Society.

Vincke, P. (1992). *Multicriteria decision-aid*. New York: Wiley.

Wolsey, L. (1998). *Integer programming*. Wiley.

Yager, R. (1988). On ordered weighted averaging aggregation operators in multicriteria decision making. *IEEE Transactions on Systems, Man, and Cybernetics*, *18*(1), 183–190. doi:10.1109/21.87068

Yager, R. R. (1991, March). Connectives and quantifiers in fuzzy sets. *Fuzzy Sets and Systems*, *40*(1), 39–75. doi:10.1016/0165-0114(91)90046-S

ENDNOTES

[1]   See http://www.mancoosi.org

[2]   Apache maven project. http://maven.apache.org/ (2008)

[3]   Compromises between these two approaches exist, e.g., OWA operators, and Choquet integral (Grabisch, Orlovski, & Yager, 1998; R. Yager, 1988).

[4]   This assumes the commensurateness of the criteria.

[5]   This means that the solving time scales exponentially as the problem size increases in the worst case.

[6]   The prefix *Meta* means that this constraint takes as a parameter other constraints.

[7] $\hat{v}(X)$ denotes a complete instantiation of variables in X, and $\hat{v}(f_i(X))$ the objective value for the ith criterion.

[8]   Values of the *Leximax* objective vector are computed in decreasing order, since we assume that the objective functions are to be minimized. Thus, the *Leximax* solution is given with the vector $[\hat{v}(f_{\sigma_{(1)}}(X)),...,\hat{v}(f_{\sigma_{(n)}}(X))]$, where $\hat{v}(f_{\sigma_{(s)}}(X)) = max\{\hat{v}(f_i(X)), i = 1,...,n\}$, and $[\sigma_{(1)},\sigma_{(2)},...,\sigma_{(n)}]$ is a permutation of $[1,2,...,n]$. So, the first component corresponds to the best value for the most unsatisfied objective function, and so on.

[9]   Reified constraints reflect the validity of a constraint C into a 0/1 finite domain.

[10]   Available at: http://scip.zib.de/

[11]   Problems are available at http://www.mancoosi.org

[12]   See http://www.mancoosi.org/misc.html

[3]   A versioned package p is represented by a variable p_v that gives the status of p available with version s.

[4]   Utility is designed as a way to describe Decision Maker's preferences. These values are chosen to ensure the commensurateness of the criteria.

This research was previously published in the International Journal of Open Source Software and Processes (IJOSSP), 9(2); pages 18-38, copyright year 2018 by IGI Publishing (an imprint of IGI Global).

Chapter 8
Finding Influential Nodes in Sourceforge.net Using Social Network Analysis

K.G. Srinivasa

Chaudhary Brahm Prakash Government Engineering College, India

Ganesh Chandra Deka

M. S. Ramaiah Institute of Technology, India

Krishnaraj P.M.

M. S. Ramaiah Institute of Technology, India

ABSTRACT

The contribution of volunteers in the development of Free and Open Source Software in Sourceforge.net is studied in this paper. Using Social Network analysis, the small set of developers who can maximize the information flow in the network are discovered. The propagation of top developers across past three years are also studied. The four algorithms used to find top influential developers gives almost similar results. The movement of top developers over past years years was also consistent.

INTRODUCTION

Social Network Analysis (SNA) has been an important tool for analyzing vari- ous domains of human behaviour. By bringing human interactions into graph structures they have helped gain new insights. Basic measures like betweenness, centrality, cohesion, reach etc can unveil lot of information about the modelled scenario. Concepts like 'Small World Phenomenon' are empirically verified across different cases. With the emergence of new computational tools there has been renewed interest in the application of Social Network Analysis into new domains. FOSS is primarily a global network of volunteers and thus makes for an ideal case to study using SNA Tools. The rich research available in SNA can be helpful in understanding the complex phenomenon which makes FOSS work. The present work focuses

DOI: 10.4018/978-1-7998-9158-1.ch008

on one aspect of SNA namely the influence maximization problem. The main objective here is to find a small set of most influential nodes in a social network so that their aggregated influence in the network is maximized. In the context of FOSS, the most influential nodes correspond to developers who are very well connected in FOSS ecology and therefore have maximum chance to propagate information in the network. Four well known algorithms namely High Degree, LDAG, SPS-CELF++ and SimPath are used to find top 5 influential developers. The propagation of top developers during past three years are also studied.

Early attempts of applying social network analysis to Free and Open Source Software phenomenon was undertaken by studying the properties such as degree distribution, diameter, cluster size and clustering coefficient. The emergence of the small world phenomenon in such networks was also studied (Xu, Christley, & Madey, 2006). The issue of finding the most influential nodes in social networks is treated in the literature as problem of centrality. In one of earliest comprehensive study on the centrality of social networks nine centrality measures were proposed. Among them three were based on degrees of points, next three on betweenness of points and last three on closeness. These different conceptions give three different views of centrality namely control, independence and activity (Freeman, 1979). The first natural greedy strategy solution which performed better than node selection heuristics based on notions of degree centrality and distance centrality continues to influence the studies in this domain (Kempe, Kleinberg & Tardos, 2003). A greedy algorithm for the target set selection problem where an initial set of nodes are selected to maximize the propagation in a social network was also proposed by same authors (Kempe, Kleinberg, & Tardos, 2005).

The later works have used variety of approaches to find top-k nodes in social networks. Finding top influential nodes using bond percolation method is tried (Kimura, Saito & Nakano, 2007). Using the metaphor of 'Outbreak Detection' the problem of informa- tion diffusion was discussed in different way. The novel solution was proposed as CELF algorithm which is reported to perform 700 times faster than simple greedy algorithm (Leskovec et al., 2007). Effective heuristics derived from the independent cascade model was comparable or better then greedy algorithms in finding top nodes for influ- ence maximization problem (Chen, Wang & Yang, 2009). Most of the studies on influence maximization assume single degree of influence across the network. In contrast, the study of topic level social influence on large networks is also undertaken (Tang et al., 2009). A novel algorithm using the concept of Shapley value from cooperative game theory is also proposed to find top influential nodes in social network (Narayanam & Narahari, 2010).

Greedy algorithm for mining top-K influential nodes which works by identifying communities within the network and then detecting the influential nodes is also reported (Wang et al., 2010). A recent attempt to improve the CELF algorithm by exploiting the property of submodularity of the spread function for influence propagation models is reported as SPS-CELF++ (Goyal, Lu, & Lakshmanan, 2011). While most solutions for influence maximization depend on the social graph structure a data based approach using historical data and avoiding the need for learning influence probabilities is also proposed by same authors (Goyal, Bonchi & Lakshmanan, 2011). They also propose another efficient algorithm SIMPATH for influence maximization under the linear threshold model (Goyal, Lu & Lakshmanan, n.d.). The first scalable influence maximization algorithm specific for the linear threshold model was proposed using LDAG algorithm (Chen, Yuan & Zhang, 2010). Identifying influential nodes using Principal Component Centrality is also proposed (Ilyas & Radha, 2011). A comprehensive survey of the development in this area is also reported (Bonchi, 2011).

Finding Top-k Developers

The crucial aspect in social network analysis is to determine the weight of the edges in the graph. For the present discussion, the weight of an edge corresponds to the influence a node has on related node. Instead of randomly assigning the edge weight two methods were contemplated. The first was to use outdegree of each node as a means to determine influence of each node as follows:

$$Influence_{A \to B} = 1 \big/ deg^+ (A)$$

where in graph

$deg^+(v) \leftarrow out\_degree\ of\ developer\_no\_dev$

The above method has a shortcoming that all related nodes will be assigned same weight. That means if a developer is working on many projects it is assumed that he is equally active in all projects. In a more realistic scenario as a developer involves himself in more number of projects his contribution to each of those should decline. Therefore, a different method to calculate the weight of the influence called 'Shared Project Model' was formulated. The Procedure to calculate influence edge from developer node A to node B is as follows:

$$Influence_{A \to B} = w * \frac{|P_A|}{|U_{ab}|}$$

where $w = \sum_{p \in I_{ab}} \frac{1}{|p|}$

$U_{ab} = P_A \cup P_B$

$I_{ab} = P_A \cap P_B$

$P_X \leftarrow \{p_1, p_2, p_3 \dots p_n\}$ where p_i is a project of developer X

The partial structure of the graph thus obtained is shown in Table 2. This was used to find the top-5 influential nodes using the four algorithms High Degree, LDAG, SPS-CELF++ and SimPath. The result obtained for the month of Dec 2011 is given in Table 3. As it can be seen from the results except High Degree all algorithms almost give same results for top two nodes. The developer with id 2909886 emerges as the top most influential developer. This set of developers can be considered as seed nodes for maximizing the information flow in the sourgeforge.net community. This has huge implications regarding targeted marketing campaigns or simple information dissemination among the developer community.

The runtime performances of these four algorithms are given in Figure 1 and Figure 2. LDAG algorithm trades memory for speed because it constructs LDAG for each node. HighDegree requires very little computation over represen- tation of the graph in memory. The parameters used for each algorithm are k = 20 and the propagation model is Linear Threshold. LDAG has threshold of 1/320, Cutoff for SimPath and SPS-CELF++ is 0.001 and its topl is 4 for Look Ahead Optimization.

[1] $G = (V, E, b)$

$S \leftarrow \varnothing$

Find the k nodes with the highest out-degree(deg^+) and add each node to set S

```
S
[1]
/* preparation phase */
S = ∅
∀v ∈ V, IncInf (v) = 0
each node v ∈ V
generate LDAG(v, θ)
/* Inf Set(v)'s are derived from LDAG(v, θ)'s */
∀u ∈LDAG(v, θ), set ap_v (u) = 0
∀u ∈LDAG(v, θ), compute α_v (u)
each u in LDAG(v, θ)
IncInf (u)+ = α_v (u)
/* main loop for selecting k seeds */ i = 1 to k
s = argmax_{v∈V\S} {IncInf (v)}
each v ∈ Inf Set(s)\S
/* update α_v (u) for all u's that can reach s in LDAG(v, θ) */
Δα_v (s) = -α_v (s); ∀u ∈ S, Δα_v (u) = 0
```

Topologically sort all nodes that can reach s in LDAG(v, θ) in a sequence ρ, with s sorted first. Compute $\Delta\alpha_v (u)$ for all $u \in \rho$), where $\rho\backslash (S \cup \{v\})$ is replaced by $\rho\backslash (S \cup \{s\})$ and $\alpha_v ()$ is replaced by $\Delta\alpha_v ()$.

```
α_v (u)+ = Δα_v (u), for all u ∈ ρ
IncInf (u)+ = Δα_v (u) · (1 - ap_v (u)) for all u ∈ ρ
/* Update ap_v (u) for all u's reachable from s in LDAG(v, θ) */
Δap_v (s) = 1 - ap_v (s); ∀u ∈ S, Δap_v (u) = 0
```

Topologically sort all nodes reachable from s in LDAG(v, θ) into a sequence ρ, with s sorted first. compute $\Delta ap_v (x)$ for all $u \in \rho$, where $\rho\backslash S$ is replaced by $\rho\backslash (S \cup \{s\})$ and $ap()$ is replaced by $\Delta ap_v ()$

```
ap_v (u) += Δap_v (u), for all u ∈ ρ
IncInf (u) - = α_v (u) · Δap_v (u) for all u Î ρ
S = S ∪ {s}
S
[1] G, k seed set S
S ← ∅; Q ← ∅; last seed = null; cur best = null.
```

```
each u ∈ V
u.mg1 = σ({u}; u.prev best = cur best; u.mg2 = σ({u, cur best}); u.flag = 0.
Add u to Q. update cur best based on mg1.
|S| < k
u = top (root) element in Q. u.flag == |S|
S ← S ∪ {u}; Q ¬ Q - {u}; last seed = u.
continue; u.prev best == last seed
u.mg1 = u.mg2.
u.mg1 = Δ_u(S); u.prev best = cur best; u.mg2 = Δ_u(S ∪ {cur best}).
u.flag = |S|; Update cur_best
Reinsert u into Q and heapify.
[1] G = (V, E, b), η, l
```

Find the vertex cover of the input graph *G*. Call it *C*. each $u \in C$

```
U ← (V - C) Ç N^{in}(u).
Compute α(u) and α^{v -v}, ∀v ∈ SIMPATH -SPREAD(u, η, U).
Add u to CELF queue.
each v ∈ V - C
Compute α(v) .
Add u to CELF queue.
S ← ∅. spd ← 0
|S| < k
U ← top-l node in CELF queue.
Compute α^{v -x}(S), ∀x ∈ SIMPATH-SPREAD(S, η, U).
each x Î U
x is previously examined in the current iteration
S ← S + x; Update spd.
Remove x from CELF queue. Break out of the loop.
Call BACKTRACK(x, η, V - S, E) to compute α^{v -s} (x).
Compute α(S + x) using Eq. 6
Compute marginal gain of u as α(S + x) - spd.
Re-insert u in CELF queue such that its other is maintained.
return S
```

The procedure mentioned above to find top 5 developers was applied to all datasets from Feb 2009 to Dec 2011. The results are shown in Figure 3, Figure 4, Figure 5 and Figure 6. The graphs show remarkable consistency of some developers to remain in top 5 positions over many years. This is an indication that the select group of developers remain active for long time thus confirming that few developers do most of the work in FOSS ecology (Raj & Srinivasa, 2011, 2012).

Table 1. Structure of Table USER_GROUP

Column	Type	Modifiers
User_group_id	integer	not null
User_id	integer	not null default 0
Group_id	integer	not null default 0
Admin_flags	character (16)	not null
Forum_flags	integer	not null default 0
Project_flags	integer	not null default 2
Doc_flags	integer	not null default 0
Member_role	integer	not null default 100
Release_flags	integer	not null default 0
Artifact_flags	integer	not null default 0
Added_by	integer	not null default 100
Grantcvs	integer	not null default 1
grantshell	integer	not null default 1
Row_modtime	integer	not null
News_flags	integer	not null default 0
Screenshot_flags	integer	not null default 0
Grantsvn	integer	not null default 1

Table 2. Structure of social network graph

Node1	Node2	Edge Weight
0	51680	0.222222
0	16458	0.222222
1	60747	0.500000
2	19263	0.133333
2	21267	0.057143
2	30770	0.100000
2	20935	0.080000
3	22251	0.074074
3	6431	0.055556

Table 3 Top 5 developers in Dec 2011

Algorithm	Top Developers
High Degree	783089 405789 1632 11084 438768
LDAG	2909886 454395 11058 597819 918951
SPS-CELF++	2909886 454395 72656 45353 597819
SimPath	2909886 454395 72656 45353 597819

Figure 1. CPU utilization of algorithms

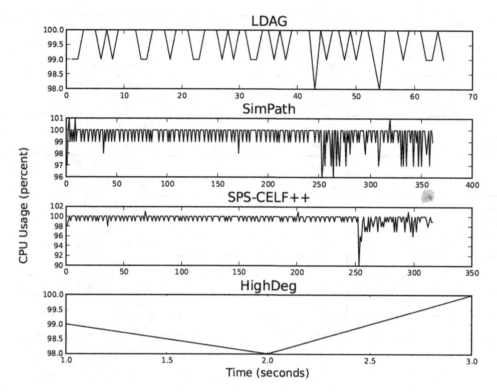

Figure 2. Memory utilization of algorithms

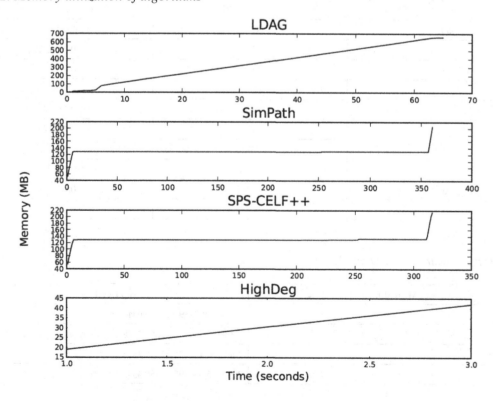

Figure 3. Top 5 developers: high degree algorithm

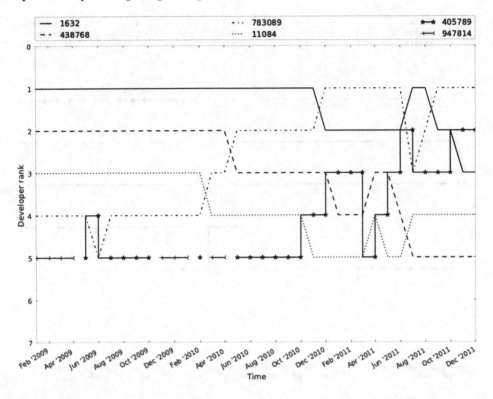

Figure 4. Top 5 developers: LDAG algorithm

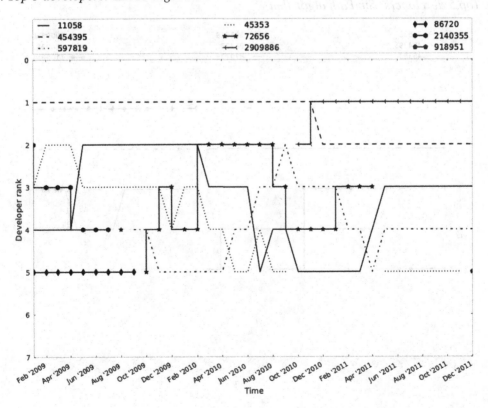

Figure 5. Top 5 developers: SPS-CELF++ algorithm

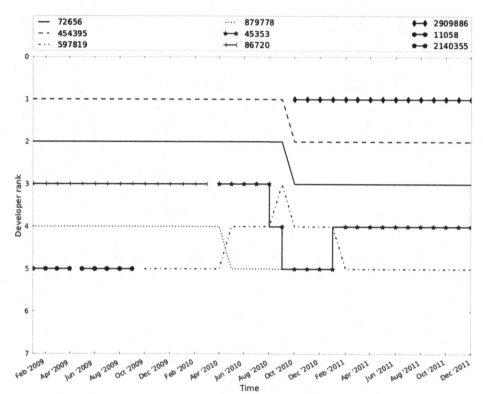

Figure 6. Top 5 developers: SimPath algorithm

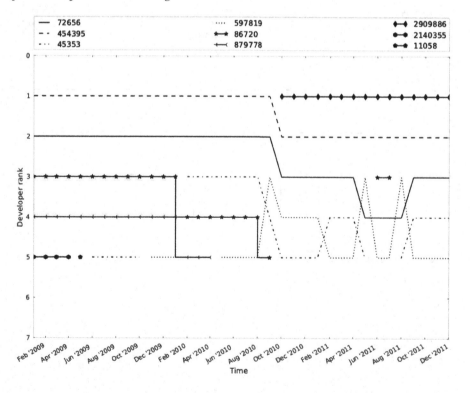

CONCLUSION

In this work, a novel attempt to find most influential nodes in the Free and Open Source Software developer network using Social Network Analysis approach was attempted. The influential developers were discovered using four different algo- rithms namely High Degree, LDAG, SPS-CELF++ and SimPath. It was found that except High Degree all other algorithms mostly agree on top developers. Identification of this influential set of developers is important because they can be the seed nodes for targeted marketing. The study of their movement across time line establishes the consistency of the top developers. Overall this work adds to the growing literature in this domain by making new contributions using theories from Social Network Analysis.

The future directions are to verify the presence of same results across different FOSS project sites. It should be interesting also to check the validity of these results in large, single project like GNU-Linux. Another way forward is to change the way weights are assigned to the edges in the graph. This can have huge implications regarding the results. The algorithms tried in this work can also be optimized to perform better. There are many interesting opportunities that are opened up with this work which should bring more clarity in understanding the phenomenon of FOSS.

REFERENCES

Bonchi, F. (2011). Influence propagation in social networks: A data mining perspective. In *Proceedings of the 2011 IEEE/WIC/ACM International Conferences on Web Intelligence and Intelligent Agent Technology*. IEEE.

Chen, W., Wang, Y., & Yang, S. (2009). Efficient influence maximization in social networks. In *Proceedings of the 15th ACM SIGKDD international conference on Knowledge discovery and data mining* (pp. 199–208). ACM.

Chen, W., Yuan, Y., & Zhang, L. (2010). Scalable influence maximization in social networks under the linear threshold model. In *Proceedings of the 2010 IEEE 10th International Conference on Data Mining (ICDM)* (pp. 88–97). IEEE.

Freeman, L. C. (1979). Centrality in social networks conceptual clarification. *Social Networks*, *1*(3), 215–239. doi:10.1016/0378-8733(78)90021-7

Goyal, A., Bonchi, F., & Lakshmanan, L. V. S. (2011). A data-based approach to social influence maximization. *Proceedings of the VLDB Endowment*, *5*(1), 73–84. doi:10.14778/2047485.2047492

Goyal, A., Lu, W., & Lakshmanan, L. V. S. (2011). Celf++: optimizing the greedy algorithm for influence maximization in social networks. In *Proceedings of the 20th international conference companion on World Wide Web* (pp. 47–48). ACM. 10.1145/1963192.1963217

Goyal, A., Lu, W., & Lakshmanan, L.V.S. (n.d.). Simpath: An efficient algorithm for influence maximization under the linear threshold model. Academic Press.

Ilyas, M. U., & Radha, H. (2011). Identifying influential nodes in online social networks using principal component centrality. In *Proceedings of the 2011 IEEE International Conference on Communications (ICC)*. IEEE.

Kempe, D., Kleinberg, J., & Tardos, E. (2003). Maximizing the spread of influence through a social network. In *Proceedings of the ninth ACM SIGKDD international conference on Knowledge discovery and data mining* (pp. 137-146). ACM. 10.1145/956750.956769

Kempe, D., Kleinberg, J., & Tardos, E. (2005). *Influential nodes in a diffusion model for social networks* (pp. 99–99). Automata, Languages and Programming. doi:10.1007/11523468_91

Kimura, M., Saito, K., & Nakano, R. (2007). Extracting influential nodes for information diffusion on a social network. In *Proceedings of the National Conference on Arificial Intelligence* (Vol. 22, p. 1371). London: AAAI Press.

Leskovec, J., Krause, A., Guestrin, C., Faloutsos, C., & VanBriesen, J. Glance (2007) - Cost-effective outbreak detection in networks. In *Proceedings of the 13th ACM SIGKDD international conference on Knowledge discovery and data mining* (pp. 420–429). ACM.

Narayanam, R., & Narahari, Y. (2010). A Shapley value-based approach to discover influential nodes in social networks. *IEEE Transactions on Automation Science and Engineering*, (99), 1–18.

Raj, P. M. K., & Srinivasa, K. G. (2011, March). Analysis of projects and volunteer participation in large scale free and open source software ecosystem. *ACM SIGSOFT Softw. Eng. Notes*, 36.

Raj, P. M. K., & Srinivasa, K. G. (2012, March). Empirical studies of global volunteer collaboration in the development of free and open source software: Analysis of six top ranked projects in sourceforge. net. *ACM SIGSOFT Softw. Eng. Notes*, 36, 1–5.

Tang, J., Sun, J., Wang, C., & Yang, Z. (2009). Social influence analysis in large-scale networks. In *Proceedings of the 15th ACM SIGKDD international conference on Knowledge discovery and data mining* (pp. 807–816). ACM. 10.1145/1557019.1557108

Wang, Y., Cong, G., Song, G., & Xie, K. (2010). Community-based greedy algorithm for mining top-k influential nodes in mobile social networks. In *Proceedings of the 16th ACM SIGKDD international conference on Knowledge discovery and data mining* (pp. 1039–1048). ACM. 10.1145/1835804.1835935

Xu, J., Christley, S., & Madey, G. (2006). Application of social network analysis to the study of open source software. Elsevier Press.

Chapter 9
The Cultural and Institutional Barrier of Knowledge Exchanges in the Development of Open Source Software

Ikbal Maulana

(iD) https://orcid.org/0000-0002-3727-3809

Indonesian Institute of Sciences, Indonesia

ABSTRACT

Open source software (OSS) gives developing countries inexpensive or free alternatives to proprietary software. It gives them the opportunity to develop software and software industry without starting from scratch. This chapter discusses the diffusion and development of OSS in Indonesia especially after the government took "Indonesia, Go Open Source" (IGOS) initiative. This initiative united government organizations, communities, R&D institutions, and universities. While the government's concern was to tackle piracy by replacing illegal software with OSS, the others sought to develop their own OSS. However, the openness of their software is only in terms of that they were developed using OSS development tools, while their mode of development remained closed, which was caused by cultural barrier and institutional incompatibility between government's regime of project administration and the governance of OSS development.

INTRODUCTION

Industry has developed to be increasingly relying on technology rather than on workers. In the past or today in craftsmanship traditions, technology is manifested as tools that are only useful in hands of skillful workers, whereas in modern production systems workers "becomes a mere appendage to an already existing material condition of production" (Marx, 1906, p. 421). As machineries becoming more sophisticated, because knowledge which was previously possessed by workers is increasingly embedded into them, they can be operated by much less skillful workers. This development allows capitalists to better

DOI: 10.4018/978-1-7998-9158-1.ch009

control their production systems and even transport their machineries to any developing country to find low-cost labors to operate them. The transfer of sophisticated machineries to developing countries does not automatically lead to the transfer of knowledge of production. When the machineries are moved to other countries, the workers' involvement in production does not develop necessary skills that allow developing countries to make the same production. Their skills of operating machineries apparently are necessary but easily replaceable parts of production process.

Software industry has given new promises to developing countries, because software can be produced on inexpensive machines. Software programmers can develop their skills by experimenting on widely available computers. Software industry, as part of information and communication technology (ICT) industries, seems to give the sense of promise because it periodically experiences transformation caused by the emergence of, what Christensen (Christensen, 2000) calls, disruptive technology. The disruption of technology demands industry players to play with new knowledge and technology, because the old one is not only irrelevant, but can be a liability to those who use it. It also explains why the innovations that direct this industry has been created by young people who have no significant experience in business and industry. This fact seems to give hope to entrepreneurs in developing countries as well. "Although it is dominated by firms based in major industrialized countries of the world, it continues to offer great prospects for economic growth and industrial development within developing economies" (UNCTAD, 2002, p. 3).

The strong reliance on knowledge rather than on technology may deceive people to underestimate the complexity of the development of software industry, as if knowledge can be easily acquired through simple learning and softwares can be easily produced through mere thinking in front of a computer. The intangibility of software gives them the illusions that the development of software and software industry are easy and inexpensive, and that both developed and developing countries have the same opportunities because this industry does not rely on expensive production capital. Indeed, if every country has the same opportunity, then the competition must be very high, and even higher for software industry, which produces products that are "costly to *produce* but cheap to *reproduce*" (Shapiro & Varian, 1999, p. 3), and can be inexpensively distributed throughout the world. Consequently, having the capability to create a working software is not sufficient, competition demands producers to create it better than similar products competing in the same marketplace. India has often been mentioned as the best exemplar of a developing country that can take advantage of the opportunity in global software industry (Nagala, 2005), but most of other developing countries can only dream of that achievement.

Opportunities in software industry for developing countries have become elusive if we see that the market leaders, which are from advanced countries, can make their clients dependent on them, because users of software "are notoriously subject to switching costs and lock-in: once you have chosen a technology, or a format for keeping information, switching can be very expensive" (Shapiro & Varian, 1999, p. 11). And as current softwares are also very complex, consisting of thousands to hundred thousand of codes which require time consuming, hence expensive, development and testing, it becomes more difficult for new software companies to challenge market leaders. So proprietary software industries from advanced countries have erected a high barrier for new entrants from developing countries.

The above barrier is irrelevant in the development of open source software (OSS). One of the basic tenets of OSS is that you do not have to develop anything from scratch, because it is legal for you to modify what others have developed, and, hence, "open source developers enjoy a great productivity gain from code reuse" (DiBona, 2006, p. 22). In OSS development, you do not need to reinvent the wheel, rather use the wheel invented by others and modify it when it is necessary. This principle is practiced by any OSS developer, including developers working for large corporations. "You can still build platforms today, of course, but for practical considerations, it only makes sense to build them on top of open source infrastructure. Amazon and Google are familiar platform businesses (one for retailing, the other for advertising), built on cheap or free open source building materials" (Polese, 2006, p. xi).

Adopting OSS will benefits developing countries because it is "a means of reducing licensing costs and of promoting indigenous technological development by having access to the source code of these products" (Câmara & Fonseca, 2007, p. 121). This claim is also supported by the reports of United Nations, by adopting OSS developing countries can prevent themselves to be the hostage of proprietary software (UNCTAD, 2004), and by having access to the source code, they can advance knowledge more quickly (UNCTAD, 2003), or adapt existing OSS to their needs, and further the adoption may lead to the development of their software industries (Weerawarana & Weeratunge, 2004).

The benefits of and opportunities from OSS for developing countries have often been mentioned, how to realize the benefits and opportunities is not always clear and easy, even when it is supported by government policy, such as what has happened in Indonesia. This chapter will discuss the barriers that limit the success of OSS diffusion and development in Indonesia by using various perspectives, from knowledge to cultural to institutional perspectives.

LITERATURE REVIEWS

The Role of Software in Economic Development

The utilization of software, together with other elements of ICT, has become unavoidable for any country, including developing countries (Avgerou, 2010). Many businesses and government administrations cannot be carried out without ICT. The increasing complexity and pace of production systems cannot be managed without ICT (Beniger, 1986). The progress of a country depends on how best they can allocate their resources, which in turn depends on how best they utilize various information and knowledge about the resources which is not given to anyone in its totality (Hayek, 1945, p. 520). The performance of a country, therefore, depends on the quality and flow of information from one element to another in their national system of production, which necessitates the utilization of ICT (Stiglitz, 2002). In today's world ICT cannot be ignored, because it is a major driving force of the globalization of economy. "More than any other technology ICTs drive economic and financial globalization as they facilitate rapid transactions and global market transparency" (Miranda et al., 2007, p. 17).

The potentials of ICT in modern economy has promised great opportunities, but with accompanying complex policy challenges in realizing those opportunities. Without having to develop their own ICT industry sector, but by effectively utilizing ICT in any part of their economy, they can boost the productivity of the other industry sectors (Arora & Athreye, 2002). "As every sector of the global economy and nearly every facet of modern society undergoes digital transformation, the ICT industry community is focused on opportunities that spur not only the development of ICT innovations but also, and more importantly, their adoption and use throughout the economy" (Martin, 2016, p. 24). The utilization of ICT requires more than just the implementation of technology, but also demands the changing of business processes or even organizational forms. Many people in developing countries view ICT as magic bullet for development. They are enthusiast to adopt e-government and expect their public administration will run effectively just by putting technology in their offices. However, effective e-government implementation requires bureaucratic reform (Cordella, 2007), which is unlikely to happen voluntarily due to organizational inertia. Effective ICT utilization demands more than just the use of technologies, but the reorganization of internal and interorganizational information flows (Cordella, 2007), which will significantly affect culture, structure and power relations within organization.

Effective utilization of software in other economic sectors is no simpler than the development of software industry. The success of Singapore, a tiny country, which has become one of the most important financial service and economic hubs in the world, is due to the systematic integration of ICT into its government and economic activities (Angelidou, 2014). The incorporation of ICT into various business and government processes were carefully and systematically crafted, and seriously implemented in Singapore's 10-year masterplan entitled Intelligent Nation 2015 (iN2015 Steering Committee, 2006). So, developing countries can take advantage from either the utilization or development of software. Neither is easier than the other. Utilization and development pose different challenges that need to be addressed differently by government policy. OSS reduces the investment cost burdening developing countries, also reveal the algorithmic secret of sophisticated softwares and give economic and engineering benefits of reusable open source codes. That is why "Within the last decade, more than 60 countries and international organizations have developed nearly 275 policy documents related to the use of an open-source approach in the public sector" (Dener, Watkins, & Dorotinsky, 2011, p. 78).

Software as Knowledge

Technology is not merely material objects, but also embeds particular knowledge that enables it to perform particular functions. Therefore, it can be viewed as "a form of knowledge created by humans" (Parayil, 1991a, p. 235), or "as the organization of knowledge for practical purposes" (Mesthene, 1997, p. 74). Technology can also be seen "as a spectrum, with ideas at one end and techniques and things at the other, with design as a middle term" (Layton Jr, 1974, pp. 37–38). If this view is applied to software technology then the spectrum ranges from ideas to designs to softwares, all of which are different kinds of information. While ideas are information that guide people what they should do, softwares are information that dictate computers what they have to do. The development of software can be seen as a translation of human knowledge into the knowledge understood by computers.

Translating human knowledge into software is not easy, not only because a computer speaks different language from human, but it also needs to be told step by step what to do. Developing software is more than just making human knowledge explicit, but also utilizing it to tackle specific problem in systematic and step-wise ways. There is additional complexity, the knowledge that needs to be translated may not be available in one single mind. Currently many softwares have to deal with complex business processes, of which no single individual comprehends the whole processes in their entirety. Before being translated into computer program, a set of human knowledge need to be negotiated and integrated. The common challenge to deal with complex knowledge is how "to make sensible use of what knowledge we think we have, to find ways of combining it effectively with the knowledge that we think other people have, and to protect ourselves against the consequences of our own and other people's ignorance" (Loasby, 1999, p. 7). What makes it difficult is that knowledge is not a mental commodity that can be easily codified and exchanged between individuals (Visser, 2010), and also it is difficult to recognize our own lack of knowledge.

OSS development is an open, and mostly also virtual, collaboration among people who might not know each other personally. The openness and virtuality of the collaboration create opportunities as well as challenges in integrating knowledge and ideas. While richness of knowledge and ideas might flow in from all around the world, transforming that richness into a working OSS is of a great challenge, because not every suggestion can be accommodated. What has to be attempted by OSS project leaders is that while they should keep encourage people's contributions, they also have to prevent chaotic situation due to the unmanageability of crowded involvements. An institution, rule of the game (North, 1990), has to be established to structure the collaboration, to make it more manageable (Parayil, 1991b), even though the collaborative structure of a community of voluntary developers will be different from and more complex than that of a business organization.

The Nature of OSS Development

OSS is open in two senses. First, by definition and in practice, the source code of OSS is open to be examined by anyone with knowledge of programming. The openness of OSS allows people who can read software codes to see the internal working of OSS, which not only allows them to find bugs and propose suggestions, they can also revise it by themselves, modify it, or even develop something else on top of it. Second, an OSS project can be made open to volunteers from any stage of its development, even from the beginning before starting to write any code. Currently, there are many OSS projects that are open for anyone's participation even from the very beginning of ideas which are hosted by SourceForge, GitHub, Google Source Code and many others. Each of these sites can host from as many as thousands to millions of OSS projects. SourceForge claims to host more than 430,000 projects; whereas GitHub claims to host millions of OSS projects (Slashdot Media, 2018; GitHub, 2018). OSS is a model of global peer production, sharing, revision, and review (Vaidhyanathan, 2005).

For popular and complex OSS, such as operating system or office suite, which can be acquired for free, it is common that there are communities of users and developers around the softwares. Since they are free, consequently, there is no vendor that is responsible to help you when you face any problem with that free OSS. Therefore, you must rely on the help of communities of OSS users and developers. It is common practice that users assist each other to utilize OSS (Câmara & Fonseca, 2007). Adopting OSS will encourage users to share more knowledge among themselves than if they use commercial propriety softwares. Not only users are willing to help each other, even some developers are eager to listen and help users. Problems faced by users or suggestion given by users are sources of ideas of improvement for OSS developers. That is why that "The open source development process is somewhat reminiscent of the type of `user-driven innovation' seen in many other industries" (Weber, 2004, p. 3).

Software is different from tangible products. When someone creates the same bicycle as what another person has made, mostly the latter does not mind, because it takes a lot of effort to create that same bicycle. But, it is different for software, making a copy of a software that took weeks or months to create requires just a few mouse clicks, therefore, it is easy for software developers to quickly occupy the whole market with their products, whereas producers of tangible products need to firstly invest in machineries before increasing the production. The nature of software production and reproduction and its market potential makes proprietary software adherents prefer to impose strong IPR protection on software.

The institutionalization of proprietary software development, which has been so intense and influential since 1980s, makes people consider this as the only way of developing software (Vaidhyanathan, 2005). In fact, OSS development was the only way of developing software in the early history of computing. Just as what has been told by one of its pioneers, Richard Stallman, "When I started working at the MIT Artificial Intelligence Lab in 1971, I became part of a software-sharing community that had existed for many years. Sharing of software was not limited to our particular community; it is as old as computers, just as sharing of recipes is as old as cooking" (Stallman, 1999, p. 53).

OSS is certainly not the first type of open innovation. In the past, or even now in traditional society, innovation has been developed openly to public, "…. throughout most of human history all information technologies and almost all technologies have been open source. And we have done pretty well as a species with tools and habits unencumbered by high restrictions on sharing, copying, customizing, and improving" (Vaidhyanathan, 2005, p. 342). Anyone can see what others have developed and improve it without worrying of being complaint about intellectual property right. Even in the beginning of software development, it was very common that software was developed openly and people learned from each other and developed upon what had been developed by others. "The practice of sharing source code is not an entirely novel feature in the software industry. The first "intensive" users of mainframe computers were universities and corporate research laboratories. In that environment, computer programs were eminently seen as research tools, and it was seen as a normal practice to share code with other developers" (Nuvolari, 2005). Sharing source code of a program, which is a manifestation of technical knowledge, was perceived as normal as sharing any kind of knowledge which is until now common in universities.

The Culture of OSS Development

In a global software industry dominated by proprietary softwares, open source mode of development might be considered as a strange way of software development, contradicting common economic reasoning (Nuvolari, 2005). Many people perceive that OSS is developed by a community of altruistic programmers having no commercial interests. This is considered as the only rational explanation of their willingness to sacrifice an enormous amount of time to develop products that later can be freely distributed by other people. What puzzles them is the fact that many large corporations, including IBM and Google, have also participated in OSS development. Indeed, there are many voluntary developers actively contribute to the development of software that can compete against proprietary ones, which shows that the altruistic side of OSS development community, however "altruism is neither the only nor the most important motivation" (DiBona, Cooper, & Stone, 2006, p. xxx).

Modern market economics will find it difficult to comprehend that thousands of top-notch programmers dispersed in many loosely organized virtual community contribute freely to the development of a public good (Lerner & Tirole, 2002, p. 198). And the beneficiaries of their contribution are not only "poor users" from developing countries, but also large corporations in advanced countries. OSS developers are no different from other innovators, many of them are also selfish individuals. "The apparent paradox rests on the assumption that acts of charity necessarily conflict with acts of self-interest. From the point of view of a modern market economy, it often appears that charity and self-interest do conflict against each other. What drives the open source developer, however, is clearly self-interest—even if it is based on an older notion of self-interest not easily captured by modern market economics" (DiBona et al., 2006, p. xxx).

DiBona et al (2006), argue that the paradox can be explained away if reputation is regarded as important currency as money. By becoming important contributors to OSS projects, people can gain reputation among OSS communities as well as in ICT industry in general. Indeed, OSS activists and evangelists, such as Linus Thorvalds and Richard Stallman can never gain wealth as the leaders of proprietary software corporations, but their reputation will provide them with survival resources, their OSS accomplishments could provide them with the opportunities to earn a living from their expertise.

The development of OSS is not always smooth, peaceful and successful. The openness of OSS allows "open development and decentralized peer review to lower costs and improve software quality" (Raymond, 2001, p. xi), but it can also lead to be chaotic and full of conflict and result in dysfunctional softwares. To be successful, certain level of order must be established in OSS project. Therefore, the process of a successful OSS project "is not a chaotic free-for-all in which everyone has equal power and influence. And it is certainly not an idyllic community of like-minded friends in which consensus reigns and agreement is easy. In fact, conflict is not unusual in this community; it's endemic and inherent to the open source process" (Weber, 2004, p. 3).

The ideas proposed by the initiators of OSS project were not immediately understood or accepted by joining volunteers. During the period of development of complex software, a loosely group of independent developers, who are not bound by contract of employment and might have never seen and developed close and warm friendship with each other, would have to struggle to reach consensus. Intensive and harsh discussion were often being carried out before actual codes have been written. "One of the common and most misleading fallacies about the open source process is that it involves like-minded geeks who cooperate with each other in an unproblematic way because they agree with each other on technical grounds" (Weber, 2004, p. 81). Sometimes the discussions were not easy to manage, because it can range from discussion about bugs that give false result, new ideas that need to be incorporated, to conspiracy theory of the intervention of proprietary software industry into OSS projects. Since the discussions were carried out in mailing-lists, the proto-form of social media we know today, people were not constrained by ethics and norms, so the discussions may go wild and lead to interpersonal conflicts.

OSS project is different from what is generally understood as community of practice. In the latter, "knowledge exchange is motivated by moral obligation and community interest rather than by narrow self-interest" (Wasko & Faraj, 2000, p. 155). It is assumed that individuals can submit to community interest without expecting "intangible returns such as reputation and self-esteem" (2000, p. 159). While in OSS projects, ego is considered as the driving force of active participation. "In trying to create a legacy as a great programmer, many developers believe deeply that "scientific" success will outstrip and outlive financial success" (Weber, 2004, p. 140).

The different role of ego in an OSS project and a community of practice can be understood from different commitment and involvement demanded by the two. In the community of practice, people just share knowledge and help one-another with their advices, which do not need to be followed, and hence the competition among members of the community is relatively low. That is why members of the community can easily look good to one another, or at least they do not need to show their ego or self-interest. In an OSS project, developers do not just share their technical knowledge, they also compete and fight to make their technical contribution accepted by others. An OSS project often grows to be a competition for creating memorable legacy. The problem is that there is a limited space that cannot adopt all those legacies. Therefore, criticism against each others' codes is a common game in any OSS project. "The norm in the open source community is to criticize the code, not the individual who wrote it, which may reduce a little bit how badly it hurts. But because code is precisely identified with an author, a virtuous circle of ego-boosting can easily become a much messier status competition, in which one person's ego boost becomes another person's insult" (Weber, 2004, p. 141).

Probably, because what OSS developers pursue is not financial, but the intangible and unmeasurable reputation, the knowledge sharing in OSS projects is more politically complicated than any other form of software development or knowledge sharing. Leaders of OSS projects have to balance the conflicting interests against the progress of OSS development. It is not easy when they have to deal with developers' ego who work voluntarily. "If egos can be boosted, they can also be damaged, which raises the question of what kinds of behavior will follow. The person with the hurt ego has choices: She can leave the project, she can fork the code, she can retaliate against the leader or against other developers" (Weber, 2004, p. 141). Success OSS development requires leadership that can deal with the social dynamic of a loosely group, of which norms and cultures are strongly shaped by the different norms and cultures of participating volunteers as well as by the virtual nature of their interactions. This unprecedented and unique way of doing OSS projects makes this practice not easily transferable to different communities having different values and cultures.

THE INTRODUCTION OF ICT IN INDONESIA

Personal computers were introduced in the early 1980s to Indonesian people when proprietary software had already dominated global software industry. People did not mind to be dependent on proprietary softwares, because they could easily use the illegal copy of any software, which cost just a little more than the the cost of the floppy disk on which the software was recorded. They did not have the sense that it was illegal, because the shops that sold illegal software were open to public, not hiding from law enforcement institutions. The widespread availability of pirated softwares made people not interested in public domain, or free and open source softwares.

Even though piracy had prevented the development of mass market software industry, people had high expectation in ICT professions, including software developers. Many ICT higher educations were established, probably because they attracted a lot of students and were very inexpensive to establish compared to other engineering educations. The education institutions only needed to provide class rooms and computer labs, and even increasingly more students preferred to use their own computers rather than to use their university's computers. Today there are 354 ICT departments belong to universities, and 388 departments belong to ICT specialized higher education institutions (Utami, 2018). What belong to ICT departments are computer engineering, information system, and informatics (software development). Many of the above education institutions have become the fertile ground for the growth of OSS communities. The difficulty of installing and modifying OSS is an attractive challenge for showing off the geekiness of OSS activists.

Government's Commitment on ICT

Formally, ICT has taken special position in Indonesian government since two decades ago. Except the current president, all the previous five presidents had established a council to give advice or formulate ICT-related policy to the president. That the council had never delivered significant policy recommendation was probably due to the fact that the core members of the teams were ministers who actually had already had heavy tasks in their specific areas of duties. While business leaders and top academics who were appointed to assist them were also already busy with their own duties.

The proliferation of ICT educations indicates that government and society regard software development as important capability for the nation. Yet, the strong protection of intellectual property right (IPR) which is required for the development of software industry has never entered public discourse, hence, has never been their concern. While Indonesian government have long sought to formally promote ICT utilization and development, their commitment to protect software copyright has been the target of criticism from overseas until today. Even though copyright law has a history of over a century, for it was introduced by the Dutch colonial government in 1912 (Susanti, Nurjaya, Safaat, & Djatmika, 2014). Indeed, the enactment of this law was for the interest of the colonizers rather than the colonized. Not long after the independence from the Dutch colonialism, in 1950 Indonesia ratified Bern Convention, an international agreement governing the protection of copyright. However, they seemed to see this law just gave the young country unnecessary limitation. In 1958 they abandon their membership to this convention for the reason of promoting national interest in education, namely, to allow local book publishers to print foreign books without paying royalty (Susanti et al., 2014).

The lack of, or weak protection of copyright and other intellectual property rights does not only disadvantage foreign businesses, but also many Indonesian, from authors, musicians, to film producers. Representing only a tiny fraction of Indonesian people, they could neither give sufficient pressure to the government nor effectively raise their concern in public arena.

Indonesia has not reached IPR-based economy, that is the level of economy where local players can derive commercial benefits from their IPR. Currently the IPR system is seen as burden instead of opportunity. Therefore, it was not due to the local interest to protect IPR, but due to the pressure by developed countries. In 1997, Indonesia ratified Bern Convention again through Presidential Decree Number 18. However, until now the protection of copy right is still disappointing many parties. For example, in Indonesia, according to the joint study by Business Software Alliance (BSA) and the International Data Corporation (IDC), the commercial value of illegal software installed on personal computers reached $1.32 billion in 2010, and the illegal users were not just personal users but also companies, which seemed not to realize that they used illegal softwares (Ratri Adityarani, 2011).

Indeed, there have been pressures on Indonesian government to take strong measures against software piracy. In 1995 two US industry associations, the Business Software Alliance (BSA) and the International Intellectual Property Alliance (IIPA), called for the office of United States Trade Representative (USTR) to impose trade sanctions against Indonesia, which they reiterated in the following year (Rosser, 2012). At that time, the source of concern was not only software piracy, but also other informational goods, from books to musics. In May 1996, the USTR responded to this call by moving Indonesia from its 'watch list' to 'priority watch list,' and made the country just one step away from being hit by trade sanctions. Since the US was its major trading partner, Indonesia had no choice but to move ahead with copyright law reform, at least by imposing the use of legal software among its ministries and state-owned enterprises.

The OSS Movements in Indonesia

Since the mid-1990s, the beginning of widespread diffusion of the Internet, many Linux user groups were established in Indonesian cities where there were universities having computer science departments. But membership of the groups soon expanded beyond the confines of the computer departments and universities. Linux and its various tools were attractive because they could be readily used to develop Internet servers and applications. The success stories of American Internet based companies in the second half of the 1990s also got wide coverage in Indonesian media and might inspire Indonesian software developers and businesses to imitate their success.

Virtual interactions among Linux enthusiasts were probably much more intensive than were their off-line interactions. Virtual interactions could engage people nationwide, but also encouraged further formation of Linux user groups in many other cities. Through virtual interactions which were sometimes continued by face-to-face meeting, some people have emerged as Linux evangelists who gained nation-wide popularity among Indonesian Linux communities. In 2005 the Linux user groups were spread over 35 cities. Some activists were not satisfied just expanding the user base of Linux, they also aimed to develop their own versions of Linux. Some versions, namely, WinBI and IGOS Nusantara, were funded and developed by government institutions. While the others, such as BlankOn, Trustix Merdeka, RimbaLinux, were developed by communities or private companies. The Linux communities later promoted the term "open source" to refer to the expansion of their interests which were no longer limited to the operating system.

Among government institutions, the Agency for the Assessment and Application of Technology (BBPT) has been most active in OSS development. Their active role was probably because they were headed by Minister of Research and Technology who was actively promoting high technology industries, such as aircraft and ship building industries. Prior to year 2000, ICT was not perceived as priority by the government which regarded sophisticated technology only tangible and expensive products, such as aircraft technology. In the era when people could easily used illegal softwares, it was difficult to sense the urgency of developing their own softwares. Around 2000s ICT and other buzzwords such as ecommerce, ebusiness and egovernment entered public discourse, national as well as international. The head of BPPT, who was also the Minister of Research and Technology, often accompanied the president to go overseas, which probably made him exposed to the popular awareness of the importance of ICT. Therefore, he increased the budget of software development, which was used to develop the first Indonesian Linux Distro, named WinBi, which literally means Windows in Indonesian language. BPPT has also developed applications that have been widely used by local governments, such as Kantaya (virtual office) and applications for serving local governments' one-stop service. BPPT also saw that the slow diffusion of ICT due to the expensive cost of computer hardwares. In order to decrease the cost of computers and use legal software, BPPT developed a system consisted of a set of old, and therefore cheap, computers and one new computer used as server. The cheap computers were used as terminals, connecting to the server where all data were stored. This system was named KOMURA, the abbreviation of Indonesian phrase which means "cheap computers". This system was intended to be used at school or universities.

Strong pressure on Indonesian government from overseas to respect copy right, had been used by OSS proponents from both inside and outside government institutions to push government to take a major OSS initiative. The IPR regime of OSS gives developing countries chances to free themselves from the market power and monopolistic conditions imposed by large proprietary software firms. Either as users or developers, people from developing countries can benefit from the abundant stock of existing OSS. The reduction of IT investment cost, but without violating IPR protection law, is regarded as the reason that gather the momentum in the utilization of OSS in developed and developing countries (Weerawarana & Weeratunge, 2004, p. 7). The availability of many off-the-shelf OSS that could be used legally for free was often communicated by OSS proponents to the government and society, even though they knew that OSS is not necessarily free (zero cost), because some of them were developing OSS and providing OSS services as their sources of income. The idea of using legal but free software increasingly attracted the government which could not find effective way to tackle software piracy. In 2000s two ministries had been the strong supporters of OSS, namely ministry of research and technology and ministry of communication and information. Ultimately, on June 30, 2004, five ministries declared "Indonesia, Go Open Source" (IGOS) initiative, which was then being followed by various government programs promoting the utilization of OSS. By adopting OSS, at least government institutions can use legal software without spending a lot of money.

To many proponents, the OSS movement was ideological, not just mere technical replacement of proprietary softwares. In many IGOS events, the narrative of nationalism, "OSS for national independence" was occasionally stated. OSS developers, in both communities and government research institutions, wanted more than just promoting the utilization of OSS. They wanted to develop their own OSS. Local Linux distros and various open source applications have been developed by communities as well as government institutions. And rather than using already existing Linux distro, government developed its own Linux distro, namely, IGOS Nusantara. The openness of OSS enables Indonesian developers to dwell into the complexity of sophisticated source code, whereas in proprietary software industry, the source code has become the secret of the company which owns it.

As part of IGOS initiative, supporting organizations were established to help general users to smoothly adopt OSS. Government institutions that committed to adopt OSS established help desk teams in their offices. OSS Empowerment Centers (POSS) were established by a number of major universities to promote OSS, and IGOS Centers were established as business activities to help people or organizations, who previously used proprietary software, to migrate to OSS. Then the support of government was strong, but to be sustainable, both government and OSS activists were aware that OSS movement also needed business supports (Maulana & Handoko, 2006). OSS based industry needed to be developed.

Government's OSS policy to deal with software piracy did not make the critics happy, because it did not recover their losses. Microsoft's strong responses was apparent. When in 2005 ministry of research and technology held IGOS Open House which consisted of lectures and exhibitions of open source companies and communities, Microsoft took part in the exhibition, even though this corporation did not exhibit any open source product. Ironically, its booth became the most crowded, because it gave door prize of some Xbox game consoles to audiences. The participation of Microsoft in this open source event actually surprised many activists. But, in the same year, when some government institutions and communities sought to bundle their efforts to promote OSS, the Indonesian President Yudhoyono met Bill Gates in the United States, and in the following year Indonesian government signed Memorandum of Understanding (MoU) with Microsoft, which became a contract that required the government to buy over 35 thousand licenses of Microsoft Windows and over 177 thousand licenses of Office Suites. In terms of price, Indonesia got big discounted prices, but it was estimated at $40 millions and payment would be due in June 2007 (Oxford Business Group, 2007). It was a very high cost which OSS proponents regarded as unnecessary. This MoU was also criticized by the Business Competition Supervisory Agency (KPPU), which regarded that the MoU contradicted a number of government organizations' initiative to adopt OSS. After the MoU was signed by the Indonesian Ministry of Communication and Information, Sofyan Djalil, who was before a strong supporter of OSS, some OSS activists sought to meet and demand him to give the explanations. They also met Kusmayanto Kadiman, Minister of Research and Technology, who had been successful in forcing his ministry to adopt OSS. It seems that there were conflicting views or interests within the government. However, despite some disappointment, good relationship between government and OSS communities still continued.

Proponents of OSS within government institutions and communities continued to support one another. They established Indonesian Association of Open Source (AOSI) in June 2009 to further push OSS movement. Even though government officials actively support the establishment of the association, formally they kept distance from it to allow strong initiatives from communities and private sectors. Betti Alisjahbana, former country general manager of IBM, was appointed as the first chairperson. Within the same year, in November 2008, they held Asia-Africa Conference on Open Source, which was actively supported by the government.

Some elements in government still showed their support for OSS as a way to reduce software copy right violation. In March 2009, the Ministry of Administrative Reform (MenPAN) issued Circular Letter No. 1 of 2009 to all government organizations and State-owned enterprises, endorsing the adoption and use of OSS. But, it made International Intellectual Property Alliance (IIPA) not happy and regarded that it "will create additional trade barriers and deny fair and equitable market access to software companies" (IIPA, 2010, p. 51). IIPA responded to it by recommending that Indonesia remain on the Priority Watch List.

THE ACHIEVEMENTS AND FAILURES OF OSS INITIATIVES

The Adoption of OSS After the End of Formal Campaign

Through the IGOS initiative the government expected that by the end of December 2011 all government institutions would have adopted OSS. To further stimulate the use of OSS among government organizations and communities, Ministry of Communication and Information presented Indonesia Open Source Award (IOSA) to government organizations, educational institutions, individuals and communities. Despite the lively ceremonies of many OSS events as well as formal promotion of OSS, proprietary softwares could easily sneak into government organizations through the procurement of computers, which usually have been installed with proprietary operating systems. Beside that, the MoU between the government and Microsoft was regarded as the permission to allocate budget to procure proprietary softwares which were considered more user-friendly than OSS. The MoU had weakened government's messages of support for OSS.

Today, there is no longer any program that explicitly support the diffusion and development of OSS. The government organizations that were in the past actively promoting OSS, have switched their attentions to something else, for example, creative industry, mobile technologies, Internet of Things or the fourth industrial revolution. OSS is no longer an attractive terrain. Communities of Linux Users and AOSI do still exist, even though they are not as active or enthusiast as a decade ago. The current development of technologies and ICT industry have posed different challenges. Mobile technologies and businesses based on those technologies attract more attentions. Fighting for OSS seems to be out of fashion in the current technological discourse.

However, several local governments have successfully maintained their adoption of OSS, either of off-the-shelf applications or of specially developed applications for egovernment services. Even though their ICT skills are relatively lower than central government organizations, but when their leaders show strong visions and commitments, employees of local governments seem to be relatively easier to lead to adopt OSS. BPPT, a technology development state organization, have strongly supported these local governments in developing their back-office applications. But BPPT admitted that most of the ideas came from their local government partners which interacted with them intensively. Without strong commitment from the management, the complexity of massive OSS migration at organizational scale might be unbearable and unsustainable. Since there was no vendor that could provide post-sale services, then the organization that adopted OSS must establish their own help desks. In fact, part of the IGOS initiative was the setting up of various supporting institutions, from help desks at the organizational level, to Linux or OSS communities to commercial supporting units. But the establishment of such supporting units and making them sustainable were quite a challenge. Many local government could not establish their own help desks, while the cooperations with communities were often difficult to establish due to the institutional and cultural incompatibility between the former and the latter. OSS communities relied on voluntarism which gave their members freedom, while dealing with government organizations required them to go through administrative and bureaucratic hurdles.

As the government's formal supports of OSS ceased and then ended, OSS seemed to be immediately forgotten in many places. Except in several local governments, OSS has returned to their previous positions, the toys and tools of geeks and computer enthusiasts. The ideological narrative of OSS proponents that OSS could make the country technologically more independent and advanced failed to spread throughout society and government.

Cultural and Institutional Incompatibility of OSS Development

Government's supports for both OSS and e-government should consequently stimulate the growth of an exciting and vibrant OSS industry, not just of hobbyists' activities. There have been many open source applications being developed, however, most of them are OSS in the sense that they were developed using OSS development tools, such as PHP, Python, etc and running on Linux operating system. Their mode of development was as closed as the development of proprietary softwares. The three proceedings of national conferences of OSS held by Indonesian Institute of Science (LIPI) in 2006, 2007 and 2009 shows the papers describing OSS developed by universities and research organizations which did not engage people outside their organizations to contribute and did not provide links to the source codes of the applications. Even, the major work of developing two Linux distros were carried out as closed activities by two separate government R&D organizations. They took advantages of the available OSS but did not apply OSS as a mode of development, which opened the process of development to public. OSS as a governance structure of software development (Jensen & Scacchi, 2010) was not adopted.

There has never been any specific policy to promote and deal with the complexity of OSS development. The intangibility of softwares might deceive people to underestimate the complexity of its development. Regardless of the level of complexity, from a few lines of code to a complex operating system, the skill to develop software is called programming, and it just looks like typing on a computer, without any visible sophistication like working in a laboratory or in manufacturing plant. OSS development is much more than just knowledge sharing, such as what happens in virtual discussion forums or Wikipedia. In discussion forums each member can have different opinions without affecting each other's opinions, in Wikipedia people seek to produce a coherent article, but the system allows incoherency and contradiction, whereas in OSS, any part of the code can affect the working of the whole system, therefore even a small error in any part of the software cannot be tolerated and must be corrected.

Coordinating collaboration of software development is very complicated due to the intangibility of the product they seek to produce. The more people involved in software development, the more difficult to reach the consensus in determining the architecture of a software, identifying its building blocks, and implementing it in programming language. Therefore, OSS production could be more complicated than the closed production of a proprietary software, but this complication could be compensated by the voluntary contributions of enthusiast and experienced programmers from any part of the world (Rusovan, Lawford, & Parnas, 2005).

The involvement of programmers from around the world can give the projects access to abundance of technical knowledge, however, it can also pose severe problems. Besides the increasing complexity of managing those people and incorporating their contributions, online communication can lead to unfriendly interactions. "Successful collaboration among these highly talented people is not simple.

Conflict is customary. It will not do to tell a story about the avoidance of conflict among like-minded friends who are bound together by an unproblematic technical rationality, or by altruism, or exchanges of gifts" (Weber, 2004, p. 88). From the Indonesian cultural perspective, there is a paradox in an OSS project. The project has a noble goal, that is to deliver a software that can be used by anyone. But, in the process of developing the software, conflict is often unavoidable. For many Indonesian people who generally seek to maintain harmony at work, participating in voluntary work full of conflict is just unacceptable. However, the conflict can be much reduced if the goal of the project is clear, the design of technical solutions has been clearly established. So, the initiators of the project should have already solved their design problems before inviting others to contribute to the project.

It can be claimed that there have been a number of successful OSS applications being developed and funded by the government, but the OSS as a mode of development has been failed to develop. Besides culture, the other cause of the failure is institutional incompatibility. Government funded OSS projects were usually carried out by a small team from single government organizations or universities without engaging external communities, because the regime of administration of government projects did not give sufficient flexibility to engage OSS communities that would contribute voluntarily. According to the administration, everything – the number of people who would participate, what would be delivered, the time it would be finished, and the budget being allocated, should be clearly specified in detail and in advance. IGOS initiative, which was formally aimed at promoting the development of OSS, did not address the inflexibility of the administration regime. So the incompatibility of government administration and OSS development governance remained unaddressed and hence unsolved.

There are different opportunities from OSS each of which poses different challenges. The opportunity mostly taken by the government was of the least resistance, namely, diffusing generic applications that would be widely used by end-users, such as operating system and office suite. They were already available, well-proven and widely used by OSS-familiar users. Adopting them at organizational scale could relieve government from great expenses, as has been shown by a number of local governments. OSS proponents wanted the government to do more than just the diffusion of existing OSS. The opportunity was there, because the OSS initiative went simultaneously with the e-government initiative. Together, both initiatives would trigger local OSS development. Given the e-government budget of all government organizations, it should be enough to boost local OSS industry. Unfortunately, OSS based companies are mostly small and could not participate to bid in government projects. While rhetorically the government and others often mention about encouraging startup companies, they did not address the problem of how to engage OSS businesses in government's projects.

People tended to focus on overcoming technical problems and underestimating the rest. Technology was not the only determining factor in the development and diffusion of innovation. To be sustainable, the initiative should develop a well-functioning industry. What the OSS providers should deliver is not a mere product, but solution. When their clients are organizations/businesses, not individual users, the complex utilizations of software often demanded the creation of innovative business models, to make their products/services more flexible and affordable for their clients. "In a commodity world, technologists need to think about innovating in their business models as much as (if not more than) innovating in their technology. Of course, it's a natural trap for the technologist to think about technology alone, but technology is but a small part of the technology business" (Murdock, 2006, p. 102).

CONCLUSION

OSS gives computer users inexpensive or even free alternatives to proprietary softwares. OSS also removes the wall that constrains developing countries to enter into developing their own software industry. The openness of OSS allows software developers to examine the internal working of softwares as well as to freely modify and distribute it. The openness does apply for all, hence the benefits given by OSS is widely and equally distributed, rather than concentrated on a few business players. Different policy approaches are needed to take the advantages of OSS, because the development and business of OSS have different nature from that of proprietary softwares.

Indonesian government has taken major OSS initiative, the IGOS initiative, which was intended to support the diffusion and development of OSS. This initiative allowed the government to combine their power and resources with the knowledge and creativity of communities, R&D organizations and higher educations. While the major concern of government was to overcome the problem of widespread software piracy by replacing illegal softwares with OSS, the others wanted more than just the diffusion of OSS, but also the development of local OSS.

The IGOS initiative soon triggered unhappy responses from overseas businesses, which was suspected to cause the government's signing an MoU with Microsoft. This MoU has weakened the government's messages of support for OSS and made others raise question about the commitment of the government in supporting OSS. Nevertheless, some government organizations have actively organized events and implemented programs to promote the diffusion and development of OSS. But after all these were over, OSS seems to be forgotten in many government organizations, except in few local governments where OSS has strong presence to support not only routine office or administrative works but also back office applications that underly their public services.

Many OSS have been developed and funded by the government. But, they are only open in the sense that they were developed using OSS development tools, while the governance of development itself remain closed, preventing the involvement of volunteers that is usual in common OSS projects. The development of OSS demands for the adoption of special norms and cultures, but also the openness toward the behaviors that violate any norm and culture. It is culturally challenging for society that are used to seek harmony among themselves, especially among people who participate in voluntary works, such as OSS projects. Another source of constraint that prevented open mode of development was the incompatibility between the rigid administration regime of government's project and the open participation of volunteers in common OSS projects.

OSS is the product of people who are not only willing to share their knowledge, but also confront their ideas with one another, and struggle to reach the agreement on technical solutions. All volunteers may bring their own ideas/solutions into an OSS project, for the used ideas/solutions must logically and technically fit with one another, there is high possibility that many ideas/solutions would be abandoned. The involvement in OSS projects can be intellectual, emotional as well as political struggle. Managing OSS projects and being involved in an OSS project demands more than just knowledge and programming skills, but also attitudes and mental toughness, because the norms and cultures of virtual OSS project can be very harsh and totally different from those faced people in their daily life.

REFERENCES

Angelidou, M. (2014). Smart city policies: A spatial approach. *Cities (London, England)*, *41*, S3–S11. doi:10.1016/j.cities.2014.06.007

Arora, A., & Athreye, S. (2002). The software industry and India's economic development. *Information Economics and Policy*, *14*(2), 253–273. doi:10.1016/S0167-6245(01)00069-5

Avgerou, C. (2010). Discourses on ICT and Development. *Information Technologies and International Development*, *6*(3), 1–18.

Beniger, J. R. (1986). *The Control Revolution: Technological and Economic Origins of the Information Society*. Cambridge, MA: Harvard University Press.

Câmara, G., & Fonseca, F. (2007). Information Policies and Open Source Software in Developing Countries. *Journal of the American Society for Information Science and Technology*, *58*(1), 121–132. doi:10.1002/asi.20444

Christensen, C. M. (2000). *The Innovator's Dilemma*. New York, NY: HarperBusiness.

Cordella, A. (2007). E-government: Towards the e-bureaucratic form? *Journal of Information Technology*, *22*(3), 265–274. doi:10.1057/palgrave.jit.2000105

de Miranda, A., Peet, D.-J., Mulder, K. F., Berkman, P. A., Ruddy, T. F., Pillmann, W., & Bijker, W. E. (2007). ICT for Development: Illusions, Promises, Challenges, and Realizations. In W. Shrum, K. R. Benson, W. E. Bijker, & K. Brunnstein (Eds.), *Past, Present and Future of Research in the Information Society* (pp. 13–31). New York, NY: Springer. doi:10.1007/978-0-387-47650-6_2

Dener, C., Watkins, J. A., & Dorotinsky, W. L. (2011). *Financial Management Information Systems: 25 Years of World Bank Experience on What Works and What Doesn't*. Washington, DC: The World Bank. doi:10.1596/978-0-8213-8750-4

DiBona, C. (2006). Open Source and Proprietary Software Development. In C. DiBona, D. Cooper, & M. Stone (Eds.), *Open Sources 2.0: The Continuing Evolution*. Sebastopol, CA: O'Reilly.

DiBona, C., Cooper, D., & Stone, M. (2006). Introduction. In C. DiBona, D. Cooper, & M. Stone (Eds.), *Open Sources 2.0: The Continuing Evolution 2.0*. Sebastopol, CA: O'Reilly.

GitHub. (2018). *The Largest Open Source Community in the World*. Retrieved from https://github.com/open-source

Hayek, F. A. (1945). The Use of Knowledge in Society. *The American Economic Review*, *35*(4).

IIPA. (2010). *2010 Special 301: Indonesia. iN2015 Steering Committee. (2006)*. Singapore: Innovation. Integration. Internationalisation.

Jensen, C., & Scacchi, W. (2010). Governance in Open Source Software Development Projects: A Comparative Multi-level Analysis. In P. Ågerfalk, C. Boldyreff, J. M. González-Barahona, G. R. Madey, & J. Noll (Eds.), *Open Source Software: New Horizons: 6th International IFIP WG 2.13 Conference on Open Source Systems, OSS 2010, Notre Dame, IN, USA, May 30 -- June 2, 2010. Proceedings* (pp. 130–142). Berlin: Springer Berlin Heidelberg. 10.1007/978-3-642-13244-5_11

Layton, E. T. Jr. (1974). Technology as Knowledge. *Technology and Culture*, *15*(1), 31–41. doi:10.2307/3102759

Lerner, J., & Tirole, J. (2002). Some Simple Economics of Open Source. *The Journal of Industrial Economics*, *L*(2).

Loasby, B. J. (1999). *Knowledge, Institutions and Evolution in Economics*. London: Routledge. doi:10.4324/9780203459096

Martin, C. (2016). Shaping the Industry Agenda. In *Annual Report 2015-2016*. Geneva: World Economic Forum.

Marx, K. (1906). *Capital: A Critique of Political Economy*. New York, NY: Random House.

Maulana, I., & Handoko, D. (2006). Tantangan dalam Pengembangan Industri OSS. In Prosiding Seminar Nasional Strategi Pemasyarakatan Open Source Software di Indonesia. Academic Press.

Mesthene, E. G. (1997). The Role of Technology in Society. In K. S. Shrader-Frechette & L. Westra (Eds.), *Technology and Values* (pp. 71–86). Lanham, MD: Rowman & Littlefield Publishers, Inc.

Murdock, I. (2006). Open Source and the Commoditization of Software. In C. DiBona, D. Cooper, & M. Stone (Eds.), *Open Sources 2.0: The Continuing Evolution*. Sebastopol, CA: O'Reilly.

Nagala, S. V. (2005). India's Story of Success: Promoting the Information Technology Industry. *Stanford Journal of International Relations*, *6*(1). Retrieved October 21, 2017 from https://web.stanford.edu/group/sjir/6.1.05_nagala.html

North, D. (1990). *Institutions, Institutional Change and Economic Performance*. Cambridge, MA: Cambridge University Press. doi:10.1017/CBO9780511808678

Nuvolari, A. (2005). Open source software development: Some historical perspectives. *First Monday*, *10*(10). doi:10.5210/fm.v10i10.1284

Oxford Business Group. (2007). *The Report: Emerging Indonesia 2007*. Author.

Parayil, G. (1991a). Technological Change as a Problem-Solving Activity. *Technological Forecasting and Social Change*, *40*(3), 235–247. doi:10.1016/0040-1625(91)90054-J

Parayil, G. (1991b). Technological Knowledge and Technological Change. *Technology in Society*, *13*(3), 289–304. doi:10.1016/0160-791X(91)90005-H

Polese, K. (2006). Foreword: Source Is Everything. In C. DiBona, D. Cooper, & M. Stone (Eds.), *Open Sources 2.0: The Continuing Evolution* (pp. ix–xii). Sebastopol, CA: O'Reilly.

Ratri Adityarani. (2011). *Indonesia Ranks As The 11th Worst Pirating Nation*. Retrieved August 21, 2017, from https://www.techinasia.com/indonesia-pirating-nation

Raymond, E. S. (2001). *The Cathedral and the Bazaar: Musings on Linux and Open Source by an Accidental Revolutionary* (Revised Edition). Sebastopol, CA: O'Reilly.

Rosser, A. (2012). *The Politics of Economic Liberalization in Indonesia: State, Market and Power*. Abingdon, UK: Routledge.

Rusovan, S., Lawford, M., & Parnas, D. L. (2005). Open Source Software Development: Future or Fad? In J. Feller, B. Fitzgerald, S. A. Hissam, & K. R. Lakhani (Eds.), *Perspectives on Free and Open Source Software*. Cambridge, MA: The MIT Press.

Shapiro, C., & Varian, H. R. (1999). *Information Rules: A Strategic Guide to the Network Economy*. Boston, MA: Harvard Business School Press.

Slashdot Media. (2018). *SourceForge*. Retrieved from https://sourceforge.net/about

Stallman, R. (1999). The GNU Operating System and the Free Software Movement. In C. DiBona, S. Ockman, & M. Stone (Eds.), *Open Sources: Voices from the Open Source Revolution*. Sebastopol, CA: O'Reilly.

Stiglitz, J. E. (2002). *Globalization and Its Discontents*. London: Allen Lane.

Susanti, R. D. I., Nurjaya, I. N., Safaat, R., & Djatmika, P. (2014). The Problem of Copyright for Traditional Cultural Expression in Indonesia: The Example of the "Malang Masks." *Journal of Law, Policy and Globalization, 29*, 57–71.

UNCTAD. (2002). Changing Dynamics of Global Computer Software and Services Industry: Implications for Developing Countries (UNCTAD/ITE/TEB/12). New York: UNCTAD.

UNCTAD. (2003). E-commerce and development report (No. UNCTAD/SIDTE/ECB/2003/1). New York: UNCTAD.

UNCTAD. (2004). Road maps towards an information society in Latin America and the Caribbean (No. LC/G.2195/Rev.1-P). Santiago, Chile: UNCTAD.

Utami, M. S. (2018). *28 Universitas Jurusan Kompter Teknik Informatika Terbaik di Indonesia*. Retrieved from http://www.ban-pt-universitas.co/2015/04/universitas-jurusan-komputer-teknik-informatika-terbaik-di-indonesia.html

Vaidhyanathan, S. (2005). Open Source as Culture - Culture as Open Source. In C. Brandt (Ed.), *Open source annual*. Berlin: Technische University. Retrieved November 4, 2017 from https://ssrn.com/abstract=713044

Visser, M. (2010). Constructing organisational learning and knowledge socially: An interactional perspective. *International Journal of Knowledge and Learning, 6*(4), 285–294. doi:10.1504/IJKL.2010.038650

Wasko, M. M., & Faraj, S. (2000). "It is what one does": Why people participate and help others in electronic communities of practice. *The Journal of Strategic Information Systems, 9*(2-3), 155–173. doi:10.1016/S0963-8687(00)00045-7

Weber, S. (2004). *The Success of Open Source*. Cambridge, MA: Harvard University Press.

Weerawarana, S., & Weeratunge, J. (2004). *Open Source in Developing Countries*. Sida.

KEY TERMS AND DEFINITIONS

Copyright: The exclusive legal right, given to an author, a creator, or an assignee to print, publish, perform, film, or record literary, artistic material, or software, and to authorize others to do the same.

Intellectual Property Rights: The rights given to persons over their creations, which are different from those having been created before. The rights give the persons an exclusive right over the use of their creations for a certain period of time, and encompass a collection of rights that include copyrights, trademarks, and patents.

Linux: An operating system that was initially created by Linus Torvalds as a personal project, and then being made open to contributions from thousands of other programmers.

Open Mode of Development: A process of software development which is open to anyone to participate in writing and testing codes, writing manuals, or just giving suggestions and comments. People having Internet access, if they have the necessary skills and knowledge, can participate in open mode of development. Most of open source softwares have been developed through open mode of development.

Open Source Software: A software that is distributed with source code that anyone can read, modify, and compile into a new open source software.

Operating System: A computer software that is running underneath all other softwares on a computer, manages computer hardware and software resources, and provides common services requested by other softwares.

Proprietary Software: A commercial software that is the opposite of open source software, its source code is kept secret by the developers or company that developed it.

Source Code: A text listing of commands written in a programming language to be compiled or assembled into an executable computer program. A source code is understood by human programmers and cannot directly be executed by computers. In order for a source code to be executable by computers, it has first to be converted into a machine executable code.

This research was previously published in The Role of Knowledge Transfer in Open Innovation; pages 139-157, copyright year 2019 by Information Science Reference (an imprint of IGI Global).

Chapter 10

Understanding Users' Contributions in Open Source Software Communities:
A Social Influence Perspective

Tao Zhou

School of Management, Hangzhou Dianzi University, China

ABSTRACT

User contributions are crucial to the success of open source software (OSS) communities. As users conduct frequent interactions between each other, their contribution behaviour may receive the social influence from other members. Drawing on the social influence theory, this research examined user contributions in OSS communities. The results indicated that contribution intention is significantly affected by social identity, which includes cognitive, affective and evaluative identity. In addition, the researchers found that the subjective norm has a negative effect on contribution intention. The results imply that service providers need to enhance user identification with the community in order to facilitate their contribution in OSS communities.

INTRODUCTION

Open source software (OSS) has received wide adoption among enterprises in recent years (Ghapanchi, 2015). For example, Taobao, which is the largest e-commerce website in China, has applied OSS in its operation systems, servers and databases. The OSS has helped Taobao to burden the huge amount of views and transactions, especially on November 11, which is similar to Black Friday in US. A few reputable companies such as Google and Facebook have also actively adopted OSS in their business operations (Spaeth, von Krogh & He, 2015). OSS communities provide a platform for programmers to effectively interact with each other and collectively develop software. They can release projects, discuss with other members and optimize project codes. Github is a representative OSS community. Compared to these well-known OSS communities, other communities face a few problems such as inactive user

DOI: 10.4018/978-1-7998-9158-1.ch010

participation, lack of quality OSS projects, and poor maintenance of projects (Ho & Rai, 2017). Among these, users' contribution is crucial to the success of OSS communities (Spaeth et al., 2015). If users contribute little to a community, the service provider cannot survive in the intense competition as the community loses its value to users. Service providers need to understand the factors affecting user contribution. Then they can take effective measures to facilitate user contribution and ensure the continuous development of OSS communities.

Previous research has examined OSS user behaviour from multiple perspectives, such as the motivational theory (Choi & Pruett, 2015; Spaeth et al., 2015), flow (Csikszentmihalyi & Csikszentmihalyi, 1988; Daniel and Stewart, 2016), reputation (Cai and Zhu, 2016), and network structure (Choi & Chengalur-Smith, 2015; Behfar, Turkina & Burger-Helmchen, 2018). Various factors such as intrinsic motivation, attention, and user reputation are found to affect OSS users' behaviour. In addition to these internal factors, users may also receive external social influence from other members as they actively interact with each other in a community. For example, users may comply with other important members' opinions to contribute their knowledge on a project. They may also internalize group values into their own beliefs and develop a strong identification with the community, such as membership, belongingness, and attachment. These social influences may affect a user's behaviour in OSS communities.

The purpose of this research is to draw on the social influence theory to examine users' contribution in OSS communities. As users conduct frequent social interactions with other members in a community, they may form close social networking relationships between each other. Then their behavioural decision such as contribution may receive social influence from others. According to the social influence theory, an individual user's behaviour is affected by three social processes: compliance, identification and internalization, which is represented by subjective norm, social identity and group norm, respectively (Dholakia, Bagozzi & Pearo, 2004). In addition, social identity consists of three dimensions: cognitive, affective and evaluative. This research will identify the relative effect of these social influence factors on user contribution in OSS communities. The results enrich extant research on OSS user behaviour and advance our understanding of OSS community users' contribution. As noted earlier, although extant research has identified the effect of internal factors such as motivations (Spaeth et al., 2015) and flow (Daniel & Stewart, 2016) on user behaviour, it has seldom examined the effect of external social influence on user contribution in OSS communities. However, as a member of communities, individual user behaviour may receive social influence from other members. This research tries to fill the gap. The results imply that service providers need to consider the effect of social influence when facilitating users' contribution in OSS communities.

RESEARCH MODEL AND HYPOTHESES

OSS Community User Behaviour

As an emerging service, OSS community user behaviour has received attention from information systems researchers. They have examined the intrinsic motivations affecting user behaviour. found that both credibility and openness affect social identification, which in turn affects users' intrinsic motivation to participate in OSS projects. reported that library OSS users have a high level of intrinsic motivations, which include altruism and fun.

Other researchers examined OSS user behaviour from the perspectives of reputation, socialization and user experience. noted that an OSS user's reputation is determined by coding quality, community experience and collaboration experience. In addition, reputation affects project success. suggested that both socialization factors of social identification and social integration affect contributor performance in OSS projects. noted that both core and peripheral members in OSS communities use positive politeness strategies. stated that interactive discussion and externally focused user attention affect a project's success. found that two quality controls, which include accreditation and code acceptance, influence users' continued participation.

A few studies have investigated the effect of network structure on user behaviour. suggested that user support network, which includes structural and junctional embeddedness, affects OSS popularity, which reflects the number of active users and downloads of the software. noted that direct and indirect network effects influence the characteristics of OSS projects for the general population. found that intragroup density and users' centrality affect intergroup coupling in OSS communities.

As we can see from these studies, they have examined OSS community user behaviour from multiple perspectives, such as user motivations and reputation. However, in addition to these internal factors, the external social influence may also affect an individual user's behaviour as the user interacts with other members in a community. This research will examine users' contribution in OSS communities from a social influence perspective.

Social Influence Theory

Social influence reflects that an individual's attitudes, beliefs and behaviors are influenced by referent others (Kelman, 1958). Social influence consists of three processes: compliance, identification and internalization (Dholakia et al., 2004). Compliance reflects that a user accepts influences to gain rewards or avoid punishments (Wang, Meister, & Gray, 2013). Identification reflects a user's identification with a community, such as attachment and belongingness. Internalization reflects that a user assimilates group norms into his or her own beliefs.

Social influence theory has been attached great importance in the information systems research. It has been applied to examine user behaviour in various contexts, which include knowledge management (Wang et al., 2013), virtual communities (Tsai & Bagozzi, 2014; Chou, Wang, & Tang, 2015; Wang, Hsiao, Yang, & Hajli, 2016b), social networking services (Zhou & Li, 2014; Cheung, Lee & Chan, 2015; Wang & Chou, 2016), electronic health records (EHR) (Wang, Zhao, Sun & Zhou, 2016a), knowledge sharing (Liao, 2017), and online travelling (Sedera, Lokuge, Atapattu & Gretzel, 2017). Prior research has focused on the single effect of compliance (Venkatesh, Morris, Davis & Davis, 2003). Recently, it has also paid attention to the other two processes of social influence: identification and internalization (Tsai & Bagozzi, 2014; Zhou & Li, 2014). In this research, we will examine the effects of these three social influence processes on users' contribution in OSS communities.

Subjective Norm

Subjective norm reflects that a user's behaviour is influenced by those people who are important to him or her. When a user's social circle members such as friends or colleagues suggest him or her to share codes in a community, the user may comply with their opinions even if he or she has not formed a positive attitude toward the community. This represents a compliance process as users feel an urge to behave in accordance with these external pressures. Subjective norm has been identified to be a significant factor affecting user behaviour in the information systems research (Venkatesh et al., 2003; Luarn, Yang, & Chiu, 2015; Yoon & Rolland, 2015). Thus, we suggest:

H1: Subjective norm is positively related to users' contribution intention in OSS communities.

Social Identity

Social identity reflects a user's identification with a community. That is, the user accepts influences to build a beneficial relationship with the community (Wang et al., 2013). When users have participated in a community for a long time, they may gain a good understanding of the community norms and develop identification with the community, such as membership, attachment and belongingness. This may promote their commitment and contribution behaviour (Chou & Hung, 2016).

According to, social identity includes three dimensions: cognitive, affective and evaluative. This measurement has been adopted in much research (Wang et al., 2013; Tsai & Bagozzi, 2014). Cognitive social identity means that a user's self-identity and value are consistent with those of a community. For example, online OSS communities always encourage users' contribution or sharing. When a user finds that this is also their own belief, they may volunteer to share codes in the community. In contrast, if the user feels that contribution is not in their interest, they may lurk in the community. Affective social identity reflects a user's emotional connections with a community, such as attachment and belongingness. These emotional feelings may enhance a user's relationship with the community and facilitate his or her continuance (Kordzadeh & Warren, 2017; Lin, Featherman & Sarker, 2017). Evaluative social identity reflects a user's feelings of influence in a community. When users find that the software or codes, they contribute are valuable to other members, they may feel a sense of accomplishment and importance. This may in turn facilitate their continued contribution. Evaluative identity is similar to peer recognition, which is found to affect knowledge contribution in online question and answer communities (Jin, Li, Zhong & Zhai, 2015). Previous research has found that social identity affects social commerce users' purchasing behaviour (Wang, Yeh & Yen, 2015), co-creation activities between customers and firms (Wang et al., 2016b), e-learning (Hwang, 2016), and social networking usage (Koohikamali, Peak & Prybutok, 2017; Pan, Lu, Wang & Chau, 2017). In line with these studies, we suggest:

H2: Social identity is positively related to users' contribution intention in OSS communities.

Group Norm

Group norm reflects the shared values and beliefs held by community members (Dholakia et al., 2004), which may guide a user's behaviour in a community. It is often used to represent an internalization process. When users assimilate group norms into their own beliefs, they may be motivated to contribute in a community. They may feel an obligation to contribute their knowledge in the community as this reflects their own value. In contrast, if users have not recognized group norm, they may be unwilling to share codes in a community. Previous research has found the effect of group norm on physicians' use of EHR (Wang et al., 2016a) and consumers' continuance of social networking applications (Wang & Chou, 2016). Consistent with these results, we suggest:

H3: Group norm is positively related to users' contribution intention in OSS communities.

According to the theory of reasoned action and the theory of planned behaviour, behavioural intention is a significant determinant of actual behaviour (Fishbein & Ajzen, 1975; Ajzen, 1991). Thus:

H4: Contribution intention is positively related to contribution behaviour.

Figure 1 shows the research model. As a second-order factor, social identity is composed of three reflective factors: cognitive, affective and evaluative social identity.

Figure 1. Research model

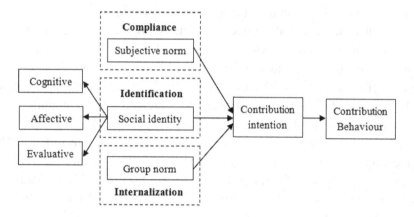

METHOD

Data were collected at a university campus. University students are an appropriate sample for the study as they represent an important group of internet users (CNNIC, 2017). In addition, they are young and well-educated. This enables them to have the knowledge and expertise necessary to share codes in OSS communities. The questionnaires were distributed to graduate students majoring in computer science, who have a good understanding of computer-related knowledge and a relatively rich experience of coding. They were asked to fill the questionnaire based on their usage experience of OSS communities. We scrutinized all responses and dropped those with missing values. In addition, we only included those responses that had actual contribution experience as we measured actual behaviour in this research. As a result, we obtained 351 valid responses. Among these samples, 71.23% were male and 28.77% were female. The frequently used OSS communities include Github, CSDN (China Software Developer Network), Oschina, and Linux China, which represent a few popular OSS communities in China. The results indicated that a majority of users (66.4%) have contributed more than twice in OSS communities during the latest half year.

The research model includes seven factors. Except contribution behaviour, other factors were measured with multiple items. All items were adapted from extant literature to ensure content validity. When the instrument was developed, it was sent to three information systems researchers for their advice. Then based on their suggestions, we revised a few items to improve the clarity and comprehensibility. The final items and their sources are listed in the Appendix. Each item was measured with a seven-Likert scale ranging from strongly disagree to strongly agree.

Items of subjective norm were adapted from to reflect the influence of those important people on an individual user's behaviour. Items of cognitive social identity were adapted from to reflect that a user's value and working style are consistent with those of a community. Items of emotional social identity were adapted from to measure a user's feelings of closeness, membership and proudness. Items of evaluative social identity were adapted from to measure a user's perceived importance and influence in a community. Two items of group norm were adapted from to reflect a user's perceived strength of holding shared values by community members. Items of contribution intention were adapted from to measure a user's intention to share software or codes in a community. Contribution behaviour was measured with an item reflecting the frequency of sharing codes in the community.

We conducted two tests to examine the common method variance. First, we performed a Harman's single-factor test (Podsakoff, MacKenzie, Lee & Podsakoff, 2003). The results indicated that the largest variance explained by an individual factor is 19.27%. Thus, none of the factors can explain the majority of the variance. Second, we modeled all items as the indicators of a factor representing the method effect and re-estimated the model. The results indicated a poor fitness. For example, the Goodness of Fit Index (GFI) is 0.506 (<0.90). The Adjusted Goodness of Fit Index (AGFI) is 0.374 (<0.80). The results of both tests indicated that common method variance is not a significant problem in our research.

RESULTS

We followed a two-step approach to conduct data analysis. First, we examined the measurement model to test reliability and validity. Then we examined the structural model to test research hypotheses.

First, we performed a confirmatory factor analysis to examine the validity, which includes both convergent and discriminant validity. As Table 1 lists, all item loadings are larger than 0.7 and significant at 0.001. Each AVE (the average variance extracted) exceeds 0.5 and each CR (the composite reliability) exceeds 0.7. This suggests good convergent validity (Gefen, Straub & Boudreau, 2000). In addition, all Alpha values are larger than 0.7, suggesting good reliability.

To examine the discriminant validity, we compared the square root of AVE and factor correlation coefficients. As listed in Table 2, for each factor, the square root of AVE is significantly larger than its correlation coefficients with other factors, suggesting good discriminant validity.

Second, we employed structural equation modeling software LISREL to estimate the structural model. The results are presented in Figure 2. Table 3 lists the recommended and actual values of a few indices. All of them are within the threshold values. The explained variance of contribution intention and contribution behaviour is 50.9% and 11.6%, respectively.

DISCUSSION

As shown in Figure 2, social identity has a significant effect on contribution intention, which in turn affects contribution behaviour. Thus, H2 and H4 are supported. We did not find any effect of group norm on contribution intention.

Table 1. Standardized item loadings, AVE, CR and Alpha values

Factor	Item	Standardized Loading	AVE	CR	Alpha
Subjective norm (SN)	SN1	0.928	0.86	0.92	0.92
	SN2	0.921			
Cognitive social identity (CSI)	CSI1	0.856	0.74	0.92	0.92
	CSI2	0.850			
	CSI3	0.881			
	CSI4	0.853			
Affective social identity (ASI)	ASI1	0.859	0.80	0.92	0.92
	ASI2	0.937			
	ASI3	0.887			
Evaluative social identity (ESI)	ESI1	0.911	0.80	0.94	0.94
	ESI2	0.900			
	ESI3	0.890			
	ESI4	0.869			
Group norm (GN)	GN1	0.891	0.77	0.87	0.87
	GN2	0.864			
Contribution intention (CI)	CI1	0.880	0.74	0.90	0.89
	CI2	0.911			
	CI3	0.786			

Table 2. The square root of AVE (shown as bold at diagonal) and factor correlation coefficients

Factor	SN	CSI	ASI	ESI	GN	CI
SN	**0.925**					
CSI	0.601	**0.860**				
ASI	0.585	0.643	**0.895**			
ESI	0.528	0.496	0.629	**0.893**		
GN	0.356	0.428	0.538	0.546	**0.878**	
CI	0.379	0.592	0.485	0.527	0.519	**0.861**

Figure 2. The results estimated by LISREL

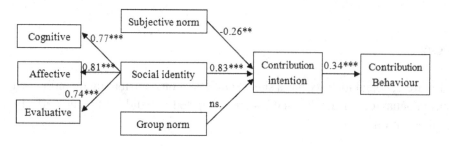

Table 3. The recommended and actual values of fit indices

Fit Indices	GFI	AGFI	CFI	NFI	NNFI	RMSEA
Recommended value	>0.90	>0.80	>0.90	>0.90	>0.90	<0.08
Actual value	0.940	0.895	0.977	0.967	0.966	0.079

Note: GFI is Goodness of Fit Index, AGFI is the Adjusted Goodness of Fit Index, CFI is the Comparative Fit Index, NFI is the Normed Fit Index, NNFI is the Non-Normed Fit Index, RMSEA is Root Mean Square Error of Approximation

The results indicated that subjective norm has a significant but negative effect $(\gamma = -0.26, P < 0.01)$ on contribution intention. This is contrary to our hypothesis, which suggests the positive effect. This demonstrates that when users receive great pressure from their social circle, they may have low intention to contribute their knowledge in a community. This may be for three reasons. First, the strong effect of social identity on contribution intention may attenuate that of subjective norm. We removed social identity from the research and re-estimated the model. The results indicated the positive effect of subjective norm on contribution intention. Second, previous research has found that when users have gained more experience, the effect of subjective norm on their behavioural intention may gradually diminish to be insignificant (Venkatesh & Davis, 2000; Xiao & Wang, 2016). Our results disclosed that users not only ignore external pressure when determining their behaviour, but also dislike this pressure to some extent. Third, our sample is composed of graduate students. They represent junior members that are not well-established in their field. They are desperate for the approval of their seniors. When they are not sure that they can obtain this approval, they may be tentative to contribute their knowledge in an OSS community.

Social identity has a strong effect $(\gamma = 0.83, P < 0.001)$ on contribution intention. This suggests that users attach great importance to identification when deciding their contribution in a community. This result is consistent with previous research (Lin et al., 2017; Wan, Lu, Wang & Zhao, 2017), which has identified the significant effect of identification on user behaviour. Social identity may act as a social sanction that prevented their inactive participation. If users contributed little in an OSS community, they may lose their membership and influence in the community. To some extent, social identity is similar to sense of community including four factors of membership, influence, needs satisfaction and emotional connection, which has been found to affect social networking users' behaviour (Zhang, 2010; Mamonov, Koufaris & Benbunan-Fich, 2016). In addition, our results indicated that three factors of cognitive, affective and evaluative identity have high loadings (0.77, 0.81, and 0.74, respectively) on the second-order factor. This suggests that it is appropriate to measure social identity with these three reflective factors. Thus, when developing users' social identity, service providers need to be concerned with these three factors simultaneously. They need to enhance users' feelings of membership, attachment, belongingness and influence in the community.

We did not find the significant effect of group norm on contribution intention. This indicates that users are not concerned with shared values and beliefs when deciding their contribution in a community. They pay more attention to their identification with the community rather than group norm that is held by community members. In addition, we removed the path from social identity to contribution intention and re-estimated the model. The results disclosed the significant effect of group norm on contribution intention. This suggests that the effect of social identity on contribution intention overshadows that of group norm on contribution intention.

IMPLICATIONS AND LIMITATIONS

From a theoretical perspective, this research examined users' contribution in OSS communities from a social influence perspective. Although previous research has found the effect of user perceptions such as intrinsic motivations, reputation and flow on OSS users' behaviour, it has seldom examined the effect of social influence received from community members on an individual user's behaviour. This research tries to fill the gap. The results revealed that social influence has a significant effect on OSS community users' contribution. These results advance our understanding of OSS user behaviour. Second, we found that among three factors representing social influence, social identity has the strongest effect on contribution intention. This highlights the central role of identification in facilitating users' contribution behaviour. In addition, we found that subjective norm has a negative effect on user contribution. This result is contrary to previous findings. Future research can validate the effect of subjective norm in other contexts such as social commerce. Third, social influence theory has been examined in various contexts such as knowledge management, social networking and EHR. This research generalizes it to an emerging context: online OSS communities. We found that about half of the variance of contribution intention is explained by social influence. These results enrich extant research on social influence.

From a managerial perspective, the results imply that service providers need to be concerned with social influence when facilitating users' contribution in OSS communities. As social identity is the main factor affecting user contribution, service providers need to enhance users' identification with the community. For example, in addition to building online membership, they may organize offline activities to increase users' social identity. They may also improve community platforms such as system quality and service quality in order to develop users' emotional connection with the community (Zhang, 2010).

This research has a few limitations. First, our sample is composed of university students. Although they represent an important group of internet users, future research needs to generalize our results to other samples such as enterprise employees. In addition, our results need to be generalized to other reputable OSS communities, such as SourceForge. Second, besides the social influence, there are other factors possibly affecting users' contribution, such as culture and consumerist tendency. Future research may consider their effects. Third, we mainly conducted a cross-sectional study. However, user behaviour is dynamic. Thus, a longitudinal research may provide more insights into user behaviour development.

ACKNOWLEDGMENT

This work was supported by National Natural Science Foundation of China (71771069).

REFERENCES

Ajzen, I. (1991). The theory of planned behavior. *Organizational Behavior and Human Decision Processes*, *50*(2), 179–211. doi:10.1016/0749-5978(91)90020-T

Behfar, S. K., Turkina, E., & Burger-Helmchen, T. (2018). Knowledge management in OSS communities: Relationship between dense and sparse network structures. *International Journal of Information Management*, *38*(1), 167–174. doi:10.1016/j.ijinfomgt.2017.09.004

Cai, Y., & Zhu, D. (2016). Reputation in an open source software community: Antecedents and impacts. *Decision Support Systems, 91*(Supplement C), 103–112. doi:10.1016/j.dss.2016.08.004

Carillo, K., Huff, S., & Chawner, B. (2017). What makes a good contributor? Understanding contributor behavior within large Free/Open Source Software projects – A socialization perspective. *The Journal of Strategic Information Systems, 26*(4), 322–359. doi:10.1016/j.jsis.2017.03.001

Cheung, C., Lee, Z. W. Y., & Chan, T. K. H. (2015). Self-disclosure in social networking sites The role of perceived cost, perceived benefits and social influence. *Internet Research, 25*(2), 279–299. doi:10.1108/IntR-09-2013-0192

Chiu, C.-M., Hsu, M.-H., & Wang, E. T. G. (2006). Understanding knowledge sharing in virtual communities: An integration of social capital and social cognitive theories. *Decision Support Systems, 42*(3), 1872–1888. doi:10.1016/j.dss.2006.04.001

Choi, N., & Chengalur-Smith, I. (2015). Characteristics of open source software projects for the general population: Reciprocity and network effects. *Journal of Computer Information Systems, 56*(1), 22–30. doi:10.1080/08874417.2015.11645797

Choi, N., & Pruett, J. A. (2015). The characteristics and motivations of library open source software developers: An empirical study. *Library & Information Science Research, 37*(2), 109–117. doi:10.1016/j.lisr.2015.02.007

Chou, C. H., Wang, Y. S., & Tang, T. I. (2015). Exploring the determinants of knowledge adoption in virtual communities: A social influence perspective. *International Journal of Information Management, 35*(3), 364–376. doi:10.1016/j.ijinfomgt.2015.02.001

Chou, S. W., & Hung, I. H. (2016). Understanding knowledge outcome improvement at the post-adoption stage in a virtual community. *Information Technology & People, 29*(4), 774–806. doi:10.1108/ITP-05-2015-0121

CNNIC. (2017). *The 40th China Statistical Report on Internet Development*. China Internet Network Information Center.

Csikszentmihalyi, M., & Csikszentmihalyi, I. S. (1988). *Optimal experience: psychological studies of flow in consciousness*. Cambridge: Cambridge University Press. doi:10.1017/CBO9780511621956

Daniel, S., & Stewart, K. (2016). Open source project success: Resource access, flow, and integration. *The Journal of Strategic Information Systems, 25*(3), 159–176. doi:10.1016/j.jsis.2016.02.006

Dholakia, U. M., Bagozzi, R. P., & Pearo, L. K. (2004). A social influence model of consumer participation in network- and small-group-based virtual communities. *International Journal of Research in Marketing, 21*(3), 241–263. doi:10.1016/j.ijresmar.2003.12.004

Fishbein, M., & Ajzen, I. (1975). *Belief, Attitude, Intention and Behavior: An Introduction to Theory and Research*. Reading, MA: Addison-Wesley.

Gefen, D., Straub, D. W., & Boudreau, M. C. (2000). Structural equation modeling and regression: Guidelines for research practice. *Communications of the Association for Information Systems, 4*(7), 1–70.

Ghapanchi, A. H. (2015). Investigating the interrelationships among success measures of open source software projects. *Journal of Organizational Computing and Electronic Commerce, 25*(1), 28–46. doi :10.1080/10919392.2015.990775

Ho, S. Y., & Rai, A. (2017). Continued voluntary participation intention in firm-participating open source software projects. *Information Systems Research, 28*(3), 603–625. doi:10.1287/isre.2016.0687

Hwang, Y. (2016). Understanding social influence theory and personal goals in e-learning. *Information Development, 32*(3), 466–477. doi:10.1177/0266666914556688

Jin, J., Li, Y., Zhong, X., & Zhai, L. (2015). Why users contribute knowledge to online communities: An empirical study of an online social Q&A community. *Information & Management, 52*(7), 840–849. doi:10.1016/j.im.2015.07.005

Kelman, H. C. (1958). Compliance, identification, and internalization: Three processes of attitude change. *The Journal of Conflict Resolution, 2*(1), 51–60. doi:10.1177/002200275800200106

Koohikamali, M., Peak, D. A., & Prybutok, V. R. (2017). Beyond self-disclosure: Disclosure of information about others in social network sites. *Computers in Human Behavior, 69*, 29–42. doi:10.1016/j. chb.2016.12.012

Kordzadeh, N., & Warren, J. (2017). Communicating personal health information in virtual health communities: An integration of privacy calculus model and affective commitment. *Journal of the Association for Information Systems, 18*(1), 45–81. doi:10.17705/1jais.00446

Liao, T. H. (2017). Developing an antecedent model of knowledge sharing intention in virtual communities. *Universal Access in the Information Society, 16*(1), 215–224. doi:10.100710209-016-0452-5

Lin, M.-J. J., Hung, S.-W., & Chen, C.-J. (2009). Fostering the determinants of knowledge sharing in professional virtual communities. *Computers in Human Behavior, 25*(4), 929–939. doi:10.1016/j. chb.2009.03.008

Lin, X., Featherman, M., & Sarker, S. (2017). Understanding factors affecting users' social networking site continuance: A gender difference perspective. *Information & Management, 54*(3), 383–395. doi:10.1016/j.im.2016.09.004

Luarn, P., Yang, J. C., & Chiu, Y. P. (2015). Why people check In to social network sites. *International Journal of Electronic Commerce, 19*(4), 21–46. doi:10.1080/10864415.2015.1029353

Mamonov, S., Koufaris, M., & Benbunan-Fich, R. (2016). The role of the sense of community in the sustainability of social network sites. *International Journal of Electronic Commerce, 20*(4), 470–498. doi:10.1080/10864415.2016.1171974

Pan, Z., Lu, Y. B., Wang, B., & Chau, P. Y. K. (2017). Who do you think you are? Common and differential effects of social self-identity on social media usage. *Journal of Management Information Systems, 34*(1), 71–101. doi:10.1080/07421222.2017.1296747

Podsakoff, P. M., MacKenzie, S. B., Lee, J. Y., & Podsakoff, N. P. (2003). Common method biases in behavioral research: A critical review of the literature and recommended remedies. *The Journal of Applied Psychology, 88*(5), 879–903. doi:10.1037/0021-9010.88.5.879 PMID:14516251

Sedera, D., Lokuge, S., Atapattu, M., & Gretzel, U. (2017). Likes—The key to my happiness: The moderating effect of social influence on travel experience. *Information & Management*, *54*(6), 825–836. doi:10.1016/j.im.2017.04.003

Spaeth, S., von Krogh, G., & He, F. (2015). Perceived firm attributes and intrinsic motivation in sponsored open source software projects. *Information Systems Research*, *26*(1), 224–237. doi:10.1287/isre.2014.0539

Sutanto, J., Kankanhalli, A., & Tan, B. C. Y. (2014). Uncovering the relationship between OSS user support networks and OSS popularity. *Decision Support Systems*, *64*(Supplement C), 142–151. doi:10.1016/j.dss.2014.05.014

Tiwana, A., & Bush, A. A. (2005). Continuance in expertise-sharing networks: A social perspective. *IEEE Transactions on Engineering Management*, *52*(1), 85–101. doi:10.1109/TEM.2004.839956

Tsai, H.-T., & Bagozzi, R. P. (2014). Contribution behavior in virtual communities: Cognitive, emotional, and social influences. *Management Information Systems Quarterly*, *38*(1), 143–163. doi:10.25300/MISQ/2014/38.1.07

Venkatesh, V., & Davis, F. D. (2000). A theoretical extension of the technology acceptance model: Four longitudinal field studies. *Management Science*, *46*(2), 186–204. doi:10.1287/mnsc.46.2.186.11926

Venkatesh, V., Morris, M. G., Davis, G. B., & Davis, F. D. (2003). User acceptance of information technology: Toward a unified view. *Management Information Systems Quarterly*, *27*(3), 425–478. doi:10.2307/30036540

Wan, J., Lu, Y., Wang, B., & Zhao, L. (2017). How attachment influences users' willingness to donate to content creators in social media: A socio-technical systems perspective. *Information & Management*, *54*(7), 837–850. doi:10.1016/j.im.2016.12.007

Wang, E. S. T., & Chou, N. P. Y. (2016). Examining social influence factors affecting consumer continuous usage intention for mobile social networking applications. *International Journal of Mobile Communications*, *14*(1), 43–55. doi:10.1504/IJMC.2016.073358

Wang, T., Yeh, R. K. J., & Yen, D. C. (2015). Influence of customer identification on online usage and purchasing behaviors in social commerce. *International Journal of Human-Computer Interaction*, *31*(11), 805–814. doi:10.1080/10447318.2015.1067481

Wang, W., Zhao, X. P., Sun, J. L., & Zhou, G. Q. (2016a). Exploring physicians' extended use of electronic health records (EHRs): A social influence perspective. *The HIM Journal*, *45*(3), 134–143. doi:10.1177/1833358316651764 PMID:27246917

Wang, Y., Hsiao, S.-H., Yang, Z., & Hajli, N. (2016b). The impact of sellers' social influence on the cocreation of innovation with customers and brand awareness in online communities. *Industrial Marketing Management*, *54*, 56–70. doi:10.1016/j.indmarman.2015.12.008

Wang, Y. L., Meister, D. B., & Gray, P. H. (2013). Social influence and knowledge management systems use: Evidence from panel data. *Management Information Systems Quarterly*, *37*(1), 299–313. doi:10.25300/MISQ/2013/37.1.13

Wei, K., Crowston, K., Eseryel, U. Y., & Heckman, R. (2017). Roles and politeness behavior in community-based free/libre open source software development. *Information & Management*, *54*(5), 573–582. doi:10.1016/j.im.2016.11.006

Xiao, X., & Wang, T. N. (2016). The implications of social influence theory on continuance intention for social networking among Chinese university students. *Journal of Organizational and End User Computing*, *28*(4), 55–72. doi:10.4018/JOEUC.2016100104

Yoon, C., & Rolland, E. (2015). Understanding continuance use in social networking services. *Journal of Computer Information Systems*, *55*(2), 1–8. doi:10.1080/08874417.2015.11645751

Zhang, Z. (2010). Feeling the sense of community in social networking usage. *IEEE Transactions on Engineering Management*, *57*(2), 225–239. doi:10.1109/TEM.2009.2023455

Zhou, T., & Li, H. (2014). Understanding mobile SNS continuance usage in China from the perspectives of social influence and privacy concern. *Computers in Human Behavior*, *37*, 283–289. doi:10.1016/j.chb.2014.05.008

This research was previously published in the International Journal of Technology and Human Interaction (IJTHI), 16(4); pages 105-117, copyright year 2020 by IGI Publishing (an imprint of IGI Global).

APPENDIX: MEASUREMENT SCALE AND ITEMS

Subjective norm (SN) (adapted from Venkatesh and Davis (2000))

SN1: Most people that influence my behaviour think that I should share open source software or codes in this community.

SN2: Most people that are important to me think that I should share open source software or codes in this community.

Cognitive social identity (CSI) (adapted from Lin et al. (2009))

CSI1: Sharing open source software or codes in this community is consistent with my values.

CSI2: Sharing open source software or codes in this community can meet my learning or working needs.

CSI3: Sharing open source software or codes in this community is consistent with my previous experiences.

CSI4: Sharing open source software or codes in this community is consistent with my working style.

Affective social identity (ASI) (adapted from Chiu et al. (2006))

ASI1: This community gives me a feeling of solidarity and closeness.

ASI2: I feel that I am a member of this community.

ASI3: I am proud of being a member of this community.

Evaluative social identity (ESI) (adapted from Tiwana and Bush (2005))

ESI1: Other members of the community think that the open source software or codes I provided are valuable.

ESI2: Other members of the community think that the open source software or codes I provided are useful.

ESI3: Other members of the community think that the open source software or codes I provided are helpful.

ESI4: Other members of the community think that the open source software or codes I provided are important.

Group norm (GN) (adapted from Dholakia et al. (2004))

Promoting codes sharing in the community can be considered a goal. For each of the members in the community, please estimate the strength with which each holds the goal.

GN1: Strength of the shared goal by yourself.

GN2: Average of the strength of the shared goal by other members.

Contribution intention (CI) (adapted from Venkatesh and Davis (2000)):

CI1: I will continue sharing open source software or codes in this community.

CI2: In the next half year, I intend to share open source software or codes in this community.

CI3: If possible, I will share open source software or codes in this community.

Contribution behaviour (CB) (adapted from Dholakia et al. (2004))

The frequency of my sharing open source software or codes in this community during the latest half year is: none, one time, two or three times, four or five times, six or seven times, eight or nine times, ten times or more.

Chapter 11

Trust in Open Source Software Development Communities:
A Comprehensive Analysis

Amitpal Singh Sohal

Research Scholar, IKG Punjab Technical University, Kapurthala, Punjab, India

Sunil Kumar Gupta

Department of Computer Science and Engineering, Beant College of Engineering and Technology, Gurdaspur, Punjab, India

Hardeep Singh

Department of Computer Science, Guru Nanak Dev University, Amritsar, Punjab, India

ABSTRACT

This study presents the significance of trust for the formation of an Open Source Software Development (OSSD) community. OSSD has various challenges that must be overcome for its successful operation. First is the development of a community, which requires a healthy community formation environment. Taking into consideration various factors for community formation, a strong sense of TRUST among its members has been felt. Trust development is a slow process with various methods for building and maintaining it. OSSD is teamwork but the team is of unknowns and volunteers. Trust forms a pillar for effective cooperation, which leads to a reduction in conflicts and risks, associated with quality software development. This study offers an overview of various existing trust models, which aids in the development of a trust evaluation framework for OSSD communities. Towards the end of the study, various components of the trust evaluation along with an empirical framework for the same have been proposed.

DOI: 10.4018/978-1-7998-9158-1.ch011

1. INTRODUCTION

Open source software development (OSSD) is an ideology, which has paved the way for which dedicated teams of volunteer software developers participate and contribute in various areas of software engineering. The aim of OSSD communities is to make a high quality and reliable software, no matter how complex an application may be (Asundi, 2001). The project is initiated by the core team and is made open for developers across the globe to contributing code and feature enhancements. The core team of the project analyzes the contributions from various contributors. The core team may have single or number of coordinators. Coordinators are project creators and are responsible for the evolution and growth of the community. They would take the final decision to incorporate the received code into the final build and release the next test version of the software. After rigorous testing and debugging when the required quality of software is achieved, test versions of software are promoted to be the next stable release. Further, with the passage of time new contributions in form of bug fixes and feature enhancements for the software are received. The same cycle of thorough testing and integration of code into existing software is followed. Every effort is done to attract more and more people towards the project and with the passage of time the community grows. The team members of the OSSD community provide feedback, which acts as a base for the planning of future project managing strategies. With constant efforts, gradually, the project attains high quality and upcoming issues are dealt with even better ways. The ways in which development work is coordinated and communicated amongst the developers makes it different from existing software development strategies and this is what is unique. It is intended to perform a study for improvement of the relationship among the virtual team members of an OSSD community, which in turn enhances the quality of the developed open source software. We move ahead with this work, keeping in mind the following research objectives.

1.1. Research Objectives

This study is performed to accomplish the following research objectives:

- To formulate various challenges associated with OSSD;
- To study the relevance of trust for open source systems;
- To study various methods for building and sustaining trust;
- To propose a trust evaluation framework for OSSD communities.

To achieve the aforementioned objectives of our research, a comprehensive literature analysis has been conducted. Various papers covering the nature of OSSD, existing models of software production, challenges associated with OSSD have been analyzed. Trust related aspects like trust characteristics, importance to OSSD communities, methods for building and sustaining trust in OSSD communities, existing OSSD trust models, contributions and suggestions of various researchers for trust building in virtual teams have been also analyzed.

To collect the relevant literature for this study, following search terms or keywords were used:

- Trust;
- Trust framework for open source software development communities;
- Trust in virtual teams;

- Trust in social networks;
- Trust evaluation frameworks;
- Trust enhancement mechanism.

About one hundred research papers, articles, primary studies, and few HTML pages had been downloaded. Those research papers and articles (about 60) were selected and reviewed which covered various aspects of trust, its need, importance, trust building methods, and various existing trust models. The special consideration was given to the literature related to trust building in virtual teams. It has been felt that in order to bind the virtual teams involved in OSSD, a strong need for trust amongst the team members is essential.

This research paper has been organized into eight sections each covering different aspects of OSSD movement. Section 1 provides a brief introduction to the process of OSSD including various research objectives of this study. The keywords used for searching the relevant literature are presented in the same section. Section 2 presents various challenges associated with OSSD. These challenges must be subjugated for the success of OSSD. This section ends with consequences of lack of trust amongst OSSD community members. Section 3 presents relevance of trust in OSSD including trust definitions given by various authors and methods for building and maintaining trust. Trust characteristics and contributions of various authors in this field are then analyzed along with studying of various trust models. Section 4 presents the review of various existing trust evaluation models, their evolution and feature addition with time. Section 5 presents commentary on trust after literature review. Then a set of research questions for future study has been formulated. Section 6 illustrates various components of the proposed trust evaluation along with the empirical model for the same. Section 7 presents future work directions followed by conclusions in section 8.

2. CHALLENGES OF OPEN SOURCE SOFTWARE DEVELOPMENT

Open Source Software Development is altogether a different approach of software development and hence is associated with number of challenges which must be overcome for its success. Some of the challenges of OSSD are as listed below.

1. The development team is globally distributed and may not have face to face interactions ever;
2. Team members are volunteers so cannot be forced to work and are free to quit anytime;
3. Software development is governed by formation of a community, therefore, healthy environment for community formation is required (Lewicki & Bunker, 1996);
4. Mechanism must be in place for effective communication, coordination and feedback among community members (Kasper-Fuehrer & Ashkanasy, 2001; McAllister, 1995);
5. Participant's enthusiasm (Kogut & Metiu, 2001) and positive leadership (Pavlidis, 2011) has to be maintained;
6. Trust among members in open source teams will take more time to develop due to frequent change in team composition;
7. Mechanism to overcome trust betrayal due to someone else's provocation or communication gap. System for detection of lying and ditching by the members have to developed;
8. Mechanism for conflict avoidance, handling and regaining the lost trust should be in place;

9. Mechanism for mutual support, response in newsgroup, FAQs, time needed for response, etc.;
10. Every effort must be done to increase team commitment and to reduce conflicts and associated risks;
11. Another factor to be taken into consideration is that members of community belong to different part of the world, understand different languages and belong to various cultures. Members have to understand other languages and familiarize them with each other in order to work together;
12. Third party betrayal have to be detected and handled;
13. Preserve the interaction history, dynamic trust ratings and graphical representation of trust over time.

Keeping above factors into consideration and for effective working and governance of OSSD communities, a strong bond of TRUST among community members is essential. The intend of this work is to propose a framework for development and enhancement of trust among the community members. The lack of trust among team members may cause the following effects:

1. Reduce the effectiveness of individual contribution to team (Dasgupta & Partha, 2000);
2. Concentrating on individual goals rather than team goals (Bulman, 1992);
3. Reduces trust on other team member contributions and make them feel recheck the work performed by others (Lee, 2009);
4. Insecurity (Dasgupta & Partha, 2000) and ultimately productivity and quality go to lower level (Jarvenpaa et al., 2004);
5. There is absence of any central rule enforcement authority;
6. Rule enforcement is made possible by the presence of large number of motivated people who may punish rule-breakers by 'flaming', 'kill-filing' or 'shunning'.

3. RELEVANCE OF TRUST IN OPEN SOURCE SOFTWARE DEVELOPMENT

3.1. Definitions of Trust

Trust is taken from a German word, "TROST", meaning comfort. Trust is a relationship among individuals in which one person takes risk to communicate and cooperate with the other to create a collaborative development environment (Asundi, 2001; Lane et al., 2004; Stewart & Gosain, 2006). Trust is abstract and operates at various levels. Trust among two or mode individuals can be interpersonal. Trust among groups is termed as intergroup. Organization have organizational trust whereas societal trust exists in societies. Trust is applicable in all areas and people belonging to economics, sociology, psychology, management, marketing and personality developers have explored it.

According to Mui et al. (Mui et al., 2002) trust develops with time and is based on past encounters. Such trust is also termed as "reputation-based": "Trust is a subjective expectation an agent has about another's future behavior based on the history of their encounters."

Grandison and Sloman (Grandison & Sloman, 2000) added the concept of context to trust as one cannot trust other without it. According to them "Trust is the firm belief in competence of an entity to act dependably, securely, and reliably within a specified context." It is competence to act instead of actions.

Olmedilla et al. (Olmedilla et al., 2005) defined trust in terms of actions. According to them "Trust of a party A to a party B for a service X is the measurable belief of A in that B behaves dependably for a specified period within a specified context (in relation to service X)."

3.2. Methods for Building and Maintaining Trust

Zucker (Zucker, 1986) proposed three methods in which trust can be developed in a relationship. According to the author trust can be characteristics based trust which aims for development of social culture and norms for welfare of people. It is just like member-ship of any professional organization. Second form of trust is institutions based, just like technical or professional standards which one is bound to adhere. Third type of trust is process based, in which trust is developed slowly with time. Trust develops after experience gained from social interactions, mutual adaptation and learning by doing. Virtual teams cooperate over the web and usually do not know each other. They can interact and work together effectively only if they have trust among themselves. Trust is a combination of four components (Bergquist & Ljungberg, 2001). One who trusts another is termed as Trustor. Trustor creates trust by providing some benefits to the beneficiary. Second component is, trustee, one who is trusted. Trustee holds some authority, responsibility or position due to which it is trusted and is for public benefit. Third is reason for trust and the fourth is conditions based on which one is trusted.

Trust acts as pillars for team work as it increase the extent of co-operation among members of community. Trust enhancement would help in reduction of conflicts among members, thereby, improving the software development pace and processes. Communication and cooperation help in improving the quality of software. But trust alone may not be able to improve and sustain team performance, every team member has an allocated job which it must perform. Role allocation is based on capabilities, but work done is based on intentions of the member. Trust is the measure of interdependence but has associated risks. Higher trust values existing among community members encourages new members to join the community. As membership of community increases, team performance will improve. The communities are large and open, any team member can join or quit without any obligation. This leads to a problem that long-time interactions among same members may not be there. Members may not get long time to know others and develop trust over considerable period of time (Piccoli & Ives, 2003).

Keeping in mind the changing nature of membership of open source community a quick form of trust called *Swift Trust* (Michlmayr et al., 2005) was introduced. Swift trust binds together teams that work for short interval of time, they do not meet each other and do not have any personal relationship among themselves (Kasper-Fuehrer & Ashkanasy, 2001). First type of swift trust exists in situations where the second person need first more than the first needs second. It is in interest of second person not to deceive the first one. Such type of trust is based on the self-interest of first party (Hardin, 2002). Second person must get enough incentives and should not think of deceiving the other. Such type of trust would ensure that it is in personal interest of community members to participate and contribute to the project. Second is cognitive swift trust in which the second party do not let the first party down. First party trusts the second based upon some already known characteristics. Such type of trust ensures that there are internally motivated contributors attracted towards a project (Piccoli & Ives, 2003). Both types of trust ensure a strong bond among the contributors and corresponding project.

Osterloh and Rota (Osterloh & Rota, 2004) proposed setting up of institutions or some central mechanism to ensure trust is not hampered in relationship and to keep the contributors motivated. In order for contributors to contribute to any public repository, cost of contributions must be kept low.

Costa (Costa, 2003) classified trust factors into three categories. First is team composition consisting of factors like team cohesion, technical skills of members, type of job allocated and willingness to work together in the team etc. Second is characteristics of work which covers aspects like task ambiguity, communication mechanism to work together, information requirements and dependency on others etc. Third is nature of the organization, its reputation, management principles and powers allocated to team members.

Various types of trust proposed by authors in different articles are - calculus based trust. knowledge based trust, identification (Lewicki & Bunker, 1996) based trust, cognition based and affect based trust (McAllister, 1995).

The nature of OSSD suggests that success of open source projects depend upon information exchanged among core members and other contributors of the community. The sustainability of open source software projects greatly depends upon the level of trust among its members (Sirkkala et al., 2010). Trust plays an important role in this process therefore required trust information must be renewed and updated regularly (Howison & Crowston, 2004). Non-availability of dedicated tools for communication and information exchange among members of open source communities account for decrease in trust among members of the community (Dasgupta & Partha, 2000). The success of any open source software depends upon cooperation among its community members which in trun depends upon trust among members.

Therefore, trust enhancement should start as soon as contributions from various developers are received and proper trust management system should be in place (Michlmayr et al., 2005; Bulman, 1992). Feedbacks help in trust enhancement and makes the communication more effective (Lee, 2009; Jarvenpaa et al., 2004). Every relationship has associated expectations with it which must be communicated as soon as a team is formed (Bandow, 2004). Every team member may not be quick, some may take more time to communicate. Delays and long communication times should be minimized for success of the community (Pinyol et al., 2012). Increasing trust takes long time but decrease can be sudden. Gaining lost trust may take considerable amount of time. Context of trust is very important, therefore, trust and distrust can exist together in a relationship. Certain changes are expected during the life time of a project and are usually covered by formal contracts which incorporate those changes into the project. But large number of unexpected changes also occur and are covered by trust among members which is psychological contract based on goodwill (Lewicki & Bunker, 1996; Samoladas & Stamelos, 2003). Therefore, both trust and distrust in a balanced form are required to make a healthy relationship.

Open source software development is not entirely planned but involves mutual understanding and adjustments for success of the project. When hundreds of developers coordinate then conflicts are bound to happen so a proper conflict avoidance, handling and resolution mechanism is required. Rocco (Rocco, 1998) proposed that trust would play a vital role and hence must be strengthened through meetings, social and other team formation activities. Trust develops with time and interactions but in open source environment people across the globe are part of development team. Open platforms must have mechanism to handle diverse cultures, languages and writing skills (Barbar et al., 2006). Trust cannot be built free of cost but considerable amount of effort, time and money are to be involved (Cubranic, 2001). Trust of a developer depends upon the nature and amount of contributions made to the community (de Laat, 2010).

4. EXISTING TRUST EVALUATION MODELS

In the model proposed by Yu and Liu (Yu & Liu, 2001) trust is deemed to be a non-functional requirement and should be considered at requirement gathering level phase of software development. Trust is some combination of attributes based upon which quality of the system under development could be ascertained. Approach followed was demonstrated by studying the behaviour of a Multi-Agent system under attack and examine defense mechanism needed for maintenance of trust.

According to Yan and Cofta (Yan & Cofta, 2003) trust can be described as a set of goals and statements. All the entities in a system have well defined domains. Entities are represented in form of a graph to get clear understanding of interconnections among them in the system. Representation of trust is subjective in nature and some new elements are required to bridge gaps existing in trust domains. This study was performed for Mobile Communication System. Giorgini (Giorgini et al., 2004) explained a model termed as Tropos in which a framework to evaluate trust in information systems was developed. The work aimed at securing such systems. Trust in relationships was captured at individual and social levels. Concept of trust provisioning and delegation was added. Trust owership was also proposed by the author.

Other authors like Bimrah (Bimrah, 2009) also developed trust model for information systems and included number of other relevant factors for enhancing trust computation. Concept of action based on request is proposed. Requesting others depends upon already existing trust in the relationship and knowledge about previous actions based on request acts as a guiding factor for communication. Concept of recommendation by someone known is added and it helps to locate trustworthy agent with ease. Another concept proposed by the author is trusting intention as one may trust others in specific situations only. Consequence of trust may not always be positive, and one must be prepared to deal with it. Uddin and Zulekerninr (Uddin & Zulekernine, 2008) developed a UML based trust model which takes into consideration the concept of trust from initial phases of software development and advocates trust based upon various scenarios evolving out of interactions among various agents.

The work of Avizienis et al. (Avizienis et al., 2004) proposed that systems developed have to be trustworthy and it should be assured that the system have to fulfill the expectations of its users. Research work performed was related to construction of dependable software systems. Pavlidis (Pavlidis, 2011) illustrated that most of the above said approaches are based upon some subset of trust parameters. One parameter that can further improve the trust mechanism is context dependency of trust. Another aspect stated is that the aim of developing and following software engineering principles is to design trustworthy information systems with capability of addressing stated, unstated and even unanticipated needs of customers.

Hoffman et al. (Hoffman et al., 2006) developed a trust framework and added the concept of privacy (with sub-components as anonymity, un-observability, pseudonmity and unlink-ability), security (with sub-components as integrity, confidentiality, availability, authentication and authorization), safety, availability, reliability, user expectations and usability as its components. Rohm and Milne (Rohm & Milne, 2004) presented that information systems like e-commerce, e-banking etc. collect, store and manipulate personal information like credit card numbers very easily and provide a very wider access to it. There is increase in risk that such vital data may fall into the hands of unauthorised or malicious users. This will result into decrease in trust of the information system.

Bhattacharya et al. (Bhattacharya et al., 1998) proposed another trust building model. According to this model, factors affecting trust must have some logical values and trust should be calculated based upon it. Proposed model is based upon world of two individuals that can engage in actions, which jointly determine outcomes. The actions randomly determine outcomes according to random translation functions. There is a finite set of all the possible actions and respective outcomes of persons. The outcomes have consequences on two parties. Two types of interactions are allowed in the model. Individuals interact and can either follow certain sequence of actions or simultaneous actions. Two types of situations are taken care off. First in which two parties do not know which action the other would take based upon its actions. But in second situation each party know how the other would react based upon its action. Throughout the interactions of teams involved in open source software development confusions and conflicts emerge and efforts are made to resolve them during this creative software development process.

Zacharia (Zacharia, 1999) explained SPORAS model that had proposed an open multi-agent system which takes into consideration the rating aggregation based upon regular updating of reputation after obtaining feedback from the involved parties. New user entering the system have lowest reputation. Feedback is provided by interacting parties. Reputation of new users is updated in accordance with the obtained feedback. It takes time to build reputation. Bad reputation users may leave the system and join as fresh users but would be discouraged as they have to start with lowest reputation value again. However, this may discourage new agents from entering the system even though they were most trusted in their previous societies. Most recent ratings are given higher priority while evaluating the trustworthiness.

Pinyol et al. (Pinyol et al., 2012) discussed model proposed by Jurca and Faltings with the concept of providing incentives, using a payment scheme, to agents who truthfully report about other agents when asked upon. Dishonest agents will continue to lose money whereas honest agents would gain. It introduced broker agent called as R-agents which are responsible for buying and aggregation of reputation reports from other agents in a centralised manner. They sell the reputation information to other agents whenever it is asked to do so. The main contribution of this study was to introduce a mechanism for honestly reporting. But the use of value 0 to represent cheating agents and 1 for cooperating agents would make the model unable to adapt to situation where reputation reports are represented by values like 0.1 or 0.75.

E-Bay reputation model (Hong & John, 2015) determines the trustworthiness of an agent based on its past behaviour. It is a centralised rating system which rates its partners by allocating 1, 0 or -1 as rating valves. If rating is positive then rating value 1 is assigned, 0 is assigned for neutral and in case rating is negative then -1 is assigned. Reputation value can be further supported by textual comments and past behaviour is put in public domain. Value of reputation is calculated as a single value based on summation of ratings of past six months. Centralized mechanism handles and stores all the rating values. Users need to go through textual comments for getting more information about the agent. This model keeps no check on user that may cheat after obtaining high trust value. Therefore, such mechanism may not suit well for open community-based systems.

Sabater and Sierra (Sabater & Sierra, 2002; Sabherwal, 1999) proposed a model called REGRET which is a decentralized trust evaluation reputation model. Every agent rates the performance of its partner after every interaction and record it in its local ratings database. Trust value is calculated using stored ratings and its associated weight. Recency of ratings is taken into account while allocating weights to a rating. Trust predictive power has an associated reliability value which is based upon the number of ratings taken for calculating the trust values and deviation of those ratings. Regret also have a sophisticated method to calculate witness reputation based upon witness reports which prevents dishonest reporting. Social networks are used by Regret to identify witnesses to be consulted to assess and weight witness opinions. But Regret does not specify the method to build a social network. Trust calculation in Regret is not only based upon direct trust and witness reputation but also on system and neighbourhood reputation. Regret follows a decentralised approach in which agents are empowered to evaluate trust with other agents. Efforts are done to minimise disinformation by comparing information obtained from multiple sources. Therefore, we can say that Regret follows an appropriate approach which can be used to develop a trust model for open source software development communities. Trust evaluation as per Regret model depends upon social network but it does not show the processes of building a social network.

Luketeacy et al. (Luketeacy et al., 2006) proposed a model called TRAVOS which employ probability theory to evaluate trust in a relationship. History of previous interactions is maintained and they assist in trust development. Interactions are simplified into binary ratings where value 1 is used for successful interaction and value 0 for unsuccessful rating. Further beta family of probability density function (Asundi, 2001) is used by TRAVOS to find the probability of successful interactions. Probability values hence obtained becomes that agent's trust value. Probability density function is further used to evaluate confidence level of trust values. In this model, past performance of the target agent is asked from a witness agent when computed level of confidence of target is found to be less than minimum level. Any agent which had previous interactions with target acts as witness agent and shares information in form of successful and unsuccessful interactions. To evaluate truth in trust value, received witness report is compared with own observed trust values by the evaluator. Future reliability of witness will depend upon the amount of matching of witness and own observed trust value. This process also helps to develop trust between the evaluator and witness thereby improving relationship for future interactions.

Huynh et al. (Huynh et al., 2006) proposed FIRE model which evaluates trust based upon four parameters which are Weighted direct experience, witness information, role-based trust, and third-party references. Direct experience is used to evaluate trustworthiness of the target agent and is based upon the experience of evaluator gained from their previous interactions. It is also termed as interaction trust. Witness information is gathered from other agent if they wish to share their previous experiences. This is just like asking people about the reputation of someone before personally interacting with him. This is known as witness reputation. Role-based rules are the result of certain relationships existing between target, evaluator and its domain knowledge. System may have certain rule base which will set an agent with preset trust value, e.g., there may be a parent – child relation between evaluator and target agent. Child is bound to trust his parent. There may be a trustworthy group (like some branded product) which the evaluator trusts without any question. This is termed as role-based trust. Above discussed three types of trust is calculated by the evaluator after finding the required information about trustworthiness of target agents. But there can be a situation where target agent may prove its trustworthiness to the evaluator by providing some arguments (like previously generated trust certificates from some older interactions). Before any further communication target may also want to know about reputation of the evaluator. This is termed as certified reputation and is bidirectional trust relationship between requester and provider of information. As illustrated by FIRE model, trust may originate from different sources like witness information, direct contact, some policies, regulations or rules. Taking into consideration an open community of software developers rarely have any personally association, knowledge level of peers vary greatly and certain sources of information may not always be available or adequate for evaluation of trust.

Schillo et al. (Schillo et al., 2000) proposed a trust model in which trust emerging out of interactions between two agents can be good or bad and is treated as a boolean value. Degree of satisfaction is not taken into account. The model uses probability theory to evaluate trust. Schillo evaluated the probability of an agent to be honest in coming interactions and is given by an equation $T(A, Q) = e/n$ where e is the number of times target agent was honest and n is number of situations to be observed. Every agent uses a data structure called TrustNet which is in form of a directed graph in which witnesses are represented as nodes of the graph. Parent agent would convey about the honesty of his child agent to the root node of TrustNet graph and is represented in form of information carried by edges of the graph. This model is based upon assumption that witness agents may hide positive information but would not lie at all. Information would be analysed and reported to all if found to be negative. Lying and biasing must be taken into account so as to get the exact trust values. Hiding of information is modelled in terms of probability *p* for informing about positive facts of an agent and probability *(1-p)* for hiding that information. Hidden amount of positive information is estimated using probability theory. This process can be applied from target node to the root node through all ancestoral nodes of the TrustNet. This model is used to detect deceitful agents in Artificial Societies.

Marsh (Marsh, 1994) gave one of the oldest proposed trust model. It takes into account three types of trust, i.e. basic trust, general trust and situational trust. Basic trust is calculated based upon all the experiences gathered over time by an agent. General trusting disposition is modelled using Basic trust component of this model. Good experience leads to greater trust disposition and the other way. Second component which is general trust is simply trust that an agent has over other irrespective of any situation. Situational trust is trust based upon a specific situation. Situational trust is calculated based upon general trust, its importance and utilization of the situation. Model takes into consideration optimistic, pessimistic and realistic agents. Optimistic agents take maximum value out of set of experiences, pessimistic takes minimum value whereas realistic agents takes sources of reputation into consideration. Decision of cooperation with other agents is taken based on utility of the performed action, associated risk and competence of target agent. Concept of reciprocation is introduced in which agent *x* reciprocates to agent *y* as agent *y* had helped it in the past.

Zacharia (Zacharia, 1999) elaborated on HISTOS model which deals with direct information and witness information in a very simple way. Reputation value is treated as a subjective property of the system alloted by individuals of community. It evaluates reputation based on ratings resulting out of most recent interactions. Directed graphs based TrustNet used earlier by Schillo et.al (Schillo et al., 2000) is employed for reputation evaluation. Pair wise ratings are depicted using directed graphs in which agents are represented by nodes and edges carry reputation value provided by the agent based on most recent interaction between two agents. Reputation value of an agent is recursively calculated at any level in the graph in terms of weighted mean of previous rating values that an agent received from agents below it. Model does not take context of provided reputation into consideration and there is no mechanism for detection of cheaters.

Two trust acquisition mechanisms are proposed by Esfandiari and Chandrasekharan (Esfandiari & Chandrasekharan, 2001). First mechanism is based on observation which uses Bayesian networks for representation and Bayesian learning for trust acquisition. Bayesian network structure is known and fully observable and the learning process consists only of statistical values. Second trust mechanism uses two protocols and is based on interactions among agents. First protocol is the exploratory protocol in which one agent asks the other agent for known parameters to calculate the trust degree. Trust between two interacting agents *A* and *B* is calculated by formula $T(P,Q) = $ *(number of true replies)/(total number of such replies)*. Second is the query protocol in which agent asks for advice from already trusted agents. To take care of witness information, a directed graph is built by an agent where agents are represented by nodes of the graph and edges represent trust value between the two interacting agents. Edge between two nodes in the graph is not drawn if trust value of nodes is not known. Multiple paths between two agents in a graph may give contradictory values. This problem is solved by using the largest and smallest value among all the paths which are without cycle in graph. Further author claims that trust flows in trust graph in a similar way as data is routed in a network. Therefore, we can apply algorithms used for distributed networks successfully in this situation. Trust always have an associated context. The author proposes to represent multi-context nature of trust by using colored edges in the trust graph with one color per type of trust. One type of trust would only propagate through a particular color only. In the end author proposes to get the trust value using trust acquisition through interactions with environmental structure of the residing agents.

Yu and Singh (Yu & Singh, 2001; Yu & Singh, 2002b; Yu & Singh, 2002a) proposed the concept of quality of interactions for purpose of trust calculation based on set of values of direct interactions. The trust calculation is based upon most recent experiences with the partner agent. Upper and lower threshold values are defined by agents corresponding to QOS (Quality-of-Service) assigned to trustworthy agents, non-trustworthy agents and agents with no clear classification. Type of the service provided by fellow agent is calculated using Dempster-Shafer theory based upon historic data. If the calculated value is larger than some minimum trust value, the target agent is considered to be trustworthy agent. Target agent may not be found in the very first interaction. Witness agent can provide two kinds of information when queried about target agent. If the target agent is one whom we are interested to find, then it returns its own address otherwise referral to another agent from whom information about target can be obtained is returned. Referrals will lead to the desired agent or new referrals till the intended agent is found or depth limit is reached. The set of referral chain generated in the query process will form a graph similar to TrustNet. Information from multiple witnesses may be aggregated using Dempster's rule of combination. Direct information if available with respect to the target agent will be given preference.

The model proposed by Dasgupta (Dasgupta & Partha, 2000) is based on expectation or the belief that a party will act benignly and cooperatively. The model can be deployed for sociological problems, making and breaking of cooperative relations. Rahman and Hailes (Rahman & Hailes, 2000) in their model calculate trust based upon experiences gained from direct interactions and communications received from third party regarding the same. Agent trustworthiness is classified in form of a discrete set *{vt, t, u, vu}*. This set represents four tuples which are very trustworthy, trustworthy, untrustworthy and very untrustworthy. An agent *A* having a tuple like (0,0,3,4) for agent *B* means that during interactions *A* has experienced 3 untrustworthy and 4 very untrustworthy experiences. Therefore, final trust value is the largest value corresponding to the trust set which here is very untrustworthy. In case two values are same system returns a neutral output value. Information coming from an agent is not blindly trusted, but it is compared with earlier information received from it. If an agent communicates that a particular agent is very trustworthy but according to our own previous experience, it is untrustworthy then witness information has to be adjusted. The problem that arises is that it is not possible to detect agent who are speaking truth and provide different answers but are not lying at all. Witness information requiring least adjustment would be for agents having similar perspective for a situation which may not always be correct.

Mass and Shehory (McAllister, 1995) proposed a trust model based on concept of generation of trust certificates by an authentic neutral third party. The aim of a neutral third party was to minimize biasing. The model was validated by computing trust in open multi-agent systems. Sen and Sajja (Sen & Sajja, 2002) developed a trust model by incorporating experiences gained from direct and observed interactions. It is employed in situations where noisy observations exists which means that observed behaviour is different from actual behaviour of target agent. Fact is that direct interaction only provides the real picture. Reputation values are updated using reinforcement learning. More importance is given to updated reputation value based on interaction than the update that takes place when reputation value is updated based on observation. Reputation values lie between 0 and 1. Value larger than 0.5 is awarded as good performers and value less than 0.5 represents poor performers. One agent may ask the other about reputation of its partner. This model assumes liar agents to lie consistently about other agents. This model gives a method to evaluate the number of witnesses to be queried before a particular agent is trusted. There is only a likelihood of selection of good partner as the witnesses are randomly selected. The author has not given any mechanism to club direct experience and witness observation to compute the final reputation value.

Carbo et al. (Carbo et al., 2002) compared SPORAS with Fuzzy based reputation model in which reputation values are represented in terms of Fuzzy sets. The reputation is calculated based on some degree of satisfaction corresponding to latest interactions among partners. The new satisfaction values are aggregated with old reputation values using weighted aggregation. Weights are evaluated based on an already predicted value called remembrance or memory. The remembrance factor is based on similarities between old reputation value and satisfaction level of previous experiences. Relevance of previous experience is incremented when satisfaction level of older experience matches trust value of partner. But if satisfaction level and assigned reputation values differ then relevance value of latest interaction is incremented. Recommendations coming from a high reputation recommender are relied upon just as if they are based upon direct interactions. Recommendations of agent having bad reputation are not considered. Apart from the above discussed trust models, number of other trust models were also studied. A new evidential trust model for open communities is proposed by Wang and Sun (Wang & Sun, 2009). This model is an improvement over Yu and Singh (Yu & Singh, 2002a) model. This model used Dezert-Smarandache theory for trust acquisition. The proposed model can be used for computing trust in open communities. Gomez et al. (Gómez et al., 2006) proposed Anticipatory trust model which is based on advertisement based trust, direct trust and recommendations based trust. Another approach to ensure honest interactions among parties is to employ a trusted third party whom both the interacting parties trust. It is the duty of third party to review every aspect of communication taking place between two parties and ensure transparency.

Xiong and Liu (Xiong & Liu, 2004) proposed PeerTrust model which uses feedback obtained from peers to determine trust. Peer experience and credibility is vital as entire trust is based upon their feedback. Community members earn incentives if the provided feedback matches the real time experience. Trust is evluated and a composite trust metric if formed. This model evaluates Peer-to-Peer trust in ecommerce communities. Vercouter and Muller (Vercouter & Muller, 2010) proposed LIAR model which can be employed for Liar Identification in the community. An agent may provide higher trust rating for less rated agent or vice-versa but in both the cases an agent had given wrong trust values which is not good for any system. LIAR model ensures true value of Agent Reputation. This model ensures that social norms and other communication rules are respected. It is used for implementation of a social control of agent interaction.

Albuquerque at al. (Albuquerque et al., 2014) proposed a trust model termed as 3Gtrust which is developed for distributed systems and is based on groups of peers. This model is used to ensure that group of peers can be trusted or not. Chubin et al. (Carbo et al., 2002) discussed a trust model called CREDIT and it used fuzzy sets to evaluate trust value. It combines direct exchanges among agents together with the agent reputation. Clifford (Clifford, 2002) proposed SOLAR trust model which have a number of independent certification authorities perform the job of trust computation. Each certification authority acts as sun in solar system and other trusted parties act as planets revolving around it. Reputation value is calculated and represented using digital certificates. Chong et al. (Chong et al., 2013) proposed a multi valued trust evaluation model for cloud computing based applications. Malicious feedbacks are filtered and a trust metric to evaluate the trustworthiness of service provider is developed. This model is suitable for use in E-commerce trading partners in cloud environment. Josang et al. (Josang & Haller, 2007) developed a Bayesian Reputation System. This model is used in open dynamic environment and it calculates trust value using Dirichlet Probability Density Function. This model is binomial and multinomial rating models.

After going through different aspects of existing reputation and trust models presented by various researchers, the applicability of certain trust features to open source software development trust model are summarized in Table 1.

5. COMMENTARY ON REVIEWED WORK

Following the analysis of literature pertaining to OSSD, Trust and various Trust models, following inferences regarding the development of OSSD community trust model are drawn. The software development virtual communities have to ensure that all its members are registered. Trust helps in improving relationships and binds the virtual teams. Trust must be considered as an integral part of software development and trust requirements must be strictly incorporated into every phase of software development starting with requirement gathering stage. Otherwise, it results in conflicts with other functional and non-functional requirements of the system. Trust should be a combination of certain attributes which must be quantitatively determined and graphical represented to have a better insight into it. Trust model to be developed will calculate trust at the individual level for every contributor which in turn ensures the trustworthiness of the community. The aim of this work is to design a trustworthy system to incorporate security, authentication, reliability, usability, safety, availability and to meet all user expectation concerns.

The trust enhancement framework to be developed will have a centralized trust computation system in which every aspect of software production is finalized by a core team. Every community member must have a finite set of actions to be performed with the corresponding outcomes. Regular updating of reputation based on feedback is to be incorporated. New members enter the community with the lowest reputation which is updated with time. Trusted members of other communities must be taken care off. They should be provided with relatively higher trust values than other new community members provided they bring with them old trust certificates from their previous community. The community member may be alleviated to higher levels or may be made part of the core team if very high trust value is maintained by that member over a considerable period of time. This possible only if a mechanism for honestly trust computation is at the place. The past behavior of the community member should be in the public domain. The skill levels of the contributors differ as someone may be a good code contributor, other may be very good at debugging while someone else may be very good document writer. This leads to the conclusion that trust should be multi-valued based on different types of past contributions like contributed code, amount of code tested, help provided to other users, documentation provided etc. The correctness of the contributions has to be inspected by certain minimum numbers of community members before incorporating them into the final build of software and only then it would add to their trustworthiness. Trust development is a continuous process in which trust value is an aggregate of old and new trust values. Feedback obtained from peers will be given due importance. Framework for OSSD community will take care of all the above-stated facts.

Table 1. Key features of trust models

Author	Key Characteristics of the Proposed Trust Model	Whether Applicable to OSS Trust Model
Yu and Lin	Trust to be considered at requirement gathering level.	Yes
Yan and Cofta	Reputation in form of goals and statements with a graphical representation.	No
Giorgini et al.	Trust delegation, provisioning and ownership for developers.	Yes
Bimrah	Intention of Trust relationship among interacting parties.	Yes
Avizienis	Trust-Worthiness to be assured.	Yes
Pavlidis	Context added with trust.	Yes
Lawson and Blum	Privacy, Security, Reliability, usability, safety, availability and user expectation.	Yes
Rohm and Milne	Information systems to be highly trustworthy.	Yes
Bhatta-charya	Finite set of actions and outcomes.	Yes
Zacharia	Reputation updated after Feedback, Recency of rating.	Yes
Pinyol et al.	Incentive for Trustful agents.	Yes
E-Bay reputation model	Centralized rating system, Past behavior in public domain.	Yes
Sabater and Sierra	Decentralized trust evaluation model.	No
Luketeacy et al.	Uses probability theory.	Yes
Huynh et al.	Weighted direct experience, witness reputation, role-based trust, third party reference	No
Schillo	Trust as good or bad only.	No
Marsh	Basic trust, General trust, Situational trust, Concept of reciprocation.	No
Zacharia	Directed graph based TrustNet.	No
Esfandiary and Chandrasekharan	Multi Context nature of Trust based on observation.	Yes
Yu and Singh	Intended agent is found by chain of referrals.	No
Rahman and Hailes	Agent ranked very trustworthy, trustworthy, untrustworthy or very untrustworthy.	No
Mass and Shehory	Generation of trust certificates.	Yes
Sen and Sajja	Reinforcement learning is used where observations are noisy.	No
Carbo et al.	Fuzzy sets used, Recommendations from higher reputation agent.	No
Xiong and Liu	Feedback determines trust, Composite trust metric formed.	Yes
Vercouter and Muller	Liar identification in community.	No
Albuquerque et al.	Group of peers can be trusted or not	No
Chubin et al.	Use fuzzy sets	No
Clifford	Digital certificates used.	Yes
Josang et al.	Framework for open dynamic environment.	Yes

Finally, after going through all the aspects of OSSD methodology, the need of trust for community formation and existing trust models, the following research questions have been formulated.

RQ1: To become familiar with various processes and methodologies adopted by OSSD communities.

RQ2: To determine the challenges associated with the formation of virtual software development teams.

RQ3: To understand the importance of trust as a binding force among virtual team members.

RQ4: To identify the basic attributes based upon which trust in OSSD environments could be computed.

RQ5: To develop a relational database system (repository) for preserving the above attributes corresponding to community members.

RQ6: To develop a trust evaluation framework based on above-found trust attributes.

RQ7: To implement the proposed framework.

RQ8: To validate the proposed framework.

6. PROPOSED TRUST EVALUATION FRAMEWORK AND ITS COMPONENTS

6.1. Components of Trust Evaluation Framework

Various components of the proposed trust evaluation framework based upon which the OSSD community can evaluate the trust of its community members are:

- Code contributed by a particular OSS developer/volunteer;
- Code reviewed by a particular OSS developer/volunteer;
- Help requested by other members and relevant information provided to them by a volunteer/developer;
- Number of trustworthy members referred for joining the community;
- Amount of documentation written for the community;
- Active time spent for the betterment of the community;
- Awards/ honors received by the community members;
- Amount of monetary contributions;
- Active OSSD projects on which a particular OSS developer/volunteer is working.

The proposed trust evaluation framework also preserves the personal information of the community member and his/her login details.

6.2. The Proposed Trust Evaluation Framework

The proposed trust evaluation framework (Figure 1) starts operating as soon as a member enters into the community. The members entering into the community are always monitored by a trust calculation and update module. This module takes care of new as well as existing members of the community. Trust development is a continuous process, therefore, the trust value is updated after every interaction of member with the community. The member is marked trustworthy only if trust value is more than some minimum threshold value. The member joining the community may already be a trustworthy member of some other established community. Such member may be given higher initial trust value provided that member furnishes trust certificate from the community he is already working with. In case no such certificate is there, the member has to start afresh in the community.

As soon as the member enters the community, a decision is taken to determine whether the member is new or existing. New members are required to register themselves. Space is reserved for them in the repository, personal and professional information is taken, the user is registered, login id and password is generated and besides other things, the trust value is set to minimal. The new member now can interact with the community. Existing members can log into the system by providing a login id and password. Whenever a member logs into the system time elapsed since the last interaction is determined. If the time elapsed is less than the prescribed limit, the member is allowed further interact in the system. But if the time elapsed is more than the prescribed limit, then the member is asked about whether the member wants to retain the membership or not. If a member says yes, then control is passed to member interaction and handling interface. But if the member says no, then old trust values are preserved. Before any other operation is performed, it is ensured whether the member was trustworthy or not. If a member is trustworthy then some incentives are offered to retain him. If the incentive is accepted, control is passed to member interaction and handling interface. If the incentive is not accepted or member is found out to be non-trustworthy then trust certificate is generated and goodbye message is printed. The data of members who leave the community is stored in a different repository containing details of migrated members. This is done to ensure that only active members remain in the database. Throughout the interaction, various attributes affecting the trust value are updated which leads to the latest trust value of the member.

Figure 1. Flow of the proposed trust evaluation framework

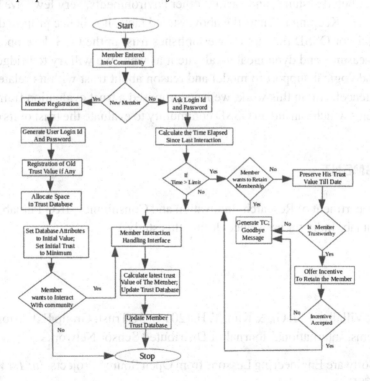

7. FUTURE WORK

The future research would aim to find answers to the research questions as illustrated above. Henceforth, one can work towards the development of a set of well-optimized databases for storage and retrieval of data corresponding to all the above-given components for trust evaluation. The process of trust computation with respect to community members can also be developed. Various algorithms to handle the process of code submission and review, documentation submission and review, member activity handling, response handling, bug tracking, and member activity analysis can be developed as a part of future work. The proposed system can then be implemented in any supporting language followed by its verification and validation by taking real-time data as an input from certain existing open source communities for analyzing trust exhibited by their members.

8. CONCLUSION

The OSSD paradigm suggests that a team of connected persons develops the intended product. It becomes very essential for a member of the development team to have trust in the other members of the team. If trust levels among team members are high, then coordination between them also raises to a higher level, which results in a higher quality of the product. Another dimension of OSSD is the geographically diverse location of its team members. It, therefore, becomes very important to install trust in such a geographically dispersed team. Ongoing through the literature, it has been found that although a large number of trust studies have been carried out in development of information systems, mobile communication, distributed systems, and various other environments, very few have been worked upon for OSSD communities. Keeping in view, the above-stated facts, it is hence proposed to develop a trust model and framework for OSSD that not only establishes trust in the OSS developers and community members but also measures and dynamically validate it as well. We will try to bridge the deficit of ontological and methodological support to model and reason about trust with its related concepts in one allied framework. Henceforth, in this work, we have proposed a trust evaluation framework along with its various components which can aid an OSSD community to evaluate the trust of its existing members.

ACKNOWLEDGMENT

Sincere thanks to Department of Research, Innovation and Consultancy, IKG Punjab Technical University, Kapurthala, Punjab, India for assistance during this study.

REFERENCES

Albuquerque, R. O., Villalba, L. J. G., & Kim, T. H. (2014). 3GTrust: Group Extension for Trust Models in Distributed Systems. International Journal of Distributed Sensor Networks.

Asundi, J. (2001). Software Engineering Lessons from Open Source Projects. *In: 1st Workshop on Open Source Software. ICSE.*

Avizienis, A., Laprie, J. C., & Randell, B. (2004). *Dependability and its Threats: A Taxonomy. In 18th IFIP* (pp. 91–120). Kluwer Academic Publishers.

Bandow, D. (2004). Time to Create Sound Teamwork. *Journal for Quality and Participation, 24*(2), 41–47.

Barbar, M. A., Verner, J. M., & Nguyen, P. T. (2006). Establishing and Maintaining Trust in Software Outsourcing Relationships: An Empirical Investigation. *Journal of Systems and Software*, *80*(9), 1438–1449. doi:10.1016/j.jss.2006.10.038

Bergquist, M., & Ljungberg, J. (2001). The power of gifts: Organizing social relationships in open source communities. *Journal of Information Systems*, *1*(1), 305–320. doi:10.1046/j.1365-2575.2001.00111.x

Bhattacharya, R., Devinney, T. M., & Pillutla, M. M. (1998). A Formal Model of Trust Based on Outcomes. *Academy of Management Review*, *23*(3), 459–472. doi:10.5465/amr.1998.926621

Bimrah, K. K. (2009). A Framework for Modeling Trust during Information Systems Development [PhD Thesis]. University of East London.

Bulman, R. J. (1992). *Shattered Assumptions: Towards a new psychology of trauma*. New York: Free Press.

Carbo, J., Molina, J., & Davila, J. (2002). Comparing predictions of SPORAS vs. a Fuzzy Reputation Agent System. In *3rd International Conference on Fuzzy Sets and Fuzzy Systems* (pp. 147-153). Interlaken.

Chong, S. K., Abawajy, J., Ahmad, M., Rahmi, I., & Hamid, A. (2013). A Multilevel Trust Management Framework for Service Oriented Environment. In *International Conference on Innovation, Management and Technology Research ICIMTR 2013*, Malaysia (pp. 22 – 23).

Clifford, M. A. (2002, Dec 9-13). Networking in the Solar Trust Model: Determining Optimal Trust Paths in a Decentralized Trust Network. In *Proceedings of 18th Annual Conference on Computer Security Applications*. IEEE. doi:10.1109/CSAC.2002.1176298

Costa, A. C. (2003). Understanding the Nature and the Antecedents of Trust within Work Teams. In B. Nooteboom & F. Six (Eds.), *The Trust Process in Organizations: Empirical Studies of the Determinants and the Process of Trust Development* (pp. 105–124). Cheltenham: Edward Elgar. doi:10.4337/9781843767350.00012

Cubranic, D., & Murphy, G. C. (2001). The Ramp-Up Challenge in Open Source Software Projects. In *Workshop on Open Source Software, IEEE/ACM International Conference on Software Engineering (ICSE 01)*.

Dasgupta & Partha. (2000). Trust as a Commodity. In D. Gambetta (Ed.), *Trust: Making and Breaking Cooperative Relations. Electronic edition* (pp. 49–72). Department of Sociology, University of Oxford.

de Laat, P. B. (2010). How can Contributors to Open-Source Communities be Trusted? On the Assumption, Inference and Substitution of Trust. *Ethics and Information Technology*, *12*(4), 327–341. doi:10.100710676-010-9230-x

Esfandiari, B., & Chandrasekharan, S. (2001). On How Agents Make friends: Mechanisms for Trust Acquisition. In *Proceedings of the Fourth Workshop on Deception, Fraud and Trust in Agent Societies*, Montreal, Canada (pp. 27-34).

Giorgini, P., Massaci, F., Mylopoulos, J., & Zanone, N. (2004). Requirements Engineering for Trust Management. *International Journal of Information Security*, *5*(4), 257–274. doi:10.100710207-006-0005-7

Gómez, M., Carbó, J., & Earle, C. B. (2006). An Anticipatory Trust Model for Open Distributed Systems. In *Workshop on Anticipatory Behavior in Adaptive Learning Systems* (pp. 307-324).

Grandison, T., & Sloman, M. (2000). A Survey of Trust in Internet Applications. *IEEE Communications Surveys and Tutorials, 4*(4), 2–16. doi:10.1109/COMST.2000.5340804

Hardin, R. (2002). *Trust and Trust-Worthiness*. New York.

Hoffman, J. L., Jenkins, K. L., & Blum, J. (2006). Trust Beyond Security: An Expanded Trust Model. *Communications of the ACM, 49*(7), 95–101. doi:10.1145/1139922.1139924

Hong, X., & John, C. S. L. (2015, September). Modeling eBay-like reputation systems: Analysis, Characterization and Insurance Mechanism Design. *Performance Evaluation, 91*, 132–149. doi:10.1016/j.peva.2015.06.009

Howison, J., & Crowston, K. (2004). The Perils and Pitfalls of Mining SourceForge. In *Proceedings of the International Workshop on Mining Software Repositories (MSR 2004)*, Edinburg, UK (pp. 7-11). 10.1049/ic:20040467

Huynh, T. D., Jennings, N. R., & Shadbolt, N. R. (2006). An Integrated Trust and Reputation model for open Multi-agent systems. *Journal of Autonomous Agents and Multi Agent Systems, 13*(2), 119–154. doi:10.100710458-005-6825-4

Jarvenpaa, S. L., Shaw, T. R., & Staples, D. S. (2004). Toward Contextualized Theories of Trust: The Role of Trust in Global Virtual Teams. *Information Systems Research, 15*(3), 250–264. doi:10.1287/isre.1040.0028

Josang, A., & Haller, J. (2007, April 10-13). Dirichlet Reputation Systems. In *ARES' 07 Proceedings of The Second International Conference on Availability, Reliability and Security* (pp. 112-119). IEEE Computer Society. 10.1109/ARES.2007.71

Kasper-Fuehrer, E. C., & Ashkanasy, N. M. (2001). Communicating Trustworthiness and Building Trust in Inter-organizational virtual organizations. *Journal of Management, 27*(3), 235–254. doi:10.1016/S0149-2063(01)00090-3

Kogut, B., & Metiu, A. (2001). Open Source Software Development and Distributed Innovation. *Oxford Review of Economic Policy, 17*(2), 248–264. doi:10.1093/oxrep/17.2.248

Lane, M. S., Vyver, G., Basenet, P., & Howard, S. (2004). Interpretative Insights into Interpersonal Trust and Effectiveness of Virtual Communities of Open Source Software Developers. In ACIS 2004 Proceedings.

Lee, C. (2009, May). Utilizing Open Source Tools for Online Teaching and Learning: Applying Linux Technologies. In *Strengths and Weaknesses of Open Source Software*. Hershey, PA: IGI Global.

Lewicki, R. J., & Bunker, B. B. (1996). Developing and Maintaining Trust in Work Relationships. In T. R. Tyler & R. M. Kramer (Eds.), *Trust in Organizations: Frontiers of Theory and Research* (pp. 114–139). Thousand Oaks, CA: Sage Publications. doi:10.4135/9781452243610.n7

Luketeacy, W. T., Patel, J., Jennings, N. R., & Luck, M. (2006, February 24). TRAVOS: Trust and Reputation in the Context of Inaccurate Information Sources. *Journal of Autonomous Agents and Multi-Agent Systems, 12*(2), 183–198. doi:10.100710458-006-5952-x

Marsh, S. P. (1994). Formalising Trust as a Computational Concept [Doctoral Thesis]. University of Stirling, United Kingdom.

McAllister, D. J. (1995). Affect and Cognition Based Trust as Foundations for Interpersonal Cooperation in Organizations. *Academy of Management Journal, 38*(1), 24–59.

Michlmayr, M., Hunt, F., & Probert, D. (2005, July 11-15). Quality Practices and Problems in Free Software Projects. In *Proceedings of the First International Conference on Open Source Systems* (pp. 24-28).

Mui, L., Mohtashemi, M., & Halberstadt, A. (2002). A Computational Model of Trust and Reputation. In: *Proceedings of the 35th International Conference on System Science* (pp. 280–287). 10.1109/HICSS.2002.994181

Olmedilla, D., Rana, O., Matthews, B., & Nejdl, W. (2005). Security and Trust Issues in Semantic Grids. In *Proceedings of the Dagsthul Seminar, Semantic Grid: The Convergence of Technologies.*

Osterloh, M., & Rota, S. (2004). Trust and Community in Open Source Software Production. *Analyse & Kritik*, 279–301.

Pavlidis, M. (2011). *Designing for Trust, CaiSE* (pp. 3–14). Doctoral Consortium.

Piccoli, G., & Ives, B. (2003). Trust and the Unintended Effects of Behavior Control in Virtual Teams. *Management Information Systems Quarterly, 27*(3), 368–395. doi:10.2307/30036538

Pinyol, I., Sabater Mir, J., Dellunde, P., & Paolucci, M. (2012). Reputation-based Decisions for Logic based Cognitive Agents. *Autonomous Agents and Multi-Agent Systems, 24*(1), 175–216. doi:10.100710458-010-9149-y

Rahman, A. A., & Hailes, S. (2000, January 4-7). Supporting Trust in Virtual Communities. In *Proceedings of the Hawaii's International Conference on Systems Sciences*, Maui, HI.

Rocco, E. (1998, April 18-23). Trust Breaks Down in Electronic Context but can be repaired by Some Initial face-o-face Contact. ACM. 10.1145/274644.274711

Rohm, J. A., & Milne, R. G. (2004). Just what the Doctor Ordered: The Role of Information Sensitivity and Trust in Reducing Medical Information Privacy Concern. *Journal of Business Research, 57*(9), 1000–1011. doi:10.1016/S0148-2963(02)00345-4

Sabater, J., & Sierra, C. (2002). Reputation and Social Network Analysis in Multi-Agent Systems. In *AAMAS-2002 Proceedings of the first International Joint Conference on Autonomous agents and Multi-agent Systems* Bologna, Italy(475-482). . 10.1145/544741.544854

Sabherwal, R. (1999). The Role of Trust in Outsourced IS Development Projects. *Communications of the ACM, 42*(2), 80–86. doi:10.1145/293411.293485

Samoladas, I., & Stamelos, I. (2003). *Assessing Free/Open Source Software Quality*. Greece: Aristotle University of Informatics.

Schillo, M., Funk, P., & Rovatsos, M. (2000). Using Trust for Detecting Deceitful Agents in Artificial Societies. *Applied Artificial Intelligence.*

Sen, S., & Sajja, N. (2002). Robustness of Reputation-based Trust: Boolean Case. In *Proceedings of the first International Joint Conference on Autonomous Agents and Multi-agent Systems* (pp. 288-293). Bologna, Italy.

Sirkkala, P., Hammounda, I., & Aaltonen, T. (2010). From Proprietary to Open source: Building a Network of Trust. In *OSCOMM 2010 Proceedings of Second International Workshop on Building Sustainable Open Source Communities* (pp. 26-30).

Stewart, K. J., & Gosain, S. (2006). The Impact of Ideology on effectiveness in open source software development teams. *Management Information Systems Quarterly, 30*(2), 291–314. doi:10.2307/25148732

Uddin, M. G., & Zulekernine, M. (2008). UML-Trust: Towards Developing Trust Aware Software. In: *Proceedings of the ACM Symposium on Applied Computing,* Brazil (pp. 831-836).

Vercouter, L., & Muller, G. (2010). L.I.A.R. Achieving Social Control in Open and Decentralized Multi-agent systems. *Applied Artificial Intelligence, 24*(8), 723–768. doi:10.1080/08839514.2010.499502

Wang, J., & Sun, H. J. (2009, September 1). A New Evidential Trust Model for Open Communities. *Computer Standards & Interfaces, 31*(5), 994–1001. doi:10.1016/j.csi.2008.09.025

Xiong, L., & Liu, L. (2004, July). PeerTrust: Supporting Reputation-Based Trust for Peer-to-Peer Electronic Communities. *IEEE Transactions on Knowledge and Data Engineering, 16*(7), 843–857. doi:10.1109/TKDE.2004.1318566

Yan, Z., & Cofta, P. (2003). Methodology to Bridge Different Domains of Trust in Mobile Communications. In *Proceedings of the First International iTrust Conference* (pp. 211-224). Springer. 10.1007/3-540-44875-6_15

Yu, B., & Singh, M. P. (2001). Towards a Probabilistic Model of Distributed Reputation Management. In *Proceedings of the Fourth Workshop on Deception, Fraud and Trust in Agent Societies,* Montreal, Canada (pp. 125-137).

Yu, B., & Singh, M. P. (2002a). Distributed Reputation Management for Electronic Commerce. *Computational Intelligence, 18*(4), 535–549. doi:10.1111/1467-8640.00202

Yu, B., & Singh, M. P. (2002b). An Evidential Model of Distributed Reputation Management. In: *AAMAS-02 Proceedings of the first International Joint Conference on Autonomous Agents and Multi-agent systems,* Bologna, Italy (pp. 294-301). 10.1145/544741.544809

Yu, E., & Liu, L. (2001). Modeling Trust for System Design Using the i* Strategic Actors Framework. In *Proceedings of the International Workshop on Deception Fraud and Trust in Agent Societies* (pp. 175-194). Springer.

Zacharia, G. (1999). Collaborative Reputation Mechanisms for Online Communities.

Zucker, L. G. (1986). Production of trust: Institutional sources of economic structure. In B.W. Staw & L. L. Cummings (Eds.), Research in Organizational Behavior. Greenwich, CT: JAI Press.

This research was previously published in the International Journal of Open Source Software and Processes (IJOSSP), 9(4); pages 1-19, copyright year 2018 by IGI Publishing (an imprint of IGI Global).

Chapter 12
The Impact of Project Initiators on Open Source Software Project Success:
Evidence From Emerging Hosting Platform Gitee

Ling Wang

School of Business, China University of Political Science and Law (CUPL), Beijing, China

Jinxiao Wang

School of Economics and Management, Tsinghua University, Beijing, China

ABSTRACT

This paper focuses on studying the role of open source software project initiator in affecting the OSS project success from the perspective of individual and collective behaviors. The authors collected the data from an emerging OSS hosting platform Gitee in China. This research indicates that the success mode for open source software projects in China relies a lot on the project initiators. Project initiators not only contribute codes to aid the project directly, but also use their social capital to facilitate the project success. But no full play has been given to social network's effect on mass production and collaborative innovation. The authors suggest collaborative innovation which could lead to coherence of global collective wisdom, reduced development costs, and expanded source of innovation should be the further direction for the OSS project in emerging platforms.

1. INTRODUCTION

Open Source Software (OSS, or Open Source Code Software) refers to any software that is permitted to be used, modified and distributed by anyone in accordance with relevant protocols on open sources (see https://opensource.org/osd). After nearly 5 decades of development, OSS has long been an essential

DOI: 10.4018/978-1-7998-9158-1.ch012

part of the software field. Many excellent OSS projects such as Linux, Apache, and Eclipse, have been widely applied in the global IT industries due to their advantages such as high quality, low development cost, and short development cycles (Jin, Zhou & Zhang, 2016). According to the analysis by International Data Corporation and Trend Force, OSS is closely related to emerging industries such as mobile Internet, servers, cloud computing, big data, and artificial intelligences. The development of OSS in China began in 1995. With its prosperous Internet-based industry and software development industry in China, open source has become a key element to support high-speed iterations of software products (Liu, 2013). Technology companies such as Huawei and Alibaba have raised the application of OSS to the strategic level of development and regard it as an important means of their enterprises to gain competitive advantages in the future (Wang, Dai & Feng, 2009). At present, a large number of in-depth studies have been done on OSS, covering many disciplines such as software engineering, economics, management science, and science of law (Aksulu & Wade, 2010). OSS research topics in China are more concentrated in applications (Feng, 2010).

OSS projects developers volunteer to produce free public products (Lerner & Tirole, 2002). These developers gained private benefits such as knowledge and fun by investing in OSS project development (Hippel & Krogh, 2003). Unlike proprietary software which is developed in the firm-based production model, OSS is developed depending on the online-community-based self-organization behaviors (Garzarelli, 2003). The proprietary software development was vividly compared by Raymond (1999) to an elitist and closed cathedral construction, while the OSS development was compared to a chaotic and open marketplace. Though without explicit organizational structure and process arrangements, OSS projects can develop software that may be on a par with or better than traditional commercial software, thus offering a completely new concept of production and innovation for software development. However, despite the great success of several OSS projects such as Linux and Apache, most OSS projects are facing various development challenges (Bai, 2014). To illustrate, in Source Forge, an international OSS community, there are a huge amount of outcast OSS projects with few user download and voluntary developers.

The study of OSS project success has attracted widespread attention in the academic community. In the burgeoning stage of the open source movement, there were fewer OSS projects. Scholars mainly performed qualitative analysis on individual success cases. For example, the founder of Fetch mail summed up a large number of practical experiences based on his own experience in open source, and thus subverted the traditional software engineering concept (Raymond, 1999). With constantly improving OSS development tools, professional OSS projects cooperative development communities have integrated a large number of OSS projects of different natures and sizes (Zhang et al., 2015). The massive information and data on open software and developers in the Internet create good conditions for the quantitative analysis of the success of OSS projects. Social network analysis, based on a large amount of collaborative interaction data, has become an emerging perspective to study OSS projects development and to focus on the impact of network relationships formed among individuals, groups, organizations, and communities on the success of OSS projects.

This paper investigates the role of OSS project initiator in affecting the OSS project success via two different influencing mechanisms. From the individual behavior level, we view OSS development as an investment model and theorize that when the OSS project initiators contribute more work, the OSS projects would become more successful. From the collective behavior level, we put our emphasis on the effect of the social capital of the OSS project initiator on the project success. Based on the social capital theory, we propose that different dimensions of the project initiators' social capital could have diverse promotive functions for the OSS project success. The study described in this paper can make four important contributions: (1) Our research on the mechanisms of the success of OSS projects could contribute to the study of "private-collective" innovation model, which has drawn wide attention in the industry and academia; (2) The existing researches mainly focused on the large international open source communities. Prior work has exclusively focused on the collective behaviors in the OSS development process, but the role of important nodes in the network, taking the project initiator as a typical example, has not been fully explored; (3) China's open source community is still in its early stage of development, relatively small, and absent of large OSS projects, which provide a perfect condition for investigating the role of OSS project initiators; (4) In particular, this paper investigates the effect of the social capital of OSS project initiator on the project success and takes both the individual behavior level and the collective behavior level into account, which could offer deeper insights into in the OSS project development in emerging OSS hosting platform.

2. HYPOTHESES

OSS projects development is a paradigm of the "private-collective" innovation model. When exploring the success model for OSS projects in the open source community in China, our research focuses on the OSS project initiators, combines the theoretical analysis on individual behaviors and collective behaviors, and puts forward hypotheses about relations between OSS project initiators and project success.

2.1 Individual Behaviors Level

At the individual behavior level, the OSS projects can be regarded as a private investment behavior of developers. The OSS project initiators establish the initial framework and general development direction for their projects at the beginning and continue to contribute code in the subsequent OSS project development. The OSS project initiators invest time, energy, knowledge and so on, and get project returns such as improved quality of their software. Based on the above analysis, the paper proposes the following hypotheses:

Hypothesis H1: Individual commitment from OSS project initiators has a positive impact on project success.

2.2 Collective Behavior Level

The developer groups in the open source community are not subject to the information about market price or hierarchical management, but rather by developing OSS project through voluntary collaboration (Benkler, 2002). At the collective behavior level, developers and users form a cooperative network by participating in common projects. In addition, under the influence of social network services websites such as Facebook and Twitter, the new-generation open source communities are not limited to the functions of any platform for collaborative development of projects any longer but become a social platform of geeks. Taking Gitee, the largest open source technology community in China (China version of GitHub) as an example, registered users can pay attention to not only the progress of a project but also the developer's personal dynamics through the "follow" function. The project initiators, developers, and users interact via online channels to form a complex relational network and create valuable social capital

(Bourdieu, 1986), thus impacting the success of OSS projects. Within the domain of management science, social capital mainly developed from the network of interpersonal relationships among groups as well as resources brought to actors (Luo, 2010). Its connotation can be divided into three dimensions:

(1) Structural dimension. The structural dimension mainly refers to the network ties established among people. Individuals could obtain social resources by establishing ties with others. OSS is not born in a socially isolated environment. The network embeddability of projects and their developers have strong impacts on the success of OSS projects (Grewal, Lilien & Mallapragada, 2006). This paper takes into account the interactive characteristics of the new generation of open source communities on the basis of previous research, and comprehensively examines cooperative ties and following ties. When it comes to cooperative ties, previous partnerships could help recruit developers for the OSS. Hahn, Moon & Zhang (2008) studied the impact of previous partnerships on formation of new project teams and found that developers are more inclined to join the team led by project initiators who have cooperated with them. Developer participation is the driving force behind the success of OSS projects. Besides, cooperative ties could promote efficient collaboration, which is good for the project success. Active interaction among community members could contributed a lot of ideas and suggestions to the project (Moon & Sproull, 2000). Through collaborative ties, knowledge could be transferred and integrated, which is positively related with project success (Chou & He, 2011; Chen et al., 2016; Mclure & Faraj, 2005). After considering the heterogeneity of individuals' roles in different OSS projects, Méndez & García (2009) found that social networks constructed on this basis have played a significant role to promote project success through knowledge circulation. Chen, Zhou, & Su (2016) conducted a quantitative analysis on large samples using 403 valid questionnaires and found that distributed innovations using knowledge sharing as the medium affect the performance of OSS projects, in which social networks have the greatest influence on knowledge sharing among members. As for the following ties, we propose that if the OSS project initiators have established more following ties in the OSS community, the information about the projects they initiate will be better known and recognized by more potential developers, thus attracting more potential developers to work for the OSS projects and facilitate the project success.

In view of the theoretical analysis, this paper proposes the following hypotheses:

Hypothesis H2: Social networks of OSS project initiators have a positive impact on project success.

Hypothesis H2a: Cooperative ties between OSS project initiators and other developers have a positive impact on project success.

Hypothesis H2b: Connections triggered by behaviors following project initiators have a positive impact on project success. If project initiators gain more followings of people, this will bring more collaborative opportunities and resources, thus increasing the probability of project success.

(2) Cognitive dimension. The cognitive dimension refers to the subjective consensus that leads individuals to behaving collectively, including common language and values. Cognitive social capital is a resource channel that is built on a common culture. Since the open source community is an open organization formed from the gathering of all users involved in the development and improvement of OSS projects based on recognition of the open source spirit, the paper does not consider the impact of cognitive social capital on specific projects.

(3) Relational dimension. The relational dimension covers the network content established through the network and cognitive consensus, including trust and recognition. Since trust and recognition are core elements of social capital, a person who is trusted and recognized can get more opportunities for

cooperation and people are also willing to provide him (her) with resources and expect rewards. Chou & He (2010) showed that the relational social capital attached to social networks have a positive impact on knowledge integration in OSS projects, thus improving the performance of OSS projects. Therefore, we posit:

Hypothesis H3: Trust and recognition of OSS project initiators have a positive impact on project success.

3. THE MODEL

To analyze the link between OSS project initiators and project success and to verify the above-mentioned hypotheses, in the paper, the regression method has been selected where the dependent variable is the OSS project success, and the independent variables include the commitment of the project initiator, collaborative tie of the project initiator, follow to the project initiators, trust and recognition on the project initiator and the commitment of other project participants as described below in details.

3.1 Dependent Variable

OSS project success, a concept involving multiple dimensions, has been measured by referencing largely studies on traditional software success (Crowston, Howison & Annabi, 2010). For traditional software, the focus is on the ultimate quality and its outcome (Delone & McLean, 1992). While for OSS project, it involves a dynamical development process for continual improvement because of no need of predetermined users. Further, the description on its success is more focused on the indices of various activities in the development process (Sen, Sing & Borle, 2012), as shown in Table 1.

Table 1. Index system of OSS PROJECT success

Dimension	Presentation	Index	Literature
Market success	User	User engagement (user feedback; user innovation); user interest (downloads; mail subscriptions);	Rebeca (2006); Grewal et al. (2006);
Technical success	Developer	Code quality; developer engagement (developer population; bug-fixing frequency; software-updating frequency); developer interest (number of follow; number of collection, number of calls);	Crowston (2003); Stewart, Ammeter & Maruping (2006); Subramaniam, Sen & Nelson (2009); Gu (2009);

In this paper, OSS project success refers to the overall extent to which the OSS project is both recognized by the user community and developer community. Given all that, the principal component analysis has been processed on multiple variables of OSS projects success to obtain the composite index y to evaluate OSS project success. Based on this way, a multivariate regression model has been established.

3.2 Independent Variables

(1) Commitment of the project initiator: Submitting codes is the main form of commitment to OSS development, therefore in the paper, the number of times for code submissions by initiators in the development process has been used to measure the commitment of project initiators.

(2) Collaborative tie of the project initiator: Though it may be assumed that the collaborative tie set up in the open source community by initiators is roughly in normal proportion to the number of projects that initiators initiate or participate in, seeing that members of different projects are in different conditions, the total number of initiator-involved projects cannot accurately reflect the collaborative tie established by initiators. As a result, the number of all other collaborative developers participating in initiator's projects has been accumulated to measure the collaborative tie of initiators. In this method, two developers' jointly participating in development of one OSS project is regarded as the basis for the tie between two nodes, to reflect undirected collaborative network. This is also a most common approach in existing studies.

(3) Follow to the project initiator: The follow in Gitee is similar to that of social network services, e.g., Twitter. By following registered users, a user's activity feeds for initiating and participating in OSS projects can be tracked. In the paper, the followers displayed at the initiator's personal homepage is regarded as the measuring indicator of the follow to the initiator. Besides, the follower of the initiator in the OSS community can be viewed as a proxy of his reputation and influence.

(4) Trust and recognition to the project initiator: There are two kinds of stars in Gitee. On the one hand, it gives a start to OSS at its homepage and the number of stars shows its success or failure; on the other hand, giving a star to an individual at the personal homepage in the open source community. The number of stars that an initiator gets reflects the trust and acceptance to the initiator in the open source community. And the star of the initiator can represent the extent to which his technical knowledge and experience have been recognized.

3.3 Control Variables

Commitment of the developers: Considering the commitment of other participants other than the initiator, the number of times for code submissions by other developers has been selected as a control variable. In particular, it's found out that in the data collection process, a small amount of non-initiator developers in China's open source community are mostly entrants whose social capital plays a very small role compared with the initiator's social capital. Moreover, for the OSS projects in China, it's a wheel communication network centering on initiators. Social capital influences the OSS projects in the way of knowledge integration and sharing. When in a project, knowledge integration and sharing are achieved by initiators, social capital for other participants is negligible to a project's success. Therefore, in the paper, the social capital of other participants has not been considered in the model.

Above all, in the paper, the developer group which is developing an OSS project has been abstracted as a wheel network centering the initiator, as Figure 1 shows: inside the circle, it's the developing team led by the initiator; outside the circle, it's the developers in the open source community, also the potential developers of the project; solid lines represent strong undirected collaborative ties established with an OSS initiator through previous project collaboration, while the broken line with an arrow represents weak unidirectional follow ties established with an OSS project initiator.

Figure 1. Developer network of OSS project

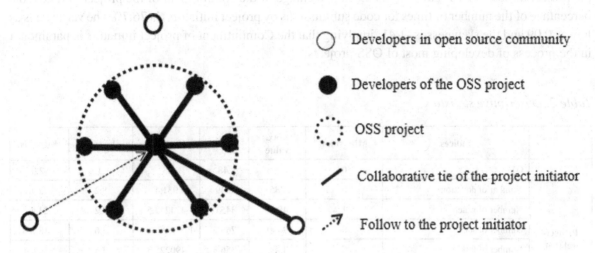

4. EMPIRICAL TEST AND ANALYSIS

4.1 Samples and Data Sources of Research

Since massive data is generally involved in an OSS project, the project data in the open-source China Gitee hosting platform are used in this research in order to avoid data overflow in the process of computing. As of February1st 2018, 80 pieces of very excellent OSS projects were selected as GVP (Gitee Most Valuable Projects). Since the research in this paper focus on the projects initiated by individuals of GVPs., all projects that were initiated by individuals (48 projects in total) were selected as one of research subjects. Additionally, 52 non-GVPs were randomly selected. Themes of sampled projects (N = 100) are wide, involving enterprise applications, mobile applications, games and entertainments; the programs of projects are written by languages, such as, Java, PHP, C#, C++ and Python.

4.2 Descriptive Statistics

Table 2 shows the descriptive statistic results of 100 sampled projects and the indices related to their initiators. In terms of projects, the skewness of all indices concerning project situation is higher than 0, meaning that the peak of the index frequency distribution is at the left and its long-tail extends towards the right side. Considering the sum of project developers, the mean sum of project developers is 8.4. However, the larger skewness suggests that developer sum of most projects is less than the mean. The successful projects, though in a small amount, can attract more developers, thus increasing the overall mean. And this view is also demonstrated in the frequency distribution diagram and the histogram of developer sum (see Figure 2).

In terms of project initiators, project initiators have long joined the open-source community, and all have been recognized and followed in the open-source community to a certain degree. By comparing the number of projects initiated by project initiators and that of those that they participated in, it is easy to find out that project initiators tend to be more likely to initiate their own projects than participate in development of any OSS led by others in the open-source community. Regarding the commitment of the project initiator (see Figure 3), the mean percentage of the commitment of the project initiator (the percentage of the number of times for code submissions by project initiators) is 76.7% The variance is as low as 0.09 and the skewness is -1.41, implying that the Commitment of project initiators is paramount in the process of developing most of OSS projects.

Table 2. Descriptive statistics

	Indices	Min. value	Max. value	Mean	Variance	Skewness	Kurtosis
Project-related index	GVP	0	1	.48	.3	.1	-2.0
	Number of donations	0	285	6.49	931.4	8.2	72.7
	Number of watch	1	4800	345.0	424253.5	4.2	23.4
	Number of star	0	9400	763.5	1796893.9	3.6	18.2
	Number of folk	0	4300	356.3	490225.3	3.5	14.0
	Size of warehouse (MB)	0	260	48.4	4513.8	1.7	1.7
	Sum of developers	1	142	8.4	238.650	7.0	57.6
	Total number of times for code submissions	2	5356	413.7	468014.7	4.4	27.4
Initiator-related index	The number of times for submissions by project initiators	1	2390	284.1	182117.4	2.8	8.9
	Percentage of commitment of the project initiator	.00	1.00	.8	.1	-1.4	.9
	Duration in the community (year)	.00	5.00	2.9	2.2	-.1	-1.0
	Number of star	0	172	13.5	740.210	4.1	18.7
	Number of follow	0	1700	120.5	79950.5	3.7	14.5
	Number of initiated project	1	79	9.5	177.4	3.4	13.3
	Number of participated projects	0	10	.5	2.0	4.1	21.4
	Collaborative tie of the project initiator	0	400	14.6	3040.9	6.9	49.4

4.3 Variance Analysis

All samples are divided into two groups: GVP group (N1=48) and non-GVP group (N2 = 52), and data of both groups are analyzed for the variance. In these samples, if the value is 0, it belongs to the non-GVP group, and if the value is 1, it belongs to the GVP group. Table 3 shows the descriptive statistic results on project-related indices of the GVP group and the non-GVP group, where the numbers of donations, watches, stars, folks and the developer sum of the GVP group are far larger than those of the non-GVP group.

The results from analysis of the project-related indices of the GVP group and the non-GVP group indicate that the differences in indices reflecting projects (success) between both groups are statistically significant, suggesting the objectivity of appraisal and selection of GVPs in the Gitee platform to a certain degree.

Figure 2. Histogram for sum of project developers

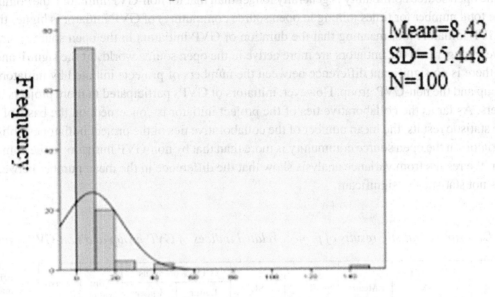

Figure 3. Histogram for percentage of the commitment of the project initiator

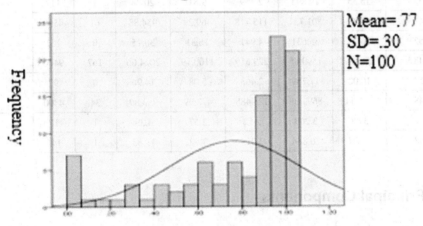

Table 4 shows the descriptive statistic results of initiator-related indices of GVP group and non-GVP group. Table 6 shows the results from variance analysis of initiator-related indices of GVP group and non-GVP group. By comparing the means and its CI 95%, it is not difficulty to find that the follow level and the number of stars of the GVP initiators are far greater than that of non-GVP initiators in the open source community. In terms of project inputs, the number of times for code submission by GVP initiators are far more than those by non-GVP initiators, meaning that GVP initiators input more in software development. But the difference in the percentage of the number of times for code submissions by project initiators between both groups is not significant, implying that no matter whether any OSS is developed successfully or not, project initiators are generally the most important developer and developer in the process of development. In terms of the open source community, the number of years for GVP initiators joining the open source community is generally longer than that for non-GVP initiators, the commitment level (the total number for times joining in open source community) of GVP initiator is higher than that of non-GVP initiators too, meaning that the duration of GVP initiators in the open source community is relatively longer, and the initiators are more active in the open source world. At the significance level of 0.05, there is no significant difference between the numbers of projects initiated by initiators of the GVP group and the non-GVP group. However, initiators of GVPs participated in more projects by other developers. As far as the collaborative ties of the project initiator is concerned, on the basis of the descriptive statistic results, the mean number of the collaborative ties of the project initiator established by GVP initiators in the open source community is more than that by non-GVP initiators in the community. However, the results from variance analysis show that the difference in the mean number between both groups is not statistically significant.

Table 3. Descriptive statistic results of project-related indices of GVP group and non-GVP group

| | | N | Mean | SD | SE | CI 95% of means | | Min. value | Max. value | Variance Analysis Significance |
						Lower limit	Upper limit			
Number of donations	0	52	.04	.277	.038	-.04	.12	0	2	.027
	1	48	13.48	43.195	6.235	.94	26.02	0	285	
Number of watch	0	52	15.35	19.893	2.759	9.81	20.88	1	117	.000
	1	48	702.08	801.721	115.718	469.29	934.88	61	4800	
Number of star	0	52	26.23	35.631	4.941	16.31	36.15	0	151	.000
	1	48	1562.13	1590.85	229.619	1100.19	2024.06	167	9400	
Number of folk	0	52	10.02	17.759	2.463	5.08	14.96	0	99	.000
	1	48	731.44	869.408	125.488	478.99	983.89	34	4300	
Developer sum	0	52	3.48	3.263	.452	2.57	4.39	1	17	.001
	1	48	13.77	20.854	3.010	7.72	19.83	1	142	

4.4 Analysis of Principal Components

On the basis of the success model of the OSS projects, this paper analyzed the principal components, and then, using the dimension reduction method, analyzed the five indices which reflect OSS projects success from different perspectives - the number of project donations (the number of times that projects got donations of users in the open source community), the number of project watches (the number of users in the open source community who are watching the progress of project development), the number of project stars (the number of users in the open source community who star a project), the number of project contributors (the number of users in the open source community who have intention to improve an OSS project) and the size of the warehouse (the capacity of codes) - and finally got comprehensive quantitative indices on project success y_1. The results from the tests by KMO and Bartlett verified the principal components were extracted rationally. On the basis of the interpreted total variance table (Table 5) (text reserved, and the Table to be deleted) and the scree plot (Fig. 4) from the analysis of principal components, only one principal component was extracted from above-mentioned five specific indices as a comprehensive index which can reflect variation of 61.99% data in original variables and better represent the success of the OSS projects.

Table 4. The descriptive statistic results of initiator-related indices of GVP group and non-GVP group

		N	Mean	SD	SE	CI 95% of means		Min. value	Max. value	Significance from variance analysis
						Lower limit	Upper limit			
Number of initiator follow	0	52	14.12	54.324	7.533	-1.01	29.24	0	384	.000
	1	48	235.67	373.01	53.839	127.36	343.98	8	1700	
Number for initiator star	0	52	3.94	7.524	1.043	1.85	6.04	0	33	.000
	1	48	23.75	35.908	5.183	13.32	34.18	0	172	
Number of times for submissions by project initiators	0	52	95.12	181.76	25.205	44.51	145.72	1	1170	.000
	1	48	488.88	515.19	74.361	339.28	638.47	18	2390	
Percentage of commitments of project initiators	0	52	.7299	.37441	.05192	.6257	.8341	.00	1.00	.200
	1	48	.8073	.18678	.02696	.7531	.8615	.32	1.00	
Numbers of years in the community	0	52	2.5927	1.4804	.20529	2.1806	3.0048	.00	5.00	.017
	1	48	3.2917	1.3985	.20185	2.8856	3.6977	1.00	5.00	
Commitment level	0	52	220.34	434.45	60.2478	99.390	341.295	.0	2131.0	.003
	1	48	502.06	497.60	71.8223	357.575	646.550	2.0	1702.0	
Number of initiated projects	0	52	7.37	9.053	1.255	4.84	9.89	1	54	.095
	1	48	11.81	16.560	2.390	7.00	16.62	1	79	
Number of participated projects	0	52	.21	.696	.096	.02	.41	0	3	.023
	1	48	.85	1.879	.271	.31	1.40	0	10	
ColTie	0	52	14.577	55.144	7.64717	-.7754	29.9292	.00	400.00	.444
	1	48	21.292	25.933	3.74307	13.7616	28.8218	.00	165.00	

4.5 Multivariate Regression Analysis

The result from multivariate regression analysis is as shown in Table 6. The regression coefficient of project IniCommit is positive and significant ($\dot{\beta}$ =0.001, p=0.000), suggesting that the project IniCommitment has a significant positive impact on project success (H1 valid). The number of times for submissions by other project developers poses no significant impact on project success ($\dot{\beta}$ =0.000, p=0.113). The follow to project initiators poses significant positive impact on project success (H2 and H2b valid). However, the numbers of stars and collaborative ties gained by project initiators have insignificant impact on project success (H2a and H3 invalid). VIF (Variance Inflation Factor) is far less than 10 indicating that there is no problem concerning multicollinearity present between interpreted variables.

Table 5. Interpreted total variance

Component	Initial eigenvalue			Square extraction and loading		
	Total	Variance, %	Accumulation, %	Total	Variance, %	Accumulation, %
1	3.099	61.99	61.988	3.099	61.988	61.988
2	.981	19.622	81.610			
3	.804	16.072	97.682			
4	.104	2.071	99.754			
5	.012	.246	100.000			

Figure 4. Scree pilot

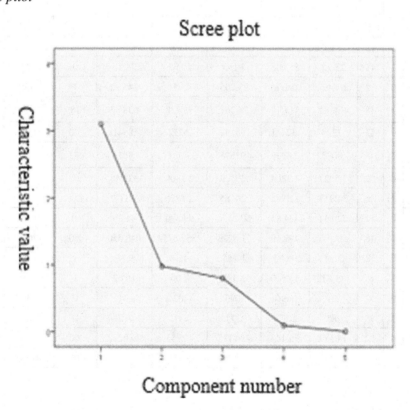

To sum up, the model verified that the commitment of the project initiators has a significant positive impact on OSS projects while the number of times for code submissions by other project developers has no significant impact. This indicates that, in China, project initiators are in general the most important code developer of OSS projects. The greater the number of times the project initiators provide codes for projects, the higher the software quality is, thus the more successful the projects will be. The impact of collaborative tie of the project initiator on project success failed in the significance test, which may have bearing on the fact that deep cooperation has not yet formed in the open source community of China. Also, the model verified that the follow level gained by project initiators in the open source community has a significant positive impact on project success.

In addition, in this paper, by verifying the model with the endogenic test, it is found that the correlation between the residual and the explanatory variable is 0, which negates the two-way impact between the follow of project initiators and project success. In other words, the follow of project initiators has positive impact on project success and it is not project success that brings high follows to project initiators. This will give new inspirations to the management strategy of OSS projects. Project initiators may catch the eyes of fans by multiple means, such as participating in construction of the open source community, thus pulling in supporters to OSS projects indirectly. However, the results from analysis show that the capability approval of the open source community gained by project initiators has no significant impact on project success, similar to the conclusion drawn by Zhang (2008), in other words, the main approaches of project initiators to pull in new developers are social cues rather than status cues.

Table 6. Results from multivariate regression analysis

	Nonstandard coefficient		Standard coefficient	t	Sig.	Statistical amount of colinearity	
	B	SE	Trial version			Tolerance	VIF
(Constant)	-.422	.091		-4.655	.000		
The number of times for submissions by project initiators	.001	.000	.327	4.218	.000	.801	1.248
Number of times for submissions by other developers	.000	.000	-.124	-1.601	.113	.797	1.254
Collaborative tie of the project initiator	-.001	.002	-.049	-.663	.509	.885	1.130
Initiator follow	.002	.000	.670	7.853	.000	.662	1.510
Initiator star	-.001	.003	-.040	-.463	.644	.662	1.511

From the perspective of the indices of the whole model (shown in Table 7), the larger square of R is, the better goodness-of-fit of the linear model is. It indicates that the multivariate regression model allows for better interpretation of the success of OSS projects. F test shows that the model is significant as a whole. The result from DW test demonstrates that no first-order autocorrelation exists in the error terms of the regression model.

Table 7. Summary of the multivariate regression model

R	Square of R	Adjusted square of R-	Error estimated by standard	Revised statistic number					Durbin-Watson
				Revised square of R	Revised F	df1	df2	Revised Sig. F	
.740	.547	.523	.690419	.547	22.737	5	94	.000	1.591

5. ROBUSTNESS ANALYSIS

We conducted a robustness test. First, we used another measurement method of the dependent variable. And then we ran a logistic regression model to test the hypothesis. Since appraisal and selection of GVPs reflects lots of information about the success of OSS projects, only those projects that submit complete files, reach to a certain activity of development (at least 10 updates every year), respond actively to user's feedback, gain high appraisal (the number of stars > 100) and are recognized by the expert panel of the open source China Gitee are eligible to become a GVP. For this reason, whether an OSS project is a GVP may be used to determine whether it is a successful one, and the binary variable y' is used as dependent variable to build a logistic regress model (if a project is one of Gitee GVPs, then $y' = 1$; if it is a non-GVP, then $y' = 0$), which reflects the comprehensive information concerning project success. It is found by analysis that such classification shares very high coincidence degree with the positive/negative sign of project success (y) obtained by analyzing principal components, corroborating that the above-described index structure of dependent variables is rational once again. The binary variable is used as dependent variable to get the results from logistic regression as shown in Table 8, which could provide a robustness check. The assumptions are tested again through empirical testing by building a multivariate regression model and a logistic regression model, both leading to results which are highly consistent with the multivariate e.

It is observed that the number of times for submissions by project initiators is most important for the project success (H1 valid), followed by the follow level gained by project initiators (H2 and H2b valid). At the significance level of 0.05, the ColTie of project initiators and their gained cognition still have insignificant impact on project success ((H2a and H3 invalid). If the significance level is set as 0.1 loosely, the number of stars that project initiators get has a positive impact on project success (H3 valid).

Table 8. Summary of the logistic regression model

	B	S.E,	Wals	df	Sig.	Exp (B)
The number of times for submissions by project initiators	.006	.002	8.040	1	.005	1.006
Number of times for submissions by other developers	-.001	.002	.515	1	.473	.999
Collaborative tie of the project initiator	-.009	.009	1.197	1	.274	.991
Initiator follow	.016	.007	5.225	1	.022	1.016
Initiator star	.054	.033	2.786	1	.095	1.056
Constant	-2.238	.495	20.447	1	.000	.107

The classification table (see Table 9) indicates the built logistic regression model allows to better predict the project success (the prediction success rate up to 85%), which also indicates that the model has a high degree of interpretation.

Table 9. The classification table

Observed		Predicted		
		GVP or not		Corrected percentage
		0	1	
GVP or not	1	11	37	77.1
	0	48	4	92.3
Total percentage				85.0

6. SUMMARY AND IMPLICATIONS

In this research, we investigated the main effects of OSS project initiators on project success in China and the influencing mechanisms. More specifically, we studied whether and how the OSS project initiators can affect the project success in China. In the theoretical part, we view OSS projects development as a "private-collective" innovation model and explore the relationship between OSS project initiators and project success from both the individual or private level and the collective level. In the empirical section, this paper extracts comprehensive indices that reflect project success by analyzing principal components. Based on this, a multivariate regression model to test these hypotheses is established. In addition, the results from this study are verified through Logistic regression analysis.

Through this research, we found that a vast majority of OSS projects in China's open source community are small and hard to sustain. Furthermore, we also explored the mechanisms through which the OSS project initiators can contribute to the project success. The project initiators, in most cases, make their own efforts to be devoted to the vast majority of codes while implementing their projects. In particular, we found that the social capital of OSS project initiators can promote the project success. However, success of OSS projects in China is mainly ascribed to the project initiators, in absence of voluntary participation of other developers.

These findings mainly generate theoretical insights into OSS project development in emerging OSS platforms. This research extends the extant research by studying on the effect of the important protagonist in the OSS developing network, combining the individual behavior level and the collective behavior level through the social network lens. This research also has practical implications. The rise of the OSS project development mode brings a new concept and opportunities to develop the IT industry in China and therefore must be given greater attention by relevant enterprises and government agencies. This paper explored the developing situation of OSS projects in China and found that the success of OSS projects in China relies a lot on the project initiators instead of peer production, which is an immature mode. Hence, it's urgent for the OSS development in China to give full play to the effect of social networks on mass production and collaborative innovation. Based on the research, we suggested that the open source software platform in China should encourage more collective collaboration mode which could lead to coherence of global collective wisdom, reduced development cost and expanded source of innovation. One important implication of this research for management is to promote the willingness and efforts to develop OSS projects in the emerging hosting platform. Since there is no salient distinction between the code contribution of project initiators and other developers in the project, we should encourage more developers besides the project initiators to become active contributors of the OSS project, making

OSS development a real collective product. Another significant implication for OSS projects is to take advantage of the power of social capital catalyze the success of the OSS project.

The major limitation of this study is that the scope of the analysis of OSS development is the emerging hosting platform. Further study will extend the distinction between the developing mode of the OSS projects in emerging OSS platforms and advanced OSS community. In addition, the specific mechanisms of the effect of the OSS project initiators, which include the mediation mechanisms and moderation mechanisms, need more exploration.

ACKNOWLEDGMENT

The research for this paper has been supported by the National Natural Science Foundation of China (No: 71272215) and the Beijing Social Science Fund (No: 17GLB024).

REFERENCES

Aksulu, A., & Wade, M. (2010). A comprehensive review and synthesis of open source research. *Journal of the Association for Information Systems, 11*(11), 576–656. doi:10.17705/1jais.00245

Bai, H. (2014). *Research on the avalanche effect of the open source community failure project*. South China University of Technology.

Benkler, Y. (2002). Coase's Penguin, or Linux and" The Nature of the Firm. *The Yale Law Journal, 2002*(3), 369–446. doi:10.2307/1562247

Benkler, Y., & Nissenbaum, H. (2010). Commons-Based Peer Production and Virtue. *Journal of Political Philosophy, 14*(4), 394–419. doi:10.1111/j.1467-9760.2006.00235.x

Bourdieu, P. (1986). The forms of capital. Handbook of Theory & Research of for the Sociology of Education, 280-291.

Chen, X., Zhou, Y., & Su, J. (2016). Relationship between distributed innovation, knowledge sharing and performance of Open Source Software projects. *Studies in Science of Science, 34*(2), 228-235+245.

Chou, W., & He, Y. (2011). The factors that affect the performance of Open Source Software development-the perspective of social capital and expertise integration. *Information Systems Journal, 21*(2), 195–219. doi:10.1111/j.1365-2575.2009.00347.x

Crowston, K., Howison, J., & Annabi, H. (2010). Information systems success in free and Open Source Software development: Theory and measures. *Software Process Improvement and Practice, 11*(2), 123–148. doi:10.1002pip.259

DeLone, H., & McLean, R. (1992). Information systems success: The quest for the dependent variable. *Information Systems Research, 3*(1), 60–95. doi:10.1287/isre.3.1.60

Feng, G. (2010). Bibliometric Analysis of Open Source Software Published During the Period of 2000 -2009. *Library and Information Service, 54*(2), 50–54.

Garzarelli, G. (2003). Open Source Software and the economics of organization. *Industrial Organization*, *1*, 51–56.

Grewal, R., Lilien, G., & Mallapragada, G. (2006). Location, location, location: How network embeddedness affects project success in open source systems. *Management Science*, *52*(7), 1043–1056. doi:10.1287/mnsc.1060.0550

Gu, Z. (2009). *Research on key success factors of Open Source Software projects*. Fudan University.

Hahn, J., Moon, J., & Zhang, C. (2008). Emergence of new project teams from Open Source Software developer networks: Impact of prior collaboration ties. *Information Systems Research*, *19*(3), 369–391. doi:10.1287/isre.1080.0192

Hippel, E., & Krogh, G. (2003). Open Source Software and the "private-collective" innovation model: Issues for organization science. *Organization Science*, *14*(2), 209–223. doi:10.1287/orsc.14.2.209.14992

Jin, Z., Zhou, M., & Zhang, Y. (2016). Open Source Software and its eco-systems: Today and tomorrow. *Science & Technology Review*, *34*(14), 42–48.

Kogut, B., & Metiu, A. (2001). Open Source Software Development and Distributed Innovation. *Oxford Review of Economic Policy*, *17*(2), 248–264. doi:10.1093/oxrep/17.2.248

Lerner, J., & Tirole, J. (2002). Some simple economics of open source. *The Journal of Industrial Economics*, *50*(2), 197–234. doi:10.1111/1467-6451.00174

Liu, K. (2013). *The present and the Future of Open Source Software Industry in China*. Central China Normal University.

Luo, J. (2010). *Social Network Analysis Handout* (2nd ed.). Social Sciences Academic Press.

Mclure, M., & Faraj, S. (2005). Why should share? Examining social capital and knowledge contribution in electribution in electronic networks of practice. *Management Information Systems Quarterly*, *29*(1), 35–57. doi:10.2307/25148667

Méndez-Durón, R., & García, E. (2009). Returns from social capital in Open Source Software networks. *Journal of Evolutionary Economics*, *19*(2), 277–295. doi:10.100700191-008-0125-5

Moon, J., & Sproull, L. (2005). Essence of distributed work: The case of the Linux kernel. *First Monday*.

Raymond, E. (1999). The cathedral and the bazaar. *Philosophy & Technology*, *12*(3), 23.

Sen, R., Sing, S., & Borle, S. (2012). Open Source Software success: Measures and analysis. *Decision Support Systems*, *52*(2), 364–372. doi:10.1016/j.dss.2011.09.003

Stewart, J., Ammeter, P., & Maruping, M. (2006). Impacts of license choice and organizational sponsorship on user interest and development activity in Open Source Software projects. *Information Systems Research*, *17*(2), 126–144. doi:10.1287/isre.1060.0082

Subramaniam, C., Sen, R., & Nelson, L. (2009). *Determinants of Open Source Software project success: A longitudinal study*. Elsevier Science Publishers B.V.

Wang, H., Dai, W., & Feng, Y. (2009). Open Source Strategy and Intellectual Property Protection for China's Telecommunication Enterprises. *Electronic Intellectual Property*, *9*, 18–22.

Zhang, C. (2008). *A network perspective on Open Source Software development: team formation and community participation*. Purdue University.

Zhang, D., Li, B., He, P., & Zhou, H. (2015). Research on the Characteristics of Open Source Community Based on Software Ecosystem. *Computer Engineering*, *41*(11), 106–113.

This research was previously published in the International Journal of Information Systems in the Service Sector (IJISSS), 12(1); pages 28-43, copyright year 2020 by IGI Publishing (an imprint of IGI Global).

Chapter 13
Does an Open Source Development Environment Facilitate Conventional Project Management Approaches and Collaborative Work?

Richard Garling
American Military University, USA

ABSTRACT

Open source software (OSS) is very well known for allowing free access to the source code of the application. The idea is to allow for the creation of a better product. The more people working to make each aspect of an application better, more minds create more ideas, create a better project. OSS runs the internet since all of the protocols—network time protocol (NTP), HTTP, amongst many others—are OSS projects with many years of use. These projects are run by volunteers worldwide. But, none of these projects are run using the traditional methodologies of project management: Waterfall and Agile. This chapter asks: How does an open source development environment facilitate conventional Waterfall project management approaches? and How does an open source development environment facilitate Agile project collaborative work? The method used to determine the answers used surveys and questionnaires involving actual participants in a variety of OSS projects from across the United States (US). The questions asked concerned the organization OSS projects, did they use a particular traditional methodology or some other non-defined method of organization? The answers received by this study centered on non-defined methods of organization; traditional methodologies were considered too restrictive and not agile enough to allow for the freedom cherished by their volunteers.

DOI: 10.4018/978-1-7998-9158-1.ch013

INTRODUCTION

Information and communicating are keys to managing projects to a successful conclusion. There are major differences in the management of information and communication between traditionally managed projects using traditional management techniques and methodologies such as Waterfall or Agile and the management styles that Open Source Software (OSS) projects use. Knowing the work and the risks are the best defense for handling problems and delays. Assessing potential overall project risks brings to the forefront the need for changing project objectives. It is these risk analysis tools that allows the Project Manager (PM) to transform an impossible project into a successful project (Campbell, 2012). Project risks become increasingly difficult when dealing with an unrealistic timeline or target date when given insufficient resources, or insufficient funding. Knowing the risks can help to set realistic expectation levels of deliverables, and the work required given the resources and funding provided. Managing risks means communicating and being ready to take preventive action. The PM cannot be risk-averse; accepting risk will happen remains part of the job, doing nothing is not an option (Gido & Clements, 2012). The PM needs to set the tone of their projects by encouraging open and frank discussion on potential risks. The PM needs to encourage identifying risks, the potential impact of the project, and the likelihood of occurrence, develop risk response plans and monitor those risks. OSS seems to want to do it differently. It claims to be more collaborative, yet it is also very closed in many ways, to the point of being very possessive, not willing to share.

This chapter will explore the various properties of traditional project management and how they are, or are not, applied to OSS projects. Examples abound showing real-life case studies from both traditionally managed projects from the corporate world, and from open source software projects currently active in the OSS world. The key in this comparison is in showing how it is that OSS has become successful, even to the point of literally running the internet as we know it today. What makes OSS so successful in spite of the way projects are managed?

Starting a new project can be a very interesting experience, and yet it can also be a terrifying experience. Interesting or horrifying depends greatly on your level of experience. The most interesting and challenging part is putting the team together. There are many aspects to consider such as what are the tasks to complete the project? What level of expertise will be needed? What amount of time will be required to complete each task? What if the task requires certain expertise for a short time, is that expertise available when you needed?

Other questions that need to be considered involve governing the project. The processes that will need to be established will need to be considered by both the team and by management. Processes that involve communicating, conflict management, risk management; all need to be considered and planned. Many of these processes are not practiced initially in many OSS projects. Most leaders of OSS projects consider this type of organization to be cumbersome at best; more a chore to be avoided.

Project Oversight

The Project Management Office (PMO) provides the integration of procedures, technology, organizational structure, staffing, and guidance that ensures projects are in alignment with company strategy and goals. The three tiers of management in the PMO model form the relationship between project, the project's resources, and company strategy. Project management concentrations are on the successful completion of selected projects. Program management serves to coordinate projects and the resources of each project. Usually, these projects share a similar goal and processes. Project portfolio management links the selection of projects and programs to the strategic goals of the company.

Program management is the management of numerous related projects. Each project is managed by individual project managers, and one Program Manager oversees the whole. The goal is to remove the confusion characteristic of many related projects by efficiently organizing limited resources between each project. Project portfolio management (PPM) makes sure that projects and programs meet the organizational strategies and goals of the company. It does this by managing the limited resources available within the company. It requires well-organized decisions compelled by priorities established by the Project Management Office or Executive decision. The benefits of PPM are in choosing the right projects with the right resources to complete those using strategic priorities to direct resource allocation.

Program Management

Program Management is similar to, yet very different, from project management. Program managers coordinate groups of related projects rather than manage individual projects themselves. The program manager manages horizontally across the functional projects involved with the program. The program manager ensures that cross-project work effort remains feasible from a business standpoint and realizes benefits. The goal is to leverage ROI and control not available from managing projects separately helping organizations achieve strategic results. (Ward, 2009).

Program Managers already have years of experience as Project Managers, but they need to keep the big picture in mind when guiding the individual projects towards the company goals. They need to understand leadership and team building. The ability to communicate, especially in the negotiation of contracts, and influencing outcomes, is highly important. Program Managers have to be strong in conflict resolution, in stakeholder management, possess superior analytic abilities allowing them to plan the effective use of resources, and, of course, understand how to use all the tools available to their Project Managers.

Project Scope

The Program Manager uses the scope of the project to define the needs of the organization to the various project teams. The project scope document is the most important document that can assure success in a project. The scope serves as the explanation for why the project exists. It is impossible to determine if the project is "done" if you don't know the definition of "done." The team cannot possibly determine if there is progress made if there is no defined goal. The scope is that defined goal, it is the definition of done. It is the Program Manager's job to help management define the scope so that it meets the strategic goals of the organization. The Program Manager's next responsibility is to explain the scope so that the project team can meet the goal successfully.

The scope is the process of developing a detailed description of the project and product. The key benefit of this process is that it describes the product, service, or result in boundaries by defining which of the requirements collected will be included in and excluded from the project scope (PMBOK, 2013).

Project Schedule

Posting the defined scope into a stationary time frame so that performance can be measured throughout the life of the project determines an important level of success. A well-defined scope and the timeframe to complete the project are fundamental to all successful projects. The project schedule is one of the best tools the Program Manager has for managing the overall activities and resources available to a project. The project schedule can be used to monitor project performance regularly; even day-to-day. The schedule contains the order of authorized work and what resources will be needed and for how long. The schedule, with the WBS, identifies the milestones, the tasks, the resources and the timeframe required to complete each task.

The points in the schedule will be used to measure progress, identify the differences between planned and actual schedule performance, planned and actual costs, and provide the explanations for the variances in the detail needed by program management. The Program Manager can use this information to make decisions to ensure successful project conclusion.

Work Breakdown Structure Development

The Work Breakdown Structure (WBS) is used to categorize and establish all tasks needed in which to complete a project according to the scope of the project. It only calls for those tasks needed, and only those tasks needed, in which to complete the project (PMBOK, 2013). The WBS is a decomposition of the work deliverables into manageable work packages; it organizes and defines the total scope of the project. The WBS shows, in ordered form, the activity required to complete the project. Work packages are time measured by duration, commonly one day to one week. Packages are then ordered sequentially to determine a project schedule. The WBS will also include the resources required to be used to complete the work on a specific package.

The WBS framework provides a common method with which to organize all the identified tasks needed to complete the project. The WBS is made up of different levels that determine project needs. The first three levels will usually reflect the integrated efforts of the project. Level one called the "home" level, concerns the authorization and release of work. Level two is for budgetary information; level three is for scheduling the tasks; lower levels are the work packages of the project. The sum of the work of each child level must equal 100% of the work at the parent level. Each level is ordered sequentially to identify dependencies while keeping in mind that some tasks can be done in parallel to others (Kerzner, 2009).

The Budget

The budget is what gives the Program Manager and the project team the hard currency to measure success. Once the project has determined overall project costs from the WBS and the schedule, the project has the means to measure its progress. This measurement of progress is what the Program Manager and upper management will use to determine if the project is on track, on time and within the defined budgetary constraints. Project performance will be measured using earned value metrics, expressed as a cost or schedule performance variance from the baseline. Variances will give an early warning of looming problems; can be used to determine needed corrective action to be taken to keep the project within defined parameters. The Performance Measurement Baseline (PMB), a baseline against which performance may be measured, is an important aspect of project management. The PMB references the point in which a project can measure actual completed work. It will tell whether the project is on the planned schedule, and within budget.

Resource Allocation and Management

Network analysis can provide vital information for planning, scheduling, and execute projects. The reason for network planning is to avoid emergency management by using picture illustrations (graphs) displaying the total project activities in a logical order. These graphic depictions aid in determining sequencing and duration of activities and the project. The following information can obtain from such a graphical picture. Interdependencies of activities, project completion time, the impact of late starts the impact of early starts, trade-offs between resources and time, performance slippages, performance evaluations are some of the benefits derived from network analysis.

The Critical Path Method (CPM) was mainly worried about creating activity prerequisites and determining simple network solutions. It was primarily useful for keeping track of activities and identifying activity conflicts or sequencing flexibilities which could affect project completion. The Project Evaluation and Review Technique (PERT) was designed to overcome characteristic problems in assuming activity time estimates deterministically (Kerzner, 2009). Using CPM and PERT to analyze the project the Program Manager can determine the interdependencies of each activity and thus can sequence these activities in a logical order. From this information, the Program Manager can determine the Critical Paths of the projects he controls. Through network analysis, the Program Manager can determine how to utilize resources effectively and to track how the project progresses thus keeping control on time and costs.

Team Development and Management

Team members working together is an important part of team development, and it helps make management of a project much easier. A challenge for the PM and the Program Manager is when the team is made up of diverse cross-functional resources from different departments and geographic locations. Getting such a group to work together has many of its issues. Besides different rules or procedures, there are time zones and cultural difference to consider. Each department could have different forms for requesting their services. There could be internal accounting charges to track, especially if each department has its budget to maintain. The Program Manager has to help ensure that each group communicates with one another to provide the needed resources at the required time and place.

Processes are very important to managing projects and groups of projects. These processes are needed to ensure that each of the projects within a program is going in the direction needed to reach the company goals. There are five attributes that help to ensure the processes are effectively developed and managed by the team. These attributes include depersonalizing issues or topics; make the environment participative and inclusive; makes discussions objective, not emotional; and increase team transparency (Wong, 2007).

Encouraging each team member to contribute shows each team member their opinion matters. When the team member is allowed to speak freely, ideas flow freely. And when ideas flow freely, solutions are soon to follow. The Program Manager's first duty is to encourage an atmosphere for free-flowing discussions on how best to solve all project issues so that it benefits the company. The important aspect here is that the Program Manager and the PM have set up an atmosphere for the team to create their processes that they will use to self-mange the project (Wong, 2007). Developing processes as you go along only leads to disaster with the team trying to decide the procedure for how to solve issues when they occur. A pre-planned process allows the team to put simply into action when unanticipated events or issues occur. This transparency encourages full involvement in an inclusive atmosphere.

The six core areas that require effective processes to manage projects successfully include many day-to-day activities. They include running meetings, communications, decision making, performance measuring, roles and responsibilities, and feedback (Wong, 2007). Regularly scheduled status meetings with the team, upper management, and with the sponsors of the project is a major part of planning a project. The project team needs to meet regularly to review the status of the project, discussing completed tasks and upcoming tasks in the plan, and to determine a course of action for any issues or blockers (PMBOK, 2013). All of this gathered information is reported to the Program Manager.

Team lead's and facilitators' roles need to be spelled out, defined and assigned at the beginning of a project. By the act of defining and assigning decision-making and receiving feedback is easier. Once responsibility is defined issue resolution is quick.

The very first order of business in any project is to develop a communication plan. The communication plan outlines what, where, when, how, and to whom information gets communicated in the project. The plan outlines responsibility for sending a communique and who receives it. It should outline if there is to be any expected response (PMBOK, 2013). Status reports are an example of a communique in a project. Status reports are driven from the bottom up with the final summarized version being received by upper management. Each status report delivers information to the next level that is vital for ensuring the project work is completed within the allotted time. These reports provide information which allows the managers to make decisions that can adjust the direction of the project to ensure success. Each report is formatted to allow for the easy dissemination of the information needed that conveys the status message.

Program Managers need to be aware of the content of the message they're delivering to the project teams under their watch. The information within the message, the content of the message, tells the team why they're being asked to do this project. It tells the team why this project exists and the expected result. The objective, the assumptions made, and the company's strategic goals are all spelled out very carefully to the team to ensure maximum impact. Within this communique the company vision is shared. The vision tells the team what the company's aim is, what it seeks by completing this project successfully. A company's vision should inspire, motivate its people toward a goal, and provide direction that moves the team forward because they see themselves as part of something bigger they can share. By understanding the content, the vision, the mission, the team can create the plan and the answer that delivers that promise.

Conflict happens in a project. Sometimes it's the best way to arrive at the best solution to a problem. The key is in defining the process used to confront conflict productively. Conflict is likely, especially if the project team comes from diverse geographic locations and cultures. Differences in values, perceptions, and personalities all play a role in how conflict occurs. Program Managers and PM's need appropriate skills in which to handle conflict (Ohlendorf, 2001).

Often there are hidden agendas, based on individual needs, sometimes caused when members of the team do not share information with the team. Sometimes this is due to mistrust amongst teammates, perhaps due to not feeling comfortable with working together; sometimes referred to as the formative stage of group dynamics. Building trust through open and honest communications can establish a trusting environment for the project team leading to successful project conclusions (Herzog, 2001).

What Is a Process?

Processes are the tools and procedures used to complete projects successfully. In team space, the project team usually defines processes that fit the needs of the specific project. These can be temporary or for the life of the project.

Some processes are determined by the company. These types of processes are considered to be permanent processes and all projects have to abide by them. An example could be financial reporting procedures, timekeeping, status reports, or procurement policies as processes the company decides, not the project.

Good Team Processes

Rules of engagement and processes help keep a project running smoothly. The team and management need to agree on what these rules or processes are because without them projects will go off in many different directions losing control, leading to failure. There are many attributes that effectively develop and manage the rules and processes the team should follow. They include five key attributes: 1) depersonalize issues or topics; 2) increase team transparency; 3) make discussions objective, not emotional; 4) make the environment participative and 5) inclusive by giving each team member equal weight and power in decision making (Wong, 2007).

These key attributes make certain the smooth running of the project. Encouraging contribution shows team members that it is safe to speak up. When the team openly contributes, ideas come out and they discover better solutions. Discouraging equal contributions from team members leads to an unsuccessful project. Inclusiveness, encouraging participation, gives each team member a sense of ownership and willingness to help make decisions. The key is the team decides on the rules of engagement on how it will manage itself. And these processes need to be decided early in the project (Wong, 2007). When the team decides on the rules of engagement, breaking those rules means they're lying to themselves and their teammates. Breaking their word means they break the bond of trust with the team. Determining rules on the fly lead to chaos and an unsuccessful project. Predetermining rules of engagement and putting processes in place that determine how to manage unanticipated issues or needs is just good thinking on the part of the team.

Important Processes

The important processes needed to manage the main day-to-day activities of a successful project include team meetings, roles and responsibilities, communications, decision making, measuring performance, and feedback (Wong, 2007). Each project team needs to set regularly scheduled status meetings with the team as a whole, no matter their location, and with upper management and the sponsors of the project. The team, depending on the project schedule should meet at least weekly, daily if necessary, to review the status of the project, discuss what work is completed and planned, and to determine a course of action for any issues or blockers (PMBOK, 2013).

Depending on how the team organizes determines the frequency of meeting. If the team is geographically spread out across the world, New York and Beijing, for example, the team could meet twice a day since there is a twelve-hour difference between each city. Both of these meetings could be considered a stand-up meeting as is used in Scrum projects. The team could decide to limit these meetings to fifteen minutes each meeting session so as to maintain good status communications.

The project needs to define roles and responsibilities of the team leaders and facilitators as this will help expedite decision making and feedback. This definition is important because it will help to determine which team member takes the lead when issues occur. Defining these roles helps the team, and management, determine who to go to if a crisis arises and decisions need to be made quickly without the luxury of meeting to discuss options thoroughly. A communication plan needs to be established right from the start of any project. The communication plan determines how and what gets communicated and to whom. It determines who is responsible for what gets communicated and how that communication gets delivered (PMBOK, 2013). For example; there are many different types of status reports. Status reports come from the project team and go up to management, stakeholders, or the sponsors of the project. Each report requires different levels or amounts of information in different formats. The team needs to determine the information required for each report, the delivery method, and feedback required. These are reports needed to manage the project. Not everyone needs the same information or as much information.

Content

Content tells the team what it is that is being asked of them. It explains why this project is being put together, what the objective is, what assumptions are being made, and how it affects the strategy of the company.

Vision is a major part of content as it tells the team what it is we're all aiming for. Vision shows what is possible by completing this project. Vision can be inspiring and shared by everyone on the team. Vision can be a motivator that provides direction moving the team forward because it understands the opportunities and the strategies presented.

To accomplish the goals of the project the team needs to understand the content in order to create the processes that will help deliver that vision. Without the content the team has no idea what is expected or being asked of them.

Remote Teams

Many of the problems remote project management faces deals with determining how the team will work together. The team needs to determine the tools available to them, and if those tools work effectively in the environment in which they work. If you're a collection of contractors, the tools you can use that are readily available to a corporate employee may not be available to you. As such, the rules of engagement need to be determined. How is the team going to communicate? How often will they meet, and when? What tools will they use to conduct the meeting? What are the document requirements for each meeting? The team has to consider how the technology runs in the locales they live. While the United States is relatively wide open, China has restrictions that need consideration. There is also the time differences, language barriers, cultural differences that need to be carefully considered by the team.This paper will give a brief discussion on the importance of setting the rules and processes, as well as the tools used by the team so they can properly manage a project to success with a remote team.

Risks of Remote Team Project Management

As with anything in our world today, there are risks. One problem deals with the use of technology when it's spread out to locations not easily accessible for tech support to access. A team member may be good at planning, but they can be technology challenged in not having the experience to use the tools the team has agreed on using. When the project depends on utilizing personal equipment owned by the team member the challenge is using available tools that work on the equipment available and within the experience of the team members. While Skype is relatively easy to install and use, it can be persnickety when the connection isn't good. If the team member uses dial-up ISP connection versus broadband, many applications won't work because they use massive amounts of broadband space. Cloud-based applications can lose their connection simply because their cloud-based applications; even with broadband, there is no guarantee the connection will be consistent.

Listening

One of the top skills that the Project Manager needs throughout these approaches is their ability to listen. And keep in mind that listening works both with the Project Manager and with the team member. Many times team members are busy trying to figure out how to win the argument rather than listening to what the other team member is saying. This behavior is particularly prevalent when the project has been doing a lot of avoidance or when the issue has been forced due to an uncompromising party to the conflict. Recently a conflict arose in my current project due to a decision forced on one team by another team impacted by the needs of the project. The team that had forced the original decision was now finding itself in the position to have to defend that decision to the sponsors of the project. They were trying to wiggle their way out of it and just kept digging that hole deeper and deeper. They weren't listening, even when the team they had forced the original decision on was offering a face-saving compromise. Listening would have led them to resolving the issue. Not listening almost caused irreparable damage the project as well as to relationships and reputations.

Interpersonal Skills

There is no doubt that the best PM's are also exceptional leaders. They inspire, they bring people together by giving them the vision of what's down the road, people trust them, and they achieve countless things. To successfully lead a project to completion requires a strong leader with people skills in leadership, teamwork and team behaviors, decision making, problem solving, and conflict resolution. Without these interpersonal skills the project will lack strong leadership and direction which could cost the organization tremendously.

There are three skills, broadly speaking, that good leaders should have:

1. Technical skills because the team will trust and believe in you if you can participate one-on-one with them in finding a solution; or at least can talk the talk and walk the walk. In the IT world it's knowing programming, it's knowing how the pieces of the system fit together in order to make it work. The team wants to know that if need be, you can make it work on your own.

2. Human skill knows how to work with people. It's very different from technical skill which has to do with working with things. These skills allow a leader to work with people to help them achieve their goals which helps the project achieve its goals. People skills allows a leader to work with groups of people, especially useful in project management since the object is to get a group of people to work as one towards a common goal.

3. Conceptual skills involves possessing the intelligence trait as it deals with the ability to work with ideas and concepts. It is central to creating the vision and plans for the project and conveying those thoughts effectively to the team and stakeholders.

Good leaders need to possess a certain trait like intelligence; basically, the ability to express ones-self verbally, perceptually and with sound reasoning brings people to trust in your ability to lead. They need to be self-confident. Self-confidence is the ability to be certain about one's skills and competencies. This includes self-esteem. But a good leader is not arrogant. Influencing others is part of being leader and having the self-confidence to influence allows the leader to feel that their attempts to influence are correct and good for the project. Integrity is highly important because it is the quality trait of honesty and trustworthiness. Leaders who adhere to a strong set of principles taking responsibility for their actions exhibit integrity. Sociability is the trait of seeking positive pleasant social encounters. Good leaders like to talk with people, especially in intelligent stimulating conversations. They are polite, sensitive to others needs, outgoing, tactful and diplomatic (Northouse, 2004).

Leadership

Leadership involves concentrating the efforts of a group of individuals and moving them toward a collective goal, empowering them to work as a team. Leadership is the talent to get things done through others. It's very much like herding a bunch of cats. Respect and trust are keys of actual leadership. Fear and compliance only lock the door to future cooperation. Although important in every project phase, good leadership is critically important during the initiation and planning phases of a project. This is the time to bring the team onboard by telling them the importance of the goal, using that vision to motivate and inspire a group of individuals to come together formulating a team to achieve success. Good leaders always have the end in mind.

All through a project, the PM has to establish and reinforce the vision and strategy by continuously communicating the message. This communicating helps to build trust; build team; influence, mentor, and monitor project and team performance. After all, it is people, not plans that complete projects. The PM, by inspiring others to find their voice, keeps the goals and objectives front and center. A successful project is a result of everyone agreeing on what needs to be done and then doing it. From initiation to closing, the project depends on the willingness of all involved to come to agreement, to synchronize action, to solve problems, and to react to changes. Communication amongst everyone is all that is required (Verzuh, 2012).

Team Building

Team building is the process of helping a group of individuals to work together as a cohesive unit, to work with their leader, to work with external stakeholders, and the organization. In the end, good leadership with good team building makes teamwork. PM's have to remember that running a project is not a one-person effort; it takes a team to complete a project. Team building really does require all the interpersonal skills a PM can muster, as well as the five success factors for a project. To know and like a PM is to trust them. It's not likely the team will trust their leader if they don't really like him, they can't really like him if they don't know him, and in the end they won't trust him if they don't like or know him.

A project team is a group of people with complementary but diverse skills and experiences who are asked to work together to accomplish the goals and objectives of the project. The purpose of the team is to develop and execute a work plan that will meet the goals and objectives of the project. Everyone on the team needs to be committed and dedicated to the same thing: meeting the goals of the project. Although the goals may be same, how the team elects to execute the work plan is variable.

Team-building activities consist of a series of tasks that establish the goals of the project, clearly define the roles and responsibilities of each team member and establish the procedures and processes the team will work under.

Some of these processes include how the team will communicate, how it will interact with each other in meetings; the PM needs to lead the team to agreement on establishing the rules for conflict management. Establishing these rules allows the developing of an environment in which the team can work. Part of developing a team environment involves handling project team problems and determining how these issues will be discussed. The PM puts these processes together with their team because the PM knows that the team needs to take ownership and have buy-in for it to work.

Team building helps build commitment from your team. They have to choose to become a member of the team. The PM cannot make them commit, the individual has to decide. The PM, as a leader, has to figure out what is the best way to get that true commitment from you. He has to figure out how to empower you to decide to commit to the project, its goals and its objectives. Some people prefer committing to a team rather than as an individual; it makes it easier for individuals to join. Some people just have trouble committing to a decision except when in a group. Some call this group think where one individual does all the talking and everyone else just follows along. The talker is given a false sense of empowerment believing they have control. The wise leader will learn what it takes to motivate this individual and what it will take to bring the best out in the rest of the team.

Team building involves bringing out the best in each member. Some members can be timid allowing other members to make the decision and they're along for the ride. The problem here is that there are a select few who are actually running the team rather than having involvement from all. If all are not participating it makes it tough to get strong commitment for all because decisions are being made that some might find objectionable. But because the team leader didn't allow the opportunity for them to speak up, they go along half-heartedly accepting the direction the project is taking even though they might know a better course of action. Changes are inevitable in a project, and the PM has to manage them effectively with a continual team-building efforts. The PM should continually monitor team functionality and performance to determine if any actions are needed to prevent or correct various team problems. With team building, as the PM develops the team, team performance should increase. One model of team building involves five distinctly different stages of maturation in the team (Tuckman, 1965):

1. Forming is when the team is getting to know each other. They're interested in who each member of the team is and what they bring to the table. Questions like, what do they know, and will they be able to help me if I have a problem. Teammates also want to know that the other teammates will carry their weight

2. Storming is where the team begins to dig into the project goals and objectives. They begin to define and divide the tasks needed to be done and who will be responsible for completing those tasks as well as when. Technical decisions are made during this period. Gaining an understanding of the project processes also occurs. Cooperation can become counterproductive if the team does not collaborate well.

3. Norming is the beginning of cooperation amongst the members of the team. They begin to trust one another, especially each other's abilities.

4. Performing is when the team begins to work as a well-oiled machine. Trust is attained and production increases. Conflict is minimal but productive as they work through issues easily.

5.   Adjourning brings the project to a close. The final product is approved for production and the team moves on to the next project.

Team building can be additionally enriched by gaining top management support; encouraging team member commitment to the goals and objectives of the project; introducing appropriate rewards, recognition, and ethics; creating a team identity; managing conflicts effectively; promoting trust and open communication among team members; and providing leadership. While team building is essential during the front end of a project, it is an ongoing process. Changes in a project environment are inevitable. Maintaining ownership and buy-in form the team will be difficult. To manage these changes effectively, a continued or renewed team-building effort is required. Outcomes of team building include mutual trust, high quality of information exchange, better decision making, and effective project management.

Motivation

Project team members come from diverse backgrounds. Each has their own expectations, and individual objectives that they want to meet. The overall success of the project depends upon the project team's commitment. This commitment is directly related to their level of motivation. Motivating your team in a project involves creating an environment to enable your team to meet project objectives while also enabling them to meet their objectives and what they value most. These values will likely include job satisfaction, challenging work, a sense of accomplishment, achievement and growth, perhaps even money.

The PM must determine how best to meet the need of each team member by learning what does motivate each of them. One way to do this is by listening every day to how they respond to different interactions. Meeting with each team member individually will be time consuming in the beginning, but will prove to beneficial later in the project when you get to crunch time. By learning early on what it takes to motivate that team member the leader will be able to know how to ask them to step up to the plate when it becomes necessary (Spreitzer & Quinn, 2001).

One motivation tool to use is letting your team do their own communicating with stakeholders, so long as they can do so reliably. What this does is to build confidence in the team member that you as the leader believe in their ability to do their job. If the PM is constantly hovering over the team member, especially in meetings with business Subject Matter Experts (SME), interrupting and over explaining, it brings a level of distrust in to the relationship. The PM has to allow for the team member to rise or fall on their own. Setting the expectation that the team member has to work with the SME's raising the level of confidence in the team member. More importantly; it takes a load of work off of the PM by letting the team do their jobs.

Communication

Today, business is changing faster than ever, and most of those changes are being implemented through projects that require even stronger project management. However, just using sound project management methods does not ensure success, as many a PM has learned. Many PM's have learned that while their project is a technical success; everything works as the business requirements document, the functional requirements documents, and the technical drawings stated; but the project is deemed a failure because it didn't meet the business objectives of the company (Campbell, 2009).

The biggest reason a project fails was because communication, identified as one of the single biggest reasons for project success or failure, failed. Real communication is essential not only within the project team, but between the PM, team members, and all external stakeholders. Open communication is the opening to building team, creating teamwork and getting high performance from team members as well as your stakeholders. Communications helps build relationships among project team members which helps to create mutual trust. Building trustful relationships helps to move the project along enabling it to meet the goals and objectives all have agreed to. The PM needs to be aware of the communication styles of all involved in the project; He needs to know the cultural nuances/ norms, relationships, personalities, and the overall context of the situation in order to communicate effectively. Awareness of these factors leads to mutual understanding and thus to effective communication. Identifying various channels of communications helps the PM to better understand what information they need to provide, what information they need to receive, and the interpersonal skills that will help them communicate successfully with various project stakeholders.

Stakeholder satisfaction can be met through a clearly defined project scope. In the scope the object and the goals of the project need to be clearly defined to meet the expectations of the business and the stakeholders. Ultimately they are the ones who approve the scope of the project. The PM needs to ensure that the scope defines how the object of the project will be met. He needs to ask and get answered the question of what is the purpose of the project: What need or problem is the project supposed to fulfil or solve? What business outcome is the end result? The definition of the scope is the first means by which the team begins to make the connection between the stated business goal and the means by which to achieve that goal. One of the tools that incorporate the scope is the project plan, including the Work Breakdown Structure (WBS). In the WBS the project team defines the work needed to achieve the business goal. It breaks the work down into manageable work packages, sometimes referred to as activities. The duration of time it takes to perform these work packages is estimated which ultimately helps to formulate our budget. The stakeholders will have to review and approve the WBS, the budget, and the schedule that gets produced. All this activity brings a greater understanding of the strategic business goal of the project.

With the Communication plan the project determines what types of communication would be required including status reports, Business Requirements documents, Functional Requirement documents, Project Plan, Project Schedule, Financial Communications, and as you can see, the forms and types of communication are many (Westland, 2006).

Many of these types of communication were determined by utilizing other documents such as the Stakeholder Register, the Charter and Scope, as well as the Project Management Plan. The Project Management Plan helps put all the relevant structure under one document; it helps us to define how we were going to communicate; manage certain events in the project such as change management, and risks: Verzuh points out that the Change Management Plan should be tailored to fit your specific function (Verzuh, 2009). PM's should carry out team building activities to help determine and understand team member styles of communication such as by email, phone, types of reports, and texting. This allows managers to plan their communications with understanding towards relationships and cultural differences. Listening is always an important part of communication. Both active and passive listening techniques give the user awareness of problem areas, management strategies for conflict and negotiations, decision making, and problem resolution.

What happens if you ignore project communications? You do so at your own risk. As stated earlier, many projects fail due to poor communications. Poor communications could be the result of weak leadership. Not wanting to be the bearer of bad news you will hope the issue goes away. Of course it never does go away. The issue just becomes worse until when you finally decide you need to tell upper management, it's too late to solve the issue except at tremendous cost of time and money. You, as the PM, look bad because it's your job to raise these issues so that can be solved; obviously the earlier the better. Part of your job is to solve these problems. Being the bearer of bad news comes with the job. The PM cannot be afraid to raise the red flag when a management decision is the only way to resolve the issue.

One area of communication the PM should consider is with the key roles of members of the project. Would your Business Systems Analyst be able to connect with business stakeholders? Can the Tech Lead deal with outside vendors in communicating technical requirements? Good salespeople learn early on that they can land a sale if they bring in a Subject Matter Expert (SME) to talk with the customer. It's not like the sales person, or PM, doesn't have the technical know-how; it's that the business stakeholder, or customer, will have a tendency to believe the SME over the PM or sales person. The PM has to realize that if what it takes is the SME talking with the stakeholder to get the issue resolved, so be it. True leadership never lets their ego get in the way.

Political and Cultural Awareness

Politics are inevitable in projects due to the variety of backgrounds, and expectations of the people involved with a project. Skillful use of politics and power helps the PM to bring the project to a successful end. Ignoring or avoiding project politics and incorrect use of power can mean trouble in managing projects. Because PM's operate globally in many projects, and many projects operate with a mix of cultures they are expected to be able to handle a multitude of different situations. By being appreciative and making the most of cultural differences, the PM is more likely to create an atmosphere of mutual trust and a highly performing atmosphere. Cultural differences are not just individual; they can be corporate in nature and may involve internal and external stakeholders. One way to manage cultural variety is getting to know the various team members. Developing a good communication plan goes a long way towards reaching that goal. Culture behavioral awareness includes those behaviors and expectations that occur outside of geography, ethnicity, or language differences. Culture can either slow or increase the speed of working, decision-making process, and the urge to act without appropriate planning or permission. Conflict and stress can occur in some organizations as a result of these differences unless addressed appropriately (Kerzner, 2001).

Politics, handled effectively, can help smooth the road in a project. The level in the hierarchy your sponsor has can be the difference between moving forward with the tools and the authority needed or finding brick walls in front of you. Having a sponsor of equal footing with other department managers within the hierarchy of the organization makes bringing in the big gun easier if needed. Having upper management support certainly helps to remove a lot of political obstacles as it gives greater authority to the PM. If the CEO of the company is supporting your project everyone in the company knows it and will usually bend over backwards to ensure you get what you need to reach the project goal.

Negotiation

Negotiation is a strategy of consulting with various parties of shared interests with a view toward reaching an agreement. Negotiation is an important part of project management and if done well, increases the chances of project success. The following skills and behaviors are useful in negotiating successfully:

Analyzing the situation, and differentiating wants and needs. By focusing on the interests and issues rather than on positions you stand a chance of concluding successful negotiations. Be realistic when negotiating: ask high and offer low. When conceding, make it sound like a really valuable concession, don't just hand it to them. The negotiations should always be a win-win proposition (Katz, 2009).

Decision Making Styles

There are four basic decision styles normally used by PM's: command, consultation, consensus, and coin flip (random). There are four major factors that affect the decision style: time constraints, trust, quality, and acceptance. PM's may make decisions individually, or they may involve the project team in the decision-making process. PM's and project teams use a decision-making model or process such as the six-phase decision model (PMBOK, 2013):

1. **Problem Definition:** Fully explore, clarify, and define the problem.
2. **Problem Solution Generation:** Prolong the new idea-generating process by brainstorming multiple solutions and discouraging premature decisions.
3. **Ideas to Action:** Define evaluation criteria, rate pros and cons of alternatives, select best solution.
4. **Solution Action Planning:** Involve key participants to gain acceptance and commitment to making the solution work.
5. **Solution Evaluation Planning:** Perform post-implementation analysis, evaluation, and lessons learned.
6. **Evaluation of the Outcome and Process:** Evaluate how well the problem was solved or project goals were achieved (extension of previous phase).

Trust

The ability to build trust across the project team and other key stakeholders is a critical component in team leadership. Trust is connected to cooperation, information sharing, and problem resolution. Without trust it is near impossible to establish the positive relationships necessary between the various stakeholders engaged in the project. When trust is compromised, relationships deteriorate, people disengage, and collaboration becomes near impossible. Some actions PM's can take to help build trust (Verzuh, 2012):

1. Engage in open and direct communications to resolve problems.
2. Keep all stakeholders informed, especially when fulfilling commitments is at risk.
3. Spend time directly engaged with the team asking non-assumptive questions to gain a better understanding of the situations affecting the team.
4. Be direct and explicit about what you need or expect.
5. Do not withhold information out of a fear of being wrong, be willing to share information admitting you may be wrong.
6. Be open to innovation and address any issues or concerns in an upfront manner.
7. Look beyond your own interests.
8. Demonstrate a true concern for others and avoid engaging in non-productive pursuits detrimental to the project or others.

Conflict

Conflict is inevitable in a project environment. Incongruent requirements, competition for resources, breakdowns in communications, and many other factors could become sources of conflict. Within a project's environment, conflict may yield dysfunctional outcomes. However, if actively managed, conflicts can actually help the team arrive at a better solution. The PM must be able to identify the causes for conflict and then actively manage the conflict thus minimizing potential negative impacts. The project team is then able to deliver better solutions and increase the probability of project success. PM's have to develop the skills and experience necessary to effectively manage to the situation. Managing conflict in a projects involves building trust with all involved parties early in the project; being open and honest, and to seek a positive resolution to the situation causing the conflict. PM's make every effort to establish a collaborative approach among the team members to achieve full resolution of the problems. When the collaborative approach isn't working, the PM must then use other methods for handling the conflict; forcefulness, accommodation, avoidance, or compromise. Managing conflict is one of the biggest challenges a PM must deal with on a regular basis. It requires use of all the other interpersonal skills of a PM in order to bring the conflict to a successful conclusion (Kerzner, 2001).

CONCLUSION

Agile project methodologies would seem to be a perfect fit for OSS projects. Agile Project methodologies come in many flavors; Scrum, Extreme Programming (XP), and Kanban for example. Agile, like OSS, encourages people over process. It encourages self-organizing and cross-functional teams within a single team. Agile encourages collaboration between the development team and the business. It is software project management that many project managers experience, even when using waterfall methodologies to manage their projects. It is inevitable that a different direction needs to be taken in software development. What was thought to work when the project first started, will likely change mid-way through. Technology will have changed; someone will have made a better widget, the business will have changed their mind.

Planning, developing, testing, and deploying are consolidated into a sprint. Within each sprint, the business defines the high-level requirement within an epic. The requirements to meet the epic are further defined stories where the business details their wishes. These stories are entered into a product log where they are categorized as to importance. The developing team takes these stories and estimates how long it will take to meet the requirement described in the story. A group of these stories will be categorized as to similarity and organized into a sprint. Within each sprint, the developing team will develop the code to meet the requirement, and fully test until they have produced working software.

Studies done by Adarsh Kakar (2017), show that while the level of self-management would vary across Agile projects, found that self-organization was substantially higher when compared to planned projects. And they had a more positive effect on the success of the project (Kakar, 2017). In planned driven projects, the project manager is expected to deliver a defined scope, plan, schedule and list of tasks for each project. In self-managed projects, the requirements give the team direction; they determine how they will get there. Business has come to realize that they need only explain the requirements; how the team produces the end product is entirely up to them. OSS strives for quality, as does Agile; an example would be stressing unit testing during each sprint over full validation testing at the end of the project as is done in waterfall. Both Agile and OSS push for flexibility in the process with a preference towards self-managed teams over hierarchical management. OSS and Agile both stress continual improvement in the software package (Highsmith, 2010).

The difference between Agile and OSS management styles centers around time. Agile believes in time-boxing the processes used to manage a project; daily stand-up meeting limited to 15 minutes; two to four-week sprints depending on the teams burn rate are two examples. OSS projects run in the open-governance mode have no set time frame. Volunteers participate at their own speed, not by a time-frame as dictated by traditional project methodologies. Misra and Sing (2015) propose there is a way for OSS projects to utilize Agile methods effectively; they advocate that the similarities in the two styles allow for a new methodology to emerge. This new methodology would merge the best of the Software Development Life Cycle (SDLC) with the best of Agile and OSS forming Open Agile Software Development Life Cycle (OASDLC) model (Misra and Singh, 2015).

One of the key questions concerns if waterfall project methodology applies to managing OSS software projects. OSS doesn't lend itself to the controlling aspects of a waterfall methodology. Many programmers choose to fix a perceived problem in a software application on their own because of the freedom it allows them. Waterfall demands to define project goals and scope of the proposed project. Waterfall stresses the need to document each task; defining it, determining the order of occurrence, identifying the dependencies, determine the critical path. OSS looks at waterfall methodologies as too much unnecessary work that gets in the way of producing working software (Highsmith, 2010).

Business need for flexibility in software development increasingly requires the need for methodologies such as Agile, Kanban, and Scrum due to their ability to adapt to change on short notice (Stoica, Ghilic-Micu, Mircea, and Uscatu, 2016). Adapting to an ever-changing market requires the flexibility of Agile methods to remain competitive. Many companies can adapt to methodologies like Agile; Allstate Insurance, Walgreens, and CVS are examples of companies adopting Agile methods successfully. But some companies are unable to adapt the Agile or OSS methods successfully. AbbVie, due to heavy Federal Government regulations, has found it difficult to adopt Agile methods.

The apparent envy of many a waterfall project manager is the self-inspiration and dedication shown by many an OSS programmer. These Project Managers continually seek to copy the style of OSS projects and the mindset possessed that produces high-quality software (Harzl, 2017).

Prior research has concentrated on the governance of OSS projects. Prior research has also concentrated on the effectiveness of using Agile due to the similarities in the OSS and Agile mindset. Using waterfall methodologies woefully lacks any significant research finding as of this writing.

What needs determining is how effectively Agile or waterfall facilitates collaboration in OSS projects. While OSS development has been very successful, it has not been conducive to traditional project management nor agile project management methodologies. This paper proposes to study further the question of whether waterfall or Agile project methodologies are conducive to collaboration in OSS projects, or, is there a describable methodology being used to manage these OSS projects.

REFERENCES

Agile Manifesto for Software Development. (2017, November 15). Retrieved April 8, 2018, from https://www.agilealliance.org/agile101/the-agile-manifesto/

Campbell, P. M. (2012). *Communications skills for project managers*. New York, NY: Amacom American Management.

Fleming, Q. W., & Koppelman, J. M. (2010). *Earned value project management*. Newtown Square, PA: Project Management Institute.

Gido, J., & Clements, J. P. (2012). *Successful project management*. South-Western Cengage Learning.

Harpham, B. (2015, March 30). *ProjectManagement.com - Leveraging the Best Knowledge Management Practices*. Retrieved from http://www.projectmanagement.com/articles/293355/Leveraging-the-Best-Knowledge-Management-Practices

Highsmith, J. A. (2010). *Agile project management: creating innovative product* (2nd ed.). Academic Press.

Kendrick, T. (2012). *Results without authority: Controlling a project when the team doesn't report to you* (2nd ed.). New York, NY: AMACOM.

Kerzner, H. (2014). *Project recovery: Case studies and techniques for overcoming project failure*. Hoboken, NJ: John Wiley & Sons, Inc. doi:10.1002/9781118841617

Kerzner, H. (2015). *Project management 2.0: Leveraging tools, distributed collaboration, and metrics for project success*. Hoboken, NJ: John Wiley & Sons. doi:10.1002/9781119020042

Marchewka, J. T. (2015). *Information technology project management* (5th ed.). Hoboken, NJ: John Wiley & Sons, Inc.

Mullaly, M. (2011, March 1). *ProjectManagement.com - A Critical Look at Project Initiation*. Retrieved from http://www.projectmanagement.com/articles/262617/A-Critical-Look-at-

Project Management Institute. (2013). *A guide to the project management body of knowledge (PMBOK guide)* (5th ed.). Newtown Square, PA: Author.

Robertson, S., & Robertson, J. (2013). *Mastering the requirements process: Getting requirements right*. Upper Saddle River, NJ: Addison-Wesley.

Schwalbe, K. (2014). *Information technology project management*. Boston, MA: Course Technology.

The High Cost of Low Performance: The Essential Role of Communications. (2013, May). [Web log post]. Retrieved from http://www.pmi.org/~/media/PDF/Business-Solutions/The- High-Cost-Low-Performance-The-Essential-Role-of-Communications.ashx

Verzuh, E. (2012). *The fast forward MBA in project management* (4th ed.). Hoboken, NJ: John Wiley & Sons.

Wurzler, J. (2013). *Information risks and risk management*. Retrieved from Sans Institute website: https://www.sans.org/reading-room/whitepapers/dlp/information-risks-risk-management-34210

This research was previously published in Information Technology as a Facilitator of Social Processes in Project Management and Collaborative Work; pages 99-123, copyright year 2018 by Business Science Reference (an imprint of IGI Global).

Chapter 14
Prospects of Open Source Software for Maximizing the User Expectations in Heterogeneous Network

Pushpa Singh

Accurate Institute of Management & Technology, Greater Noida, India

Rajeev Agrawal

G.L.Bajaj Institute of Technology & Management, Greater Noida, India

ABSTRACT

This article focuses on the prospects of open source software and tools for maximizing the user expectations in heterogeneous networks. The open source software Python is used as a software tool in this research work for implementing machine learning technique for the categorization of the types of user in a heterogeneous network (HN). The KNN classifier available in Python defines the type of user category in real time to predict the available users in a particular category for maximizing profit for a business organization.

1. INTRODUCTION

Free and open source software (FOSS) is one of the effective tools that can be easily utilized in business, research and academia. FOSS is a movement started way back in 1980 to provide reliable software at low cost/free of cost to the users (FOSS A General Introduction, 2018). These softwares could be used, modified, redistributed without any permission required. FOSS insists on ethical and moral importance of users' freedom and hence has strict norms on how to aggregate free and proprietary software together. Open Source Software has a pragmatic view on this matter and allows proprietary software to be easily aggregated with open source software. These two terms (free and open source) are used for the unique development model and innovative distribution policy of software. The software can be mostly free,

DOI: 10.4018/978-1-7998-9158-1.ch014

but not open source and can also be open source but not free. FOSS provides both free and open source software for the use of people. FOSS has drawn the attention of people from various backgrounds who have labelled it as an opportunistic software development model (Umarji, Sim & Lopes, 2008).

The FOSS developers can modify the software to make it trustworthy for the future users. Today FOSS is growing with the large number of open source software projects and the amount of open source code in the world at an exponential rate. The total amount of source code and the total number of projects double about every 14 months (Deshpande & Riehle, 2008).There are various example of FOSS product such as Linux, KDE, GCC, Android, Apache, MySQL, Perl, PHP and Python, etc. These FOSS' products are changing the shape of the current digital world. Python become very popular and get no. 1 position in all other parallel and similar solutions. Python is an open source and free to use even for commercial applications because of its high regard and ubiquitous nature (Srinivasa & Deka, 2017).

A HN provides integration of WLAN, WMAN and WPAN-adhoc peer-to-peer networks. These standards operate on a different set of service parameters such as data rates, distance (signal range), bandwidth, frequency band, and modulation technique (Simek et al., 2007). However, the concept of HN requires the whole network to operate in an efficient and seamless manner. As each standard supports different types of data rate as mention in Table 2, a mobile user can select any of the available networks as per his need from the set of HN.

As there are approximately 7.2 billion mobile devices /customers worldwide (Okeleke, Rogers & Pedros, 2017). The QoS experience of a customer is crucial for a service provider to retain its existing customers. Nowadays adding a new customer to its base is a difficult and costly affair than to retain an existing loyal customer (Jain, 2005; Sanchez, 2003). Here customer loyalty is a subjective term which can be defined by the segment of mobile user according to their payoff toward the service provider or a profit received by the customer in terms of service provider perspective and may differ case to case as per the subject. The customer retention is defined as the intention to stay with the current network provider quantified in terms of time span, whereas customer loyalty is defined as the intention to maintain the business relationship with the current service provider (SP) measured in the revenue acquired by the SP. Many research papers have been reported to define the term customer loyalty in different aspects and parameters. It is important to understand that why should a customer be loyal to service providers. Taking a general view a customer will continue with the same service provider if he is getting the value of its money and its experience is good with this, the customer will develop a faith of trust towards that provider.

FOSS provides liberty to individual, researchers and developer to design its own program for the beneficiary of their own business. Thousands of companies have placed open source software at the center of their business (Igor Faletski, 2013). This paper focus to identify the suitability of open source technologies as a tool to optimize a formulated problem and establishes its potential. A problem statement to identify the loyal customer based on the revenue generated or other parameters as per the case and provides them the uninterrupted network services to gain the customer trust and subsequently increase the revenue of the service provider. This research work introduces to predict the category of customer for the service provider and the telecom industry is used as a case study.

The paper is organized with following section. After the introduction, Section 2 discusses about the related works and section 3 gives the problem formulation in conventional programming and introduced the requirement of python with KNN classifier. Next section uses python for the classification of customers as a proposed framework with result and discussion. The next section discusses the application of proposed work in a heterogeneous network. Section 6 gives a brief application of proposed work in HN. Last section concludes the paper.

2. RELATED WORK

A number of tools/ literature are available to define the importance of customer loyalty in the service industry. The objective is to identify the loyal mobile users in a given network and to retain them by providing the best available services as per their requirements. Customer retention has become a decisive factor in the world of mobile telecommunications business (Shafei & Tabaa, 2016) service providers passes multiple offers and promotional schemes for their active user along with assured QoS. Determinants of customer loyalty and customer satisfaction were discussed by Deng et al. (2010) for Mobile Instant Messages (MIM) in China. Dudin et al. (2017) analyzed a multi-server priority retrial queue with many types of customers such as a primary customer and secondary customer. They discussed several types of primary customers having different requirements for the service time and preemptive priority over secondary customers. Aydin and Özer (2005) proposed a loyalty measurement model for the telecom industry that included the corporate image, perceived service quality, trust and customer switching costs as major antecedents of customer loyalty. Seth, Momaya, and Gupta (2008) analyzed the relative importance of service quality attributes and shown that responsiveness was the most importance dimension followed by reliability, customer perceived network quality, assurance, convenience, empathy and tangibles. John J. (2011) analyzed the factors that influenced customer loyalty to the company.

Several metrics can be obtained to measure customer loyalty quotient based on multiple factors such as based on time period (retention period): how long a customer is with the same service provider, high data usage rate, Net Promoter Score (NPS): customers also use or refer the same providers for his family, friends and colleagues, depth: The customer usage several different services such as voice, video, VoIP and background services, from the same operator. The service providers can create competitive advantage by providing a high level of service quality to their loyal customer (Yoo & Park, 2007). There may be several combinations of metrics or attributes with different possible values which can be utilized in the computation of customer loyalty. These computations are complex but need quick answers to a query. Machine learning (ML) provides such opportunity to learn without being explicitly programmed. Machine learning utilized mathematical models, heuristic learning, knowledge acquisitions and decision trees for decision making. Machine learning is playing a vital role in almost all the areas such as medical (Mandal & Sairam, 2014), manufacturing process (Wuest et al., 2016) and wireless network (Bastug, Bennis, & Debbah, 2014). Dullaghan and Rozaki (2017) analyzed C.5 algorithm, within a naive Bayesian modeled for the segmentation of telecommunication customers according to their billing and socio-demographic aspects. Vafeiadis and et al. (2015) proposed machine learning methods to the challenging problem such as a customer churning prediction in the telecommunications industry. Poor network QoS services are a major cause of customer churning (Diaz-Aviles, Pinelli, Lynch et al., 2015). Exponential growth of mobile user and limited number of resources can easily affect network performance. Nath and Behara (2003), developed a working database system by using data mining technique to predict the churn of customer for the wireless industry.

This paper proposed a machine learning framework implemented in python to compute category of a user or customer within a service provider network so as a loyal customer can be extended to avail best network services from given set of network from the HN.

2.1. Why Python?

Python implements the OOPs concept in very simple manner. Developers can easily produce readable and functional code in a very short period of time and become the center of attraction for programmers and researchers. Numerous libraries provide the needed functionality for scientific purpose. The library scikit-learn offers machine learning features to python. Scikit-learn have features of classification, regression, and clustering algorithm and also are designed to interoperate with the Python numerical and scientific libraries NumPy and SciPy (Pedregosa-Vanderplas, 2011). This pair of libraries provides the array and matrix structures, linear algebra routines, numerical optimization, random number generation, statistics routines, differential equation modeling, Fourier transform and signal processing, image processing, sparse and masked arrays, spatial computation, and numerous other mathematical routines. Scikit-learn implements two different nearest neighbor classifiers: K Neighbors Classifier (KNC) and Radius Neighbors Classifier (RNC). The K Nearest Neighbors (KNN) algorithm in KNC is the more commonly used of the two classifiers. Proposed work utilizes a pair of libraries NumPy and SciPy along with Pandas. Panda library can easily read/write data from different data structures and different formats: CSV and text files, Microsoft Excel, SQL databases and others. It is data modeling and analysis tool. For the data analysis, one can store data as a csv (comma delimited value) file and import by pandas.

3. PROBLEM FORMULATION

Revenue generated, usage, and time duration, etc. are important attributes which are identified and discussed in the previous works (Singh & Agarwal, 2017) for the customer loyalty. In that paper author proposed an agent that collects the current value of the attributes which is then normalized by the utility function. The overall weighted score W' (g), is obtained by the average weighted score of parameter usage (U), time duration (T), and revenue generated (R_v). The parameter x_i, represents attribute in user grade selection criteria, n is the number of the decision criteria and W (x_i) is the weighted value of each criterion i, which is computed by a utility function. Final weighted value is the average value of recent value W_r (g) and previous weighted value $W_p(g)$. As the type of user cannot be fixed. Type of user is dynamic and is changing every time on the basis of U, T, and R_v. So there is a need of an average, weighted value to define type of user.

After a specific time interval, the agent will collect the value of U, T & R_v attribute from user equipment calculates the type of user by algorithm 1. It is important to note here that it is difficult to predict customer loyalty, according to the attribute U, T and R_v only. There may be another parameter that can also affect the type of user (u_type). However, agent based model based on previous programming methods can add complexity in order to predict u_type for an exponential user and adding another parameter in u_type computation.

Algorithm 1. Pseudocode for computing type of user

```
for i← 1 to no. of users  do
W_p(g)  = 0
```

$$W'(g) = \frac{1}{n}\sum_{i=1}^{n} W\left(x_i\right)$$

$$W_r(g) = \frac{W(u) + W(r) + W(t)}{3}$$

$$W(g) = \frac{W_p(g) + W_r(g)}{2}$$

```
if (W (g) ≥ 0.9 &&W (g)≤ 1)   then  u_type= 'VL'
else if (W (g) < 0.9  && W(g)≥ 0.6)   then u_type=  'L'
else if (W(g)< 0.6  && W (g)≥ 0.3)    then u_type= 'N'
else      u_type= 'R'
w_p(g) = W_r(g)
end
```

As the systems and devices are becoming more powerful, pervasive, multi-domain and diverse in applications so as the requirements of the users, it's a challenging task to meet the growing demand and expectation of the customer along with utilization of the resources in a manner so as to maximize profit/revenue. Machine learning can be one of the promising artificial intelligence tools to solve such multi objective optimization problem. In fact, with machine learning one can also record the network usage and bandwidth utilization on real time and can able to predict the usage in time instant $t + \Delta t$ and accordingly balance the network load and adjust its demand and usage so as to gain maximum rather than leaving the resources idle. The proposed work takes into consideration KNN classification to classify their type of user.

3.1. Overview of K-Nearest Neighbor (KNN) Classification Algorithm

KNN has been used in statistical estimation and pattern recognition already in the beginning of 1970's as a non-parametric technique. KNN is widely used classification, estimation and prediction algorithm in the area of data mining (Han & Kamber, 2011). The basic idea is that, in a sample space, if most of its nearest neighbor samples belong to a category, then the sample belongs to the same category. The nearest neighbor refers to the single or multidimensional feature vector that is used to describe the sample on the closest, and the closest criteria can be the Euclidean distance of the feature vector. The KNN is a simple algorithm to understand and implement, and a powerful tool to predict the type of user (u_type). The optimal choice of the value k is highly data-dependent: in general a larger k suppresses the effects of noise, but makes the classification boundaries less distinct. The author has taken following parameter value for KNN classifier.

```
KNeighborsClassifier(algorithm='auto', leaf_size=30, metric='minkowski', met-
ric_params=None, n_jobs=1, n_neighbors=5, p=2,  weights='uniform')
```

Algorithm ='auto', means that the most appropriate algorithm based on the values passed to knn fit method. Other choices of algorithms are 'ball_tree', 'kd_tree', and 'brute'. Parameter leaf_size can affect the speed of the construction and query, as well as the memory required to store the tree and default value is 30. P is a power parameter for the Minkowski metric. The default metric is Minkowski, and with p=2 is equivalent to the standard Euclidean metric.The metric_params is additional keyword parameters for the metric function. n_jobs shows the number of parallel jobs to run for neighbor search. Parameter n_neighbors is the number of neighbors for queries and by default value of this parameter is 5.

If n_neighbors=1 then the object is simply assigned to the class of that single nearest neighbor. Weights ='uniform' means all points in each neighborhood are weighted equally. Except weight and the metric parameter rest of the parameter is optional.

4. PROPOSED FRAMEWORK

Let (A_i, C_i) where $I = 1, 2 ..., n$ be data points. A_i denotes attribute values and C_i denotes labels for A_i. Assuming the number of classes for each u_type $\in \{L, N, R\}$ for all values of i. Label L belongs to the loyal category user whose usage is very high, and generated high revenue to SP, label N belongs to those users who are regular or can call as Normal, while label R, denoted for recent user, who occasionally use the system. The type of user is measured on the basis of parameter U, T and R_v and NPV. NPV is a net promoted value which is calculated on the basis of how a user recommends his service provider to his family/ colleague. U, T, R_v and NPV is normalized between 0 to 1 according to the Equation (1).

$$N(A_i) = \frac{A_a}{A_{max}} \qquad A_a \leq A_{max} \tag{1}$$

Where A_a is actual value collected by user equipment and A_{max} is the maximum expected value of that parameter. Maximum expected value can be set by different service providers. For example, service providers can set his maximum desired value of usage is 2GB or 3GB per day, and similarly for the other parameter. Author proposed a data set (DS), consisting of labeled instance to predict u_type. The data set is designed as a comma separated value (csv) file. A CSV file is a human readable text file where each line has a number of fields, separated by commas or some other delimiter. The data set is based on following assumption:

1. If $U \geq 0.7$ && $T \geq 0.7$ && $R_v => 0.7$ && $NPV_i \geq 0.7$ then u_type= 'L'
2. If U is between (0.7 to 0.5) && T is between (0.7 to 0.5) && R_v (0.7 to 0.5) && NPV_i is between (0.7 to 0.5) then u_type= 'N'
3. If $U < 0.5$ && $T < 0.5$ $R_v < 0.5$ && $NPV_i < 0.5$ then u_type= 'R'

Let x be a point for which label is not known, and we would like to find the label class using k-nearest neighbor algorithms. If the user data is A (0.6,0.6,0.55,0.6), then programmatically u_type is predicted as 'N'. The user data can be in any combination such as A (0.3, 1, 0.2, 1), According to algorithm 1, this sample would predict 'L' category as average value is more than 0.6. But logically, this sample should belong to 'N' category. Because that sample is not contributing considerably in revenue generation. Which attributes can more affect marketing strategy is the part of interest of SP. There may be several factors or single factor for a service provider. For this type of prediction machine learning is identified as one of the important tools. Consider the pseudo code for u_type prediction in the next section.

4.1. Making Predictions with KNN

KNN is used to predict u_type directly from the training data set. Predictions are made for a new instance A (U_i, T_i, R_{vi}, NPV_i) by searching through the entire training set for the K most similar instances (the neighbors) and summarizing the output variable for those K instances.

To determine which of the K instances in the training dataset are most similar to a new input a distance measure is used. There are many distance measures such as Euclidean, Hamming, Manhattan and Minkowski distance. For real-valued input p, the most popular distance measure is the Euclidean distance. But we have used Minkowski distance because Minkowski distance is a normed vector space which is considered as a generalization of Euclidean and Manhattan distance. The Minkowski distance defines a distance between two points in a normed vector space.

$$d(x,y) = \left(\sum_0^{n-1} \|a_i - b_i\| \right)^{1/p} \tag{2}$$

If $p=1$, the distance is called as the Manhattan distance and if $p=2$, the distance is called as the Euclidean distance as shown in Equation (2).

The data set consists of 100 samples from each of three type of user u_type = {'L','N','R'}. Out of 100 samples, 70 samples are for training and 30 samples is for testing purpose. The average accuracy of the Scikit-Learn neighbors by using KNN classifier has plotted for different value of n_neighbors. In scikit-learn a random split into training and test sets can be quickly computed with the train_test_split () helper function with state parameters as shown in Equation (3). This function splits arrays or matrices into the random train and test subsets. That means that every time you run it without specifying random_state, you will get a different result, this is expected behavior.

train_test_split(X, y, test_size=0.3, random_state=7) (3)

Where X represents a list of features set involved in u_type i. e. $A(U_i, T_i, R_{vi}, NPV_i)$, y is the target set such as {'L','N','R'} and random_state is the seed value used by random number generator.

Pseudo code for u_type prediction

1. Reading the csv file which has a data set for training and testing. A csv file is comma-separated values (CSV) file to store tabular data.
2. Splitting csv file into training & testing sets by using the function (3).

X_train, X_test, y_train, y_test =Train_test_split(X, y,test_size=0.3, random_state=7)

3. Use the KNN classifier to find the target label:

knn = KNeighborsClassifier (n_neighbors = K)

y_pred=knn.predict (X_test)

4. Find the knn prediction accuracy for different value of n_neighbors.
5. Set the maximum value of each attribute (features) in the dataset and normalized the each attribute value of (0-1), by equation 1.

$$N\left(A_i\right)=\frac{A_a}{A_{max}} \qquad A_a \leq A_{max}$$

Where A_i is U_i, T_i, R_{vi}, & NPV_i.

6. After getting the normalized value of each sample, $A(U_i, T_i, R_{vi}, NPV_i)$, predict the category of u_type by knn.predict (sample).

Figure 1, is plotted for various value of K which range 1 to 30. Figure 1, shows that maximum accuracy achieves at K=1 or n_neighbours=1.

Figure 1. KNN Accuracy for different value of K

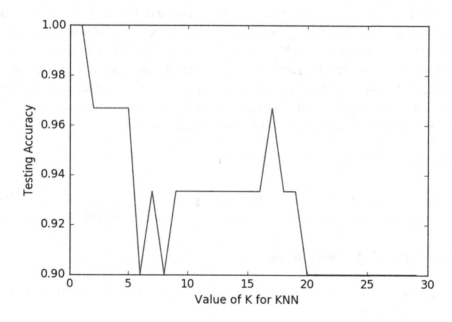

4.2. Simulation and Result Discussion

Further, we have generated sample A (U, T, R_v, NPV) by using a different distribution for simulation purpose rather than generated individually for different value of A_{max}. The value of U, T, R and NPV are generated separately that is normalized between 0 to 1 and predicted u_type. Figure 2, is plotted for the generation of total no. of loyal customer out of 50 customers by using a different distribution. The maximum number of loyal customer is generated 15 by using a uniform distribution as shown in Table 1.

Table 1. Loyal customer generated in various distributions

S. No.	Distribution Name	No. of loyal customer
1.	GammaVariate	1
2.	Random	10
3.	Triangular	14
4.	Uniform	15

Figure 2. No. of loyal customer generated in various distributions

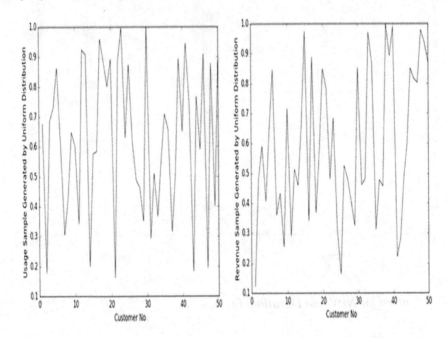

Maximum numbers of loyal customers are generated by uniform distribution. The Sample pattern generated by the uniform distribution for the individual attributes U_i, T_i, R_{vi}, and NPV_i is shown in Figure 3 and Figure 4.

5. APPLICATION OF PROPOSED WORK IN HETEROGENEOUS NETWORK

HN is future mobile network (Glisic, 2016) in which multiple users are connected to numbers of wireless networks such as Cellular, WLAN, WMAN and WPAN and other related network. FOSS is widely used for network monitoring, diagnosis, and vulnerability testing tools. To control the complexity of HN (Nam & et al., 2004), introduced a new object called the virtual Domain Controller (VDC) in a 3G core network. The VDC can be extended to control the complexity of HN, where complete environment is heterogeneous in term of usage, application, type of user and service provider. The task of Designing future adaptable HN that provide QoS guarantees to users is extremely complex and challenging task, especially for those customers who are loyal towards their service provider. To identify loyalty quotient of a customer is crucial and proposed work will simplify this task. VDC is a conceptual and virtual object that can be physically constructed with several servers in a distributed manner. Proposed machine learning (ML) code which is written in FOSS :python is available on the VDC.

Figure 3. Sample Pattern for Usage(U) and Revenue (R)

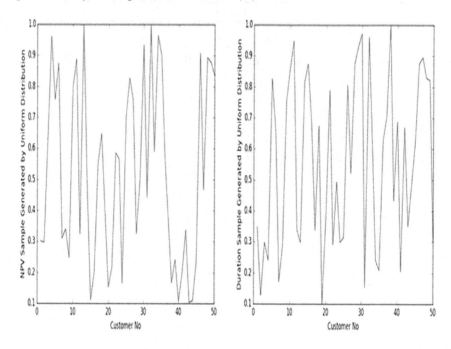

Figure 4. Sample Pattern for NPV and Duration(T)

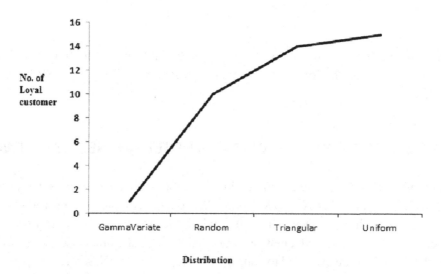

Consider a HN environment as depicted in Figure 5. VDC is implemented on core network (CN). The basic components of HN are mobile stations (MSs), Base Station (BSs), Access Point (APs), and a core (IP) network (CN). CN serves as the backbone network with Internet connectivity and packet data (Cavalcanti & et al., 2005). Which in turn connected with another HN. The next generation network will witness an exponential growth in terms of user and traffic volumes. The real time application such as voice, data, and video have different QoS requirement. Current QoS resource allocation scheme is based on customer loyalty and priority based queuing control mechanism. ML code is used to identify the type of customer and shift the customer in a priority queue if they are loyal. Otherwise, the customer will be in a waiting queue. The request in priority non-preemptive queue means that loyal customer has high priority packet and will not wait as lower priority packet, which is categorized or tagged during the process of transmission.

Figure 5. Heterogeneous network environment

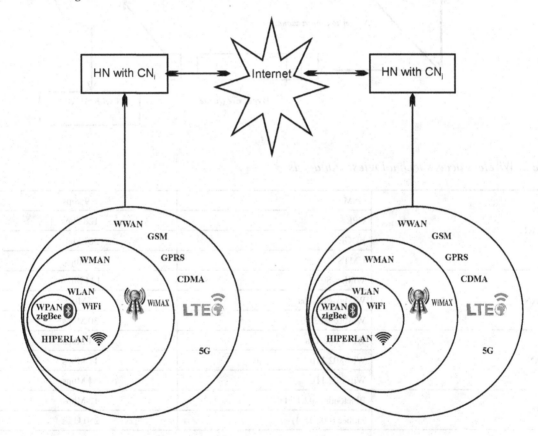

Consider the scenario presented in Figure 6, where CN_i is a source heterogeneous network and CN_j is a destination heterogeneous network of a customer. CN_i is characterized by the behavior of the arrival of data and pattern of arrival of data at the system size. The Poisson distribution is a discrete probability distribution of the number of data arriving in some time interval. Data in arriving at the service system stays in the system until served.

Figure 6. Queuing environment between two HN

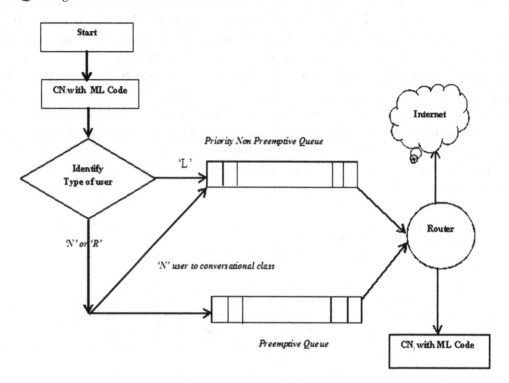

Table 2. Wireless access technologies: standards

WMAN	GSM	6,9 kbps
	GPRS	128 kbps
	EDGE	384 kbps
	UMTS	2 Mbps
WMAN	WiMax-802.16	134 Mbps
	WiMax-802.16a	75Mbps
	WiMax -802.16e	30 Mbps
WLAN	Wi-Fi-802.11a	54 Mbps
	Wifi-802.11b	11 Mbps
	Wifi-802.11g	54 Mbps
WPAN	Bluetooth (802.15.1)	12 Mbps
	Zigbee (802.15.4)	250 kbps

The Customer can have different type service class requirement such as conversational, streaming, interactive and background. These types of services are mixture of voice and data traffic. Voice traffic or conversational services are less delay sensitive compare to data service. All types of request of a loyal customer is placed in nonpreemptive priority queue along with conversational request of regular customer. Receiving Router search the destination core network. CN_j in turn, on receiving the loyal customer request selects the best possible network on the basis of service requirement. For an instance if user service requirement is 11 Mbps, then best network is Wifi-802.11b and if required data rate is 54 Mbps then select Wifi-802.11a, standards. Table 2 represents data rate support in different standards of HN.

6. CONCLUSION

The proposed work uses a FOSS set up to identify the type of user as per the category defined in terms of different service aspects. Based on the type of user a priority queue for their services is extended. In the proposed model a separate queue prioritizes the valued customer, so as to gain the trust of the customer through seamless access to services with minimum delay and blockage. This in turns maximizes the revenue of the service provider. The application of the work can be extended to many of the service related sectors where the retention of the customer is important, a queue is to be modelled as per the requirement and type of service which is future and extended the work of the proposed model.

REFERENCES

Aydin, S., & Özer, G. (2005). The analysis of antecedents of customer loyalty in the Turkish mobile telecommunication market. *European Journal of Marketing*, *39*(7/8), 910–925. doi:10.1108/03090560510601833

Bastug, E., Bennis, M., & Debbah, M. (2014). Living on the edge: The role of proactive caching in 5G wireless networks. *IEEE Communications Magazine*, *52*(8), 82–89. doi:10.1109/MCOM.2014.6871674

Cavalcanti, D., Agrawal, D., Cordeiro, C., Xie, B., & Kumar, A. (2005). Issues in integrating cellular networks WLANs, AND MANETs: A futuristic heterogeneous wireless network. *IEEE Wireless Communications*, *12*(3), 30–41. doi:10.1109/MWC.2005.1452852

Deng, Z., Lu, Y., Wei, K. K., & Zhang, J. (2010). Understanding customer satisfaction and loyalty: An empirical study of mobile instant messages in China. *International Journal of Information Management*, *30*(4), 289–300. doi:10.1016/j.ijinfomgt.2009.10.001

Deshpande, A., & Riehle, D. (2008, September). The total growth of open source. In *IFIP International Conference on Open Source Systems* (pp. 197-209). Boston, MA: Springer.

Diaz-Aviles, E., Pinelli, F., Lynch, K., Nabi, Z., Gkoufas, Y., Bouillet, E., . . . Salzwedel, J. (2015, October). Towards real-time customer experience prediction for telecommunication operators. In *2015 IEEE International Conference on Big Data (Big Data)* (pp. 1063-1072). IEEE.

Dudin, A. N., Lee, M. H., Dudina, O., & Lee, S. K. (2017). Analysis of priority retrial queue with many types of customers and servers reservation as a model of cognitive radio system. *IEEE Transactions on Communications*, *65*(1), 186–199.

Dullaghan, C., & Rozaki, E. (2017). Integration of Machine Learning Techniques to Evaluate Dynamic Customer Segmentation Analysis for Mobile Customers. arXiv:1702.02215

Igor Faletski. (2013, January 15). Yes, You Can Make Money with Open Source [Blog post]. *Harvard Business Review*. Retrieved from https://hbr.org/2013/01/yes-you-can-make-money-with-op

FOSS A General Introduction. (2018, March 8). Retrieved https://en.wikibooks.org/wiki/FOSS_A_General_Introduction/Introduction#A_Brief_History_of_Free/Open_Source_Software_Movement

Glisic, S. (2016). *Advanced Wireless Networks: Technology and Business Models*. John Wiley & Sons. doi:10.1002/9781119096863

Han, J., Pei, J., & Kamber, M. (2011). *Data mining: concepts and techniques*. Elsevier.

Jain, S.C. (2005). CRM shifts the paradigm. *Journal of Strategic Marketing, 13*(4), 275–291. doi:10.1080/09652540500338329

John, J. (2011). An analysis on the customer loyalty in telecom sector: Special reference to Bharath Sanchar Nigam limited, India. *African Journal of Marketing Management, 3*(1), 1–5.

Mandal, I., & Sairam, N. (2014). New machine-learning algorithms for prediction of Parkinson's disease. *International Journal of Systems Science, 45*(3), 647–666. doi:10.1080/00207721.2012.724114

Miao, G., Zander, J., Sung, K. W., & Slimane, S. B. (2016). *Fundamentals of Mobile Data Networks*. Cambridge University Press. doi:10.1017/CBO9781316534298

Nam, M., Choi, N., Seok, Y., & Choi, Y. (2004, September). WISE: energy-efficient interface selection on vertical handoff between 3G networks and WLANs. In *15th IEEE International Symposium on Personal, Indoor and Mobile Radio Communications PIMRC 2004* (Vol. 1, pp. 692-698). IEEE.

Nath, S. V., & Behara, R. S. (2003, November). Customer churn analysis in the wireless industry: A data mining approach. In *Proceedings-annual meeting of the decision sciences institute* (pp. 505-510).

Okeleke, K., Rogers, M., & Pedros, X. (2017). The Mobile Economy 2017.

Pedregosa, F., Varoquaux, G., Gramfort, A., Michel, V., Thirion, B., Grisel, O., ... Vanderplas, J. (2011). Scikit-learn: Machine learning in Python. *Journal of Machine Learning Research, 12*(Oct), 2825–2830.

Sanchez, J. G. (2003). Customer relationship marketing: Building customer relationships for enduring profits in a wired economy. Atthapholj.net.

Seth, A., Momaya, K., & Gupta, H. M. (2008). Managing the customer perceived service quality for cellular mobile telephony: An empirical investigation. *Vikalpa, 33*(1), 19–34. doi:10.1177/0256090920080102

Shafei, I., & Tabaa, H. (2016). Factors affecting customer loyalty for mobile telecommunication industry. *EuroMed Journal of Business, 11*(3), 347–361. doi:10.1108/EMJB-07-2015-0034

Simek, M., Mica, I., Kacalek, J., & Burget, R. (2007). Bandwidth efficiency of wireless networks of wpan, wlan, wman and wwan. *Elektrorevue*.

Singh, P., & Agrawal, R. (2018). A Customer Centric Best Connected Channel Model for Heterogeneous and IoT Networks. *Journal of Organizational and End User Computing, 30*(4), 32–50.

Srinivasa, K. G., & Deka, G. C. (Eds.). (2017). Free and Open Source Software in Modern Data Science and Business Intelligence: Emerging Research and Opportunities. Hershey, PA: IGI Global.

Umarji, M., Sim, E. S., & Lopes, C. (2008). Archetypal internet- scale source code searching. In *Open source development, communities and quality* (pp. 257–263). Springer. doi:10.1007/978-0-387-09684-1_21

Vafeiadis, T., Diamantaras, K. I., Sarigiannidis, G., & Chatzisavvas, K. C. (2015). A comparison of machine learning techniques for customer churn prediction. *Simulation Modelling Practice and Theory, 55*, 1–9. doi:10.1016/j.simpat.2015.03.003

Wuest, T., Weimer, D., Irgens, C., & Thoben, K. D. (2016). Machine learning in manufacturing: Advantages, challenges, and applications. *Production & Manufacturing Research, 4*(1), 23–45. doi:10.10 80/21693277.2016.1192517

Yoo, D. K., & Park, J. A. (2007). Perceived service quality: Analyzing relationships among employees, customers, and financial performance. *International Journal of Quality & Reliability Management, 24*(9), 908–926. doi:10.1108/02656710710826180

This research was previously published in the International Journal of Open Source Software and Processes (IJOSSP), 9(3); pages 1-14, copyright year 2018 by IGI Publishing (an imprint of IGI Global).

Section 2
Multi-Industry Applications

Chapter 15
Open Source Software Usage in Education and Research:
Network Traffic Analysis as an Example

Samih M. Jammoul
Bauman Moscow State Technical University, Russia

Vladimir V. Syuzev
Bauman Moscow State Technical University, Russia

Ark M. Andreev
Bauman Moscow State Technical University, Russia

ABSTRACT

Information technology and telecommunication is considered a new and quickly evolving branch of science. New technologies and services in IT and telecommunications impose successive changes and updates on related engineering majors, especially in practical qualification that includes using software facilities. This chapter aims to join the efforts to spread the use of open source software in academic education. The chapter consists of two main sections. The first presents the trend of using open source software in higher education and discusses pros and cons of using open source software in engineering education. The second section presents network traffic analysis as an example of recent effective research topics and provides a set of open source tools to perform the research's practical steps. The research example with the suggested tools is valid as practical lab work for telecommunication and IT-related majors.

OPEN SOURCE SOFTWARE IN EDUCATION AND RESEARCH

Tendency to Use Open Source Software in Higher Education

By definition, open source software (OSS) is software that is available to everyone, including the source code, along with the copyright license that permits using, studying, modifying, or redistributing the software (Beal, 2008). OSS covers a wide range of user needs, ranging from simple programs such as

DOI: 10.4018/978-1-7998-9158-1.ch015

editing utilities, to very advanced software such as operating systems. The most famous successes in OSS are the operating systems Linux and Android.

Using OSS in education is a current tendency in some of the leading universities around the world, including the USA and Europe (Wilson, 2013; Roach, 2016). Some of these universities, such as MIT and Stanford, effectively participate in developing open source projects through their dedicated research labs. The main reasons for choosing OSS in many educational institutions are the cost, which plays a key role especially in limited-budget educational systems; its high effectiveness and success with some important educational platform systems such as Moodle (Cole & Foster, 2008); and better suitability than closed software for research environments in higher education. Nowadays, there is a tendency in some countries to share information and make education available to everyone (e.g., the #GoOpen campaign in the USA) (Office of Educational Technology, 2016). Open source and open education complement each other, and both focus on transparency and sharing information. The next section presents pros and cons of using OSS in engineering education.

Pros and Cons of Using OSS in Engineering Education

Due to the particularity of the learning activities in engineering education, specifically in IT and tele-communications engineering, the advantages and drawbacks of using OSS are not the same as in other domains. In engineering institutions, the students and professors use the software as an educational tool, and, at the same time, they may develop it as a part of practical training. Table 1 shows a summary comparison of using OSS and closed software in engineering education.

Table 1. Comparison between OSS and closed software in engineering education

Criteria	OSS	Closed Software
The cost	-OSS is free -No limitation on usage duration or number of copies	-Not free of change -Limited number of copies -Could be for limited duration
Cooperation between Academic Institutions	-Valid to be used as a common platform for joint projects	-Less likely to be used for joint projects
Interoperability with other Systems	-Possibility to compile different versions for different OSs -Possibility to change the source code and the input/output format	-Software is intended to work on specific OS -Limited or fixed input/output format
Fit Lab Needs	-Predefined options and scenarios -Possibility to change the source code to adapt lab needs	-Predefined options and scenarios
Availability for Specific Research Purposes	-Many OSS has been developed in academic institutions for specific research purposes	-Closed software development is based on market needs
Support	-Support depends on contributors (not guaranteed) -Lack of documents and materials	-the software companies support their products -Availability of documents, help, and support materials
User Interface Quality	-In general, has a poor GUI quality, especially in the old versions (command line only)	-Most commercial software has a good GUI quality

Table 1 shows that OSS is better than closed software with respect to cost, fitting lab needs, possibility of using the software as a common platform for joint projects, interoperability with other systems, and availability for specific research purposes. Closed software is better for support and graphical user interface (GUI). In the following section, advantages and drawbacks of using OSS in engineering education are discussed in more detail.

Advantages of Using OSS in Engineering Education

- Cost: The educator can choose whatever he/she needs from the available OSS to enhance the quality of the practical work, without concern for the cost; and can also change and update lecture content according to the emerging technologies and available resources. Students too can benefit from using the OSS to perform their projects without any charge. The total cost of closed software is not a negligible amount of money, considering the limited budget of educational institutions.

- Cooperation between Academic Institutions: Scientific cooperation between academic institutions requires using similar teaching environments, such as educational contents, technologies, and software. The availability of no-cost OSS enhances the chance to establish such cooperation in practical terms. Furthermore, OSS can be used as a common software environment to establish joint scientific and research projects among universities and research groups, which enhances the educational level and the scientific experience of both the educators and the students.

- Interoperability with Other Systems: The possibility of interoperating various kinds of commercial software is low if they are issued by various companies. Moreover, some versions of commercial software are intended to work under a specific version of operating system. Unlike commercial software, the OSS shows more interoperability. The developer can get the suitable executable version for his/her operating system by compiling the source code on the specified operating system. Moreover, the developer can modify the input/output format, data structure, parameters, and other necessary conditions to make the OSS interoperate properly with other installed software.

- Fit with Lab Needs: OSS can fit lab needs more readily than commercial software, for two reasons. First, the educator can choose the OSS based solely on its functionalities and features. Second, the educator, as well the students, can develop the software source code to meet research or laboratory requirements.

- Availability of OSS for Specific Research Purposes: Much OSS was originally developed in research laboratories or in academic institutions, for the purpose of completing specific scientific tasks, regardless of the number of eventual users or the returned value. On the other hand, commercial software is developed to get a good return on investment, which is related to the expected number of eventual sold copies and software cost.

Drawbacks of Using OSS in Engineering Education

- Lack of Support: Usually, commercial companies provide a good level of support for their products. The support may include training, new updates, and fixing bugs. On the other hand, OSS is developed by various contributors, and may not have the same level of support as closed software (Wilson, 2014). Usually, the OSS support comes from the contributors themselves, but it is notable that recently documentation and support for OSS has been enhanced. Some commercial companies offer support for specific kinds of OSS, including training, installation, and fixing bugs, but such support is not free of charge.

- Poor User Interface Quality: Users frequently complain about OSS interfaces; most do not have good quality GUI (Wilson, 2014); some even use command-line interface for installation and configuration, which is not easy for a nontechnical user. On the other hand, commercial software usually has a user-friendly interface, and in most cases the installation and configuration are straightforward processes. In fact, the primitive versions of the Linux operating system and OSS were not that easy to use, with problems of library dependency and compilation issues. Current versions are much easier for nontechnical users, and most have been supported with GUI.

OSS for Research Environments

OSS is preferred more than the closed software in academic research. The nature of research tasks imposes extra constraints on the software, for example, the need to understand and evaluate the internal work methods or develop a specific part of the code. In some cases, the researcher must either develop the needed software locally or use OSS directly, as in the case of unavailability of qualified commercial software, or high cost of software. For most research domains, several available kinds of OSS can be used to perform research tasks, though they differ from each other in features and performance. The comparison of available OSS may facilitate the task of choosing the appropriate tool for specific tasks.

Network traffic analysis is getting more attention in recent years, due to rapidly evolving telecommunication infrastructure and services. This subject could be a useful part of engineering preparation in the network's lab, as it is a current issue in the industry. The next section presents motivations of network traffic analysis for the industry. Then, traffic-analysis methods are presented. Finally, traffic-analysis steps with a complex of available OSS for each step are explained.

NETWORK TRAFFIC ANALYSIS AS EDUCATIONAL LAB MATERIAL

Network Traffic Analysis Motivation

Network traffic analysis is one of the most researched topics in the last decade (Li, Springer, Bebis, & Gunes, 2013), due to its importance to Internet service providers (ISP) and network administrators. Network traffic analysis is the process of recording, reviewing, and extracting information on network traffic. Network traffic analysis enables getting statistics on user activities, the performance of the network, and the used protocols. Network traffic classification is a part of network traffic analysis, which focuses more on recognizing traffic according to certain levels—e.g., according to application type, such as web, streaming, peer to peer; or according to the used protocol, such as HTTP, FTP, or Skype's protocol.

Controlling Internet traffic is one of the most important and difficult tasks, due to the extensive usage of Internet applications and diversity of contents, as well as the evolution of concealing methods to escape monitoring and filtering. Network traffic analysis is required to enhance the quality of service, network security, investigating issues, and for business trends.

Example of Practical Issues in ISPs

BitTorrent is one of the most widely known peer-to-peer file-sharing applications. ISPs try to block this application, because it uses Internet resources, and because of the nature of the exchanged contents. The users of BitTorrent may exchange legal contents without the license of the original owner, including movies, software, or any e-materials; or exchange illegal e-materials such as those related to drug trade or violence.

ISPs use different methods to block this application, such as blocking the application ports, the seeds websites (the information files), or the traffic that contains the BitTorrent signature (pattern recognition). On the other hand, BitTorrent developers constantly create new methods to avoid filtering, using different port numbers and encryption. As a result, BitTorrent traffic still has a very high percentage of Internet traffic—for example, 24.02% of the fixed Internet access in the Asia-Pacific area in 2016 is BitTorrent traffic (Sandvine, 2016).

Network Traffic Analysis Methods

Port-Number Method

The port number is the first method used to classify network traffic. It is based on the assigned port numbers for standard Internet applications and services, as defined by the Internet Assigned Numbers Authority (IANA, 2017).

The port-number method is simple and fast, but it is not considered an accurate method for classification, for two reasons. First, many current applications are not standard IANA applications (i.e., have no registered port number). Second, some forbidden applications dynamically change their port numbers, using ports of legal applications to avoid filtering; or a tunnel application, such as Skype, that could be configured to use TCP ports 80 and 443 if the original port is blocked by the firewall (see Figure 1).

Figure 1. Example of applications that use different protocols

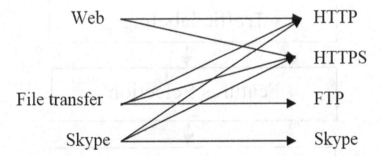

Deep Packet Inspection Method

Deep packet inspection method is based on finding an application's pattern recognition within the traffic (White, Daniel, & Teague, 2012). Most known applications have pattern recognitions (application signature) in their payload. Usually, the pattern recognition consists of a sequence(s) of bytes in specific order and of specific value. The advantage of this approach is that it recognizes the application regardless of the port number. The two main drawbacks of this method are that it violates user privacy, since the content of the packets is considered confidential information; and this method does not work in cases of encrypted traffic.

Machine Learning Method

The most recent traffic-analysis studies are based on machine learning method, which overcomes the issues of user privacy, application tunneling, and encryption technique (Dainotti, Pescape, & Claffy, 2012). Machine learning method is based on discovering common flow features that belong to the same application. A flow feature is any characteristic value of the flow (e.g., mean packet size, number of packets within the flow, acknowledgment [ACK] number). Moore, Crogan, and Zuev (2005) state that the complete number of flow features is 249.

In network traffic analysis, the most widely known method is supervised learning, where the relationship between the applications and flows can be derived from learning examples (training data sets).

Recent research shows that machine learning methods can identify many known applications with a very high rate of accuracy (e.g., BitTorrent can be identified with accuracy over 95%) (Wang, Zhang, & Ye, 2015).

Figure 2. Traffic classification steps using machine learning

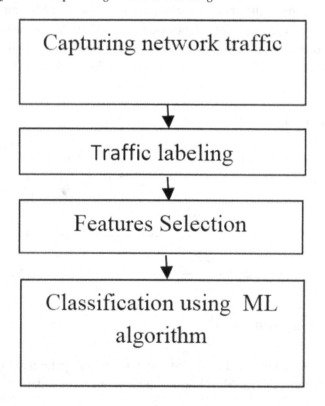

Practical Steps of Network Traffic Classification for New Lab Development

This section presents practical steps of a traffic-classification process using the machine learning method. Figure 2 presents traffic-classification flow, which consists of capturing network traffic, traffic labeling, features extraction, and classification using machine learning steps.

Capturing Network Traffic

Capturing network traffic (logs) is the first step in traffic classification. Depending on the purpose of the study, traffic capturing can be done at different levels of the network hierarchy (e.g., network interface of a local machine for studying local applications behavior; network switches to study distributed attacks; or at the ISP level to study global bandwidth usage). Capturing network traffic on the local machine can be done using special software called a sniffer. There are two ways to capture traffic on the local network switch. First, by using port forwarding on the main switch from all ports to a specific port, the sniffer captures the traffic at that specified port. Second, traffic can be captured at the exit firewall or the exit router directly.

The sniffer can work in two modes. The first is called promiscuous mode, where the sniffer collects all traffic running through the network. The second mode is the usual mode, where the sniffer captures only the traffic that belongs to the local host. Table 2 shows the available OSS for network sniffing.

Table 2 shows the available open source sniffers, with some general information about each. The most simple and efficient sniffer is Tcpdump (Sloan, 2001). Network and system administrators frequently use this tool, as it is fast, simple, and an essential GNU package. For academic use, the most widely known and recommended tool is Wireshark (Chappell, 2014). It can capture and monitor traffic both online and offline, and is provided with a wide range of filtering options, with detailed graphical display for protocols (headers and payload) at various network levels. Students can use it as well, to monitor and analyze the traffic directly in various formats (ASCII, hexadecimal, and binary).

Tools for Labeling Data Sets

The second step of the traffic-classification process using machine learning method is labeling the training data set. This step is very important since the training data set is used as ground truth (learning model) for the learning algorithm.

The most widely known open-source tools for traffic labeling are LibProtoIdent (Alcock & Nelson, 2012), "L7 Filter" (Santos, 2008), and nDPI (Deri, 2014). They use different classification methods to classify traffic, like deep packet inspection, port number, and simple statistical methods.

Table 3 shows a list of available open-source tools for traffic classification, most of them based on deep packet inspection technique. The precision of protocol identification depends on the studied protocol. A detailed comparison between popular DPI tools for traffic classification (Bujlow, Carela-Españolb, & Barlet-Ros, 2014) shows identification accuracy of the most used protocols using the chosen tools. Velan, Cermak, Celeda, and Drasar (2015) mention that LibProtoIdent generally has the highest classification accuracy among the other tools. It identifies the maximum number of protocols among the other open-source classification tools (375 protocols), and is very fast and designed to work in a limited-resources environment.

Table 2. The available open-source tools for network sniffing

Capturing Network Traffic Tools	Developer	User Interface	Last version/ date	Available for OS	License	Supported protocol level	Brief info
Wireshark	The Wireshark team	GUI, CLI	2.2.7/ Jun 01, 2017	Linux, BSDs, MacOSX, MS Win, Solaris	GNU General Public License	App. level – wide range of protocols	Most popular tool, practical and easy with several display and filtering options
Tcpdump	The Tcpdump team	CLI	4.9.0/ Jan 18, 2017	Linux, BSDs, MacOSX, MS Win, Solaris	BSD License	TCP/IP	An essential package of Linux OS releases, well known for network admin
Netsniff-ng	Daniel Borkmann	CLI	0.6.3/ Apr 11, 2017	Linux	GNU General Public License	TCP/IP	Used for protocol analysis, reverse engineering, and network debugging
Junkie	The Junkie team	CLI	2.6.4/ Oct 15, 2013	Linux	GNU General Public License	App. Level, Limited number of Protocols	Packet reordering, reassembling tracking connections
CapAnalysis	Gianluca Costa	Web	1.2.2/ Aug 22, 2016	Linux	GNU General Public License	TCP/IP	Gives geographical representation of connections
EtherApe	Juan Toledo	GUI	0.9.15/ Feb. 10, 2017	Linux	GNU General Public License	Application level, Wide number of protocols	Network monitoring and analyzing connections
Ettercap	Contributors	GUI and CLI	0.8.2 -Ferri/ March 14, 2015	Linux, BSDs, MacOSX	GNU General Public License	App. Level, Limited number of protocols	Can be used to perform Man in Middle Attack
Snoop	Sun Microsystems	CLI	Solaris10/ Dec. 11, 2006	Solaris	Common Development and Distribution License	TCP/IP	Similar to tcpdump

Table 3. The available open-source tools for network traffic classification and traffic marking

Traffic Labeling Tools	Developer	Last Version/date	User Interface	Number of identified protocols	Available for Operating system
LibProtoIdent	the University of Waikato WAND research group	2.0.10/ Jan. 06, 2017	CLI	375	Linux, MacOS X, FreeBSD
nDPI	ntop - Deri Luca	1.16 May 31, 2015	CLI	185	Linux, FreeBSD, MacOSX
L7 Filter	L7 Filter	May 28, 2009	CLI	110	Linux
Traffic Identification Engine TIE	TIE Team - University of Napoli Federico II	v1.2.0-alpha Jul 30, 2014	CLI	297	Linux, FreeBSD, MacOS X
NeTraMark	NeTraMark	Dec 8, 2010	GUI	93	Linux
Tstat	Tstat	3.1.1 May 30, 2016	Web	38	Linux

Extracting Flow Features

Flow feature is any characteristic value of the flow that can be used to predict the application or application type. For example, flow duration, mean packet size, and total packets number are flow features that can be calculated from traffic logs.

Features selection is the third step in the traffic classification process using machine learning method. In this step, the selected flow features are studied based on their efficiency in predicting the expected results. Most of the flow features can be extracted (calculated) from the flow trace directly, but some of them, such as the statistical features, need more processing. If the machine learning tool is supported by mathematical and data-processing libraries, then the flow features can be calculated using the machine learning tool itself; otherwise, they should be processed in separate steps using an appropriate tool.

Some special open-source tools for extracting flow features from raw traffic are used mostly for research purposes. However, there are no dedicated commercial tools for extracting flow features, the available open source tools for this task are:

- **Fullstats:** Fullstats (Moore & Zuev, 2005) is an open-source tool to extract flow features from raw data logs (.pcap) or directly from local network interface (online). This tool was developed at Cambridge University using C language. The output of the tool contains 268 flow features in comma-separated values format. The output can be used directly as an input for machine learning tools.
- **NetMate:** NetMate (Zander & Schmoll, 2009) is OSS, used to extract flow features from raw network logs (.pcap format) or from local network interface (online). The output of NetMate consists of only 40 features that are the most effective features among the others. A subset of the features collection can be specified using the configuration file. The output file can be used directly as an input feature file for machine learning software.

Table 4. The most widely known open-source machine learning tools

ML Tools	Developer	Supported language	Operating system	Support statistical analysis	Deep learning	Distributed computing	GUI	GPU acceleration
Scikit-Learn	multiple; support: INRIA, Google	C, C++, Python, Cython	Linux, MacOSX, Windows	+	-	-	+	-
R-Programming	John Chambers and colleagues - AT&T	C, Fortran, R	Linux, Unix, MacOSX, Windows	+	-	+	+	+
H2O	H2O.ai	Java, Python, R, Scala, JSON	Linux, MacOSX, Windows	+	+	+	+	-
Weka	Univ. of Waikato, New Zealand	Java	Linux, Unix, MacOSX, Windows	-	-	+	+	-
Apache Spark MLlib	Apache Spark-Berkeley's AMPLab	Java, Scala, Python, R	Linux, MacOSX, Windows	+	-	+	-	+
TensorFlow	Google Brain team	Python, C/C++, Java, Go	Linux, MacOSX, Windows	+	+	+	+	+
Theano	Montreal University	Python	Linux, Unix, MacOSX, Windows	+	+	-	+	+
Accord.NET	Contributors	C#	Windows, Linux	+	-	-	+	+
Apache Singa	Apache Incubator	Python, C++, Java	Linux, MacOSX, Windows	+	+	-	-	-
Shogun	Contributors	C, C++, Python, R, Matlab	Linux, MacOSX, Windows	-	-	-	-	+

Classification Based on Machine Learning Method

Machine learning is the most promising approach for traffic analysis and classification; it classifies encrypted network traffic very effectively, and it does not violate user privacy. Table 4 shows a list of most featured and used machine learning tools; most of them support statistical and deep learning solutions. These tools have been developed and used in academic institutions, e.g., Weka (Witten, Frank, & Hall, 2011) and MLlib (Pentreath, 2015). In addition, they support the famous programming languages, including Python, Java, and C++.

Most of the famous learning algorithms (Naïve Bayes, Support vector, decision tree, and others) are implemented in most of the software listed in Table 4. Machine learning algorithms differ from each other in learning model, speed, accuracy, and method of classification.

According to Jovic, Brkic, and Bogunovic (2014), Weka is one of the most featured tools for general data-mining solutions. Weka offers developers a graphical and command-line interface, and is provided by several utilities for importing and transforming data through simple wizards. Weka is a suitable tool to use in student laboratories, as the students can start their lab work and monitor their results quickly. For more profound professional research projects, using more specialized software is preferable, depending on the project type. For example, H2O could be a good choice for big-data solutions, as it has an efficient parallel processing engine (Cook, 2016).

Summary of Network Traffic Analysis

This chapter may help interested people start practical network traffic classification, which can be very useful for preparing practical work for the student lab. The educator can create various scenarios for student lab work, such as performing a practical study on using social media on the local network, or identifying remote login services from/to the local network. The needed tools for each scenario depend on the aim of the study and the methods used. For example, when the statistical features are used in a learning method, it is better to use scikit-learn (Brownlee, 2014) or R-programming (Lantz, 2013) as machine learning software. For general or simple student lab work, using the tools (Wireshark, LibProtoIdent, NetState, and Weka) is recommended.

FUTURE RESEARCH DIRECTIONS

OSS is an essential part of current and future research tools, as well using OSS is a global tendency in many educational systems around the world, specifically in engineering preparation. Therefore including the OSS in the educational process seems to be an inevitable step due to its increasing role in this domain. Adoption of OSS in higher education, especially in engineering preparation, requires collaboration between different entities like governments, educational institutions, and OSS developers. The government usually gives the financial support, the strategies of education and issues the related rules and regulations to organize the work of the educational institutions, which may include a plan or a policy to involve more OSS in the educational process, or at least gives recommendations to use and support OSS in higher education. The education institutions play the most effective role to adopt the OSS in engineering education, as they can allocate the necessary resources and efforts to achieve this purpose like:

- Dedicate OSS research and development lab(s) to support the engineering preparation laboratories in different specialties, as well this lab(s) can provide the required software for special research purposes.
- Organize conferences and workshops on OSS In education, usage, benefits, challenges etc.
- Include OSS in IT engineering curriculum as an essential part of engineering preparation.

OSS developers as well can play an important role in adoption OSS in educational process, as they allocate more efforts to respond to educational software needs, for example, they can provide software for a specific lab activity and take into consideration the specific nature of the education process, like graphical user interfaces, interactive exercises, educational manuals, resolved examples etc.

CONCLUSION

Using OSS in engineering preparation enhances student skills and strengthens the sense of collaboration and sharing information. OSS is a very rich environment, which helps students to better understand the lab's goals and enhance creativity. Already OSS has become an obvious option in research, and more familiar in engineering preparation. The availability and diversity of OSS, given the trend toward open education, will make OSS a primary option in preparing the next generation of engineers. However, despite the success and great features of OSS, there is no concrete decision to adopt it in the education process of many educational institutions; choosing such software is still a professor's personal decision.

This chapter aims to present a brief study of using OSS in academic education and proposes an open source tools' set to perform practical steps of network traffic analysis. The chapter also provides a brief feature comparison of the open-source tools for each step, which may help the researcher/professor to choose the convenient ones for his/her research. The research example introduced, with the suggested tools, can be used as a platform for the networks lab for telecommunication and IT majors.

ACKNOWLEDGMENT

The work is being supported by the Russian Ministry of Education and Science (Project #2.7782.2017/BC dated 10/3/2017).

REFERENCES

Alcock, S., & Nelson, R. (2012). *Libprotoident: Traffic classification using lightweight packet inspection.* Technical report, University of Waikato. Retrieved from https://wand.net.nz/sites/default/files/lpi.pdf

Brownlee, J. (2014). *Gentle introduction to Scikit-Learn: A Python machine learning library.* Retrieved April 21, 2017, from http://machinelearningmastery.com/a-gentle-introduction-to-scikit-learn-a-python-machine learning-library/

Bujlow, T., Carela-Españolb, V., & Barlet-Ros, P. (2014). *Extended independent comparison of popular deep packet inspection (DPI) tools for traffic classification*. Retrieved from http://people.ac.upc.edu/pbarlet/reports/extended_dpi_report.pdf

Chappell, L. (2014). Troubleshooting with Wireshark: Locate the source of performance problems. Reno, NV: Protocol Analysis Institute (dba "Chappell University").

Cole, J., & Foster, H. (2008). *Using Moodle* (2nd ed.). Sebastopol, CA: O'Reilly Media, Inc.

Cook, D. (2016). *Practical machine learning with H2O: Powerful, scalable techniques for deep learning and AI*. Sebastopol, CA: O'Reilly Media, Inc.

Dainotti, A., Pescape, A., & Claffy, K. (2012). Issues and future directions in traffic classification. *IEEE Network, 26*(1), 35–40. doi:10.1109/MNET.2012.6135854

Deri, L., Martinelli, M., Bujlow, T., & Cardigliano, A. (2014). nDPI: Open-source high-speed deep packet inspection. In *Proceeding of Wireless Communications and Mobile Computing Conference (IWCMC) 2014 International*. IEEE Xplore. 10.1109/IWCMC.2014.6906427

Internet Assigned Numbers Authority. (2017). *Service name and transport protocol port number registry*. Retrieved April 4, 2017, from http://www.iana.org/assignments/service-names-port-numbers/service-names-port-numbers.xhtml

Jovic, A., Brkic, K., & Bogunovic, N. (2014). An overview of free software tools for general data mining. In *Proceedings of the 37th International Convention on Information and Communication Technology, Electronics and Microelectronics (MIPRO) 2014*. IEEE Xplore. 10.1109/MIPRO.2014.6859735

Lantz, B. (2013). *Machine learning with R*. Retrieved from https://www.packtpub.com/big-data-and-business-intelligence/machine learning-r

Li, B., Springer, J., Bebis, G., & Gunes, M. H. (2013). A survey of network flow applications. *Journal of Network and Computer Applications, 36*(2), 567–581. doi:10.1016/j.jnca.2012.12.020

Moore, A., Crogan, M., & Zuev, D. (2005). *Discriminators for use in flow-based classification*. London, UK: Intel Research Tech.

Moore, A. W., & Zuev, D. (2005). Internet traffic classification using Bayesian analysis techniques. In *Proceedings of the 2005 ACM SIGMETRICS international conference on Measurement and modeling of computer systems*. Association for Computing Machinery. 10.1145/1064212.1064220

Office of Educational Technology. (2016). *Openly Licensed Educational Resources*. Retrieved from https://tech.ed.gov/open/

Pentreath, N. (2015). *Machine learning with Spark*. Birmingham, UK: Packt Publishing Ltd.

Roach, N. (2016). Open Source in Higher Education: Top 10 Universities [Blog post]. Retrieved March 26, 2017, from https://www.axelerant.com/blog/open-source-in-higher-education

Sandvine. (2016). *Global Internet phenomena, Africa, Asia-Pacific, and Middle East*. Retrieved from https://www.sandvine.com/downloads/general/global-internet-phenomena/2016/global-internet-phenomena-apac-mea.pdf

Santos, R. (2008). *Intrusion prevention with L7-Filter.* Retrieved from InfoSec Reading Room WebSite: https://www.sans.org/reading-room/whitepapers/intrusion/intrusion-prevention-l7-filter-32868

Sloan, J. D. (2001). *Network troubleshooting tools.* Sebastopol, CA: O'Reilly & Associates, Inc.

Beal, V. (2008). *What is open source software?* Retrieved March 28, 2017, from http://www.webopedia.com/DidYouKnow/Computer_Science/open_source.asp

Velan, P., Cermak, M., Celeda, P., & Drasar, M. (2015). A survey of methods for encrypted traffic classification and analysis. *International Journal of Network Management, 25*(5), 355–374. doi:10.1002/nem.1901

Wang, C., Zhang, H., & Ye, Z. (2015). A peer to peer traffic identification method based on wavelet and particle swarm optimization algorithm. *International Journal of Wavelets, Multiresolution, and Information Processing, 13*(6), 1550048. doi:10.1142/S0219691315500484

White, C. M., Daniel, E. J., & Teague, K. A. (2012). A real-time network analysis tool to aid in characterizing VoIP system performance. *International Journal of Electrical Engineering Education, 42*(2), 119–131. doi:10.7227/IJEEE.42.2.1

Wilson, S. (2013). Open source in higher education: How far have we come? [Blog post] Retrieved March 28, 2013, from https://www.theguardian.com/higher-education-network/blog/2013/mar/28/open-source-universities-development-jisc

Wilson, S. (2014). *Tackling the challenges of open source adoption in education.* Retrieved from https://opensource.com/education/14/5/choosing-open-source-education

Witten, I. H., Frank, E., & Hall, M. A. (2011). *Data mining: Practical machine learning tools and techniques* (3rd ed.). San Francisco, CA: Elsevier Inc.

Zander, S., & Schmoll, C. (2009). *Calculating flow statistics using Netmate.* Retrieved April 12, 2017, from https://dan.arndt.ca/nims/calculating-flow-statistics-using-netmate/

ADDITIONAL READING

Abu Talib, M. (2016). Open Source Software in the Arab World: A Literature Survey. *International Journal of Open Source Software and Processes, 7*(1), 49–64. doi:10.4018/IJOSSP.2016010103

Barry, B. I. A. (2009). Using open source software in education in developing countries: The Sudan as an Example. *In International Conference on Computational Intelligence and Software Engineering (CiSE 2009)*, 1–4. DOI: 10.1109/CISE.2009.5364872

Hai-Jew, S. (2012). *Open-Source Technologies for Maximizing the Creation, Deployment, and Use of Digital Resources and Information.* Hershey, PA: IGI-Global; doi:10.4018/978-1-4666-2205-0

Hanandeh, F., Al-Shannag, M. Y., & Alkhaffaf, M. M. (2016). Using Data Mining Techniques with Open Source Software to Evaluate the Various Factors Affecting Academic Performance: A Case Study of Students in the Faculty of Information Technology. *International Journal of Open Source Software and Processes*, 7(2), 72–92. doi:10.4018/IJOSSP.2016040104

Hancock, M. (2007). The Impact of Open Source Software on Education. Open Source Software and the User Experience in Higher Education. Retrieved from http://cnx.org/content/m14762/latest/?collection=col10431/latest

Kong, X. (2013). Improving OOS Usability of Software Technology in Higher Education in China. *Journal of Theoretical & Applied Information Technology*, 48(1), 655–660.

Sooryanarayan, D. G., Gupta, D., & Smrithi Rekha, V. (2014). Trends in Open Source Software Adoption in Indian Educational Institutions. *In 2014 IEEE Sixth International Conference on Technology for Education*, DOI: 10.1109/T4E.2014.26

Williams van Rooij, S. (2011). Higher education sub-cultures and open source adoption. *Computers & Education*, 57(1), 1171–1183. doi:10.1016/j.compedu.2011.01.006

Wyles, R. (2007). *Innovation for Education: OSS and Infrastructure for NZs Education System*. Retrieved from http://cnx.org/content/m14647/latest/

KEY TERMS AND DEFINITIONS

Application Tunneling: A method of encapsulating the traffic of a prohibited application in the payload of a legal application.

Commercial Software: Any developed software for commercial purposes and that has a price and a license.

Data Mining: A computer process that discovers hidden information or relations in a large amount of data, using artificial intelligence and machine learning methods.

Deep Learning: A recent method of machine learning based on neural networks with more than one hidden layer.

Engineering Preparation: The process of teaching and qualifying the students with the basic knowledge and skills in specific engineering domain.

Flow Features Extracting: The process of getting specific flow metrics from network traces, these metrics are used to identify the application (or application type) which generated the flow.

Free Software: A kind of software that available for everyone without any constraints on usage, modification or redistribution.

Laboratory's Software: The used software in laboratory to teach students.

Machine Learning Tools: A software which implements learning algorithms to resolve prediction problems.

Network Traffic Analysis: A process of network logs manipulation in order to know the used applications, protocol addresses, or to get statistics of network usage.

Network Traffic Identification: A kind of network traffic classification with interests in one or more specific applications.

Network Traffic Labeling: A process which maps the network flows with the convenient application or application type.

Open Source Software (OSS): A free computer program, available with its source code for everyone to use, modify, and redistribute to the others under some terms of usage.

Sniffer: A kind of software is used to capture network traffic.

This research was previously published in the Handbook of Research on Engineering Education in a Global Context; pages 331-345, copyright year 2019 by Information Science Reference (an imprint of IGI Global).

Chapter 16
Open Sourcing the Pedagogy to Activate the Learning Process

Alan Rea
https://orcid.org/0000-0003-0082-6630
Haworth College of Business, Western Michigan University, Kalamazoo, USA

Nick Yeates
UMBC, Baltimore, USA

ABSTRACT

Information systems graduates increasingly need to understand the collaborative, technology-driven practices inspired by open source software development that are fundamentally changing today's workplace. To meet this challenge, instructors must bring open source principles and technologies to active learning experiences. In this paper, the authors describe how nineteen undergraduates in a web development and design course at a Midwest university worked collaboratively with leading open-source software provider, Red Hat, to revamp the Teaching Open Source website. Accommodating this semester-length project required making significant revisions to course structure, instructional strategy, and assessments. The authors also describe the challenges of integrating these practices into the classroom and conclude with project reflections, including cautions and suggestions for instructors considering similar initiatives to move away from the "instructor as expert" paradigm to "meritocracy rule" thereby enabling students to make decisions with impacts beyond the classroom.

INTRODUCTION

The information systems department offers an undergraduate web design and development class at least once a year. The course is a degree requirement for juniors or seniors majoring in Digital Marketing and an elective for Information Systems majors. Instruction focuses on client-side scripting such as HTML5, CSS3 and JavaScript, and web design theory.

DOI: 10.4018/978-1-7998-9158-1.ch016

To practice what they are learning, students typically work in small groups on a semester-length project to develop websites for local small businesses or nonprofit organizations. However, at the outset of a fall semester, an opportunity presented itself for students to collaborate on a more substantial project: building a website for the only billion-dollar open source company, Red Hat (redhat.com).

This paper describes how an instructor and Red Hat consultant developed a course structure that enabled nineteen undergraduates to use open source software (OSS) development principles and technologies as they redesigned, developed, and implemented the Teaching Open Source website (teachingopensource. org) according to Red Hat's specifications and input. Students worked within an agile development environment much like they would in the real world (Turnu, et al., 2006) and were encouraged to make their own decisions to meet project expectations.

In the rest of Section 2, the authors describe the project's context and learning strategies. Section 3 contrasts it with previous attempts at collaboration. Section 4 explains the division of labor (into five student groups) and the means of motivating them. Section 5 describe new processes put in place to ensure the students succeeded at collaboration. Section 6 summarizes how technologies allowing virtual collaboration were applied. Section 7 reviews overall findings, including successes and shortcomings, and Section 8 offers suggestions for replicating the learning experience. Finally, Section 9 offers conclusions and future directions.

Open Source and Inner Source Approaches

To examine how the concepts and practices that the authors used diverged from established class projects and pedagogies, this subsection summarizes the industry strategies and practices that the class employed.

Open source typically refers to how source code is distributed and shared publicly via open source licensing (Koohang & Harman, 2005; Kamthan, 2007; OSI, 2019). Similarly, a new business practice--the "open source way"--applies to the work environment the same methodologies, best practices, processes, tools and culture that have transformed software development. The open source way empowers a workforce to collaborate freely as a community of people; new priorities include transparency, communal work, meritocratic rewards, and rapid prototyping (Red Hat, 2009).

These methods also may be used when the code will not be released to the public, or at least not to more than a select few (InnerSource Commons, 2019). The InnerSource approach describes communal, transparent, and iterative methods applied to in-house platform development (O'Reilly, 2000; Stol & Fitzgerald, 2015). Inner source provides the benefits of open source for circumstances in which company culture, technical reasons, legal uncertainties, or business secrets prevent disclosing the source code outside the company (Capraro & Riehle, 2016). Another instance is when a government has restricted the material from open source licenses.

We classify the project results as inner source because students worked with the authors in an online meeting space accessible only to themselves and project facilitators from Red Hat and the Professors Open Source Software Experience group (POSSE). The website was inner source because its code has not yet been released, but open source because it will be freely available after its completion and approval by Redhat and POSSE.

Project Origins

The authors met at a POSSE (foss2serve.org) workshop for computer science and computer information systems professors sponsored by Red Hat and run by POSSE member faculty with support from the National Science Foundation. Without participating in initiatives designed to foster partnerships between academia and industry, projects such as this one do not easily occur. The authors encourage instructors who want to implement classroom projects such as this one to attend meetings of local AITP chapters (aitp.org) or contact organizations looking for project assistance, such as the Free Software Foundation (fsf.org)

During the workshop Red Hat and POSSE spoke of an initiative to revamp the Teaching Open Source website. One of the authors (the instructor) saw an opportunity to engage his students in the redesign and offered to take on the project in the fall. After discussions with Red Hat managers and POSSE leadership, the instructor and Red Hat consultant left the workshop as project leaders and agreed that the collaboration would be:

- Implemented by students in a classroom project environment;
- Managed by Red Hat via the consultant and the university via the instructor; and
- Overseen by stakeholders and facilitators from Red Hat and POSSE.

Project Approach

The project would be considerably larger than the instructor's previous web projects, which had small teams of three to five students using limited deliverables to design websites for local clients. For this more substantial undertaking, the authors agreed that the class should function as an open source community in which diverse people collaborate for an improved outcome (Sack, et al., 2006).

Revisions to the course structure, instructional strategy, schedule and assessments would be necessary. The authors first planned the project's approach and expectations, which would take their cues from the IT industry's complex and multifaceted processes both in OSS development (Stewart & Gosain, 2006) and recently, InnerSource development (Capraro & Riehle, 2016; Stol, Babar, Avgeriou, & Fitzgerald, 2011). The authors soon determined:

- Everyone would work on the same project;
- Everyone would get the same project grade;
- Five work groups would have three to five students each;
- Each group would have a subfocus;
- Groups would work with Red Hat to implement the website;
- Email responses would be expected within three days;
- Weekly group sprints would be a check-in with everyone;
- The consultant would make an in-person visit at kick-off.

Project Expectations

The student team was asked to begin the project by investigating the existing site, evaluating its content and writing a site analysis. The student team's first deliverable report states:

The original Teaching Open Source website was put together to encourage students to learn about open source projects and software by reaching them through teachers. The site was mainly a teaching resource to allow teachers to view projects, recent open source events, and blogs regarding open source. Changes in management of the site led to lowered upkeep, whereupon spam accounts and poorly structured data led to most users leaving the site...[The client] looks to relaunch the website to better facilitate the original concept of promoting education and problem solving with open source...

After summarizing the tasks at hand, the analysis delineated objectives for each student group (as discussed in Section 4.1) as well as for the overall team. It also offered a preliminary timeline to meet the assigned delivery date. After feedback from the authors, students discussed the report at length and made revisions. By allowing students to set expectations and work through them with the instructor and consultant, the team had a sense of ownership from initial stages (Stewart & Gosain, 2006).

PREVIOUS COLLABORATION APPROACHES

Case studies have focused on team building among students pursing different college majors and with programming levels ranging from beginner to advanced, as were the challenges with the students. Sahin (2011) recommends taking students' preferences and instructor's considerations into account when forming teams for software engineering courses. Kruck & Teer (2009) advocate the use of interdisciplinary teams as an advantage in a group technical project and describe how a professor can adjust a course to accommodate it. Fortunately, the authors were able to incorporate this knowledge using the CATME system (CATME, 2019; Layton, Loughry, Ohland, & Ricco, 2010) for generating a questionnaire that classified each student's skills and knowledge as well as attitudes toward team projects (catme.org).

Team building is only the first hurdle in many classroom projects; despite being part of a traditional in-person class, the project required online collaboration. In seeking to replicate an efficient interactive learning environment as outlined by Uzunboylu (Uzunboylu, Bicen, & Cavus, 2011), the authors' experience was that Google Docs, Hangouts, and Sheets, as well as LucidChart and Trello were invaluable. The Google offerings, in particular, made the project possible (as explained in Section 6).

A final goal of student teamwork in a virtual environment is to motivate students to become active rather than passive learners (Pundak, Herscovitz, Shacham, & Wiser-Biton, 2009; Schiller, 2009; Coldwell, Craig, & Goold, 2011; Drake, 2012). While sharing goals with the team during the semester, the authors encouraged students to determine how they would reach them, in particular by deciding which tools and components best fulfilled the client's requirements (Teel, Schweitzer, & Fulton, 2012; Kamthan, 2007; McComb, Green, & Compton, 1999). This was validated when students disputed the client's suggestions. Some, but not all, of their arguments were adopted. During post-project feedback, one student noted that the authors hearing and giving serious consideration to their ideas and suggestions during sprint meetings (explained Section 5.3) was positive. Such support is critical to OSS development teams because it "fosters trust and good communication practices by encouraging behaviors and orientations that are beneficial to the team's work" (Stewart & Gosain, 2006, p. 292).

Previous Classroom Attempts

Semester-length, real-world projects are core to the web design and development class and identified as such in the course description. However, preceding projects were smaller scoped and less complicated; a few students at a time had been able to manage the information architecture, design, development and implementation of a local organization's website assigned to their team.

Yet, previous projects also had overly depended on self-generated initiative from both clients and students. Some clients had been generous--and others uncharitable--in volunteering time and assistance to project teams. Moreover, past projects lacked iterative deliverables or checkpoints to help teams stay on schedule and on task. Ultimately, these learning experiences lacked community, cooperation, and a strong sense of identification with the project team: three concepts essential for OSS development to be effective (Stewart & Gosain, 2006).

Taking this into account, the authors improved the class structure and assessments through smaller deliverables, planned revisions of deliverables, weekly check-ins with the client and flexible objectives. Many of these techniques mirror tenets of agile development in software engineering (Kamthan, 2007; Teel, et al., 2012). Most worked well, but Section 7.3 of this paper describes times when the project deviated from its goals.

Industry's Shifting Paradigm

The course's new strategy borrowed from the Open Source, InnerSource, Agile, and DevOps approaches: all new models for software development as modern IT projects get bigger and more complicated. Industry use of organizational and cultural practices taken from open source originated with the software itself in the late 1990s and became a trend along with the InnerSource model in the following decade (Capraro & Reihle, 2016; InnerSourcing, 2019). Written in 2001, The Agile Manifesto (Beck, et al., 2001) created a new trend in project management that has benefited software development-based organizations by promoting iterative, cooperative, and frequent feedback practices.

More recently--beginning in 2009 in Belgium (Edwards, 2012)--the rapidly-growing DevOps movement has helped software organizations resolve the conflict between product development (feature creation) and operations (systems administration) that often delays getting software to the marketplace. DevOps principles are being embraced by large, complex IT organizations worldwide.

Today, large industry players such as IBM, Intel, Facebook, and Microsoft are more committed than ever to open source software. In recent years they have begun to allow their own developers to share high-potential code via company-sponsored initiatives, such as IBM's developerWorks Open, or by joining existing open source software communities (Capraro & Riehle, 2016). Preparing students to work in these new fast-paced approaches to software and system development is important for their continued success. However, it does require instructors to shift the overall classroom focus and become more of a guide rather than the sole expert. The next section outlines how the semester project created an environment where this could happen.

PROJECT FRAMEWORK

The semester began with forming student groups, setting up project architecture, and familiarizing students with the context of the project, as detailed in the following subsections.

Group Focus Within the Team

While intending to encourage the entire class to collaborate on activities such as brainstorming and problem solving, the authors also saw value in forming smaller groups to accomplish specific tasks. Therefore, by applying an accepted approach to OSS development that uses loosely prescribed roles (Sack, et al., 2006), the authors devised the following groups of three to five students each:

- **Information Architecture / User Experience (IA):** After first harvesting material from the old site, the IA group focused on content organization and usability, resulting in a new information structure and improved site navigation. Its members created an impressive 1,188-cell spreadsheet mapping old content to new, which helped the entire team rearrange the site;
- **Project Management (PM):** This group managed schedules and deliverable dates and ensured collaboration across groups. One of its members attended each of five sprint meetings per week, during which they logged progress and assisted the team with reminders and next steps;
- **System Administration, Programming, Development (SysAdmin):** This group was responsible for cloud infrastructure implementation, shell-level administration tasks, and verifying that the site was secure, robust and reliable. The group installed and tested all platforms, modules and plugins, and managed user roles. Moreover, the group independently learned OpenShift (openshift.com), an open source cloud-based containerized application hosting system, and implemented and configured Wordpress (wordpress.org), the content management system (CMS) platform selected for the new site;
- **Systems Analysis (SysAnalysis):** This group researched and tested seven platforms with the potential to meet client requirements and worked with the authors to create a 1,640-cell spreadsheet analyzing these findings. After recommending a CMS, the group documented and explained the system to both potential system administrators and users. This accomplishment should not be minimized given the lack of clear documentation in many open source projects (Izquierdo-Cortazar, González-Barahona, Robles, Deprez, & Auvray, 2012);
- **User Interface and Design (UI):** This group was responsible for design, layout and color theme, as well as the site achieving client standards for usability and branding. Dozens of designs were sketched on paper and then built in LucidChart (lucidchart.com), a collaborative online diagram maker similar to Microsoft Visio. Additionally, group members independently learned Wordpress's theme and plugin framework to take their art from idea to implementation.

Although forming groups helped to break a complex project into more manageable pieces, specialized groups also risked creating a silo effect within the team. The authors avoided this by requiring collaboration on all documents and group reports at weekly sprints (discussed in Section 5.3). For example, the class received proposed designs from the UI group, organizational revisions from the IA group, and summaries of sprints from the PM group. All of these items were presented to the class as a whole and could be viewed at any time in the shared project folders. Peer cooperation throughout the semester was a critical component to ensure collaborative work (Poindexter, 2003).

Figure 1. Old to new information architecture mapping

Hierarchy	New Page Name	Old Page Name(s)
Teaching Materials	Teaching Guides	currently on github, Teaching Materials Catalogue
	Teaching Materials Catalogue	Teaching Materials Catalogue
	In-Class Learning Activities	currently on foss2serve
	Academic Papers List	Articles, OSS education papers in scholarly journals
	Textbook	POSSE Textbook
	List of Courses	Course Content
	Schools That Teach OS	Programs That Teach OS
	Intro to FOSS	
	Promote POSSE / Foss2Serve	Programs About Teaching OS
	Presentations	Presentations
Participate	Join IRC Chat	Join TOS IRC Channel
	Participate in Initiative	Participate in Project
	Presentations	Presentations
	Promote POSSE / Foss2Serve	Programs About Teaching OS
	Edit this site	Join Wiki
	Events	Upcoming Events
	Blog Feed	Planet, Blog onto Planet / Planet Feed List, How to n
	Join Mailing List	Mailing List Archives
Connect with Others	Roll Call	Roll Call
	Join Mailing List	Mailing List Archives
	Blog Feed	Planet, Blog onto Planet / Planet Feed List, How to n
	Events	Upcoming Events
	Promote POSSE / Foss2Serve	Programs About Teaching OS
Friendly Projects	OSS Project List	FOSS Mentor Projects
	Dating Site Stub... coming in 2016	
	Promote POSSE / Foss2Serve	Programs About Teaching OS

Collaboration Motivators

If the student groups failed to work in a joint-delivery environment, and siloed outputs had to be assembled at the project's end, there likely would be compatibility issues (Stol, Avgeriou, Babar, Lucas, & Fitzgerald, 2014). Therefore, each student had to understand collaboration benefits. Although there were many motivational factors inherent in the course structure, the three most important were:

- Shared project grade;
- Shared document space; and
- Shared project knowledge.

Ideally, students were motivated by interests that *they* cared about, and not simply told to collaborate. Still the authors found these three shared areas to be the most important when facilitating open source interdependence throughout the course.

Figure 2. Content management system analysis

Major Requirements				
Features / Abilities	**Description**	**Joomla**	**Wordpress**	**Silverstripe**
CMS Overview				
FOSS/ License	Free/Open Source? What License does the software operate on?	Pass: GPL	Pass: GPL	Pass: BSD License
Developer/Community Strength	Developer commits often and recent? What is the community support like? [1]	Pass+ Timeline for release into 2016	Pass+ very popular with routine commits	Pass: Commits often, different versions available
OpenShift Hosting capability	OpenShift Immediate Compatibility	Pass [2]	Pass	Depends [3]
Platform	Platform (java, php)	php	php	php
Subjective usability of CMS by admins and editors				
Content Editor	Content editor usability- preferrably low barrier to entry [4]	Pass	Pass+	Pass
Developer	Developer usability [5]	Pass	Pass	Depends
Publishing & Content Management				
Wiki-like Editing UI	WYSIWYG (What You See is What You Get) On/Off [6]	Depends	Pass++	Pass- [7]
Customizable to our CSS	Can we use custom CSS, or use a theme [8]	Pass	Pass	Pass
Images in Content	Ability to insert images to content	Pass	Pass	Pass
Define Access/Permissions Based on Roles	Control privilege to content by defining roles, access, or editing rights [9]	Pass	Pass	Pass
Restrict Content editing by Type/Directory Structure	Control content access by content type/directory structure, such as static pages like Contact Us [10]	Pass [11]	pass	Pass
Broken Links	Detect and Notify broken links across site [12]	Pass	Pass [13]	Pass [14]
Mobile View and Nav	Viewable and Navigable on Mobile platforms	Pass	Pass	Pass [15]
Page/Title rename or move	Page or Title rename/move [16]	Pass	Depends- [17]	Pass [18]
Document Mgmt				
User-Defined Metadata	Metadata types can be user defined	Pass	Pass	Pass
Archiving & Auditing				
Track Site Changes	Track Changes to documents, version types	Pass	Pass [19]	Pass [20]

Figure 3. Proposed site designs

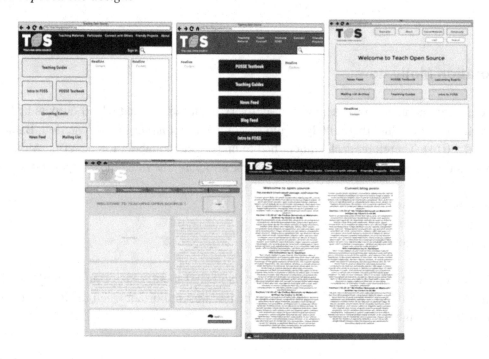

Shared Grade

Arguably the single most important motivator was the shared project grade. The class earned a single mark for the all of the project deliverables, which accounted for 50% of each student's final grade for the course. Early in the process, the authors considered whether the instructor should grade separately on certain deliverables from each group (e.g., site hierarchy analysis by the IA group), but rejected this to encourage cooperation and avoid a silo effect. It worked well. Asked about the benefits of participating in the project, a student noted:

It was, to be blunt, scary just letting go of all control over more than half of my points [for the course] on this project by allowing others to work towards it instead, but it was a great learning experience.

Shared Document Space

"Default to open," or transparency in decision-making, is a principle that Red Hat applies to its entire work culture. Students were strongly encouraged to work only in shared spaces. The authors told them, "If it is not written down for all to see, it didn't happen." If during sprint meetings a student disclosed working apart from the group, the authors asked him or her to post the work--even as a rough draft--in a shared space. This occurred only once or twice before all work was shared by default.

To enhance teamwork further, edit privileges were granted across the collaborative cloud platform. No one misused or abused these privileges, an issue of common concern in open source processes. Shared document space allowed students to follow the overall progress and find opportunities to contribute to content not assigned to their group (Poindexter, 2003). This permitted meritocracy, a unique benefit of open source communities. At any point in time a student was able to provide feedback on any area of the project. This leads to process openness.

Shared Knowledge

Transparency is another much-touted advantage to open source communities; it helps members multiply their personal skills to achieve a greater result than if they had worked separately (Stol, et al., 2011, 2014). Creating a culture of openness in the Red Hat project transcended students simply knowing what others were doing or being able to monitor real-time progress on deliverables and provide input. Students had to understand that helping each other *was* in their own personal interest because a better project would be the result. As the project progressed, the authors saw an increase in peers giving feedback on other group deliverables either via the shared space or in class sessions.

Project Processes

However, an increase in peer cooperation would not have happened without an adequate atmosphere to encourage collaboration (Poindexter, 2003). Without careful planning and facilitation, students will become frustrated and ultimately stymie the learning experience for all. The following subsections describe how the project was allocated adequate weekly time and resources to enable peer cooperation and increased collaboration beyond what students are accustomed in a more traditional classroom environment. Although many smaller course adjustments are always necessary, the authors assert that without a shift in course scope and weekly sprints, this project would not have been completed.

Class Scope

Collaboration typically requires more "overhead" efforts, such as planning and meetings, which do not directly result in a student's measurable progress on a project deliverable (Pundak, et al. 2009). As such, the project with Red Hat required significant changes to the instructor's strategy for the course, including grading procedures.

Modifying the class schedule to allow more classroom time for the project was slightly easier than deciding how much it should influence final grades. In previous semesters, a smaller group project counted for 35% of a student's final grade with the remaining 65% comprised of exercises, hands-on labs, and exams. After a discussion with students that ended in a show of hands, the Red Hat project was adjusted to become 50% of the grading component for the course. The instructor accomplished this change by removing exams from the course. Ultimately this change enabled the authors to increase the number of iterative sub-deliverables for the project in order to commit early, commit often (Red Hat, 2009), as well as allocate more time to enable group peer cooperation and team collaboration on the project in class.

Client Visit is Critical

Because the project was to be a major class focus, a client-team meeting early in the process was essential. Fortunately, the consultant was able to travel on short notice and became an "executive in residence" for three days at the university. Besides meeting with various student groups, he led in-class workshops to discuss open source and Red Hat. In the Web class the authors conducted workshops to help students understand the project though question and answer sessions, set benchmarks, and help students begin to brainstorm about the project (Kamthan, 2007).

This face-to-face meeting fostered trust between the team and the consultant that would boost students' motivation to collaborate throughout the semester. As Stewart & Gosain (2006) noted, "Affective trust stems from emotional attachment between a trustor and a trust target and may, therefore, be most relevant to potential developers' psychological and emotional reasons for joining, staying with, and contributing to OSS teams" (p. 296).

Sprint Meetings Are Anchors

To maintain the close interaction, a weekly sprint conducted in a round robin format was scheduled with each group and the consultant. During the sprint, group members each shared what they worked on that week and what they anticipated doing the next. The consultant led the initial group sprint, but after the first meeting asked each group leader to take it over, thus maintaining the culture and pace of the weekly sprint.

During the weekly sprint, in addition to the consultant, a PM group member also was present. This requirement was a highly effective means to record and disseminate information among the groups and the team as a whole. The PM group kept a detailed log of all meetings, resulting in a virtual project history that would benefit anyone wanting to learn from reviewing the process (Teel, et al., 2012). Open source culture advocates such transparency because it allows new developers, transient bug fixers, curiosity seekers, and researchers alike to delve deep into a project knowledge base and culture as if they were participants from the onset. Thus, OSS can expand beyond its progenitors (Stallman, 1992).

Asked at the end of the project to share what worked well, nearly every student named the weekly sprints:

The thing that worked well the most with this project were the weekly sprint meetings...[The sprints] allowed us to get feedback on our work very quickly which in turn allowed us to make decisions on what to do next. I have taken part in many large projects where a deliverable is given and there is very little to zero communication up until the day before a deliverable is due. This causes everyone to scramble at the very last second, which usually results in low quality work. I also believe the workshop days where the entire class was able to collaborate and speak to [the consultant] were equally as important. I also believe this more accurately represents a scenario you would face in the real world.

The consultant's availability to each student group via its weekly sprint required him to attend five Google Hangouts per week, an exceptional commitment that contributed greatly to the project's success. Although the authors realize a large commitment such as this may not be possible for every class project, it was necessary for one of this scope. However, sprint meetings could be scaled back depending on the client's goals for the project.

COLLABORATIVE TECHNOLOGIES

Project commitment and open lines of communication (Stewart & Gosain, 2006) are tenets of successful open source projects. Collaborative technologies enabled the students to accomplish the latter despite most of their communication and work taking place apart from their twice weekly classes.

Cross-platform compatibility enabled students to interact using any operating system or modality, including Chrome OS and smartphones. The class defaulted to productivity tools offered by Google Apps for Education (google.com/edu) because of its availability and Google's strong communal-oriented creation abilities. Google enabled the students to collaborate on the same documents to create, share, and edit files in real-time; however, any other multifaceted development environment would work.

Another preference was open source platforms such as OpenShift, Git, and Wordpress. The following table summarizes how technologies allowing virtual collaboration were applied to the project. Each is rated (High, Medium, Low) in terms of importance.

Collaborative technologies allowed students to witness project elements evolve and helped them to contribute in real time rather than waiting for a deadline. These communal social motivators are critical to the success of open source and other collaborative projects (Krogh, Haefliger, Spaeth, & Wallin, 2012).

OVERALL PROJECT FINDINGS

Given the fluid nature of open source processes in play not only in the project components and interaction but also the pedagogical shifts to encourage them, we offer both the major successes and the shortcomings for those who might want to implement similar initiatives. In this section, the authors distill the primary motivators and potential sticking points in regard to replicating similar learning opportunities.

Table1. Collaborative technology used

Tool	Explanation	Importance
Google Docs	All work was to be placed in shared folders with edit/revision privileges extended to all. This included the contents of group subfolders and even a folder for turning in specific deliverables. Because Google Docs logs edits with attribution, students could see who made any changes, including deletions. To address potential conflicts, the Project Management (PM) group wrote policies for handling revisions, code commits, and other project needs; this group also was responsible for quality control on all final submissions.	High
Google Hangouts	Weekly sprint meetings were held as group video chats on Google Hangouts, giving students with busy schedules the flexibility of attending via smartphones. For workshops throughout the semester, Google Hangouts allowed the consultant to address the class from a projection system, and later to move around the room on a laptop screen to meet with groups.	High
Google Calendar	Students could check deadlines and conveniently join Hangouts via links from Google Calendar. PM members and all group leaders had edit privileges to share dates and times.	Medium
Trello (trello.com)	Early in the semester a Trello board was useful to organize deliverables, group formation, and other information. Its use diminished as the project progressed.	Low
LucidChart (lucidchart.com)	The UI group and IA group extensively used LucidChart for collaboration on site schematics, theme building and CSS frameworks. An educational version made LucidChart available to students without cost to them or the university.	High (Select Groups [IA and UI]) Low (Remaining Groups)
Git and GitHub (github.com)	All code was hosted in a private Git repository; students used GitHub to share code, documents and other materials. Using Git and GitHub was challenging for students and required in-class instruction using tutorials and practice exercises. Concepts such as fork, push, and pull denote actions that are confusing for first time users. GitHub recognizes the challenge many face and has developed detailed guides and tutorials at its website (education.github.com).	High (Select Groups [SysAdmin])
OpenShift (openshift.com)	The project's development and production sites were housed by OpenShift, which is Red Hat's open source cloud-based Platform as a Service (PaaS) hosting system. It provides quick access to a Linux shell prompt and can automatically set up development environments such as PHP and a MySQL or PostgreSQL database. Other free PaaS offerings such as Heroku (heroku.com) are also available. The SysAdmin group, in particular, used OpenShift to test multiple Content Management Systems (CMS), and to stand up a development and production copy of Wordpress for the project. OpenShift and other PaaSs let students access as many virtual servers as needed to experiment with and deploy project technologies.	High
Email	All groups and the team as a whole relied on email sometimes to its detriment (Section 7.3).	High

Instructional Shift

Collaborative and cooperative learning requires not only students but also instructors to take on new roles. Early in the semester the instructor abdicated power as content expert of the classroom in favor of becoming the designer or architect of a learning experience (Poindexter, 2003). The quality of the collaborative process became the instructor's priority as he helped students make decisions (Lakhani & von Hippel, 2003). At times this included letting the students fail, learn how to recover, and return to the project's critical path.

Even if the instructor's hands-off instructional approach resulted in a less-than-perfect final project, students benefitted from having observed the ramifications of poor decision-making in a real-world

OSS development process. Krogh, et al. (2012) note that the potential impact of the work is a strong motivator. As one student observed:

The most important experience of this project was the real-world work environment we participated in. There are not nearly enough courses that truly apply a real-world environment to the curriculum and this class was an exception. This project allowed us to proactively learn what working in a web development position would be like. … Overall this gave us valuable career applicable knowledge we can take with us to a professional environment.

The consultant first expected to function as "client" for the project but soon took a more active project manager role that added another level of real-world authenticity. In addition to being an open source business strategist at Red Hat, he also had previously worked on an InnerSource project at the Naval Air Systems Command (NAVAIR) of the U.S. Department of Defense. He interacted with students in a truly open source collaborative manner in which the merit of ideas and approaches influenced decisions (Raymond, 2001). For example, the UI group used research and examples to convince the consultant that the client should go with a different site design than the preferred one. His willingness to allow ideas to flourish contributed to student ownership and the project's ultimate success.

Project Successes

From student, industry, and instructor viewpoints, the project worked well. The authors note as examples:

- **Student ownership and excitement:** Encouraged to make team decisions, listened to as valued team members, and trusted to proceed on their own in groups and in a team (Stewart & Gosain, 2006), students responded by making it their mission to complete a successful project;
- **Real world lessons and output:** The project extended the relevance of doing web design and development well beyond the classroom, allowing students to learn course content by *doing* rather than by only reading and practicing. Although coursework besides the project included labs, the potential for real-world results made the OSS learning experience indelible because it enabled students to try diverse approaches as they engineered the product (Kamthan, 2007);
- **More employable graduates:** Completing the project gave students an industry-sponsored project to put on their resumes and to help build their professional identities on LinkedIn (linkedin. com). Long notes that OSS experience on student resumes has a major impact when students are looking for their first job (2009). Additionally, the consultant was asked to submit recommendations that led to students getting technology jobs and internships. As one student shared:

I lack internship experience and most of my job experience is in entry level service industry positions. Having been part of this project gives a great experience to list on my resume, something I consider highly important as I write this paper not a week removed from taking my walk at commencement.

- **Benefits to client:** Red Hat and POSSE received an improved product created by a team of nineteen aspiring professionals, any of whom could be recruited as interns or future employees. Red Hat also was able to encourage good software practices, a benefit to the entire industry (Long, 2009);

- **Benefits to university:** Well beyond a press opportunity, the project further helped to foster a culture of collaboration between the college and its industry technical partners beyond those in the local community. Additional university entrepreneurial ventures are now considering open source collaborations as potential venues;
- **Proof of open source success:** The authors offer this project as an example that open source, coupled with collaborative and peer learning, can be successful. Though a significant departure from traditional instruction-based classrooms, projects such as this one should be more common-place on campuses wanting to prepare students for today's workplace (Long, 2009). The project accomplished this while also applying the principles of OSS software development, as the best enterprise development organizations also do (Capraro & Riehle, 2016). The authors' hope is that other instructors, familiar with this project's success, consider the viability of open source in the classroom not only with technology but also with pedagogy.

Project Shortcomings

Although successes outweighed shortcomings, a few problems did impact student collaboration and project deliverables, as described below:

- **Feature bloat and scope creep:** In the IT industry, project management suffers when the product accrues too many features or changes uncontrollably. In the students' project, the team wasted time studying features such as user management that were outside of the project scope and thus counterproductive. In hindsight, the authors should have moved more quickly to define the project scope rather than permit the team to promote features that were not required;
- **Critical path slowdown:** In feedback at the project's conclusion, nearly every student said it had taken too long at the project's outset to decide which CMS to use:

...what we could have done better was the time comparison between researching the different parts, especially the CMS, and actually developing the prototype...too much time was spent on it, leaving the [team] very little time to create and implement the actual prototype.

At the time, the authors were not aware of the slowdown and encouraged some of the research. Care should be taken to start work into developing technical aspects early on, versus spending too much time weighing which paths to go down.

- **Group arguments:** Although minimal, there were instances of group conflict. For example, the SysAdmin group argued for a certain CMS that the SysAnalyst group did not value from its research. The authors let the students work through their conflicts without interference in order to maintain open source governance structures (O'Mahoney & Ferraro, 2007);
- **Email miscommunication:** Students relied on Google docs to stay abreast of collaboration on the deliverables, perhaps to the neglect of email. Discussion lists were not created for each student group or for the overall class. As a result, forgetting an email address in the *Cc:* field would leave a student uniformed. Discussion lists also would have contained a record of communications similar to the virtual project history described in Section 5.3. Future replications must have robust communication systems such as email lists or newer technologies such as Slack (slack.com);

- **Privacy rights / FERPA:** Getting students' consent to use personally identifiable information for educational or promotional purposes should not be overlooked. Consider checking with university counsel in terms of what FERPA items can be released or waived by the students. If survey instruments will be used, contact the university's human subjects research board.

The overall project was successful because students learned OSS processes and techniques, and as well how to collaborate with a major technology company. Ultimately, the Teaching Open Source website the students developed was not adopted, but the students' research, design, as well as deliverables influenced its re-development by Red Hat.

SUGGESTIONS FOR IMPLEMENTATION

In this section the authors offer additional considerations for instructors or partner organizations preparing to undertake a student learning experience that will use open or inner source development practices:

- **Organization buy-in:** Success at short-term projects of a semester length requires that companies actively embrace the opportunity for open exploration of a business challenge or problem with a university and its students. Instructors who are uneasy about the potential for a single client failure might instead consider working with an established open source project team at the Free Software Foundation (fsf.org/campaigns/priority-projects), Apache Foundation (www.apache.org), or GitHub (github.com/explore);
- **Organization active contact:** Instructors should look for the client who has interest in the university and program. An experienced industry professional who sits on a college or program advisory board would be a great resource to help in the project or to refer a colleague who would actively engage the students as their trusted mentor;
- **Organization time allocation:** One of the most precious assets a mentor can offer students is his or her time. To do so, a mentor may need to relinquish or delegate other work duties. Of course, an ideal collaboration would let the professional volunteer a substantial amount of his or her work week, but this is not usually possible (as it was in our case). At a minimum, instructors should advocate the project as a short-term commitment allowing the company to build relationships and gain access to undergraduates' talent and skills to increase company participation in projects;
- **Organization project need:** Which OSS projects should the IT industry consider appropriate for collaboration with university partners? The optimal scenario would be a relatively low-risk idea or unfinished project that has not yet warranted much corporate investment or time. If the students fail to deliver a result meeting all client requirements, the organization can continue with the next semester's class, recruit interns from the students, or use internal resources to finish it;
- **Course time and scope fit:** Project success depends on the student team being given the time and resources to succeed. The aforementioned project, for example, dominated a fifteen-week semester and demanded half of the course evaluation. If the university calendar is short, or the coursework cannot accommodate a large project, the authors suggest reducing the project scope. Consider improving an aspect of an existing open source project. Many projects need help with documentation, particular feature sets, etc. SourceForge (sourceforge.net/p/forge/helpwanted/) provides a listing to start the process.

CONCLUSION AND FUTURE DIRECTIONS

This paper describes how student-led collaboration with a large technology provider enhanced the learning experience for an undergraduate web design and development class. Instead of small teams of students using limited deliverables to design websites for local businesses or nonprofits (as in previous semesters), a decision to "open source the pedagogy" challenged the class to collaborate on a more substantial project, building a website for an S&P 500 company.

Success, however, required major classroom changes to accommodate the open source principles of cooperation, collaboration, and meritocracy, as well as Agile project management. To replicate this active learning opportunity, instructors must be willing to shift their primary responsibility from presenting course content to becoming the facilitator of a learning process that may exceed their comfort zone. The client must be able to provide a mentor to work with students for the duration.

Similarly, students must forgo the familiarity of exams and predetermined deliverables, as well as their direct correlation to a final grade, while gaining considerable control of their deliverables and the final project outcome. Accordingly, they participate in intense teamwork, new technologies, and daily checkpoints and communication. Students may not fully perceive the real-world benefits of such an undertaking until they seek internships and jobs. However, learning projects based on open or inner source principles do prepare students for today's workplace.

Future collaboration between open source and academic realms is promising, and the authors want to see such initiatives become fundamental to undergraduate coursework. They continue to develop the best practices applicable to replicating the experience described herein.

REFERENCES

Beck, K., Beedle, M., van Bennekum, A., Cockburn, A., Cunningham, W., Fowler, M., & Thomas, D. (2001). *Manifesto for Agile Software Development*. Retrieved June 21, 2016, from http://agilemanifesto.org/

Capraro, M., & Riehle, D. (2016). Inner Source Definition, Benefits, and Challenges. *ACM Computing Surveys*, *49*(4), 36. doi:10.1145/2856821

CATME. (2019). Retrieved on February 13, 2019 from http://info.catme.org/

Coldwell, J., Craig, A., & Goold, A. (2011). Using eTechnologies for Active Learning. *Interdisciplinary Journal of Information, Knowledge, and Management*, *6*, 95–106. doi:10.28945/1367

Drake, J. (2012). A Critical Analysis of Active Learning and an Alternative Pedagogical Framework for Introductory Information Systems Courses. *Journal of Information Technology Education: Innovations in Practice*, 39–52.

Edwards, D. (2012, September 21). *The History of DevOps*. Retrieved from http://itrevolution.com/the-history-of-devops/

Hat, R. (2009). *The Open Source Way*. Retrieved from http://www.theopensourceway.org/book/index.html

InnerSource Commons. (n.d.). Retrieved February 13, 2019, from https://paypal.github.io/InnerSource-Commons/

Innersourcing. (n.d.). Retrieved February 13, 2019 from http://www.inner-sourcing.com/

Izquierdo-Cortazar, D., González-Barahona, J., Robles, G., Deprez, J., & Auvray, V. (2012). *FLOSS Communities: Analyzing Evolvability and Robustness from an Industrial Perspective*. Retrieved from https://hal.inria.fr/file/index/docid/1058788/filename/izquierdo-cortazar-etal.pdf

Kamthan, P. (2007). On the Prospects and Concerns of Integrating Open Source Software Environment in Software Engineering Education. *Journal of Information Technology Education*, 6, 45–64. doi:10.28945/201

Koohang, A., & Harman, K. (2005). Open Source: A Metaphor for E-Learning. *Informing Science Journal*, 8, 75–86. doi:10.28945/488

Kruck, S. E., & Teer, F. P. (2009). Interdisciplinary Student Teams Projects: A Case Study. *Journal of Information Systems Education*, 20(3), 325–330.

Lakhani, K. R., & von Hippel, E. (2003). How open source software works: "free" user-to-user assistance. *Research Policy*, 32(6), 923–943. doi:10.1016/S0048-7333(02)00095-1

Layton, R. A., Loughry, M. L., Ohland, M. W., & Ricco, G. D. (2010). Design and validation of a web-based system for assigning members to teams using instructor-specified criteria. *Advances in Engineering Education*, 2(1), 1–28.

Long, J. (2009). Open Source Software Development Experiences on the Students' Resumes: Do They Count? - Insights from the Employers' Perspectives. *Journal of Information Technology Education*, 8, 229–242. doi:10.28945/618

McComb, S., Green, S., & Compton, W. (1999). Project goals, team performance, and shared understanding. *Engineering Management Journal*, 11(3), 7–12. doi:10.1080/10429247.1999.11415033

O'Mahony, S., & Ferraro, F. (2007). The Emergence of Governance in an Open Source Community. *Academy of Management Journal*, 50(5), 1079–1106. doi:10.5465/amj.2007.27169153

O'Reilly, T. (2000). *Response to Matt Feinstein on Open Source and OpenGL*. Retrieved June 25, 2016, from http://archive.oreilly.com/pub/a/oreilly/ask_tim/2000/opengl_1200.html

Open Source Initiative (OSI). (2019). *Licenses & Standards*. Retrieved January 31, 2019, from https://opensource.org/licenses

Poindexter, S. (2003). Assessing Active Alternatives for Teaching Programming. *Journal of Information Technology Education*, 2, 257–265. doi:10.28945/326

Pundak, D., Herscovitz, O., Shacham, M., & Wiser-Biton, R. (2009). Instructors' Attitudes toward Active Learning. *Interdisciplinary Journal of E-Learning and Learning Objects*, 5, 215–232. doi:10.28945/74

Raymond, E. S. (2001). *The Cathedral & the Bazaar: Musings on Linux and Open Source by an Accidental Revolutionary*. O'Reilly Media, Inc.

Sack, W., Détienne, F., Ducheneaut, N., Burkhardt, J.-M., Mahendran, D., & Barcellini, F. (2006). A Methodological Framework for Socio-Cognitive Analyses of Collaborative Design of Open Source Software. *Computer Supported Cooperative Work*, 15(2-3), 229–250. doi:10.100710606-006-9020-5

Sahin, Y. (2011). A team building model for software engineering courses term projects. *Computers & Education*, *56*(3), 916–922. doi:10.1016/j.compedu.2010.11.006

Schiller, S. Z. (2009). Practicing Learner-Centered Teaching: Pedagogical Design and Assessment of a Second Life Project. *Journal of Information Systems Education*, *20*(3), 369–381.

Stallman, R. (1992). *Why Software Should Be Free - GNU Project - Free Software Foundation*. Retrieved June 11, 2016, from https://www.gnu.org/philosophy/shouldbefree.html

Stewart, K. J., & Gosain, S. (2006). The Impact of Ideology on Effectiveness in Open Source Software Development Teams. *Management Information Systems Quarterly*, *30*(2), 291–314. doi:10.2307/25148732

Stol, K. J., Avgeriou, P., Babar, M. A., Lucas, Y., & Fitzgerald, B. (2014). Key factors for adopting inner source. *ACM Transactions on Software Engineering and Methodology*, *23*(2), 1–35. doi:10.1145/2533685

Stol, K. J., Babar, M. A., Avgeriou, P., & Fitzgerald, B. (2011). A comparative study of challenges in integrating Open Source Software and Inner Source Software. *Information and Software Technology*, *53*(12), 1319–1336. doi:10.1016/j.infsof.2011.06.007

Stol, K. J., & Fitzgerald, B. (2015). Inner Source–Adopting Open Source Development Practices in Organizations: A Tutorial. *IEEE Software*, *32*(4), 60–67. doi:10.1109/MS.2014.77

Teel, S., Schweitzer, D., & Fulton, S. (2012). Teaching Undergraduate Software Engineering Using Open Source Development Tools. *Issues in Informing Science and Information Technology*, *9*, 63–73. doi:10.28945/1604

Turnu, I., Melis, M., Cau, A., Setzu, A., Concas, G., & Mannaro, K. (2006). Modeling and simulation of open source development using an agile practice. *Journal of Systems Architecture*, *52*(11), 610–618. doi:10.1016/j.sysarc.2006.06.005

Uzunboylu, H., Bicen, H., & Cavus, N. (2011). The efficient virtual learning environment: A case study of web 2.0 tools and Windows live spaces. *Computers & Education*, *56*(3), 720–726. doi:10.1016/j.compedu.2010.10.014

von Krogh, G., Haefliger, S., Spaeth, S., & Wallin, M. W. (2012). Carrots and Rainbows: Motivation and Social Practice in Open Source Software Development. *Management Information Systems Quarterly*, *36*(2), 649–676. doi:10.2307/41703471

This research was previously published in the International Journal of Information and Communication Technology Education (IJICTE), 16(2); pages 1-17, copyright year 2020 by IGI Publishing (an imprint of IGI Global).

Chapter 17
Optimization Scenarios for Open Source Software Used in E-Learning Activities

Utku Köse

Suleyman Demirel University, Turkey

ABSTRACT

Using open software in e-learning application is one of the most popular ways of improving effectiveness of e-learning-based processes without thinking about additional costs and even focusing on modifying the software according to needs. Because of that, it is important to have an idea about what is needed while using an e-learning-oriented open software system and how to deal with its source codes. At this point, it is a good option to add some additional features and functions to make the open source software more intelligent and practical to make both teaching-learning experiences during e-learning processes. In this context, the objective of this chapter is to discuss some possible applications of artificial intelligence to include optimization processes within open source software systems used in e-learning activities. In detail, the chapter focuses more on using swarm intelligence and machine learning techniques for this aim and expresses some theoretical views for improving the effectiveness of such software for a better e-learning experience.

INTRODUCTION

With the transformation of the society into information society, all fields of the life have started to change form according to needs of this new society form. Now, it is more important to reach to desired information rapidly and adapt it to the problems – tasks by using specific approaches of the digital world. Among all the improvements, the field of education has a unique place because it is both among objective fields to be changed and supportive fields to grow up individuals, who are appropriate members of the information society. At this point, the field of education has received many revolutionary changes in time and the educational experiences has become some type of special processes, which are done even we do not take place face-to-face in a real classroom environment. In this sense, the approach of

DOI: 10.4018/978-1-7998-9158-1.ch017

Distance Education and the E-Learning, which is a type of Distance Education as supported with computer, communication and multimedia technologies, have become very popular leading an unstoppable trend towards the future (Bates, 2005; Klašnja-Milićević et al., 2017a; Moore, 2013; Welsh et al., 2003).

E-Learning is today's effective form of education with its features and mechanisms to eliminate limitations regarding time and place. But as a result of rapid improvements in especially computer and communication technologies, it has become more common to run E-Learning processes just simply and considering other factors directly in order to improve effectiveness and efficiency of this process. As general, both teachers and students may need different supportive factors to make E-Learning better for them. Although it is more considerable to run E-Learning solutions instead of traditional educational approaches before, it is now more widely followed to find alternative ways of improving E-Learning experiences.

It is possible to see many different types of ways for improving effectiveness of E-Learning activities. In the associated literature, this issue is even widely discussed (Burgess, 2017; Dascalu et al., 2014; Hamburg et al., 2008; Johnson et al., 2008; Kalyuga & Sweller, 2005; Kechaou et al., 2011; Korres, 2017; Liaw, 2008; Macleod & Kefallonitis, 2017; Romero & Ventura, 2006; Shen et al., 2009; Song et al., 2004; Sun et al., 2008; Zhang et al., 2006). At this point, using open software in E-Learning application is today's one of the most popular ways of improving effectiveness of E-Learning based processes without thinking about additional costs and even focusing on modifying the software according to needs. Because of that, it is important to have idea about what is needed while using an E-Learning oriented open software system and how to deal with its source codes. Generally, it is a good option here to add some additional features and functions to make the open source software more intelligent and practical to make both teaching - learning experiences during E-Learning processes. That can be achieved better thanks to a strong scientific field: Artificial Intelligence. Approaches, methods, and techniques in Artificial Intelligence has a remarkable place in a multidisciplinary manner with all effective and efficient solution that have been provided so far, even for the most complex, and advanced types of problems. So, in the intersection of E-Learning and open source software systems, applications from Artificial Intelligence could be very effective to improve E-Learning. In the associated literature, we can see many different examples of Artificial Intelligence applications within E-Learning and Distance Education in a general manner (Aroyo & Dicheva, 2004; Brusilovsky & Peylo, 2003; Colchester et al., 2017; Herder et al., 2017; Klašnja-Milićević et al., 2017b; Kose & Koc, 2014; Schiaffino et al., 2008; Tang & McCalla, 2003; Van Eck, 2007; Villaverde et al., 2006; Wen-Shung Tai et al., 2008; Wenger, 2014; Woolf, 2010). But as an alternative, it will be a good way to think about some 'butterfly effects' by considering improve of open source based E-Learning software systems.

Considering the explanations so far, objective of this chapter is to discuss about some possible applications of Artificial Intelligence to include optimization processes within open source software systems used in E-Learning activities. Here, the main issue is achieving an actual mathematical optimization model or a solution process that can be accepted as 'optimizing something' in the active E-Learning habitat towards an improved E-Learning experience for both teachers and students. In detail, the chapter focuses more on using Swarm Intelligence and Machine Learning techniques for this aim and express some theoretical views for improving effectiveness of such software for a better E-Learning experience. It is believed that this research work will be a good opportunity to have ideas about possible optimization oriented applications within open source software systems of E-Learning and lead the interested readers to realize further investigations in this manner.

In the context of the chapter subject and scope, remaining content of the chapter is organized as follows: The next section is devoted to some brief introduction of today's known open source software solutions for E-Learning activities. With this section, it is aimed to give some essential information the readers for having idea about what types of open source E-Learning software systems are generally used. Following to that section, some examples of optimization scenarios are discussed – explained theoretically under the third section. In detail, there are some alternative scenarios supported by Swarm Intelligence and Machine Learning techniques to improve E-Learning processes over open source software systems. Here, more consideration has been tried to be given for achieving optimization by considering possible codes used within open source software systems. Next, some ideas derived for future research directions are expressed briefly under the fourth section and the chapter is ended by discussing about conclusions under the last section.

A BRIEF VIEW FROM OPEN SOURCE E-LEARNING SOFTWARE SYSTEMS

For a long time, there is a remarkable effort on developing open source E-Learning software. In this context, it is important that majority of such software systems are focused on ensuring learning management system (LMS) platforms to combine important features and functions useful for a typical E-Learning processes. On the other hand, there are also some software systems, which can be used as supportive actors to achieve a better organization of E-Learning. So, we can think about modular E-Learning approaches in which different open software systems are connected each other (In this chapter, such connection is associated with intelligent optimization scenarios as it can be understood). Because of that, we can provide some examples of open source E-Learning software by providing a categorization according to essential features provided by them.

The author has provided an example categorization before in order to list some free and open source software systems regarding E-Learning 2.0 (Kose, 2014). Because today's open source software systems are already based on principles regarding to Web 2.0, Web 3.0, and even Web 4.0, it is more important to use just the categorization approach here (For more information regarding the concepts of E-Learning 2.0, Web 2.0, Web 3.0, and Web 4.0, readers are referred to Aghaei et al., 2012; Downes, 2005; Ebner, 2007; Kose, 2010; Kose, 2014). Considering the categorization by Kose (2014), it is possible to examine the open source E-Learning software (as considering them also even services sometimes) under four categories as: (1) E-Learning Portals, (2) File Sharing Environments, (3) Social-Network Based Services, and (4) Specific – Special Applications and Services (Figure 1).

E-Learning Portals

Some well-known open source E-Learning software systems that can be examined as 'E-Learning Portal' can be explained briefly as follows:

Moodle

Moodle is one of the most popular E-Learning portals – learning managements systems with its stable, flexible and fast using style. The system is based on PHP programming language and uses MySQL or PostgreSQL for database management. It comes with many different features including dashboards, stu-

Figure 1. Categories regarding open source E-Learning software (Kose, 2014)

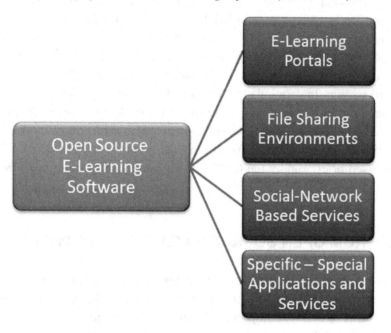

dent tracking mechanisms, examinations – quizzes, organizing tools, course content sections, and many other ones as supported with multimedia elements. All over the world, there is a remarkable community of developers – supporters, so it is always possible to find alternative components – plug-ins, pre-made course contents, translations for the whole system, wide documentation on its use and development, and also instant help from different users – experts, who have mastered E-Learning experience with Moodle (Pappas, 2015; Web Resources Depot, 2009).

ATutor

ATutor is another alternative of open source E-Learning portal with its fast and user-friendly interface. ATutor employs a common interface in which teachers and students can perform their own tasks. As general, the system employs different features – functions including development and providing of courses – course content, arranging assessments, preparing polls, performing analyses over the data regarding performed E-Learning activities (Pappas, 2015).

Eduslide.Open Source

Eduslide.Open Source is a software system developed by The Virtual Training Company located in Virginia, USA. Over the system teachers can share their knowledge by creating custom courses by using Eduslide. Eduslide employs many different features for creating a whole online learning community. It comes with different tools such as wikis, forums, chats and quizzes. At this point, wikis, forums and chat tools can be employed for collaboration between teachers and students. Furthermore, it is also possible for teachers to use integrated project management tools for controlling students' learning process. On the other hand, it is also possible for teachers to create lesson objectives for task based learning activities over Eduslide. Another feature of the Eduslide is supporting the invitation based learning (Kose, 2014).

Claroline

Claroline is another portal based open source solution for E-Learning processes. In detail, the system has been designed by teachers and it provides all necessary needs for an effective and collaborative E-Learning experience for both teachers and students. As developed over PHP and use with MySQL database management, Claroline also has a wide support all over the world with translations into many languages. Some remarkable features of the system are related to online exercise preparing, learning path determination for students and also communication options over online chat or forums (Web Resources Depot, 2009).

eFront

As based on an Ajax structure, eFront is an E-Learning portal with many features and functions to organize flow of an E-Learning process. In detail, the system provides wide content authoring tools supported with multimedia elements, file managers and also digital libraries to store files, and some other tools like quiz, survey generators to achieve an effective E-Learning environment for both teachers and students (Web Resources Depot, 2009).

File Sharing Environments

File sharing environments are actually useful for not only E-Learning activities but also for all works associated with online file share over the Web. But here, it has been tried to give some idea about open source solutions for explaining the opportunities on providing own-service for file share among teachers and students within an E-Learning habitat.

YouTransfer

YouTransfer is a free and open source self-hosted file sharing solution that may be used along E-Learning activities. It seems that it has also some pricing options in some alternative using approaches but generally it can be used accordingly fast and easily as a file sharing module of a formed E-Learning structure. Except from its features and functions regarding file share, YouTransfer comes with also support regarding Firewalls in order to achieve a more secure and controllable self-hosted file share system on the back (Nesbitt, 2017).

FileDrop

FileDrop is another open source solution regarding file share but in order to run it, the software systems of Sandstorm.io or Sandstorm Oasis should be used, too. Generally, the FileDrop is a rapid and simple software to be used for sharing files directly to people over their e-mail addresses (Nesbitt, 2017).

LinShare

As another file sharing service as open source, LinShare provides more security features and functions to achieve a flexible and fast file sharing environment. With the use of well-known features like drag-n-drop, it is possible to share files with varying sizes with people. So, it is another alternative form of open source file sharing that may be used through an E-Learning plan (Nesbitt, 2017).

ProjectSend

ProjectSend is an open source, self-hosted solution for file share and it comes with again security features – options to achieve a more secure, self-hosted file sharing environment. In detail, this system also enables users to share their files and even folders with people or groups, which can be adjusted before (Nesbitt, 2017).

Social-Network Based Services

Nowadays, there is no certain line between having social-network based features and just traditional using features within open source software systems. Because, today's trendy using features generally promote social interaction among users even it is the simplest system located over the Web, for particular tasks – activities. But in order to meet with the classification made before, some alternative open source solutions having more social features – functions have been combined here. Of course, these systems can be accepted as also E-Learning portals.

Elgg

Elgg is a generally a social-networking based open source solution as developed by Curverider Ltd. and open source community, for educational processes. Elgg employs some interactive tools like blogs, podcasting applications, file sharing applications, and even a RSS reader. In detail, it is possible for both teachers and students to search for other ones by using tags over the system and finally create some type of active learning communities – groups over the system environment. The tagging approach is a remarkable feature used widely over the system. As multimedia support, Elgg enables teachers and students to upload their photos, audio, and video files within blog posts easily, and even make comments and open discussions on objective topics (Kose, 2014).

OLAT

OLAT is an open source E-Learning software system, which provides a use oriented solution for getting more effectiveness in E-Learning experiences. In addition to the provided calendar tools, course pages, certificate system and approaches regarding file storage, the system also focuses on the use of social learning. The system also supports different types of devices so that teachers and students can experience the E-Learning activities over even their mobile devices (Pappas, 2015).

Opigno

Opigno is an E-Learning environment, which provides more interaction by using multimedia elements to some other tools that can used by system users. As general, it is possible over Opigno to use E-Learning authoring and course development tools, arrange course time tables and control – manage objective students' activities over the system. The system also comes with video galleries and thanks to some communication tools like chat and instant messaging, it promotes a collaborative teaching – learning experience (Pappas, 2015).

ILIAS

ILIAS is another open E-Learning platform, which comes with many features and functions to achieve a collaborative environment. In this context, the system employs a simple, fast, and flexible interface in order to organize a common E-Learning environment in which it is more effective to communicate each other and perform any other tasks (i.e. document share, reaching to other teachers – students, performing time based tests) regarding the planned E-Learning flow (Pappas, 2015; Web Resources Depot, 2009).

Dokeos

As based on PHP and MySQL to run database, Dokeos is more than just traditional E-Learning portal. Briefly, Dokeos employs a flash-based video conferencing system as integrated to enable teachers – students to experience online, interactive communication sessions. With also its coaching features – functions, the system employs assignment feedback, online chat, agenda, and forum tools to ensure a general E-Learning environment (Web Resources Depot, 2009).

Specific: Special Applications and Services

In addition to the mentioned open source software systems, there are many other E-Learning oriented tools that can be examined out of the categories considered before. Especially nowadays, there are many different types of specific E-Learning applications – services to support general E-Learning flow with their interactive features. Some remarkable ones are:

Fedena

Rather than just E-Learning oriented environment, Fedena allows users to manage the whole school with its wide analyzing tools. As developed by using Ruby on Rails, the system employs a flexible, fast interface to deal with all tasks regarding a school by including also tracking students, examinations, and many other statistical data associated with teachers and students (Morpus, 2016). It is remarkable here that use of general school management software systems can enable educational institutions to have more then they desired and achieve a more effective E-Learning experience by organizing the whole structure with some other software systems and as according to their needs. In addition to Fedena, some other remarkable open source school management software systems are: FeKara, SchoolTime, TS School, and Gibbon (Morpus, 2016).

Annotum

Annotum is an open source solution for writing and organizing scholarly articles over a Web platform supported with WordPress. In Annotum, it is possible to arrange articles by using many writing tools like document styles, citations, and even mathematical equations. From a general perspective, the system forms a general, blog based, article platform to support educational collaborations and information share (Pappas, 2011).

Open Meetings

As a specific and important need among E-Learning systems, OpenMeeting is a Web conferencing system, which tries to complete this need of online conferencing with an open source approach. In detail, the system supports also instant messaging, online whiteboard, document sharing and editing, audio based features, and even screen sharing in order to improve interactivity over active Web conferencing sessions (Pappas, 2016).

Big Blue Button

Big Blue Button is another open solution for Web conferencing through E-Learning activities. It is popular as like the Open Meetings and widely supported by the open source community as hosted over Google Code platform. As general, Big Blue Button provides all necessary Web conferencing tools like whiteboards, screen and document sharing, audio based features, and also some additional tools to perform zoom in, highlighting, and notes drawing over active white boards (Pappas, 2016).

In addition to open source Web conferencing solutions like Open Meetings and Big Blue Button, there are also many other open source software systems to achieve online, Web conferencing over an organized E-Learning process. Some of them are: MConf, VMukti, Jitsi, and WebHuddle (Pappas, 2016).

OPTIMIZATION SCENARIOS OVER OPEN SOURCE E-LEARNING SOFTWARE

Considering the open source software systems for E-Learning, it is possible to think about some optimization scenarios, which include use of Artificial Intelligence techniques. At this point, it is important here to adapt different open software systems in a modular manner to run an optimized way of E-Learning experience, which is beneficial for both teachers and students.

It is possible to derive many different optimization scenarios by using different features and functions of the related open source software systems. But some remarkable ones, which will direct the interested readers to think about more, can be explained briefly as follows:

Optimum Content: Data Providing

By making necessary code additions and adjusting database structure, it is possible for the E-Learning environments having course content to determine which course content can be provided to a specific student. At this point, it is possible to use a Machine Learning technique: Artificial Neural Network model to get some input data regarding student (i.e. exam results, content viewing information, course difficulty, student's academic success level) and receive output(s) indicating which content can be provided to the objective student. This can be done under a flexible Artificial Neural Network model in which number of artificial neurons, hidden layers, number of input / output neurons can be updated according to additional E-Learning tasks – activities done over the system. The author has already some example of optimizing research works introduced to the associated literature before (Kose, 2013; Kose & Arslan, 2017). At this point, this scenario of optimum content receiving can be done in even E-Learning plans using open source software systems in a modular manner. For example, outputs of specific E-Learning tools can be used as students' input data and an Artificial Neural Network among different types of E-Learning software systems can be used as a 'regulator' for determining the most optimum course content (even maybe quiz, file…etc.) to be provided for the objective student. Readers interested in having more information about Artificial Neural Networks are referred to (Kubat, 2015; Wang, 2003; Yegnanarayana, 2009; Zhu, 2017).

Figure 2. A representative simple scheme for the scenario of optimum content – data providing

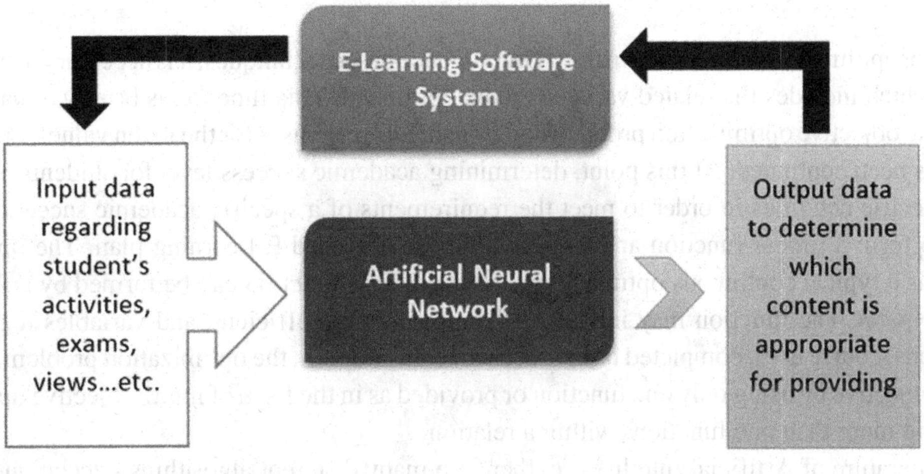

Optimizing Activities Students Can Perform

Whether it is included in an E-Learning portal or not, some specific activities can be enabled or disabled according to students' performance over the system. Of course, this scenario is not for limiting students' activities but an encouragement way to make them more active over the system environment. At this point, the same Artificial Neural Network model approach explained under the previous sub-title can be followed to determine weights of each activity for the associated student. These data can be within the system so its database and the related codes of using features – functions should be revised. On the other hand, if some activities are done by using external software systems out of the main E-Learning system, their data can be used within again in a regulator Artificial Neural Network in the middle of the whole E-Learning plan. As it is explained under the following sub-title(s), a mathematical fitness function can also be used to do same thing via intelligent optimization algorithms.

Figure 3. A representative simple scheme for the scenario of optimizing activities students can perform

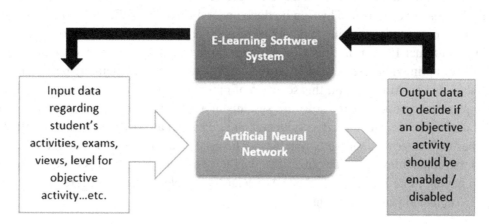

Optimization of Academic Success Over Fitness Functions

In intelligent optimization done with Artificial Intelligence based techniques, it is necessary to use a fitness function, which includes the related variables to be optimized. This function is briefly a mathematical model of the objective optimization problem and by using its responses for the given values, optimization process has been continued. At this point, determining academic success level for students or directing them to specific activities in order to meet the requirements of a specific academic success level, it is possible to form a fitness function and use it within the designed E-Learning plan. The optimization done here is a typical continuous optimization and the fitness function can be formed by collaboration of many experts. The function may include different kind of coefficient, and variables regarding i.e. examinations, course uses, completed tasks – activities. In addition, the optimization problem model can be single-objective by using only one function or provided as in the form of multi-objective optimization by including more than one functions within a relation.

In the literature of Artificial Intelligence, there are many different algorithms – techniques that can perform an optimization process iteratively, according to given inputs. It is important that the source codes of the used E-Learning software systems require to be updated according to complexity of the considered mathematical optimization problem. The related updates can be done according to the structure of the plan as it includes modular software systems or not. Another issue that should be discussed here is the diversity of intelligent optimization techniques. Nowadays, there are many different types of intelligent optimization algorithms – techniques. Even a separate research interest called as 'Swarm Intelligence' has an active flow through the scientific community as including majority of such algorithms – techniques. Some examples of intelligent optimization algorithms are: Particle Swarm Optimization, Artificial Bee Colony, Cuckoo Search, and Genetic Algorithms. Readers are referred to (Bai, 2010; Blum & Li, 2008; Brownlee, 2011; Garnier et al., 2007; Karaboga & Akay, 2009; Reeves, 2009; Yang & Deb, 2010; Wang, 2001; Whitley, 1994) in order to have more information about these algorithms – techniques, the concept of intelligent optimization, and Swarm Intelligence.

Figure 4. A representative simple scheme for the scenario of optimization of academic success over fitness functions

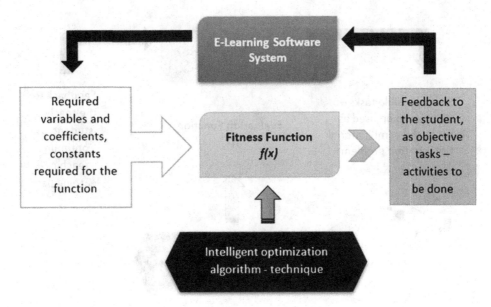

Optimum Teaching-Learning Path With Combinatorial Optimization

As different from continuous optimization, task – activity outputs of the used E-Learning software systems can be used to determine a specific teaching-learning path for both teachers and students. According to their performances, it is possible for both teachers and students to find an optimum way of teaching or learning, by using the already provided E-Learning tasks, documents, data, and any other elements having active role in the process. The most important thing to do here is defining a good function, which will evaluate possible teaching-learning paths according to teachers' or students' needs – tasks. In the open source software systems, it is again needed to update source codes and even it may be required to form new relations, define triggers or procedures according to the current structure of the database included within objective software systems.

Again, Artificial Intelligence comes with specific algorithms – techniques to deal with combinatorial optimization problems. For example, Ant Colony Optimization, Intelligent Water Drops Algorithm, and Algorithmic Reasoning Optimization are some examples of them. Readers are referred to (Blum & Roli, 2003; Dorigo et al., 2006; Kose & Arslan, 2016; Shah-Hosseini, 2009) to have more information about the algorithms and the intelligent combinatorial optimization.

FUTURE RESEARCH DIRECTIONS

Under the previous sections, more consideration was given to the state of currently employed open source E-Learning software solutions and also Artificial Intelligence based optimization ways. It is important that the future has a great potential to move the open source E-Learning to different kinds of application types and maybe transforming it into another revolutionary version of open distance education that we

Figure 5. A representative simple scheme for the scenario of optimum teaching-learning path with combinatorial optimization

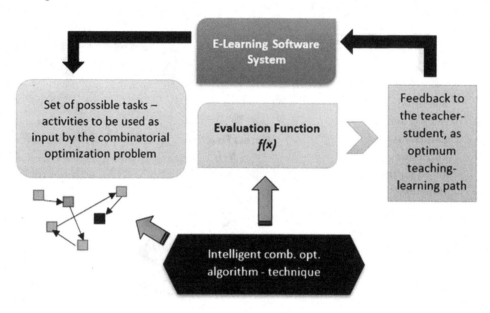

cannot imagine well enough for now. But at this point, it could be also a good start to derive some ideas by thinking about current developments within alternative technologies and also focusing on possible applications of intelligent optimization towards open source E-Learning software systems for at least near future.

By considering the explanations provided under previous sections and also thinking the state of the associated literatures nowadays, some remarkable future research directions can be explained briefly as follows:

- Although we have thought about continuous and combinatorial optimization while introducing some example scenarios before, near future may have the potential of using more complicated application types of these optimization methods in order to improve open source software systems for E-Learning. It is certain that the literature associated with intelligent optimization techniques is greatly active and because of that, there will be always an open door for new types of optimization scenarios done by i.e. newly introduced optimization algorithms or newly thought optimization problem applications regarding E-Learning processes.
- Artificial Intelligence is not the only supportive technology taking active place in today's E-Learning applications. Considering the open source software structure, it is possible to adapt different types of multimedia technologies for improving E-Learning processes from different sides. For example, Augmented Reality has a great popularity in today's E-Learning applications and because of that there will probably be specific optimization problem settings for open source E-Learning software systems including also Augmented Reality. Readers interested in Augmented Reality are referred to (Azuma, 1997; Azuma et al., 2001; Hainich, 2009; Höllerer & Feiner, 2004; Leighton & Crompton, 2017; Pasaréti et al., 2011; Sánchez-Acevedo et al., 2017; Van Krevelen & Poelman, 2010; Wu et al., 2013) for getting more information about Augmented Reality.

- As indicated under the previous paragraph, Augmented Reality has a remarkable place in the future of education and so an intelligent E-Learning over open source software systems. That may means less use of hardware but it is also important that the Augmented Reality or any other alternative supportive technology within E-Learning can come with alternative types of hardware that can be used by teachers and students. At this point, optimization scenarios regarding optimizing such hardware for better E-Learning experience can be foreseen and thus, possible optimization oriented adjustments between hardware and open source software systems can be considered as under important research directions in the future.

- As it was expressed before, Object Oriented Programming has a valuable place in today's software development processes by including even strong relations with intelligent optimization techniques. But it is not clear that the future will bring us new types of programming approaches with the changed hardware and software technologies and the ways of processing data. So, the future research directions in this manner will always include adaptations to newly introduced programming approaches and directing the current optimization techniques to new types of optimization problems that may appear while designing effective ways of better E-Learning over open source software systems developed thanks to these new programming approaches.

- Since their first developments, open source software systems in E-Learning have become more specific as aiming to solve a particular problem of the teaching – learning process. So, as it is understood from the explanations under this chapter, it has become a common thing to combine different types of software systems for the same E-Learning process. That means hybridization of open software systems will be increasingly popular in the future and research directions will continue to be focused on designing specific optimization scenarios by considering that hybridization factor of E-Learning oriented software systems.

- Scenarios explained under this chapter are some essential types of examples for improving features and functions of open source software systems in order to improve E-Learning experiences in this way. Of course, there can be many different types of optimization problem settings regarding designed E-Learning habitat, code structures of the employed software systems or even data used as input or output for the open source software systems. So, there will be always an active effort on designing alternative ways of optimization scenarios in the future of open source oriented E-Learning.

CONCLUSION

This chapter has focused on open source E-Learning software systems and tried to answer the question of how intelligent optimization scenarios can be employed for improving open source E-Learning systems. In detail, it is important for anyone interested in open source E-Learning software systems to know which types of software oriented approaches are generally followed currently to support E-Learning processes realized by both teachers and students. So, the chapter has firstly provided a brief look at to some examples of open source E-Learning software systems. In the chapter, it was claimed that one effective and efficient way of improving open source software based E-Learning experiences is to employ intelligent solutions within open source software systems. At this point, Artificial Intelligence has been taken into consideration and also more focus was given to intelligent optimization, which is an important research interest of Artificial Intelligence. It is clear that the whole problem solution mechanisms and even naturally occurred dynamics over the world are associated with some optimization processes and because of that they can be formulated or imagined in the form of optimization problems. Moving from that, some example scenarios of optimization for improving using features – functions of the objective open source E-Learning software or just combining more than one system to have more advanced, 'intelligent' E-Learning habitat have been explained briefly under this chapter. The provided scenarios have been some typical theoretical views (but practically applicable) with the use of Swarm Intelligence and Machine Learning techniques to achieve optimization oriented solutions.

It is clear that the scientific developments and improvements have many hidden things waiting for us to be used for designing and developing innovative solutions for real-world based problems. In this context, the field of education has a remarkable popularity for applying innovative applications supported by new technologies. As an important example of them, E-Learning seems to be always active field in even future thanks to employment of new technologies and even scientific approaches, methods, and techniques. Nowadays, employment of Artificial Intelligence is one of the most remarkable factor in achieving positive results within E-Learning processes and at this point, using small steps of solutions has an effective role to get desired educational outputs. As associated with this philosophical view, this chapter has discussed about some examples of intelligent mechanisms, which use optimization for improving the E-Learning experience at the top level by affecting maybe small building blocks of an E-Learning system with open source support. On the other hand, it is important that the chapter has given more emphasis on software coding oriented factors while designing the related optimization scenarios.

REFERENCES

Aghaei, S., Nematbakhsh, M. A., & Farsani, H. K. (2012). Evolution of the world wide web: From WEB 1.0 TO WEB 4.0. *International Journal of Web & Semantic Technology*, *3*(1), 1–10. doi:10.5121/ijwest.2012.3101

Aroyo, L., & Dicheva, D. (2004). The new challenges for e-learning: The educational semantic web. *Journal of Educational Technology & Society*, *7*(4).

Azuma, R., Baillot, Y., Behringer, R., Feiner, S., Julier, S., & MacIntyre, B. (2001). Recent advances in augmented reality. *IEEE Computer Graphics and Applications*, *21*(6), 34–47. doi:10.1109/38.963459

Azuma, R. T. (1997). A survey of augmented reality. *Presence (Cambridge, Mass.)*, *6*(4), 355–385. doi:10.1162/pres.1997.6.4.355

Bai, Q. (2010). Analysis of particle swarm optimization algorithm. *Computer and Information Science*, *3*(1), 180.

Bates, A. T. (2005). *Technology, e-learning and distance education*. Routledge. doi:10.4324/9780203463772

Blum, C., & Li, X. (2008). Swarm intelligence in optimization. In *Swarm Intelligence* (pp. 43–85). Springer Berlin Heidelberg. doi:10.1007/978-3-540-74089-6_2

Blum, C., & Roli, A. (2003). Metaheuristics in combinatorial optimization: Overview and conceptual comparison. *ACM Computing Surveys*, *35*(3), 268–308. doi:10.1145/937503.937505

Brownlee, J. (2011). *Clever algorithms: nature-inspired programming recipes*. Jason Brownlee.

Brusilovsky, P., & Peylo, C. (2003). Adaptive and intelligent web-based educational systems. *International Journal of Artificial Intelligence in Education, 13*, 159–172.

Burgess, E. O. (2017). *Attrition and Dropouts in the E-learning Environment: Improving Student Success and Retention* (Doctoral dissertation). Northcentral University.

Colchester, K., Hagras, H., Alghazzawi, D., & Aldabbagh, G. (2017). A survey of artificial intelligence techniques employed for adaptive educational systems within E-learning platforms. *Journal of Artificial Intelligence and Soft Computing Research, 7*(1), 47–64. doi:10.1515/jaiscr-2017-0004

Dascalu, M. I., Bodea, C. N., Lytras, M., De Pablos, P. O., & Burlacu, A. (2014). Improving e-learning communities through optimal composition of multidisciplinary learning groups. *Computers in Human Behavior, 30*, 362–371. doi:10.1016/j.chb.2013.01.022

Dorigo, M., Birattari, M., & Stutzle, T. (2006). Ant colony optimization. *IEEE Computational Intelligence Magazine, 1*(4), 28–39. doi:10.1109/MCI.2006.329691

Downes, S. (2005). E-learning 2.0. *E-learn Magazine, 2005*(10), 1.

Ebner, M. (2007). E-Learning 2.0= e-Learning 1.0+ Web 2.0? In *Availability, Reliability and Security, 2007. ARES 2007. The Second International Conference on* (pp. 1235-1239). IEEE.

Garnier, S., Gautrais, J., & Theraulaz, G. (2007). The biological principles of swarm intelligence. *Swarm Intelligence, 1*(1), 3–31. doi:10.100711721-007-0004-y

Hainich, R. R. (2009). *The End of hardware: augmented reality and beyond*. BookSurge.

Hamburg, I., Engert, S., Anke, P., Marin, M., & im IKM Bereich, E. C. A. (2008). Improving e-learning 2.0-based training strategies of SMEs through communities of practice. *Learning, 2*, 610-012.

Herder, E., Sosnovsky, S., & Dimitrova, V. (2017). Adaptive Intelligent Learning Environments. In Technology Enhanced Learning (pp. 109-114). Springer International Publishing. doi:10.1007/978-3-319-02600-8_10

Höllerer, T., & Feiner, S. (2004). *Mobile augmented reality. In Telegeoinformatics: Location-Based Computing and Services* (p. 21). London, UK: Taylor and Francis Books Ltd.

Johnson, R. D., Hornik, S., & Salas, E. (2008). An empirical examination of factors contributing to the creation of successful e-learning environments. *International Journal of Human-Computer Studies, 66*(5), 356–369. doi:10.1016/j.ijhcs.2007.11.003

Kalyuga, S., & Sweller, J. (2005). Rapid dynamic assessment of expertise to improve the efficiency of adaptive e-learning. *Educational Technology Research and Development, 53*(3), 83–93. doi:10.1007/BF02504800

Karaboga, D., & Akay, B. (2009). A comparative study of artificial bee colony algorithm. *Applied Mathematics and Computation, 214*(1), 108–132. doi:10.1016/j.amc.2009.03.090

Kechaou, Z., Ammar, M. B., & Alimi, A. M. (2011). Improving e-learning with sentiment analysis of users' opinions. In *Global Engineering Education Conference* (pp. 1032-1038). IEEE. 10.1109/EDUCON.2011.5773275

Klašnja-Milićević, A., Vesin, B., Ivanović, M., Budimac, Z., & Jain, L. C. (2017a). Introduction to E-Learning Systems. In E-Learning Systems (pp. 3-17). Springer International Publishing.

Klašnja-Milićević, A., Vesin, B., Ivanović, M., Budimac, Z., & Jain, L. C. (2017b). Recommender Systems in E-Learning Environments. In E-Learning Systems (pp. 51-75). Springer International Publishing.

Korres, M. P. (2017). The Positive Effect of Evaluation on Improving E-Learning Courses Addressed to Adults: A Case Study on the Evolution of the GSLLLY Courses in Greece over a Decade. *Journal of Education and Training Studies*, 5(1), 1–11. doi:10.11114/jets.v5i1.1940

Kose, U. (2010). *Web 2.0 Technologies in E-learning. In Free and Open Source Software for E-learning: Issues, Successes and Challenges* (pp. 1–23). Hershey, PA: IGI Global.

Kose, U. (2013). An Artificial Neural Networks Based Software System for Improved Learning Experience. In *Machine Learning and Applications (ICMLA), 2013 12th International Conference on* (Vol. 2, pp. 549-554). IEEE. 10.1109/ICMLA.2013.175

Kose, U. (2014). On the State of Free and Open Source E-Learning 2.0 Software. *International Journal of Open Source Software and Processes*, 5(2), 55–75. doi:10.4018/ijossp.2014040103

Kose, U., & Arslan, A. (2016). Optimization with the idea of algorithmic reasoning. *Journal of Multidisciplinary Developments*, 1(1), 17–20.

Kose, U., & Arslan, A. (2017). Optimization of self-learning in Computer Engineering courses: An intelligent software system supported by Artificial Neural Network and Vortex Optimization Algorithm. *Computer Applications in Engineering Education*, 25(1), 142–156. doi:10.1002/cae.21787

Kose, U., & Koc, D. (2014). *Artificial Intelligence Applications in Distance Education*. IGI Global.

Kubat, M. (2015). Artificial neural networks. In *An Introduction to Machine Learning* (pp. 91–111). Springer International Publishing. doi:10.1007/978-3-319-20010-1_5

Leighton, L. J., & Crompton, H. (2017). Augmented Reality in K-12 Education. In Mobile Technologies and Augmented Reality in Open Education (pp. 281-290). IGI Global.

Liaw, S. S. (2008). Investigating students' perceived satisfaction, behavioral intention, and effectiveness of e-learning: A case study of the Blackboard system. *Computers & Education*, 51(2), 864–873. doi:10.1016/j.compedu.2007.09.005

Macleod, J., & Kefallonitis, E. (2017). Trends Affecting e-Learning Experience Management. In Strategic Innovative Marketing (pp. 753-758). Springer International Publishing. doi:10.1007/978-3-319-33865-1_93

Moore, M. G. (Ed.). (2013). *Handbook of distance education*. Routledge.

Morpus, N. (2016). The Top 6 Free and Open Source School Administration Software. *Capterra – Blog*. Retrieved from http://blog.capterra.com/the-top-6-free-school-administration-software/

Nesbitt, S. (2017). *4 open source tools for sharing files*. Retrieved from https://opensource.com/article/17/3/file-sharing-tools

Pappas, C. (2011). *Top 10 Free and Open Source eLearning Projects to Watch for 2012*. Retrieved from https://www.efrontlearning.com/blog/2011/12/top-10-free-and-open-source-elearning.html

Pappas, C. (2015). *The Top 8 Open Source Learning Management Systems*. Retrieved from https://elearningindustry.com/top-open-source-learning-management-systems

Pappas, C. (2016). *Top 6 Open Source Web Conferencing Software Tools for eLearning Professionals*. Retrieved from https://elearningindustry.com/top-6-open-source-web-conferencing-software-tools-elearning-professionals

Pasaréti, O., Hajdin, H., Matusaka, T., Jambori, A., Molnar, I., & Tucsányi-Szabó, M. (2011). Augmented Reality in education. *INFODIDACT 2011 Informatika Szakmódszertani Konferencia.*

Reeves, C. R. (2009). Genetic algorithms. Encyclopedia of Database Systems, 1224-1227.

Romero, C., & Ventura, S. (Eds.). (2006). *Data mining in e-learning* (Vol. 4). Wit Press. doi:10.2495/1-84564-152-3

Sánchez-Acevedo, M. A., Sabino-Moxo, B. A., & Márquez-Domínguez, J. A. (2017). Mobile Augmented Reality. *Mobile Platforms, Design, and Apps for Social Commerce, 153.*

Schiaffino, S., Garcia, P., & Amandi, A. (2008). eTeacher: Providing personalized assistance to e-learning students. *Computers & Education, 51*(4), 1744–1754. doi:10.1016/j.compedu.2008.05.008

Shah-Hosseini, H. (2009). The intelligent water drops algorithm: A nature-inspired swarm-based optimization algorithm. *International Journal of Bio-inspired Computation, 1*(1-2), 71–79. doi:10.1504/IJBIC.2009.022775

Shen, L., Wang, M., & Shen, R. (2009). Affective e-learning: Using" emotional" data to improve learning in pervasive learning environment. *Journal of Educational Technology & Society, 12*(2), 176.

Song, L., Singleton, E. S., Hill, J. R., & Koh, M. H. (2004). Improving online learning: Student perceptions of useful and challenging characteristics. *The Internet and Higher Education, 7*(1), 59–70. doi:10.1016/j.iheduc.2003.11.003

Sun, P. C., Tsai, R. J., Finger, G., Chen, Y. Y., & Yeh, D. (2008). What drives a successful e-Learning? An empirical investigation of the critical factors influencing learner satisfaction. *Computers & Education, 50*(4), 1183–1202. doi:10.1016/j.compedu.2006.11.007

Tang, T. Y., & McCalla, G. (2003). Smart recommendation for an evolving e-learning system. *Workshop on Technologies for Electronic Documents for Supporting Learning, International Conference on Artificial Intelligence in Education*, 699-710.

Van Eck, R. (2007). Building artificially intelligent learning games. In *Games and simulations in online learning: Research and development frameworks* (pp. 271–307). IGI Global. doi:10.4018/978-1-59904-304-3.ch014

Van Krevelen, D. W. F., & Poelman, R. (2010). A survey of augmented reality technologies, applications and limitations. *International Journal of Virtual Reality, 9*(2), 1.

Villaverde, J. E., Godoy, D., & Amandi, A. (2006). Learning styles' recognition in e-learning environments with feed-forward neural networks. *Journal of Computer Assisted Learning, 22*(3), 197–206. doi:10.1111/j.1365-2729.2006.00169.x

Wang, L. (2001). Intelligent optimization algorithms with applications. Tsinghua University & Springer Press.

Wang, S. C. (2003). Artificial neural network. In Interdisciplinary computing in java programming (pp. 81-100). Springer US. doi:10.1007/978-1-4615-0377-4_5

Web Resources Depot. (2009). *7 Widely-Used and Open Source E-Learning Applications*. Retrieved from https://webresourcesdepot.com/7-widely-used-and-open-source-e-learning-applications/

Welsh, E. T., Wanberg, C. R., Brown, K. G., & Simmering, M. J. (2003). E-learning: emerging uses, empirical results and future directions. *International Journal of Training and Development, 7*(4), 245-258.

Wen-Shung Tai, D., Wu, H. J., & Li, P. H. (2008). Effective e-learning recommendation system based on self-organizing maps and association mining. *The Electronic Library, 26*(3), 329-344.

Wenger, E. (2014). *Artificial intelligence and tutoring systems: computational and cognitive approaches to the communication of knowledge*. Morgan Kaufmann.

Whitley, D. (1994). A genetic algorithm tutorial. *Statistics and Computing, 4*(2), 65–85. doi:10.1007/BF00175354

Woolf, B. P. (2010). *Building intelligent interactive tutors: Student-centered strategies for revolutionizing e-learning*. Morgan Kaufmann.

Wu, H. K., Lee, S. W. Y., Chang, H. Y., & Liang, J. C. (2013). Current status, opportunities and challenges of augmented reality in education. *Computers & Education, 62*, 41–49. doi:10.1016/j.compedu.2012.10.024

Yang, X. S., & Deb, S. (2010). Engineering optimisation by cuckoo search. *International Journal of Mathematical Modelling and Numerical Optimisation, 1*(4), 330–343. doi:10.1504/IJMMNO.2010.035430

Yegnanarayana, B. (2009). *Artificial neural networks*. PHI Learning Pvt. Ltd.

Zhang, D., Zhou, L., Briggs, R. O., & Nunamaker, J. F. Jr. (2006). Instructional video in e-learning: Assessing the impact of interactive video on learning effectiveness. *Information & Management, 43*(1), 15–27. doi:10.1016/j.im.2005.01.004

Zhu, A. (2017). *Artificial Neural Networks. The International Encyclopedia of Geography*. Wiley.

ADDITIONAL READING

Abraham, A. (2005). *Artificial neural networks. Handbook of measuring system design*. Wiley.

Alpaydin, E. (2014). *Introduction to machine learning*. MIT Press.

Arora, J. S., & Baenziger, G. (1986). Uses of artificial intelligence in design optimization. *Computer Methods in Applied Mechanics and Engineering*, *54*(3), 303–323. doi:10.1016/0045-7825(86)90108-8

Atkins, D. E., Brown, J. S., & Hammond, A. L. (2007). A review of the open educational resources (OER) movement: Achievements, challenges, and new opportunities (pp. 1-84). Creative common.

Aydin, C. C., & Tirkes, G. (2010). Open source learning management systems in distance learning. TOJET: The Turkish Online Journal of Educational Technology, 9(2).

Azuma, R., Baillot, Y., Behringer, R., Feiner, S., Julier, S., & MacIntyre, B. (2001). Recent advances in augmented reality. *IEEE Computer Graphics and Applications*, *21*(6), 34–47. doi:10.1109/38.963459

Azuma, R. T. (1997). A survey of augmented reality. *Presence (Cambridge, Mass.)*, *6*(4), 355–385. doi:10.1162/pres.1997.6.4.355

Boettcher, S., & Percus, A. (2000). Nature's way of optimizing. *Artificial Intelligence*, *119*(1-2), 275–286. doi:10.1016/S0004-3702(00)00007-2

Bonabeau, E., Dorigo, M., & Theraulaz, G. (1999). *Swarm intelligence: from natural to artificial systems (No. 1)*. Oxford university press.

Braunschweig, B. L., Pantelides, C. C., Britt, H. I., & Sama, S. (2000). Process modeling: The promise of open software architectures. *Chemical Engineering Progress*, *96*(9), 65–76.

Brusilovsky, P. (1999). Adaptive and intelligent technologies for web-based eduction. KI, 13(4), 19-25.

Brusilovsky, P., & Peylo, C. (2003). Adaptive and intelligent web-based educational systems. *International Journal of Artificial Intelligence in Education*, *13*(2), 159–172.

Cavus, N. (2016). Development of an Intellegent Mobile Application for Teaching English Pronunciation. *Procedia Computer Science*, *102*, 365–369. doi:10.1016/j.procs.2016.09.413

Cohen, E., & Nycz, M. (2006). Learning objects and e-learning: An informing science perspective. *Interdisciplinary Journal of E-Learning and Learning Objects*, *2*(1), 23–34.

Coppola, C., & Neelley, E. (2004). Open source-opens learning: Why open source makes sense for education.

Cusumano, M. A. (2004). Reflections on free and open software. *Communications of the ACM*, *47*(10), 25–27. doi:10.1145/1022594.1022615

Dagger, D., O'Connor, A., Lawless, S., Walsh, E., & Wade, V. P. (2007). Service-oriented e-learning platforms: From monolithic systems to flexible services. *IEEE Internet Computing*, *11*(3), 28–35. doi:10.1109/MIC.2007.70

Dalziel, J. (2003). Open standards versus open source in e-learning. *EDUCAUSE Quarterly*, *26*(4), 4–7.

Engelbrecht, A. P. (2006). *Fundamentals of computational swarm intelligence*. John Wiley & Sons.

Evans, J., Jordan, S., & Wolfenden, F. (2016). Developing academics' assessment practices in open, distance and e-learning: an institutional change agenda.

Feller, J., & Fitzgerald, B. (2002). *Understanding open source software development* (pp. 143–159). London: Addison-Wesley.

Fisler, J., & Bleisch, S. (2006). eLML, the eLesson Markup Language: Developing ustainable e-Learning Content Using an Open Source XML Framework. In In WEBIST 2006-International Conference on Web Information Systems and Technologies, April 11th-13th 2006 (Setubal).

Goldszmidt, M., Cohen, I., Fox, A., & Zhang, S. (2005). Three Research Challenges at the Intersection of Machine Learning, Statistical Induction, and Systems. In HotOS.

Graf, S., & List, B. (2005). An evaluation of open source e-learning platforms stressing adaptation issues. In Advanced Learning Technologies, 2005. ICALT 2005. Fifth IEEE International Conference on (pp. 163-165). IEEE. 10.1109/ICALT.2005.54

Hauger, D., & Köck, M. (2007). State of the Art of Adaptivity in E-Learning Platforms. In LWA (pp. 355-360).

Hernández-Leo, D., Bote-Lorenzo, M. L., Asensio-Pérez, J. I., Gocmez-Sanchez, E., Villasclaras-Fernández, E. D., Jorrín-Abellán, I. M., & Dimitriadis, Y. A. (2007). Free-and open-source software for a course on network management: Authoring and enactment of scripts based on collaborative learning strategies. *IEEE Transactions on Education*, *50*(4), 292–301. doi:10.1109/TE.2007.904589

Jennings, N. R. (2000). On agent-based software engineering. *Artificial Intelligence*, *117*(2), 277–296. doi:10.1016/S0004-3702(99)00107-1

Keegan, D. (2004). *Foundations of Distance Education*. New York: Routledge.

Kennedy, J. (2006). Swarm intelligence. In Handbook of nature-inspired and innovative computing (pp. 187-219). Springer US.

Kounavis, C. D., Kasimati, A. E., & Zamani, E. D. (2012). Enhancing the tourism experience through mobile augmented reality: Challenges and prospects. *International Journal of Engineering Business Management*, 4.

Kumar, S., Gankotiya, A. K., & Dutta, K. (2011). A comparative study of moodle with other e-learning systems. In Electronics Computer Technology (ICECT), 2011 3rd International Conference on (Vol. 5, pp. 414-418). IEEE. 10.1109/ICECTECH.2011.5942032

Kunene, M. F., & Barnes, N. (2017). Perceptions of the Open Distance and E-Learning Model at a South African University. *International Journal of Education and Practice*, *5*(8), 127–137.

Lantz, B. (2015). *Machine learning with R*. Packt Publishing Ltd.

Lee, H., Sin, D., Park, E., Hwang, I., Hong, G., & Shin, D. (2017). Open software platform for companion IoT devices. In Consumer Electronics (ICCE), 2017 IEEE International Conference on (pp. 394-395). IEEE.

Leung, E. W. C., & Li, Q. (2007). An experimental study of a personalized learning environment through open-source software tools. *IEEE Transactions on Education*, *50*(4), 331–337. doi:10.1109/TE.2007.904571

Li, S., Zhang, J., Yu, C., & Chen, L. (2017). Rethinking Distance Tutoring in e-Learning Environments: A Study of the Priority of Roles and Competencies of Open University Tutors in China. *The International Review of Research in Open and Distributed Learning*, *18*(2). doi:10.19173/irrodl.v18i2.2752

Littlejohn, A. (Ed.). (2003). *Reusing online resources: a sustainable approach to e-learning*. Psychology Press.

Lujara, S., Kissaka, M. M., Trojer, L., & Mvungi, N. H. (2007). Introduction of open-source e-learning environment and resources: A novel approach for secondary schools in Tanzania. *The International Journal of Social Sciences (Islamabad)*, *1*(4), 237–241.

Marsland, S. (2015). *Machine learning: an algorithmic perspective*. CRC Press.

Papadimitriou, C. H., & Steiglitz, K. (1998). *Combinatorial optimization: algorithms and complexity*. Courier Corporation.

Pavlicek, R., & Foreword By-Miller, R. (2000). *Embracing insanity: Open source software development*. Sams.

Pawlowski, J. M., Ras, E., Tobias, E., & Snezana, Å. Ä., DÃ3nal, F., Mehigan, T., ... & Moebs, S. (2016). Barriers to open e-learning in public administrations. *Technological Forecasting and Social Change*, *111*(C), 198–208.

Pfenninger, S., DeCarolis, J., Hirth, L., Quoilin, S., & Staffell, I. (2017). The importance of open data and software: Is energy research lagging behind? *Energy Policy*, *101*, 211–215. doi:10.1016/j.enpol.2016.11.046

Prlić, A., & Procter, J. B. (2012). Ten simple rules for the open development of scientific software. *PLoS Computational Biology*, *8*(12), e1002802. doi:10.1371/journal.pcbi.1002802 PMID:23236269

Read, T., Barcena, E., Traxler, J., & Kukulska-Hulme, A. (2017). Toward a Mobile Open and Social Language Learning Paradigm.

Reyes, N. R., Candeas, P. V., Galan, S. G., Viciana, R., Canadas, F., & Reche, P. J. (2009). Comparing open-source e-learning platforms from adaptivity point of view. In *EAEEIE Annual Conference*, 2009 (pp. 1-6). IEEE. 10.1109/EAEEIE.2009.5335482

Russell, S. J., Norvig, P., Canny, J. F., Malik, J. M., & Edwards, D. D. (2003). *Artificial intelligence: a modern approach* (Vol. 2). Upper Saddle River: Prentice Hall.

Scacchi, W. (2001). Software development practices in open software development communities: a comparative case study. In Making Sense of the Bazaar: Proceedings of the 1st Workshop on Open Source Software Engineering.

Soman, K. P., Loganathan, R., & Ajay, V. (2009). *Machine learning with SVM and other kernel methods*. PHI Learning Pvt. Ltd.

Stracke, C. M. (2017). Open education and learning quality: The need for changing strategies and learning experiences. In *Global Engineering Education Conference (EDUCON)*, 2017 IEEE (pp. 1049-1053). IEEE. 10.1109/EDUCON.2017.7942977

Stracke, C. M. (2017). Why We Need High Drop-Out Rates in MOOCs: New Evaluation and Personalization Strategies for the Quality of Open Education. In Advanced Learning Technologies (ICALT), 2017 IEEE 17th International Conference on (pp. 13-15). IEEE.

Strobl, C., & Neteler, M. (2016). Open Data with Open Software-the EU Copernicus Programme.

Tsolis, D., Stamou, S., Christia, P., Kampana, S., Rapakoulia, T., Skouta, M., & Tsakalidis, A. (2010). An adaptive and personalized open source e-learning platform. *Procedia: Social and Behavioral Sciences*, *9*, 38–43. doi:10.1016/j.sbspro.2010.12.112

Wagner, N., Hassanein, K., & Head, M. (2008). Who is responsible for e-learning success in higher education? A stakeholders' analysis. *Journal of Educational Technology & Society*, *11*(3).

Woolf, B. P. (2010). *Building intelligent interactive tutors: Student-centered strategies for revolutionizing e-learning*. Morgan Kaufmann.

KEY TERMS AND DEFINITIONS

Artificial Intelligence: (1) Artificial intelligence is a sub-field of computer science dealing with research studies on developing intelligent systems simulating the human-thinking behavior and intelligence or specific mechanisms in nature. (2) Artificial intelligence is a concept used for describing the feature, function, or characteristic of computer systems or machines that are able to simulate human-thinking behavior and intelligence or specific mechanisms from nature.

E-Learning: E-learning is a type of learning activity supported and performed with electronic media sources by directing individuals to experience learning while eliminating limitations caused by time or place.

Intelligent Optimization: Intelligent optimization is a type of optimization that is done by using artificial-intelligence-based approaches, methods, or techniques.

Machine Learning: Machine learning is a sub-field of artificial intelligence, including approaches, methods, and techniques, that has the mechanism of learning from pre-data in order to be trained for dealing effectively with new problem states and solving them.

Open Source (Software): Open source is a type of software system or program of which source codes are freely available to use, change, or adapt.

Optimization: Optimization is the process of finding the most appropriate value or state of a mathematical function or a specific decision variable.

This research was previously published in Optimizing Contemporary Application and Processes in Open Source Software; pages 102-123, copyright year 2018 by Engineering Science Reference (an imprint of IGI Global).

Chapter 18
DuBot:
An Open-Source, Low-Cost Robot for STEM and Educational Robotics

Avraam Chatzopoulos
iD https://orcid.org/0000-0002-2569-4147
University of West Attica, Greece

Michail Kalogiannakis
iD https://orcid.org/0000-0002-9124-2245
University of Crete, Greece

Stamatios Papadakis
iD https://orcid.org/0000-0003-3184-1147
University of Crete, Greece

Michail Papoutsidakis
University of West Attica, Greece

Dethe Elza
iD https://orcid.org/0000-0002-4422-5928
Richmond Public Library, Canada

Sarantos Psycharis
School of Pedagogical and Technological Education, Greece

ABSTRACT

This chapter presents the design and development of an open-source, low-cost robot for K12 students, suitable for use in educational robotics and science, technology, engineering, mathematics (STEM). The development of DuBot is a continuation of previous research and robot's innovation is based on three axes: (a) its specifications came from the 1st cycle of action research; (b) robot's visual programming language is integrated into the robot, taking advantage of the fact that it can be programmed from any device (smartphone, tablet, PC) with an internet connection and without the need to install any software or app; (c) is low-cost with no "exotic" parts robot than anyone can build with less than 50€. Furthermore, the robot's initial evaluation is presented -from distance due to emergency restrictions of Covid-19 is presented by the University of Crete, Department of Preschool Education's students.

DOI: 10.4018/978-1-7998-9158-1.ch018

INTRODUCTION

Today, we are experiencing the *4th Industrial Revolution (IR)*, that more and more academics, businessmen, politicians, and media outlets refer to (Marr, 2016, 2018), and directly affects the worldwide workforce as it requires workers with new skills (Chatzopoulos, Papoutsidakis, Kalogiannakis, Psycharis, & Papachristos, 2020). In this context, the *P21's Frameworks for 21st Century Learning*, a framework developed by the non-profit organization *"Battelle for Kids"* with input from teachers, education experts, and business leaders, suggests and defines the following skills and knowledge students need to succeed in work and life (Battelle for Kids, 2019):

1. creativity and innovation
2. critical thinking and problem-solving,
3. communication, and
4. collaboration,

STEM education and Educational Robotics appear to support (Papadakis, 2020; Psycharis, 2018) and prepare students for the 21st century and 4th IR requirements. STEM and Educational Robotics are increasingly considered as the newest trends in education (Zygouris et al., 2017), offering real practical experiences to the students, while hands-on robotic activities and tasks -due to their *play aspect*- are fun and attractive for them (Atmatzidou, Markelis, & Demetriadis, 2008; Papadakis & Kalogiannakis, 2020).

Robots and educational robotic platforms are the tools to apply Educational Robotics and STEM and can be considered an excellent vehicle for students to demonstrate fundamental engineering problems as they help them develop the above skills (Wagner, Hohmann, Gerecke, & Brenneke, 2004). To apply them in such a variety of subjects and different scenarios, these educational platforms have to meet several technical as well as educational requirements such as flexibility, modularity, scalability, ease of use (Wagner et al., 2004) and should be affordable enough, so that low-income students will not be excluded.

This paper describes the overall process of designing and developing an *Education Robotic Platform (ERP)* that aims to STEM education and Education Robotics activities for K12 students. This ERP's technical aspects and specifications did not come from the researchers' personal preferences, but the systematic data collection and analysis as they came from the 1st cycle of an Action Research.

Besides, this research's proposed robot innovates in a total of three axes:

1. Robot's specifications came from the 1st cycle of action research.
2. Robot's visual programming language is integrated into itself, taking advantage of being programmed from any device (smartphone, tablet, PC) with an Internet connection and without the need to install any software or app.
3. It is low-cost with no "exotic" parts robot than anyone can build with less than 50€.

THEORETICAL BACKGROUND

STEM Education Definition

In the literature (Ioannou & Bratitsis, 2016; Texley & Ruud, 2018; Tsupros, Kohler, & Hallinen, 2009), there is a variety of *STEM* or *STEM Education* definition, which is an abbreviation for *Science, Technology, Engineering,* and *Mathematics* and refers to teaching and learning in the fields of the above derivatives (Chatzopoulos, Papoutsidakis, Kalogiannakis, & Psycharis, 2020). Moreover, STEM is used as a generic label for any educational program or practice, policy, or action, that involves one or more of its disciplines (Gonzalez & J.Kuenzi, 2012).

Educational Robotics Definition

In recent years, *robots* and specifically *educational robots* have become increasingly popular due to their playful nature. As a result, their integration –a STEM integration- into the educational activities is described by *Educational Robotics (ER)*. ER is more than "robots in education," a broad term referring to a collection of educational programs, resources and activities, technology, and pedagogical learning theories inside and outside schools (Daniela & Lytras, 2018). Moreover, in Greece, the main mobility currently seen in STEM education in schools concerns ER applications (Chatzopoulos et al., 2019).

STEM and ER Benefits

STEM and ER are collaborative environments that engage students in tackling grand challenges and learning through the process of exploration, discovery, and invention using real problems and situations (Chatzopoulos et al., 2019). According to researchers (Alimisis, 2013a; National Academies of Sciences, Engineering, 2018; Wagner et al., 2004) and educators, STEM and ER have numerous benefits:

1. STEM and ER motivate students in curiosity and learning (Chin, Hong, & Chen, 2014; Mondada et al., 2006).
2. Students are encouraged to create ideas expression, problem thinking, and thinking differently and become problem solvers, innovative, self-conscious, and reasonable thinkers (Morrison & Bartlett, 2009).
3. They are fostered teamwork, socialization, learning how to learn from and with others, and building a cooperative environment (Ronsivalle, Boldi, Gusella, Inama, & Carta, 2018).
4. They improve their concentration (Kucuk & Sisman, 2017) and the overall learning process even with specific difficulties (Chin et al., 2014; Daniela & Lytras, 2018).
5. STEM and ER offer hands-on exposure (such as mechanical, electrical, and computer engineering) to a wide range of subjects and are a useful aid for learning computer programming, technology, mathematics, and science (Wagner et al., 2004).
6. Hands-on STEM and ER activities are fun and attractive, retain students' high levels of attention and curiosity (Ronsivalle et al., 2018), and they can help capture their interest in future STEM studies (Chalmers, 2018; Kucuk & Sisman, 2017).

7. Through STEM and ER, students develop new skills such as critical thinking, teamwork, problem-solving, creativity, and cognitive-social skills and become technologically literate (Xatzopoulos, Papoutsidakis, & Chamilothoris, 2013),

8. Furthermore, STEM and ER contribute to the bridging of ethnic and gender differences and eliminate gender stereotypes about girls' role with and technology (Kalogiannakis & Papadakis, 2019a, 2019b; Kalogiannakis, Papadakis, & Dorouka, 2020).

PROBLEM STATEMENT

This research's innovation is based on the fact that *Education Robotic Platform's (ERP)* specifications have emerged from an *Action Research (AR)* focused on the educational community. AR involves community members in the research process with the ultimate goal of contributing effectively to interventions and actions that promote change (Chatzopoulos et al., 2019). While AR's definitions and concept are different, numerous, and vary according to space, place, and context (Billett, Harteis, & Gruber, 2010; Kemmis, Nixon, & McTaggart, 2014), researchers agree that AR seeks to exploit data to solve practical problems (Smith, 2007; Villanueva, 2016). It can also be considered a continual professional development to improve teaching and learning or improve educators' practice (Calhoun, 2002; Carr & Kemmis, 2004). Moreover, AR allows teachers to derive their theories from an action (Li, 2008). In the literature (Elliott, 1991; Kemmis et al., 2014; Santos, Ali, & Hill, 2016), several AR models are available. However, most of them use a *circular* or *spiral* process (Figure 1) of the four following main stages (Manesi & Betsi, 2013):

1. *Planning*
2. *Acting*
3. *Observing*
4. *Reflecting*

Figure 1. Action research cycles (Chatzopoulos et al., 2019)

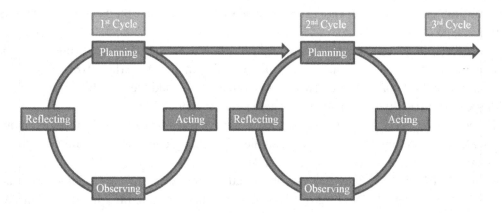

This AR model (Figure 1) is a self-reflective spiral of cycles where every cycle includes the stages of (i) planning, (ii) acting or action, (iii) observing or observation, and (iv) reflecting or evaluation, which then leads into further cycles where the stages are repeated (Carr & Kemmis, 2004; Gibbs, Kooyman, Marks, & Burns, 2015; Santos et al., 2016). Consequently, in this research, a slightly modified AR model was adopted where every cycle has the following four stages (Figure 2):

1. *Data collection to define ERP's initial specifications and to redefine them.*
2. *ERP's design and development.*
3. *ERP's application in ER and STEM seminars.*
4. *ERP's evaluation, reflection, and proposal for improvements.*

Till now, the research has already gone through the 1st AR cycle where: (i) data collection received (from the events presented below) and analyzed to define the initial ERP's specifications, (ii) a prototype ERP was designed and developed, (iii) an ERP's presentation was implemented, (iv) and last but not least, the first ERP evaluation and proposal for improvements were completed.

Figure 2. This research's AR cycles

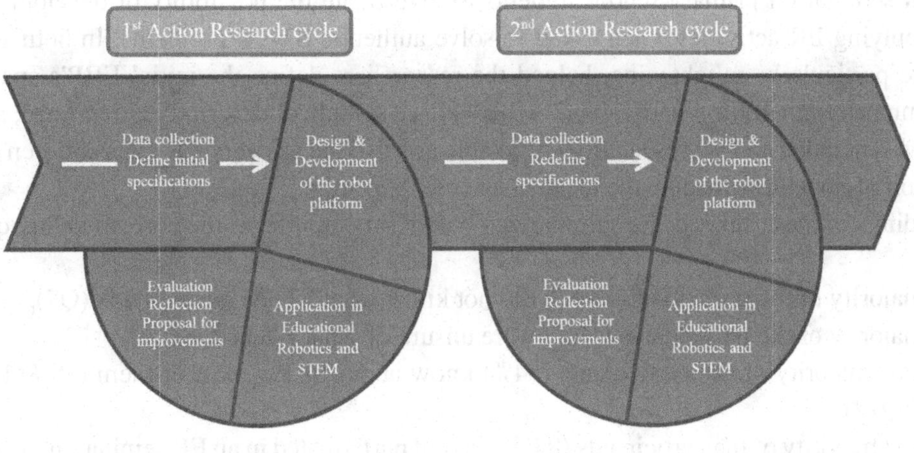

For this purpose, qualitative and quantitative data were obtained from surveys, specifically from:

1. An ER event was handled in Athens-Greece, which aimed to help students and their parents learn about STEM Education and ER and measure their interest in future ER seminars within their municipality (Municipality, 2019; Vamvakopoulos, 2019).
2. Pilot research on students in the form of an experiential seminar and workshop to investigate the possibility of developing their CT skills by applying ER activities when they are asked to solve authentic STEM problems (Chatzopoulos, Papoutsidakis, Kalogiannakis, Psycharis, et al., 2020).

This data collection guided researchers to articulate the technical aspects and specifications of the ERP with the ultimate goal of making this educational tool useful and practical for the educational community, especially for primary education.

THE SURVEYS

In November 2019, the University of West Attica, in collaboration with the relevant Municipality of Agia Varvara, handled a successful ER event to present ER and STEM Education to students, parents, and teachers and to measure their interest in future STEM and ER seminars within the municipality (Municipality, 2019; Vamvakopoulos, 2019). For a relatively small municipality, as Agia Varvara is, with a total number of 1800 students, this event turned out to be very successful as the event's venue "Ioannis Ritsos" theater - cinema (400 people capacity) was unexpectedly filled. Pre and post questionnaires were distributed to record participants' (students, parents, teachers) views and measure their interest in ER, STEM education, and *Computational Thinking (CT)*.

In this survey, many questions related to STEM, ER, and ERPs were included, particularly about the participants' intention to get involved in the construction of their own ERP, participate in STEM Education, and engage in ER seminars. So, this ER event was the spark to conduct a pilot study and an experiential seminar on primary school students to investigate the possibility of developing their CT skills by applying ER activities when asked to solve authentic STEM problems. In both surveys, the results were particularly enlightening, helped the researchers define the initial ERP's specifications, and are summarized in Table 1 and Table 2 -where also a sample of descriptive, free-form, and "other" questions was included and is presented. Remarkable are also the answers - designs children drew in the Q28 question of how they imagine the ideal robot (see Appendix: Figure 11).

The findings of these surveys are summarized below (in parenthesis the corresponding question):

1. The majority of the participants (49%) did not know what STEM education is (Q7).
2. The majority of the participants (50%) were unsure of what ER is (Q8).
3. The vast majority of the participants (84%) know about ERPs; most of them (68%) know about Lego (Q12).
4. The vast majority of the participants (83%) had not participated in an ER seminar in the past (Q11).
5. The vast majority of them (88%) would like to develop their ERP (Q14), and they (55%) would have unlimited time to complete its construction (Q17).
6. The vast majority (67%) of the participants' parents want to get involved in robots' development along with their children (Q18).
7. For the participants that answer the following questions, the majority of them (54%) want to program their ERP with any device such as PC/Laptop, tablet, smartphone (Q22), they want (92%) ERP to be open-source (Q19), they prefer (50%) to build it using a 3D printer (Q21), and they like (40%) their ERP to be compatible with old devices (Q23).
8. Concerning ERP's total cost, participants' answers summed in the following Table 3.

Table 1. Pre and post sample questions and their summarized results

Question (No. & Description)	Answers	
	Yes (n,%)	
Q11. Have you participated in an ER/STEM seminar in the past?	21 (16%)	

Question (No. & Description)	**Answers**		
	No (n,%)	**Neutral (n,%)**	**Yes (n,%)**
Q7. Do you know what STEM Education is?	65 (49%)	35 (27%)	32 (24%)
Q8. Do you know what Educational Robotics is?	24 (18%)	66 (50%)	42 (32%)
Q10. Do you know what Free and open-source software (FOSS) is?	75 (57%)	32 (24%)	25 (19%)

Question (No. & Description)	**Answers**				
	Completely Disagree (n,%)	**Disagree (n,%)**	**Neither Agree / Disagree (n,%)**	**Agree (n,%)**	**Strongly Agree (n,%)**
Q14. Would you like to build your own robot?	1 (1%)	3 (2%)	7 (5%)	31 (23%)	86 (55%)
Q.18. You will be involved in building/planning robots together with your child?	9 (7%)	7 (5%)	26 (20%)	46 (35%)	42 (32%)

Question (No. & Description)	**Answers**				
	I do not know (n,%)	**No / Not at all (n,%)**	**A little (n,%)**	**Moderate (n,%)**	**Very (n,%)**	**Very much (n,%)**
Q.19. Should the robot be accompanied by Free Software / Open Source Software?	76 (58%)	1 (1%)	9 (7%)	10 (8%)	18 (14%)	16 (12%)
Q.20. In order for the robot to be programmed, should it be necessary to connect to the Internet?	42 (35%)	30 (23%)	14 (11%)	7 (5%)	22 (17%)	15 (11%)
Q.21. Will the robot be able to be built with a 3D printer?	61 (46%)	12 (9%)	6 (5%)	14 (11%)	25 (19%)	11 (8%)
Q.23. Would you like your robot to be compatible with older computer technology, tablets, smartphones?	25 (19%)	18 (14%)	20 (15%)	25 (19%)	30 (23%)	10 (8%)

Question (No. & Description)	**Answers**				
	I do not want to waste time; I want it ready.	**1 - 2 hours**	**3 - 4 hours**	**4 - 8 hours**	**I will spend unlimitted hours, as long as I complete it**
Q17. If you could build your own robot, how much time would you have to build it?	0 (0%)	20 (15%)	27 (20%)	9 (7%)	72 (55%)

335

Table 2. A sample of the descriptive, free-form and other questions

Q15. If you want to build your own robot: Q15a. what shape do you want it to have? ...... Q15b. what form do you want it to have? Q15c. what size do you want it to have? ...... Q15d. what color do you want it to have?
Q16. Choose which of the adjacent materials you have dealt with / created / worked with: **Answers:** Q16.1 Paper / Cardboard, ... Q16.2 Plasticine / Clay, ... Q16.3 Wood, ... Q16.4 Plastic, ... Q16.5 Metal / Wire
Q12. Choose which of these educational platforms you know. **Answers:** Q13a. Lego, Q13b. Thymio, Q13c. Edison, Q13d. BBC Microbit, Q13e. Makeblock, Q13f. BeeBot, Q13g. Arduino, Q13h. Raspberry, Q13i. Parallax, Q13j. I haven't dealt with it, Q13k. Another (please clarify)
Q13. Choose which of these educational platforms you have dealt with. **Answers:** Q13a. Lego, Q13b. Thymio, Q13c. Edison, Q13d. BBC Microbit, Q13e. Makeblock, Q13f. BeeBot, Q13g. Arduino, Q13h. Raspberry, Q13i. Parallax, Q13j. I haven't dealt with it, Q13k. Another (please clarify)
Q.22. Which of these devices would you prefer to program your robot with? **Answers:** Q22.a. I don't know, Q22b. Smart Phone, Q22c. Tablet, Q22d. Laptop/PC, Q22e. On all devices
Q28. How do you imagine the ideal robot (for results see Appendix: Figure 12).

Table 3. Participants' views about ERP's cost

Question:	Answers								
"How much money would you spend to buy an ERP (ready-made or the materials for making your own)?"	0€	less than 30€	31€ to 50€	51€ to 100€	101€ to 150€	151€ to 200€	201€ to 350€	351€ to 500€	more than 500€
	3,6%	3,6%	35,7%	32,1%	7,1%	14,3%	3,6%	0%	0%

The majority (39,3%) of the participants want the ERP's cost to be under 50€. Specifically, 35,7% of them want it to range between 31€ to 100€, and 32,1% of them prefer ERP's cost to be between 51€ to 100€. Hence, researchers set a goal for the ERP's cost to be around 50€ instead of the higher cost (usually between 100€ - 200€) of other corresponding ERPs in the market. This last specification was critical as it influenced the strategic choices made in Dubot's hardware design. Remarkably, DuBot's parts cost were calculated based on retail prices, so in mass production, the cost will be less than half.

Last but not least, the survey showed a wide variety of answers regarding shape, form, and color (Q15). Researchers choose to develop an easy to build, two-wheel vehicle with a differential drive to achieve mobility in two-dimensional space, so the ERP can move in all possible directions by controlling the direction and speed's rotation of its DC motors (Xatzopoulos et al., 2013). In future ERP versions, the researchers plan to redesign and/or build robots in different shapes/forms, such as humanoids.

Summarizing, the above findings formed the Dubot's initial specifications: it has to be low-cost, open-source, to can be built using a 3D printer, it has to be programmed by any device, to be compatible with old technology devices, and should not depend on an Internet connection in order to work.

EDUCATIONAL ROBOTIC PLATFORM DESIGN

ERP design and development was based on its easy construction, assembly, and use. ERP is aimed at the educational community, and therefore the following assumptions had been made to fulfill its needs and preferences:

1. ERP's cost should be as low (< =50€) as possible.
2. ERP hardware's electronic parts should be easy to find in the market (common, not "exotic").
3. ERP's hardware and software should be free to download and open-source.
4. ERP's assembly should be easy enough for students, teachers, and parents.
5. ERP should be easily programmed by almost any device: PC, tablet, and smartphone.
6. ERP's programming language should be embedded in the robot, so the user does not need todownload and install any extra software. For this reason, a custom *Visual Programming Language (VPL)* will be embedded into the ERP.

ERP's Shell

ERP's first edition's shell (robot's shape and form) is based on the Juno Rover by Explore Making and is licensed under the Creative Commons – Attribution license (Anderson & Li-Leger, 2016b). This shell was selected as a "starting shell" because it is open-source, 3D printed, easy to assembly, low-cost, accompanied with assembly instructions, and according to users' feedback, it is quite cute. However, in future versions, the ERP's shell will be replaced by a new one according to the educational community's preferences. Figure 3 and Figure 4 show that Juno Rover's photo, 3D parts, and assembly are shown.

Juno Rover is designed for in-house 3D printing. The largest component is the body, which requires a 3D printer with a 125x100 mm print bed. Its designers recommend a 200uM or more acceptable 3D printing resolution; however, our test printing with less resolution provided a working robot shell. It will be needed 15 printing time hours to print the Juno Rover with the recommended resolution; however, there are maybe time deviations depending on the used 3D printer.

Figure 3. Juno Rover's assembly, and photo (Anderson & Li-Leger, 2016a)

Figure 4. Juno Rover's photo, and assembly (Anderson & Li-Leger, 2016a)

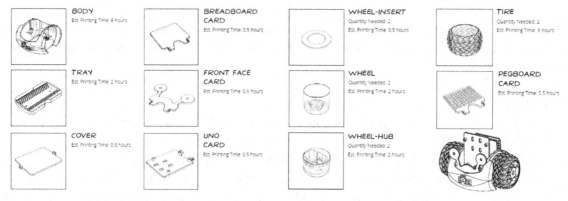

ERP's Electronics and Hardware

The ERP's construction consists of the Juno Rover's 3D parts, two servo motors (converted to DC), sensors (hypersonic sonar, LDR, button), actuators (led, buzzer), an ESP 8266 microcontroller, electronic parts for interfacing (resistors, L293 motor driver), battery holder, batteries and various parts such as screws, jumper wires, pin connectors, shrink tube, etc. A complete part list with indicative purchase prices is shown in Table 3. The total cost of the ERP's construction is 33,5€, much less than the target price of 50€. The full assembly instructions of the Juno Rover can be found at the following link: https://www.thingiverse.com/download:2677311.

Table 4. ERP's components list with indicative purchase prices (€)

Qty	3D Parts	€	Qty	Electronic Part	€
1	Body (approx. 36m PLA)	2,75	1	ESP 8266 microcontroller	2,65
1	Tray (approx. 8m PLA)	0,61	1	L293D motor driver	0,33
1	Cover (approx. 5m PLA)	0,37	1	LDR (Light Dependent Resistor)	0,10
1	Breadboard Cards (approx. 2,9m PLA)	0,21	1	Led (Red color)	0,02
1	Front Face Card (approx. 2,2m PLA)	0,17	2	Servo Motors (converted to DC)	3,60
2	Wheel inserts (approx. 3,2m PLA)	0,24	1	Sonar HC-SR04 (for distance meter)	1,10
2	Wheels (approx. 19m PLA)	1,45	1	Push button	0,10
2	Wheel hubs (approx. 28m PLA)	2,14	1	Buzzer	0,80
2	Tires (approx. 44,6m PLA)	3,41	6	Resistors (1x100Ω, 1x220Ω, 1x1K, 1x1.2K, 1x2.2K,1x10K)	0,03
1	Pegboard Card (approx. 3m PLA)	0,23	1	Battery holder for 4xAA batteries	0,35
			4	AA batteries NiMH 2700mAH	8,20
Qty	Hardware Parts		1	PCB electronics board	2,00
1	Shrink Tube 1m	0,09	1	Breadboard (to connect experimental electronic circuits)	0,85
12	Screws	0,10	20	Jumper Wires (male to male, female to female, various cm)	0,85
1	Pin Connectors Series	0,10	1	USB cable type B to micro USB (for ESP programming)	0,65

All the electronic schematics, mechanical designs, and software would be freely available to the educational community under the Attribution-By Creative Commons (CC-BY) license (Neil Butcher, 2015). In contrast to Arduino UNO (or other cheap Arduino boards), the ESP 8266 was primarily chosen as the ERP's main microcontroller because it has native Wi-Fi support, good specifications (32-bit RISC CPU running at 80 MHz, 32 KB RAM, 32 KB cache RAM, 80 KB user-data RAM, 16 KB ETS system-data RAM, External QSPI flash: up to 16 MiB, IEEE 802.11 b/g/n Wi-Fi, 16 GPIO pins, SPI, I²C, I²S, UART, 10-bit ADC), has a low cost (approximately 2,65€ less than the Arduino's cost), and high availability (Vordos, Chatzopoulos, Papoutsidakis, & Piromalis, 2018).

Figure 5. ERP's block diagram

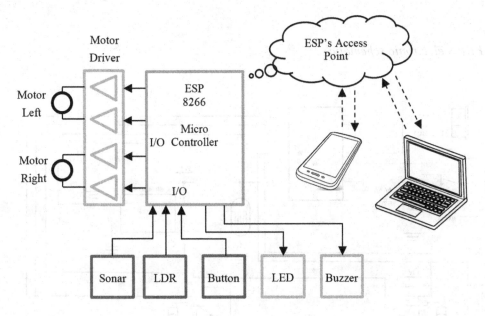

ESP can be programmed in C/C++ through the well-known Arduino IDE (Xatzopoulos et al., 2013). However, this implementation uses a different innovative approach; it uses the ESP (Papoutsidakis, Chatzopoulos, & Piromalis, 2019) as an intermediate webserver to integrate a custom made VPL and program the ESP's movements scenario. In previous ERP's experiments, an Arduino UNO board was used in conjunction with a Wi-Fi shield; however, the overall cost was much more than the final choice with ESP implementation.

In Figure 5, the ERP's electronic block diagram is presented. ESP is connected to motors through a motor driver to support the needed current (at least 350–500mA/motor) and the different motors' voltage (5V instead of 3.3V) (Mavrovounioti, Chatzopoulos, Papoutsidakis, & Piromalis, 2018). It is also connected to the sensors (Sonar, LDR, and buttons) and the actuators (LEDs, buzzer) through electronic-circuit interfaces (Papoutsidakis, Chatzopoulos, Drosos, & Kalovrektis, 2018). ESP microcontroller has a multi-role in the ERP's development:

1. to create a *wireless access point* (*WAP*), so users' devices (PC, tablets, smartphones) will connect to,
2. to act as a *web server*,
3. to establish the client-server connection,
4. to listen and answer client's requests,
5. to send ERP's VPL code (HTML, CSS, and JS) to the client,
6. to convert Blocks to ERP's robot directions, and
7. to read sensors (LDR, Sonar) and control motors and actuators (button, led, buzzer). In this way, ESP is used for every ERP task. In Figure 6, ERP's full electronic schematic is presented.

Figure 6. ERP's electronic schematic

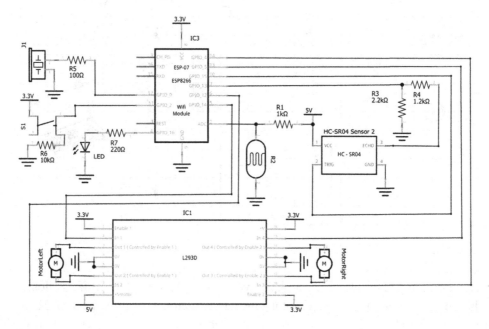

ERP's Software and VPL

ERP's software includes all the necessary firmware plus an integrated custom VPL. The ERP's firmware is responsible for:

1. reads its sensors data (sonar, LDR, button),
2. drives its actuators (motors, led, buzzer),
3. creates the ESP's WAP,
4. hosts a web server (Figure 7) to serve client (devices) requests, and
5. incorporates all the necessary functions for the cooperation and smooth operation of the above operations.

Figure 7. Flow chart of a web server's part

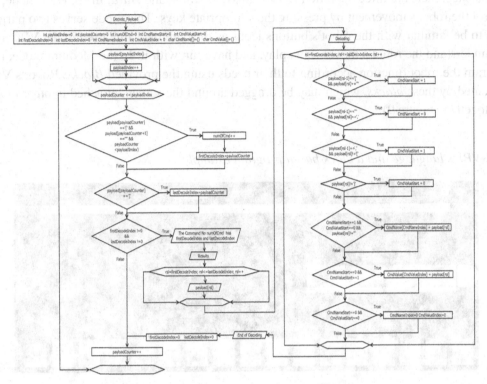

ESP's VPL is based on Dethe Elza's Block code (Elza, 2020b, 2020a) in contrast to other powerful VPLs such as Blockly, mainly because it has a minimal memory footprint (500 lines of code) and its simplicity that is particularly suitable for use in a microcontroller, leaving its RAM for students ERP's experiments. Moreover, Block code is custom made, implemented in HTML, CSS, JavaScript, and provides ERP's ability to be programmed without the client's need to download and install a piece of software or app. The VPL creates an easy to use, slick *User Interface (UI)* that user can see and navigate using his device's browser.

In Figure 8 and Figure 9, VPL's introductory screen and Block–based language allow users to create their program through graphical manipulation- are respectively presented. After the client's device is connected to the ERP's WAP established, the user opens the device's browser, and the introductory page is loaded.

Figure 8. VPL's intro screen

On this page, there are three operation modes: *Easy*, *Medium*, and *Hard*. In the Easy mode, the user can control the robot's movement by pressing the appropriate keys. This mode serves two purposes, (i) for users to be familiar with the robot's buttons icons as they are the same used in the VPL, (ii) users learn to understand the robot's movements, play, and have fun with it. In the Medium mode, the users can program the robot function according to their needs using the provided *Blocks*. Robot's VPL code is represented by these *blocks*, which may be dragged around the screen, attached to other *blocks,* and chained together (Figure 9).

Figure 9. VPL's language and a block based program example

Blocks are non-text representation, are using icons and input numbers. When the program is ready, the user may press the *Start Block* to execute his ERP program.

In the Hard mode, more advanced blocks are introduced, sensors' data are printed into the screen, and there is also a simulation area where the program operation is immediately shown. However, this model is under continuous development, according to the users' feedback. Figure 10 shows that an older version of the ERP's *Graphical User Interface (GUI)* and its simulation area are shown; GUI is under continuous development.

Figure 10. Older version of the ERP's software

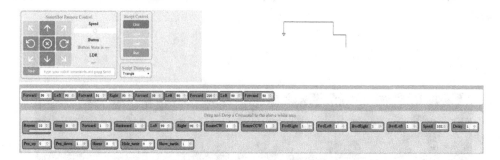

VPL's main philosophy is for users to follow an overall evolutionary learning process. They become more familiar with the ERP and its software: (i) they discover more features, (ii) they motivate their curiosity and learning and keep their interest and engagement alive. In this way, users (students) are encouraged to express creative ideas, problem thinking, and thinking differently. At the same time, VPL's GUI is designed to be fun and attractive and retain students' high levels of attention and curiosity.

EVALUATION

According to this research's proposed AR model (see *Problem Statement*), the next stage after the ERP's specifications define and developed is its application on ER and STEM seminars (Figure 2), to be evaluated by the whole educational community (students, teachers, parents, stakeholders). Their suggestions for improvements and notes will later be utilized to lead to a new AR cycle. However, coronavirus' pandemic temporarily canceled all the scheduled live events (STEM - ER seminars for students, teachers, presentations for parents), so the researchers conducted an initial from distance Dubot's evaluation to the Department of Preschool Education's students by the University of Crete. For this purpose, three short online videos were produced describing Dubot's functional parts, user interface, and the program language environment. Later, students recorded their evaluation of online forms. Form's questionnaire (Figure 11) included questions about demographics, general interest, e.g., about STEM, ER, ERPs, and –of course- questions about DuBot's evaluation.

Figure 11. Dubot's evaluation form's block diagram

Dubot's evaluation set of questions is based on the WAMMI model (Kirakowski & Cierlik, 1998), a 60-item reliable and valid evaluation tool for assessing user satisfaction with web sites. This model was selected because both Dubot's GUI and program language are web-based and developed using websites' languages and tools (e.g., HTML, CSS, JavaScript). A subset of 12 questions of a demo WAMMI model was selected (Kirakowski & Cierlik, 2016), and others added to clarify participants' views about the overall design of the Dubot it is GUI, and Blocks' design and use. A small sample of the questionnaire is presented below in Table 5.

The results were particularly enlightening, helped the researchers spot future improvements for the new version of Dubot's development, and are summarized below (in parenthesis, the corresponding question number).

Table 5. Sample questions of the Dubot's evaluation form

Question (No. & Description)	Answers				
	Strongly Agree (n,%)	**Agree (n,%)**	**Neither Agree / Disagree (n,%)**	**Disagree (n,%)**	**Completely Disagree (n,%)**
Q14. It's hard to move through the software.	1 (5%)	2 (9%)	3 (14%)	11 (50%)	5 (23%)
Q15. I can quickly find whatever I want in the software.	13 (59%)	5 (23%)	4 (18%)	0 (0%)	0 (0%)
Q16. My software seems to follow a logic.	15 (68%)	4 (18%)	3 (14%)	0 (0%)	0 (0%)
Q17. This software needs more introductory explanations.	0 (0%)	6 (27%)	9 (41%)	4 (18%)	3 (14%)
Q18. Software design is very attractive.	11 (50%)	4 (18%)	4 (18%)	3 (14%)	0 (0%)
Q19. I don't like using this software.	1 (5%)	0 (0%)	3 (14%)	9 (41%)	8 (35%)
Q20. It's hard to say if this software has what I want.	2 (9%)	2 (9%)	9 (41%)	7 (32%)	2 (9%)
Q21. Using this software for the first time is easy.	8 (36%)	10 (45%)	1 (5%)	3 (14%)	0 (0%)
Q22. This software has some annoying features.	0 (0%)	2 (9%)	3 (14%)	9 (41%)	8 (36%)
Q24. Remembering where I am in this software is difficult.	0 (0%)	2 (9%)	4 (18%)	12 (55%)	3 (14%)
Q25. Using this software is a waste of time.	0 (0%)	0 (0%)	0 (0%)	5 (23%)	15 (68%)
Q26. Everything in this software is easy to understand.	7 (32%)	9 (41%)	4 (18%)	2 (9%)	0 (0%)
Q27. The symbols used in this software are understandable.	14 (64%)	6 (27%)	2 (9%)	0 (0%)	0 (0%)
Q28. I like the choice of colors used in this software.	8 (36%)	(14%)	6 (27%)	4 (18%)	1 (5%)
Q29. Fill in the interpretation next to the symbol as you perceive it.					
Q30. Fill out what you liked about the DuBot robot.					
Q31. Feel free to fill out what you didn't like about the DuBot robot.					
Q32. Fill in what you would like to change in the DuBot robot.					
Q33. Complete some educational activities / educational scenarios that you would like to be implemented with the DuBot robot.					
Q34. Describe how you imagine the "ideal" training robot. You can refer to its construction (size, shape, color, etc.), its mode of operation, its software (programming) and / or its accompanying educational content.					

The vast majority of the participants (n=22) were women (Q1, 95%), aged between 22-34 years old (Q2, 73%), and students (Q3, 82%). The majority of them (54%) did not know (27%) or know a little (27%) about STEM education (Q5), while 32% knew a moderate about it. In respect to ER (Q6), 41% moderate knew, and 36% very knew what it is. This may be evidenced by the fact that about half of the participants (48% instead of 52% who disagreed) had previously participated in an ER seminar (Q8). While a moderate (45%) and a very (41%) percentage of them answered that they knew well the new technologies such as computers, smartphones, apps, etc. (Q9), a significant 41% of them knew nothing about Free/Open Software (Q7). The participants proposed various specifications (questions: Q10.1 – Q10.4, Q11.1 – Q11.6) concerning a future Dubot version. The vast majority of them (59%) preferred an animal shape for Dubot, to be medium-size between 15-25cm (59%), and multi-colored (68%). They also confirmed the previous ER event's survey data regarding the Dubot's ideal cost (Q13) and the time it would take to build one (Q12). 55% of them want Dubot to cost between 31€ - 50€, and the vast majority of them (59%) would spend unlimited hours as long as to build it.

The overall valuation of Dubot's software, according to the WAMMI model, was especially positive. The vast majority of the participants (73%) found it easy to move through the software (Q14), and 82% could found quickly whatever they want in it (Q15). The vast majority of them (86%) believed that Dubot's software follows a logic (Q16), and 68% found its design very attractive (Q18). They agreed (81%) that using the software for the first time is easy (Q21), and 87% liked to use it (Q19). While 87% disagreed that Dubot's software has some annoying features, many participants came with suggestions concerning Dubot's software aesthetics. They proposed Dubot's software to use different colors and shades and become more playful and attractive to attract students' interest. The latter also justifies the dispersion of answers to Q28 question "I like the choice of colors used in this software," where 36% of the participants totally agreed, 14% agreed, 27% neither agreed/disagreed, a significant of 18% disagreed and 5% totally disagreed. Last but not least, in the free-form questions, Q29.1 - Q29.10 ("Fill in the interpretation next to the symbol as you perceive it"), the majority of the participants understood the meaning of the Blocks' symbols. They also provided researchers with valuable feedback in terms of what they like most (Q30), what they did not like (Q31), what changes they prefer to be done in the future Dubot's version (Q32), and suggested future educational scenarios that you would like to be implemented with the robot (Q33).

DISCUSSION AND CHALLENGES

In the literature (Alimisis, 2013b; Chatzopoulos et al., 2019; Daniela & Lytras, 2018; Miller & Nourbakhsh, 2016; Papadakis, 2020; Papadakis & Kalogiannakis, 2020), researchers seem to agree on the numerous benefits of ER and STEM education. Although there is numerous research on unplugged ER and STEM applications using visual programming tools (Menon, Bp, Romero, & Viéville, 2019), there is a need to choose hands-on applications and use an ERP. This research shows a lack of students' engagement in ER due to the high ERPs cost, so a low-cost ERP implementation was thoroughly presented, where its specifications came from the 1st cycle of an AR results. The educational community's needs shaped Dubot's (this research's proposed ERP) specifications to be the following: low-cost (<50 €), open-source, and should be easily programmed by any (old or new) device (PC, tablet, smartphone), and can be built by a 3D printer. Dubot's evaluation showed that this ERP fully meets the initial specifications that came from the AR's 1st cycle and provided a rich proposal for improvements. However, evaluation came exclusively from a small group of the educational community (Preschool Education Department's students) due to emergency restrictions of Covid-19 and is completely absent the evaluation by the students themselves and other stakeholders (teachers, parents) of the educational community.

CONCLUSION AND FUTURE WORK

The next step of this research is a complete evaluation of the proposed ERP (Dubot). For this purpose, future workshops and seminars are scheduled to introduce Dubot to students and teachers and finally measure their acceptance, thoughts, and suggestions (Dubot's evaluation). These results will guide the researchers to change or form the new Dubot's specifications, improve its design and development, and repeat the stages of a new AR cycle (Chatzopoulos et al., 2019). This research's goal is for Dubot to have widespread acceptance by the educational community, so after improvements, a new large scale evaluation study to collect quantitative and qualitative data will be scheduled.

Moreover, future work could include Dubot's minor or major modifications, e.g.:

1. re-production using a CNC machine (Koikas, Aggelis, & Chatzopoulos, 2015) for higher resistance to time and stress,
2. converting to a 2-wheels balancing educational robot (Melkonian, Chatzopoulos, Papoutsidakis, & Piromalis, 2018),
3. converting to an educational quadcopter (Louros, Papoutsidakis, Chatzopoulos, & Drosos, 2018), so it can be used for other purposes and other target groups.

Dubot still ensures the efficiency of a robot platform for many and beyond educational applications. It could be programmed by high-level languages, e.g., C/C++ and -after light modifications- it could be used in conjunction with other programming environments (e.g., Arduino IDE, MATLAB, etc.), so to be used by secondary education and/or university students.

REFERENCES

Alimisis, D. (2013). Educational robotics: Open questions and new challenges. *Themes in Science & Technology Education, 6*(1), 63–71. doi:10.1109/FIE.2014.7044055

Anderson, C., & Li-Leger, N. (2016a). *IMA Juno Assembly Instructions. Explore Making.* Retrieved from https://www.thingiverse.com/thing:1720394

Anderson, C., & Li-Leger, N. (2016b). *Juno Rover intro to electronics and coding by ExploreMaking - Thingiverse.* Retrieved January 12, 2020, from https://www.thingiverse.com/thing:1720394

Atmatzidou, S., Markelis, I., & Demetriadis, S. (2008). The use of LEGO Mindstorms in elementary and secondary education : game as a way of triggering learning. *Workshop Proceedings of International Conference on Simulation, Modeling, and Programming for Autonomous Robots (SIMPAR)*, 22–30.

Battelle for Kids. (2019). Framework for 21st Century Learning. *Partnership Fo 21st Century Learning.* Retrieved from https://www.battelleforkids.org/networks/p21/frameworks-resources

Billett, S., Harteis, C., & Gruber, H. (2010). *Learning Through Practice Models, Traditions, Orientations and Approaches* (S. Billett, C. Harteis, & H. Gruber, Eds.). Springer. doi:10.1007/978-90-481-3939-2

Butcher. (2015). A Basic Guide to Open Educational Resources (OER). In Wirtschaftsinformatik. Paris, France: United Nations Educational, Scientific and Cultural Organization. doi:10.100711576-012-0326-2

Calhoun, E. (2002). *Action Research for School Improvement Action Research at Work: A Teacher's Story*. Academic Press.

Carr, W., & Kemmis, S. (2004). *Becoming Critical. Education, Knowledge and Action Research*. Taylor & Francis e-Library. Retrieved from https://enotez.files.wordpress.com/2011/09/becoming-critical.pdf

Chalmers, C. (2018). Robotics and computational thinking in primary school. *International Journal of Child-Computer Interaction, 17*, 93–100. doi:10.1016/j.ijcci.2018.06.005

Chatzopoulos, A., Papoutsidakis, M., Kalogiannakis, M., & Psycharis, S. (2019). Action Research Implementation in Developing an Open Source and Low Cost Robotic Platform for STEM Education. *International Journal of Computers and Applications, 178*(24), 33–46.

Chatzopoulos, A., Papoutsidakis, M., Kalogiannakis, M., & Psycharis, S. (2020). Innovative Robot for Educational Robotics and STEM. In V. Kumar & C. Troussas (Eds.), *16th International Conference on Intelligent Tutoring Systems, ITS 2020* (pp. 95–104). Athens, Greece: Springer.

Chatzopoulos, A., Papoutsidakis, M., Kalogiannakis, M., Psycharis, S., & Papachristos, D. (2020). Measuring the impact on student's Computational Thinking skills through STEM and Educational Robotics projects implementation. In M. Kalogiannakis & S. J. Papadakis (Eds.), *Handbook of Research on Tools for Teaching Computational Thinking in P-12 Education* (pp. 234–284). IGI Global. doi:10.4018/978-1-7998-4576-8

Chin, K. Y., Hong, Z. W., & Chen, Y. L. (2014). Impact of using an educational robot-based learning system on students' motivation in elementary education. *IEEE Transactions on Learning Technologies, 7*(4), 333–345. doi:10.1109/TLT.2014.2346756

Daniela, L., & Lytras, M. D. (2018). Educational Robotics for Inclusive Education. *Technology, Knowledge and Learning*. doi:10.100710758-018-9397-5

Elliott, J. (1991). *Action Research for educational change* (1st ed.). Philadelphia: Open University Press; Retrieved from https://books.google.gr/ books?hl= el&lr= &id= faDnAAAAQBAJ&oi= fnd&pg= PP1&dq= %22Action+ research+for+ educational+change %22+Elliot+ J&ots=r2MYO 4taR9&sig= ogxcUXN1AT 257byPeGnrF 7iexQY& redir_esc= y#v=onepage&q= %22Actionresearch foreducationalchange %22ElliotJ&f=f

Elza, D. (2020a). *500 Lines or Less Blockcode A visual programming toolkit*. Retrieved April 10, 2020, from http://www.aosabook.org/en/500L/blockcode-a-visual-programming-toolkit.html

Elza, D. (2020b). *GitHub - dethe_bloc A fork of my blocklib code from Architecture of Open Source Applications 500 Lines or Less*. Retrieved May 15, 2020, from https://github.com/dethe/bloc/

Gibbs, C., Kooyman, B., Marks, K., & Burns, J. (2015). Mapping the Roadmap: Using Action Research to Develop an Online Referencing Tool. *Journal of Academic Librarianship, 41*(4), 422–428. doi:10.1016/j.acalib.2015.05.004

Gonzalez, H. B., & Kuenzi, J. J. (2012). Science, technology, engineering, and mathematics (STEM): A Primer. *Congressional Research Service*, 1–15. Retrieved from https://www.ccc.edu/departments/Documents/STEM_labor.pdf

Ioannou, M., & Bratitsis, T. (2016). Utilizing Sphero for a speed related STEM activity in Kindergarten. *Hellenic Conference on Innovating STEM Education.*

Kalogiannakis, M., & Papadakis, S. (2019a). Evaluating a course for teaching introductory programming with Scratch to pre-service kindergarten teachers. *International Journal of Technology Enhanced Learning*, *11*(3), 231. doi:10.1504/ijtel.2019.10020447

Kalogiannakis, M., & Papadakis, S. (2019b). Evaluating pre-service kindergarten teachers' intention to adopt and use tablets into teaching practice for natural sciences. *International Journal of Mobile Learning and Organisation*, *13*(1), 113–127. doi:10.1504/IJMLO.2019.096479

Kalogiannakis, M., Papadakis, S., & Dorouka, P. (2020). Tablets and apps for promoting robotics, mathematics, STEM education and literacy in early childhood education. *International Journal of Mobile Learning and Organisation*, *14*(2), 255. doi:10.1504/ijmlo.2020.10026334

Kemmis, S., Nixon, R., & McTaggart, R. (2014). *The Action Research Planner. Doing Critical Participatory Action Research.* Singapore: Springer Science+Business Media. doi:10.1007/978-981-4560-67-2

Kirakowski, J., & Cierlik, B. (1998). Measuring the usability of web sites. In *Human Factors and Ergonomics Society 42nd annual meeting* (pp. 424–428). HFES. Retrieved from https://www.tib.eu/en/search/id/TIBKAT%3A253751101/Proceedings-of-the-Human-Factors-and-Ergonomics/

Kirakowski, J., & Cierlik, B. (2016). *Web Site Analysis and Measurement Inventory.* Retrieved March 4, 2020, from http://www.wammi.com/samples/index.html

Koikas, D., Aggelis, P., & Chatzopoulos, A. (2015). Rebuilding a CNC Milling Machine. In *International Conference eRA - 10* (pp. 52–58). Pireaus. Retrieved from era.teipir.gr

Kucuk, S., & Sisman, B. (2017). Behavioral patterns of elementary students and teachers in one-to-one robotics instruction. *Computers & Education*, *111*, 31–43. doi:10.1016/j.compedu.2017.04.002

Li, Y. L. (2008). Teachers in action research: Assumptions and potentials. *Educational Action Research*, *16*(2), 251–260. doi:10.1080/09650790802011908

Louros, A., Papoutsidakis, M., Chatzopoulos, A., & Drosos, C. (2018). Design of an Innovative Flight Controller for Quadcopter Robust Handling. *Journal of Multidisciplinary Engineering Science and Technology*, *5*(10), 8968–8972.

Manesi, S., & Betsi, S. (2013). Collaborative action research projects: The role of communities of practice and mentoring in enhancing teachers' continuing professional development. *Action Researcher in Education*, *4*(4), 109–121.

Marr, B. (2016). Why Everyone Must Get Ready For The 4th Industrial Revolution. *Forbes*, 4–6. https://www.forbes.com/sites/bernardmarr/2016/04/05/why-everyone-must-get-ready-for-4th-industrial-revolution/print/

Marr, B. (2018). What is Industry 4.0? Here's A Super Easy Explanation For Anyone. *Forbes*, 4–7. https://www.forbes.com/sites/bernardmarr/2018/09/02/what-is-industry-4-0-heres-a-super-easy-explanation-for-anyone/#5b3ba6539788

Mavrovounioti, V., Chatzopoulos, A., Papoutsidakis, M., & Piromalis, D. (2018). Implementation of an 2-wheel Educational Platform for STEM Applications. *Journal of Multidisciplinary Engineering Science and Technology*, *5*(10), 8944–8948.

Melkonian, S., Chatzopoulos, A., Papoutsidakis, M., & Piromalis, D. (2018). Remote Control via Android for a Small Vehicle ' s 2-Wheels Balancing. *Journal of Multidisciplinary Engineering Science and Technology*, *5*(10), 8964–8967.

Menon, D., Bp, S., Romero, M., & Viéville, T. (2019). *Going beyond digital literacy to develop computational thinking in K-12 education. In Smart Pedagogy of Digital Learning. Taylor&Francis*. Routledge.

Miller, D. P., & Nourbakhsh, I. (2016). Robotics for Education. Springer Handbook of Robotics, 2115–2134. doi:10.1007/978-3-319-32552-1_79

Mondada, F., Bonani, M., Raemy, X., Pugh, J., Cianci, C., & Klaptocz, A. … Martinoli, A. (2006). The e-puck, a Robot Designed for Education in Engineering. *9th Conference on Autonomous Robot Systems and Competitions, 1*(1), 59–65.

Morrison, J., & Bartlett, R. V. (2009). *STEM as a Curriculum*. Retrieved from papers3://publication/uuid/48C36DF6-30CA-42ED-876D-0D4214A1F890

Municipality, A. V. (2019). *Educational Robotics Event for Elementary-High School-High School Students*. Retrieved January 2, 2020, from https://agiavarvara.gr/event/ekdilosi-ekpaideytikis-rompotikis-gia-mathites-dimotikoy-gymnasioy-lykeioy/

National Academies of Sciences, Engineering, and Mathematics. (2018). English Learners in STEM Subjects: Transforming Classrooms, Schools, and Lives (2018). Washington, DC: National Academy of Sciences. doi:10.17226/25182

Papadakis, S. (2020). Evaluating a Teaching Intervention for Teaching STEM and Programming Concepts Through the Creation of a Weather-Forecast App for Smart Mobile Devices. In M. Kalogiannakis & S. J. Papadakis (Eds.), *Handbook of Research on Tools for Teaching Computational Thinking in P-12 Education* (pp. 31–53). IGI Global. doi:10.4018/978-1-7998-4576-8.ch002

Papadakis, S., & Kalogiannakis, M. (2020). Exploring Preservice Teachers ' Attitudes About the Usage of Educational Robotics in Preschool Education. In M. Kalogiannakis & S. J. Papadakis (Eds.), *Handbook of Research on Tools for Teaching Computational Thinking in P-12 Education* (pp. 335–351). IGI Global. doi:10.4018/978-1-7998-4576-8.ch013

Papoutsidakis, M., Chatzopoulos, A., Drosos, C., & Kalovrektis, K. (2018). An Arduino Family Controller and its Interactions via an Intelligent Interface. *International Journal of Computers and Applications*, *179*(30), 5–8.

Papoutsidakis, M., Chatzopoulos, A., & Piromalis, D. (2019). Distance Control of Water Temperature via Android Devices. *Journal of Multidisciplinary Engineering Science and Technology*, *6*(12), 11240–11244.

Psycharis, S. (2018). STEAM in educations: A literature review on the role of Computational Thinking, Engineering Epistemology and Computational Science. *Computational STEAM Pedagogy*, *4*(2), 51–72. doi:10.5281/zenodo.1214565

Ronsivalle, G. B., Boldi, A., Gusella, V., Inama, C., & Carta, S. (2018). How to Implement Educational Robotics' Programs in Italian Schools: A Brief Guideline According to an Instructional Design Point of View. *Technology, Knowledge and Learning*. doi:10.100710758-018-9389-5

Santos, I. M., Ali, N., & Hill, A. (2016). Students as Co-designers of a Virtual Learning Commons: Results of a Collaborative Action Research Study. *Journal of Academic Librarianship*, *42*(1), 8–14. doi:10.1016/j.acalib.2015.09.006

Smith, M. K. (2007). *Action research*. Retrieved June 2, 2018, from http://infed.org/mobi/action-research/

Texley, J., & Ruud, R. M. (2018). *Teaching STEM Literacy A Constructivist Approach for Ages 3 to 8*. Redleaf Press.

Tsupros, N., Kohler, R., & Hallinen, J. (2009). *STEM Education in Southwestern Pennsylvania the missing components*. Retrieved from https://www.cmu.edu/gelfand/documents/stem-survey-report-cmu-iu1.pdf

Vamvakopoulos, P. (2019). *Event for Educational Robotics, with great interest*. Retrieved January 2, 2020, from http://proodeutiki.gr/?p=85159

Villanueva, J. (2016). Flipped inclusion classroom : An action research. *21st Annual Technology, Colleges and Community Worldwide Online Conference*, 1–16. Retrieved from https://scholarspace.manoa.hawaii.edu/bitstream/10125/40822/1/Flipped_Inclusion_Classroom_Action_Research_Jeanette_Villanueva.pdf

Vordos, G., Chatzopoulos, A., Papoutsidakis, M., & Piromalis, D. (2018). Balance Control of a Small Scale Sphere with an Innovative Android Application. *Journal of Multidisciplinary Engineering Science and Technology*, *5*(10), 8957–8963.

Wagner, B., Hohmann, P., Gerecke, U., & Brenneke, C. (2004). Technical Framework for Robot Platforms in Education. In *International Conference on Engineering Education and Research "Progress Through Partnership"* (pp. 699–703). Academic Press.

Xatzopoulos, A., Papoutsidakis, M., & Chamilothoris, G. (2013). Mobile Robotic Platforms as Educational Tools in Mechatronics Engineering. In *International Scientific Conference eRA – 8* (pp. 41–51). Pireaus. Retrieved from era.teipir.gr

Zygouris, N. C., Striftou, A., Dadaliaris, A. N., Stamoulis, G. I., Xenakis, A. C., & Vavougios, D. (2017). The use of LEGO mindstorms in elementary schools. *IEEE Global Engineering Education Conference, EDUCON*, 514–516. 10.1109/EDUCON.2017.7942895

ADDITIONAL READING

Dorouka, P., Papadakis, St., & Kalogiannakis, M. (2020). Tablets & apps for promoting Robotics, Mathematics, STEM Education and Literacy in Early Childhood Education. *International Journal of Mobile Learning and Organisation*, *14*(2), 255–274. doi:10.1504/IJMLO.2020.106179

Kalogiannakis, M., & Papadakis, S. (2017). Pre-service kindergarten teachers acceptance of "ScratchJr" as a tool for learning and teaching computational thinking and Science education. In *proceedings of the 12th Conference of the European Science Education Research Association (ESERA), 'Research, practice and collaboration in science education' (pp. 21-25)*. Dublin City University and the University of Limerick, Dublin, Ireland.

Kalogiannakis, M., & Papadakis, St. (2018). A proposal for Teaching ScratchJr Programming Environment in Preservice Kindergarten Teachers. In *Finlayson, O., McLoughlin, E., Erduran, S., & Childs, P. (Eds.), Electronic Proceedings of the ESERA 2017 Conference. Research, Practice and Collaboration in Science Education, Part 15/Strand 15 (co-ed. Bodil Sundberg & Maria Kallery, Early Years Science Education)*, (pp. 2095-2105). Dublin, Ireland: Dublin City University. ISBN 978-1-873769-84-3

Kalogiannakis, M., & Papadakis, S. (2019). Pre-service kindergarten teacher's acceptance of "ScratchJr" as a tool for learning and teaching computational thinking and Science education. [JES]. *The Journal of Emergent Science, 15*, 31–34.

Kalogiannakis, M., & Papadakis, S. (2020). The Use of Developmentally Mobile Applications for Preparing Pre-Service Teachers to Promote STEM Activities in Preschool Classrooms. In S. Papadakis & M. Kalogiannakis (Eds.), *Mobile Learning Applications in Early Childhood Education* (pp. 82–100). IGI Global., doi:10.4018/978-1-7998-1486-3.ch005

Kanaki, K., Kalogiannakis, M., & Stamovlasis, D. (2020). Assessing Algorithmic Thinking Skills in Early Childhood Education: Evaluation in Physical and Natural Science Courses. In M. Kalogiannakis & S. Papadakis (Eds.), *Handbook of Research on Tools for Teaching Computational Thinking in P-12 Education* (pp. 103–138). IGI Global., doi:10.4018/978-1-7998-4576-8.ch005

Papadakis, S. (2020). Apps to Promote Computational Thinking Concepts and Coding Skills in Children of Preschool and Pre-Primary School Age. In S. Papadakis & M. Kalogiannakis (Eds.), *Mobile Learning Applications in Early Childhood Education* (pp. 101–121). IGI Global., doi:10.4018/978-1-7998-1486-3.ch006

Papadakis, S., & Kalogiannakis, M. (2017). Using Gamification for Supporting an Introductory Programming Course. The Case of ClassCraft in a Secondary Education Classroom. In *Interactivity, Game Creation, Design, Learning, and Innovation* (pp. 366–375). Springer.

Papadakis, St., & Kalogiannakis, M. (2019). Evaluating a course for teaching introductory programming with Scratch to pre-service kindergarten teachers. *Int. J. Technology Enhanced Learning, 11*(3), 231–246. doi:10.1504/IJTEL.2019.100478

Papadakis, St., & Kalogiannakis, M. (2019). Evaluating a Course for Teaching Advanced Programming Concepts with Scratch to Preservice Kindergarten Teachers: A Case Study in Greece. In D. Farland-Smith (Ed.), *Early Childhood Education* (pp. 1–19). IntechOpen Limited., https://www.intechopen.com/online-first/evaluating-a-course-for-teaching-advanced-programming-concepts-with-scratch-to-preservice-kindergart/ doi:10.5772/intechopen.81714

Papadakis, S., & Kalogiannakis, M. (2020). A Research Synthesis of the Real Value of Self-Proclaimed Mobile Educational Applications for Young Children. In S. Papadakis & M. Kalogiannakis (Eds.), *Mobile Learning Applications in Early Childhood Education* (pp. 1–19). IGI Global., doi:10.4018/978-1-7998-1486-3.ch001

KEY TERMS AND DEFINITIONS

Blockcode: Is a visual programming tookit developed by Dethe Elza. It is a tool for block-based programming (like Lego WeDo, Blockly, AppInventor, Tynker), web-native open-source, written in HTML, CSS, and JavaScript, in order to work in most browsers and platforms.

Educational Robotic Platform: Used in educational robotics, is a robot technology platform of hardware, software accompanied by educational material.

Educational Robotics: Is a broad term that refers to a collection of educational programs, resources and activities, technology (robotic) platforms, and learning pedagogical theories.

ESP: Is a family of low cost and power system on chip microcontrollers based on a (single-core or dual-core variation) Tensilica Xtensa LX6 microprocessor, with integrated -depending on the model- Wi-Fi, dual-mode Bluetooth, built-in antenna switches, power-management modules, low-noise receive amplifier, power amplifier, RF balun, filters developed by Espressif Systems.

Microcontroller: MCU (MicroController Unit) or microcontroller is a small computer on a single integrated circuit (IC or chip), usually used in embedded systems for a dedicated application rather than a general-purpose application.

STEAM: An acronym (Science, Technology, Engineering, Arts, and Mathematics) that used to refers to teaching and learning in the fields of science, technology, engineering, arts, and mathematics. However, there are other less know variations of "A" definitions.

STEM: An acronym (Science, Technology, Engineering, and Mathematics) that used to refers to teaching and learning in the fields of science, technology, engineering, and mathematics.

VPL: An acronym for Visual Programming Language is a programming language for creating programs by manipulating graphic elements rather than use text code. In VPL visual expression, graphic symbols and spatial arrangements are used as elements of syntax.

This research was previously published in the Handbook of Research on Using Educational Robotics to Facilitate Student Learning; pages 441-465, copyright year 2021 by Information Science Reference (an imprint of IGI Global).

APPENDIX

Figure 12. Indicative answers to the Q28 question of how participants imagine the ideal robot

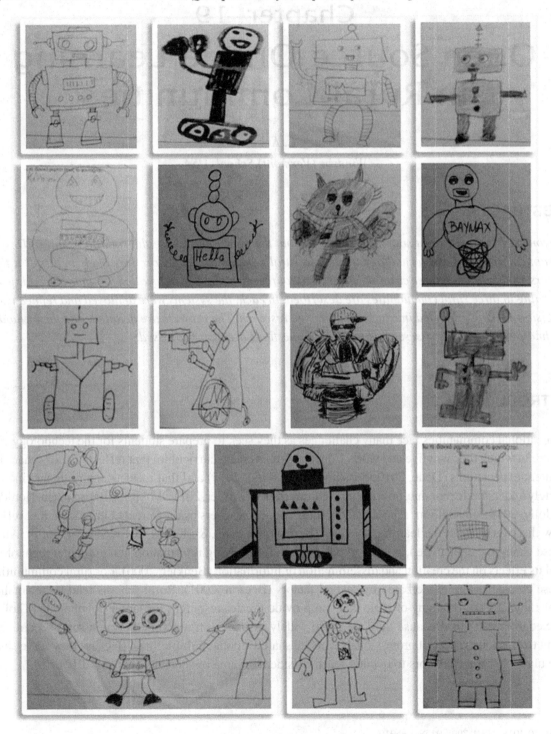

Chapter 19
Open Source Online Learning in Rural Communities

Gary L. Ackerman
Windsor (Vermont) School, USA

ABSTRACT

Anyone is free to use open source software without the need to purchase the right to install it. Despite its appeal to school and technology leaders in rural communities, they are less likely to install it than others. In this chapter, three cases in which open source technology was installed to support teaching and learning in three rural communities are described. In each, the systems were deployed and refined using decision-making grounded in educational design research. The projects are detailed, and the method of technology planning is assessed. Unanswered questions are also addressed.

INTRODUCTION

Educational communities face many challenges as they seek to prepare students for the technology-rich future in which they will live and work. Educators must create curriculum that reflects rapidly changing content expectations (Dede, 2010; Susskind & Susskind, 2015) and that reflects emerging and incompletely understood economic, political, and cultural norms (Miller, 2011; Wokurka, Banschbach, Houlder, & Jolly, 2017). In addition, school leaders must support teachers as they create classrooms that reflect new discoveries from the learning sciences (Benassi, Overson, & Hakala, 2014; Sawyer, 2008). All of these changes can be traced, at least in part, to rapidly evolving information and computer technology and its effects on the creation and dissemination of information (Benkler, 2006). For rural communities, these challenges are exacerbated by several factors (Beeson, 2001). Rural schools tend to be smaller, thus they lack the economy of scale that can provide greater resources for larger populations (Tholkes & Sederberg, 1990). Because they are more widely dispersed, travel time between rural schools can limit the responsiveness of professionals who are shared among multiple sites. Because they serve small populations, rural educators frequently teach outside their area of specialty (Miller, 2012).

DOI: 10.4018/978-1-7998-9158-1.ch019

Advocates suggest the technology used to deliver online learning can be adapted to address many problems faced by educators and school leaders. For example, school leaders can use online learning to expand opportunities for students (Dabrowski & Lodge, 2017), facilitate teachers' professional learning (Baran & Correia, 2014), and support authentic learning and assessment (Herrington, Reeves, & Oliver, 2006). Platforms for online learning are available from both proprietary publishers and from open source communities; open source platforms can be obtained and installed at no cost to the user. Ostensibly, open source tools will have wide appeal to school and technology leaders in rural communities because of the minimal costs. Despite this, there is evidence rural schools are less likely than suburban and urban schools to use open source tools to manage information and to promote learning (Kimmons, 2015). In this chapter, the author describes three projects in which open source distance learning technologies were applied to the professional needs of educators working in rural communities in the northeast United States; the planning and decision-making that focused the projects were grounded in educational design research (McKenny & Reeves, 2012).

Open Source Technology

A growing community produces open source software and open educational resources (OER) communities have grown and their products have begun to compete with and complement commercial products. They are also increasingly used in both K-12 and higher education. Baker (2017) suggested open resources are defined by dimensions of transparency and freedom, and these characteristics can be traced through the information products created by educators for many generations. Transparency is that characteristic of open resources that allows users to access and modify the original works; freedom is that characteristic that allows use of the products without the need to purchase or license the work. More importantly, however, freedom entails the rights to create and distribute derivative works.

The software used in these projects is published and licensed under the GNU General Public License (Free Software Foundation, 2016); the Apache License, Version 2.0 (Apache Software Foundation, 2017); or the Creative Commons Attribution-ShareAlike 3.0 Unported License (Creative Commons, n.d.). All of these licenses fit Baker's (2017) dimensions of transparency and freedom. In the cases described in this chapter, school and technology leaders obtained copies of open software, installed it per the conditions of the license, and customized it using the options available in the software. In no case did the author or any other individuals involved with the projects vary the source code of the software or create derived works.

Educational Design Research

This chapter describes both the software used to support virtual teaching and learning as well as the planning decisions and processes that led to changes in the ways the technology was configured and used. In these cases, the school and technology leaders followed a multi-step process grounded in educational design research (McKenny & Reeves, 2012) Educational design research is a variety of user-based research (Stokes, 1987) in which researcher-practitioners seek to simultaneously understand phenomena and to design interventions that meet human needs. McKenny and Reeves (2014) described educational design research as "the iterative development of solutions… to practical and complex educational problems" which leads to "new knowledge that can inform the work of others" (p. 133). The iterative processes are undertaken for three distinct phases (see Figure 1), and each phase finds researcher-practitioners

Figure 1. Phases of educational design research
Adapted from McKenny & Reeves (2012).

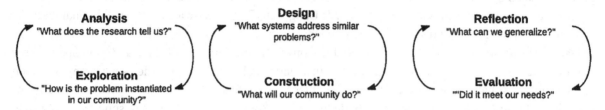

consuming (or creating) literature for the wider community and also reconciling the literature with the local circumstances.

Analysis/ exploration comprises both literature review and deconstructing local situation to clarify the problem and identify relevant factors that are unique to local the instantiation; this work leads to deeper understanding of the problem. The product that emerges from this phase is a description of the problem and the nature of the anticipated solution. Design/ construction includes the development of interventions; existing technology and practices become the basis for the initial designs and further iterations improve them according to the local circumstances. Evaluation/ reflection finds researcher-practitioners both determining the degree to which the intervention met local needs and articulating new knowledge that can be applied to other problems and that can be used by other researcher-practitioners.

PURPOSES

Qualitative data are provided for two purposes. The first is to illustrate the iterative analysis/ exploration and design/ construction phases of educational design research (McKenny & Reeves, 2012) and to describe how the process influenced planning decisions and outcomes. The second is to articulate several generalizations about the practice of using open source online learning platforms in rural schools that appear to be supported by this data.

METHODS

As part of the author's duties as either an internal or external consultant, he facilitated projects to use open source online learning technologies in six schools between 2013 and 2015; planning and decision making followed the generic model of educational design research (McKenny & Reeves, 2012). During analysis/ exploration, the author engaged school leaders in a two-part semi-structured interview (Drever, 2006) held in a single session; the interview was focused by the prompts, "tell me about the situation you seek to improve" and "tell me what you want students and teachers to experience." The author summarized these into a problem statement and a statement of anticipated outcomes; these were revised with the leader or leaders until they were satisfied it accurately summarized the situation. These statements gave direction to the groups convened to begin design/ construction of interventions to solve the problem.

Once the leader deemed the problem was sufficiently understood and the expected outcomes accurately defined; other professionals (including licensed and non-licensed teachers and educational technology professionals) engaged with the author to develop an initial intervention. From the beginning, it was made clear to those involved with design/ construction that the work would be iterative so the interventions would be redesigned and reconstructed based on observations made and feedback gathered during the process. Participants understood also they would keep journals that would be used as data to research the projects.

The primary role of the author in the design/ construction phase was investigating open source solutions that appeared to solve the identified problem and that were compatible with extant information technology systems. In some cases, the author installed and configured the initial open source solution, then provided training while it was first deployed. The author also provided technical advice and support for expanding the open source solutions and refining configurations as the iterative phases of design/ construction proceeded.

In 2016, the author contacted the schools in which these interventions had been deployed. In three cases, the leaders who initiated the projects were still employed and the project was still active. In those three cases, transcripts and summaries of the original exploration/ analysis interviews with leaders, agendas and minutes from planning meetings, and journals kept by participants during the design/ construction phase were reviewed to describe the work. These descriptions were composed by reviewing minutes that recorded meetings to identify decisions that were made, then analyzing participants' research journals and other documents to describe the situations that led to the decisions. Finally, the leaders reviewed the descriptions and marked any sections they identified as potentially inaccurate; those were rewritten after the leader and the author reviewed and agreed on the meaning of the original documents.

The leaders who initiated the three cases described in this chapter were also interviewed in 2016. These two-part interviews were conducted via video conference; each was scheduled for thirty minutes and the two sessions separated by about one week. The first session was focused on the degree to which the project had solved the original problem and the second focused on generalizations about the process and project. In addition, a school leader who initiated a fourth project, which had been abandoned, was interviewed. Transcripts of these interviews were analyzed using the constant comparative method (Glaser, 1965); the author and another researcher who was enrolled in a graduate level education research course at the time coded the transcripts. The themes that were common to both reviewers are elucidated in the findings.

THE PROJECTS

The three projects described in this chapter were undertaken by school leaders and professionals working in public schools located in rural areas of New England. The schools are all members of larger organizations that provide a similar range of clerical and administrative support, including technology support, to member schools. In this chapter these organizations will be called "alliances," and schools in the same organization will be "allied" schools. One case occurred in a single school with no alliance to other schools in the study; one case included several allied schools, and the third case comprises data from two different communities of allied schools that deployed similar solutions and that found professionals from non-allied schools collaborating.

Replacing and Expanding a Learning Management System

Northern Middle and High School enrolls approximately 300 students in grades seven through 12. Most students who attend Northern attend one of two allied elementary schools. Three years prior to the initiation of this project, Northern had begun a one-to-one initiative, so it was undertaken in the first year that each student in the high school grades (nine through 12) had access to a laptop computer.

Coincident with the beginning the one-to-one initiative, teachers started using a proprietary learning management system (LMS). The version of the LMS used by the school was free to use, but had limited functions; it was not transparent, thus is was not open source (Baker, 2017). The principal articulated the coincident goals of the LMS and one-to-one initiatives, "with the one-to-one computers, teachers will use [the LMS] post materials so we can replace textbooks. They can lead discussions and share files for creative purposes, and move towards online materials and collaboration." He recognized, however, this had not been realized. The LMS had been adopted by about half of the faculty, but it served primarily as a digital drop box for and a file repository. The principal recorded a conversation during which "students said their online classroom was 'like a big filing cabinet for handouts' and they usually printed files from the site or they uploaded files the teacher printed out to grade." The principal further pointed to questions posed when broken copier which also served as a scanner broke; teachers asked, "How are we supposed to get out handouts online if we can't scan them?" For the principal, the LMS should, "be a space where students and teachers interact and collaborate, but this is not happening." It was clear the LMS was being used, but not in the intended manner.

It was not clear from the documents available if the limited use of the LMS by teachers was the result of the limited functionality of the version they were using or if the functions were available, but unused. The decision to replace the free version of the propriety LMS was motivated the discovery that an online classroom had become corrupted and work was lost. Because they were using the free version of the LMS, there was neither a backup copy of the course nor was the school entitled to technology support from the provider. After that incident the principal reported, "we need a more professional system so this does not happen again." In replacing the LMS, the principal insisted "it be flexible so teachers can do more things with students online, plus they need to be able to share assessment rubrics with others, and we need backups to prevent loss of work." It was clear the cost of subscribing to the proprietary LMS at the level necessary for support and flexibility was beyond the budget, so the principal accepted the recommendation that and open source solution be deployed.

A design/ construction committee comprising two teachers who had been using the proprietary LMS, the technology coordinator for the allied schools, and the author was convened to recommend a replacement LMS. At the first meeting, the technology coordinator resigned from the group reasoning, "I have no time, budget, or server resources to dedicate to this project, and other projects need my attention this year." He did recommend to the group, "Get a web hosting service that meets the system requirements, install the LMS you want, and have teachers manage it all." The reduced committee advised the principal to purchase space on a virtual private server (VPS) with storage, bandwidth, and processing that exceeded the estimated need and that fell within the budget identified by the principal. The committee also

reviewed the features of several open source learning management systems. The demonstration sites all appeared to provide the features we want and could be installed on the VPS service we recommend. The committee suggests we install Moodle, because the three people on the committee all have experience using it.

Within one week, the principal had secured space on a virtual private server, and the author had installed Moodle (Version 2.7) (Moodle, 2014), an open source learning management system that is widely used in both K-12 and higher education, and configured the database. As an initial test, committee members confirmed: a) the Moodle site was available from the school's network, b) it was available off-campus, c) teachers could create courses, d) several users could administer the site. Once the initial test was successful, the two teachers on the design/ construction committee began using Moodle with their students. Within days of learning it was available, three teachers (who were still using the proprietary LMS) requested access to Moodle. This was granted, so the test installation and the committee participating in its development quickly expanded.

The design/ construction committee now comprised five teachers, and they recorded observations of Moodle before reconvening to "discuss changes to Moodle before extending the pilot project any further." The first recommendations focused on navigation and appearance. The teachers reported that students complained about the appearance of the site and found it "hard to use," but those complaints dissipated as students became familiar with the interface. One teacher observed, "I can't see the menus without scrolling and I can't see the names of students who posted in the discussions" The committee was able to resolve the navigation problems by changing the theme which controlled the appearance of the site (including the behaviors of menus and discussion boards).

The committee also recognized Moodle allowed more sophisticated grading than the replaced propriety LMS. While teachers wanted to use those features, they felt unprepared, so they shared a word processing document on which they recorded the steps to filter submissions, display a single individual's assignments, update grades for multiple students at once, and otherwise manage grades. One teacher also described a feature she had used at another school that allowed teachers to add comments to portable document format (PDF) files that students had uploaded. The plugin that added the PDF mark-up functionality was located and the author installed and configured it.

Less than one month after the initial test of Moodle, the first redesign/ reconstruction iteration was complete. By deploying a different theme, the committee improved navigation of Moodle for all users within minutes by editing the settings that were provided by the producers. Using advanced grading features was developed over several days and included both the deployment of a new plugin (a technology solution) and effort by teachers to share new learning (a non-technology solution).

About four months into the project, it had expanded to a total of eight teachers and over 100 students who were enrolled in more than 20 sections. It was nearing the end of the school year, so the principal asked for recommended next steps. The teachers described the minor changes that had been made to the installation of Moodle during the first iteration. When asked directly about the original goals of using more advanced features of the LMS, the teachers shared examples of threaded discussions, embedded media, and examples of PDF assignments with comments; none of which had been used on the replaced LMS. Convinced it was used for more types of activities than the previous LMS, the principal charged the committee with "rolling this out so the whole school can use Moodle when we return to school at the end of summer."

Meeting minutes indicated the committee members were satisfied the functionality of Moodle met the previous uses of the LMS (a drop box and a collection of shared files) and advanced features were sufficiently understood and supportable that the Moodle could be "promoted to teachers as the 'new and improved' online platform." The committee noted, however, "students have too many usernames and passwords—the network, their email, the student information system, and now Moodle", so it recommended, "a single sign-on is necessary so students do not have to remember another username and password, and teachers don't have to know how to reset them." It further recommended, "allowing self-enrolling in Moodle courses, so teachers don't have to 'do all of that clicking' to get students in their courses."

Both of those recommendations were incorporated into the next design/ construction iteration. Another plugin was added to Moodle to allow users to log on using their Google Applications for Education accounts, which were already used for other purposes by both teachers and students. To address security concerns, only accounts controlled by Northern Middle and High School were allowed to be used to log on to Northern's installation of Moodle. The configuration of Moodle was also changed to allow authenticated users to self-enroll in courses; when teachers returned for the start of school, they were given directions on how to utilize this feature.

At the same time the LMS replacement was underway, the faculty was undertaking a separate initiative to add authentic learning (Herrington, Oliver, & Reeves, 2013) into the curriculum. Associated with that initiative was the decision to replace the existing electronic portfolio platform. A group of faculty who were working on the authentic learning initiative met with the Moodle committee. The first meeting of this combined committee found the team returning to the explore/ analyze phase of educational design research. The combined committee articulated the goal of "designing a single online space where students' work could flow easily between the online classroom and the online portfolio."

During the initial design/ construction iteration, the team identified Mahara (Mahara, n.d.) as an open source portfolio platform that that could be installed on the same virtual private server use to host Moodle. Once the system was installed and configured, the combined committee spent time "sandboxing, so the teachers can determine it Mahara fits the assessment and data collection needs of the authentic learning initiative." After they concluded Mahara provided the necessary portfolio functions, the combined committee directed the author to configure Mahara so that students and teachers could use their Moodle accounts, which were actually users' GAFE accounts, to authenticate into Mahara. This configuration also allowed for documents and portfolios to be shared between the two platforms.

Northern Middle and High School's full development of the Moodle/ Mahara system began with an initial decision to replace the proprietary LMS, this decision was made to improve the performance of the technology and to provide more flexible teaching and learning. Several iterations of design/ construction based on users' feedback made the LMS easier to use and expanded its functionality while easing management. Further design/ construction iterations resulted in the LMS and the electronic portfolio system being integrated so that they appeared to be a single system. In each step, the combined Moodle/ Mahara complex more closely reflected the teaching and learning goals the principal had originally articulated.

Algebra 1 at a Distance

Dan is the principal at Crossroads Elementary School which enrolls just over 100 students in grades K-8. More than half of the students who attend the school live in the village that extends about one mile in each direction from the intersection where the school is situated. Most of the other students live on the farms that are scattered throughout the town. He recognized, "the community takes great pride in nurturing young people and providing excellent opportunities, but the tightening budget and some personnel changes have made continuing that tradition very challenging."

One particular problem was providing Algebra 1 for the students who were ready to take that course for high school credit. Dan explained the process recently adopted by the allied high school, "students can take Algebra 1 in their home school, but they take the same final exam as the high school students. If they pass, they get credit, if not they take it again." In the letter that explained the new policy, the principal of the allied high school and the chairperson of the mathematics department had explained, "we need more control over who enrolls in advanced mathematics courses."

Dan further described the situation in which he found his faculty, "We have one science and math teacher for our middle school. Her schedule was full and we had three kids who were ready for Algebra, but we had no teacher." When Dan learned an allied K-8 schools had hired a new part-time math teacher who was very experienced, he contacted the principal and asked how his students might be able to access that teacher. With the cooperation of the curriculum coordinator who was shared among the allied K-8 schools and the high school, Dan arranged for the schools to teach eighth grade math at a time that coincided with the Algebra 1 class taught by the new math instructor. At Crossroads Elementary, the instructional problem was summarized as, "Providing Crossroads students access to a highly qualified Algebra teacher who teaches at a location other than our school," and the "instruction is to be synchronous."

The first solution to having remote students participate in the Algebra 1 course was to set up a web camera in the classroom where the teacher was and to use a free, but proprietary, video chat tool to connect the teacher with students at Crossroads and the other schools. It was clear during the first session, however, it was not an adequate solution. Dan observed the first session and noted, "all of the students agree they cannot see the board well enough and there is little chance for them to ask questions. Plus, the teacher had his back to the students much of the time." The technology integration specialist employed by the allied K-8 schools observed the session from a different remote site and confirmed students at that site had the same experience. Dan noted, "this solution will not work for our students. We need another way for kids to work with [the Algebra teacher]." The initial design/ construction iteration in this case was deemed a failure; so it was immediately abandoned.

Dan convened a group (the composition of which is unclear) to reopen the analysis/ understanding of the problem of, especially to reexamine the need for Algebra to be taught via synchronous meetings. That group asked the author and the technology integration specialist to "test other technology systems that will resolve the connections between the teacher and the remote sites, specifically: a) unclear transmission of visuals, b) unclear transmission of spoken information, and c) lack of two-way communication between the remote sites to the location of the teacher." It was proposed that sites be connected through a video conferencing tool rather than simply a camera, and the author and the technology integration specialist suggested, "screen sharing, an open audio channel between the sites, and reliable chat between the sites will improve interaction."

The next iteration of the design/ construction of the video conferencing link connecting the K-8 schools found a group of people at each location for a "test activity in which we will try to replicate an Algebra lesson, but with a focus on refining the system rather than learning math." At each site, one of the students taking the Algebra course, along with the school's principal, connected to a video conference that was initiated by the Algebra teacher from his school. The technology integration specialist was at the site with the teacher and the author was at Crossroads. The connection was established using a free to use version of a proprietary video conferencing platform. Further, the remote Algebra teacher had constructed a system whereby a digital camera pointed at the whiteboard where he wrote.

Upon completion of the trial, Dan and the student at his school concurred, "this is a much better system. We could see and hear what was said and written and we could ask questions by both chat and speaking." The individuals who participated at all of the sites further concurred that several practices needed to become standard for the course, including "a) sites need to mute their microphones unless they are speaking, b) the teacher needs to watch for chat requests, and c) there needs to be a seamless method for switching between the white board camera and the camera on the computer." While the video conferencing platform was deemed an improvement over the web camera, the arrangement of the digital camera and whiteboard was determined to need further improvement before the system was used for teaching and the limits placed on users of the freemium software were deemed to pose a significant obstacle to its effective use. Prior to using the system to teach Algebra again, the author and the technology integration specialist along with the teacher completed a second design/ construction phase in which two changes were implemented.

First, the team (in collaboration with the technology coordinator employed by the allied school) deployed Jitsi (n.d.), an open source video conferencing platform. Tests of this platform determined it appeared to resolve the video, audio, and interaction problems that prompted the decision to abandon the original web camera solution. Second, the video transmission of the visuals drawn on the whiteboard were improved by devising a method whereby a camera was poised over a whiteboard on a table where the teacher wrote and drew. The method of viewing the whiteboard through the video conference was even adopted by the students in the room where the teacher taught, so they would connect to the same video conference and watch the same whiteboard presentations as the students at the remote sites. The teacher also reported the students in the classroom with him began using the same chat channels to interact as the remote students, as well.

Unlike the case of Northern Middle and High School, in which the feedback that led to design/ construction decisions were largely informed by students and teachers who were actively using the systems for their work and which took place over weeks, Crossroads and its allied schools made decisions based on small groups of users who tested the system prior to its being deployed again. Dan noted, "the web camera thing was terrible, we needed to fix all of it before we tried it again." In the notes he kept as the system was used in the following months, Dan further noted, "as the teacher got better at using it, the lessons seemed to flow much better and students and got better at asking questions using the chat feature."

Two unpredicted outcomes arose from this project. First, the chairperson of mathematics department at the allied high school attended some distance Algebra classes by connecting to the video conference, so it had more oversight by the high school mathematics department than had been reasonable previously. She noted, "We did not want to be intrusive, but we wanted to be sure student were getting what they needed because we were essentially giving credit for what happened in those schools. It worked well, and we even had some of our students participate in some of the sessions." Second, the teacher began recording parts of the sessions and those became a resource for several purposes including a collection of worked examples and posted them for students and parents to use as a reference during homework and they became a focus of professional development for the mathematics teachers at the high school.

Supporting New Teaching via Online Classrooms

Peter is the assistant superintendent for an alliance of six schools that extends "more than 25 miles from end to end," and Joan is a part-time technology coordinator working in an adjoining alliance of four schools including three small elementary schools. In each of those jurisdictions, curriculum initiatives were underway. Peter was engaged in an initiative to increase problem-based learning in all grades, but especially in the secondary grades. Joan was engaged in an initiative to refresh technology-based teaching and learning to coincide with the arrival of new Chromebooks in the elementary schools. This project started when the two began to collaborate with the author to support teachers' learning.

Both Peter and Joan sought to include teacher-leaders to provide leadership to their peers. One of the teacher-leaders from Joan's schools described the problem and her motivation as "finding technology resources that are appropriate for my students, we have been inheriting old technology from the high school. Now, we get new stuff and we want to show what we can do." Joan explained that most of the computers in the district's elementary schools had been "hand-me-downs from the high school, but a new superintendent insisted the elementary students get better technology to use." A teacher-leader in Peter's high school said he had been motivated by "the excessive focus on standardized testing, and the need to give students the chance to dig deeper into our subjects." These two projects had similar goals as they both sought to support teachers who were developing previously untaught curricula and using unfamiliar methods and tools; the support was to include both access to instructional materials and collaborative development of teaching methods.

Peter's district had been using Moodle to provide online classrooms for students; Peter explained,

most of our teachers were at least familiar with Moodle and used it for at least some things. Middle school and elementary teachers less so than high school, and we wanted them to use it more, so we decided to start an online classroom dedicated to project-based learning and we enrolled all of the teachers in it.

Joan described her decision to follow a similar approach to Peter's, "when I heard what they were doing, I decided to steal the idea, and Peter's 'tech guy' was very helpful in helping me get Moodle up running much quicker than I could have because I am only part-time." For the teachers in Joan's schools, this would be the first and only use of Moodle in their professional lives; she noted, "when this was introduced at a faculty meeting, no one said they had used Moodle before. Some younger teachers have done some online courses in college, but it was very limited." The first iteration of the design/ construction phase concluded when Joan's schools had Moodle installed and teachers could access a classroom for teachers to "explore how the Chromebook can help you teach and share ideas."

Because Joan's teachers were using Chromebooks, many of the materials they shared on Moodle were links to web sites. One problem they soon encountered was reported in an email sent to one of the teachers-leaders; "the sites are great, but the list is getting too big and it is kind of disorganized. It takes too long to scroll through them and it would help if we could keep some notes on them, so we know how to find the ones we need." Teachers in Peter's schools encountered a similar problem. A teacher recorded, "We share good sites, like [an art museum's] online collection, but it would be more useful if we could see just the stuff we need for our classes." Joan and Peter identified "finding an easy method of organizing the materials on the Moodle site, so users can quickly find what they need" as a problem that needed to be resolved through design/ construction. Peter and Joan each assigned one teacher-leader to collaborate to find a solution. That pair of teacher-leaders met with the author to explore different options for categorizing or filtering materials in Moodle. The group prepared three different options; specifically, they demonstrated a) adding tags to items using that feature which is part of Moodle, b) organizing materials into folders, and c) organizing resources with a wiki. Screen recordings of each method were posted on the World Wide Web and teachers in both jurisdictions were invited to review the methods. One week later, the teacher-leaders hosted an afterschool meeting in two locations (one in each jurisdiction and connected via a video conference tool) at which teachers discussed the method they preferred.

In the report to Peter and Joan that followed that session, the teacher-leaders noted, "The teachers recommend tagging as the preferred method for organizing resources. The primary reason was the ease for teachers—they just type the words they want to use or they select from existing tags." In addition, the group had expressed concern over the potential of a teacher deleting items added by others. The teacher-leader from Peter's schools met with the technology coordinator who served those allied schools, and who had the greatest experience administering Moodle of anyone in the group, to discuss the concern about teachers editing or deleting items. The teacher-leader reported, "solutions were possible, but we concluded any changes were too much work to develop and test. Basically, we just need to be careful, and if [accidental deleting] becomes a problem, then we can worry about preventing it."

In the weeks after tagging was introduced as a strategy for organizing resources, the pair of teacher-leaders worked within their schools to ensure teachers knew how to tag; concurrently, they asked teachers to cull and tag the remaining resources. One of the teacher-leaders recorded, "Mrs. Smith was a teacher who was overwhelmed by the disorganized resources, but she is now using tags and is always reminding others to add tags. The site is much more useful to her now." Although there are no other data regarding teachers' perceptions of the process or the value it added to the collection in either jurisdiction, in October 2016 Joan and Peter tallied the 50 most recent additions to the Moodle site he or she manages and at least 45 on each had been tagged with at least one term.

As project-based learning was becoming a focus of teaching in his schools, Peter had led many in-person curriculum development workshops to introduce the method and to provide teachers with experience in preparing materials. As the initiative entered its third year (which was the first year that Moodle was introduced to support the work) teachers were becoming increasingly independent in the work and found others' input on their ideas helped, but the face-to-face sessions seemed less important. Peter observed, "teachers are impatient with the time to schedule face-to-face reviews, so they wanted to move that work online." Peter described how "teachers started a forum where they posted projects they were thinking about and they gave each other feedback and found connections between the projects in one subject areas and those in another."

Because Joan and Peter communicated frequently on this work, Joan decided to add forums to her installation of Moodle as well. Joan sent an email to teachers indicating she had added a "forum for questions and answers about how to use the Chromebooks in classrooms." About a month after the forum was added to Moodle, Joan noted there were fewer than five posts on the forums and none had responses. Peter observed a similar situation when his schools first deployed forums to Moodle, "three of our teachers were absent from the forums. It turns out they were unsure of what to do. But after a tutoring session, they were participating along with the others." Using this as a cue, Joan decided to provide a brief in-person training session in how to use forums for teachers in her schools. Immediately afterwards, she noted far greater participation in the forums, with teachers posting suggestions, asking questions, and answering others' questions.

In the case of online professional development in these two jurisdictions, several iterations of design/ construction led to an improved online environment for teaching and learning. The decision to adopt Moodle for professional development purposes by Joan and her school was largely informed by the similar decision made by Peter and the collaborative relationship Joan and Peter had established. In the same way improvements to the LMS at Northern Middle and High School were made in response to feedback from individuals who were actively using the system, Joan and Peter convened groups to design/ construct solutions in response to the feedback from active users. Using that feedback to identify deficiencies in the configuration or the manner of professionals' use of the system, decisions were made and improvements were deployed.

FINDINGS

This final phase of educational design research (McKenny & Reeves, 2012) is evaluation/ reflection. This finds researcher-practitioners evaluating the work to determine if the intended outcomes were realized and also to articulate generalizations that can inform their further work in the field, that can be applied by others in other settings, or that can be applied to different problems. The data from these cases support generalizations with regard to the use of educational design research as a strategy to inform planning decisions and also the application of open course technologies to the support of teaching and learning in rural schools.

Educational Design Research as Technology Planning

Educational design research (McKenny & Reeves, 2012) is simultaneously a research methodology and a method for designing interventions. In the semi-structured interviews conducted with the school leaders who initiated these projects that were conducted in 2016, the leaders where asked about educational design research as a method of designing interventions. In each case, the leaders differentiated these planning processes from those they typically employed. They identified these as more satisfactory than others and described specific aspects of educational design research that appeared to contribute to the value of the interventions. There is evidence the improvement are grounded in the iterative nature of the process and in the clearly defined roles of different individuals in the process.

Understanding Improvement

Researchers adopt an objective stance towards the measurements they make and the data they analyze and interpret; through objective analysis, they seek to use evidence to support and elucidate theories that accurately predict and explain observations. In contrast, designers of interventions adopt a subjective stance towards data; designers seek to achieve outcomes that are defined by the designers or others, and data is interpreted to ascertain the degree to which the outcomes were achieved. While there appears to be a contradiction in these two approaches to data and evidence, there is a tradition of applying research methods, including sophisticated data collection and analysis procedures, to the design of interventions.

Bereiter (2002) described progressive discourse as a planning method that is simultaneously grounded in a research and intended to improve conditions. For Bereiter, progressive discourse depends on a shared understanding of activity that will constitute the intended outcome (simply agreeing on language is insufficient), and interventions are defined and refined so that what is observed more closely resembles what the planners want to observe. Like progressive discourse, educational design research (McKenny & Reeves, 2012) is intended to be iterative and improving; planners deploy an intervention, observe its effect, then refine and redeploy it so that its performance improves according to the designers' perceptions.

Dan, the principal who initiated the Algebra at a distance project, contrasted the planning he was taught as a graduate student to the planning he experienced in this project. "I was taught planning was a step-by-step process. Once you have a goal, you plan to meet it, then decide if you met it. It is step at a time and slow," but he observed in this project "we failed at first, we quickly went back to much quicker planning than I am used to." Dan further described how the iterative processes were connected, and the first failure helped to revise his understanding.

I knew we wanted 'a good way to have our students take the class, but I didn't really know what that meant... I thought I did... but it wasn't until I saw how bad our first solution was that I could break it into the parts.

For Dan, the lens of the failure was essential to defining improvement, "Once I saw the bad images on the screen, I knew what we needed to improve."

It became immediately clear to Dan what would constitute improvement, but for other leaders, the improvements were less obvious at first. The principal at Northern admitted the problem was originally unclear in his school; "using online courses to replace textbooks and the authentic learning stuff we were doing were both good ideas—teachers were on board the community was too—but we really didn't know what it was going to look like." Because the initiatives were unfamiliar to most faculty, there was little agreement about the technology capacity and functionality necessary. "For us," he said, "we moved from non-technology to technology," and he clarified that with the example of electronic portfolios,

we talked about what we did [previously] and what we wanted to do with portfolios to document learning, then we looked to the tech people who were on the committee to build it. Our work then became better organized as we followed the procedures for using the technology.

In Northern Middle and High School, the activity of compiling portfolios to document students' authentic learning was improved by the process of designing a technology solution for that work; specific improvements included more teachers documenting more work than had been done previously.

Iterations

The iterative nature of planning the followed educational design research (McKenny & Reeves, 2012) also changed the approach to planning experienced by these school leaders. The principal at Northern described how iterations were essential to the progress and improvements that he observed as the proprietary LMS was replaced and as the open source LMS was configured to provide better service. He noted, "Our school had a long history of making technology decisions, but then never revisiting them. The response from the technology coordinator was always, 'I built what you asked for, it is your problem you didn't ask for the right thing.'" The principal described a sense of relief when that technology coordinator removed himself from the LMS planning process, "the committee had permission to keep working and keep fixing until it was right which is important in education, because you can't always know what you will need until you are using it with students."

For Peter, also, the explicit nature of planning that followed educational design research led to iterative and continuous planning. "Too often, we try to change things all at once in education and that can be uncomfortable for teachers," Peter said. He contrasted that with how the Moodle classrooms had been refined in his schools. "We started with one step, and when it got to where it wasn't working the question we asked was, 'how do we improve what we have?' rather than 'what do we replace [Moodle] with?'" Joan concurred with the view of the manner in which Moodle was implemented and she described the approach as "a slow process, but it never restarted. Once teachers were comfortable, we took the next step. It is unusual to improve professional development slowly with each step 'a step up' from where we were."

The Need for Expertise

The open source technology solutions deployed in these cases were all designed to improve the use of technology for teaching and learning. Educational technology is a multidimensional aspect of school planning and it requires expertise in multiple areas to be effectively deployed. In each of these cases, technical expertise was needed to identify and initially evaluate then install and configure open source software. Much of the feedback that informed the iterative design/ construction cycles originated in observations and criticisms from teachers or others who lacked the technical expertise to reconfigure the technology, but whose experience using it was deeply connected to how it was configured. In these cases, effective open source solutions resulted from systems that were properly configured by those with technical expertise and appropriately configured to reflect the needs of teachers and learners.

The lack of sufficient technical expertise appears to be an impediment to the improvements that were illustrated in these cases. The one principal who was interviewed, but who abandoned the project she had initiated fewer than 18 months previously noted, "we used Moodle for curriculum development work and it was great. Our part-time technology person made some changes to it, but something went wrong. He found a full-time job, and he wasn't able to fix it before leaving." She did contrast managing content and courses with configuring Moodle; "we had a teacher who had been doing lots with Moodle try to fix the problems but there was a setting that he could not figure out, so we switched our work over to Google Drive so we could get better technology support." For that principal, access was limited by the expertise necessary to perform the duties; she was unable to secure an individual with the necessary knowledge given the time and salary limits of her budget.

Access to technology expertise is also a challenge to Joan's initiative, but the access appears to have been in time, not knowledge. She observed,

Working with [the technology coordinator from Peter's schools], I have learned how to manage Moodle. It was not much different from the work I have done for years as a web master for schools, but I just don't have the time to tend to problems in a timely manner.

These data also appear to confirm the need for greater levels of technological expertise in communities using open source tools compared to those using proprietary tools (Kimmons, 2015). Budgets limit the level of expertise that can be hired in some rural communities; while in others, individuals with sufficient expertise have other duties or reduced schedules which limit the degree to which their expertise can be used.

Collaboration Among Experts

Stefaniak (2015) noted the tendency to perceive educational technology to be primarily technical in nature, so projects and improvements are assigned to technical experts. Once technologists assume responsibility for a project, there tends to be a sharp boundary separating educators from technologists who receive little oversight from school leaders. This can contribute to a challenging situation in schools where the individual with the greatest expertise in implementing technology changes are the individuals with least experience using it with students, so the systems they build or the changes they make can pose an obstacle to students' use of technology. Wegner, White, and Smith (2009) observed the most effective technology leaders are often those whose experience is based in the operation of the organization. As was demonstrated in these cases, effective technology was designed only with the input of both educators and technologists.

When the faculty in Peter and Joan's schools identified the need to organize resources on the LMS, a small number of teachers with greater than usual technical skill collaborated with the author (who served as a technology expert) to develop three potential solutions. After the potential solutions had been tested, they were presented to the full faculty to make the final decision. In this way, there was a division of labor that led to improvement, but the division was collaborative as the final decision was made by the teachers and it was further refined following their feedback. The committee that met to develop those options was charged with "bring to the committee multiple methods of organizing the things teachers add to the site, so the teachers can agree on the one that seems best." Peter recorded, "the resulting collaboration worked—people with tech expertise built [the solutions], but the teachers selected the best one." These are examples of how collaboration between educators and technologists produced a solution that was both easy and effective for the teachers and easy to deploy for the technologists.

The principal at Northern recorded a similar observation early in the planning of the initial LMS project. "It is probably good that [the technology coordinator] is not on the team. He is known to build what we first say we want, but then to react badly when the plan changes." The principal compared the typical progress with technology projects with sharp divisions of labor to the work that led to the Moodle-Mahara system, "We needed both tech people and teachers to get this to work... and they needed to listen to each other and to change their thinking based on what the others were saying." At Northern, the iterative and collaborative nature of the planning allowed for an effective solution to be developed by excluding an individual who had avoided collaboration in the past; the principal noted, "when [the technology coordinator] resigned from the committee before it even met, his excuse was [a lie,] but it was good that he understood he would not do well on that team."

In these cases, the decision that led to new cycle of design/ construction decisions were informed by educators who sought to improve or expand the function of the technology systems. Technologists were largely responsible for configuring the systems to reflect the design/ construction decisions, then the solutions were evaluated by educators before they were deployed for all users. The role of the teacher-leaders whose recommendation led to organizing resources in the Moodle installations deployed by Peter and Joan via tagging explained, "School administrators left it to us, as long as it worked, they wanted 'hands-off.' We sat with [the author] to research options on the Moodle site, then configure them, but if teachers didn't like it, we would fix it."

Open Source Technology in Rural Communities

The projects undertaken for this study were designed to improve technology-rich teaching and learning in schools located in rural areas. Because the solutions made us of open source technologies, which are available at no cost to users, the findings regarding the successful development of the tools are of particular interest to educators in rural areas. The decision to use these tools is likely to alleviate some of the financial challenges faced by school and technology leaders in rural areas. Further, the nature of the technology use and the changes in educators' interaction with these tools indicate educators may become more sophisticated users of technology if they are deployed in a collaborative and iterative manner.

Technology Acceptance

Technology acceptance model (Davis, 1989) was first elucidated to identify the factors positively associated with the decision to use technology; it was later combined with eight other theories the predict technology use into the unified theory of acceptance and use of technology (UTAUT) (Venkatesh, Morris, Davis, & Davis, 2003). In general, technology acceptance predicts tools that are perceived to be easy to use (high effort expectance), effective (high performance expectancy), and that is used by others (high social expectancy) are more likely to be used than tools that do not demonstrate these characteristics.

Two decisions captured in this data support the observation that effort expectancy is influenced redesign decisions. In the case of Northern Middle and High School, the selection of Moodle (and then the subsequent decision to install Mahara) was motivated by the fact that the systems could be connected to students' existing accounts on the Google domain already managed by the school technologists and used daily by the students. The principal described his observations of students' work in classes using the replaced LMS, "before we rolled this system out, I watched teachers spend 20 minutes getting passwords reset because they forgot them, and it was a system not everyone used—in part because of the password problems." Although there is no evidence that his "20 minutes" assessment is accurate, it does capture effect that using a single-sign on exerted on increasing effort expectancy, thus improving the system.

Ease of use also contributed to expanded use project-based learning and other authentic learning activities at Northern. Some resistance from teachers to incorporating authentic assessments was that grounded in the perception that documenting it was too much work and it was done inconsistently by teachers. The principal described how authentic learning was documented prior to the Moodle-Mahara system,

we used to take pictures of projects, but some teachers put them on a server, others used [Google Drive,] and still others did who knows what. When we had students try to compile a portfolio, it was a mess trying to find everything they needed.

Dan described how ease of use affected the distance-based Algebra course at Crossroads Elementary School, as well.

One of the challenges we faced as the course progressed was testing. We started out scanning tests to the teacher, but that was a very slow process. The Algebra teacher worked with some of his former colleagues to learn how to use the free version of [a propriety learning management system] for online tests. It was much easier to have students just go take tests online, but we kept scanning the projects and more challenging problems he had them do.

The decision to recommend tagging as a means of organizing content in the LMS's provided for professional development in the schools led by Peter and Joan also supports the observation that perceived effort expectancy is associated with the intention to use technology. The primary decision to adopt tagging was made because it was going to be the easiest of the three options for the teachers, and Joan noted, "one of our teachers who was reluctant to use the site at first now introduces it to new teachers and she tells them all the time how easy it is to use."

A second factor associated with increased use of technology according to UTAUT (Venkatesh et al., 2003) is performance expectancy; that factor is grounded in several characteristics including job fit.

The principal at Northern described a situation in which the technology influenced teachers' curriculum decisions in a manner that was perceived as improvement by school leaders. He observed "teachers can have students create portfolio pages, then hand them in on Moodle, so there seems to be a stronger connection between the projects in portfolios and the content of the courses." With the greater amount of authentic learning being compiled in the system, the principal observed, "we are taking it more seriously, and finally having conversations about broad learning expectations that go across all courses," and he also noted, "we seemed to be struggling with both authentic learning and using the online classrooms, but once both were built and connected, there has been increased use of each."

UTAUT (Venkatesh et al., 2003) further posits that use of technology is increased in those instances in which there are strong social influences. Specifically, one is more likely to use technology used by others whose opinions are valued. In these cases, this was illustrated in the active role of teacher-leaders in Norther Middle and High School and in Joan's and Peter's schools. When asked about the quick spread of the initial tests of Moodle in his school, the principal at Northern said,

looking back, that was important, the few teachers who started using Moodle were really mentors to others, and they just started sharing without me or anyone else telling them to. Others saw what they were doing and wanted to join the club.

Joan noted the importance of the teacher-leaders in the wide adoption of the Moodle site to support Chromebook-based teaching in her schools as well. "I knew I could not be the full time leader and principals were all too busy, so I thought carefully about the teachers who I asked to be leaders." Joan detailed the characteristics she wanted in the teacher-leaders, "They needed to be perceived as strong teachers, have technical skill, and be able to work with colleagues in a patient manner."

Teo (2011) observed, "teachers spend much of their planning time to consider how technology could be harnessed for effective lesson delivery and assessment" (p. 1). In these cases, there appears to be support for the conclusion that planning can be more efficacious and solutions perceived to be improving if they are designed to increase factors associated with technology acceptance.

Participatory Cultures

In 2009, Jenkins and his colleagues defined participatory cultures as those "with relatively low barriers to artistic expression and civic engagement, strong support for creating and sharing creations, and some type of informal mentorship whereby experienced participants pass along knowledge to novices" (p. xi). While Jenkins' participatory culture is largely understood to be a phenomenon of younger generations, scholars have identified an increasing expectation that users of digital information assume a more active role in creating and consuming information compared to those generations that experienced only print media and electronic mass media (Deuze, 2006). One of the defining characteristics of participatory cultures is the collaborative nature of the creative processes (Halverson, 2012). The interventions described in each of the cases in this chapter were produced by collaborative interactions among the professionals. All school leaders in the schools described this chapter played an active role in both initiating the projects and ensuring they were adequately supported. Their active support included scheduling time for professionals to meet, arranging for the purchase of necessary materials and technologies, and ensuring other professionals participated as appropriate. Teachers ensured that the interventions were tested under appropriate situations and they gave focused and informative feedback to those with technological expertise who configured and reconfigured the open source technology to provide necessary functions.

Two of the cases described in this chapter appear to have contributed to on-going consumption and creation of open educational resources by the teachers who were initially engaged in them. The Algebra 1 teacher who taught remotely for students at Crossroads became interested in other remote teaching. Dan explained the teacher originally wanted to put recordings of his lectures online but the teacher decided against that; "he saw there was plenty of other good lectures online already, so he shifted his focus." Dan noted as well the Algebra course has shifted "from a traditional course just taught via video conference to a problem solving course." The teacher has created a web site to show students how to work problems," and "the video conferences have become students talking about complex problems and sharing their own solutions." In addition, the students are "using some new tools to show off their own solutions." In effect, Dan noted, "we have transitioned away from using the technology to deliver the content to using the technology as a place where students explore the content."

In addition, Dan described how the experience with Algebra 1 motivated him, along with the principals of the allied schools, to explore the use of the distance learning infrastructure for other projects. "We had a virtual science fair before the actual science fair, [students] discussed their projects before we all got on a bus and took the displays boards to [an allied school]" and "teachers get students together to discuss books on Jitsi." At Crossroads and the allied schools, the distance learning activities tended to be for specific projects, and each teacher adopted the platforms for single projects rather than as the primary method of instruction. Dan noted, "last year students did maybe five or six distance learning activities in different units in different classes. Teachers have shared the load without overdoing it, but students use distance learning in many contexts."

The teachers in Peter's schools discovered that textbooks were a weak resource for the authentic learning projects they sought to include in the curriculum; textbooks often did not provide sufficient coverage to meet students' needs when they researched topics of their own interest. In response, two of the teacher-leaders in Peter's schools began to explore open educational resources (OER) and to include resources from several open providers in their classes. Peter noted, "one science and one English teacher have become leaders in our expanded use of open educational resources." Their participation in the OER communities has expanded as well. While presenting workshops for their colleagues these two teachers illustrated the similarities between our use of Moodle and their participation in the extended OER communities.

Peter further described what he had observed in these teachers' classrooms, "the students were writing their own materials to repost to the OER site." According to Peter, this project appeared to be engaging students on multiple levels. "Some students were double-checking their materials against the novel to make sure details were accurate, but other students were working as copy editors." Peter also recounted the conversation he had with the teacher after the lesson, "he told me that students had become heavily invested in the work once someone downloaded an early draft of one piece [from the OER site] and they got some critical feedback."

DISCUSSION

Data reported in the chapter illustrate the use of decision-making processes grounded in educational design research (McKenny & Reeves, 2012) to develop and deploy open source technology solutions.

The schools in which these projects were undertaken were rural, and demonstrated many of the characteristics of rural schools, including difficulties in staffing and limited access to support staff. These appear to have been limiting factors in previous school planning initiatives. Among the effects of these limiting factors were terminal interruptions to efforts toward school improvement. In these cases, there appears to be evidence that school leaders perceived interventions designed through educational design research (McKenny & Reeves, 2012) to have improved technology-rich teaching and learning, the improvements include both results that more closely reflect the intended outcomes and more sustained efforts to continue the improvements compared to previous planning strategies.

In addition to illustrating the application of design as an effective planning strategy, the data reported in this chapter appear to support several generalizations the are consistent with other findings. Hew & Bush (2007) observed technology integration, which they described as the use of computer and information technologies for instructional purposes, is a practice that is affected by many and interconnected factors. According to Hew & Bush, overcoming these barriers, and improving the level of technology integration is accomplished when barriers are identified and there is a strategy for overcoming them. Further, the strategy must be informed by a clear vision for technology which gives "school leaders and teachers an avenue to coherently communicate how technology can be used as well as a place to begin, a goal to achieves, and a guide along the way" (p. 234).

This research suggests that a vision is insufficient to completely support technology integration. In this data, there is evidence that the school leaders had a vision, but the iterative nature of this planning led them to clarify the vision and to guide not only the beginning place but also a strategy and framework that encouraged refining the vision and the improving the practices as technology was deployed. In addition to clarifying the problem, and contributing to effective evaluation of efforts, the method allowed school leaders to identify needs that previously would have remained hidden to them. The planning strategies provided a framework for how the work would proceed so the vision could be realized. In this way, the planning and decision-making described in this chapter supports the conclusion that iterative planning in which observation of activity is the data that informs further decisions leads to improved performance of the systems.

Davis (1989) observed that white collar workers did not always use technology that was available to facilitate their work. When originally elucidating technology acceptance model, he found that the intention to use technology was affected by several factors, especially the degree to which the user perceived the technology to be easy to use and to be useful. In 2003, Venkatesh, Morris, Davis, & Davis combined eight theories that had been used to predict technology use into the unified theory of acceptance and use of technology (UTAUT). UTAUT posits that technology perceived to be easy to use (high effort expectancy), useful (high performance expectancy), and used by others (high social expectancy) is more likely to be used than other technologies. While originally designed to predict and explain decisions to use technology in setting other than education, there is growing evidence that it describes the use of technology in these populations (Holden & Rada, 2010; Hu, Clark, and Ma, 2003; Smarkola, 2007) and also that efforts to increase technology acceptance can improve the degree to which technology is used in K-12 schools (Ackerman, 2017; Straub, 2009). These data further support the applicability of technology acceptance as a heuristic for predicting and explain technology use in schools. Educators in rural schools tend to adopt multiple roles, and those school tend to have fewer resources to support professional development. When planning increased technology acceptance, the systems tend to be easier to use, thus reducing the need for training, so these data describe planning that will reduce the need for this already limited resource in rural schools.

A final conclusion that appears to be supported by this data describes the changing nature of educators' engagement with educational technology. Blumenfeld, Kempler, and Krajik (2006) define autonomy to include the "perception of a sense of agency" (p. 477), which arises from awareness and understanding of problems and solutions, as well as capacity and authority to implement solutions. The conclusion that educators exerted greater than usual autonomy in these planning efforts arises from the observation that the iterative process led to deeper understanding of the problem and the solutions than other planning efforts. Further, there is evidence in each case that the educators who were participating in the process had been given authority to make decisions. In these case of Northern Middle and High School's adoption of Moodle, there were budgetary limits placed on the decision to purchase space on a web server to host Moodle. In the decision to adopt tagging in Joan's schools, the teachers were given choice of limited options. In these examples, the authority to make decisions was limited by school leaders' decisions, but within those limits authority was given. There is evidence that teachers may exert limited autonomy with regards to regarding instructional practices (Range, Pijanowski, Duncan, Scherz, & Hvidston, 2014), however, so additional research in the emerging role of autonomy is necessary.

LIMITATIONS

The school leaders associated with these cases articulated differences between these planning methods and those used in other activities. Despite these observations, it cannot be determined from these data if those perceptions were the result of the planning methods or other factors. There are no data available to compare these planning efforts with those envisioned by the leaders when they identified differences. There is also no evidence that the problems solved in these cases would not have been solved using different planning methods. In each case, the problem was perceived to be real and efforts of multiple professionals were focused on solving it, so a sufficient solution might have emerged from any planning processes. Given the perceptions that educational design research was effective because it recognized improvement of students' and teachers' experiences as a worthy outcome, it was iterative, and it focused the work of the various types of experts in the design/ construction of technology-rich interventions; it appears those aspects of planning grounded in educational design research deserve additional inquiry.

This research also did not gather data regarding the application of planning methods derived from educational design research (McKenny & Reeves, 2012) to other planning problems encountered by the participants in this research. Schools are places where leaders constantly seek to make improvements. If this approach to planning was perceived to be more effect than other approaches, then it would be reasonable to expect these school leaders to have applied these methods to other aspects of school management. This study gathered no data to investigate other planning; it is also reasonable to expect evidence of this approach to school planning would be observed in other areas of school planning if the school leaders did find it more effective than other methods.

The data appear to support the conclusion that teaching and learning was improved in these cases. Improvement is a very difficult construct to define as it is based in individuals' perceptions, thus the same situation can be perceived differently by different people (Rittel and Weber, 1973). In these cases, improvements were judged only from the perspective of the school leaders who were both involved with the projects and were interviewed many months after the project began. It is unknown if the improvements were manifest in any other data sources or if the improvements were perceived to be improvements by other stakeholders.

The three cases described in this chapter are a subset of projects begun between 2013 and 2015; the author began collecting data for six projects when they were initiated, but only three met the inclusion criteria of being still active and under the original leaders. This research leaves unanswered questions regarding the sustainability of projects developed using educational design research. The three cases described in this chapter are still active, but they appear to have evolved since they were initiated. This research does not indicate what factors affected continuation and modification decisions. Data were collected from one of the projects that was abandoned, and it appears to suggest the lack of sufficient technical expertise contributed to that decision. It is unclear what other factors might cause a leader to abandon a project that was begun using planning grounded in educational design research. It is not known if the projects continued beyond the tenure of the leaders who initiated the project.

CONCLUSION

As illustrated in these cases, iterative planning undertaken to understand how a problem is instantiated and to design and deploy technology solutions appears to be and effective strategy for school and technology leaders. For professionals working in these rural communities, open source technology was deployed and efforts to improve instruction through sustained iterative planning were demonstrated.

REFERENCES

Ackerman, G. (2012). *Measuring technology acceptance: Adapting an instrument.* Paper presented at the New England Educational Research Organization Annual Conference, Portsmouth, NH.

Ackerman, G. (2017). Strategies to increase technology acceptance. In M. Grassetti & S. Brookby (Eds.), *Advancing next-generation elementary teacher education through digital tools and applications.* Hershey, PA: IGI Global, Inc. doi:10.4018/978-1-5225-0965-3.ch001

Apache Software Foundation. (2017). *Licenses.* Retrieved March 28, 2017, from https://www.apache.org/licenses/

Baker, F. (2017). An alternative approach: Openness in education over the last 100 years. *TechTrends, 61*(2), 130–140. doi:10.100711528-016-0095-7

Baran, E., & Correia, A.-P. (2014). A professional development framework for online teaching. *TechTrends, 58*(5), 95–101. doi:10.100711528-014-0791-0

Beeson, E. (2001). Rural schools: Facing unique challenges. *Principal, 8*(1), 22–24.

Benassi, V., Overson, C., & Hakala, C. (2014). *Applying science of learning in education: Infusing psychological science into the curriculum.* Retrieved from the Society for the Teaching of Psychology web site: http://teachpsych.org/ebooks/asle2014/index.php

Benkler, Y. (2006). *The wealth of networks: how social production transforms markets and freedom.* New Haven, CT: Yale University Press.

Bereiter, C. (2002). *Education and mind in the knowledge age.* Mahwah, NJ: L. Erlbaum Associates.

Blumenfeld, P., Kempler, T., & Krajcik, J. (2006). Motivation and cognitive engagement in learning environments. In R. Keith Sawyer (Ed.), *The Cambridge Handbook of Learning Science* (pp. 475–488). New York: Cambridge University Press.

Creative Commons. (n.d.). *Creative Commons — Attribution-ShareAlike 3.0 Unported — CC BY-SA 3.0.* Retrieved March 28, 2017 from https://creativecommons.org/licenses/by-sa/3.0/

Dabrowski, A., & Lodge, J. (2017). Pedagogy, practice, and the allure of open online courses: Implications for schools and their students. In A. Marcus-Quinn & T. Hourigan (Eds.), *Handbook on digital learning for K-12 schools* (pp. 443–454). Cham, Switzerland: Springer International Publishing. doi:10.1007/978-3-319-33808-8_27

Davis, F. (1989). Perceived usefulness, perceived ease of use, and user acceptance of information technology. *Management Information Systems Quarterly*, *13*(3), 319–340. doi:10.2307/249008

Dede, C. (2010). Comparing frameworks for 21st century skills. In J. Bellanca & R. Brandt (Eds.), 21st century skills: Rethinking how students learn (pp. 51-76). Bloomington, IN: Solution Tree Press.

Deuze, M. (2006). Participation, Remediation, Bricolage: Considering Principal Components of a Digital Culture. *The Information Society*, *22*(2), 63–75. doi:10.1080/01972240600567170

Drever, E. (2006). *Using semi-structured interviews in small-scale research: a teacher's guide*. Glasgow, UK: The SCRE Centre.

Free Software Foundation. (2016, November 18). Retrieved March 28, 2017, from https://www.gnu.org/licenses/gpl.html

Glaser, B. (1965). The constant comparative method of qualitative analysis. *Social Problems*, *12*(4), 436–445. doi:10.2307/798843

Halverson, E. (2012). Participatory media spaces: A design perspective on learning with media and technology in the 21st Century. In C. Steinkuehler, K. Squire, & S. Barab (Eds.), *Games learning & society: Learning and meaning in a digital age* (pp. 244–270). New York: Cambridge University Press. doi:10.1017/CBO9781139031127.020

Herrington, J., Oliver, R., & Reeves, A. (2013). Authentic learning environments. In Handbook of research on educational communications and technology (4th ed., pp. 401-412). New York, NY: Springer New York.

Herrington, J., Reeves, T. C., & Oliver, R. (2006). Authentic tasks online: A synergy among learner, task, and technology. *Distance Education*, *27*(2), 233–247. doi:10.1080/01587910600789639

Hew, K., & Brush, T. (2007). Integrating technology into K-12 teaching and learning: Current knowledge gaps and recommendations for future research. *Educational Technology Research and Development*, *55*(3), 223–252. doi:10.100711423-006-9022-5

Holden, H., & Rada, R. (2011). Understanding the influence of perceived usability and technology self-efficacy on teachers' technology acceptance. *Journal of Research on Technology in Education*, *43*(4), 343–367. doi:10.1080/15391523.2011.10782576

Hu, P., Clark, T., & Ma, W. (2003). Examining technology acceptance by school teachers: A longitudinal study. *Information & Management*, *41*(2), 227–241. doi:10.1016/S0378-7206(03)00050-8

Jenkins, H. (2009). *Confronting the challenges of participatory culture: media education for the 21st century*. Cambridge, MA: The MIT Press.

Jitsi [Computer Software]. (n.d.). Retrieved from https://jitsi.org/

Kimmons, R. (2015). Open online system adoption in K-12 as a democratising factor. *Open Learning: The Journal of Open. Distance and E-Learning*, *30*(2), 138–151. doi:10.1080/02680513.2015.1077109

Mahara [Computer Software]. (n.d.). Retrieved from https://mahara.org/

McKenney, S., & Reeves, T. (2012). *Conducting educational design research*. New York: Routledge.

McKenney, S., & Reeves, T. (2014). Educational design research. In J. M. Spector, M. D. Merrill, J. Elen, & M. J. Bishop (Eds.), *Handbook of research on educational communications and technology* (pp. 131–140). New York, NY: Springer New York. doi:10.1007/978-1-4614-3185-5_11

Miller, L. (2012). Situating the rural teacher labor market in the broader context: A descriptive analysis of the market dynamics of New York state. *Journal of Research in Rural Education*, *27*(13), 1–31.

Miller, V. (2011). *Understanding digital culture*. Los Angeles, CA: SAGE.

Moodle [Computer Software]. (2014). Retrieved from http://www.moodle.org

Range, B., Pijanowski, J., Duncan, H., Scherz, S., & Hvidston, D. (2014). An analysis of instructional facilitators' relationships with Teachers and Principals. *Journal of School Leadership*, *24*(2), 253.

Rittel, H., & Webber, M. (1973). Dilemmas in a general theory of planning. *Policy Sciences*, *4*(2), 155–169. doi:10.1007/BF01405730

Sawyer, K. (2008). Optomising learning: Implications of learning sciences research. In *Innovating to learn, learning to innovate* (pp. 45–65). Organisation for Economic Co-operation and Development Publishing. doi:10.1787/9789264047983-4-en

Smarkola, C. (2007). Technology acceptance predictors among student teachers and experienced classroom teachers. *Journal of Educational Computing Research*, *37*(1), 65–82. doi:10.2190/J3GM-3RK1-2907-7U03

Stefaniak, J. (2015). Promoting learner-centered instruction through the design of contextually relevant experiences. In B. Hokanson, G. Clinton, & M. W. Tracey (Eds.), *The design of learning experience* (pp. 49–62). Cham, Switzerland: Springer International Publishing. doi:10.1007/978-3-319-16504-2_4

Stokes, D. (1997). *Pasteur's quadrant: basic science and technological innovation*. Washington, DC: Brookings Institution Press.

Straub, E. (2009). Understanding technology adoption: Theory and future directions for informal learning. *Review of Educational Research*, *79*(2), 625–649. doi:10.3102/0034654308325896

Susskind, R., & Susskind, D. (2015). *The future of the professions: how technology will transform the work of human experts*. Oxford, UK: Oxford University Press.

Teo, T. (2011). Technology acceptance research in education. In T. Teo (Ed.), *Technology acceptance in education: Research and issues* (pp. 1–5). Rotterdam, The Netherlands: Sense Publishers. doi:10.1007/978-94-6091-487-4_1

Tholkes, R., & Sederberg, C. (1990). Economies of scale and rural schools. *Journal of Research in Rural Education, 7,* 9–15.

Venkatesh, V., Morris, M., Davis, G., & Davis, F. (2003). User Acceptance of Information Technology: Toward a Unified View. *Management Information Systems Quarterly, 27*(3), 425–478. doi:10.2307/30036540

Wenger, E., & White, N., Smith, J. (2009). *Digital habitats: Stewarding technology for communities.* Portland. OR: CPSquare.

Wokurka, G., Banschback, Y., Houlder, D., & Jolly, R. (2017). Digital culture: Why strategy and culture should eat breakfast together. In G. Oswald & M. Kleinemeir (Eds.), *Shaping the Digital Enterprise* (pp. 109–120). Springer International Publisher. doi:10.1007/978-3-319-40967-2_5

This research was previously published in Learner Experience and Usability in Online Education; pages 61-84, copyright year 2018 by Information Science Reference (an imprint of IGI Global).

Chapter 20
Open Source Software Virtual Learning Environment (OSS–VLEs) in Library Science Schools

Rosy Jan
University of Kashmir, India

ABSTRACT

A Virtual Learning Environment (VLE) is a software system designed to facilitate teachers in the management of educational courses. The system can often track the learners' progress, which can be monitored by both teachers and learners. While often thought of as primarily tools for distance education, they are most often used to supplement the face-to-face classroom as well as blended learning. Plethora of research conducted on VLEs has reported positive impacts from various contexts. Keeping in view the benefits, the work has been initiated to review concept, features and issues of virtual learning environments. Some of the most used OSS VLEs are discussed. Further it determines the suitability of a VLE for higher education. The chapter also explore and identify the recent contributions to the concept by analyzing ongoing virtual learning initiatives and projects by different organizations and information centres to stimulate future Research and development trend in the field.

INTRODUCTION

The cost of higher education with the attrition of formal learning and the rise and evolution of informal learning presents a unique challenge to academic institutions. Students can no longer afford the cost of textbooks, and the use and embracement of proprietary software limits the freedom of knowledge exchange. The situation is further stimulated by considerably changed attitude and skills of students in IT over the last few years. The transformation of web from static to dynamic has changed the perception of the younger generation towards information presentation and availability. The younger generation now expect to be in 'constant connectivity' with friends and family taking the benefit of participatory and interactive nature of the web. They increasingly expect technology to have a significant role in their learning also. Learning styles are growing fast as the technology grows in the world. New techniques are forthcoming

DOI: 10.4018/978-1-7998-9158-1.ch020

within the higher education system to get the better student's presentation, tutors philosophy and the institution enlargement. Information and Communication Technology innovates the new technologies for conversing the information and knowledge to have a different transform for teachers to teach and for students to learn Ruíz, Martínez & López (2016). So, need emerged to rethink how we teach and how we use learning technologies and how education is delivered. In response to this changing environment, e-learning is being implemented more and more frequently in higher education, creating new and exciting opportunities for both educational institutions and students. E-learning means "instructional content or learning experience delivered or enabled by electronic technologies" (Ong, Lai & Wang, 2004). Which more recently, include mobile and wireless learning applications. E-learning is increasingly adopted in the workplace for supporting professional development and continuing education; however, in higher education, the use of e-learning is predominantly used as a tool support teaching (King & Boyatt, 2015).

The variations in the configuration of e-learning offerings can be described through a number of attributes. One of such attributes is the use of VLEs. A Virtual Learning Environment (VLE) is a software system designed to facilitate teachers in the management of educational courses. The system can often track the learners' progress, which can be monitored by both teachers and learners. While often thought as primarily tools for distance education, they are most often used to supplement the face-to-face, classroom as well as blended learning. VLEs are defined as "computer-based environments that are relatively open systems, allowing interactions and knowledge sharing with other participants and instructors" and providing access to a wide range of resources (Wilson, 2006). "The Joint Information Systems Committee (JISC) considers a Virtual Learning Environment (VLE) an online environment in which learners and tutors participate in "on-line" interactions of various kinds" (JISC, 2000). Besides many more names VLEs are also referred as online learning environments, learning management systems or collaborative learning software (Britain & Liber, 2000). The first systems that fitted the criteria of VLEs as we know them now started to emerge between 1995 and 1997 (Stiles, 2007). VLE is a boxed system that mediates between teacher(s) and student(s). They have a consistent and customizable interface and a clear navigational structure (Stiles, 2007). Access to the environment is often ubiquitous and supports anywhere learning with the support of internet connection (Jacobsen & Kremer, 2000).

The value of a VLE is to fully bring out the characteristics of both "Learning Any Where" and "Learning Any Time," and the purpose of a VLE is to emphasize and diffuse thinking models, diverse viewpoints, independent thinking, etc. (Chou& Liu, 2005). Plethora of research conducted on VLEs has reported positive impacts from various contexts. They can; increase enthusiasm and confidence, improved readiness to learn, promote reflection, accommodate the needs of students and broadly reported improved course assessment performance (Means, Toyama, Murphy, Bakia and Jones, 2009). More recently, the research targets at using on Web 3.0 – based personalisation of learning objects (LOs) while learning in virtual learning environments (Kurilovas, Kubilinskiene & Dagiene, 2014).

Keeping in view the benefits, the work has been initiated to review concept, features and issues of virtual learning environments. Some of the most used OSS VLEs are discussed. Further it determines the suitability of a VLE for higher education. The chapter also explore and identify the recent contributions to the concept by analyzing ongoing virtual learning initiatives and projects by different organizations and information centres to stimulate future Research and development trend in the field."

BACKGROUND

Technologies are affecting almost all facets of life be it business, entertainment or social activity. Commentators and futurists suggest that there are profound implications for education as well. They argue that because the "Net Generation" of learners is so engrossed in a networked world of digital technology, they behave differently, have different social characteristics, different ways of using and making sense of information, different ways of learning, and different expectations about life and learning. So, need emerged to rethink how we teach and use learning technologies and how education is delivered.

In response to this changing environment, one of the means of education that has been propagated with internet revolution is e-learning. e-learning is being implemented more and more frequently in higher education, creating new and exciting opportunities for both educational institutions and students. E-learning means "instructional content or learning experience delivered or enabled by electronic technologies" (Ong, Lai & Wang, 2004). Naresh and Reddy (2015) identified the key factors of successful implementation of e-learning in both developing and developed countries and concluded that financial support from governments, students' motivation and well trained tutors are important for such implication. In addition, user perception and readiness also play an important role in e-learning effectiveness. The barriers faced to a larger extent by developing countries than developed ones are as follows: lack of infrastructure, trained instructors, lack of financial support, government policies and less student readiness. Developed countries, on the other hand, have a strong infrastructure and face the following challenges: student engagement, student motivation, and high student drop out ratio. It has been observed that the variations in the configuration of e-learning offerings can be described through a number of attributes. One of such attributes is the use of VLEs.

A VLE is a web-based communications platform that allows students, without limitation of time and place, to access different learning tools, such as program information, course content, teacher assistance, discussion boards, document sharing systems, and learning resources Martins and Kellermanns (2004). VLEs electronically support training and development in higher educational and vocational training settings. These are frequently used and preferred over the traditional systems keeping in view the benefits like ubiquity, timeliness, efficiency, individuality and learning task orientation. They do so by offering a repository for course documents, discussion forums, chat boxes, mass communication options, etcetera.

Within the overwhelming amount of technology acceptance studies Sun and Zhang (2006). The number of those studying the acceptance and use of VLEs is small but growing (Martins and Kellermanns 2004; Ngai, Poon &chan, n. d.; Ong et al, 2004; Pituch&Lee, 2006&Selim,2003). VLEs are rapidly becoming an integral part of the teaching and learning process (Pituch& Lee, 2006). Ahmed and Morley (2010) qualitative and quantitative explored how a Virtual Learning Environment (VLE) can be supported in a Higher Education setting. Findings revealed that holistic support strategies were capable of targeting larger groups of teachers effectively via staff development workshops and strategies. Study by Mimirinis and Bhattacharya (2007) presents the results of a case study which explore the relationship between approaches to learning and studying, and perceptions of use of a VLE in a Higher Education taught module. Further the study investigates the requirements for appropriate design of VLEs. Recommendations are aiming to highlight the importance of specific elements in the design and delivery of online courses through VLEs. Graham, Woodfield & Harrison (2013) observed that there has been rapid growth in blended learning implementation and research focused on course-level issues such as improved learning outcomes, but very limited research focused on institutional policy and adoption issues.

Comparisons of traditional classroom learning and studying with a VLE have been carried out by Piccoli, Ahmad and Ives (2001), Kekkonen-Moneta and Moneta (2001), Marandi and Luik (2003), Zhang et al. (2004) and McDonald et al. (2004). VLEs have advantages compared with traditional teaching. When different teachers lecture on the same topic, no two lectures are ever exactly the same. Furthermore, the same teacher hardly ever repeats the same lecture in exactly the same form or with exactly the same content (Walker & Harrington,2004). Lecturers can de-motivate students with their routines. On the other hand, VLEs are a flexible way of teaching (Walker & Harrington,2004) because VLEs can be used at the most convenient time (Clarke,2001). The learners learn beyond the timetable routines and guidelines, and therefore chances of missing a lecture is rare (Walker & Harrington, 2004). Lee et al. (2002) found in their study that positive attitudes towards using computers were the key factor in the VLE's success. Students' positive relationship to computers helps also the learning process (Lee et al., 2002). Costello (2014) highlighted that Virtual learning environments (VLEs), such as Moodle, have become an integral part of the complex infrastructure of higher education systems throughout the world. However, Babic (2012) argued that both educational practice and scientific research indicate that teachers' insufficient use of VLEs in higher education teaching still represents a problem. It would not be honest to claim that virtual learning environments will improve the quality of education or reduce the costs of educational systems. These environments have some potential effects. However, the past tells us that it is very difficult to set up the conditions that turn potential into actual effects. Nonetheless, even if there were no proof of superiority in terms of learning outcomes, the evolution would not stop. The issue is not to prove the effects but to understand them.

Coppola (2005) highlighted and focused the e-learning platforms (both LMS and LCMS). Author concluded that the platforms currently available are based on either proprietary e-learning software (PES) or open source e-learning software (OSS). Further it was observed that OSS usage in implementing e-learning systems is more emphasized due to the challenges faced when implementing the PES. Open source software offers the potential to reduce the cost of the software while providing the universities greater control over its destiny. Elimination or reduction of license leaves more budgets available to invest in adapting and managing the software; offers reliability, performance and security over proprietary software due to the availability of the source code, which allows vulnerabilities to be identified and resolved by third parties and it is easy to customize. Some of the widely used open-source e-learning software programs are the Claroline and Moodle. Littlejohn et al (2006) found that with the merger of Blackboard and WebCT, the selection of the open source system Moodle is an increasingly attractive alternative for many institutions. The Open University (OU) recently choose Moodle as a core component of its virtual learning environment after an extensive requirement-gathering process and evaluations of commercial and open source products demonstrate the way of using the Moodle in the education process at the Gaia Vocational School (GVS). The platform was characterized and promoted among the School members of GVS. The impact of this new platform (e-Courses) on the learning institution activities was evaluated through an online questionnaire, which showed high satisfaction levels with e-Courses. Thus, regarded MOODLE an excellent example of learning management system (Syed, 2009). Report from the Croy, Smelser and McAlpin (2009) describes the results of an evaluative comparison of the Moodle Learning Management System with the Blackboard system. Recommends that the University of North Carolina adopt Moodle as its sole Learning Management System; and Outlines the consequences of doing so in conjunction with a plan for making the transition from Blackboard to Moodle. Hodhod et al. (2010a) found that current market place for VLEs in HEIs is dominated by two products Blackboard and WebCT, each offering a variety of tools and functionality. Many other products are available and in wide use such as First-Class and LearnWise. More recently the advent of open source has offered the academic community Moodle. This VLE is fast superseding the proprietary products as being the most popular and easy to use system of choice apart from many licensed VLEs like BlackBoard, desire2learn, CyberExtension or It's Learning; there are few open source VLEs as well in the market. Adoption to open source VLE is very much dependent on requirements of the organizations. Famous open source VLEs are Bodington & Moodle. A comparison between the available free VLEs Claroline, Moodle and Atutor by Hodhod.et al (2010b) to assure that Moodle is really the suitable choice and it holds the suitable features for a good learning environment. White paper by Luzet (2010) provides brief overview of the usability of the main features of Moodle and Fronter. The results of this work reveal that Fronter wins out from a usability perspective in its simplicity: it offers fewer options and is therefore easier to grasp for a novice user. On the other hand, Moodle's help system scores highly for its comprehensive and content-specific help documentation. Further Moodle is more flexible and scalable which makes it popular as the educational institutions become more demanding in their needs. A comparative study of Moodle with other e-learning systems by Kumar, Gankotiya& Dutta (2011) focused on the Moodle Architecture and presents some authentication plug-in that Moodle supports. LMS Moodle has been adopted by many people and organizations around the world because it offers a tightly integrated set of tools said to be designed from a social constructive perspective. Moodle has been developed under the general public license and many of its components were developed without a specific design documentation including its security services. Ajlan (n. d.) in a book chapter study, analyze, and explore the right decision when choosing a suitable VLE platform to meet the requirements of Qassim University. It focused on a comparison between Moodle and other VLE systems, and is based on two kinds of comparison. This study has proved that the best platforms are Moodle and Sakai, which have missed just two out of forty features. Other than the comparative studies recent studies focused on the development process different experiences and perspectives of the staff involved. Study by Buus (2016) highlighted the development process and some of the didactic considerations undertaken for the implementation of VLE. The evaluations undertaken during the process was presented, along with the results collected in the use of Moodle to highlight the educational changes. While as Sinclair & Aho (2016) presents initial, qualitative research aimed at understanding how Moodle is being used and the different experiences and perspectives of the staff involved. To generate themes and areas of interest for future investigation the paper uses interview data from two "expert witnesses" having a deep understanding of how the platform is used. Emergent themes include: divergence between confident and basic users; the spread of usage within an academic community; lack of progression to innovative teaching methods.

VLE IN LIS SCHOOLS

The field of library and information science is presently passing through a phase of rapid changes. This situation demands an educational system of continuing or life-long learning for new technologies, methods and service procedures. The augmentation of traditional classroom activities with electronic learning objects along with the rise of the free and open source software based course management systems is changing the way faculty and students access, create and use learning objects, information and knowledge FERL (2005). It is providing new opportunities for libraries to design and to disseminate new services. Library schools are also investigating the use of VLE in imparting traditional classroom based courses as well focused and continuing education and/or training programmes for LIS professionals. In fact, the relationship between VLE and LIS profession may be viewed from two angles – application of LIS services in virtual learning environment and use of VLE in design & delivery of traditional as well as focused courseware. OCLC in its white paper McLean (2003) prescribes following library supported services for a typical VLE: Consecutive display and integration of a variety of information windows as part of a learning activity, Aggregation of access to content in any given learning context, Provision of bibliographic tools, Integration of plagiarism software into course management systems, Integration of library resources in course management systems, Customization of portal facilities for storing personal preferences. Paper by (Singh & Devi, 2009) highlighted VLE, Virtual Community, Characteristic features, objectives, Issues, Essentialities, Choice of content, etc. LIS Education in VLE emphasizes on the American Experience, IGNOU initiatives in India concluded that Indian LIS Schools should adopt virtual learning system. However, paper by Mukhopadhyay (2006) concentrates on use of VLE in managing LIS courseware. The author has experimented the design of vidyaOnline, the prototype web-based modular and interactive learning system, aimed to produce a Virtual Learning Environment (VLE) for library and information science courses as well as for other distance and traditional courses of Vidyasagar University. The structure of VidyaOnline extends support for all three forms of VLE – web-based training, supported online learning and informal e learning. Chowdhury and Chowdhury (2006) describe the findings of the initial phase of the eLLIS that aims to study the current practices and support for e-learning available in the Library and Information Science departments in UK. The paper provides a snapshot of the current practices, highlighting the most interesting ones, of e-learning supports provided by the LIS departments and the libraries of the corresponding universities. This paper shows that all the LIS departments and the corresponding university libraries provide some supports for e-learning, though the nature of these support services varies significantly. Most LIS departments in UK currently offer a blended learning environment. Islam, Chowdhury and Islam (2009) examine the LIS education in e-learning environment and its implications in other areas. This study also gives an overview of e-learning education systems in Bangladesh and finds out problems of e-learning in LIS educations in Bangladesh. The findings reveal that Bangladesh needs a proposal to acquaint with this system. It provides a proposal to apply distance and e-learning modes adopted by different LIS institutions in Bangladesh making some recommendations for implementing the proposal. Paper by Lihitkar (2010) attempts to provide a conceptual idea to build-up a prototype model for VLE@DLISc,RTMNU in ICT environment by integrating the two software i.e. Moodle and GSDL.Paper by Arora and Lihitkar (2015) endeavours to discuss the need of VLE in the present LIS education, its pros and cons and also some issues that one will face while implementing it for university, college, or any educational institute. While as Qutab, Shafi-Ullah, Safdar & Khan (2016) explores the use of Virtual Learning Environment tools by professional library associations for career development, collaboration, networking, and building communities across the globe. The paper further emphasised that Continuing Professional Development is the dire obligation of the practising library and information professional in the challenging information society, ever-changing user needs, and advancing support tools. The national and international library associations carry the responsibility of the CPD for the librarians. Traditional face-to-face training, discussions and conferences are supplementary with eLearning platforms, making acquisition of knowledge easy, accessible, economical and thus possible across the geographical limits for career advancement. While as Watkins & Sheu (2016) presented the concept of open knowledge diffusion and the effects of social inertia in preserving constrained learning environments. Authors identified and explained Open Knowledge Diffusion Tools (OKDT) such as Open Educational Resources (OER), Open Textbooks (OT), Massive Open Online Course (MOOC), and Free and Open Source Software (FOSS).

FUTURE RESEARCH DIRECTIONS

The future of learning is outside the traditional campus and classroom. There are profound advances and changes in technology resulting in rapid and unparalleled changes in learning and teaching. The default access points will be mobile phones, laptops and tablets keeping in view the plethora of new devices and APIs as well as super-fast internet speeds available around the world. The future will turn and twist the whole gamut of educational system. Thus, the changes and disruptions to traditional form of university teaching in general and teaching in LIS School in particular will be wide and profound. The LIS schools that mainly rely on disseminating information in traditional classrooms will have fewer resources to such an evolution and therefore will be pressured to bring changes. So, the only way to deal with that will be by investing in blended learning, using the flipped classroom model. The future lies in the use of Open Knowledge Diffusion Tools and the potential of Three-Dimensional Multi-User Virtual Environments (3-D MUVES) such as Second Life (SL) in the service of learning

That leads towards infinite imaginative educational possibilities. The future lies in extending classrooms practice, curriculum enhancement, engagement of students, teachers and administrators to support learning, promote collective creativity and shared leadership and unite learning groups with shared values, vision and practices in a global perspective.

CONCLUSION

Open Knowledge Diffusion Tools, MUVES and other latest leaning technologies of the future will offer a very different set of features and tools. The recent merger and ongoing development of various VLEs like SAKAI and other open source products, which offer the promise of easily shared learning tools, and new techniques such as AJAX, will drive the change process. Eventually, a more responsive set of learning tools will be a demand of upcoming generation of students. Just as they are quickly moving beyond the traditional institutional environment to create their own virtual social realms, they may one day create and utilize their own learning tools and communities. Of course, institutions will always hold the upper hand in these developments as they maintain the formal credentials students require for future careers. But this exercise of power is an illusion in a rapidly changing society and we want to engage our students through experiences that are both empowering and transformative. Doing this will require that we rethink about our teaching model, and grasp the reality that the underlying paradigms are, indeed, changing faster than we think.

REFERENCES

Syed Adnan Adil. (2009). Virtual Learning Environment (VLE) at a Glance. *PLAP News Online: A Bimonthly Newsletter of the Pakistan Library Association, 12.*

Ahmed, J., & Morley, G. (2010). VLE a blessing or a curse: VLE use by HE Academic Staff. In *Global Learn Asia Pacific 2010 - Global Conference on Learning and Technology*. Retrieved from http://eprints. hud.ac.uk/8901/

Arora, D., & Lihitkar, S. (2015). *Need of Virtual Learning Environment for Educating Library & Information Science*. Retrieved from http://ir.inflibnet.ac.in/handle/1944/1880

Britain, S., & Liber, O. (2004). *A framework for pedagogical evaluation of virtual learning environments*. Retrieved from https://hal.archives-ouvertes.fr/hal-00696234/

Chou, S. W., & Liu, C. H. (2005). Learning effectiveness in a Web-based virtual learning environment: A learner control perspective. *Journal of Computer Assisted Learning, 21*(1), 65–76. doi:10.1111/j.1365-2729.2005.00114.x

Chowdhury, G., & Chowdhury, S. (2006). *E-learning support for LIS education in UK*. Retrieved from http://strathprints.strath.ac.uk/40628/

Clarke, A. (2001). *Designing Computer-Based Learning Materials*. Aldershot Gower Company.

Coppola, C. D. (2005). *Will open source unlock the potential of e-learning?*. Campus Technology. Retrieved from eprints.hud.ac.uk/8901/

Croy, M., Smelser, R., & McAlpin, V. (2009). *Report to the provost from the learning management system evaluation committee*. Retrieved from http://lmseval.uncc.edu/index.php

FERL. (2005). *Designing online courses – good practice guidelines*. Retrieved from http://ferl.ngfl.gov.uk

Hodhod, R., Ibrahim, M., Khafagy, M., & Abdel-Wahab, M. S. (2010). Issues of Choosing the Suitable Virtual Learning Environment. *Research Journal of Information Technology, 2*(1), 24–29.

Islam, S., Chowdhury, S., & Islam, A. (2009). LIS education in e-learning environment: problems and proposal for Bangladesh. In *Asia-Pacific Conference on Library & Information Education & Practice*. Retrieved from http://ir.inflibnet.ac.in/dxml/handle/1944/1470

Jacobsen, M., & Kremer, R. (2000). Online testing and grading using WebCT in computer science. Academic Press.

Kekkonen-Moneta, S., & Moneta, G. B. (2001). Online Learning in Hong Kong: A Preliminary Comparison of the Lecture and Online Versions of a Computing Fundamentals Course. In *WWW Posters*. Retrieved from http://www10.org/cdrom/posters/1081.pdf

King, E., & Boyatt, R. (2015). Exploring factors that influence adoption of e-learning within higher education. *British Journal of Educational Technology, 46*(6), 1272–1280. doi:10.1111/bjet.12195

Kumar, S., Gankotiya, A. K., & Dutta, K. (2011). A comparative study of moodle with other e-learning systems. In *2011 3rd International Conference on Electronics Computer Technology (ICECT)* (Vol. 5, pp. 414-418). IEEE. 10.1109/ICECTECH.2011.5942032

Kurilovas, E., Kubilinskiene, S., & Dagiene, V. (2014). Web 3.0–Based personalisation of learning objects in virtual learning environments. *Computers in Human Behavior, 30*, 654–662. doi:10.1016/j.chb.2013.07.039

Lee, J., Hong, N. L., & Ling, N. L. (2002). An analysis of students' preparation for the virtual learning environment. *The Internet and Higher Education, 4*(3), 231–242. doi:10.1016/S1096-7516(01)00063-X

Lihitkar, S. R. (2010). Virtual Learning Environment for DLISc, RTMNU, Nagpur: A Prototype Design. *Proceeding of one day National Workshop on Digital Library Initiative and Applications in Indian Context*.

Littlejohn, A., Cook, J., Campbell, L., Sclater, N., Currier, S., & Davis, H. (2006). Managing educational resources. In *Contemporary perspectives in e-learning research* (pp. 134-146).

Marandi, T., & Luik, P. (2003). Teacher Training – With or Without Computers?. In *Proceedings of the 2nd European Conference on eLearning*. Academic Conferences International.

Martins, L. L., & Kellermanns, F. W. (2004). A model of business school students acceptance of a web-based course management system. *Academy of Management Learning & Education*, *3*(1), 7–26. doi:10.5465/AMLE.2004.12436815

McDonald, M., Dorn, B., & McDonald, G. (2004). A Statistical Analysis of Student Performance in Online Computer Science Courses. In *Proceedings of the 35th SIGCSE technical symposium on Computer science education*. ACM Press. 10.1145/971300.971327

McLean, N. (2003). *OCLC e-learning task force: libraries and the enhancement of e learning*. OCLC Online Computer Library Center. Retrieved from http://www5.oclc.org/downloads/community/elearning.pdf

Means, B., Toyama, Y., Murphy, R., Bakia, M., & Jones, K. (2009). *Evaluation of Evidence-Based Practices in Online Learning: A Meta-Analysis and Review of Online Learning Studies*. US Department of Education.

Mimirinis, M., & Bhattacharya, M. (2007). Design of Virtual Learning Environments for Deep Learning. *Journal of Interactive Learning Research*, *18*(1), 55–64.

Mukhopadhyay, P. (2006). VidyaOnline: Design and Development of a FOSS based Virtual Learning Environment on Library and Information Science. *DRTC – ICT Conference on Digital Learning Environment*.

Ngai, T., Poon, L., & Chan, C. (n.d.). Empirical examination of the adoption of WebCT using TAM. *Computers & Education*. doi:10.1016/j.compedu.2006.11.007

Ong, L., Lai, J.-Y., & Wang, Y.-S. (2004). Factors affecting engineer's acceptance of asynchronous e-learning systems in high-tech companies. *Information & Management*, *41*(6), 795–804. doi:10.1016/j.im.2003.08.012

Piccoli, G., Ahmad, R., & Ives, B. (2001). Web-based virtual learning environments: A research framework and a preliminary assessment of effectiveness in basic IT skills training. *Management Information Systems Quarterly*, *25*(4), 401–426. doi:10.2307/3250989

Pituch, K. A., & Lee, Y.-K. (2006). The influence of system characteristics on e-learning use. *Computers & Education*, *47*(2), 222–244. doi:10.1016/j.compedu.2004.10.007

Selim, H. M. (2003). An empirical investigation of student acceptance of course websites. *Computers & Education*, *40*(4), 343–360. doi:10.1016/S0360-1315(02)00142-2

Singh, I., & Devi, M. (2009). *Virtual learning environment: issues and challenges before LIS schools and libraries*. Retrieved from http://hdl.handle.net/1944/1470

Stiles, M. (2007). Death of the VLE?: A challenge to a new orthodoxy. *Serials, 20*(1), 31–33. doi:10.1629/20031

Sun, H., & Zhang, P. (2006). The role of moderating factors in user technology acceptance. *International Journal of Human-Computer Studies, 64*(2), 53–78. doi:10.1016/j.ijhcs.2005.04.013

The Joint Information Systems Committee (JISC). (2000). *Circular 7/00: MLEs in Further Education: Progress report*. Retrieved from http://www.jisc.ac.uk/index.cfm?name=news_circular_7_00

Venkataraman, S., & Sivakumar, S. (2015). Engaging students in Group based Learning through e-learning techniques in Higher Education System. *International Journal of Emerging Trends in Science and Technology, 2*(01).

Walker, B. L., & Harrington, S. S. (2004). Can nursing facility staff with minimal education be successfully trained with computer-based training? *Nurse Education Today, 24*(4), 301–309. doi:10.1016/j.nedt.2004.02.004 PMID:15110440

Wilson, S. (2006). Personal Learning Environments: Challenging the dominant design of educational systems. *Journal of e-Learning and Knowledge Society, 3*(2), 27-38. Retrieved from www.sciencedirect.com/science/article/pii/S0378720603001265

Zhang, D., Zhao, J. L., Zhou, L., & Nunamaker, J. F. Jr. (2004). Can e-learning replace classroom learning? *Communications of the ACM, 47*(5), 75–79. doi:10.1145/986213.986216

ADDITIONAL READING

Britain, S. (1999). A Framework for Pedagogical Evaluation of Virtual Learning Environments. JISC Technology Applications Programme: Report. 41.

Dawley, L., & Dede, C. (2014). Situated learning in virtual worlds and immersive simulations. In *Handbook of research on educational communications and technology* (pp. 723–734). Springer New York. doi:10.1007/978-1-4614-3185-5_58

Hamada, M. (2007). Web-based active e-learning tools for automata theory. Paper published in the Proceedings of Seventh IEEE International Conference on Advanced Learning Technologies, Niigata, Japan, July 18–20, 2007. Doi: 10.1109/ICALT.2007.283

Haythornthwaite, C., Kazmer, M. M., Robins, J., & Shoemaker, S. (2000). Community development among distance learners: Temporal and technological dimensions. *Journal of Computer-Mediated Communication, 6*(10). Retrieved from http://jcmc.indiana.edu/vol6/issue1/haythornthwa ite.html

Hölbl, M., & Welzer, T. (2015). Students' feedback and communication habits using Moodle. *Elektronika ir Elektrotechnika, 102*(6), 63-66.

Hotline, W. (2014). Top trends in academic libraries: A review of the trends and issues affecting academic libraries in higher education. *College & Research Libraries News, 75,* 294–302.

Islam, M. S., Kunifuji, S., Miura, M., & Hayama, T. (2014). How library and information science academic administrators perceive e-learning in LIS schools A qualitative analysis. *IFLA Journal, 40*(4), 254–266. doi:10.1177/0340035214541401

Niemi, H., Harju, V., Vivitsou, M., Viitanen, K., Multisilta, J., & Kuokkanen, A. (2014). *Digital Storytelling for 21st-Century Skills in Virtual Learning Environments.* Creative Education.

Secker, J. (2004). *Electronic Resources in the Virtual Learning Environment.* Chandos Publishing. doi:10.1533/9781780630700

Stichter, J. P., Laffey, J., Galyen, K., & Herzog, M. (2014). iSocial: Delivering the social competence intervention for adolescents (SCI-A) in a 3D virtual learning environment for youth with high functioning autism. *Journal of Autism and Developmental Disorders, 44*(2), 417–430. doi:10.100710803-013-1881-0 PMID:23812663

KEY TERMS AND DEFINITIONS

E-Learning: Education via the Internet, network, or standalone computer. It is essentially the network-enabled transfer of skills and knowledge. E-learning applications and processes include Web-based learning, computer-based learning, virtual classrooms and digital collaboration.

Massive Open Online Course (MOOCS): An online course aimed at unlimited participation and open access via the web. In addition to traditional course materials such as filmed lectures, readings, and problem sets, many MOOCs provide interactive user forums to support community interactions among students, professors, and teaching assistants (TAs). MOOCs are a recent and widely researched development in distance education which were first introduced in 2008 and emerged as a popular mode of learning in 2012.

Moodle: Moodle is free and open-source software learning management system written in PHP and distributed under the GNU General Public License. Developed on pedagogical principles. It is used for blended learning, distance education, flipped classroom and other e-learning projects in schools, universities, workplaces and other sectors.

Open Source Software: Software with source code that anyone can inspect, modify, and enhance.

Virtual Learning Environment (VLEs): A system for delivering learning materials to students via the web. These systems include assessment, student tracking and collaboration and communication tools.

This research was previously published in the Encyclopedia of Information Science and Technology, Fourth Edition; pages 7912-7921, copyright year 2018 by Information Science Reference (an imprint of IGI Global).

Chapter 21
A Multi–Step Process Towards Integrating Free and Open Source Software in Engineering Education

K.G. Srinivasa
Chaudhary Brahm Prakash Government Engineering College, India

Ganesh Chandra Deka
M. S. Ramaiah Institute of Technology, India

Krishnaraj P.M.
M. S. Ramaiah Institute of Technology, India

ABSTRACT

Free and Open Source Software (FOSS) is a phenomenon which has overgrown its software origins. From being viewed as a cheaper software alternative, it has become a fountain head of ideas which are adopted cheerfully by people across many domains. From a collaborative effort to build world's biggest encyclopaedia to artists sharing their works under liberal licences, FOSS has become a reference for global, peer-reviewed, volunteer based production model of creating knowledge commons. With everyone from governments to big corporates displaying keen interest in FOSS, it is high time educationalists too take FOSS into classrooms. The ecology of FOSS is filled with more than just a set of software from which a teacher can choose from. He can bring the rich set of coding practices, licensing options, production model and importantly a different world-view by adopting FOSS in teaching. The benefits for students too are many ranging from using modern tools to participating in real world software development. There are many scholarly papers reporting the innovative use of FOSS in teaching graduate courses. By combining these studies with our experience of delivering courses in FOSS, we present a three-stage process which can be adopted by teachers and institutes to utilise the benefits of FOSS to the fullest.

DOI: 10.4018/978-1-7998-9158-1.ch021

INTRODUCTION

The freedoms provided to users by Free Software have their roots in academic culture (Foltin et al., 2011). Education system has a long history of practices like distributed development, peer review and revision based on feedback which are also found in FOSS and therefore education sector is but the natural home for FOSS (Carmichael & Honour, 2002). FOSS is attractive to educators because as scientists they are used to share and allow others to modify their ideas (O'Hara & Kay, 2003). Just like scientists are interested in various phenomenons for the case of curiosity, FOSS developers too get involved in projects that interest them. While scientists share their results publicly, FOSS developers too share the source code (Bezroukov, 1999). So, FOSS should be the natural choice of educators.

The utilitarian idea of teaching is often reflected upon and a writer comments it is strange to convince educators that it is good to share information. Educators should use FOSS because software industry discriminates access to software on economic grounds.

Figure 1. The process of integration FOSS in education

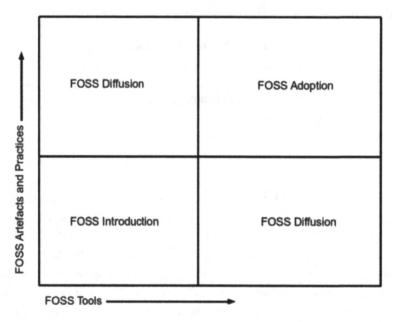

As software forms important part of knowledge in modern age, it should not be allowed to be dominated by commercial players. Hence using FOSS becomes not merely an economic but moral obligation for teachers (Hart, 2003).

There is rich literature available on why and how of FOSS usage in educational institutes. UNDP published a primer on FOSS in education discussing various issues like the potential benefits of using FOSS, various FOSS tools for common academic and administrative usage and legal issues which should be considered while switching over to FOSS (Tong, 2004). But introducing FOSS in institutes can be long and daunting experience for educators as there is FUD (Fear, Uncertainty and Doubt) surrounding FOSS usage. Therefore, we propose a three step process for integrating FOSS in education system. We focus on Engineering education as we are involved in this sector but we hope this approach can be customised to other domains as well. The process is depicted in Figure 1 and is detailed in the following sections.

Stage 1: FOSS Introduction

FOSS is making its presence felt in education sectors of developed countries. In UK, 38% of higher education reported that their institutions have an IT strategy which explicitly considers FOSS (Attwell, 2005). 57% of higher education sector in US use FOSS products (Abel, 2006). But some advanced nations and many developing nations are yet to identify the advantage FOSS brings to education system. A study reported that it is highly unlikely that a wide adoption of FOSS to replace incumbent systems will sweep through educational institutions in emerging markets like India, Brazil, Russia, South Africa, and China (Gangadharan & Butler, 2012). In another study, it was found that many schools in Sweden also seem unaware of the potential with FOSS as enablers for innovative use of IT (Lundell & Gamalielsson, 2013).

In a systematic review, it was found that the drivers of FOSS adoption in US higher education sector were:

1. Social and philosophical benefits;
2. Software development methodology benefits;
3. Security and risk management benefits;
4. Software adoption life cycle benefits;
5. Total cost of ownership benefits (Rooij, 2009).

While educators are attracted to FOSS due to increased student engagement and active learning support, administrators love FOSS because it reduces licence fees (Rooij, 2011). Though institutes have concerns regarding security, support and longevity of FOSS, the potential advantages like cost reduction and vendor independence help matters turn towards FOSS (Rooij, 2007). In addition to providing the possibility of using different tools, the definite advantage of FOSS in education is that it allows innovation. With the availability of open content and open standards, it is possible for educators to experiment with different pedagogic applications (Attwell, 2005).

These and many such reports prompt us to suggest that the first step regarding FOSS usage in classroom should be to provide holistic introduction of FOSS to students. That is because first, many countries are yet to understand the potential of FOSS and second, even if they are using FOSS they do it mainly for technical and economic reasons. This limits the discussion of FOSS as a cheaper alternative and hides the moral and ethical urgency of embracing FOSS. Also, educators cannot be blind to the increasing commercialisation of every aspect of software which hinders the growth and reach of knowledge in digital world. FOSS has the potential to bridge the digital divide (Krogh & Spaeth, 2007) and therefore it is necessary to use FOSS in education.

More specifically, we recommend that in addition to encouraging the usage of FOSS tools, it is necessary that they are aware of its history and culture. Bringing in the narratives of FOSS heroes like Richard M Stallman and Linus Torvalds will help students absorb the spirit of FOSS. They will appreciate Wikipedia more if they learn the collaborative nature of its development. The philosophy of Unix and the ethics of hackers will lay solid foundation to the increased usage and ultimately contribution to FOSS movement. Otherwise students will treat FOSS as just another tool with same or maybe better quality than its counterparts.

Stage 2: FOSS Diffusion

The real advantage of FOSS in education sector is beyond its role as a supplier of development and application tools for students. It can play a constructive role in transforming the teaching methods through what has been identified by pedagogues as 'active learning' (Howison, Conklin & Ossmole, 2005). We propose that the next stage of using FOSS in curriculum should focus on utilising the FOSS artefacts and FOSS practices.

Since FOSS development is a public affair, the entire data covering the lifecycle of software development is now freely available. Educators should bring these valuable resources into classroom so that students get to know how software is created in the real world. For example, FOSS repositories like Sourceforge (Slashdot Media, 2017) and Freecode (Slashdot Media, 2015) give away development data about the software hosted by them including the communication trails. There are also aggregated project data available through projects like FLOSSMOLE (Howison, Conklin & Crowston, 2006). These data can be used to bring qualitative difference in teaching many courses.

In Elon University, USA, FLOSSMOLE data was used in Database course to give real time experience to students. It was also used in Management Information System course to evaluate FOSS projects using established quality methods like Business Readiness Rating (BRR). FLOSSMOLE data was also used in Artificial Intelligence courses to parse the project details using Natural Language Programming techniques (Squire & Duvall, 2009). Linux source code can be used to deliver Operating System course in a better way. The large data sets are ideal to be used in Database and Data Mining course. Availability of source code will help teachers to explain the concepts by 'dissecting' the real projects and teach the 'software anatomy'.

Software Engineering educators are always in search of relevant materials and novel pedagogies that will provide life-long learning experiences and improve the quality of students learning outcomes (Sowe, Stamelos & Deligiannis, 2006). FOSS is both interesting and intriguing from Software Engineering perspective. At first, the practices followed in its development seem to contradict the established norms prescribed in software engineering textbooks. But a careful study will reveal that the differences are just superficial. Increasingly many educators have used FOSS in interesting ways to deliver Software Engineering courses. In the context of increased use of FOSS components in modern software, there are attempts to reorient the Software Engineering education to help students acquire the required skills (Hawthorne & Perry, 2006). In Aristotle University, Greece, students used the real projects hosted in Sourceforge in Software Testing course. They found bugs, reported them to the community and got a first-hand experience of real time quality assurance procedures (Sowe, Stamelos & Deligiannis, 2006). At the University of Skvde, students were first involved in contributing to Wikipedia to understand collaborative development model. Then they selected a FOSS project to participate. They were not only making code commits or fix bugs, but were encouraged to write design documents and help manuals (Lundell, Persson & Lings, 2007). In Western Oregon University and Oregon State University, USA, students were asked to join and contribute to FOSS projects (Morgan & Jensen, 2014).

But joining a FOSS project directly and start contributing may be difficult for many students because each project follows its own unique practice and tools. Therefore, in Tampere University of Technology, educators developed a reputation model and a concrete reputation environment known as KommGame that mimics real FOSS projects (Goduguluri, Kilamo & Hammouda, 2011). Based on our experience in similar attempts, we highly recommend that students be hand-held in initial stages by using controlled environment like this one.

FOSS projects allow students to contribute to an ethical and worthwhile cause in addition to learning good practices of global software development models. University of Lincoln identified the One Laptop Per Child (OLPC) project as a potentially excellent way of getting students involved in collaborative software development (Boldyreff, Capiluppi, Knowles et al., 2009). The Humanitarian FOSS project across multiple universities is an example of successful use of FOSS in education system. The faculty members involved in these projects underlined the importance of sensitising the students regarding the philosophical and ethical roots of FOSS which helped them attract more students to their works (Morelli, Tucker, Danner et al., 2009). In another case, a popular FOSS disaster management solution, Sahana, was used as a basis of teaching Software Engineering course. It is reported that students were highly motivated towards contributing for humanitarian project (Ellis, Morelli, Lanerolle et al., 2007). In Norway, students combined contribution to FOSS projects and doing empirical research regarding the same (Jaccheri & Osterlie, 2007).

Therefore, in FOSS Diffusion stage teachers should first use FOSS artefacts beyond software to bring qualitative difference in various courses. Details regarding code commits, bug lifecycle, software release and communication trails will help students relate their learning to real world. Later students should be introduced to the practices involved in FOSS development such as community collaboration, peer review, and co-creation by making them participate in real projects through careful handholding (Goduguluri, Kilamo & Hammouda, 2011). Not only will this help students gain more knowledge through active participation but it also potentially helps ensure FOSS communities have enough qualified developers to draw from to meet their needs (Morgan & Jensen, 2014).

Stage 3: FOSS Adoption

After the students are familiar with the FOSS philosophy, tools and practices teachers can start offering a separate course in this topic. More than a decade of research in FOSS has resulted in a rich body of knowledge. Multiple taxonomies are also proposed which signal the maturity of the field. With the availability of books which capture multiple aspects of FOSS, teachers have enough resources to deliver the course. More importantly FOSS presents an interesting premise which deserves a thorough investigation by academic community.

There are multiple reports of universities offering stand alone course covering various issues in FOSS. Most of these courses focus just on single dimension like development practices, legal issues like IPR or specific FOSS tools. As discussed in previous sections, it is futile if students are not introduced to ethical and moral issues regarding FOSS. It is also necessary that they study the unique development process, legal issues encountered in using FOSS and the potential areas where FOSS can bring effective changes. To address these issues, we had offered a course titled 'Free and Open Source Software Engineering' to graduate students whose details are as follows

Overview of the Subject

The subject covered the vast expanse of FOSS by critically examining five issues:

1. What conditions led to the emergence of FOSS?
2. What motivates volunteers to contribute to FOSS?
3. What are the Software Engineering processes followed in FOSS?

4.   How can FOSS be used effectively in public administration, business, education, and research?
5.   What are the legal and economic issues surrounding the usage of FOSS?

Text Books

1.   Steve Weber, *The Success of Open Source*, Harvard University Press, 2004.
2.   Joseph Feller et al. (Eds.), *Perspectives on Free and Open Source Software*, MIT Press, 2005.

Delivery Model

Classroom lectures coupled with open discussions based on documentaries, telefilms and docu-dramas covering various issues of FOSS.

Videos of all lectures are available at http://goo.gl/ciZJlR.

Innovations in Teaching

1.   Usage of e-learn tool for collaboration.
2.   Inclusion of videos in course materials.
3.   Open discussions covering many interesting topics.
4.   Mandatory reading exercises.
5.   Encouragement to community service.

Evaluation Methods

In addition to tests and book reviews, community participation activities were also considered for evaluation. This gave enough scope for students to display their learning abilities.

Feedback From Students

For many students, this was the first exposure to FOSS. They responded positively to the course and many said they would continue to use and contribute to FOSS.

Many universities have started offering master degrees in FOSS. Though there are no such attempts in English speaking countries, Spain, Portugal, Italy, Colombia, Equadar and Mexico grant post graduate master degrees in FOSS (Leon, Robles, Gonzalez-Barahona et al., 2014). We suggest that universities in India too look at this possibility as there is increasing demand for people who can work in a globally collaborative environment which can be better taught through FOSS. The paradigm shift in the software development methods and tools are well internalised by FOSS projects. Increasingly corporates too are getting involved in FOSS development and governance. Therefore, the stage is set for offering full fledged degree in this domain.

CONCLUSION

We propose a three-stage process which will help educators and institutes to reduce the risks and increase the benefits of using FOSS. In first stage teachers should move beyond treating FOSS just as another tool and sensitise students regarding the history, philosophy, legal and economic issues of FOSS. In next stage, they should use FOSS artefacts beyond software in delivering courses like Databases and Operating System. Software Engineering teaching should be reoriented to include FOSS practices so that students learn from participating in real projects. In stage three institutes can offer stand alone courses and later start master's degree programs in FOSS.

REFERENCES

Attwell, G. (2005). What is the significance of open source software for the education and training community. In *Proceedings of the First International Conference on Open Source Systems (OSS 2005)*, Genova, Italy, July 11.

Bezroukov, N. (1999). Open source software development as a special type of academic research: Critique of vulgar raymondism. *First Monday, 4*(10), 1999. doi:10.5210/fm.v4i10.696

Boldyreff, C., Capiluppi, A., Knowles, T., & Munro, J. (2009). Undergraduate research opportunities in oss. In Open Source Ecosystems: Diverse Communities Interacting (pp. 340–350). Springer.

Carmichael, P., & Honour, L. (2002). Open source as appropriate technology for global education. *International Journal of Educational Development, 22*(1), 47–53. doi:10.1016/S0738-0593(00)00077-8

Ellis, H. J. C., Morelli, R. A., Lanerolle, T. R. D., & Hislop, G. W. (2007). Holistic software engineering education based on a humanitarian open source project. In *Proceedings of the 20th Conference on Software Engineering Education & Training CSEET'07* (pp. 327–335). IEEE.

Foltin, M., Fodrek, P., Blaho, M., & Murgaš, J. (2011). Open source technologies in education. In *Recent Researches in Educational Technologies: Proceedings of the 8th WSEAS International Conference on Engineering Education (EDUCATION'11)* (pp. 131–135).

Gangadharan, G. R., & Butler, M. (2012). Free and open source software adoption in emerging markets: An empirical study in the education sector. In Open Source Systems: Long-Term Sustainability (pp. 244–249). Springer.

Goduguluri, V., Kilamo, T., & Hammouda, I. (2011). Kommgame: A reputation environment for teaching open source software. In Open Source Systems: Grounding Research (pp. 312–315). Springer.

Hart, T.D. (2003). Open source in education.

Hawthorne, M. J., & Perry, D. E. (2006). Software engineering education in the era of outsourcing, distributed development, and open source software: challenges and opportunities. In *Software Engineering Education in the Modern Age* (pp. 166–185). Springer. doi:10.1007/11949374_11

Howison, J., Conklin, M., & Crowston, K. (2006). Flossmole: A collaborative repository for floss research data and analyses. *International Journal of Information Technology and Web Engineering*, *1*(3), 17–26. doi:10.4018/jitwe.2006070102

Howison, J., Conklin, M., & Ossmole, K. C. (2005). A collaborative repository for floss research data and analyses. In *Proceedings of the First International Conference on Open Source Systems*, Genova.

Jaccheri, L., & Osterlie, T. (2007). Open source software: a source of possibilities for software engineering education and empirical software engineering. In *Proceedings of the First International Workshop on Emerging Trends in FLOSS Research and Development FLOSS'07* (p. 5). IEEE.

Krogh, G., & Spaeth, S. (2007). The open source software phenomenon: Characteristics that promote research. *The Journal of Strategic Information Systems*, *16*(3), 236–253. doi:10.1016/j.jsis.2007.06.001

Leon, S. R. M., Robles, G., Gonzalez-Barahona, J. M. (2014). Considerations regarding the creation of a post-graduate master's degree in free software. In Open Source Software: Mobile Open Source Technologies (pp. 123–132). Springer.

Lundell, B., & Gamalielsson, J. (2013). Open standards and open source in swedish schools: On promotion of openness and transparency. In Open Source Software: Quality Verification (pp. 207–221). Springer.

Lundell, B., Persson, A., & Lings, B. (2007). Learning through practical involvement in the oss ecosystem: Experiences from a master's assignment. In Open Source Development, Adoption and Innovation (pp. 289–294). Springer.

Morelli, R., Tucker, A., Danner, N., Lanerolle, T. R. D., Ellis, H. J. C., Izmirli, O., ... Parker, G. (2009). Revitalizing computing education through free and open source software for humanity. *Communications of the ACM*, *52*(8), 67–75. doi:10.1145/1536616.1536635

Morgan, B., & Jensen, C. (2014). Lessons learned from teaching open source software development. In Open Source Software: Mobile Open Source Technologies (pp. 133–142). Springer.

O'Hara, K. J., & Kay, J. S. (2003). Open source software and computer science education. *Journal of Computing Sciences in Colleges*, *18*(3), 1–7.

Rooij, S. W. (2007). Perceptions of open source versus commercial software: Is higher education still on the fence? *Journal of Research on Technology in Education*, *39*(4), 433–453. doi:10.1080/1539152 3.2007.10782491

Slashdot Media. (2015). Welcome to Freecode. Retrieved March 12, 2017, from http://freecode.com/

Slashdot Media. (2017). Find, Create, and Publish Open Source software for free. Retrieved March 12, 2017, from http://sourceforge.net/

Sowe, S. K., Stamelos, I., & Deligiannis, I. (2006). A framework for teaching software testing using foss methodology. In *Open Source Systems* (pp. 261–266). Springer. doi:10.1007/0-387-34226-5_26

Squire, M., & Duvall, S. (2009). Using floss project metadata in the undergraduate classroom. In Open Source Ecosystems: Diverse Communities Interacting (pp. 330–339). Springer.

Tong, T. W. (2004). *Free/open source software education*. Malaysia: United Nations Development Programmes Asia-Pacific Information Programme.

Chapter 22
Development of Assessment Criteria for Various Open Sources GIS Software Packages

Shahriar Shams
Institut Teknologi Brunei, Brunei

ABSTRACT

There has been a significant development in the area of free and open source geospatial software. Research has flourished over the decades from vendor-dependent software to open source software where researchers are paying increasing attention to maximize the value of their data. It is often a difficult task to choose particular open source GIS (OGIS) software among a number of emerging OGIS software. It is important to characterise the projects according to some unified criteria. Each software has certain advantages and disadvantages and it is always time consuming to identify exactly which software to select for a specific purpose. This chapter focuses on the assessment criteria enabling developers, researchers, and GIS users to select suitable OGIS software to meet their requirements for analysis and design of geospatial application in multidisciplinary fields. This chapter highlights the importance of assessment criteria, followed by an explanation of each criteria and their significance with examples from existing OGIS software.

INTRODUCTION

There has been a noteworthy progress in the area of free and open source geospatial Software. In the past proprietary software such as ArcView, ArcGIS, Arc info, have been extensively used for teaching, learning and research purposes due to wider functionalities, the user friendliness of their interfaces, and also demand from industry for graduates having knowledge and skills of using a particular (or widely used) GIS software product. However, over the past decade there has been an intensive attempt to design and expand free, i.e. non-proprietary, desktop GIS software products (Sherman, 2008; Steiniger & Bocher, 2009; Donnelly, 2010).

DOI: 10.4018/978-1-7998-9158-1.ch022

Most of the industries are involved with solving problems related to basic needs of capture and visualization of spatial data and storage capability. Further advances in technology have increased interoperability across data repositories as well as user friendliness. These advancements have failed to address current development in Geographical Information Science (GIScience), which include research areas such as spatio-temporal data models, geographical ontologies, spatial statistics and spatial econometrics, dynamic modeling and cellular automata, environmental modeling, and neural networks for spatial data (Câmara, 2003). Developing a faster, cheaper and spatially enabled database is a major challenge for researchers and software developers than the software developed by the commercial vendors. A second important reason for developing open-source spatial analysis tools is the need to resolve the "knowledge gap" in the process of deriving information from images and digital maps. Difficulties in extracting information from images and digital maps are another important reason for developing open-source GIS tools. The complexity further arises due to sophisticated and sensitive data collecting process through remote sensing satellites, digital cameras, and GPS. In fact, very few techniques for image data mining in remote sensing archives are currently available in our large earth observation data archives (Câmara, 2003).

Studies on vendor dependent software to open source software has been increasing rapidly in the last 15 years due to growing consideration to maximize the value of spatial data so that resources can be utilised more efficiently (Shekar et al., 2001; Hartnett & Bertolotto, 2003; Morrison & Purves, 2002; Câmara & Onsrud, 2004; Purves et al., 2005). The XML and Java languages being the major languages for open source GIS software, has contributed to the advancement of the GIS software (Chen et al., 2010). Government, Academics and Developers are the major users of open source software such as web-based GIS and mapping applications as it is free of cost (Confino & Laplante, 2010). Researchers, academics and students can learn and collaborate more easily because of the open source concepts, coding, and algorithm. Robustness as well as user friendliness have made open source GIS widely popular and accepted in the industry. The continuous progress and development of free and open source software has extensively influenced and assisted in dissemination of information technology (Tiemann, 2009). Open source software will emerge as the largest distributer of software due to it continuous contribution to development of information technology leading to cheaper software and new business model (Peter Galli, 2007). Overall, the open source GIS is a great platform to share and manage the geographical related information in a ubiquity, visualization and interactive way.

It is often a difficult task to choose particular open source GIS (OGIS) software among a number of emerging OGIS software. It is essential to categorise the projects based on specific criteria. Each software has certain advantages and disadvantages and it is always time consuming to identify exactly which software to be selected for a specific purpose. Therefore, it is important to develop certain assessment criteria based on which a user can select OGIS software. This chapter focuses on the assessment criteria enabling developers, researchers and GIS users to select suitable OGIS software to meet their requirements for analysis and design of geospatial application in multidisciplinary fields. This chapter highlights the importance of assessment criteria, followed by an explanation of each criteria and their significance with examples from existing OGIS software.

CONCEPT OF OPEN SOURCE AND FREE SOFTWARE

Open source software is a freely distributed software consists of source code hidden in the software as a programming language that the developers, researchers or users can easily modify or add features for customization or any other purposes. The software is also known as "libre software" or "open software". One important features of open source software is "free software licenses", which states the legal rights to users with freedoms to amend, run, and redistribute source codes of the licensed software (http://www. fsf.org/licensing/essays/free-sw.html, Free Software Foundation). There is often misunderstanding about what 'free' software indicates. The term 'free', does not indicate that it is free-of-cost, rather it grants freedoms to the developers, users by the software license. These freedoms include the right to (i) run the program for any purposes (e.g. educational or business use); (ii) customize and selling the program; (iii) freely copy and distribute the program; and (iv) modify the program, and distribute the modified version. Typical free software licenses such as the GPL, LGPL, Mozilla, Apache, MIT-style and BSD-style licenses grant these four freedoms. The figure 1 illustrates that free downloadable software is not necessarily equivalent to open source software. For example, Google Earth is one of the most popular free Virtual Globe GIS applications that everyone can download and use for free. But Google Earth is not an open source software rather it is a proprietary software. A red box was added to represent the new boundary of public domain software as shown in Figure 1. Because some public domain software may have no copyright restrictions or licenses, the public domain software has been altered to both include and exclude the open source domain. In GIS software, GRASS GIS is a famous example of public domain software. Public domain software can be re-structured and re-packaged to sell as proprietary software or licensed as open source software (Valdes, 2008).

Figure 1. Categories of free and non-free software
(Adopted from http://www.gnu.org/philosophy/categories.html, by Chao-Kuei Hung).

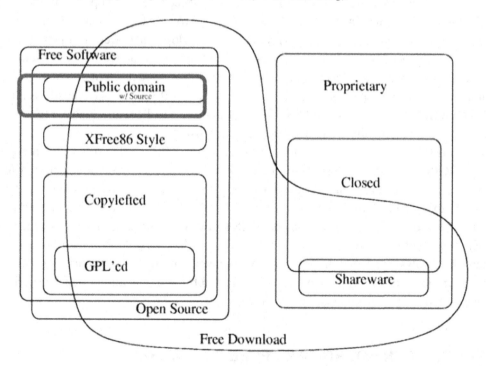

Requirements for Open Source GIS

The three major prerequisites for Open source GIS system architecture are interoperability, sharing of data, and accessibility of resource browser of heterogeneous types. Although each may be seen as a distinct set of capabilities, they all must coexist in a common framework that defines how system components interact (http://www.regis.berkeley.edu/gardels/envmodel.html).

The Open GIS Consortium has following guiding principles for geospatial information to be available across any network, application or platform:

- Geospatial information should discover with easy access to data, irrespective to its physical location.
- Data should be easy to integrate, merge, superimpose and render for display or use in spatial analyses from different geospatial sources, even when sources contain dissimilar types of data.
- Special displays and visualizations, for specific audiences and purposes, should be easy to generate, even when multiple sources and types of data are involved. (http://www.eweek.com/article2/0,4149,1184832,00.asp).

Assessment Criteria

It has been found based on various software developed for GIS utilities that there are broadly two types of open source GIS Softwares. One is developed for catering the needs of specific users which are based on Desktop Applications primarily for their modelling work; analysis of data etc. and others are Web-GIS based users who want to consume the information in a readymade mode as available for making a decision support system. As the GIS development became much simpler than before, it had promoted the development of open source GIS and a number of projects are still undergoing for utilising available resources to cater the needs of a large base of users as shown in Figure 2.

It is important to identify the key features of various existing GIS software so that important criteria can be selected based on these key features. A number of GIS software with key features is documented in Table 1.

Cross Platform Operation: Cross-platform refers to software that can be made to work on multi-platforms, such as, the UNIX systems including Linux, Windows and Mac OS. Cross-platform has been achieved in various ways. In recent years, cross-platform has been adopted by more developers as a basic requirement for software development.

Installation: The users always prefer GIS software that is easy to install. The installation procedure should be straight forward with package being unbundled and installed with minimum efforts. Some GIS software requires a number other supporting packages to be downloaded and installed simultaneously making it inconvenient for the users. Potential candidates for open sources GIS software were subsequently downloaded and installed firstly on a PC (Pentium (R), Dual-Core CPU, E5200@ 2.50 GHZ, 1.98 Gb of RAM, Microsoft Windows, XP Professional, Version 2002, Service Pack2). A relatively new Sony laptop computer with MS Windows Vista has also been used to test the Vista compliance (Chen et al., 2010). The prerequisites and outcome of the installations are demonstrated in Table 2.

Open source Operation System: As we are looking for Open source GIS, the issue of open source operation system (OS) would naturally be brought up. Linux is a well-known open source OS and is getting more popular; however MS windows are still the dominant.

Figure 2 Open source GIS tools

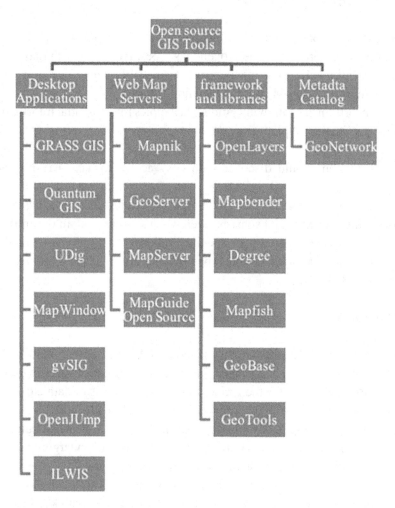

Programming languages: There are programming languages used in the development of open source GIS, like Python and Eclipse in Java programming and .NET framework in the Windows environment. A number of Open source GIS softwares with operating system and programming languages are shown in Table 3.

Maturity: Some packages may have great potential in the future but are currently still in the early or middle part of their developmental stages. Therefore each type of OGIS software need to carefully analysed in terms of maturity.

Popularity of the Software: For various reasons, there are some software packages which have drawn more attention to the user community, and they may be used more widely and developed further in the future. For example, some popular softwares mentioned in the OSGeo homepage for DeskTop GIS are GRASS GIS, OSSIM, Quantum GIS, gvSIG.

Table 1. Key features of various existing open source GIS Software

GIS Software	Key Features
Map Server	• Rendering spatial data. • Supports industry standard data formats and spatial databases. • On-the-fly projection for both raster and vector data. • Provides a wide variety of spatial and attribute-based queries. • Supports popular Open Geospatial Consortium (OGC) standards including WMS,WFS and WCS. • Integrates with popular front-end environments such as ka-Map, Chameleon, Mapbender, MapBuilder and Cartoweb.
GeoServer	• Rendering images, serving and editing geospatial data. • Outputs are available in: WMS, WFS, KML, GeoJSON, GeoRSS format. • Open standards allow publishing from any major spatial data source including: shape files, SQL Server, PostGIS, DB2, Oracle, WFS, TIFF Images, MySQL; • Integrates with existing API's like Google, yahoo, etc. • Connects to Any GeoServer- WMS services can be easily integrated with any available server for publication of web service over the web.
Map Guide	• Windows and Linux, Apache and IIS, and multiple browser support • Interactive map viewing • Quality cartographic output • Built-in storage of XML resource documents • Uniform access of vector and raster data using Feature Data Objects (FDO) API • Flexible application development: PHP, .NET, Java • Extensive server-side APIs • Fast, scalable, secure server platform
Open Layers	• Support for a variety of data sources. • Support for displaying geographic features, with markers and popups. • OpenLayers offers easy build configuration, • designed to help into other applications. • Javascript API to allow full control over • OpenLayers-powered map from within Javascript on a web page.
MapFish	• Flexible and complete framework for building rich web-mapping applications. • Extends Pylons with geospatial-specific functionality such as for creating web services that allows querying and editing geographic objects. • Compliant with the Open Geospatial Consortium standards. This is achieved through OpenLayers or GeoExt supporting several OGC norms, like WMS, WFS, WMC, KML, GML etc.
Mapbender	• Displaying, navigating, editing and querying spatial data and maps. • Map services authorization services (OWS proxy functionality). • Management interfaces for user, group and service administration. • Management of WMS and WFS. • User interface configuration and tool stored in data base.
GeoTools	• Supports OGC Grid Coverage implementation, graphs and networks. • Coordinate reference system and transformation support. • Symbology using OGC Styled Layer Descriptor (SLD) specification. • Attribute and spatial filters using OGC Filter • Encoding specification. • Java Topology Suite (JTS) - with support for the OGC Simple Features Specification used as the geometry model for vector features. • Two Renderers: Lite Renderer - a stateless, low memory renderer, particularly useful in server side environments. J2D - a state full renderer with optimizations for update rate and good for interactive client-side displays.
Geospatial Data Abstraction Library (GDAL/OGR)	• Library access from Python, Java, C#, Ruby, VB6 and Perl • Vector data model closely aligned with OGC Simple Features • Coordinate system engine built on PROJ.4 and OGC Well Known Text coordinate system descriptions • Utilities for data translation, image warping, subsetting, and various other common tasks • Highly efficiency raster data access, taking advantage of tiling and overviews • Support for large files - larger than 4GB

continues on following page

Table 1. Continued

GIS Software	Key Features
QGIS	• Create, edit, visualize, analyses and publish geospatial information for Windows, Mac, Linux, BSD and Android operating systems. With the use of QGIS • Browser, user can browse and preview data, metadata, drag and drop his data from one data store into the other one. • OGC compatible WMS and WFS services. QGIS Web Client allows publishing QGIS projects on the web with ease. • Powerful symbology, labeling and blending features helps in serving impressive maps. *(Source-* http://www.osgeo.org)
GRASS GIS	• Used for data management, image processing, graphics production, spatial modeling, and visualization of many types of data.
Open JUMP	• GIS Data interoperability via Open GIS and Cross platform • Highly efficient and reliabile
gvSIG	• user-friendly interface, being able to access the most common formats, both vector and raster ones. • features a wide range of tools (query tools, layout creation, geoprocessing, networks, etc.). • desktop application designed for capturing, storing, handling, analyzing and deploying any kind of referenced geographic information • GIS Data interoperability via Open GIS and Cross platform • Highly efficient and reliabile • Multilingual
ILWIS	• Vector and Raster capacity integrated into one package. • user-friendliness, it takes less time to learn. • Free open source software available for downloading by anyone • Some of the greatest selections of import and export modules of widely used data formats • On-screen and tablet digitizing • Comprehensive set of image processing tools, Orthophoto, image georeferencing, transformation and mosaicing • Advanced modeling and spatial data analysis, 3D visualization with interactive editing for optimal view findings • Geo-statistical analyses, with Kriging for improved interpolation, Production and visualization of stereo image pairs; Spatial Multiple Criteria Evaluation.
GeoNetwork	• Immediate search access to local and distributed geospatial catalogues • Up- and downloading of data, graphics, documents, pdf files and any other content type • An interactive Web Map Viewer to combine Web Map Services from distributed servers around the world • Online editing of metadata with a powerful template system • Scheduled harvesting and synchronization of metadata between distributed catalogues • Support for OGC-CSW 2.0.2 ISO Profile, OAI-PMH, Z39.50 protocols • Fine-grained access control with group and user management • Multi-lingual user interface

LEVEL OF COMPLEXITY: SOME SOFTWARE IS MORE COMPLEX IN TERMS OF ANALYTICAL FUNCTIONS

User Friendliness: It is an important criterion as ease of using various functions for GIS analysis can even encourage novice user to use the software. It also increases popularity among various users staring from beginners to expert users.

Data format, database and interoperability: Some software has limited capability to recognise and read wide varies of data formats. There is a need to have compliance with the openGIS standards. Also access to the database should be less time consuming. There are software packages which require less start up time to reading data while some may be faster and download large size of data as compared to other Open GIS software. The lack of an interoperable and object oriented database system are the major problems regarding storage of enormous environmental and hydrological data produced over the years. Therefore a system capable of storing data based on specific characteristics or defined schema will enable easy storage and sorting of data. Database compatibility and data format for various GIS softwares are shown in Table 4.

Functionalities: Some packages only served as tools or libraries so their functionality is limited. For example read and write access (Vector and Raster Data), database link, OGC compatibility, thematic mapping, GPS support, scripting functionality, coordinate projection are all important features based on which Open GIS software can be differentiated.

Performance, Geo-spatial simulation and visualization: The geo-spatial simulation including lines, polylines, areas, multi-areas, ellipses, circles, and rectangles as 2D graphics and visualizing them in triangulated irregular networks (TINs) and digital terrain models (DTMs), relief shading and surface draping of raster images in 3D is an added functionality for Open GIS. Following open source GIS software were tested for reading and panning an image size of 125 MB using a PC (Pentium (R), Dual-Core CPU, E5200@ 2.50 GHZ, 1.98 Gb of RAM, Microsoft Windows, XP Professional, Version 2002, Service Pack2) as shown in Table 5.

Table 2. Prerequisites and Download file size for installations of potential Open source GIS software

Name	Prerequisites	Download File Size (Mb)	Installation
DIVA GIS V6.03.0	Java and Eclipse	120	Suitable for both XP and Vista
FWTools	Java, Python	20.3	Suitable for both XP and Vista
GeoServer	Need JAVA JDK1.4 or newer	36.7	Easy to install but not run on both Vista and XP
GeOxygene	Java	10.6	Problems in installation
GRASS GIS	Python	44.3	Suitable for XP
gvSIG	VJM1.05.12, JAI 1.1, JAI image I/O 1.0 (16 + 6 + 10 Mb)	69.4	Easy, need to install 3 Java programmes. Suitable for XP,
HidroGIS	Jre1.4.2	155	but cannot read image files in Vista Installation instruction in Spanish, hard to guess
ILWIS	No	13.5	Run directly
MapWindow GIS	No need for JAVA; Net framework 2.0, is needed for XP (can be downloaded during the installation)	34.1	Easy and suitable for XP
OpenJUMP	JRE1.5.0 (happy with the jre1.05.12 for gvSIG)	11	Easy
QGIS V0.11.0	Python 2.5.2 (10.7 Mb)	73	Cannot be installed in Vista; Suitable for XP
SAGA GIS	No	7.4	Run directly
SavGIS	No	10.5	Easy
uDig	jre1.05.12 + a special uDig SDK kit (not Java SDK) including Java and Eclipse, 79.7 Mb	85.4	Easy

(Source: Chen et al, 2010)

Table 3. Operation system and programming language of various open source GIS

Name	Operating System	Programing Language
Apache Batik	Windows, Linux	Java 1.3
DIVA GIS	Windows only	Java with Eclipse
Deegree	Windows only	Java 1.5, tomcat 5.5
Fmaps	Linux and Gnome	C
FWTools	Windows, Linux	Java, python
GeOxygene	Independent	Java
GeoServer	Mac, Unix, and Windows	Java 1.4
Generic mapping tools GRASS GIS	Windows, Linux, mac Unix (Linux,) Window	C/C++ C
gvSIG	Windows, Linux, Mac OS	Java
HidroSIG	Windows and Linux	Java
ILWIS	Windows only	MS Visual 6
KOSMO	Windows, Mac OS X, Linux	Java
JTS Topology Suite	Windows, Linux	Java
Mapnik MapWindow GIS	Windows, Linux, Mac OS Windows only	C++, python, NET(VB,C++,C#),. Net framework 2.0
mezoGIS	Linux and Windows	Python
monoGIS	Linux and Windows	OGR/GDAL (C++), Shapelib (C), Net Topology Suite, (.NET, C#), Geotools.
NRDB OpenJUMP	Windows only Windows, Mac OS X, Linux	C++, Java
OpenMap	Windows, Linux, Mac OS	Java
OSSIM PostGIS	Windows, Linux, Mac OS Windows, Linux, Mac OS	C++, C
Quantum GIS	Linux, MS Windows Mac OS X, POSIX	C++
SAGA GIS SAMT	Windows and Linux Unix	C++ ?
SavGIS	Windows only	?
SharpMap	Windows only	C#,.NET, meno, Ermaper ECW SDK
Thuban	Linux, Windows and Mac OS	Python
uDig	Windows (not window2000), Mac OS X, Linux	Java with Eclipse

(Source: Adopted from Chen et al., 2010).

Security: Security is an important issue as some Open GIS may have connectivity to database allowing user to update and modify data based on particular schema. It is important to protect data, such as a database, from destructive forces and from the unwanted actions of unauthorized users.

Statistical and Geostatistical Analysis: Statistical analysis extract additional information from GIS data such as how attribute values are distributed, whether there are spatial trends in the data, or whether the features form spatial patterns. It is often used to examine the distribution of values for a particular attribute or to spot extreme high or low values. It is useful when defining classes and ranges on a map, when reclassifying data, or when looking for data errors. Geostatistical Analysis uses sample points taken at different locations in a landscape and creates a continuous surface. The sample points are measurements of some phenomenon, such as radiation leaking from a nuclear power plant, an oil spill, or elevation heights. Therefore, Statistical and Geostatistical Analysis is an important criteria for assessing the Open GIS software.

Table 4. Database compatibility and data format for various GIS softwares

Name	OpenGIS	Database	Data Format
Diva GIS	WMS, WFS	Yes	Shp, grd, tif, ipg, sid, arc
gvSIG	WMS, WCS,WFS (ArcIMS)	Yes	shp, gml, dxf, dwg, dgn, geoBD, WFS, WMS, WCS, ArcIMS
MapWindow GIS	WMS, WFS	Access, ArcXML	shp, bgd, bil, asc, ESRI grid, img,ESRI FLT, ddf, aux, dhm, bt, bmp, ecw, map, sid, LF2, kap, wmf
OpenJUMP	WMS	Yes	ESRI (shp), ecw, gml, xml, fme, jml, wkt, txt, WMS, database query
QGIS	WMS	PostGreSQL/PostGIS	ESRI (shp), mapinfo (mif), cadd, ddf, gml, tif, img, dem, asc, dt0
SAGA GIS	No	Via ODBC	ESRI E00, GPX, GDAL, DXF, SBF, ODBC
FWTools	WMS	MySQL	VPF (i.e. VMAP, VITD), RPF (i.e. CADRG, CIB), and ADRG
GeoServer	WMS, WFS	PostGreSQL/PostGIS, Oracle	VPF, MapInfo, and Cascading WFS, MrSID, ECW, JPEG2000, DTED, Erdas Imagine, and NITF
HidroSIG	WMS, WFS	MySQL	ESRI (shp), dxf, jpeg, tiff, gif, bmp
GeOxygene	WMS, WFS	Oracle and PostGreSQL/ PostGIS	ESRI (shp), dxf, jpeg, tiff, gif, bmp
SavGIS	WMS, WFS	SavGIS databases (called SavBase, proprietary format)	ESRI (shp), dxf, tiff, gif, bmp
ILWIS	WMS, WFS	PostGreSQL/PostGIS	ESRI (shp), dxf, jpeg, tiff, gif, bmp
GRASS GIS	WMS, WFS	MySQL, PostGreSQL/ PostGIS, SQLite	ESRI (shp), dxf, TINs, jpeg, tiff, gif, bmp
uDig	WMS, WFS	ArcSDE,DB2,Oracle, ArcSDE, PostGIS	ArcSDE, DB2, Map Graphic, Oracle Spatial, PostGIS, WFS, WMS

It is difficult to make a comparison among various criteria. However, a matrix and multi-criteria analysis method can be used to select specific OGIS software. This will enable users to quickly identify specific OGIS software that will satisfy the user's requirement.

Matrix Analysis

Matrix Analysis for decision making is an important tool for making a decision. It is mostly useful when many features need to be taken into consideration to select an alternative from number of potential alternatives. This makes it easy to come up with a decision when the option is not clearly understood.

Matrix Analysis enables one to take decisions smartly and logically when confusion may arise due to complexity of having too many criteria to be taken into consideration. It is very handy at a time when one might be struggling to take a decision. For example Table 6 shows the matrix anlaysis for various Open source GIS softwares.

Table 5. Performance of open source GIS

Name	Reading 125 Mb tif Image (Second)	Panning a 125 Mb Image	Time for Zooming (Second)	Comments
Diva GIS	V6.03 is very slow as uDig	Took a long time	Long	Not acceptable for large size images
gvSIG	2	Easy	<1	
MapWindow GIS	9	Easy	1	
OpenJUMP	2	Easy	<1	
ILIWS	4	Easy	<1	
HidroSIG	5	Easy	<1	
SavGIS	3	Easy	<1	
GeOxygene	11	Took longer time	Long	
GeoServer	13	Took Longer time	Long	
GRASS GIS	4	Easy	<1	
FWTools	3	Easy	<1	
QGIS SAGA GIS	2 Cannot read.tif	Easy	<1	Too few image formats
uDig	125 Mb is too big to handle, read a 47.7 Mb tif image in 317s	Took more than 350 s for a simple navigation function or zooming on a 47.7 Mb image	359s	Not acceptable for large size images

(Source: Chen et al., 2010)

Table 6. Matrix analysis for various Open source GIS softwares

OGIS Software	Cross Platform Operation	Installation	Programming Languages	Open source Operation System	Maturity	Level of Simplicity	Data format, Database and Interoperability	Functionalities	Geo-spatial Simulation and Visualization	Security	Statistical and Geostatistical Analysis
Diva GIS	+	+	+	*	--	--	+	*	*	*	-
gvSIG	+	++	*	*	+	*	++	++	+	++	+
MapWindow GIS	+	++	+	*	+	--	++	+	+	+	+
OpenJUMP	+	++	+	++	*	+	++	++	-	++	+
ILIWS	*	*	*	*	-	--	-	*	+	*	+
GRASS	+	*	++	++	++	*	-	*	++	++	++
SavGIS	+	*	*	+	*	-	-	*	*	*	+
GeOxygene	+	*	+	++	--	++	-	*	+	++	+
GeoServer	++	+	+	++	*	++	++	*	*	++	-

(Source: Modified from Chen et. al., 2010; Akbari and Rajabi, 2013).

Multi-Criterion Analysis

The multi-criterion analysis also known as weighted scoring method includes identification of all the attributes of criteria that are to be evaluated. The distribution of weights to each of them indicates their relative importance; and the obtained scores to each option represent how it performs with respect to each feature. The result is a single weighted score for each option, which may be used to indicate and compare the overall performance of the options.

This process necessarily assigns numeric values to judgements. These judgements should not be arbitrary or subjective, but should reflect expert views, and should be supported by objective information. To achieve meaningful results which decision-makers can rely on, it is important that:

- The exercise is not left to the "experts", but is undertaken by a group of people who represent all of the interested parties;
- The group possesses the relevant knowledge and expertise required to make credible measurements and judgments of how the options will impact upon the attributes;
- The group is led by an independent chairman to steer the process, probe opinions, promote consensus and avoid prejudice; and
- The justification for the group's chosen weights and scores is fully explained.

The selected software are to be evaluated based on the weight and scale as given in Table 7 and the total score is to be calculated by using the following formula:

$$\sum_{i=0}^{n} \left(CiWiSi \right) \ x100$$

where, C_i = criteria, W_i = weight for that particular criteria, S_i = scale factor or performance factor for that particular criteria.

However, a combination of both Matrix analysis and Multi-criteria analysis can be done where Matrix analysis can be used for primary criteria whereas Multi-criteria analysis using weighting and scoring can be applied for assessment of secondary criteria as shown in Figure 3.

Table 7. Selection criteria using weighted method based on the pair wise comparison

Selection Criteria	Weight (W)	Performance Scale (Very Poor-Poor-Average-Good-Excellent) (S)	Remarks
Internet connection and security (C1)	0.125		Twice as important than Operating System and programming language as it is expected WKMP will be Internet based and therefore should be well secured
Operation System (C2)	0.063		Users are less bothered about the operating system.
Programming language (C3)	0.063		Given less priority as its final users are not expected do any programming or write any codes.
Level of simplicity (C4)	0.125		As important as Internet and security as more simplicity means more user friendliness.
Data format and database (C5)	0.125	Scale (0-0.25-0.5-0.75-1)	As important as user friendliness as wider data access means more dissemination of information.
Maturity (C6)	0.125		As important as data format and database capacity as matured and well developed software are less likely to face any obstacles than those software still in its development phase
Installation and test running (C7)	0.125		Top priority given as easy installation and speed indicate wider acceptability
Functionalities (C8)	0.125		As important as data format and database as functionalities should be well defined and easy to operate

Figure 3. Stepwise screening using primary and secondary criteria

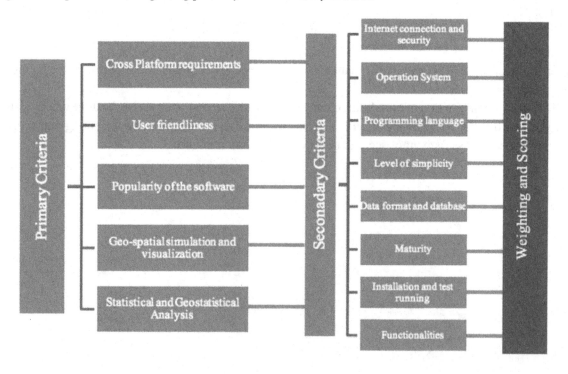

CONCLUSION

The number of open source software is emerging very rapidly due to their popularity, interoperability and cross-platform performance. A number of assessment criteria such as cross platform operation, installation and test running, programming languages, level of simplicity, data format and database, maturity, functionalities are taken into consideration. Two methods such as matrix analysis and multi-criteria analysis can be used. Matrix Analysis provides a general overview of various criteria assessed over a performance scale (very poor-poor-average-good-excellent). While multi-criteria analysis compares various criteria using weight and assigned value ranging from 0-0.25-0.5-0.75-1 for the scale (very poor-poor-average-good-excellent). Therefore, multi-criteria analysis is more specific in comparing among potential OGIS software with scored assigned to each software during the assessment process and thus making it easy to select particular software. Another approach is to apply Matrix analysis to shorten the list of potential software from a large number of software and then use Multi-criteria analysis for the shortened list to come with the most suitable software assed based on the highest scoring.

REFERENCES

Akbari, M., & Rajabi, M. A. (2013). Evaluation of Desktop free/Open source GIS software based on functional and non-functional capabilities. *Technical Gazette*, *20*(5), 755–764.

Câmara, G. (2003). *Why Open Source GIS Software?* Retrieved from http://www.directionsmag.com/entry/why-open-source-gis-software/123925

Chen, D., Shams, S., Carmona-Moreno, C., & Leone, A. (2010, October). Assessment of Open Source GIS Software for Water Resources Management in Developing Countries. *Journal of Hydro-environment Research*, *4*(3), 253–264. doi:10.1016/j.jher.2010.04.017

Confino, J. P., & Laplante, P. A. (2010). An open Source Software Evaluation Model. *International Journal of Strategic Information Technology and Applications*, *1*(1), 60–77. doi:10.4018/jsita.2010101505

Donnelly, F. P. (2010). Evaluating open source GIS for libraries. *Library Hi Tech*, *28*(1), 131–151. doi:10.1108/07378831011026742

Free Software Foundation. (n.d.). Retrieved from http://www.fsf.org/licensing/essays/free-sw.html

Galli, P. (n.d.). *Open Source Is the Big Disruptor*. Retrieved from http://www.eweek.com/article2/0,1895,2186932,00.asp

Hartnett, P., & Bertolotto, M. (2003). Developing interoperable web-based geo- spatial Digital. GIRSUK 2003. *Session*, *5b*, 185–188.

Ca^mara, G., & Onsrud, H. (2004). Open-source geographic information systems software: myths and realities. In *Open Access and the Public Domain in Digital Data and Information for Science: Proceedings of an International Symposium*. National Research Council, U.S. National Committee for CODATA.

Morrison, K. W., & Purves, R. S. (2002). Customizable landscape visualizations. Implementation, application and testing of a web-based tool. *Computers, Environment and Urban Systems, 26*(2-3), 163–183. doi:10.1016/S0198-9715(01)00033-3

Shekhar, S., Vatsavai, R. R., Sahay, N., Burk, T. E., & Lime, S. (2001). WMS and GML based interoperable web mapping system. *Proceedings of the ninth ACM international symposium on Advances in geographic information systems*, 106-111. 10.1145/512161.512185

Sherman, G. E. (2008). *Desktop GIS: Mapping the Planet with Open Source Tools*. The Pragmatic Programmers LLC.

Steiniger, S., & Bocher, E. (2009). An overview on current free and open source desktop GIS developments. *International Journal of Geographical Information Science, 23*(10), 1345–1370. doi:10.1080/13658810802634956

Tiemann, M. (2009). *How Open Source Software can Save the ICT Industry One Trillion Dollars per Year*. White paper. Retrieved from http://www.opensource.org/files/OSS-2010.pdf

This research was previously published in Emerging Trends in Open Source Geographic Information Systems; pages 33-49, copyright year 2018 by Engineering Science Reference (an imprint of IGI Global).

Chapter 23
Transmission Line Routing Using Open Source Software Q–GIS

Shabbir Uddin
Sikkim Manipal Institute of Technology, Sikkim Manipal University, Rangpo, India

Karma Sonam Sherpa
Sikkim Manipal Institute of Technology, Sikkim Manipal University, Rangpo, India

Sandeep Chakravorty
Indus University, Ahmedabad, India

Amitava Ray
Jalpaiguri Government Engineering College, Jalpaiguri, India

ABSTRACT

This article contends that planning for power systems is essentially a projection of how the system should grow over a specific period of time, given certain assumptions and judgments about the future load and the size of investment in generating capacity additions, transmission facilities expansion and reinforcements. Transmission line routing is one of the most important strategic decision-making problems for both private and public sectors. The major objective of a utility is to supply demand for power with a good quality of service, through proper planning of the system. This has led to development of methods which can be used to aid the decision-making process for selecting the best alternative. Geographical Information System (GIS)-based electricity transmission system planning strategies are proposed in this article to determine an optimum routing of feeders. Existing and proposed layouts have been drawn using a GIS-based software, Quantum Geographic Information System (Q-GIS). The developed system is based on the routing of transmission lines from Barh thermal power plant situated in Bihar, India.

DOI: 10.4018/978-1-7998-9158-1.ch023

1. INTRODUCTION

Due to the large amount of power involved, transmission normally takes place at high voltage (1150 kV, 750kV, 420 kV, 220 kV and 110 kV). Electricity is usually transmitted over long distances through overhead power transmission lines. Underground power transmission is used only in densely populated areas due to its high cost of installation and maintenance, and because the high reactive power, it produces large charging currents and difficulties in voltage management. A power transmission system is sometimes referred to colloquially as a "grid"; however, for reasons of economy, the network is not a mathematical grid. Redundant paths and lines are provided so that power can be routed from any power plant to any load center through a variety of routes, based on the economics of the transmission path and the cost of power. Much analysis is performed by transmission companies to determine the maximum reliable capacity of each line, which, due to system stability considerations, may be less than the physical or thermal limit of the line. Deregulation of electricity companies in many countries has led to renewed interest in reliable, economic designs of transmission networks.

One of the primary contributions to the advancement and improvement in man's life style over the years has been the ability to use and control energy. The socio-economic and technological development of any nation and the society is largely dependent on the supply of electricity. It is one of the most important basic needs for the smooth, meaningful and productive economic life of any nation, as the growth of the economy of nations largely depend on the effective management and control of the available generated power, effective maintenance of the equipment and efficient generation of power to meet the growing demand for electricity supply. The use of electricity as a tool for socio-economic development of the nation cannot be overemphasized. Hence, there is a need to keep a comprehensive and accurate inventory of their physical assets, spatial location, both as part of normal service provision, extending the network and undertaking maintenance by the use of geospatial technique, Geographic Information System (GIS). GIS as an emerging technology is a software application, used to create and display cartographic information. In practice, however, GIS consists of five Components: software, data, procedures, hardware, and people. These five components work together to capture, store, retrieve, analyze, and display geographically referenced information. It has an added capability to analyze spatial data, through attribute and location analysis or spatial modeling. Complexity of electrical transmission power system is only a reason for introducing new technologies, GIS is shown as a useful tool for power transmission in this paper

The proposed methodology will help power system planners to make a complete solution of planning problems by finding optimum route to replace the existing route of transmission line from Barh thermal power plant to sub-station. The method proposed can replace the traditional way of planning by mathematical calculations. Use of GIS will help to consider all the geographic impacts.

GIS software use in power transmission system planning will give planners a new and efficient way of planning and implementation of the developed model. The method will reduce man-machine effort.

GIS can be proposed and implemented in diverse field of engineering. This planning method can also help civil engineers for construction of road, bridges etc.

This article has been organized as follows: Section-2 surveys the related work in the area. Section 3 provides the background on Q-GIS. Section 4 proposes the case study and results obtained. Section 5 highlights conclusion and future work.

2. LITERATURE SURVEY

Yeh, Sumic and Venkata (1994) described a GIS based primary router for underground residential distribution (URD) design. They have presented an automated tool, Automated Primary Router (APR) for optimizing the routing of primary cables in URD systems. It also provides a full-fledged graphic user interface, along with on-line visualization and accurate cost estimation to facilitate the design process. APR employs a heuristic search algorithm to find the best primary cable routes either for new residential developments or for existing URD systems as part of the ongoing cable replacement program. Based on the test results, APR shows significant stability and efficiency in finding the optimal solution for primary cable routing. Raghav and Sinha (2006) presented an analysis that shows the power scenario and the role of GIS in spearheading the distribution reforms processes to improve the power industry's viability. They proposed that GIS has the potential to revolutionize the reform process in areas like consumer indexing, distribution network mapping, asset and work management, enhancing billing and collection efficiency and managing consumer relationships. They also suggested that GIS can help to reduce losses and improve energy efficiency through its contribution in different areas of Distribution reforms. Fleeman (1997) a project leader presented a GIS based modeling of electricity networks of midlands electricity plc, England. He gave a GIS based schematic network model, geoschematic network model, network management facilities, network optimization, normal running analysis, proposed running analysis of that area. Thus, GIS can play an important role with the use of modern tools and technology.

GIS is a valuable tool for improved decision-making through efficient Management Information System (MIS) (Trussell, 2001). The Decision Aid System (DAS) is based on the intensive use of GIS, as well as multi-criteria weighting techniques reflecting all group interests. This new DAS can be used to overcome the problems raised by initially opposing positions among different groups stemming from diverse technological, economic, environmental, and/or social interests (Monteiro, Ramirez-Rosado, Zorzano-Santamaría & Fernández-Jiménez, 2005). Work done by authors in distribution network, planning is discovered in which the spatial GIS is used for platform, the distribution network planning is tightly correlated with geographical environment and the searching process is guided by optimization algorithms (Wang & Wang, 2004). The idea for transmission network planning was generated by reading articles (Chang, Chu and & Wang, 2007).

Choosing an optimum location of a distribution sub-station and grouping the various load points to be fed from a particular distribution sub-station has always been a concern to the distribution planners. Authors have used Fuzzy c-means clustering method, which is easy to apply and implement and Analytical Hierarchy process (AHP), one of the popular optimization technique. Fuzzy c-means clustering method applied to various loads which are at different location to form a cluster so that a sub-station could be placed for each cluster for the distribution of power. Context Aware Decision Algorithm based on the AHP is then applied on each cluster comprising of load points to be fed and an optimum feeder layout is obtained depending on some reliability factors (Shabbiruddin & Chakravorty, 2011).

An expert system was proposed for power distribution system planning. Here in this paper the authors have presented a hybridization of K-means clustering method with fuzzy context aware decision algorithm for choosing the optimum location of distribution substation and its feeder layout. K means clustering has been applied to various loads which are at different location to form a cluster with load points in closer proximity so that a substation could be placed for each cluster for the distribution of power. Fuzzy Context Aware Decision Algorithm based on the AHP is then applied on each cluster to decide on the feeder layout connecting the load points in each cluster (Shabbiruddin, Ray, Sherpa & Chakravorty, 2016).

GIS platform is used to locate the load points in terms of coordinates. Soft computing based clustering algorithm is further used to divide the load points into different clusters with suitable optimum location of each substation (Shabbiruddin, Sherpa, Chakravorty & Ray, 2016).

The mission of a feeder system is to transmit power from a sub-station to the sub-station that are scattered within the service territory, always in close proximity to the customer. More than 80% of all transmission/ distribution worldwide are accomplished by using radial feeder systems, in which there are only one path between the plant and sub-station in transmission; and one path between customer and sub-station in distribution. Radial circuits are both least expensive type of transmission system, easier to analyze and to operate. Both low cost and simplicity of analysis make the radial circuits the choice of new transmission construction. Shortest route is one of the important parameter for feeder routing; optimized route with shortest path will lower both losses and cost (Wilis, 1997).

The manual design of a new power transmission feeder line with traditional methods includes the restrictions such as scale measurements, high cost, time-consumption, low speed, elimination of information, lack of information and efficient tools. The design process can be divided into two sub processes: the first, concerning feeder routing or equipment placement determination and the second, concerning sizing of all the elements. The manual design is much harder to handle, compared to automatic design which is an engineering task that optimizes the equipment installation, maintenance costs and satisfies a given set of spatial, technical, and economical constraints. Introduction of GIS in power transmission routing could find surface geography of land, restricted sites with the help of satellite images (Monteiro, Ramirez-Rosado, Zorzano-Santamaría & Fernández-Jiménez, 2005).

Interruption frequency and duration of feeder routing could be influenced by the type of design and layout of the distribution system. The standard, radial configuration used for power transmission is prone to interruptions whenever equipment fails or is otherwise out of service, because it provides only one path for power flow. Use of equipment, with good service records and careful attention on loading, and manufacturer's guidelines, results in fewer outages. Further improvement over standard radial performance could be achieved by providing rollover from another source. A rollover source would reduce duration but not frequency of outages (Wilis, 1997).

Viswarani et al. (2014) worked to get the route plan for the 110 kV cable line connecting R.A. Puram 110/33/11 kV sub-station and a sub-station which is assumed to be situated for Anna University in the campus. Authors have worked on the development of a GIS based Customized system to automate the process of path finding for routing of underground power supply cable between any two sub-stations. It combines the spatial analysis capabilities of GIS with the sophistication of one of the Artificial Intelligence technique "Ant Colony Optimization" to find shortest path for feeder line. GIS is used for getting the image of the area on which the work is planned. Ant Colony Optimization connects the two points by avoiding the obstacles in the path. Work is done on a smaller area. Path finding with the help of Ant Colony Optimization technique would be difficult for a district or state. There are few disadvantages of Ant Colony Optimization:

- Probability distribution changes by iteration.
- Time to convergence is uncertain.

Underground cabling is opted for feeder layout in the paper. Underground transmission/ distribution due to cables are costlier than overhead transmission as the ground needs to be excavated. This can be difficult when passing though geographic obstructions such as hills, marshes and rivers. Special trenches need to be constructed when passing through loose soil. Besides, heat dissipation in underground cables is an issue. Hence, the conductors have to be thicker. The insulation required for the cables are expensive in underground distribution. Hence, it is difficult to use underground cables for voltages at High Voltage (HV) levels.

Zhou et al. (2002) proposed an integrated approach of GIS platform and some mathematical steps for planning of power distribution system. GIS is used for forecasting load for different time period. Multi-period optimal selecting algorithm of sub-station is proposed, which could determine the running capacity of the sub-station depending on the load forecasted. To solve the sub-station location problem, Multi-Mid Position technique is applied to site selection. Computer automatically searches the possible location of sub-station location of sub-station, capacity and time that are put into the running of the sub-station. Authors have located the sub-station in the centre of the load points. Location of sub-station could also be sited geographically with the help of GIS software. However, an alternate sub-station location could also be sited for non-feasibility of sub-station located at first instance.

Dominguez and Amador (2007) presented a vision of GIS applications that are state of the art in the renewable energy field. The objective is to analyze the main qualities and problems of these applications, focusing on specific samples, and to carry out a methodological proposal in this genre. From this point of view, the study synthesizes the analyzed applications in three big groups: Decisions Support Systems (DSS) based on GIS; renewable energy and distributed generation of electricity; and decentralized generation for the rural electrification. DSS is used to judge renewable energy sources on various technical factors. Finally, several conclusions and a methodological outline are contributed GIS application in the rural electrification with renewable energy. In general, a perception is made that GIS can act as an important tool in power distribution system planning.

Dixit, Sharma and Singhal (2008) developed methods which can be used to aid the decision-making process for selecting best alternative from the feeder route. GIS and remote sensing technology based electricity distribution system planning strategy is presented for determining an optimum routing. The developed system is tested on 57 buses, 56 branches, and 6 feeders of a sample sub-station of IIT Roorkee distribution system. The method proposed three different feeder layouts and then the optimum routing is selected based on shortest distance. In the feeder layouts feeder line is passed through the road footpath and also between the existing buildings. Feeder routing through congested area should be done very carefully. Feasibility of the proposed route is checked through load flow analysis however, parameters like land elevation and sag could also be checked for optimum feeder layout.

Therefore, 'strategic' feeder planning, involves determining the overall character of the feeder system associated with each sub-station. This includes determining the number of feeders from the sub-station, their voltage level, the overall service area served by the sub-station as a whole and the general assigned routes and service areas. Additionally, operating problems (voltage and reliability) and overall costs may be estimated.

Transmission planning methods proposed in research papers determine sites and routes in a plan explicitly. They literally compute or develop them automatically, independent of input sites and routes. However, from literature it can be seen that most siting and routing optimization methods determine optimal sites and routes implicitly, by assigning "zero capacity" to candidate sites and routes given as input by the users. In addition to data about loads, costs and planning goals, a sub-station siting optimization method should give number of units of sub-station transformers at every site. Proper application of optimization methods to transmission system design could reduce the overall time which is required for improving the quality and cost of the resulting plan.

3. BACKGROUND ON Q-GIS

Quantum Geographic Information System (Q-GIS) is a cross platform free and open source desktop GIS application that supports the viewing, editing, and analysis of geospatial data. Q-GIS functions as geographic information system software, allowing users to analyze and edit spatial information, in addition to composing and exporting graphical maps. Q-GIS supports both raster and vector layers; vector data is stored as point, line, or polygon features. Multiple formats of raster images are supported and the software can be used to geo-reference images.

3.1. Q-GIS Integration

- It integrates the spatial data with various utility applications (customer information, assets management, outage management and billing system).
- It must display now the particular network element and their attributes (from the consumer to the utility).

3.1.1. Optimizing Electrical Lines Routing

- Installing of the transmission lines is very expensive. It carries all the cost including conductor cost, pole cost, land cost, labor cost.
- Straight route with minimum curves is the most desirable thing. Curved routes would increase length, hence conductor cost. It would also increase losses.
- Certain parameters should be considered like population around the area and environment (soils/ trees/geologic features). Transmission line routing should not cross over any private property and should not cross through dense forest; it may lead to breakages and disruption of power.
- It can be used to analyze the areas for transmission lines with minimal environmental disruption, no health risks.

GIS could help in tackling the previously mentioned concerns of power system planners.

3.1.2. Disaster Management and Locating Faults

- It relates transmission network conditions with other relevant useful information such as weather, vegetation growth, and road networks.
- Identification of a weather moving towards an area enables to determine the transmission facilities in risks.
- Necessary actions could be taken after determining the location of contingency (emergency).

Database plays an important role in planning and executing a project. There is a relation between every spatial object and its non-spatial database, e.g. in a transmission system network the location of poles on the earth is the spatial data and the height of pole is non-spatial data. GIS provides the facility to attach the non-spatial database to the corresponding spatial data or geographic features. This database can be used by different software programs (interfaced with GIS software) which uses, stores, retrieves, modifies and perform analyses with data on the distribution network. Hence GIS keeps the data stored, works as a data analyzer with a visualization of area of interest.

GIS makes it possible to collect data on dangerous or inaccessible areas. GIS also replaces costly and slow data collection on the ground, ensuring in the process that areas or objects are not disturbed. This procedure is thus imperative to data modeling in the field of GIS and other cartographic methods. For obtaining a map on computer screen one need either a road map, topographic sheet, aerial photograph or satellite imaginary. If the area is very large and consisting a dense network of houses and transmission lines then it becomes very difficult and frustrating to re-plan anything specially routing on hand made maps. In that case GIS is proved to be useful in an effective manner. Satellite imaginary can be proved a more efficient, less man-power consuming, less time-consuming solution of finding a map of our area of interest. For establishing the real location of satellite imaginary on earth it has to be geo-referenced. To geo-reference something means to define its existence in physical space. That is, establishing a relation between raster or vector images to map projections or coordinate systems. When data from different sources need to be combined and then used in a GIS application, it becomes essential to have a common referencing system. This is brought about by using various geo-referencing techniques. The limitation of satellite imaginary is its poor resolution. If an identity is not visible in satellite imaginary then GIS can establish its location. The data collected through GIS can directly be imported on the geo-referenced map. GIS can locate a waypoint as well as can track the route also. In any transmission system the location of all the existing poles and feeders can be obtained effectively.

4. CASE STUDY AND RESULTS

A case study is done in which Barh Thermal Power plant located in Bihar (India) is considered. Existing transmission line from Barh thermal power plant to Gaurichak area is traced using Q-GIS. A new route for transmission line is proposed using Q-GIS. Main aim of the planning of any transmission system is to reduce the system losses. The new route should be feasible and should have shortest route compared to the existing one. If the new route of transmission line is feasible and shorter than the existing one it will save both money and losses.

Every time planning of a transmission system requires a map of area of interest. In this study a satellite imaginary with the help of Q-GIS has been traced from the area of Barh thermal power plant to Gaurichak area in Bihar. For good results, the resolution of the imaginary should be more. In Q-GIS based Google Earth the existing transmission line with the towers could be traced as shown in Figure 1.

Using Q-GIS existing tower and the transmission line present can be traced and marked. Q-GIS software can help in zooming the image to get clear snaps. However, it would be difficult to find the area

All the existing towers from BARH thermal power plant to Gaurichak is traced and marked as shown in Figure 2.

Figure 1. It represents the zoomed view of tower and transmission lines (Adapted from http://www.Q-GIS.org/en/site/)

Figure 2. It represents the towers marked on the existing path (Adapted from http://www.Q-GIS.org/en/site/)

These marked points are then imported to Q-GIS software after uploading the DBF (dBase table file) of Bihar state in Q-GIS. The obtained points are then connected and total distance is found out. A new path is marked from Barh thermal power plant to Gaurichak considering all the restrictions like river, mountain etc. Land elevation is an important factor while putting transmission line between two towers to avoid the problems like sag. Land elevation can be found as shown in Figure 3.

Figure 3. It represents the Land elevation shown between two towers (Adapted from http://www.Q-GIS. org/en/site/)

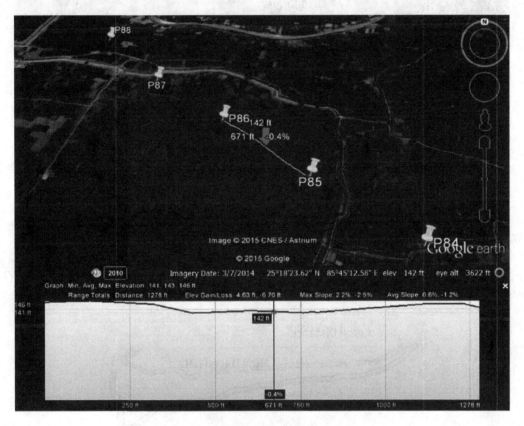

Figure 4 shows the new traced path along the existing path.

These points of the new path are again imported to Q-GIS where we first uploaded a DBF map of Bihar state and the points are connected to find the total distance of the new path which is shown in Figure 5.

Distance calculated for the transmission lines using Q-GIS are:

Total length of the transmission line for existing path using Q-GIS: 93.51 KM
Total length of the transmission line for new path developed using Q-GIS: 67.59 KM
Total length of the transmission line considering aerial distance using Q-GIS: 56.57 KM

Figure 4. It represents the New traced path is marked and shown with the existing path (Adapted from http://www.Q-GIS.org/en/site/)

Figure 5. It represents the Imported and connected points in Q-GIS (Adapted from http://www.Q-GIS. org/en/site/)

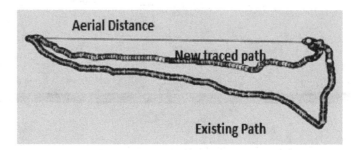

The result shows that that the new path is 25.92 KM shorter than the existing path of the transmission line. If Single core of 300 square mm for 33 KV transmission line is used its cost is Rs 2044/ meter (Havells catalogue link mentioned in reference). Total saving will be Rs 52980480. This much saving will be in transmission line cost additional saving will be through less transmission loss in power as the transmission line length is also shorter.

Q-GIS technology use in power distribution system planning of feeder routing has more advantage. Saving in losses is achieved by re-routing of the feeders by selecting shortest and feasible new route using Q-GIS based software. Route optimization has been done by adopting feasible route with shortening of feeder length. The selection of the optimum route among different technically feasible proposed layouts of power distribution system has been done on the basis of shortest route, avoiding possible restrictions like mountain and river, problems such as land elevation and sag problem has also been considered which is directly proportional to cost.

5. CONCLUSION AND FUTURE WORK

Political factor in power system planning in this paper could not be included. Widest and possible factors have been considered for feeder routing. With ever changing global environment, some more factors would arise affecting power transmission system planning. However, the proposed model developed using Q-GIS is capable to deal such scenario.

Q-GIS technology based transmission system planning of routing is an area of great importance. The whole system has been assumed to be balanced. Here saving in losses of power will make the system economically stronger. Reduced length of transmission line routing will have an economical advantage. Re-routing of the feeders by adopting shortest and feasible new route using Q-GIS based software will act as a helpful and less time-consuming tool. Feeder optimization has been done on the basis of shortening of feeder length with a feasible route. The purpose of drawing these layouts is to find shortest and feasible route. It is found that length of transmission line has been reduced in the layout. The proposed system can be of immense help to power system planners. A single approach can be presented to find optimum sub-station location, optimum feeder routing and load flow analysis. This will help to achieve the results on one platform rather using different tools and software for the complete power transmission system planning.

Applications of the proposed algorithm and methods would require considerable efforts for elaboration of more user-friendly and powerful software providing:

- **Data Collection and Processing:** Both from the data bases, which may be shared with other applications and in direct interaction with the power transmission system planners. This may include the sufficient amounts of information and therefore will require both high qualifications of the planner with convenient software. There is a large potential for creation of the new and advance tool via integration of Data Management System (DMS), Supervisory Control and Data Acquisition (SCADA), and GIS under one single platform.
- **Presentation of the Outcome:** The methodology suggested results in a set of alternatives; further, the tools or software for the convenient tradeoff between the alternatives and their analysis can be done.

The task of the power transmission system planner is to provide the set of planning options with full initial information. Development of a new technology can increase the number of alternatives. It is possible to generate technically feasible alternative through possible elaboration of an expert system. Such tools would suggest possible options along with cost associated with their realization by processing the databases. The database needs to be updated constantly.

Realization of tool based on Artificial Intelligence concepts for the generation of alternatives would engage elaboration of the corresponding algorithms. Collection and pre-processing of the required initial information may also put significant efforts.

There is possibility to obtain the larger amount of data by presence of SCADA system, which requires actual realization. Previously the conclusion was made, that the problem of power transmission system planning can be solved in a most general form without avoidable simplifications. It does not mean that further models cannot be made which are more efficient and powerful. On the other hand, the authors of this article hope for generation of more models to solve problems of power transmission system planning and wish good luck for all the researchers in this field.

REFERENCES

Chang, G. W., Chu, S. Y., & Wang, H. L. (2007). An Improved Backward/Forward Sweep Load Flow Algorithm for Radial Distribution Systems. *IEEE Transactions on Power Systems*, *22*(2).

Dixit, P., Sharma, J. D., & Singhal, M. K. (2008, December). Optimum routing of distribution system network using GIS and Remote Sensing Technology. In *Fifteenth National Power Systems Conference (NPSC)*, IIT Bombay.

Dominguez, J., & Amador, J. (2007). Geographical Information Systems applied in the field of renewable energy. *Computers & Industrial Engineering*, *52*(3), 322–326. doi:10.1016/j.cie.2006.12.008

Fleeman, P. (1997). GIS Based Modeling of Electricity Networks. In *14th International Conference and Exhibition on Electricity Distribution*.

Monteiro, C., Ramirez-rosado, I. J., Zorzano-Santamaría, P. J., & Fernández-Jiménez, L. A. (2005, August). Compromise Seeking for Power Line Path Selection Based on Economic and Environmental Corridors. *IEEE Transactions on Power Systems*, *20*(3), 1422–1430. doi:10.1109/TPWRS.2005.852149

Raghav, S. P. S., & Sinha, J. K. (2006). *Electrical Network Mapping and Consumer Indexing using GIS*. Dehradun: UPCL.

Shabbiruddin, C. (2011). Load distribution among distribution substation and feeder routing using fuzzy clustering and context aware decision algorithm. *Journal of Electrical Engineering*, *11*, 57–67.

Shabbiruddin, Sherpa, K.S., Chakravorty, S., Ray A. (2016, October). Power Sub-station Location Selection and Optimum Feeder Routing using GIS: A Case Study from Bihar (India). *Indian Journal of Science and Technology*, *9*(40).

Trussell, L. V. (2001). GIS Based Distribution Simulation and Analysis. In *16th International Conference and Exhibition on Electricity Distribution: Part 1: Contributions*.

Uddin, S., Ray, A., Sherpa, K. S., & Chakravorty, S. (2016, April-June). Design of an Expert System for Distribution Planning System using Soft Computing Techniques. *International Journal of Energy Optimization and Engineering*, *5*(2), 45–63.

Viswarani, C. D., Vijayakumar, D., Subbaraj, J., Umashankar, S., & Kathirvelan, J. (2014, July 31). Optimization on shortest path finding for underground cable transmission lines routing using GIS. *Journal of Theoretical and Applied Information Technology*, *65*(3).

Wang, C., & Wang, S. (2004, November 21-24). The Automatic Routing System of Urban Mid-Voltage Distribution Network Based on Spatial GIS. In *International conference on power system technology POWERCON '04*.

Willis, H. L. (1997). *Power Distribution Planning Reference Book* (2nd ed.). Marcel dekker, Inc.

Yeh, E. C., Sumic, Z., & Venkata, S. S. (1995, February). APR: A Geographic Information System Based primary Router for underground Residential Distribution Design. In *Transmission and Distribution Conference, Proceedings of the 1994 IEEE Power Engineering Society*. 10.1109/59.373963

Zhou, Q., Caixin, S., Guoqing, C., & Ruijin, L. (2002). GIS based distribution system spatial load forecasting and the optimal planning of substation location and capacity. In *International Conference on Power System Technology. Proceedings. PowerCon 2002* (Vol. 2, pp. 885-889). Retrieved from http://www.havells.com/content/dam/havells/brouchers/Industrial%20Cable/Industrial%20Cable%20price%20list.pdf

This research was previously published in the International Journal of Open Source Software and Processes (IJOSSP), 8(4); pages 71-82, copyright year 2017 by IGI Publishing (an imprint of IGI Global).

Chapter 24
An Open Source Software:
Q–GIS Based Analysis for Solar Potential of Sikkim (India)

Dipanjan Ghose

Sikkim Manipal Institute of Technology, Sikkim Manipal University, East Sikkim, India

Sreejita Naskar

Sikkim Manipal Institute of Technology, Sikkim Manipal University, East Sikkim, India

Shabbiruddin

Sikkim Manipal Institute of Technology, Sikkim Manipal University, East Sikkim, India

Amit Kumar Roy

Sikkim Manipal Institute of Technology, Sikkim Manipal University, East Sikkim, India

ABSTRACT

Most of the issues regarding power supply occurs due to transmission of power through long distances over diverse and unsuitable landscapes. A solar power plant, if installed within the vicinity of the diverse recipient areas, cuts short the transmission related problems by great numbers and acts like an absolute boon to hilly terrains like Sikkim. The study presented here investigates the land suitability for medium-scale solar power installations in Sikkim by using open source software - Quantum-Geographic Information System (Q-GIS) combined with Multi-criteria Decision Making (MCDM) techniques. Six exclusion criteria are identified to avoid unsuitable areas for plant installation. Analytic Hierarchy Process (AHP) is used to rank the available areas according to their suitability, which have been further presented in a technology-aided suitability map. Such a study greatly reduces the feasibility related issues for investors in such projects to visit every site available for construction of the plant, saving time and money.

DOI: 10.4018/978-1-7998-9158-1.ch024

1. INTRODUCTION

With an area of 7096 km² and a population of 653,800 inhabitants (2017) (Population of India 2018, n.d.), Sikkim accounts for a picturesque landscape on the mountain terrains of the Indian Himalayas. The geographical excellence of this place lies in the huge variety of its landscape and climatic characteristics. Despite being one of the least populated states (86 persons/km²), Sikkim has a high population growth rate, averaging 12.36% between 2001 and 2011 (Population of India 2018, n.d.) and with this increase in the population, there comes a steep rise of the demand for power. As of May 2018, nearly one-fifth of India's rural households (around 31 million by population) remain in acute or semi-acute darkness. A 2015 World Bank Study done in India entitled, *Power for all: Electricity Access Challenge in India,* mentions, "Even where electricity service has been locally available, many villages have not adopted a connection." The rapid pace of rural electrification has clearly not been matched by adoption at a household level. No states in this category are Sikkim and Tripura regions of the country ("The problem of lack of rural electricity...," 2018).

Only six states (excluding Sikkim) had an average 24-hour power supply in its rural areas ("The problem of lack of rural electricity...," 2018). Rural electrification by itself means little when load shedding and power outages are frequent enough to make those terms a mere technicality. The lack of reliability is one of the major factors which discourage households from adopting electricity, thus undermining investment and ultimately development in rural electrification ("The problem of lack of rural electricity...," 2018). Besides power theft and political factors, the transmission of uninterrupted power through remote and diverse topography from the distant sources of power is one of the major concerns faced by the distribution companies responsible for ensuring power supply to the villages.

Data from November 2015 show that Sikkim has a total allocated power capacity as: Thermal Capacity of 90 MW, Hydel capacity of 174 MW, and power capacity from other renewable energy sources (including solar) as only 52.11 MW ("States of India by installed power capacity," n.d.). Despite that, fluctuating connectivity and sometimes even hours or days without electricity is not very uncommon in the state. Conducting an energy-related research especially on renewable energy sources will clearly bridge a demanding research gap and add value to Sikkim's power system planning sector in specific. On the other hand, the fact that the current development policies of many developing nations, India being one of them, focus on the deployment of renewable energy resources, further adds value to this study (Aly, Jensen & Pedersen, 2017).

Installation of a large-scale solar plant is a project requiring huge amount of financial investments as well as manual labour. Hence ensuring that the output of such a project is at its maximum is of utmost importance. In other words, it is essential to select the plot for the installation of such a plant such that it enables the best possible output for the plant. Thus, location of the plant plays a major role in its long term working and this is the genre which this study explores. Large scale solar power plants (both Photovoltaic (PV) and Concentrated Solar Power (CSP) plants) require extensive as well as prioritized land for its establishment. Identifying the suitable land areas or regions for the same is a complex issue. Contrasting a simple overview, appropriate identification of suited geographical areas is not only dependent on the amount of solar radiation received by that area, but also on an enormous list of technical, social, economic, ecological and environmental factors that should be taken into account: such as topographical characteristics of the land considered, presence of water resources, environmental impacts and their long time effects, the alternate purpose for the considered land, urban potential of the location, proximity to demand centres and proximity to demand centres and power grids (Aly, Jensen & Pedersen, 2017).

Tackling such an issue with a complete theoretical analysis or practically visiting every land available is an extra investment both in terms of time and resources. So, to tackle this challenge, open source software - Q-GIS based approach has been used, followed by making use of MCDM techniques to develop a technology-specific suitability index for all the land terrains in the state of Sikkim to procure large scale solar power production by the plants. A large number of MCDM techniques are resourcefully available for access and amongst them; the AHP method has been used to find the weights of each of the multi-level hierarchal structure by performing pair-wise comparisons.

MCDM techniques are instrumental in handling decision-making procedures where a large number of objectives are associated. The applications of MCDM spans wide research areas, including water resources management (Zelkan, 1996), energy planning (Aydin, Kentel & Duzgun, 2013; Brewer, Ames, Solan et al., 2015; Castillo, Silva & Lavalle, 2016; Kaya & Kahraman, 2010; Loken, 2007; Omitaomu, Blevins et al., 2012; Pohekar & Ramachandran, 2004; Polatidis, Munda et al., 2006; San Cristobal, 2011), irrigation system's evaluation (Triantaphyllou, 2002), selection of site for substation (Shabbiruddin, Ray, Sherpa & Chakravorty, 2014), to jot a few. Each MCDM technique uses numeric methods to help decision makers choose among a discrete set of alternative decisions. Weights are assigned to each of the criterion considering three factors: the independency of the criterion, the variance of degree of the criterion, and the decision maker's subjective preference (Wang, Jing, Zhang & Zhao, 20090.

By far, the AHP method has already been concluded to be the most used MCDM technique (Mardani, Jusoh, Nor et al., 2015). From detection of best solar power farm locations in Karapinar district of Konya province in the Central Anatolia region of Turkey using AHP and GIS techniques (Uyan, 2013), to applying GIS modelling techniques to identify areas for wind and solar farms in Colorado, USA (Janke, 2010), proposing methodologies combining AHP with a GIS-approach for selecting optimal sites for grid connected PV solar plants at the Huescar district in the Andalusia region of Spain (Carrion, Estrella, Dols, Toro, Rodríguez & Ridao, 2008) and optimum site location for substation (Shabbiruddin, Ray, Sherpa & Chakravorty, 2013, Shabbiruddin, Sherpa, Chakravorty & Ray, 2016), there are numerous instances of using GIS and AHP oriented methods to conduct similar studies.

1.1. Related Work

Using an MCDM based approach to handle operations involving a large number of criteria or factors has not been unusual or rare, even when considering the renewable energy sector (Zhang, Xin, Yong & Kan, 2019; Hwang, Wei, Ching & Lin, 2011; Kabak & Dagdeviren, 2014; Kaboli, Aryanezhad, Shahanaghi & Niroomand, 2007). There have also been numerous instances where other MCDM techniques like PROMETHEE, different from the AHP method were implemented to achieve the goals of the research (Batali, Zahraie, Hosseini & Roozbahani, 2010).

The AHP method has by far been proven to be one of the most useful and accurate MCDM techniques (Mardani, Jusoh, Nor et al., 2015; Aly, Jensen & Pedersen, 2017) and hence finds its preference in terms of usage over the other decision making procedures, including this research. While usage of a single-way MCDM approach has been a valid methodology to handle spatial data, using a GIS based software to digitize the land data further add to the accuracy of results besides making data handling comparatively easier. Thus, the methodology used here, to combine a Q-GIS based approach with the AHP process, stands at a higher ground when compared to a simple decision-making approach. Also, there has been little research conducted on these regions of the Indian subcontinent, despite there being a beaming source of resources naturally available. As a matter of fact, a GIS based MCDM research on renewable energy will give a good platform in the area for researchers of the country.

2. METHODOLOGY FOR CALCULATION

A GIS based study for identification of suitable PV and CSP hotspots on and across Sikkim basically involves two major steps: First the selection of the criteria used to exclude the unwanted areas from the study (Exclusion criteria (EC)) and then the AHP analysis method has been implemented as a MCDM procedure to weigh the Decision Clusters (DC). The adjoining figure: Figure 1 summarises the used methodology hereafter (Aly, Jensen & Pedersen, 2017). All analysis, digitalization and conversion of data used have been done using open source software GRASS Q-GIS DESKTOP Version 2.18.22, an already established software to facilitate handling of spatial data (Shabbiruddin, Sherpa, Chakravorty & Ray, 2017).

Evaluation and working upon the entire land area available were difficult. So first, the areas which were unsuitable for establishment for construction of a solar power plant were screened out. For this, six exclusion criteria were considered, namely, Protected Areas, lands with unsuitable slope and topography, lands covered with water bodies, land which can be used for cultivation or other more resourceful uses, land very near to populated regions or cities and land receiving very low solar radiation. The exclusion procedure has been further explained under the "Exclusion of Unsuitable Areas" section.

The efficiency and work of a solar power plant depends on a number of factors as discussed earlier. Out of all the numerous factors governing the solar output of a plant, the considered factors in this study are: Availability of solar resources, water availability, proximity to roads and proximity to utility grids. These four evaluation criteria were ranked (further explained under "Ranking Criteria" section) accordingly. On the areas considered for evaluation after screening of unsuitable land, the AHP method was applied for each of the ranking criteria using pair-wise comparisons. At the end of the AHP method, each of the considered land areas had its own priority vector, which referred to the suitability index for that area for the construction of a solar power plant. The calculation procedures are further explained progressively.

2.1. Exclusion of the Unsuitable Areas

As the first step towards analysing the preferential locations for the PV and CSP hotspots, a number of Exclusion criteria topics were jotted, which, compared to relevant and spatial literature (Castillo, Silva & Lavalle, 2016; Grothoff, 2014) are comprehensive. The criteria taken into account were: Protected Areas (EC1), Topography (EC 2), Water Bodies (EC 3), Land Cover (EC 4), Urban Expansion (EC 5), and low solar radiation (EC 6) (Aly, Jensen, Pedersen; 2017). Each criterion can be further elaborated as:

2.1.1. Protected Areas (EC 1)

The International Union for Conservation of Nature and Natural Resources (IUCN) defines a protected area as "clearly defined geographical space, recognized, dedicated and managed, through legal or other effective means, to achieve long term conservation of nature with associated ecosystem services and cultural values" (Aly, Jensen & Pedersen, 2017). In Sikkim there are 8 Protected Areas comprising 1 National Park and 7 Wildlife Sanctuaries, covering about 35% of the geographical area of the state

("Forests, Energy and Wildlife Management Department," n.d.). All the mentioned protected areas under this category have been excluded from the area considered.

Figure 1. (Methodology model for calculation) Table presenting in a pictorial form, the process of calculation

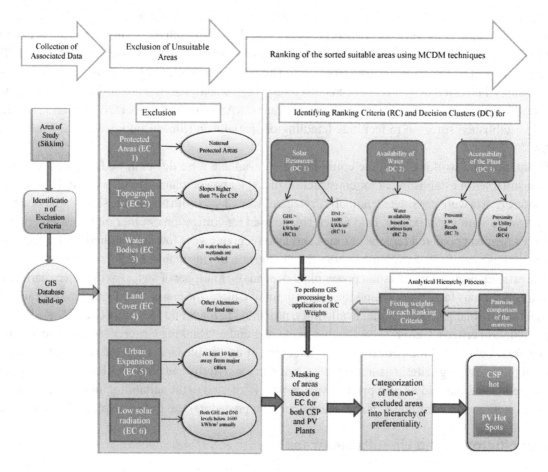

2.1.2. Topography (EC 2)

Owing to obvious reasons, large scale solar power plant installation is preferred on flat terrain. The slopes higher than 2.1% are excluded for CSP Plant installations. There is almost an accord that areas with elevation higher than 2.1% are to be excluded from CSP Plant installation sites (Kronsgae, 2001; Trieb, O'Sullivan, Pregger, Schillings & Krewitt, 2009). For PV Plants, there is no specified limit for elevation. While some studies observed excluded lands with slopes higher than 5% (Charabi & Gastli, 2011), a study of solar parabolic trough electric power plants in California, Los Angeles excluded slopes higher than 6.24% (Cohen, Skowronski & Cable, 2005) and another Iran based analysis for finding suitable land for solar farms exploitation using GIS and fuzzy AHP took into account land with slopes lower than 11% (Noorollahi, Fadai, Akbarpour Shirazi & Ghodsipour, 2016) (Aly, Jensen, Pedersen; 2017). In this study, lands with slopes higher than 7% were excluded for building solar power plants. The slope map, as shown in Figure 2 was obtained from the Geomorphological map of India from Bhuvan, Geoportal of India, which comes under the Indian Space Research Organisation (ISRO).

2.1.3. Water Bodies (EC 3)

Presence of a permanent water body like a lake or a river causes a hindrance to the construction of a solar power plant and thus, such a construction needs to be on a drier land which has no water body on it. The information on Water Bodies is based on data provided by Global Lakes and Wetlands Database (GLWD) developed as a partnership between the Centre for Environmental Systems Research, University of Kassel and World Wildlife Fund (Lehner & Doll, 2004). The aid of the Glacial Lakes Thematic Services under Bhuvan, the Geoportal of India handled ISRO was also taken to obtain the maps in Figure 3.

2.1.4. Land Cover (EC 4)

Large-scale solar power plants require extensive areas of land. Thus, those areas of land which have no other potential use need to be identified. Amongst the provided categories of land cover, the ones on which solar plant installations should not be done can be categorized as: cultivated or managed land, woody land and land covered with trees, shrub or natural aquatic vegetation. Such constraints should only be given a space for relaxation if future land management strategies can be adopted (Aly, Jensen & Pedersen, 2017). The data as depicted in Figure 4 has been obtained from Bhuvan, the geoportal base of ISRO, using Q-GIS.

2.1.5. Urban Expansions (EC 5)

Presently, as of 2017, Sikkim has a population of 653,800 ("Population of India 2018," n.d.) and in future, the existing urban areas are expected to expand in every direction. Location of a solar power project is preferentially suitable in a secluded area away from populated cities to prevent relocation and other hindrances to daily lifestyle. Thus, the areas of this study are centred at locations away from a radius of at least 8 km from the major cities of Sikkim (shown in Figure 5). The information of population is statistically calculated by considering the data provided by Census 2011 conducted by the Government of India.

2.1.6. Low Solar Radiation (EC 6)

Solar power plants need sunlight to function and clearly, areas with lower solar resources must be excluded from consideration. To obtain maximum output from the plants, the areas with Global Horizontal Irradiation levels (GHI) and Direct Normal Irradiation Levels (DNI) lower than 1600 KWh/m^2 have been excluded. The data for this criterion as shown in Figure 6 and Figure 7 for the GHI and DNI data respectively was obtained from the Global Solar Atlas.

With the aforementioned exclusion criteria, a series of exclusion layers was made, which was overlapped on each other using Q-GIS based software. From the overlapped output, the areas which do not fall under any of the exclusion categories were obtained. Only areas which do not fall under any of the exclusion categories were considered as available areas for large scale solar power plant installation.

Figure 2. (Topography of Sikkim (EC)) (extracted using Bhuvan)

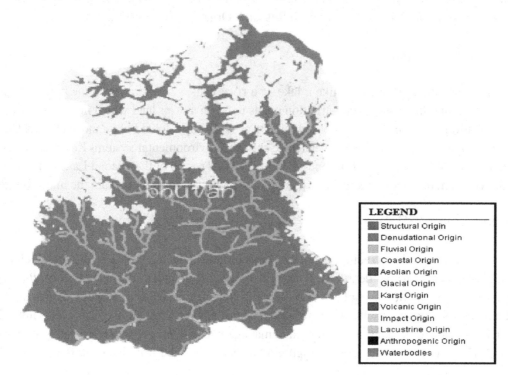

Figure 3. (Water sources of Sikkim (EC 3)) (extracted using Bhuvan)

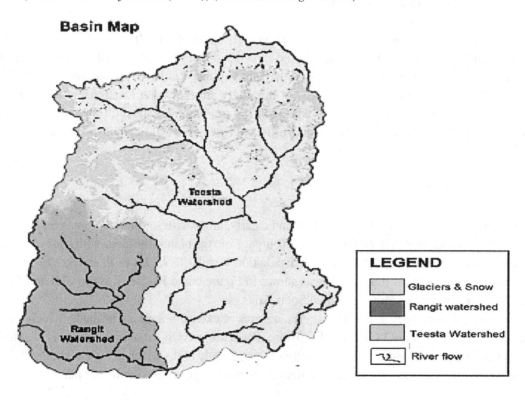

Figure 4. (Land-cover of Sikkim (EC 4)) (extracted using Bhuvan)

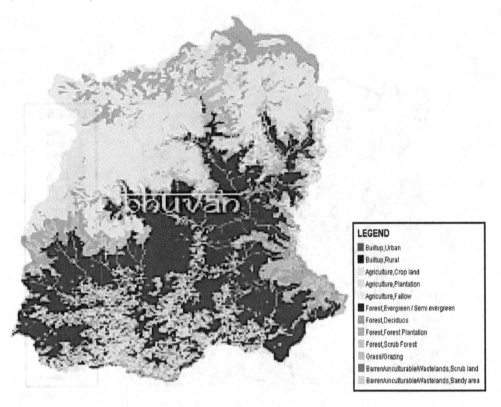

Figure 5. Major towns considered in Sikkim (EC 5)) (extracted using Q-GIS)

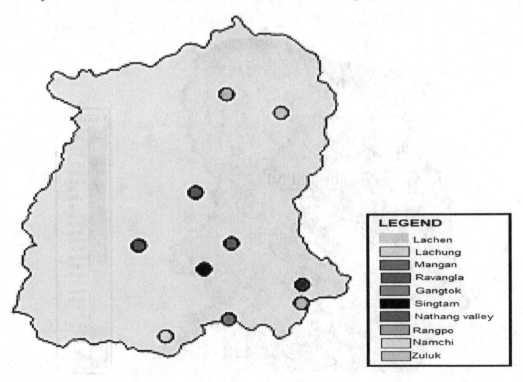

Figure 6. Annual GHI of Sikkim (EC6 (GHI<1500) / RC 1 (GHI>1600)) (Extracted using Global Solar Atlas)

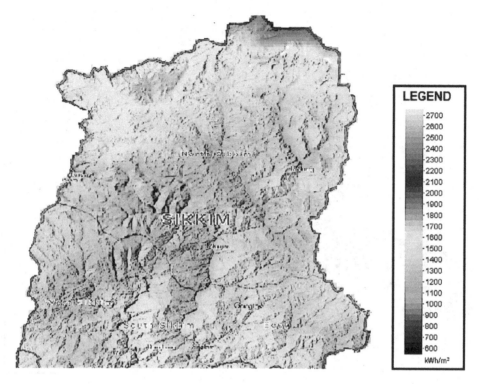

Figure 7. Annual DNI of Sikkim (EC 6 (DNI<1500) / RC1 (DNI>1600) (Extracted using Global Solar Atlas)

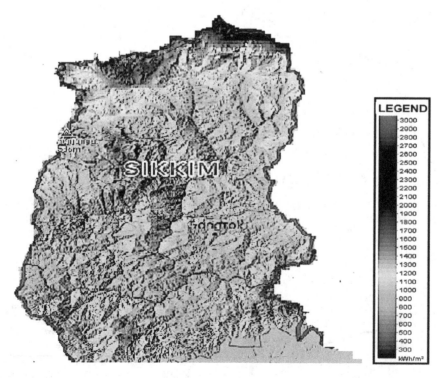

2.2. Ranking of Suitable Areas

After getting an account of the remaining non-excluded areas, MCDM technique has been used to identify the PV and CSP hotspots in the suitable areas. The ranking is an important step in the calculation, followed by distribution of justifiable weights for each of the decision-making criterion based on their preferential status in the study and the decision-makers interests.

2.3. Ranking Criteria

In total the following criteria were considered for ranking of the considered areas: Solar resources (RC1), Water availability (RC2), Proximity to roads (RC3) and Proximity to utility grid (RC4).

The relative importance of each tier within each ranking criterion decides the number of tiers for that ranking criterion. A quantitative scoring was assigned to each tier representing its relative favourability to have a large-scale solar power installation (least favourable getting the lowest score, while the most favourable ones scoring the most).

2.3.1. Solar Resources (RC1)

Solar power plants are driven by radiations from the sun. Thus, the location of a solar power plant installation will largely also depend on the amount of radiation it receives. The solar radiation received can be implemented as two criteria: GHI (Global Horizontal Irradiation) and DNI (Direct Normal Irradiation). While DNI decides the primary resource for CSP plant installations, GHI determines the location suitability for PV plants. Quite clearly, high GHI and DNI numbered areas need to be chosen as beneficial for installation of either of the plants. The information to get the GHI and DNI data for Sikkim has been obtained from the Global Solar Atlas, an open resource for obtaining solar data. To sort out the required locations, areas with both GHI and DNI radiation levels higher than 1600 kWh/m^2 have been considered, making the plant's location more techno-economically preferable with an increasing radiation level. The maps representing the solar data are shown in Figure 6 and Figure 7.

2.3.2. Water Availability (RC 2)

The considered parabolic trough CSP technology often utilizes the thermal energy generated through the solar field to drive a steam turbine and hence a water demand for cooling such plants occurs (Aly, Jensen & Pedersen, 2017). According to US National Renewable Energy Laboratory (Macknick, Newmark, Heath & Hallett, 2011), wet cooled parabolic troughs CSP plant consumes an average 3274 litres/MWh and are highly recommended to be built near water resources with high stream flow. Consequently, in this study, the various lakes of Sikkim as shown in the Figure 8 are considered along with the main river of the state, Teesta and her few tributaries as major supplies of water-based resources. The information on water resources is based on data provided by the GLWD (Lehner & Doll, 2004).

2.3.3. Proximity to Roads (RC3)

Transportation accessibility to the site of construction is crucial in construction and maintenance points of view. Thus, the nearness of the location to roads is considered a very crucial aspect as it eliminates the extra costs associated with new road constructions, and their maintenance. The data for the same was provided by the Tourism and Civil Aviation Department of the Government of Sikkim.

2.3.4. Proximity to Utility Grid (RC 4)

The preferred location of a large-scale solar power production plant is directly proportional to the presence of a utility grid in the area taken into consideration. The nearness of the plant location to a grid will put a check on its economics, by cutting off the extra charges which will otherwise get involved due to construction of power transmission lines and their associated power losses. The data for the grid lines of the state was obtained from the web portal of the Sikkim State Load Dispatch Centre (SLDC) and only the 220 kV transmission lines were considered for this study.

Figure 8. Lakes of Sikkim (RC2)0 (extracted using Q-GIS)

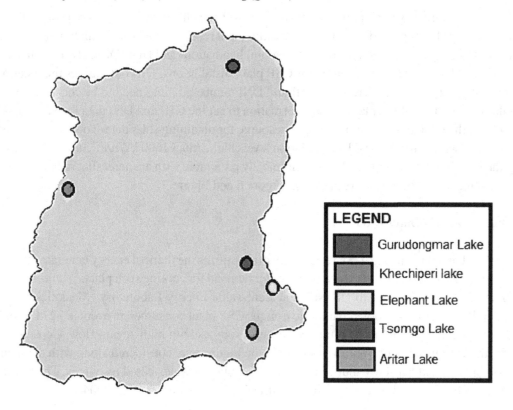

2.4. Applying the Analytic Hierarchy Process (AHP) Method

The AHP method is efficient in allowing qualitative evaluation, making it a preferable choice in this case. The AHP is a multi-criteria decision-making method that compares decision criteria through a pairwise criteria comparison to obtain a favourability scale among a set of alternatives (Vargas, 1990). The problem is first represented in a hierarchy including the factors representing the interests of the decision maker. All the decision criteria are then compared against each other in form of pairwise comparison matrices representing a way to assign relative preferences amongst the different factors, and then the criteria weights are obtained by the Eigen values and Eigen vectors of a square preference matrix.

Applying the AHP model follows a number of steps including: selecting the decision clusters and the ranking criteria, conducing pairwise comparisons at the clusters and criteria levels, performing consistency checks, and finally determining the criteria relative weight (Aly, Jensen & Pedersen, 2017).

To assign weights to the criteria, a number of studies conducted earlier in the same genre were referred to (Noorollahi, Fadai, et al., 2016; Tahri, Hakdaoui & Maanan, 2015; Sánchez-Lozano, Teruel-Solano, Soto-Elvira et al., 2013; Sánchez-Lozano, García-Cascales & Lamata, 2015; Charabi & Gastli, 2011).

Elaborating briefly on the calculations involved in the performed AHP process, firstly the pairwise comparison matrix is developed and the relative importance between each pair of alternatives is rated. Ratings are allotted by giving the highest rating to the most preferred alternative and the lowest one to the least preferred one. Immediate numeric ratings can also be assigned for the same. A reciprocal rating (i.e. 1/9, 1/8, etc.) is assigned when the second alternative is preferred to the first. The value of 1 is always assigned when comparing an alternative with itself.

Having got the comparable matrices, the relative weights of the matrices can be obtained by normalizing the matrix into a new matrix. This can be achieved by dividing the elements of each column by the sum of the elements of the same. The next step involves development of the Priority Vector, by averaging each row of the normalized matrix. The values in this vector sum to 1. The consistency of the subjective input in the pairwise comparison matrix can be measured by calculating a consistency ratio. A consistency ratio of less than 0.1 is good. For ratios which are greater than 0.1, the subjective input should be re-evaluated. To find the Consistency ratio:

For each row of the pairwise comparison matrix, a weighted sum is determined by summing the multiples of the entries by the priority of its corresponding (column) alternative. Now, for each row, the weighted sum is divided by the priority of its corresponding alternative. The average, λ_{max}, of the results is determined. The consistency index, CI, of the n alternatives is computed by:

$$CI = (\lambda_{max} - n) / (n-1) \tag{1}$$

where n is the size of the matrix (n * n). Mathematically, the consistency of a matrix X is given if:

$$X_{ij} * X_{jk} = X_{ik} \tag{2}$$

Having obtained the Consistency Index (CI), the Consistency Ratio can be estimated using:

$$CR = CI / RCy \tag{3}$$

where, the Random Consistency (RCy) of the matrix is developed using a standard table (Saaty, 1990). Having checked for the CR value to be legit, a Criteria Pairwise Development Matrix is formed, which is multiplied by the priority vector which had been obtained earlier.

3. CALCULATIONS

Table 1 lists the nine-point scale for pair-wise comparison for the AHP method.

Table 1. Nine point scale for pair-wise comparison

Intensity of Relative Importance	Definition
1	Equally important
3	Moderately preferred
5	Strongly preferred
7	Very strongly preferred
9	Extremely preferred
2,4,6,8	Intermediate importance between two values

Table 2, Table 3, Table 4, Table 5, Table 6, Table 7 and Table 8 represent the corresponding matrices for pair-wise comparisons of CSP and PV installations as well as for the mentioned criterion.

Using the priority vector matrices for each criterion, the normalised matrices were obtained for all the pairwise comparison matrices, and the calculations were carried forward to ultimately obtain the overall priority matrices for CSP and PV installations.

Table 2. Pair-wise comparison matrix for criteria for CSP installation

	GHI	Utility Grid	Road	Water
GHI	1	5.00	7.00	8.00
Utility Grid	0.20	1	8.00	0.20
Road	0.14	0.33	1	0.14
Water	0.33	5.00	7.00	1

After this, the overall priority vectors for PV and CSP installation were found out respectively, considering GHI and DNI values for calculation.

Table 3. Pair-wise comparison matrix for criteria for PV installation

	DNI	Utility Grid	Road	Water
DNI	1	5.00	7.00	8.00
Utility Grid	0.20	1	8.00	0.20
Road	0.14	0.33	1	0.14
Water	0.33	5.00	7.00	1

Table 4. Pair-wise comparison matrix Of GHI

	Lachen	Ravangla	Gangtok	Namchi	Mangan	Lachung	Rangpo
Lachen	1	7.00	5.00	7.00	3.00	1.00	5.00
Ravangla	0.14	1	0.20	0.50	0.20	0.14	0.20
Gangtok	0.20	5.00	1	5.00	0.33	0.14	0.20
Namchi	0.14	2.00	0.20	1	0.20	0.14	0.50
Mangan	0.33	5.00	3.00	5.00	1	0.20	2.00
Lachung	1.00	7.00	7.00	7.00	5.00	1	7.00
Rangpo	0.20	5.00	1.00	2.00	0.50	0.14	1

Table 5. Pair-wise comparison matrix for DNI

	Lachen	Ravangla	Gangtok	Namchi	Mangan	Lachung	Rangpo
Lachen	1	7.00	5.00	7.00	2.00	1.00	5.00
Ravangla	0.14	1	0.20	1.00	0.20	0.14	0.20
Gangtok	0.20	5.00	1	5.00	0.50	0.14	1.00
Namchi	0.14	1.00	0.20	1	0.20	0.14	0.20
Mangan	0.50	5.00	2.00	5.00	1	0.33	3.00
Lachung	1.00	7.00	7.00	7.00	3.00	1	7.00
Rangpo	0.20	5.00	5.00	5.00	0.33	0.14	1.00

4. RESULTS AND DISCUSSIONS

The obtained results for priority vector for PV and CSP installations have been shown in Tables 9a and Table 9b respectively. The maps obtained after implementing the results obtained from the above priority vectors have been shown in Figure 9 for PV plant installation hotspots and in Figure 10 for CSP plant installation hotspots.

Table 6. Pair-wise comparison matrix for proximity to utility grid

	Lachen	Ravangla	Gangtok	Namchi	Mangan	Lachung	Rangpo
Lachen	1	0.20	0.14	0.33	0.33	1.00	0.44
Ravangla	5.00	1	0.33	1.00	5.00	5.00	0.20
Gangtok	7.00	3.00	1	3.00	5.00	7.00	0.33
Namchi	3.00	1.00	0.33	1	3.00	7.00	0.20
Mangan	3.00	0.20	0.20	0.33	1	3.00	0.20
Lachung	1.00	0.20	0.14	0.14	0.33	1	0.14
Rangpo	7.00	5.00	3.00	5.00	5.00	7.00	1

Table 7. Pair-wise comparison matrix for proximity to roads

	Lachen	Ravangla	Gangtok	Namchi	Mangan	Lachung	Rangpo
Lachen	1	0.20	0.14	0.20	0.33	1.00	0.20
Ravangla	5.00	1	0.33	0.10	5.00	5.00	0.33
Gangtok	7.00	3.00	1	3.00	5.00	7.00	3.00
Namchi	5.00	1.00	0.33	1	3.00	5.00	0.20
Mangan	3.00	0.20	0.20	0.33	1	3.00	0.14
Lachung	1.00	0.20	0.14	0.20	0.33	1	0.14
Rangpo	5.00	3.00	0.33	5.00	7.00	7.00	1

Table 8. Pair-wise comparison matrix for proximity to water resources

	Lachen	Ravangla	Gangtok	Namchi	Mangan	Lachung	Rangpo
Lachen	1	7.00	0.20	7.00	3.00	5.00	0.33
Ravangla	0.14	1	0.20	1.00	0.20	0.33	0.20
Gangtok	5.00	5.00	1	7.00	5.00	7.00	1.00
Namchi	0.14	1.00	0.14	1	0.20	1.00	0.14
Mangan	0.33	5.00	0.20	5.00	1	5.00	0.33
Lachung	0.20	3.00	0.14	1.00	0.20	1	0.14
Ravangla	3.00	5.00	1.00	7.00	3.00	7.00	1

Table 9a. Priority vector for PV installation   *Table 9b. Priority vector for CSP installation*

Rangpo	0.125
Gangtok	0.118
Lachung	0.106
Lachen	0.072
Mangan	0.070
Ravangla	0.060
Namchi	0.050

Rangpo	0.14
Gangtok	0.13
Lachung	0.10
Lachen	0.08
Mangan	0.07
Ravangla	0.06
Namchi	0.04

Figure 9. Resultant map for PV hotspots (Extracted using (Q-GIS))

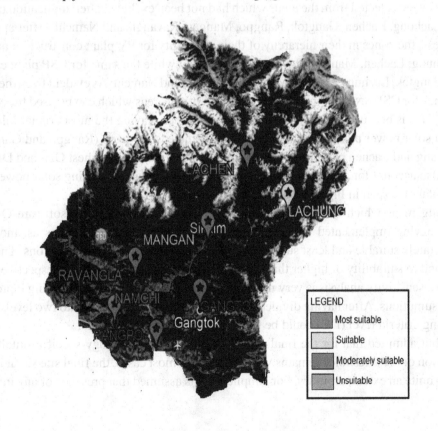

LEGEND
- Most suitable
- Suitable
- Moderately suitable
- Unsuitable

Figure 10. Resultant map for CSP hotspots (Extracted using (Q-GIS))

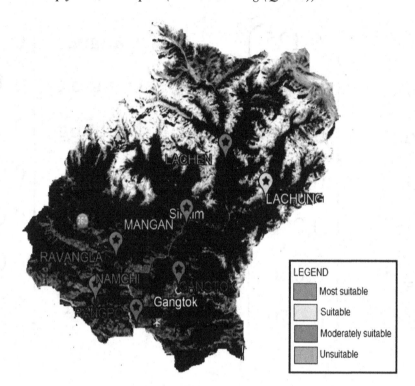

Seven zones were selected from the areas which had not been excluded after application of the exclusion criteria: Lachung, Lachen, Gangtok, Rangpo, Mangan, Ravangla and Namchi. After application of the AHP process, the zones in their hierarchy of their suitability for PV plant construction are: Rangpo, Gangtok, Lachung, Lachen, Mangan, Ravangla and Namchi while the same for CSP plant construction are: Rangpo, Gangtok, Lachung, Lachen, Mangan, Ravangla and Namchi. As evident from the results, the favourable zones for CSP installations are also inclusive of the areas which can be used for construction of a PV plant. This is because of availability of solar resources playing the most crucial role in the site suitability of a solar power plant, example, the northern and eastern parts (Rangpo and Gangtok in the East and Lachung and Lachen close to North) of Sikkim have one of the highest GHI and DNI levels of the state and also account for a high preferential rank when discussing installing solar power plants, be it CSP or PV plant (as seen in Figures 9 and 10).

The resulting maps which had been obtained after having taken an open software Q-GIS-based approach and having implemented the AHP, classifies the aforementioned zones as: most suitable, suitable, moderately suitable and least suitable for the corresponding plant installations. The classified areas correspond to suitability of higher than 80%, 60%, 35% and less than 35%, respectively. Usually, conduction on a sensitivity analysis is very much recommended for problems including inputs based on non-certain assumptions. After having divided the decision criteria weighting into two levels, the higher decision-making criteria level (DC) could be subjected to sensitivity analysis.

It is to be but admitted that for the final classification of the technology-specific suitability maps, the determination of the thresholds remains very difficult. In most cases, the final site suitability used in this study is to quite an extent, arbitrary. For simplicity, it is assumed that presence of any infrastructure also necessarily means that it is available for use. A dedicated capacity restriction assessment for all the infrastructural components is quite beyond the scope of this study.

4.1. Future Prospects

A study of this sort is greatly dependent on the availability of data for the considered criteria. The remoteness of locations, in quite some cases, acts as a hindrance to proper and satisfactory collection of data for that region. Besides, owing to continual scientific and infrastructural development, rapid modification of data with due time is not something unexpected. To further move ahead with this study, more criteria for analysis can be considered, like nearness of the site to airports, railway stations or popular tourist spots, temperature of the region, humidity, sunlight duration and so on. However, the study presented is a general approach to tackle an issue of similar sort and the procedures can be adopted by scholars working in the same field. Mere introduction of more criteria and updating of existing data will greatly benefit in any future scope for this study. Sikkim being counted as a state with an urge for development, introduction of new infrastructural facilities like new roads and new transmission lines will add up to the presence of more land for building of solar power plants. In more developed areas with higher and more comprehensive GIS based data availability, more criteria can also be included to further extend the boundaries of the scope of this study.

5. CONCLUSION

A large-scale solar power production plant demands a tremendously high investment. Thus, to provide for the success and security for such an extravagant expense by the government or any individual, it is essential to analyse the criteria governing the better performance of a power plant and decide upon the most preferable locations for its establishment. A combination of Q- GIS based analysis and MCDM technique has been applied to locate the solar PV and CSP hot spots in Sikkim.

For this study, references of a large number of similar researches were taken which had been conducted in various locations across the globe and six criteria for exclusion were decided upon: Protected Areas, Land Cover, Topography (elevation mostly, considering that Sikkim is a hilly terrain), Water Bodies, Urban Expansion, and low solar radiation received. Having removed the areas governed by the exclusion criteria, 3 decision clusters have been identified: Solar resources, Water Availability and Accessibility. While annual GHI and DNI data fell under solar resources, the accessibility cluster remained governed by Proximity to roads and Proximity to Utility Grid. From the non-excluded areas, 7 preferable areas were chosen, on which the multi criteria decision making technique (AHP method) was applied, to rank the areas on the basis of preferentiality for establishment of a solar plant. This study also explores Sikkim's progressive steps in establishing itself as a healthy utilizer of its abundant natural resources, besides providing a phenomenal solution to the problem of an insecure and inconsistent power supply across the scattered villages and cities of the state.

REFERENCES

Aly, A., Jensen, S. S., & Pedersen, A. B. (2017). Solar power potential of Tanzania: Identifying CSP and PV hot spots through a GIS multicriteria decision making analysis. *Renewable Energy, 113*, 159–175.

Aydin, N. Y., Kentel, E., & Duzgun, H. S. (2013). GIS-based site selection methodology for hybrid renewable energy systems: A case study from western Turkey. *Energy Conversion and Management, 70*, 90–106.

Balali, V., Zahraie, B., Hosseini, A., & Roozbahani, A. (2010, March). Selecting appropriate structural system: Application of PROMETHEE decision making method. In *2010 Second International Conference on Engineering System Management and Applications* (pp. 1-6). IEEE.

Bontemps, S., Defourny, P., Bogaert, E. V., Arino, O., Kalogirou, V., & Perez, J. R. (2011). GLOBCOVER 2009-Products description and validation report.

Brewer, J., Ames, D. P., Solan, D., Lee, R., & Carlisle, J. (2015). Using GIS analytics and social preference data to evaluate utility-scale solar power site suitability. *Renewable Energy, 81*, 825–836.

Carrión, J. A., Estrella, A. E., Dols, F. A., Toro, M. Z., Rodríguez, M., & Ridao, A. R. (2008). Environmental decision-support systems for evaluating the carrying capacity of land areas: Optimal site selection for grid-connected photovoltaic power plants. *Renewable & Sustainable Energy Reviews, 12*(9), 2358–2380.

Castillo, C. P., Silva, F. B., & Lavalle, C. (2016). An assessment of the regional potential for solar power generation in EU-28. *Energy Policy, 88*, 86–99.

Charabi, Y., & Gastli, A. (2011). PV site suitability analysis using GIS-based spatial fuzzy multi-criteria evaluation. *Renewable Energy, 36*(9), 2554–2561.

ENVIS Centre. (2018). Status on Environment and Related Issues. Retrieved from www.sikenvis.nic.in/Database/Energy

Forests, Energy and Wildlife Management Department, Government of Sikkim. (n.d.). Sikkim Forest. Retrieved from www.sikkimforest.gov.in/Wildlife.htm

Grothoff, J. M. (2014). *Estimating the Renewable Energy Potential in Africa. International Renewable Energy Agency*. IRENA.

Hwang, G. H., Wei, L. S., Ching, K. B., & Lin, N. S. (2011, September). Wind farm allocation in Malaysia based on multi-criteria decision making method. In *2011 National Postgraduate Conference* (pp. 1-6). IEEE.

Janke, J. R. (2010). Multicriteria GIS modeling of wind and solar farms in Colorado. *Renewable Energy, 35*(10), 2228–2234.

Kabak, M., & Dağdeviren, M. (2014). Prioritization of renewable energy sources for Turkey by using a hybrid MCDM methodology. *Energy Conversion and Management, 79*, 25–33.

Kaboli, A., Aryanezhad, M. B., Shahanaghi, K., & Niroomand, I. (2007, October). A new method for plant location selection problem: a fuzzy-AHP approach. In *2007 IEEE International Conference on Systems, Man and Cybernetics* (pp. 582-586). IEEE.

Kaya, T., & Kahraman, C. (2010). Multicriteria renewable energy planning using an integrated fuzzy VIKOR & AHP methodology: The case of Istanbul. *Energy, 35*(6), 2517–2527.

Lehner, B., & Döll, P. (2004). Development and validation of a global database of lakes, reservoirs and wetlands. *Journal of Hydrology (Amsterdam), 296*(1-4), 1–22.

Løken, E. (2007). Use of multicriteria decision analysis methods for energy planning problems. *Renewable & Sustainable Energy Reviews, 11*(7), 1584–1595.

Macknick, J., Newmark, R., Heath, G., & Hallett, K. C. (2011). A Review of Operational Water Consumption and Withdrawal Factors for Electricity Generating Technologies. *Contract (New York, N.Y.), 303*, 275–3000.

Mardani, A., Jusoh, A., Nor, K., Khalifah, Z., Zakwan, N., & Valipour, A. (2015). Multiple criteria decision-making techniques and their applications–a review of the literature from 2000 to 2014. *Economic Research-Ekonomska Istraživanja, 28*(1), 516–571.

Noorollahi, E., Fadai, D., Akbarpour Shirazi, M., & Ghodsipour, S. (2016). Land suitability analysis for solar farms exploitation using GIS and fuzzy analytic hierarchy process (FAHP)—a case study of Iran. *Energies, 9*(8), 643.

Omitaomu, O. A., Blevins, B. R., Jochem, W. C., Mays, G. T., Belles, R., Hadley, S. W., ... Rose, A. N. (2012). Adapting a GIS-based multicriteria decision analysis approach for evaluating new power generating sites. *Applied Energy, 96*, 292–301.

Özelkan, E. C., & Duckstein, L. (1996). Analysing water resources alternatives and handling criteria by multi criterion decision techniques. *Journal of Environmental Management, 48*(1), 69–96.

Pohekar, S. D., & Ramachandran, M. (2004). Application of multi-criteria decision making to sustainable energy planning—a review. *Renewable & Sustainable Energy Reviews, 8*(4), 365–381.

Population of India. 2018. (n.d.). Retrieved from www.IndiaPopulation2018.in

Saaty, T. L. (1990). *Decision making for leaders: the analytic hierarchy process for decisions in a complex world*. RWS publications.

San Cristóbal, J. R. (2011). Multi-criteria decision-making in the selection of a renewable energy project in spain: The Vikor method. *Renewable Energy, 36*(2), 498–502.

Sánchez-Lozano, J. M., García-Cascales, M. S., & Lamata, M. T. (2015). Evaluation of suitable locations for the installation of solar thermoelectric power plants. *Computers & Industrial Engineering, 87*, 343–355.

Sánchez-Lozano, J. M., Teruel-Solano, J., Soto-Elvira, P. L., & García-Cascales, M. S. (2013). Geographical Information Systems (GIS) and Multi-Criteria Decision Making (MCDM) methods for the evaluation of solar farms locations: Case study in south-eastern Spain. *Renewable & Sustainable Energy Reviews, 24*, 544–556.

Shabbiruddin, R., & Sherpa, C. (2013). Evaluation of substation location using geographical information system: A case study. *Elixir International Journal, 62*, 17464–17468.

Shabbiruddin, R., & Sherpa, C. (2014). Selection of Sub-Station site for Greater NOIDA India by Analytical Hierarchy Process (AHP). *Elixir International Journal, 66*, 20482–20486.

Shabbiruddin, S., & Chakravorty, R. (2016). Power Sub-station Location Selection and Optimum Feeder Routing using GIS: A Case Study from Bihar (India). *Indian Journal of Science and Technology, 9*(40), 1–7.

Shabbiruddin, S., & Chakravorty, R. (2017). Transmission Line Routing Using Open Source Software Q-GIS. *International Journal of Open Source Software and Processes, 8*(4), 71–82.

Solar Thermal Parabolic Trough Electric Power Plants for Electric Utilities in California. (2005). *Solargenix Energy*. Solargenix Energy.

States of India by installed power capacity. (n.d.). Wikipedia. Retrieved from www.wikipedia.org/wiki/States_of_India_by_installed_power_capacity

Tahri, M., Hakdaoui, M., & Maanan, M. (2015). The evaluation of solar farm locations applying Geographic Information System and Multi-Criteria Decision-Making methods: Case study in southern Morocco. *Renewable & Sustainable Energy Reviews, 51*, 1354–1362.

The problem of lack of rural electricity demand. (2018, May 8). Livemint. Retrieved from www.livemint.com

Triantaphyllou, E. (2000). *Multi-Criteria Decision Making Method: A Comparative Study. 2000*. Netherlands: Kluwer Academic Publishers.

Trieb, F., O'Sullivan, M., Pregger, T., Schillings, C., & Krewitt, W. (2009). Characterisation of solar electricity import corridors from MENA to Europe. Potential, infrastructure and cost. Stuttgart, Germany: German Aerospace Center (DLR).

Uyan, M. (2013). GIS-based solar farms site selection using analytic hierarchy process (AHP) in Karapinar region, Konya/Turkey. *Renewable & Sustainable Energy Reviews, 28*, 11–17.

Vargas, L. G. (1990). An overview of the analytic hierarchy process and its applications. *European Journal of Operational Research, 48*(1), 2–8.

Wang, J. J., Jing, Y. Y., Zhang, C. F., & Zhao, J. H. (2009). Review on multi-criteria decision analysis aid in sustainable energy decision-making. *Renewable & Sustainable Energy Reviews, 13*(9), 2263–2278.

Wikipedia. (n.d.). Sikkim. Retrieved from www.wikipedia.org/wiki/Sikkim

Zhang, L., Xin, H., Yong, H., & Kan, Z. (2019). Renewable energy project performance evaluation using a hybrid multi-criteria decision-making approach: Case study in Fujian, China. *Journal of Cleaner Production, 206*, 1123–1137.

This research was previously published in the International Journal of Open Source Software and Processes (IJOSSP), 10(1); pages 49-68, copyright year 2019 by IGI Publishing (an imprint of IGI Global).

Index

A

ABC algorithm 568, 580, 667-668
academic culture 390
Action Research 329-330, 332, 347-348, 350
active learning 152, 289, 304-305, 312, 391-392
agile development 289-290, 293
Analytical Hierarchy Process 415, 446
ant-1.7 596, 602, 607-608, 614
Apache Cassandra 875, 885-886, 888, 897
Apache Kafka 845, 864, 875
Apache Spark 851-852, 858, 864-865, 871-875, 877, 895-896
Apache Storm 873, 875
Application Tunneling 278, 287
Artificial Intelligence 47, 53, 134, 152-153, 171, 219-220, 261, 287, 307-308, 314, 316-328, 392, 416, 423, 506, 540, 593, 615, 789, 851, 858, 889

B

Big Data stack 827-828, 849, 859-860, 872, 875, 877
Blockcode 329, 347, 352
Bug Reports 55, 631, 676-681, 683-685, 687, 690-692, 711, 734
business intelligence (BI) 480, 482, 495, 836

C

change impact analysis 763, 765-767, 769, 779
change metrics 570, 657, 694-695, 698-699, 704-708
change point 710, 712-716, 720, 722, 731-732
change profile analysis 13
change prone classes 566-570, 572-573, 575, 578-579, 583, 592-595, 653-657, 659-661, 666-667, 671, 673, 675
change proneness 566-572, 576, 583, 592-595, 653-659, 663-664, 671, 673, 675, 694
Circle Packing Graph 840, 848, 854

class dependency 566, 570, 572, 575-579, 581, 592, 607, 612, 653, 656-657, 659, 661, 664-667, 669, 673
classroom project 289, 291
client-server 96, 99, 103-105, 340
closed standard 71, 74-75, 92
Code repositories 1, 8
Collection Building 466, 468-470
Commercial Software 2, 24, 120, 185, 222, 275-276, 287, 396, 503
Commit analysis 1, 8
Computer-Assisted Audit Tools (CAATs) 504-505, 508, 518
Concentrated Solar Power Plant 426
CouchDB 888-890, 897, 900-902
coupling metrics 569, 593, 656, 674, 762, 764-765, 767, 770-771, 775, 778-779
Cyclos 520, 526, 528, 530-536, 538

D

data measurement 826-827, 854
Data Mining 9, 126, 165-166, 259, 261, 270, 285-287, 323, 392, 399, 482, 509, 517, 540, 578, 633, 666, 758, 807, 845, 852
Data Visualization 37, 45, 813, 817, 836-837, 839, 842, 844-846, 853, 856, 858
Database 10, 20, 44-45, 67-71, 73-76, 78-81, 84-86, 89, 93-94, 99, 102-103, 106-107, 117, 126, 147, 207, 214-215, 259, 309, 311, 313-315, 317, 323, 359, 392, 398-399, 404-407, 411, 419, 423, 431, 444-445, 452-453, 455-456, 468, 482-483, 485, 499, 509, 536, 579, 597, 666-667, 743, 787, 798-799, 823, 830, 833, 836, 844, 854, 858, 863-864, 870, 873, 876, 882-885, 888-895, 897, 899-904
Debugging 201, 212, 710-715, 720, 731-734, 766, 786-787
Deep Learning 37, 61, 283, 285, 287, 386, 597
Design of Experiments (DOE) 762, 767, 778
digital collection 466, 469

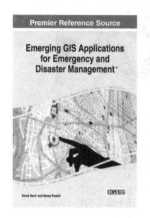
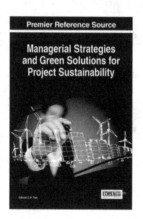

IGI Global Author Services

Providing a high-quality, affordable, and expeditious service, IGI Global's Author Services enable authors to streamline their publishing process, increase chance of acceptance, and adhere to IGI Global's publication standards.

Benefits of Author Services:

- **Professional Service:** All our editors, designers, and translators are experts in their field with years of experience and professional certifications.
- **Quality Guarantee & Certificate:** Each order is returned with a quality guarantee and certificate of professional completion.
- **Timeliness:** All editorial orders have a guaranteed return timeframe of 3-5 business days and translation orders are guaranteed in 7-10 business days.
- **Affordable Pricing:** IGI Global Author Services are competitively priced compared to other industry service providers.
- **APC Reimbursement:** IGI Global authors publishing Open Access (OA) will be able to deduct the cost of editing and other IGI Global author services from their OA APC publishing fee.

Author Services Offered:

English Language Copy Editing
Professional, native English language copy editors improve your manuscript's grammar, spelling, punctuation, terminology, semantics, consistency, flow, formatting, and more.

Scientific & Scholarly Editing
A Ph.D. level review for qualities such as originality and significance, interest to researchers, level of methodology and analysis, coverage of literature, organization, quality of writing, and strengths and weaknesses.

Figure, Table, Chart & Equation Conversions
Work with IGI Global's graphic designers before submission to enhance and design all figures and charts to IGI Global's specific standards for clarity.

Translation
Providing 70 language options, including Simplified and Traditional Chinese, Spanish, Arabic, German, French, and more.

Hear What the Experts Are Saying About IGI Global's Author Services

*"Publishing with IGI Global has been **an amazing experience** for me for sharing my research. The **strong academic production** support ensures quality and timely completion."* – **Prof. Margaret Niess, Oregon State University, USA**

*"The service was **very fast, very thorough, and very helpful** in ensuring our chapter meets the criteria and requirements of the book's editors. I was **quite impressed and happy** with your service."* – **Prof. Tom Brinthaupt, Middle Tennessee State University, USA**

Learn More or Get Started Here:

For Questions, Contact IGI Global's Customer Service Team at cust@igi-global.com or 717-533-8845

IGI Global
PUBLISHER of TIMELY KNOWLEDGE
www.igi-global.com

Publisher of Peer-Reviewed, Timely, and
Innovative Academic Research Since 1988

IGI Global's Transformative Open Access (OA) Model:
How to Turn Your University Library's Database Acquisitions Into a Source of OA Funding

Well in advance of Plan S, IGI Global unveiled their OA Fee Waiver (Read & Publish) Initiative. Under this initiative, librarians who invest in IGI Global's InfoSci-Books and/or InfoSci-Journals databases will be able to subsidize their patrons' OA article processing charges (APCs) when their work is submitted and accepted (after the peer review process) into an IGI Global journal.

How Does it Work?

Step 1: **Library Invests in the InfoSci-Databases:** A library perpetually purchases or subscribes to the InfoSci-Books, InfoSci-Journals, or discipline/subject databases.

Step 2: **IGI Global Matches the Library Investment with OA Subsidies Fund:** IGI Global provides a fund to go towards subsidizing the OA APCs for the library's patrons.

Step 3: **Patron of the Library is Accepted into IGI Global Journal (After Peer Review):** When a patron's paper is accepted into an IGI Global journal, they option to have their paper published under a traditional publishing model or as OA.

Step 4: **IGI Global Will Deduct APC Cost from OA Subsidies Fund:** If the author decides to publish under OA, the OA APC fee will be deducted from the OA subsidies fund.

Step 5: **Author's Work Becomes Freely Available:** The patron's work will be freely available under CC BY copyright license, enabling them to share it freely with the academic community.

Note: This fund will be offered on an annual basis and will renew as the subscription is renewed for each year thereafter. IGI Global will manage the fund and award the APC waivers unless the librarian has a preference as to how the funds should be managed.

Hear From the Experts on This Initiative:

"I'm very happy to have been able to make one of my recent research contributions *freely available* along with having access to the *valuable resources* found within IGI Global's InfoSci-Journals database."

– Prof. Stuart Palmer,
Deakin University, Australia

"Receiving the support from IGI Global's OA Fee Waiver Initiative *encourages me to continue my research work without any hesitation.*"

– Prof. Wenlong Liu, College of Economics and Management at Nanjing University of Aeronautics & Astronautics, China

Printed in the United States
by Baker & Taylor Publisher Services